Criminal Investigation
FORMING REASONABLE GROUNDS

FIFTH EDITION

Gino Arcaro

 2009
Emond Montgomery Publications Limited
Toronto, Canada

Emond Montgomery Publications Limited
60 Shaftesbury Avenue
Toronto ON M4T 1A3
http://www.emp.ca/college

Printed in Canada.

We acknowledge the financial support of the Government of Canada through the Book Publishing Industry Development Program (BPIDP) for our publishing activities.

The events and characters depicted in this book are fictitious. Any similarity to actual persons, living or dead, is purely coincidental.

Acquisitions and developmental editor: Tammy Scherer
Assistant developmental editor: Nick Raymond
Marketing manager: Christine Davidson
Cover designer: John Vegter

Library and Archives Canada Cataloguing in Publication

Arcaro, Gino, 1957-
    Criminal investigation : forming reasonable grounds / Gino Arcaro. — 5th ed.

Includes index.
ISBN 978-1-55239-290-4

    1. Criminal investigation—Textbooks.   I. Title.
HV8073.A7315 2009   363.25   C2008-905536-5

Contents

PHASE 1   BASIC INVESTIGATIVE STRATEGIES

CHAPTER 1   Investigative Competencies

CHAPTER 2   The Investigative Decision-Making Model: The "Base" IDM

CHAPTER 3   Basic Investigative Sequence: Theory Development Model

PHASE 2   CASE MANAGEMENT: OFFENCE VALIDATION AND WITNESS INTERVIEWS

CHAPTER 7   Validating the Offence: Criminal Investigation Analysis

CHAPTER 8   Witness Compellability and Competency

CHAPTER 9   Rules of Evidence, Part 1: Hearsay Evidence

CHAPTER 13 Applying Witness Interviews and Statements

CHAPTER 14 Evaluating Witness Credibility: Deception

PHASE 3   INTERROGATIONS AND CONFESSIONS

CHAPTER 16 Rules of Evidence: Confessions

CHAPTER 17 Preventing Charter Violations

CHAPTER 18 Interrogation Principles and Procedures

CHAPTER 19 Detecting Deception

PHASE 4   PHYSICAL EVIDENCE

CHAPTER 20 Admissibility: Rules of Evidence

CHAPTER 21 Sudden-Death Investigation

CHAPTER 22 Determining Means of Death

Preface

THE 10 PERCENT DOCTRINE

The good news: this is an era of unprecedented police hiring. The bad news: there will likely be unprecedented numbers of applicants.

There are more police jobs available than ever before, but the competition will be tough. Research shows that approximately 10 percent of police applicants are successful. That amounts to a lot of jobs, but it also means that 90 percent of applicants are unsuccessful.

THE MYTH

Contrary to popular belief, no one is born to be a police officer.

But don't take that to mean that anyone can be a police officer. Many individuals can become police officers, through training and application. But not everyone can.

Police officers are developed, through proper mentoring. Here's the key point: Mentoring is a two-way street, between a mentor and a protegé. It is a special type of coaching. Mentoring may come from one person or from several people, as well as from the young officer's experiences; experience is a mentor.

The protegé has to play his or her part in being committed and making the right decisions. These decisions, in order of priority, are as follows.

1. *Make the right character decisions.* There are a number of competencies essential to your getting hired. None are more important than "good character." If you want to be hired as a police officer, you have to meet the legislative standard of strong moral character. You are not expected to achieve sainthood. But you *are* expected to demonstrate good character. Anyone can achieve this—it's shown through your decisions. Life is about choices. Having a good character is not a static condition. Character never stops developing. It can change at any moment during a lifetime.

   The police will not hire any person with a criminal record. They will not hire any one with habits that suggest bad character. They don't have to, because there are enough suitable candidates who have good character—people who abstain from alcohol abuse, drug abuse, gambling, and general irresponsibility.

2. *Develop the right attitude.* I conducted informal research among recruiters from eight large police organizations. I asked them what was their number one reason for excluding applicants from the constable selection process. The number one reason was *arrogance*. That's not surprising, since arrogance in a candidate immediately turns off all police officers involved in the candidate interview or background investigation processes.

   Be humble. Humility is essential.

3. *Mens sana in corpore sano.* This Latin quotation means "a sound mind in a sound body."

There are four types of fitness that you have to show in order to get hired as a police officer: physical, intellectual, emotional, and psychological. Each of these is achieved through deliberate "reps." You have to practise; they don't just happen.

Real front-line policing involves potential violence. Policing always has and always will demand a high level of athleticism. You owe it to the profession. You owe it to the public. You owe it to your platoon and to the officers who need your back-up help. So get to the gym. Do manual labour. Run, lift, eat right. And once you are hired, you have no choice but to keep yourself in peak physical shape.

"Over 80" has a negative connotation in the context of drinking and driving, but it is a positive goal academically. Any police officer in training can achieve an academic goal of over 80 percent—no exceptions.

Get involved in life—that's the only way to get life experience. Get off the couch, and get away from the keyboard. Technology is great, but human interaction is the only way to gain true life experience.

Get a job. Play sports. Join a team. Join a group. Do as much community service as possible until you find some type of volunteer work that you can commit to on a long-term basis. Putting time into volunteer community service is essential to getting hired in policing. Why? It helps develop all essential police competencies. It develops *maturity* in a person—a key to getting hired. Maturity is a fundamental requirement for being selected as a constable. Community service is valuable *because the best way to improve yourself is to improve someone else.* Improving others is the best way to develop the 16 dimensions of maturation. Coach kids. Teach someone something. Share your expertise. You develop as a person by developing others.

Set big goals. Achieve big goals. Stretch yourself and extend your limits. You have to keep growing. Progress, or regress!

Each one of you controls your own destiny. There is no easy road. No one will hand it you. If you want it badly enough, you will work hard and succeed in getting hired.

INVESTIGATIVE STRATEGIES AND THEORIES

The purpose of this book is to teach how to develop investigative theories by applying strategies. Criminal investigations can be simple or complex.

THE PROFESSION

"Being a police officer is a privilege, not a right."

My boss at 33 Division, Niagara Regional Police, said this to me during one of the many occasions when I was hollered at for messing up one thing or another. In his song "Badlands" Bruce Springsteen (The Boss) is paying tribute to those who pay their dues in the anonymity and obscurity and daily struggle of front-line work. He reminds us that such work advances us and serves us well. He cautions impatient and power-hungry individuals to *learn* from and enjoy the tribulations of front-line work rather than resent it.

My boss was paying tribute to the uniform patrol branch, the front line of policing. He was reminding me to pay my dues before getting ambitious about becoming a detective; to *learn* from and enjoy the struggles of front-line police work.

Both bosses made sense—the front line is a place for learning.

Policing is arguably the most misunderstood of jobs, especially by those who aspire to work in it. A variety of factors blur and conceal the *realities* of policing and the hiring process. A healthy grasp of reality is vital for successful police work. Ignoring reality invites failure. So I offer the following *Immutable Realities of Policing* to those who are in or will be entering the police selection process:

1. "Situations which appear quite innocent, with no hostile demonstration by the person being arrested, can explode into violence, leaving the arresting officer *dead* or injured"—Alberta Court of Appeal, *R. v. Lerke* (1986). This is the most accurate, concise description of police reality that I have ever read. Policing is one of the few jobs where being murdered is an occupational hazard. It's a risky business, one that has to be taken seriously. It's not for the faint of heart. Unfortunately, this fact is inexplicitly lost on potential police recruits. The following two examples illustrate this:

   a. During mock interviews, students are asked, "What's the worst consequence that can happen in policing?" Their answers are commonly "losing a court case," "getting sued," or "getting fired." I have never heard the correct answer—"getting killed."

   b. While being interviewed by a radio talk show host about the recent murders of three police officers, I was asked if a problem existed. In response to my comments, a caller stated that she did not see a problem because it was "only three deaths." She said, "This is not like the United States." Shocking perception!

2. Policing should not be seen as an alternative to the academic challenges prerequisite to other careers. A parent recently told me that his son "screwed up" in high school and that he thought policing would therefore be a good career choice. The word "vocation" is derived from the Latin word *voca*, meaning "voice" or "calling." There should be a better reason to want to be a police officer than the misguided notion that academic success is not required.

3. You will not immediately get hired as a detective, undercover officer, SWAT team member, or chief of police. Everyone hired by a police organization is assigned to the uniform patrol branch. Everyone—no exceptions. Patrol officers represent the front line. That's where you learn real policing.

However, I have never heard any prospective candidate say, "I want to be a patrol officer." Everyone wants to be a specialist or a high-ranking officer, and they ask how the patrol branch can be avoided or bypassed. It can't. Getting promoted to a specialist branch or higher rank requires years of patrol experience in which you prove yourself by consistent performance. Goals will remain unrealized dreams without solid performance as a patrol officer.

4. The world distinguishes winners from losers. There is competition in real life. First, there is competition to get hired by a police force; they don't draft people the way the military does. Then, there is competition for advancement after being hired. Sometimes in the real world you won't get what you want the first time or even the second time. Sometimes it may take years. So don't despair if you don't get hired the first time. View it as an opportunity to get better. How you handle adversity and setbacks reveals who you really are.

5. Wearing a uniform will not make you special. A uniform cannot instill courage, intelligence, or morals. If you *need* to wear a uniform to feel bigger or more complete, do whatever it takes to rid yourself of that need. A police uniform is not intended to fill psychological voids and emptiness.

6. You will not save the world. Instead, you will solve problems—some minor, some major.

7. If your parents, teachers, or college coordinators scare you, wait until you meet *real* bad guys. Criminals will not care about your feelings, comfort, or self-esteem. They will not try to make your life easy. Some will be nasty— they may insult you, threaten to kill you and your family, and some may be violent toward you. The worst part is that there is no one to complain to if these things happen.

8. Your days as a front-line officer won't be stress-free. You will be sent to a bar fight or a domestic dispute where you will be required to think quickly, under pressure. You can't ask bad guys for more time to think about the matter when you are trying to figure out if you can arrest or search them. You can't ask to write a "make-up" case if you lose your court case. And you won't be given satisfaction surveys to express frustration about how much stress the bad guys are causing you.

9. Police forces are paramilitary organizations. A rookie's greeting an administrator with a "What's up?" or a "Hey, how's it going?" is not considered appropriate, and will not be tolerated. You'll have to get used to not being on a first-name basis with your bosses.

10. A strong bench press is not enough to succeed in policing. It helps, but there are countless other traits and skills needed.

11. You won't have summers off, you might have to work on Christmas day, you will have to work the midnight shift, you might have to spend all day in court without sleep after a midnight shift, and you won't make $100,000 per year or be given a company car.

12. People with a gun fixation are not normal. Firearms training is essential only because it may save you from being murdered. Don't get excited simply by carrying a gun. Get excited about being an expert in self-defence.

13. Although there are traditional courses called "Police Powers," this does not mean that they will give you special "powers." Laws of arrest and of search and seizure are the focus of these courses. These are *not* powers—they are *solutions* to problems.

14. Television and movies are not real life. Movies like *Lethal Weapon* should never be confused with reality or seen as a substitute for a training curriculum. Movies are not training videos. You can't chase cars at breakneck speed; you can't fire rounds of bullets wildly while chasing people on crowded streets; and you can't create bloodbaths.

15. You can't change your past. The police prefer to hire people who have no criminal tendencies. They prefer people with a proven ability to understand right from wrong, with some semblance of moral standards. They prefer to exclude substance abusers. The term "background check" understates the significance of the task. It should be named "a police investigation of your past behaviour." Before you think about trying to hide your past, think about this—the police are trained to figure out who committed a murder, robbery, or other crime. So they will not have trouble finding out if a police candidate is a substance abuser.

16. Be humble. As I have mentioned, one of the leading factors cited by recruiters as a reason for not hiring candidates is arrogance.

17. Do not do community service simply as a resumé builder. Police organizations value *sincere* volunteer work because such work significantly matures a candidate.

18. Find a mentor. A mentor is not necessarily a friend or cheerleader who simply accepts your weaknesses. A mentor imparts wisdom, develops strengths, and helps eliminate your weaknesses. A mentor is a valuable gift.

19. My boss was right—being hired as a police officer is a privilege, not a right.

NEW TO THE FIFTH EDITION

The fifth edition of *Criminal Investigation: Forming Reasonable Grounds* contains a number of new and enhanced features:

- ▸ New, easy-to-understand, reality-based strategy development models guide students in building investigative theories.
- ▸ An increased number of current, landmark case law decisions affecting front-line police procedures are outlined and explained.
- ▸ Chapters have been reorganized and restructured to better suit course structure.
- ▸ Learner Summaries have been added at the beginning of each chapter, outlining major topics and themes.
- ▸ "First officer" responsibilities are emphasized and applied in the chapter case studies.
- ▸ Includes exclusive online content for students, continually updated by the author.
- ▸ Includes Instructor's Guide and Test Bank.

About the Author

Gino Arcaro (BSc, MEd) is a professor and coordinator of the Police Foundations and Law and Security Administration programs at Niagara College in Welland, Ontario.

His unique 33-year professional career has included duties in policing in addition to those of a college program coordinator and professor, published writer, football coach, and strength training coach.

WORK EXPERIENCE

- 15 years police officer
  - nine years uniform branch
  - SWAT team
  - six years detective
- 18 years college professor
- 10 years college program coordinator
- 37 seasons football coach
- 37 years strength training
  - 23 years strength coaching
- textbook author
  - six published policing textbooks (18 editions; 2 adopted by the military police)
  - two football coaching books
- interrogation case law author for *Reid and Associates* (website)
- former journal article author for *The Canadian Journal of Police and Security Services*
- former *Blue Line Magazine* case law writer

EDUCATION

- PhD—completed one-half of dissertation in police interrogation
- MEd—organizational leadership
- BSc—criminal justice
- Ontario Police College
  - recruit diploma
  - criminal investigation diploma
- Centre for Forensic Sciences
  - homicide/forensic science certificate

VOLUNTEER COMMUNITY SERVICE

- ▸ a Level 3 NCCP coach, Gino has coached football at five different levels; his offense and defense systems have been published
- ▸ head coach of the Niagara X-Men tackle football team that competes against American NCAA Division 3 JV teams
- ▸ founder of the Niagara Colts Football Club Inc., a non-profit organization, to help Canadian student athletes get football scholarships to continue their post-secondary playing careers

PHASE 1
Basic Investigative Strategies

The Decision-Making Path

PROBLEM ▶ information/evidence ▶ analytical thinking/reasoning ▶ strategy ▶ belief ▶ discretion ▶ SOLUTION

◀─── GAP ───▶

uncertainty ◀   ▶ certainty

Decision-Making Path = The Investigation

Policing is a problem-solving profession that requires rapid decision making (RDM) within the *reality of limitations*—limited time, limited information, limited resources, and limited self-protection. Front-line police officers must be able to solve problems within an environment of uncertainty and risk.

Front-line police officers respond to countless calls for service. Like fingerprints, no two calls are exactly the same. Each call for service is unique, and each one includes some extent of a *problem*. The nature of each problem is wide-ranging, and can include violence. All risk to public safety is a problem. Each problem needs a *solution*.

Regardless of the fact that each call for service is distinct, there is one common denominator: the *gap* between the problem and the solution. The gap separates the *uncertainty* of the problem and the *certainty* of the solution.

Problems are characterized by uncertainty—who caused the problem, why, how, where, and when, it was caused, and how it can be prevented in the future. The goal of problem solving is reaching a solution.

A solution is characterized by certainty. The gap separating the problem and the solution represents a decision-making path. It involves a complex interaction of obtaining information, processing that information, and deciding: (a) what the information means (interpretation), (b) what to do (strategy), and (c) how to do it (execution).[1]

PHASE 1 LEARNING OUTCOMES

The student will be able to:

- Define the concept of investigation
- Define "beliefs"
- Explain the "duty to investigate"
- Explain the roles of the police and prosecutors
- Explain investigative goals
- Explain "investigative negligence"

The decision-making path has five elements:

1. accumulating evidence (information emerging from observation and physical items),
2. using analytical thinking (deductive, inductive, and quantitative reasoning),
3. developing strategy (designing and executing plans),
4. forming a belief (aiming for a goal of "reasonable grounds"), and
5. using discretion.

The gap and the decision-making path represent an *investigation*. In reality, an investigation is a problem-solving process that involves a series of *decisions*. The key to informed decision making is information, called **evidence**. Decisions are made in relation to information (such as responding to existing information and seeking ways to obtain more information). The ultimate goal of investigative decision making is to be able to form a specific level of belief called **reasonable grounds**, meaning strong certainty. The belief of reasonable grounds is the key to "striking the balance"—the balance between protecting public safety and protecting privacy—that the criminal justice system strives for. The goal of front-line policing stems from that balance—preventing crime while preventing the arrest and prosecution of innocent people.[2]

The decision-making path diagram above summarizes the two main objectives of this book:

1. how to develop investigative strategies, designed to lawfully obtain evidence (information), and
2. how to reach solutions by applying analytical thinking and reasoning to form lawful beliefs, while using proper discretion.

This book is divided into four phases, and is accompanied by a unique website (**www.emp.ca/ arcaro/criminvestigation5E**). The site contains an ongoing case law literature review that expands on the topics taught in all four phases.

Phase 1 is a six-chapter series that explains basic investigative strategies. Each chapter starts with a case study to introduce the strategy that will be taught in the chapter. Minimal information is given to the reader in order to make the problem as real as possible, e.g., the dispatcher's radio broadcast and only the immediate observations made by the officer on arrival.

As the reader progresses to Chapter 6, he or she will see that the strategies interact to teach an investigative foundation. This foundation applies to *unlimited* investigations; it can be used to bridge the gap from "problem" to "solution" in any type of offence or occurrence.

Chapter 6 demonstrates how the strategies are applied by completing the investigation of the case study in Chapter 1.

As a practical exercise, the reader is challenged to complete the investigations in Chapters 2, 3, and 4 by applying the same strategies. In Chapter 5, the outcome of the case study is explained to demonstrate how this actual police investigation was completed by the officers involved. The reader is asked to analyze the outcome in relation to the strategies learned.

The crucial starting point of any criminal investigation involves the "first officer." This informal title refers to the first uniform patrol officer to arrive at a crime scene. First officer duties are emphasized in Phase 1.

CHAPTER 1
Investigative Competencies

LEARNER SUMMARY

"Unknown problem, 3227 Brockport Road. Unit to back."

This is a typical radio broadcast that you will receive as a front-line police officer on patrol. It is a simple statement but it sends a powerful message of *risk and uncertainty*. You have been informed of a problem. You are responsible for solving it but you are restricted by two limitations: limited time and limited information. An *investigation* is needed to obtain as much accurate information as possible in the shortest time possible to reach an *informed solution*.

This radio broadcast starts a life-and-death rapid decision-making process. Each decision determines the extent of your safety, the safety of many other people, and the investigative pathway that you will take.

Policing is a problem-solving job. As a front-line patrol officer, you will respond to and investigate a wide range of occurrences. Some will be simple, others will be complex. The degree of urgency varies. Calls for service are classified by priority as (1) "in-progress" and (2) "belated" (not in-progress).

In your career, you will respond to countless calls of "intrusion alarm" activated. An *intrusion alarm* communicates a simple message: an offence is "in-progress" at that place. However, the frequency of false alarms creates the *alarm paradox*. A paradox refers to two sides of a concept or rule that are contradictory or conflicting. It means there is both a positive and a negative element. An alarm call warns you of potential imminent danger, but the volume of false alarms promotes complacency. Complacency is a harmful comfort zone. It puts you and the public in danger because being complacent negatively affects decision making. Complacency makes you soft. It prevents you from working at peak performance.

When you arrive, you assume a formal role—"first officer." The first officer has a number of responsibilities, all intended to achieve the overriding investigative goal of protecting the public while preventing wrongful prosecution. Investigative strategies govern first officer decision making.

Every profession includes the potential of and consequences for negligence. This sets the "accountability bar." Policing is no different. Not all negligence is equal. There are various degrees that are classified as either intentional or unintentional. The consequences for intentional police negligence have always been covered by the *Criminal Code*. However, before 2007 there was no consequence for "investigative negligence." The landmark case *Hill v. Hamilton-Wentworth Regional Police Services Board* (2007), released by the Supreme Court of Canada (S.C.C.), adds civil liability as a consequence for "investigative negligence" and sets the contemporary "investigative standards" bar of accountability.

Every police officer is an investigator, whether in the patrol branch or in the detective branch. There are a number of investigative "competencies" that define the investigators personality. "Competencies" refer to skills and personality traits needed to perform a specific task. Contrary to popular myth, every recruit must start his or her career in the uniform patrol branch. No one is hired as a detective. The only difference between a recruit's competencies and a detective's competencies is the *extent of expertise*. Although the concept of "expertise" is complex, the core is simple: expertise develops along a pathway of experience in the uniform patrol branch.

Case Study 1.1

3:00 a.m. Radio broadcast: "Intrusion alarm, Bravo Electronics, 3227 Brockport Street."

3:05 a.m. Arrival. You are the first officer to arrive at this commercial premises. You determine that the offence of break and enter with intent was committed. This offence is dual procedure and temporarily classified as indictable.

3:28 a.m. Resume patrol to search the surrounding area.

You see a pedestrian walking normally on a sidewalk 500 meters from the crime scene. You recognize him from past investigations, and you know he has a criminal record for theft. Twenty-eight minutes have elapsed since the time of offence.

A rapid decision is needed at this point, called **belief classification**. The goal of belief classification is to determine the connection between the pedestrian and the crime. There are four classifications of beliefs that may link a person to an offence:

1. find committing,
2. reasonable grounds,
3. mere suspicion, and
4. arbitrary (no belief).

What belief do you have regarding the pedestrian and the crime?

INTRODUCTION

Case Study 1.1 examines the common front-line occurrence of break and enter at a commercial premise during which an alarm is activated, and, the offender(s) leaves before police arrive. The pedestrian creates an *investigative bind*—the connection between the pedestrian and the break and enter has to be classified as either "reasonable grounds" or "mere suspicion."

The definition of reasonable grounds includes (1) a confession by the offender to any person, (2) at least one credible eyewitness, or (3) circumstantial evidence exceeding mere suspicion that leads to one logical conclusion—that the person committed the offence. Confessions and one credible eyewitness clearly constitute reasonable grounds; circumstantial evidence does not. Often, the line separating reasonable grounds and mere suspicion is blurred.

An investigative bind occurs when only circumstantial evidence exists. The bind is caused because:

- Circumstantial evidence may constitute either reasonable grounds *or* mere suspicion.
- There is no concrete formula that can be used to classify circumstantial evidence as reasonable grounds or mere suspicion.
- Circumstantial evidence includes limitless situations.

Having only circumstantial evidence forces an officer to make a decision. Within a limited time frame, limited information must be analyzed rapidly to form a conclusion or opinion about a belief—do you have reasonable grounds or only mere suspicion that the pedestrian committed the break and enter? The answer will determine your next decision.

This case study serves as a base point of reference for how to classify circumstantial evidence in order to form a belief. A base point of reference:

- refers to a simple, concrete set of circumstances that form a context for learning;
- represents a learning base—the starting point for learning how to apply complex investigative strategies; and
- dramatically reduces the investigative learning curve by simplifying basic investigative concepts and teaching how they interact to form realistic investigative strategies.

Instructions

You must make a rapid decision with regard to the pedestrian. At this point in the investigation, you have either reasonable grounds, mere suspicion, or no belief that the pedestrian is involved in the break and enter. Continue reading the remainder of Phase 1 to learn how applying investigative theory development can help you make this decision.

INVESTIGATION

> The dictum that it is better for ten guilty persons to escape than for one innocent person to go to jail has long been a cornerstone of our criminal justice system.[3]
> —Supreme Court of Canada in *Hill v. Hamilton-Wentworth Regional Police Services Board* (2007)

The starting point is defining the word **investigation** as it relates to law enforcement. An investigation is a problem-solving process intended to solve a specific law enforcement problem by answering six base questions:

1. Did an offence occur?
2. If so, what specific offence was committed?
3. Where did the offence happen?
4. When did the offence happen?
5. Exactly how did the offence happen?
6. Who committed the offence?

■ **KEY POINTS**

▸ These six questions represent the general objective of a law enforcement investigation. This general objective leads to the intended outcome or solution of an investigation. The overall goal of law enforcement is public safety, including officer safety. Achieving the investigative objectives achieves this overall goal.

▸ The intended outcome represents a precise reconstruction of an occurrence.

▸ The reconstruction of an occurrence forms a belief.

▸ There are four classifications of law enforcement beliefs that correspond with a level of certainty: The four beliefs are:

1. find committing (100 percent certainty)
2. reasonable grounds (strong certainty)
3. mere suspicion (weak certainty)
4. no belief (zero certainty)

Reasonable grounds is the important level of belief. This phrase used to be called *reasonable and probable grounds (R&PG)*. It was condensed to "reasonable grounds" but the definition and meaning remained the same.

It is the level of belief that mobilizes a number of police authorities (also called *police powers*), including: (1) arrest with and without a warrant, (2) search and seizure with and without a warrant, and (3) laying an Information (charging an offender).

Duty to Investigate

Where do the police get the authority to investigate crime? The Supreme Court of Canada answered this question in *Hill v. Hamilton-Wentworth Regional Police Services Board* (2007), stating that:

1. Police officers have multiple duties.
2. There is "no question that one of them is the duty to investigate crime."
3. The duty to investigate crime originates in common law and in provincial statutes that govern policing. For example, in Ontario, the duty to investigate is authorized in s. 42 of the *Police Services Act*,[4] which describes and lists the general duties of a police officer. According to the S.C.C., "although "investigating crime" is not specifically listed, several of the listed duties are related to, or form part of, the police investigation of crime. Section 42(1) reads as follows:

> 42(1) The duties of a police officer include,
>   (a) preserving the peace;
>   (b) preventing crimes and other offences and providing assistance and encouragement to other persons in their prevention;
>   (c) assisting victims of crime;
>   (d) apprehending criminals and other offenders and others who may lawfully be taken into custody;
>   (e) laying charges, prosecuting and participating in prosecutions;
>   (f) executing warrants that are to be executed by police officers and performing related duties;

      (g) performing the lawful duties that the chief of police assigns;

      (h) in the case of a municipal police force and in the case of an agreement under section 10 [agreement for provision of police services by O. P.P.], enforcing municipal by-laws; and

      (i) completing the prescribed training.

Police and Prosecutor Roles

The police work closely with the Crown Attorney. It is important to define their roles in relation to investigations.

The S.C.C. clarified these roles in *Hill v. Hamilton-Wentworth Regional Police Services Board* (2007)[5] by stating that:

1. Both police officers and prosecutors make decisions about whether the suspect should stand trial. However, the nature of their decision differs.
2. The police role is "gathering and evaluating evidence." The police task is "fact-based."
3. Prosecutors are "concerned mainly with whether the evidence the police have gathered will support a conviction at law."
4. "The fact-based investigative character of the police task" separates it from the Crown Attorney's role.

Investigative Goals

> When an innocent person is convicted of a crime that he or she did not commit, it is undeniable that justice has failed in the most fundamental sense.[6]
> —Supreme Court of Canada in *Hill v. Hamilton-Wentworth Regional Police Services Board* (2007)

Front-line police investigations have two goals that interact:

1. public and officer safety
2. correctly forming reasonable grounds about who committed an offence

The primary goal is called the *public safety goal*. It represents the main aim of any investigation. The secondary goal is called the *investigative goal*. Both goals are prevention strategies. The public safety goal prevents death and injury. The investigative goal prevents wrongful convictions, prosecutions, and arrests.

INVESTIGATIVE LIABILITY: INVESTIGATIVE NEGLIGENCE

Front-line law enforcement has unique challenges and demands. First and foremost of these is the risk to life. Death is an occupational hazard in law enforcement. Second, there are statutory and civil liabilities associated with negligent investigations.

Unlike many other professions, policing is governed by provincial statutes (except the RCMP, a national body) and civil law that create liabilities for negligence. Police services statutes create offences such as "Neglect of duty." Police officers may be charged, prosecuted, and convicted for wide-ranging negligent conduct. Civilly, officers may be sued for false arrests and prosecuting innocent people.

In October 2007, the Supreme Court of Canada added civil liability as a result for negligent investigations. In the landmark case *Hill v. Hamilton-Wentworth Regional Police Services Board* (2007), the S.C.C. ruled that the police may be sued if an investigation is negligently conducted.[7] This civil liability for investigative negligence is a protection against wrongful accusations and wrongful convictions. Note: an acquittal based on insufficient evidence is not enough to sue for investigative negligence. The accused has to prove he was wrongfully charged—he was not the suspect.

This groundbreaking rule makes Canada the first and only common-law jurisdiction in the world that allows persons wrongly accused or wrongly prosecuted to sue the police for investigative negligence.[8]

Investigative Standards

In addition to creating the investigative negligence liability in *Hill v. Hamilton-Wentworth Regional Police Services Board* (2007),[9] the S.C.C. raised the bar by establishing an **investigative standard of care** that the police must meet in every investigation.

This standard is defined as using reasonable investigative practices and strategies to form reasonable grounds before charging an offender. Conversely, using unreasonable investigative practices, or laying an Information based on mere suspicion, constitutes substandard investigation. In other words, charging a person without evidence that properly constitutes reasonable grounds is considered substandard, and is now subject to a civil suit for negligent investigation.

The investigative standard is not new. This case does not change the definition of reasonable grounds. However, it reinforces the importance of using proper investigative practices and provides wrongfully accused persons with a civil court remedy to substandard investigations.

The definition of "investigative standard of care" is abstract, lacking concrete guidelines. However, the circumstances of this landmark case serve as a point of reference for what does *not* make up a substandard investigation. This case involved wrongful prosecution and conviction. During the investigation, reasonable grounds were formed based on a number of investigative techniques, including:

- a Crime Stoppers tip,
- identification of the accused person by a police officer, based on a surveillance photo,
- witness interviewing, and
- a photo lineup.

The photo lineup and some aspects of witness interviewing were not conducted with total efficiency. The photo lineup was biased (it consisted of 12 photos, but 11 of them depicted persons that were not of the same race as the accused person). As well, the police failed to investigate **exculpatory evidence** (evidence that proved innocence). Despite these mistakes, the investigation was not deemed "substandard" or "negligent." The police investigation was reasonable. This point of reference will become the most important feature of this case. It creates a minimum standard for reasonable investigations, and will be used as a point of comparison in future cases where investigative negligence is the issue.

Refer to the accompanying website (**www.emp.ca/arcaro/criminvestigation5E**) for an extensive analysis of the *Hill* case.

Reactive/Proactive Investigations

A law enforcement investigation is mobilized in either a *reactive* or *proactive* way.

"Reactive" means that the police responded to a call for service. The investigation was initiated by someone other than the police, such as an individual citizen. An example of a reactive investigation is a radio broadcast of an intrusion alarm. "Proactive" means that the police initiated the investigation—no citizen report was needed. The most common example of a proactive investigation is an impaired driving investigation started by a police officer witnessing the offence.

Although the police witness a number of offences and make observations, they do not "find committing" the majority of offences that they investigate. Consequently, *forming reasonable grounds without witnessing the offence* is the most common intended investigative outcome. Essentially, after protecting the public, the investigative goal is to form reasonable grounds based on the observations of other witnesses and the finding of physical items.

INVESTIGATIVE DEVELOPMENT: THE INVESTIGATOR PERSONALITY

A *profession* is an occupation, vocation, or career where specialized knowledge is applied.[10] A *professional* is a highly skilled worker who requires extensive training, formal study, and practical experience.[11] Policing is a profession; police officers have to be professionals.

All professions feature three elements. Professions:

1. have two *performance borders*,
2. are composed of *essential competencies*, and
3. can develop *experts*.[12]

The two performance borders are (a) entry-level, and (b) expert. There are countless performance levels in between. Essential competencies are compulsory skills, abilities, and traits needed to perform entry-level professional tasks. An entry-level professional is a *novice*. Experts are professionals who have developed advanced competencies at countless levels of expertise.[13]

An investigation is the result of a team effort. It is the product of interaction among generalists (uniform patrol officers) and specialists (such as detectives, forensic officers, forensic scientists, surveillance officers, and SWAT/tactical officers). The size of the team corresponds with the size of the police organization. Every investigation requires coordination and leadership.

An investigator is a problem-solver. Every investigation is a problem-solving task, ranging from simple to complex. The term "investigator" does not refer exclusively to specialists. Every police officer, including front-line uniform patrol officers, is an investigator. The only differences are (1) the level of investigative development involved, and (2) the type of problem that needs to be solved.

No one is born with investigative skills. Investigators are *developed* by a long, complicated process involving growth and maturity. Professional development and maturation is a path toward *self-actualization*—the realization of a person's full potential. All investigator development starts at the entry-level stage; every police officer starts his or her career as a novice.

The uniform patrol branch is the place where investigative development occurs, and cannot be by-passed. The uniform patrol branch is the front line of policing. It is where you learn how to make increasingly complex decisions under severe stress. How far you develop depends on a wide range of factors, including (1) the volume and type of front-line experience, (2) the extent of your formal training, and (3) the type of mentoring you receive. The strength of your investigative development is tied to the strength of these three "base" factors—what you learn, who you learn from, and what you do with it. Contrary to the popular myth that all police careers are created equal, no two are the same. An individual police career is shaped by a specific socialization process, referring to post-hiring events and persons that influence every aspect of your investigative career.[14]

Novice officers are expected to solve simple problems by forming simple strategies, making simple decisions while learning from and being mentored by expert coach officers and veteran colleagues. Novice performance is restricted by limited experience. Limited practical experience restricts the honing of five skills and tasks:

1. processing large volumes of information,
2. rapid decision making,
3. adapting to rapidly changing situations,
4. simplifying complex information, and
5. forecasting all worst-case scenarios.

These will be developed as officers advance in their careers.

The Eight Essential Competencies

Police recruits/novices must have the minimum qualifications of strong moral character plus eight essential competencies.

Strong moral character is the most important personality trait for police recruits. It is a legal, non-negotiable requirement. Statutes that govern all levels of policing make strong moral character a mandatory, minimum-standard requirement for police hiring.

Strong moral character means having core beliefs based on knowing right from wrong, and acting in accordance with those beliefs. Police candidates must prove this trait by presenting their past conduct as evidence of their future conduct. The future obviously cannot be predicted with complete certainty. However, police recruiters need evidence that proves, with reasonable belief, that a candidate will not act with *weak* moral character after being hired as a police officer. The evidence of past conduct is generally divided into two streams of evidence: (1) existence or absence of a criminal record, and (2) opinions of persons who have relevant familiarity with the candidate. Weak moral character prevents police hiring. Recruiters cannot hire candidates with weak moral character because they would be violating statutory requirements and jeopardizing public safety.

The eight essential entry-level competencies are:

1. analytical thinking
2. self-confidence
3. communication
4. flexibility/valuing diversity
5. self-control
6. relationship building
7. achievement orientation
8. physical/medical fitness

These competencies represent the *police recruit personality*. They ensure that police recruits are simple problem-solvers, meaning that they are:

▸ low-volume processors, who are able to analyze non-complex information and circumstances;

▸ simple decision-makers;

▸ simple strategists, who are able to form *general* investigative strategies but will have difficulty improvising by adapting to changing circumstances; and

▸ capable of predicting to some degree, but not all, future consequences, referring to worst-case scenarios.

Expert Competencies

The expert investigator personality develops from the recruit personality, through the combined effects of practical experience and advanced formal learning and training. The expert personality is composed of stronger moral character plus twelve total competencies:

▸ eight *advanced* competencies (the eight essential entry-level competencies, now at an advanced level), and

▸ four *deep* competencies:

1. volume processing,
2. leadership,
3. coordinating, and
4. mentoring.[15]

These twelve competencies allow the expert investigator to **RISE**, referring to these four advanced skills:

▸ **R**apid decision making (RDM)
▸ **I**mprovisation
▸ **S**implifying complexities
▸ **E**liminating the worst consequences

Competencies interact; they work together in a complex performance network. The expert personality represents a career goal. It represents what you want to become, and what skills you must develop.

Figure 1.1   Investigative Development Model

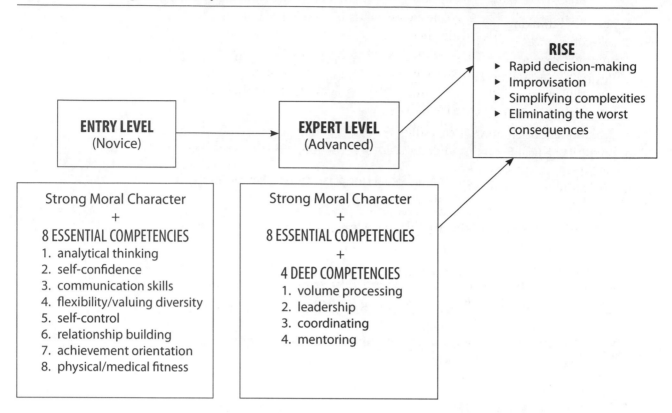

THE EIGHT ESSENTIAL COMPETENCIES: DEFINITIONS

Each competency has a formal definition.[16]

1. **Analytical thinking** is defined as:

    ▷ identifying key elements in complex situations; or

    ▷ identifying patterns or connections between situations, persons, or events.

    Analytical thinking refers to processing information and observations (evidence) for the purpose of recognizing the specific nature of the problem (e.g., a specific offence) with the goal of forming a strategy and executing the strategy to solve the problem.

    Analytical thinking is decision making. The decisions include what beliefs to form, what plans to make, and what actions to take. Analytical thinking starts with information and ends in a decision. Analytical thinking involves three types of reasoning:

    a. *deductive* reasoning (defined as the ability to process information and draw the right conclusions): Police officers have to process evidence (e.g., observations and physical items), translate their meaning, and form a belief.

    b. *inductive* reasoning (defined as the ability to process information and identify connections and common traits): Police officers obtain a significant volume of information during investigations, often in unstructured order. They have to structure that information by identifying links that create a context—a big picture of how the information correctly fits together.

c. *quantitative* reasoning (defined as the ability to apply basic math to solve problems): To create context, police officers must be able to add, subtract, multiply, and divide numbers in order to determine facts, including rates of speed and distances.

Constable selection tests, including the PATI (Police Analytical Thinking Inventory) test, measure candidates' analytical thinking skills by evaluating the three types of reasoning.[17]

2. **Self-confidence** is defined as:

   ▷ belief in one's abilities, opinions, and judgments, or

   ▷ understanding one's strengths and limitations, or

   ▷ the ability to handle failure constructively.

Policing requires a balance between knowing when you do and do not need assistance in completing a job. The balance is between two expectations: you will be expected to do simple jobs alone without always asking for assistance, but you will be expected to seek advice when complex jobs are beyond your novice experience. The entry-level standard of self-confidence refers to:

   ▷ the self-awareness of knowing when you are capable of doing something yourself and knowing when to get assistance,

   ▷ being able to learn from failure as opposed to being destroyed by it, and

   ▷ accurately knowing when your opinions are properly justified.

3. **Communication** is defined as:

   ▷ the ability to accurately express oneself, or

   ▷ the ability to present information clearly and accurately, both verbally or in writing.

Most police work involves public speaking and writing. The type of public speaking needed in police work is unique because the stakes are often very high. Your verbal communication skills will be required to solve hostile situations, interview witnesses, question suspects, and testify in court. Research has shown that next to the fear of death, the fear of public speaking is the greatest source of stress for people. The inherent risk associated with police work adds to the stress of public speaking needed in front-line policing. Equally strong skills are needed for report writing. Recruits are expected to have above-average writing skills to meet the demands of police report writing.

4. **Flexibility/valuing diversity** is defined as:

   ▷ the ability to adapt to a variety of situations, individuals, and groups, or

   ▷ having sensitivity to different and opposing perspectives, or

   ▷ the ability to work effectively with a wide cross-section of community members (of different backgrounds, cultures, and socioeconomic status).

Policing is teamwork. You will be assigned to a platoon. You will not be able to choose who you will work with and where you will work. This means you have to work with people who have different personalities, beliefs, and opinions. You will have to debate, justify, and convince in an intelligent manner.

5. **Self-control** is defined as:
   ▷ keeping emotions under control when provoked or facing stress or hostility, or
   ▷ taking constructive actions to deal with situations.

   Policing requires a balance between assertiveness and tolerance. You will be exposed to various levels of stress ranging from immediate life-threatening risk to simple nasty name-calling. You cannot underreact to the first one and overreact to the latter.

6. **Relationship building** is defined as the development and maintenance of a network of contacts.

   Police work is not done in isolation from the public. Successful police work requires partnerships with both the criminal and non-criminal communities in order to build an essential information database of *intelligence*, and to perform certain tasks that require expertise.

7. **Achievement orientation** is defined as:
   ▷ a focus on attaining a successful outcome,
   ▷ striving to improve performance, or
   ▷ committing oneself to achieving self-established or organizational goals and standards.

   The taxpaying public expects that every police officer have the strongest possible work ethic. Crime victims expect police officers to be tireless workers. A strong work ethic is synonymous with a personal desire to self-actualize. In policing, you will have goals set for you, and you will also be expected to set your own goals. Achievement orientation refers to habitual excellence and peak performance.

8. **Physical/medical fitness** is defined as a level of physical fitness that allows you to meet the demands of front-line policing.

   The challenges of police work create enormous physical demands. Physical fitness is vital for self-protection. Officers must keep in mind the Latin phrase *anima sana in corpore sano*—a sound mind in a sound body.

THE EIGHT EXPERT COMPETENCIES: DEFINITIONS

The expert personality is composed of *stronger moral character* plus eight advanced competencies that result in four deep competencies, allowing the expert to RISE. In general, experts think faster and make better decisions than novices.

During your policing career, your moral strength will be challenged repeatedly and with growing complexity. This experience will cause you to develop a higher-level moral reasoning, allowing complicated ethical decision making in situations that challenge your personal integrity.

1. Advanced analytical thinking involves the ability to process greater volumes of information.

2. Advanced self-confidence involves a deeper understanding of one's strengths and weaknesses in direct relation to a specific task in order to make rapid decisions that have greater potential consequences. It also involves the ability to work under extreme stress and to overcome adversity, failure, and disappointment. How far we go in life is directly related to how we handle disappointments. Experts view adversity as a challenge, learn from failures, and are not defeated or overwhelmed by disappointment.

3. Advanced communication involves the strengthening of three types of investigative communication skills: (a) *witness interview skills* (eliciting maximum volume of information and accurately evaluating credibility), (b) *interrogation skills* (eliciting admissible confessions), and (c) *complex court testimony.*

4. Advanced flexibility/valuing diversity involves a unique form of leadership that permits the expert investigator to both coordinate and participate within a rapidly changing environment. This means adaptive/active leadership—rapidly and concurrently working on changing personnel while setting goals, creating and executing strategy, and evaluating performance. An expert investigator often leads from the field, not the sidelines.

5. Advanced self-control involves a maturity forged by repeated exposure to unruly, uncooperative people and stressful situations, combined with the skill of improving or changing the people and events. An expert investigator cannot be overwhelmed by emotional distraction and stress that can break investigative focus. This trait is linked to adaptive/active leadership.

6. Advanced relationship building involves the development and management of two types of networks: (a) confidential informants, and (b) task experts (e.g., in the areas of science, technology, or banking). Informant development and management is a cornerstone of investigative expertise. Confidential informants usually emerge from the criminal community. They inform the police of what has happened and, more importantly, what will happen. Task experts are crucial simply because while expert investigators are experts in police work, they are not experts in wide-ranging tasks and environments where crime occurs.

7. Advanced achievement orientation involves possessing a tireless work ethic characterized by the habitual commitment and ability to achieve both *quantity* and *quality* goals. Linked to adaptive/active leadership, this skill represents an influential work ethic that consistently achieves personal and team goals of growing complexity. It is a form of leadership that demonstrates a seamless path toward reaching one's full potential—personally and professionally. Investigators have to be multitaskers. They often are assigned to a number of investigations, rather than one case at a time. Heavy workloads are common. Solving one crime doesn't allow time to celebrate and reflect.

8. Advanced physical/medical fitness involves further commitment to both sound mind and sound body.

The eight advanced competencies result in the following four deep competencies:

1. **Volume processing** refers to the ability to accurately analyze large volumes of complex information and observations because of past experience. You will become a volume processor after you have experienced a wide range of complex investigations. Experience gives you familiarity with multiple circumstances, allowing you to view a situation as a whole instead of by its separate parts.
2. **Leadership** refers to the ability to elicit peak performance from a group of people, including yourself; to achieve consistently complex goals.
3. **Coordinating** refers to a specific type of leadership that requires the ability to organize teams, set goals, design strategies and plans, instruct others, direct activities, and evaluate performance.
4. **Mentoring** refers to a specific type of coordinating where protégés are developed to full potential by means of expert instruction.[18]

The four deep competencies allow experts to RISE, referring to the following four expert skills:

1. **Rapid decision making (RDM)** refers to the ability to accurately design and select investigative strategies while being restricted by time limitations. RDM allows you to correctly decide what has to be done within seconds, without the benefit of research and consultation.
2. **Improvisation** refers to a specific type of RDM. It is the skill of modifying a general strategy to respond to rapidly changing circumstances. Improvisation means knowing exactly when to change plans in order to respond to a changing situation. Investigations involve uncertainty. You cannot always design concrete strategies that fit every situation without having to change the plan. Investigations require the ability to modify a general plan, in response to changing situations. Novices can devise general strategies and plans, but improvisation is a specific form of RDM that is needed in order to respond to the demands that accompany uncertainty.
3. **Simplifying complexities** refers to a *prerequisite* for RDM. Experts can look at complex circumstances and do two things: (a) they can simplify it for themselves, and (b) they can simplify it for others. Experts do not ignore simplicity. They create it by focusing only on what is relevant.
4. **Eliminating the worst consequence** This is the *product* of RDM. It allows an expert to see what others cannot. Experts can accurately forecast every worst-case scenario. They can predict what will happen as a result of what is or is not done.[19]

The "10-Year/Decade" Rule

A common question asked by police candidates is, "Can I start as a homicide detective?" Of course, the answer is "no." Every police career starts at the uniform patrol branch, the real front line of law enforcement. The reason for this is the "10-year/decade" rule. Research shows that at least 10 years of experience is needed to become an expert. In 2006, landmark research headed by Dr. Anders Ericsson showed that ordinary experience does not develop expertise. Instead, expertise requires deliberate, practical experience of growing complexity, under the guidance of expert mentors or coaches.[20] Conversely, ordinary practice means doing the same thing repeatedly, with no growing complexity. This has two implications for police careers: (1) a lengthy uniform career is a major benefit to becoming a specialist, and (2) doing the same thing over and over, without any added challenge, will not allow you to improve. In other words, simply showing up for work is not enough to gain expertise. Performance matters.

COMMENTARY

I have asked hundreds of police candidates about their career goals. The majority of answers have included such roles as homicide detective, SWAT, CSI, profiler, canine, and undercover. I have never heard the answer, "uniform patrol branch." I have often heard negative comments about this branch, from distinctly different sources. A high-ranking police administrator once told me that, "Some guys get promoted. Some guys spend their life as night watchmen." A student, in preparation for a police ride-along interview, told me, "I don't want to be one of those guys who spends their whole career in a cruiser."

There is absolutely nothing wrong with big goals, but denigrating the front line of policing is inexcusable. Candidates must remember where they came from; recruits have to *earn* the right to look past uniform patrol.

Uniform patrol is undoubtedly the most challenging and demanding job in policing. The reason is simple—it has the most risk with the least amount of preparation time. The uniform patrol constable is the first responder, and must constantly work in a dangerous environment characterized by both limited information and limited time in which to make decisions. In other words, the first responder has to deal with the dangers of *uncertainty*—not knowing when the next call to action will be, not knowing whether an offender will be armed, and not knowing all the details of a situation. Regardless, uniform patrol officers are expected to make rapid decisions in order to solve emergencies.

There are a number of reasons why the uniform patrol branch is not respected. The entertainment industry misleads viewers about the reality of policing. We are experiencing an age of entitlement and instant gratification. But perhaps the strongest reason has involved the removal of the rank of cadet. In 1975, most recruits were hired at age 18 as cadets, the lowest rank in policing. You had to get *promoted* to the rank of constable. Consequently, uniform patrol constable was viewed as a *goal*, not a necessary evil to be avoided. You were cautioned about looking too far ahead. If you announced your desire to get transferred out of the uniform branch too soon, the wrong message would be sent—you would be classified as too scared or too lazy to do uniform patrol work. You were constantly reminded that, "For everything there is a season." In other words, let your performance do the talking and don't try to speed up a natural process. Things happen with time.

Here is some advice: Police services, bring back the cadet rank. Make front-line policing something to aspire to, not to dread and avoid. Recruits, enjoy the uniform patrol branch. It's the best place to be. You will learn more than you can imagine. It will shape your entire career. Once you get promoted to a specialist job, you'll miss it.

Case Study 1.1 Investigation

In Chapter 6, beginning with the radio broadcast, the first officer's investigation of this break and enter offence is explained by applying the strategies and investigative theories discussed in Chapters 1–5. The actual conclusion to Case Study 1.1 is found at the end of Chapter 6.

ENDNOTES

1. G. Arcaro, "Interrogation Best Practices," Ph.D. research material, University of Regina, 2007; and G. Arcaro, "A Workable Future for Ontario Community Colleges," M.Ed. thesis, Brock University, 2005.
2. G. Arcaro, "Balancing Public Safety and Individual Freedom: Examining the Investigative Paradox" (2005) vol. 3, no. 3 *Canadian Journal of Police and Security Services.*
3. W. Blackstone, *Commentaries on the Laws of England* (1769), Book IV, chap. 27, at 352, as in *Hill v. Hamilton-Wentworth Regional Police Services Board,* 2007 SCC 41.
4. R.S.O. 1990, c. P.15.
5. *Hill v. Hamilton-Wentworth Regional Police Services Board,* supra note 3.
6. Ibid.
7. Ibid.
8. L. Sokolov, "The Police Can Be Sued for Negligence" (Spring 2008) vol. 9 *Association in Defence of the Wrongfully Convicted.*
9. *Hill v. Hamilton-Wentworth Regional Police Services Board,* supra note 3.
10. *Oxford English Dictionary,* 2nd ed. (New York: Oxford University Press, 1989).
11. Ibid.
12. Ontario Association of Chiefs of Police, "Programs: Constable Selection," http://www.oacp.on.ca/content/programs/constable_selection.html.
13. D. Leonard and W.C. Swap, *Deep Smarts: How to Cultivate and Transfer Enduring Business Wisdom* (Boston: Harvard Business School Press, 2005).
14. Ibid.
15. Ibid.
16. Ontario Association of Chiefs of Police, supra note 12.
17. Ibid.
18. Leonard and Swap, supra note 13.
19. Ibid.
20. A. Ericsson et al., *The Cambridge Handbook of Expertise and Expert Performance* (Cambridge, UK: Cambridge University Press, 2006).

CHAPTER 2

The Investigative Decision-Making Model: The "Base" IDM

LEARNER SUMMARY

In reality, every investigation emerges from a problem—a problem is the starting point of each investigation. The solution is the goal and the conclusion. The gap between the problem and the solution is a decision-making process that represents an investigation. In other words, all investigations are composed of a series of decisions.

The "base" investigative decision-making (IDM) model is a structured framework, executed by an investigative team that guides the investigation. The goal of the base IDM is to solve the problem. The base IDM consists of a relationship among seven principles that interact within an investigative team environment.

Figure 2.1 on the following page illustrates the base IDM model that will be explained in this chapter.

Case Study 2.1

You are a uniform officer on patrol.

7:00 p.m. Radio broadcast: "Alarm—robbery in progress, Alpha Corner Store, 4936 St. John Street."

7:02 p.m. Arrival.

▸ No one is seen outside the building.

▸ You can see inside the building, and only one person is inside.

▸ You enter and find Wendy (30) alone behind the counter.

▸ Wendy is Asian and cannot speak English fluently.

▸ She immediately informs you that she was robbed and points to the front door, indicating that the offender left prior to your arrival.

Instructions

1. Without reading further, and without knowing any other information, answer this question: "Was this a random crime?" Explain your answer.

2. After reading Phase 1 (Chapters 1–6), explain the following:

   ▷ all of your first officer responsibilities, beginning immediately after the radio broadcast,

   ▷ your investigative strategy, and

   ▷ your theory, applying the Basic Investigative Sequence (found in Chapter 3).

Figure 2.1   Base Investigative Decision-Making (IDM) Model

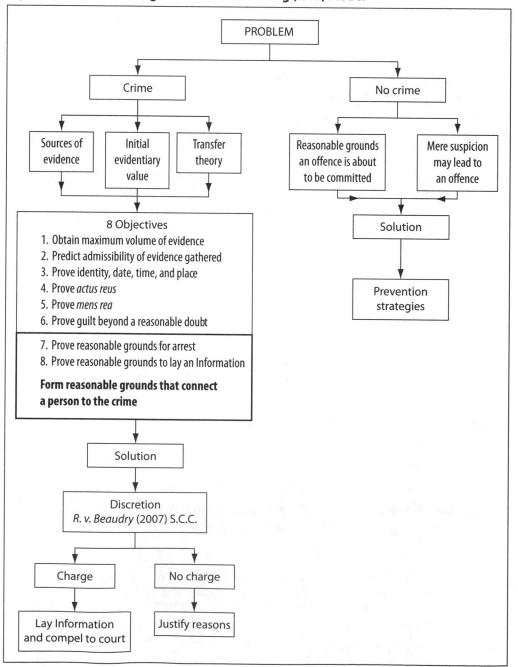

THE TEAM CONCEPT

Front-line officers work *double-crew* (with a partner) or *single-crew* (without a partner). Patrol officers work within a *team* that starts with their platoon of fellow uniform patrol officers and extends to specialists in other police branches. All police organizations are teams. Consequently, even when officers work single-crew, they never work in isolation.

All police services, regardless of size, are complex organizations composed of extensive human and physical resources. Police personnel bring wide-ranging skills and experiences to the organization. They are classified as either *generalists* or *specialists*, assigned to different *branches* within the organization. A branch is defined as a unit of personnel assigned to specific tasks and goals. The only difference between a generalist and a specialist is assignment and, in some cases, experience—not the extent of skill. Both have to be highly skilled performers in order to complete their assignments.

Investigations are a team effort. The nature of the investigation determines the nature of the investigative team. The following discusses the most common branches.

Generalists

UNIFORM BRANCH

The uniform branch is the front line of policing. It is composed of patrol officers, who hold the rank of constable. They are assigned to platoons of various sizes. Generally, platoons are supervised by *patrol sergeants* and *staff sergeants*. A patrol sergeant is a mobile supervisor. The staff sergeant is the officer in charge of a police station's "front desk."

Uniform patrol constables are generalists. The term "generalist" refers to assignments and primary tasks; it does not refer to substandard or inferior knowledge and skills. Patrol officers are first responders who require extensive general knowledge of laws and investigative strategies, but this does not mean that they never become experts if they remain in the uniform branch. The "ten-year/decade" rule[1] applies to uniform patrol officers—veteran uniform officers are experts at front-line policing. Although uniform officers are not formally classified as specialists, they have to know as much as possible about as many laws and strategies as possible.

Uniform branch responsibilities include:

- ▸ provincial investigations, including motor vehicle collision investigations, traffic enforcement, liquor offences, trespassing, and mental health investigations,
- ▸ municipal bylaw investigations, and
- ▸ criminal investigations.

The uniform officer's role includes first response duties, preliminary investigation duties, and in some cases, completing the entire investigation. Uniform officers usually complete entire investigations only when (a) an arrest is made at or in close proximity to the crime scene, (b) the offence is not a major crime, or (c) the size of the police service allows for or demands it.

Expert communication skills are crucial to uniform branch success. Report writing is arguably the most repeated task, and verbal communication is necessary to solve the countless investigative problems a first officer encounters.

The uniform branch is unique in that its personnel have the widest range of experience. It is the only branch in the police profession that contains both novices and experts. Other branches have novices particular to a specialty branch, but these officers are not novices to policing. Uniform branch novices are new recruits who work with coach officers. A complex socialization process shapes each officer's individual skill development. A wide range of experts emerge from the uniform branch, corresponding with the volume and nature of their front-line experience. In other words, a veteran uniform officer becomes an expert at his or her job, just as a specialist becomes an expert in a specialty branch after a decade of experience.[2]

"FIRST OFFICER"

This formal designation refers to the first uniform patrol officer to arrive at a crime scene. This designation is significant because of the list of responsibilities and tasks that the first officer must ensure are performed. The list represents a series of concrete goals that must be achieved. The first officer is a *coordinator*—a person who gets things done. He or she may delegate tasks, or perform each task himself or herself.

First officer responsibilities include:

- witness interviews (witness management) to determine validity, and maintenance of an "inner circle" list, referring to a list of potential suspects that corresponds with the Basic Investigative Sequence,
- radio broadcasts to other officers,
- crime scene perimeter searches, and
- crime scene protection.

Specialists

A specialty branch refers to any branch outside uniform policing. Specialist branches have a narrower focus and require more specific skills and knowledge than the uniform branch. The most common specialty branches are:

- Criminal Investigation Branch (C.I.B.),
- Forensics/Identification,
- Drug Unit,
- Intelligence,
- Surveillance, and
- SWAT.

CRIMINAL INVESTIGATION BRANCH (C.I.B.)

Commonly referred to as *detectives*, C.I.B. officers investigate criminal offences beyond the preliminary stage through to completion. They are assigned all major and non-major crimes that are beyond the scope of the uniform branch. The three most important skills, among many, needed to excel as a detective are:

1. interrogation,
2. witness interviews, and
3. informant development and management.

C.I.B. officers wear business attire, but do not conceal their profession. They are not "undercover" officers.

FORENSICS/IDENTIFICATION

Among other roles, this branch is responsible for crime scene examination. Tasks include:

- searching crime scenes for and collecting physical evidence that has been transferred, including impressions (e.g., fingerprints, shoe prints, tire prints, tool marks) and bodily substances;
- examining items recovered from other places, for transferred evidence such as fingerprints;
- photographing crime scenes and physical items; and
- making comparisons to determine the origin of transferred impressions (not bodily substances). DNA testing and other bodily substance comparisons are conducted by civilian scientists at laboratories such as the Ontario Centre of Forensic Sciences (CFS) in Toronto and the RCMP Crime Detection Lab.

"Forensics officer" is the most common term for members of this branch. The previous term, "Identification (Ident.) officer," is still used in some police services, as well as in this book.

DRUG UNIT

Drug Unit officers are undercover officers assigned to investigating *Controlled Drugs and Substances Act* (C.D.S.A.) offences. In some police services, a new branch called "Gangs, Grow, and Guns" investigates some types of substance production and the common offences associated with crime organizations and weapons.

INTELLIGENCE

This branch collects and analyzes information and data to determine findings intended to both solve past crimes and prevent future crimes.

SURVEILLANCE

This branch makes professional observations of suspects' activity, while concealing their identities as police officers.

SWAT

Also called the "emergency tactical unit" or simply "tac team," this unit primarily responds to emergencies involving the apprehension of armed offenders.

THREE CLASSIFICATIONS OF INVESTIGATIONS

All investigations have one common element—a *problem* exists that has to be solved. Although every problem is unique, there are three general classifications of investigations. These classifications are significant because they identify general types of problems and their corresponding goals:

1. reasonable grounds that a criminal offence *has* occurred or *is* occurring (past or present),
2. reasonable grounds that a specific criminal offence is *about to* occur (future), and
3. mere suspicion—possible risk; uncertain whether an offence has occurred (may lead to a criminal offence).

Reasonable Grounds That a Criminal Offence Has Occurred or Is Occurring

This classification means that a summary conviction, dual procedure, or indictable offence *has been committed* in the past or *is being committed* in the present. Either way, a crime has occurred in its entirety—there are reasonable grounds to believe that the crime occurred sometime in the past or is occurring now, in the present. The crime itself is the problem, because current and future risks and needs are present. The goals of this type of investigation include re-creating the incident to identify the offender and determining how to prevent repetition of the offence.

Reasonable Grounds That a Specific Criminal Offence Is About to Occur

This classification represents circumstances, either general or concrete, that create a strong belief that a crime is *about* to occur. This means that a there is a current *strong risk* that will likely escalate to an *actual offence.*
Examples include:

▸ information received from a confidential informant, reporting that offenders are planning to commit a specific crime; and
▸ crime analysis showing concrete tendencies that strongly predict future crimes. Offenders form habits. They often continue committing similar offences in similar ways until they are caught.

The goal of this type of investigation is prevention, which is far more challenging than the first classification of investigation because it requires changing or stopping specific human behaviour. Crime prevention is a primary goal of community policing, a model of policing from which prevention strategies emerge.

Mere Suspicion—Possible Risk

This investigation classification represents circumstances that do not constitute an actual offence or concrete indication of a future crime. Instead, the circumstances form the "mere suspicion" that an offence *may* develop into a criminal offence unless the behaviour is changed. The two most common examples are (a) domestic disputes involving non-criminal conflict, and (b) missing persons.

All domestic disputes have one common element: unresolved conflict. The outcome of the unresolved conflict is wide ranging. Some conflicts involve criminal acts; others involve no actual offence (i.e., argument only). Missing person investigations are more complicated than simply finding and returning the missing person. Disappearances cause a risk—*to* the missing person and *by* the missing person. Some missing person investigations result in the discovery of a "sudden death" (the missing person is found dead), which mobilizes an investigation to determine whether or not the death resulted from a criminal act. In most cases, the missing person is found alive (sometimes by the police); in other cases, the missing person returns on his or her own. Regardless of how the missing person is found, the investigative goal is the same—to determine whether or not an offence occurred in relation to the missing person. Specifically, the investigative goal is to answer three questions:

1. Was the missing person a *victim* of any offence?
2. Was the missing person an *offender*?
3. If the missing person was neither victim or offender, how can a future disappearance be prevented?

GENERAL PROBLEM-SOLVING MODEL

One of a police officer's goals is to become a problem-solving expert. Problem solving is a complex, challenging skill that requires strategizing and improvising. A strategy is a general plan. Improvising is making adaptations to the general plan because of rapidly changing circumstances that occur during front-line investigations. Problem solving is creative decision making, usually under extreme stress. The challenge of problem solving is that it involves the human cognitive process, not a scientific or mechanical process. Humans, not computers or machines, make law enforcement decisions; the process involves humans interacting with other humans. A solution to a problem is the product of a complex interplay among humans and their reactions and responses to events, conducts, and words. Everyone has experience in solving personal problems. Policing requires a different problem-solving skill—solving the problems of others. One of the benefits of mastering this art is dramatic personal growth. When you can solve the problems of others, solving personal problems becomes much easier.

Some problems share common features, but each problem has a degree of uniqueness. Consequently, there is no single concrete procedure that can solve all problems. However, there is a **general problem-solving model** that guides the process. A general problem-solving model provides structure and direction in the rapid decision-making (RDM) world of front-line policing. It can be applied to any investigation. The model has three steps:

1. define the problem,
2. identify the alternative solutions, and
3. choose the best alternative.[3]

Before learning the steps, the terms *problem*, *solution*, and *decision* must be understood.

A problem refers to:

▸ any wrong that needs correction, improvement, and questions answered,
▸ any situation that is not what it should be, or
▸ a negative that must become a positive.[4]

A solution is:

▸ the *goal* that is set after a problem has occurred and been identified,
▸ the *corrected state* or *condition*,
▸ the *answers* relating to the questions that were raised from the wrongdoing, or
▸ a *positive change* that corrects or improves the negative situation.[5]

A decision is:

▸ the result of analyzing *alternatives* and selecting a *belief* and *course of action*, and
▸ what people do and think as a result of analytical thinking.

All investigations include the same three elements: a *need*, a *goal*, and a *connecting path*.

Need: After a crime has been committed, several needs exist, including:

▸ the need to protect (ensure the safety of the public and the victim),
▸ the need to recover evidence, including the victim's property and items used to commit the crime, and
▸ the need to restore order in the victim's life.

Goal: The investigative goal includes preventing repetition of the offence by changing the offender's behaviour.

Connecting path: The connecting path closes the gap by converting the need to the goal. This process includes obtaining evidence, laying an Information, and court proceedings (a verdict and a sentence, depending on the verdict).

Define the Problem

Classify the problem as one of the three general types of problems, listed earlier in the chapter, before defining it. Define a problem by learning the maximum amount of information; the goal is *volume*. Witness interview skills and front-line interrogation skills are crucial to attaining this goal. There is a direct relationship between useful information and decision making. Strong information results in informed decision making and a greater likelihood of correct problem solving. Uninformed decision making has minimal chance of success.

Informed decision making requires enough information to answer the following six questions:

1. Who is being affected by the problem?
2. What are the concrete acts that constituted the problem?
3. What is the cause of the problem?

4. What is the effect or outcome of the problem?
5. Who caused the problem?
6. What are the patterns or trends that predict whether or not there will be a repetition of the problem?

In policing, defining the problem includes the skill of *offence recognition*—the ability to:

- analyze a large volume of information, and
- determine whether or not an offence has been committed—if so, identify the specific offence(s) and, if not, identify the worst possible consequences.

Offence recognition is a crucial skill used daily in front-line policing and one that must become second nature. It is the first step in correctly applying the s. 495 *Criminal Code* (C.C.) peace officer powers of arrest without a warrant.

Offence recognition requires:

- knowledge of the facts-in-issue (FII) that compose a criminal offence, and
- rapid analytical thinking, referring to the ability to process a set of circumstances, identify whether the FII of an offence(s) have been committed, and correspond those FII to an offence.

If no criminal offence has been committed, define the problem by identifying the worst possible consequence. This is done by answering the following questions: (a) What offence may occur in the future? (b) How strong is the belief? Recognize what offence the problem is leading to. The goal is then to prevent it.

After the problem has been concretely defined, maintain unbroken focus on it.

Identify the Alternative Solutions

After the problem has been concretely defined, the goal is to identify all possible alternative solutions. In law enforcement, there are two general alternative solutions to a criminal offence:

1. lay an Information and charge the offender, or
2. do not charge him (i.e., warn the offender, or, in slang terms, "give him a break").

The goals of both solutions are the same—to ensure public safety, prevent repetition, protect the victim, recover the victim's property, etc. The fundamental difference between the two general alternatives is *who* will solve the problem. When an offender is charged, an officer is placing the problem-solving responsibility on the criminal justice system. When an officer does not charge the offender, he or she is stating his or her intention to solve the problem without the intervention of the criminal justice system. How does an officer select the best alternative?

Choose the Best Alternative: Discretion

The *best* alternative means the course of action that has the strongest effect on eliminating the worst possible consequence. Choosing the best alternative is literally deciding whether or not to charge the offender. This decision is called *use of dis-*

cretion. Officers have a degree of discretion in relation to criminal offences. Discretion is authorized in s. 504 C.C. with the word "may," regarding the laying of an Information. The word "shall" is not used. Similarly, s. 495 C.C. uses the word "may" regarding arrest without warrant when lawful conditions exist.

The *Criminal Code* authorizes use of discretion, but does not explain concrete guidelines that govern how to use it. Case law research is needed to learn the use of discretion rules. Two cases are important:

1. *R. v. Beaudry* (2007) (this landmark decision explains a "use of discretion decision-making model"), and
2. *Hill v. Hamilton-Wentworth Regional Police Services Board* (2007).

The decision whether to charge has wide-ranging implications. The primary concern is future safety; the goals are protection of the public and prevention of future crimes. Consequently, the general rule that governs the selection of the best alternative is: "Eliminate the worst possible consequence." This is the golden rule of front-line RDM. The worst possible consequence that can occur is death, injury, or risk of death or injury. All other potential consequences, such as theft or damage to property, are secondary. These consequences must be eliminated, but obviously do not hold the same priority.

When deciding on an alternative solution, an officer must ask himself or herself, "What will be the worst thing that will happen after my decision is made?" In other words, if an officer chooses *not* to charge someone, he or she must be able to concretely justify that the offender will commit no future crimes and harm no one after the problem is solved. He or she must have concrete reasons that justify that the discretion used to not charge the offender was proportionate to the problem.[6]

USE OF DISCRETION: CASE LAW REVIEW

There are only three causes of problem-solving failure:

1. deficiency of knowledge (not defining the specific problem or not knowing the alternative solutions),
2. deficiency of execution (knowing which alternative solution is the right one, but not executing properly), or
3. a combination of deficiency of knowledge and execution.

Problem-solving failure is synonymous with improper use of discretion. Improper use of discretion has a number of potential consequences, including being liable for the offence of "Obstruct justice."

Shortly after I was hired as a police officer, I was at the front desk of the police station with the staff sergeant in charge of the uniform platoon. As he read a report, he lamented the decision made by an officer to charge a person with numerous offences arising from one minor incident. "This guy would charge his own mother," the staff sergeant moaned. "You have to use discretion. You can't charge everybody. It's common sense. Policing is all about common sense. You'll never get anywhere unless you use common sense. Don't forget that!" I didn't.

That same advice was conveyed to me repeatedly throughout my police career. *Discretion* and *common sense* became synonymous. They sound like simple, self-explanatory terms, but, as officers learn early in their police careers, using discretion effectively and applying common sense are not easy tasks. The use of discretion, like any other skill, has to be learned and developed through experience, but an officer also has to strictly follow guidelines created in case law.

On January 31, 2007, the Supreme Court of Canada in *R. v. Beaudry* (2007) released one of their most important decisions—one that dramatically affects every Canadian police officer. It explains how to use discretion properly and how to prevent being charged or convicted for "Obstruct justice."[7] It is likely one of the most important case law decisions you will ever read. A full version of this case can be found on the accompanying website **www.emp.ca/arcaro/criminvestigation5E**.

The following is a case law review of three S.C.C. cases. The first, *Beaudry*, creates a decision-making model that governs applied discretion. It also explains the fine line that separates the lawful use of discretion and the offence of "Obstruct justice." *Beaudry* follows *R. v. Beare* (1988), a decision in which the S.C.C. established principles to govern police discretion.[8] The last case, *Hill v. Hamilton-Wentworth Regional Police Services Board* (2007), added another step to the model created by *Beaudry*.

CASE LAW

R. v. Beaudry (2007)

Synopsis The S.C.C. upheld the conviction of a police officer who deliberately failed to gather evidence that was needed to lay criminal charges against another officer. The accused was charged after he intentionally failed to take breath samples from another police officer during an impaired driving investigation. The accused contended that his decision was a proper exercise of discretion. The trial judge convicted the accused after the Crown successfully argued that his decision was "founded on preferential treatment."[9] Appeals to the Quebec C.A. and the S.C.C. failed.

The circumstances of this case serve as a point of reference regarding improper use of discretion that constitutes "Obstruct justice."

POLICE DISCRETION

Police discretion is defined as the authority to decide to "engage the judicial process," meaning the *decision* whether or not to charge and/or arrest an offender.

The authority of police to use discretion emerges from the common law duty to investigate crimes.

> There is no question that police officers have a duty to enforce the law and investigate crimes. The principle that the police have a duty to enforce the criminal law is well established at common law.[10]

This common-law rule is codified in provincial "Police Act" statutes—the police have provincial statutory authority to both investigate crime and to use discretion.

> The ability—indeed the duty—to use one's judgment to adapt the process of law enforcement to individual circumstances and to the real-life demands of justice is in fact the basis of police discretion.[11]

> Discretion is an essential feature of the criminal justice system. A system that attempted to eliminate discretion would be unworkably complex and rigid.[12]

However, discretion is limited. All discretion must be justified.

> . . . this discretion is not absolute. Far from having carte blanche, police officers must justify their decisions rationally.[13]

The justification must have three elements:

1. an informed decision, based on evidence that constitutes reasonable grounds,

2. concrete reasons that do not constitute favouritism or bias, and

3. both subjectively and objectively logical belief. First, the officer must have a personal honest belief. Second, a trial judge must determine that the officer's belief reflected reality.

> Justification for use of discretion has to be proportionate to the offence and has to be in the interests of public safety.[14]

THE OFFENCE OF "OBSTRUCT JUSTICE"

The phrase "Obstruct justice" is a short-form, slang term that emerged from s. 139 C.C., a three-part section that creates the offence formally called "Attempting to obstruct justice."

▸ Section 139(1) creates a dual procedure offence of attempting to obstruct justice specifically relating to "sureties."

▸ Section 139(2) creates the indictable/10-year maximum offence of "Attempting to obstruct justice" in broader terms, other than sureties.

▸ Section 139(3) lists examples of how s. 139(2) is committed by the offence of obstruct justice, but is not limited to those examples.

▸ The offence is wide-ranging by virtue of the phrase "in any manner."

▸ The *actus reus* is "attempt in any manner to obstruct, pervert or defeat the course of justice.

▸ The *mens rea* is "wilful" in relation to the attempt.

▸ There is no concrete, exhaustive list of all circumstances that do and do not constitute "Obstruct justice."[15]

DISCRETION MODEL

The following seven guidelines emerge from the *Beaudry* decision and form the following summarized *discretion model*. This model applies nationwide. Arguably, nothing is more important to an officer's police career.

1. Discretion is vital for the proper operation of the criminal justice system. Not all offenders must be charged.

2. The police still have discretion, but it is not absolute—it is limited.

3. Limited discretion means that discretion must be proportionate to the severity of the offence.

4. Use of discretion to not charge an offender must be justified with concrete reasons.

5. Improper use of discretion does not automatically constitute "Obstruct justice."

6. A simple error of judgment is not "Obstruct justice."

7. "Obstruct justice" is committed when discretion is disproportionate, unjustified, and intended to obstruct, pervert, or defeat the course of justice.[16]

R. v. Beare (1988)

The leading case prior to *Beaudry* was *R. v. Beare* (1988). In the *Beare* case, the S.C.C. created the following principles relative to police discretion:

▸ Discretion is an essential feature of the criminal justice system. A system that attempts to eliminate discretion would be unworkably complex and rigid.

▸ Police may exercise discretion to start judicial proceedings, but the authority to use discretion is "not absolute." It is limited by the "subjective justification" rule.

▸ A police officer who has reasonable grounds to believe that an offence has been committed, or that a more thorough investigation might produce evidence that could form the basis of a criminal charge, may exercise his or her discretion to decide not to engage the judicial process. This discretion is not absolute. Far from having carte blanche, police officers must justify their decisions rationally.

▸ The required justification is essentially twofold. First, the exercise of the discretion must be justified subjectively—that is, the discretion must have been exercised honestly and transparently, and on the basis of valid and reasonable grounds. Thus, a decision based on favouritism, or on cultural, social, or racial stereotypes, cannot constitute a proper exercise of police discretion. However, the officer's sincere belief that he properly exercised his discretion is not sufficient to justify his decision.

▸ Hence, the exercise of police discretion must also be justified on the basis of objective factors. In determining whether a decision resulting from an exercise of police discretion is proper, it is important to consider the material circumstances in which the discretion was exercised.[17]

KEY POINTS

1. Rational justification is mandatory when discretion is used.

2. Improper discretion includes decisions based on favouritism or bias.

3. Proper justification must be relevant and proportionate to the circumstances of the offence.

Hill v. Hamilton-Wentworth Regional Police Services Board (2007)

This landmark decision allows the police to be sued for investigative negligence. The S.C.C. acknowledged that, as an easy way out of facing a potential civil suit, officers may be tempted to not charge an offender.

In this case, the S.C.C. added one more rule to the *Beaudry* discretion model: "A decision to not charge an offender only to avoid potential civil liability constitutes improper use of discretion."[18] Taking the easy way out by not laying an Information to simply avoid getting sued is the same improper use of discretion as decisions based on favouritism or cultural, social, or racial bias.

The key point that determines proper use of discretion is the combined effect of (a) forming reasonable grounds, and (b) the duty to protect the public from future risk and the suspect from a wrongful charge. The starting point in making use of discretion is the moment that reasonable grounds are formed. This standard of belief is below the standard of the "beyond a reasonable doubt" belief.

The S.C.C. called the difference separating the two standards of belief a "significant gap."[19] This means that when the lower standard of reasonable grounds is formed, the officer must then make a decision using the proportionate discretion rule established in *Beaudry*. A decision to not charge an offender cannot be based on the "selfish desire to avoid potential civil liability."[20]

THE DISCRETION MODEL: LONG VERSION

The following is the long version of the discretion model, taken from *R. v. Beaudry* (2007), with the added rule from the *Hamilton* decision.

1. A police officer who has reasonable grounds to believe that an offence has been committed, or that a more thorough investigation might produce evidence that could form the basis of a criminal charge, may exercise his or her discretion to decide not to engage the judicial process.

2. However, this discretion is not absolute. The police do not have carte blanche discretion.

3. The exercise of the discretion must be justified subjectively—that is, the discretion must have been exercised honestly and transparently, and on the basis of valid and reasonable grounds; it must also be justified on the basis of objective factors. In determining whether a decision resulting from an exercise of police discretion is proper, it is therefore important to consider the material circumstances in which the discretion was exercised.

4. The justification offered must be proportionate to the seriousness of the conduct and it must be clear that the discretion was exercised in the public interest.

5. While the administrative directives that apply to the situation in issue can shed light on the circumstances of the exercise of the discretion, they cannot be determinative. These directives do not have the force of law and cannot alter the scope of a discretion that is founded in the common law or a statute. Thus, the municipality's police practices manual cannot transform the discretion.

6. Finally, although in Quebec it is a Crown prosecutor who authorizes the laying of criminal charges, the police officer's discretion is not limited by the discretion of the Crown prosecutor. In discharging their respective duties, both the police officer and the prosecutor have a discretion that must be exercised independently of any outside influence.

7. The accused cannot be convicted of the offence provided for in s. 139(2) of the *Criminal Code* solely because he has exercised his discretion improperly.

8. Where the discretionary power is relied on, the analysis of the *actus reus* of the offence of obstructing justice must be carried out in two stages. It must first be determined whether the conduct in issue can be regarded as a proper exercise of police discretion. If so, there is no need to go any further, since it would be paradoxical to say that conduct that tends to defeat the course of justice can at the same time be justified as an exercise of police discretion. If, beyond a reasonable doubt, the answer is "no," it must then be determined whether the offence of obstructing justice has been committed. The *actus reus* of the offence will thus be established only if the act tended to defeat or obstruct the course of justice.

9. Regarding *mens rea*, this is a specific intent offence. The prosecution must prove beyond a reasonable doubt that the accused did in fact intend to act in

> a way tending to obstruct, pervert, or defeat the course of justice. A simple error of judgment will not be enough. An accused who acted in good faith, but whose conduct cannot be characterized as a legitimate exercise of the discretion, has not committed the criminal offence of obstructing justice.[21]
>
> From *Hamilton*:
>
> 10. A decision to not charge an offender only to avoid potential civil liability constitutes improper use of discretion.[22]

EIGHT OBJECTIVES OF AN INVESTIGATION

After an offence has been recognized and defined (the first step of the IDM model) and the investigation has been classified as the first type (an offence has occurred), the goal is to "solve the crime," a law enforcement term that means "correctly form reasonable grounds" to prove who committed the offence. Reasonable grounds is the standard, or level, of belief that an officer must aim for after an offence has been recognized.

The formation of reasonable grounds triggers several decisions:

- applied discretion: applying the *Beaudry* discretion model to decide whether to lay an Information to formally charge the offender,
- s. 495 C.C.: deciding whether to make an arrest without a warrant, and
- court appearance: deciding how to compel the offender to court (if an Information is laid).

In other words, after an offence is recognized, the primary goal of a criminal investigation is to form reasonable grounds that connect a specific person(s) to a specific offence. Eight investigative objectives, beginning with obtaining evidence, need to be met. These specific goals give structure to the investigation by creating an *investigative pathway*. (See Figure 2.1 on page 20.)

Sources of Evidence

Reasonable grounds is a belief formed and justified by obtaining evidence. There are only two sources of evidence: *people* and *physical items*.[23]

PEOPLE

Evidence from people (witnesses) is classified into:

1. visual observations, and
2. hearing verbal statements from the offender.

Observations seen or statements heard may be relevant to three time periods of a crime: (a) *before* (pre-offence), (b) *during* (*actus reus*), or (c) *after* (post-offence). Witnesses must be evaluated for credibility. Credibility evaluation occurs twice: (a) during the investigation, for the purpose of determining whether reasonable grounds exist, and (b) during the trial (witness testimony is evaluated as part of the process of determining whether guilt is proved beyond a reasonable doubt).[24]

The skill of *evaluating credibility* is needed to determine the accuracy and honesty of observations. Credibility evaluation is important because of three potential problems associated with witness evidence: (a) memory loss, (b) dishonesty, and (c) potential failure to appear in court.[25]

Memory decay occurs in all humans and in relation to all events. Witnesses lie and change their stories in court. Witnesses also fail to appear in court. These weaknesses of witness evidence are formally called the "frailties of eyewitness evidence," defined as the possibility of unintentional or intentional inaccuracies and potential lack of cooperation. A lengthy history of case law decisions repeatedly cautions about these frailties.[26] The accompanying website, **www.emp.ca/arcaro/criminvestigation5E**, includes some examples.

PHYSICAL EVIDENCE

Physical evidence refers to real objects/items or documents that prove any FII of the offence, directly or circumstantially.[27] Physical evidence includes:

- bodily substances (e.g., blood, hair, saliva),
- impressions (e.g., fingerprints, shoe prints, tire prints, tool marks), and
- items used to commit an offence (e.g., weapons, vehicles, writing).[28]

The evidentiary value of physical evidence depends on the investigator's ability to search, find, properly collect, and maintain *continuity* of the item until its presentation in court. Continuity refers to a chain of possession from the time of an item's seizure until the time the item is introduced in court.

Initial Evidentiary Value

In comparison with witness evidence, physical evidence provides three investigative advantages: (a) no memory loss, (b) no dishonesty, and (c) no possibility that the item will fail to appear in court. Physical evidence cannot lie, cannot forget, and cannot be uncooperative by changing its story or failing to appear at a trial to testify.[29] Consequently, physical evidence has higher initial *evidentiary value* (strength) than witness evidence.[30]

Witnesses have weaker/lower evidentiary value at the beginning of an investigation because humans forget, lie, and fail to cooperate. The evidentiary value of witnesses may be strengthened by effective witness interview techniques that will solve or minimize the three human problems. Witness interview expertise may prevent deception, failure to attend court, change of testimony, loss of credibility during testimony, and excessive loss of memory recall. There is a relationship between the *final* evidentiary value of witness evidence and the extent of the interviewer's expertise.[31]

Transfer of Evidence: The Transfer Theory (Locard's Exchange Theory)

It is impossible to commit a crime without transferring evidence.

"Transfer of evidence" is defined as the movement or exchange of physical evidence from one person, place, or item to another person, place, or item. The transfer occurs in several directions—the offender leaves, for example, fingerprints and shoe prints at a crime scene, and takes physical evidence intentionally (e.g., stolen property) or unintentionally (e.g., broken glass, carpet fibres). All transfer of physical evidence can be recognized by expert analysis. The items that are transferred can be identified by or matched to the source that caused the transfer (e.g., a shoe print may be positively matched to the shoe that caused it).

The transfer theory is formally called **Locard's Exchange Theory**. Edmond Locard was a pioneer in the field of forensic science. His research concluded that an exchange of physical evidence occurs during the commission of every offence, *without exception*.[32] Locard concluded that it is impossible to commit an offence with absolutely no transfer of evidence occurring, regardless of how careful or how experienced an offender is. According to Locard, when a person or item makes contact with another person or item, an exchange/transfer of physical evidence always occurs to some extent. The transfer represents a change—something was added or removed from the person, item, or place. No transfer is so minute that it cannot be identified. Some transfer is found through scientific analysis, while other transfer is obvious and visible without analysis.

After transfer is recognized, a comparison can be made. The items exchanged during a crime may be positively matched to the source that caused the change. The exchange or transfer proves that the two objects came into contact. The transfer of physical evidence is the cause and effect principle in reverse: the effect is observed, and the cause must be determined or concluded.[33]

Dr. Paul Kirk, a criminalistics researcher, supported Locard's transfer theory with the following conclusion:

> Wherever he steps, whatever he touches, whatever he leaves, will serve as a silent witness against him. Not only his fingerprints or footprints, but his hair, the fibers from his clothing, the glass he breaks, the tool mark he leaves, the paint he scratches, the blood or semen he deposits or collects. All of these and more bear mute witness against him. This evidence does not forget.[34]

■ KEY POINTS

1. Some extent of transfer occurs during every crime.
2. No crime can occur with zero transfer.
3. There are countless types of evidence transfer, but transfer is grouped into three *directions of movement*:
   ▷ from the offender to victim, and vice-versa,
   ▷ from the offender to the place/item, and vice-versa, and
   ▷ from the victim to the place/item, and vice-versa.

   Examples include, but are not limited to:
   ▷ item to person (injury to the victim or offender),
   ▷ item to place (damage),
   ▷ items moved at a crime scene (physical alteration of a scene),
   ▷ items removed intentionally from place or person (stolen property),
   ▷ items removed unintentionally (soil, broken glass, or fibres from a place; blood or hair from a victim),
   ▷ items unintentionally deposited at a place (fingerprints, glove prints, shoe prints, soil, tire prints, tool marks (impressions)),
   ▷ items unintentionally deposited on victim (bodily substances, clothing fibres), and
   ▷ items intentionally left at a place (weapons, writing).

An attempt to remove or conceal physical evidence at a crime scene causes identifiable transfer. For example, if an offender wipes a surface with the intention to remove fingerprints, four transfers occur: (a) fibres from the cloth to the surface, (b) substances from the surface to the cloth, (c) substances or impressions from the offender's hand to the cloth, and (d) substances from the cloth to the offender's hand.

No amount of care or expertise can prevent transfer of evidence. For example, (a) wearing gloves prevents the transfer of fingerprints, but transfers a glove impression, while (b) wearing a ski mask prevents facial recognition, but transfers fibres.

Transfer of evidence can prove (a) an offender's presence at a crime scene, (b) a victim's presence at a crime scene, (c) the source that caused the transfer, (d) possession of an item, and (e) that two items or persons came into contact. Transfer of physical evidence *corroborates* (supports) witness statements. It is one way to evaluate witness credibility.

Transfer occurs not just *during* a crime. It occurs during all three stages of a crime (pre-offence, during the offence, and post-offence. In other words, a path can be tracked from before, during, and after a crime.

When crime scene analysis reveals that no physical evidence was exchanged, two conclusions may be made:

1. The transfer was not found. Physical evidence was exchanged but the analysis failed to identify the transfer.
2. The report is invalid (fabricated), and the offence did not occur.

The reason for the absence of evidence transfer is not the professional expertise of the offender. Instead, the absence is attributed only to not finding it or to the fact that the offence never happened.

The Eight Objectives

1. OBTAIN A MAXIMUM VOLUME OF EVIDENCE, WHETHER ADMISSIBLE OR INADMISSIBLE

In accordance with the first step of the IDM model, as much information as possible is needed for informed decision making. Therefore, the goal of this first objective is to create the largest context, or biggest picture, possible. This means both admissible and inadmissible evidence will be collected.

"Rules of evidence" refers to the laws that govern the admissibility of evidence—whether an item or testimony will be admitted or excluded at a trial. An officer has to become an expert at applying the rules of evidence for accurate case management. Only admissible evidence can be used at trial. Examples of generally inadmissible evidence are hearsay evidence, opinion evidence, and bad character evidence.

Hearsay evidence, informally called "third-person evidence," is evidence that was not perceived by a person's own senses. This means that the witness did not actually see or hear the observation or statement. A *recipient* of hearsay evidence is a person who received hearsay evidence—he or she was told about an occurrence by another person who actually saw or heard the events. Police officers are often the recipients of hearsay evidence (such as in a witness's written and verbal statement during a formal interview). Another example is a radio broadcast. When a dispatcher informs a patrol officer to attend a place regarding a type of call, such as an alarm, the patrol officer is the recipient of hearsay evidence. In these cases, the officer generally cannot testify about what he or she was told. The correct way to testify regarding hearsay evidence received via a radio broadcast is as follows: "As a result of information I received, I (state what you did, e.g., responded to 41 Centrefield Drive)."[35]

Opinion is defined in case law as any inference made from observed facts.[36] An *inference* is a personal belief or conclusion that is not positively known to be an accurate fact. Examples include:

- ▸ "I think he's crazy."
- ▸ "He has anger issues, and suffers from clinical depression."
- ▸ "He meant to do it."

Generally, opinions are inadmissible. Witnesses may testify only about what they directly observed, not what they inferred or concluded. Various exceptions exist that are admissible. They are divided into two categories: non-expert and expert witnesses. Patrol officers are non-experts, just like most citizens. Examples of admissible non-expert opinions are: (a) the description of a suspect's height, weight, and age, (b) an opinion on intoxication/impairment, (c) an estimate of distance, and (d) an estimate of general rate of speed.[37]

Bad character evidence refers to past behaviour, conduct, and acts that show the accused is the type of person likely to have committed the offence that he or she is charged with. Bad character includes a wide range of past behaviour and acts such as convictions for criminal offences, violence, substance abuse, and other relevant misconduct. Generally, bad character evidence is inadmissible *during* the trial—the prosecution cannot use bad character evidence to prove any FII of the offence. Bad character evidence is usually allowed *after* the trial ends and a conviction occurs, for sentencing arguments. There are exceptions that make bad character evidence admissible during the trial.[38]

Another type of inadmissible evidence involves married couples. Legally married spouses are not competent and not compellable by the prosecution. This means that a legally married spouse cannot be subpoenaed and cannot testify against his or her spouse for the prosecution at a criminal trial.

Inadmissible evidence has no value at the trial, but it has significant value during the investigation—it may be used during the investigation to form reasonable grounds. The Supreme Court of Canada has ruled that both admissible and inadmissible evidence may be used during an investigation to form reasonable grounds.[39] This means two things: (a) *only admissible evidence may be used to form reasonable grounds to lay an Information,* but (b) *both admissible and inadmissible evidence may be used to form reasonable grounds to make an arrest without warrant under s. 495 C.C.*

The trial judge is the final decision-maker about the admissibility of evidence at a trial. Gather all possible evidence, regardless of whether it is admissible or inadmissible. Do not focus only on admissible evidence. Do not ignore inadmissible evidence, such as hearsay, bad character, and opinions. Remember that S.C.C. case law has allowed *both* admissible and inadmissible evidence to be used in the reasonable grounds formulation process, during the investigation. This rule is one of the most important investigative case law principles. It creates a significant investigative benefit because it expands the type of information that can be used to form reasonable grounds.

2. PREDICT THE ADMISSIBILITY OF EVIDENCE GATHERED

An officer has to be an expert on the rules of evidence in order to *predict* the admissibility of the evidence obtained. After a maximum volume of evidence has been obtained, predict the admissibility of the evidence by classifying it as admissible or inadmissible. After this distinction has been achieved, use both lists to prove the FII of the offence.

3. PROVE IDENTITY, DATE/TIME, AND PLACE

These three FII are the first FII group. They represent *who*, *when*, and *where*. The accused person's identity is the most important FII in all criminal offences, and must be proved beyond a reasonable doubt. Identity includes the date/time and place of the offence.

4. PROVE THE ACTUS REUS

The second FII group concerns the physical act that composes the offence. Identify the number of elements that compose the *actus reus* by reading the relevant provision.

5. PROVE THE MENS REA

The final FII is intent (*mens rea*). As with all FII, direct evidence, circumstantial evidence, or both can be used to prove *mens rea*.

6. PROVE GUILT FAR BEYOND A REASONABLE DOUBT

The goal of this objective is to make the case as strong as possible by removing all doubt and preventing any possibility of wrongful arrest and prosecution. Two levels of belief must be sought: (a) beyond reasonable doubt and (b) reasonable grounds.

"Beyond reasonable doubt" is the stronger belief. It represents the *minimum* degree of evidence/proof necessary to convict an offender at trial. It is the minimum standard of belief needed to establish a **prima facie case**. A *prima facie* case refers to a trial in which the Crown has successfully proven all the FII of the offence beyond a reasonable doubt.

"Reasonable grounds" is a weaker belief than "beyond reasonable doubt." Reasonable grounds is the minimum level of belief needed to arrest and lay an Information. This objective has a dual purpose. The first goal is to *meet* the "beyond reasonable doubt" minimum standard. The second goal is to *exceed* it by continuing the investigation and attaining the *maximum* standard. The investigation does not end when reasonable grounds are formed, when an arrest is made, or when an Information is laid. An investigation is finished when the court proceedings finish. Offenders do not stop talking to other people as soon as they are arrested. A number of *post-arrest* events are relevant to the prosecution. Strengthen the case until the trial ends.

The case-strengthening principle is: *Predict all possible defences and alibis and disprove them.* The best evidence that strengthens any case is a properly obtained confession to any person—police or citizen.[40] A confession to a citizen is automatically admissible. A confession to the police is not. Confessions to the police must be voluntary and free from Charter violations.[41]

The goal in every investigation is obtaining a confession. A confession is the best type of evidence for the following reasons:

1. It removes all reasonable doubt. Certainty is achieved.
2. It helps prevent wrongful prosecutions and convictions.
3. It helps with offender rehabilitation and reintegration into society.[42]

There is no such thing as an investigation where an interrogation is considered unnecessary because enough evidence exists. There is no such thing as a case strong enough not to require a confession. Interrogation is one of the primary skills needed to become an investigative expert.

Every interrogation has three goals:

1. Elicit an admissible confession about the original crime.
2. "Clear" all other crimes the offender committed. Offenders have often committed undetected crimes. Obtain confessions regarding all past crimes.
3. Obtain information from the offender about unrelated crimes (informant development).

7. FORM REASONABLE GROUNDS TO ARREST

This objective represents the *minimum* standard needed to make an arrest with or without warrant under the *Criminal Code*.[43] In some investigations, an officer will achieve his or her goal of obtaining the maximum strength of evidence that removes all doubt. In those cases where an officer has proven guilt (far) beyond reasonable doubt, he or she will have automatically formed reasonable grounds to arrest. Both this objective and the previous objective will have been achieved.

In other investigations, while an officer will not prove guilt beyond all doubt, he or she will form a reasonable grounds belief (beyond mere suspicion). Examples include (a) strong circumstantial evidence (without a confession or at least one credible eyewitness) that leads to only one logical conclusion, and (b) only one credible eyewitness with no confession.

The key points of this objective are:

1. Justify the reasonable grounds belief with concrete evidence.
2. Remember that both lists of evidence (admissible and inadmissible) may be used to form reasonable grounds to arrest.[44]
3. Remember the definition of "reasonable grounds." The belief must exceed mere suspicion, but it does not have to constitute 100 percent certainty. The decision to arrest corresponds with *applied discretion*. Use the discretion model to decide whether an arrest is required.

8. FORM REASONABLE GROUNDS TO LAY AN INFORMATION

The decision to charge also corresponds with applied discretion. Use the discretion model to decide whether or not to charge. Only admissible evidence may be used for this objective. In other words, only admissible evidence may justify the reasonable grounds to lay an Information.

The procedure used to lay an Information is called an ***ex parte* hearing**. When an officer lays an Information, he or she must verbally testify at this hearing, before a justice, and justify the reasonable grounds by explaining the concrete evidence that contributed to the belief. The full *ex parte* hearing procedure is taught in *Basic Police Powers: Arrest and Search Procedures*, 4th ed. (Toronto: Emond Montgomery, 2009).

Summary

Every investigation, or decision-making process, is unique. Similarities will exist, but no two investigations are exactly the same. Consequently, the "base" IDM model is not a concrete model that, when followed, will solve every investigation. Instead, it is a guide that illustrates the general pathways of all investigative problem solving. The eight objectives that structure an investigation will be discussed and explained in greater detail throughout the remainder of this text, in the context of basic investigative strategies.

Case Study 2.1 Investigation

You are the first officer. Your duties include searching and protecting the crime scene, and formulating a theory about who committed this crime—specifically, was it a "random" crime?

In Chapter 6, the strategies and investigative theories discussed in Chapters 1–5 are applied to the case study from Chapter 1 to explain how the first officer will begin the investigation. These same principles can be applied to the case study in this chapter.

ENDNOTES

1. D. Leonard and W. Swap, *Deep Smarts: How to Cultivate and Transfer Enduring Business Wisdom* (Boston: Harvard Business School Press, 2005).
2. Ibid.
3. G. Arcaro, "A Workable Future for Ontario Community Colleges," M.Ed. thesis, Brock University, 2005.
4. Ibid.
5. Ibid.
6. *R. v. Beaudry*, [2007] 1 S.C.R. 190, 2007 SCC 5.
7. Ibid.
8. *R. v. Beare* (1988), 45 C.C.C. (3d) 57 (S.C.C.).
9. *R. v. Beaudry*, supra note 6.
10. Ibid.
11. Ibid.
12. Ibid.
13. Ibid.
14. Ibid.

15. Section 139 C.C.

16. *R. v. Beaudry*, supra note 6.

17. *R. v. Beare*, supra note 8.

18. *Hill v. Hamilton-Wentworth Regional Police Services Board*, 2007 41 SCC.

19. *R. v. Beaudry*, supra note 6.

20. Ibid.

21. Ibid.

22. *Hill v. Hamilton-Wentworth Regional Police Services Board*, supra note 18.

23. H. Gross, *Criminal Investigation* (London: Sweet & Maxwell, 1924).

24. *R. v. Nikolovsky* (1996), 111 C.C.C. (3d) 403 (S.C.C.).

25. *R. v. Goran*, 2008 ONCA 195.

26. *R. v. Nikolovsky*, supra note 34.

27. *Cloutier v. The Queen* (1979), 48 C.C.C. (2d) 1, 1979 CanLII 25 (S.C.C.); *Morris v. The Queen* (1983), 7 C.C.C. (3d) 97 (S.C.C.).

28. Ibid.

29. Ibid.

30. Ibid.

31. Ibid.

32. P.L. Kirk and J.I. Thornton, *Crime Investigation*, 2nd ed. (New York: Wiley & Sons, 1974), as in B. Turvey and J. Chisum, "Evidence Dynamics: Locard's Exchange Principle and Crime Reconstruction" (2000) vol. 1, no. 1 *Journal of Behavioral Profiling*.

33. Ibid.

34. Ibid.

35. *R. v. McInroy and Rouse* (1978), 42 C.C.C. (2d) 481 (S.C.C.); *Cloutier v. The Queen*, supra note 27.

36. *R. v. Graat* (1982), 2 C.C.C. (3d) 365 (S.C.C.).

37. *R. v. B. (F.F.)* (1993), 79 C.C.C. (3d) 112, at 136 (S.C.C.).

38. *R. v. Debot* (1986), 30 C.C.C. (3d) 207 (Ont. C.A.).

39. Ibid.

40. *R. v. Oickle* (2000), 147 C.C.C. (3d) 321 (S.C.C.).

41. Ibid.

42. *R. v. Smith* (1989), 50 C.C.C. (3d) 308 (S.C.C.).

43. Sections 495 and 507(4) C.C.

44. *R. v. Debot*, supra note 38.

CHAPTER 3
Basic Investigative Sequence: Theory Development Model

LEARNER SUMMARY

To solve a crime, an officer must remain objective and open-minded during the process of theory development. *Theory development* is structured logic intended to form an exploratory path from "mere suspicion" to "reasonable grounds." It forms a list of possible suspects.

There are three fundamentals of theory development:

1. Need causes all unresolved internal and external conflict—e.g., the need for money, the need for revenge, etc.
2. Unresolved conflict (internal and external) is the cause of all crimes.
3. Minimum risk and maximum reward is the solution to all unresolved conflict.

There are three key points to forming reasonable grounds that connect a person to an offence:

1. It fulfills the dual goal of protecting the public and preventing the wrongful prosecution of innocent persons.
2. It creates an investigative focus.
3. It is the Canadian way of "solving a crime."

In some cases, forming reasonable grounds will be simple (e.g., finding the offender present at a crime scene, or the victim and witnesses know the offender and immediately identify him or her). In other cases, forming reasonable grounds is a complex task that starts with no clear suspects. When this is the case, an exploratory pathway is needed to develop theories of possible suspects.

The **Basic Investigative Sequence (BIS)** is a theory development model that can be applied to any investigation to form a list of "possible suspects" to explore and help solve the crime.

Case Study 3.1

2:00 a.m. You are a uniform officer on patrol. You receive the following radio broadcast: "unknown problem, dwelling-house, 3227 Brockport Rd." En route, you see no cars and no pedestrians.

2:02 a.m. Arrival. The house is situated in a residential urban area, six blocks from the downtown core.

You see a middle-aged woman at the front door, frantically waving for you to enter. As you walk toward her, she says, "Someone tried to attack my daughter."

You ask her, "Is the attacker still here?"

She replies, "No, he ran away. He ran out the front door, but I couldn't see what direction."

You ask how many people are inside.

She responds, "My two daughters."

You identify the woman at the door as Helen (50). Her two daughters are Phyllis (17) and Lorraine (15).

Instructions

1. Without reading further and without any additional information, answer this question: "Was this a random crime?" Explain your opinion.

2. After reading Phase 1 (Chapters 1–6), explain the following:

   a. All your "first officer" responsibilities, beginning immediately after the radio broadcast.

   b. Your investigative strategy.

   c. Your theory, applying the Basic Investigative Sequence.

BASIC INVESTIGATIVE SEQUENCE

The following is the five-step Basic Investigative Sequence. It is a theory development model structured to create lists of possible suspects. The BIS can be applied to any investigation, from minor to major crimes, to form exploratory suspicions.

Step 1. *Validate* the offence/complaint.

↓

Step 2. Suspect the possibility that a *relative*
committed the offence.

↓

Step 3. Suspect the possibility that an *acquaintance*
committed the offence.

↓

Step 4. Suspect the possibility that a *non-acquaintance*
committed the offence.

↓

Step 5. Suspect the remote possibility that a total *stranger*
committed the offence randomly.

1. Each step creates a list of potential suspects.
2. The lists are explored for:
   a. prior bad character,
   b. motive, and
   c. opportunity.

The rationale for the BIS is based on both empirical and anecdotal evidence. The remainder of this chapter provides supporting evidence for the BIS, which is crucial in learning how to apply it.

"TWO ROADS" TO REASONABLE GROUNDS

There are two roads to forming reasonable grounds: a short, easy road and a longer, more complex one.

Reasonable grounds represent a level of belief that constitutes strong certainty about who committed an offence. The definition of reasonable grounds does not require 100 percent certainty, meaning certainty beyond all doubt, but it does require a sufficient amount of concrete evidence that exceeds mere suspicion. There are three types of concrete evidence that constitute reasonable grounds—the 3 Cs: confession, credible witness, or circumstantial evidence. Specifically, the 3 Cs are:

1. a confession to anyone—police or citizen, or
2. at least one credible eyewitness, or
3. circumstantial evidence—evidence that is not a confession or an eyewitness, that forms only one *logical* conclusion—a connection between a specific person and a specific offence. If more than one logical conclusion exists, then the belief constitutes mere suspicion only. The key word is "logical."

These are the only three classifications of evidence that constitute the formation of reasonable grounds. Each one is a minimum requirement. A confession and a credible witness each include only one circumstance. Circumstantial evidence includes countless, infinite types of concrete circumstances. The three classifications represent the strategic evidentiary aim of any investigation. A minimum of one classification of reasonable grounds evidence is required in order to form strong certainty.

Although the minimum requirement is obtaining one of these types of evidence, the ultimate goal is to obtain all three groups to strengthen the belief far beyond reasonable grounds. After the minimum requirement is met, the investigation is continued until the *maximum* evidence has been obtained, referring to a combination of all three.

There are many roads that lead to the formation of reasonable grounds. A *road* is a developmental pathway, and each road has a different speed. In some cases, reasonable grounds will be formed immediately after arrival at a crime scene. In other cases, the development may take days, weeks, months, or years. All roads have the same two goals: (a) to protect the public, and (b) to prevent innocent people from being arrested and charged.

The Short Road

The *short road* is defined as an immediate reasonable grounds development path, or *simple solution*. Examples include:

1. The officer witnesses an offence being committed, therefore belief will exceed reasonable grounds.
2. The offender's presence at a crime scene is determined and evidence that immediately implicates the offender is found. For example, an officer arrives at a crime scene where a stabbing has just occurred. Claire is at the crime scene where Doug has been stabbed. Jack, a man known to police from past investigations, is present. Claire verbally reports to the officer, "I saw the whole thing. Jack stabbed Doug," and she points to Jack. Those two sentences and the act of pointing to the man constitute a *witness statement*. The statement is *verbal, informal,* and *spontaneous*, but it constitutes the definition of reasonable grounds temporarily, for the following reasons:

    ▷ Claire is an implied eyewitness with temporarily strong credibility.
    ▷ It is implied that she saw the entire offence and has prior familiarity with Jack because she called him by his given name.
    ▷ The content and the urgency of the statement allows the officer to presume Claire has strong credibility.
    ▷ Afterward, a formal witness interview will be conducted to (a) obtain all of Claire's concrete observations, (b) record her observations in a written witness statement, and (c) formally evaluate her credibility.
    ▷ The officer will then make a final conclusion about reasonable grounds in order to determine whether Claire is honest and accurate or not.

The Long Road

The *long road* is a lengthy reasonable grounds development, or *complex solution*. Long roads are required when no immediate solutions are available. The long road requires *theory development*—an objectively structured process of building a list of possible suspects, starting with logical "mere suspicions." Theory development is a way to develop investigative exploration, by forming several hypotheses to prove or disprove. It requires experience-based logic. Theories, by themselves, are insufficient to solve a crime. Whoever asserts must prove. A level of concrete evidence is needed to prove the theory and convert the theory to reasonable grounds.

Theories guide strategies and every theory has a corresponding strategy. Theories cannot be developed randomly. Structured analytical thinking is needed. The Basic Investigative Sequence provides that structure.

The BIS is a theory development model that gives officers a starting point and a proper focus for reasonable grounds development, in every investigation, regardless of how little evidence exists during the preliminary stages of an investigation. It is a system that helps form possible suspects who must be explored, using a logical step-by-step process. The BIS forms suspicions. A *suspicion* is merely a logical inference, a weak belief based on speculation or concrete evidence that leads to multiple conclusions. This is why police officers have no authority to arrest or charge people based on "mere suspicion." Mere suspicion prohibits (a) an Information from being laid, (b) an arrest warrant from being obtained, and (c) an arrest without a warrant.

The BIS prevents an officer from ever saying "I have nothing to work with" at any stage of the investigation. It structures and steers analytical thinking to develop logical theories to explore. The skill of accurate theory development separates novice investigators from expert investigators and determines an investigator's career success.

TUNNEL VISION

Although forming mere suspicion is part of an investigation, Canadian law protects people from arrest and prosecution based on mere suspicion. In other words, mere suspicion forms an investigative base only. Forming mere suspicion is a precursor to forming reasonable grounds. A suspicion is not an allegation. There is nothing unethical or illegal about forming suspicions during an investigation for exploratory purposes if the officer remains objective and open-minded throughout the investigation.

Forming logical suspicions is the police officer's job, as long as it does not cause tunnel vision. The goal is to form logical possibilities to explore, not to target one person and try to build a case to prove one's own suspicion.

Tunnel vision is defined as targeting only one suspect and ignoring the possibility of any others. It is a narrow-minded focus that tries to make all the evidence obtained match the single-target suspect. Tunnel vision is a dangerous practice that eliminates explorative investigation and may lead to wrongful prosecutions.

Preventing tunnel vision is a common theme of two major inquires and reports: (a) the Sophonow Inquiry, and (b) the Justice Campbell report on the Bernardo investigation. The following is an introduction to both reports, with an emphasis on "tunnel vision" prevention.

The Inquiry Regarding Thomas Sophonow: The Danger of Tunnel Vision

In 2001, the Sophonow Inquiry was conducted by the province of Manitoba with regard to the wrongful prosecution of Thomas Sophonow, who was charged in connection with a murder. Among the volume of recommendations that will be explained throughout this book in relevant chapters, the following quote is the most important. The quote has a dual purpose in that it defines *tunnel vision*, and warns of its consequences:

> Tunnel vision is insidious. It can affect an officer or, indeed, anyone involved in the administration of justice, with sometimes tragic results. It results in the officer becoming so focused upon an individual or incident that no other person or incident registers in the officer's thoughts. Thus, tunnel vision can result in the elimination of other suspects who should be investigated. Equally, events which could lead to other suspects are eliminated from the officer's thinking. Anyone, police officer, counsel or judge, can become infected by this virus.[1]

Bernardo Investigation Review: Report of Mr. Justice Archie Campbell

In 1996, Justice Campbell released a report that examined the murder and rape investigations that led to the conviction of Paul Bernardo. Among the volume of recommendations that will be explained throughout this book, the following relates specifically to tunnel vision:

> Another attitudinal challenge is the need to recognize, and remedy, the debilitating restrictions of tunnel vision in the investigation of mobile predatory serial killers.[2]

Tunnel vision prevention is one of the objectives of both the Sophonow and Bernardo reports. An investigative balance is needed where justified theories are formed without developing a dangerous, narrow scope. The Basic Investigative Sequence is a theory development model intended to prevent tunnel vision by developing lists of "possible suspects" for explorative investigations.

Possible Suspect

The concept of "possible suspect" has been explained in a series of complex case law decisions aimed at defining two terms—*person of interest* and *suspect*. The series of case law decisions include:

- *R. v. Dalzell* (2003)[3]
- *R. v. Nicholas* (2006)[4]
- *R. v. Morrison* (2000)[5]
- *R. v. Buchanan* (2006)[6]
- *R. v. Michaud* (2007)[7]

The website accompanying this textbook, **www.emp.ca/arcaro/criminvestigation5E**, includes a review of these cases.

The two terms and definitions are not the product of legislation. The Ontario Major Case Manual attempts to define them, as follows:

- **Person of interest** "A person whose background, relationship to the victim, or the opportunity to commit the offence may warrant further inquiry but at that time no other grounds exist to suggest culpability in the crime being investigated."[8]
- **Suspect** "A person an investigator reasonably believes may possess a degree of culpability in the commission of a criminal offence being investigated and there is some incriminating information linking the person to the crime."[9]

However, the courts found that the definitions of the two terms, which are the product of police terminology, not legislation, are too complex and confusing—they are "not well defined." They

- overlap,
- have no force in law,
- are not "terms of science," and
- possess almost identical meanings.

The conclusion of the courts is that there is "no clear difference" between the two terms; a suspect is linked to a crime by concrete circumstantial reasons; a person of interest is linked by speculation and is a possible suspect or possible witness.

Note: For the purpose of detention, specifically with regard to reading the caution and right to counsel (adult offenders), the two definitions have the same meaning: (a) the police may question by consent but cannot detain, and (b) if the person consents to questioning, the police do not have a mandatory obligation to read the caution and the right to counsel.

PRACTICAL EXERCISE

This exercise will help you understand and apply the BIS. Complete this exercise before you continue reading. Repeat the same exercise at the conclusion of this chapter after learning the BIS. The purpose is to test your current analytical thinking and compare it after reading the chapter.

Circumstances   A robbery occurs at 2:30 p.m. at a bank situated in a downtown area of a city with a population of 50,000 people. You are the first officer to arrive, eight minutes after the alarm was activated. You learn the following information:

- Fifteen employees were working in the bank; 14 were female, one was male.
- There were two customers in the bank; both were women about 40 years old.
- Three men wearing disguises entered the front door of the bank; all three were armed with long-barrelled firearms.
- One offender stood at the front entrance while the other two each approached a female bank teller, pointed weapons at them, and demanded money.
- Both tellers filled two bags with cash and gave it to the offenders; about $15,000 was stolen.
- All three offenders ran out the front door; no direction of travel or means of transportation were seen.
- Poor descriptions of the offenders were given.
- You have no other information to work on.

Exercise   Reconstruct all the events leading up to the robbery. Write your beliefs, opinions, assumptions, and suspicions about how the events *before* the robbery occurred and who committed the robbery, not by name but by relationship to the victims. Use the following questions as guidelines:

- When was the idea to rob the bank formed—shortly before the offence, or a long time before the robbery?
- Did the three offenders know each other for a long time, or did they meet shortly before the offence?
- Did extensive or minimal planning occur?
- Was this crime a spontaneous act?
- How did the offenders select the bank?
- Did the offenders have reasons for selecting this bank, or did they select it randomly?
- How did they acquire firearms?

- ‣ How did they travel to and from the bank?
- ‣ Where do they live—in the same city as the bank or in a different city?
- ‣ What are your opinions about the customers and the employees?
- ‣ Was this the first robbery that this group of offenders committed?
- ‣ Was this the first crime that this group committed?
- ‣ Have any of the offenders ever been in the bank before?
- ‣ Do the offenders know any of the employees or customers?
- ‣ Which is of greater advantage to your investigation—extensive or minimal planning by the offenders?

State reasons for your answers to justify your opinions.

_____

_____

_____

_____

_____

_____

_____

_____

_____

_____

_____

_____

_____

_____

_____

_____

_____

_____

_____

_____

_____

_____

_____

BASIC INVESTIGATIVE SEQUENCE LANGUAGE

The Basic Investigative Sequence includes eleven definitions:

- **Victim selection** a decision made by an offender about a person or place chosen as the target of a crime.
- **Victim** offender relationship—the extent of familiarity between an offender and the person selected as the victim of a crime or the place selected in which to commit the crime.
- **Random** selecting a victim without any degree of planning and without any reason; that is, spontaneous, impulsive victim selection. No thought whatsoever is given to victim selection.
- **Familiarity** knowledge of a person or place learned through (a) a prior long-term or short-term relationship, (b) planning, or (c) both.
- **Relative** a member of the victim's immediate family, including legally married or common-law spouses, parents, children, siblings, and other people actually related to the victim by blood or marriage.
- **Acquaintance** a non-relative who has any degree of prior *familiarity* with a victim, acquired *without planning*.
- **Non-acquaintance** a person who has acquired any degree of familiarity with the victim through planning.
- **Stranger** a person who has absolutely no familiarity with the victim either by prior knowledge or through planning; a person completely unfamiliar with the victim and premises; a person who commits a crime randomly.
- **Suspect** a person connected to a crime by "mere suspicion" only, referring to some degree of incriminating circumstantial evidence that needs to be explored.[10]
- **Person of interest** (a) someone who is a possible suspect because of a relationship with the victim, prior bad character, motive, or opportunity; or (b) a person who may have some relevant information related to the offence being investigated.[11]
- **Accused person** a person (a) connected to a crime by reasonable grounds, or (b) charged by formal allegation—Information laid.

Ten Fundamental Basic Investigative Sequence Key Points

The BIS builds lists of possible suspects through a progression of structured beliefs and suspicions that have to be explored and eliminated or proved. The following diagram, called the *Beam of Suspicions*, illustrates this point, using the five steps as a guide to a widening investigative focus. Broken focus is a major cause of investigative failure. The BIS prevents broken focus by building theories in logical order.

- The beam represents the chronological order of suspicions and theories.
- The widening of the beam represents the size of the group of suspects.
- The closer the group is to the offence (in the diagram), the greater the extent of familiarity, the greater likelihood of participation, and the smaller the group size.

Figure 3.1   Beam of Suspicions

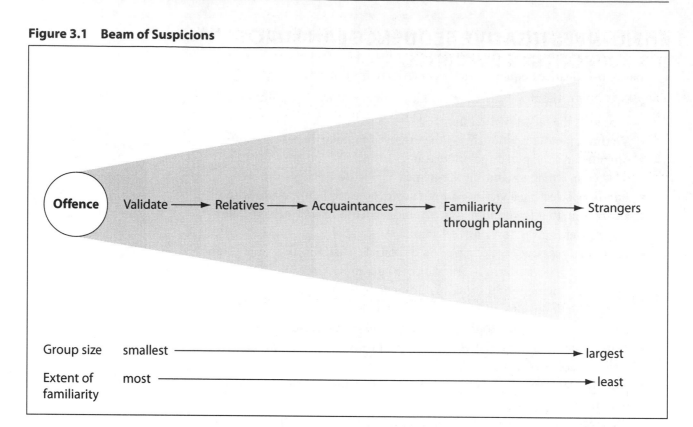

- The first step is validating the offence. *Validating* means proving that the offence actually happened, and that the report was not fabricated. In other words, proving the offence of "Public mischief" did not occur. This group is the smallest. It includes one person—the victim.
- After the offence is validated, a list of suspects is created based on familiarity—from most to least amount of familiarity. The first post-validation group of suspects are relatives. This is the smallest, most easily identifiable group who are the most logical suspects. This group is the easiest to eliminate or to prove to have participated.
- After relatives are eliminated, the focus shifts to acquaintances. This is an easily identifiable, slightly larger group who are the next most logical suspects. This group can be easily eliminated or proven to have participated.
- After acquaintances are eliminated, the focus shifts to non-acquaintances, referring to those who acquired familiarity through *planning*. This is the most challenging group to identify and investigate.
- The last to be suspected is a stranger, a person who commits an offence randomly without any planning whatsoever. This group is the least likely to be suspected because this group is the least likely to commit a crime.
- An officer can create concrete lists of relatives, acquaintances, and some non-acquaintances, but cannot create a concrete list of strangers.
- *Never reverse the order.* If you start at the fifth step you will be suspecting the least likely group, one that is extremely large, nearly infinite in size. You will never be able to completely eliminate this group and will never get around to focusing on the most logical group of suspects.

THE FOUR CONCEPTS OF THEORY DEVELOPMENT: BIS SUPPORTING EVIDENCE

The BIS is premised on empirical and anecdotal evidence. This supporting evidence serves the dual purpose of explaining the rationale for the BIS and teaching how to apply the BIS in real circumstances.

The supporting evidence is based on the four concepts of investigative theory development:

1. victim–offender selection and relationship,
2. logic,
3. coincidence, and
4. anatomy of a crime.

Victim–Offender Selection and Relationship

Victims are not selected randomly. They are selected for a reason.

> Let any (non-criminal) reader try to imagine himself in any position of being required to commit a crime—say one of the most common crimes like breaking and entering—within the next 12 hours. Few readers would select the victim completely at random, unskilled at victim selection though they might be. There will be something approaching *rationality* in the selection of the victim.[12]

ANECDOTAL EVIDENCE

The media commonly make two misleading, inaccurate statements:

1. "The crime was committed *at random*," and
2. "The police have *no leads* to work on in this case."

Both statements are myths. Random crimes are rare, and there are always "leads" to work on.

Random crimes are rare because overwhelming evidence shows that offenders select victims based on familiarity—past familiarity (long-term familiarity) or familiarity through planning (short-term familiarity).

Leads always exist because:

1. suspicions and logical theories may be made from the usual victim–offender relationship, based on familiarity, and
2. physical evidence is transferred during every crime.

An investigative theory is always possible to explore, regardless of how little evidence exists.

The BIS is both empirical and anecdotal, based on the following general principles derived from statistical research and actual investigations:

1. **Every crime has an *offender* and a *victim*** The victim may suffer either from a *personal* offence, such as an assault, or a *property* offence, such as break, enter, and theft.
2. **The usual victim–offender relationship is one of some degree of familiarity, whether through prior knowledge or planning** Relatives often have the greatest degree of familiarity with family members.

3. **Familiarity breeds contempt** Conflict often develops in relationships, among relatives and among acquaintances. Conflict with strangers is less likely than with relatives and acquaintances. Violence is the result of unresolved conflict.

4. **Some type of personal or emotional gratification motivates all crime** Crime is *benefit-oriented*. The offender needs to benefit from the offence. Nearly everything is done for a reason; rarely is anything done without reason.

5. **Offenders deliberately select victims** There is a degree of rationality and logic associated with victim selection. Victims are selected for a reason. Offenders put some degree of thought into victim selection.

6. **Committing a crime for absolutely no reason, without any degree of planning or any degree of familiarity with the victim or premises, is illogical and irrational** Offenders prefer to have some degree of familiarity with the victim and/or premises. Acquaintances have substantial familiarity with each other.

7. **Fear is the most powerful human emotion** Offenders fear three consequences: (a) getting caught, (b) being injured during the crime, and (c) failure. The greatest fear is fear of the unknown. Fear of the unknown causes significant stress. Familiarity reduces stress, develops confidence, and reduces fear. Varying degrees of familiarity are acquired by relationships and by planning. Planning and preparation are stress reducers that lead to success. The degree of planning corresponds to the degree of uncertainty. Planning produces considerable familiarity.

8. **All action is preceded by some type of thought** Acting without reason constitutes impulsivity and irrationality. Mental disturbance may cause criminal impulsivity and irrationality. A crime committed without reason often involves a *Mental Health Act* (M.H.A.) investigation and enforcement. The textbook website **www.emp.ca/arcaro/ criminvestigation5E** includes case law that explains the relationship between mental health problems and the commission of crimes.

9. **Fabricated offences are benefit-oriented acts** Some complainants mislead the police by making false reports. Intentional fabrication of an offence constitutes the dual procedure offence of "Public mischief." Fabricated offences are not rare. They are common enough to pose significant problems. False reports not only waste police time and taxpayer money, they may falsely implicate innocent people.

Five conclusions emerge:

1. Random crimes, by definition, are improbable and rarely occur. If a random crime does occur, the offender's mental health is questioned.
2. Strangers, by definition, rarely commit crimes.
3. Some degree of planning, strategy, or decision making precedes almost every offence.
4. Extensive planning by an offender represents an investigative advantage. More planning results in more transfer of evidence.
5. Every report of an offence must be verified through a validation process.

These five conclusions are the key to theory development and *applying* the BIS in actual front-line investigations.

STATISTICAL EVIDENCE

Empirical evidence overwhelmingly proves that the majority of offenders have some degree of familiarity with their victims, either by prior relationship or by planning.

Statistics Canada (StatsCan), Canada's national statistical agency, concluded that: "Criminal victimization is not a random occurrence."[13] Specifically, StatsCan research shows that:

- offenders select victims carefully,
- offenders have prior or acquired familiarity with their victims,
- strangers commit a small percentage of crimes, and
- random crimes rarely occur.

The following statistics are specific examples that illustrate the strong victim–offender relationship/familiarity:

- In 2006, 83 percent of solved Canadian homicides were committed by offenders who were relatives and acquaintances. Only 17 percent were committed by strangers. The StatsCan definition of stranger is "a person who has a range of familiarity from none to minimal." This means its definition of stranger includes persons who acquired some degree of familiarity through planning or prior knowledge. Consequently, the percentage of homicides committed randomly, with absolutely no prior planning or prior thought is likely less than 17 percent.[14]
- The 2006 stats virtually mirror those of the past two decades.[15]
- The majority of violent crimes in Canada (60–64 percent) are committed by an offender known to the victim (counting both multiple- and single-offender cases). Over one-third (34 percent) were committed by strangers, but no statistics are available to show how many of these were committed without any acquired familiarity through planning whatsoever. The 34 percent represents only those who had no prior relationship with the victim.[16]
- Only 19 percent of Canadian sexual assaults have been committed by strangers.[17]
- 87.9 percent of offenders in Canada who committed criminal harassment were known by the victim. Strangers committed only 8.1 percent of this type of crime.[18]
- Child victims of sexual assaults knew the offender in 81 percent of offences. Child victims of physical assaults knew the offender in 73 percent of offences. Strangers committed 13 percent of sexual assaults and 22 percent of physical assaults upon children.[19]

Statistics Canada, in *Juristat* (various volumes), summarized its research with the following conclusions:

- Victims of violent crimes usually know their offenders.[20]
- Like most violent crimes, homicides are more likely to be committed by an offender known to the victim than by a stranger.[21]
- Females are most likely to be assaulted, sexually assaulted, and murdered in their own homes by someone they know, most often a spouse or ex-spouse.[22]
- Males are more likely than females to be victimized by acquaintances and strangers.[23]

Strong anecdotal evidence supports this empirical data. The anecdotal evidence is explained in two sources: (a) the reality case studies at the beginning of each chapter, and (b) the case law literature review on the website that accompanies this textbook, **www.emp.ca/arcaro/criminvestigation5E.**

Logic

Logic is seeing the big picture and recognizing connections—focusing on what is relevant and not on what is irrelevant; identifying what matters and what does not matter.

Reality example 1 You are investigating a bank robbery. Two weeks later, you have a discussion about an unrelated matter with a man who has a lengthy criminal record. He informs you that he entered the bank five minutes before the robbery occurred. His girlfriend worked as a teller. He had a "bad feeling" that something was going to happen. He went to a washroom and the robbery occurred while he was in the washroom. His girlfriend was robbed during the offence.

Is this a coincidence or is the man connected to the offence?

Reality example 2 You are at a crime scene where an armed gunman committed an offence nine minutes ago. You see a man on the sidewalk, walking past the crime scene. You recognize him from past investigations. You know this man has a lengthy criminal record that includes violence and weapons.

Is this a coincidence or is he connected to the offence?

Logic refers to processing specific information and reaching the correct interpretation.[24] It means analyzing and correctly translating the meaning of circumstances. Logic includes investigative analysis of circumstances and the making of one of two conclusions: (a) connection, or (b) coincidence.

Connection means there is a link between person(s) and events. *Coincidence* means the opposite—there is no connection.

Logic is synonymous with *common sense.* Every rookie police officer has been told by a veteran officer that policing is all about common sense. This is true, but it is not as simple as it sounds. No one is born with common sense and common sense does not just happen—nothing just happens. First, one has to define common sense before it can be developed.

Common sense is defined as routine, ordinary reasonable thinking that needs no special knowledge, which results in sensible conclusions and opinions. Common sense is *experience-based intuition* and logic. It is a type of *rapid analytical thinking* that becomes second-nature.

The key characteristics of common sense and logic are:

▸ Routine, ordinary: The problems or circumstances that require processing occur daily; they are not rare.
▸ Reasonable: Although there is more than one possible conclusion, there are concrete reasons that justify the best conclusion.
▸ Thinking that needs no special knowledge: Common sense is a cognitive process—a type of thinking. It does not develop exclusively from formal training or formal education. It develops by *applying knowledge*—it develops by doing. In other words, common sense develops through

experience, referring to repeated exposure to and practice in processing information and reaching correct conclusions and opinions. Experience refers to "reps"—the repetition of applying a skill or ability.

Logic and common sense require the application of four key skills to conclude whether an event is a coincidence or not:

1. Focus on relevance.
2. Discard the immaterial (that which is not relevant).
3. Choose the conclusion with the most justification (concrete evidence).
4. Avoid the conclusion with the least justification.

Focus on relevance means identifying what matters and what does not. Recognizing what information is significant and focusing on that information. The only two sources of information (evidence) are items and humans. These sources combine to produce a three-stage event: (a) pre-offence, (b) *actus reus*, and (c) post-offence (before, during, after). Every investigation includes the interaction between events, items, and humans. The interaction is composed of a number of concrete circumstances. An officer will be able to list each individual concrete circumstance that constitutes an occurrence.

The totality of the concrete circumstances will lead to more than one possible conclusion: (a) connection and (b) coincidence. Concrete circumstances constitute justifiable reasons. The interaction either shows a connection or it does not. Either the humans, items, and events are connected or they are not. The choice of correct conclusion corresponds to the number of concrete reasons. Choose the conclusion that is supported by the greater number of reasons.

The next concept teaches how to distinguish between a connection and a coincidence.

Coincidence

Coincidence should never be one's initial belief. Coincidence is a final conclusion, but only if concrete evidence proves that a coincidence occurred.

An officer never automatically believes in coincidences during an investigation. Coincidences have to be proved to be believed. Coincidences are rare. If an officer initially believes an event is a coincidence, there is a strong likelihood they will be wrong. Events should never be dismissed as a coincidence. Coincidence should only be the last conclusion, and only after it is proved by concrete evidence.

A coincidence is an unconnected event—an event that has no link to an offence. Formally, a **coincidence** is defined as a random or chance interaction between person(s), places, and events, with *no apparent connection* or reason that links them. A coincidence has the same three elements as a connection: person(s), a place, and an event. An example of the three-way interaction is a person's proximity to a crime scene, immediately before, during, or immediately after the offence. Proximity to a crime scene may be a coincidence or a connection. An officer's job is to determine whether a person was connected or not. It can only be one or the other. If the proximity is not connected, it has to be a coincidence, and vice-versa.

The process of concluding whether an event is a connection or coincidence includes a simple strategic sequence:

1. do not arbitrarily dismiss the event as a coincidence,
2. obtain a maximum volume of evidence, including statements from the people involved in the event that prove intention, and
3. apply the definition of logic to make a final conclusion.

An initial, automatic conclusion of coincidence, before proving it with concrete evidence, is counterintuitive, illogical thinking. Coincidences are not common. They may happen, but it should not be an officer's first conclusion. Automatically believing that an event is a coincidence is a sign of inexperience. All rookie police officers start their careers with a degree of gullibility and naiveté because they have been conditioned to believe in coincidences. All rookies go through this stage. Here are three examples of how easy it is to wrongly dismiss an event as a coincidence:

1. The owners of a house unexpectedly decide to go out for only one hour. During their absence, a break and enter occurs.

   "What a coincidence"—the offenders got lucky and picked a place during a brief, unplanned absence.

2. A break and enter occurs at a house while the owners are on a three-day vacation.

   "What a coincidence"—the offender(s) got lucky and just happened to select a vacated house, by chance.

3. A robbery occurs at a gas station. No customers were present at the time of the offence. The complainant reports that it had been busy for three hours prior to the robbery with a high volume of customers.

   "What a coincidence"—the robbery happened just at the right time for the offender, when no witnesses were present, instead of earlier when several witnesses were present.

The first case was completely fabricated—the owner confessed that she falsely reported the break and enter. The second offence was committed by a person who knew that the house was unoccupied during the day—he confessed that he learned about it from the complainants' sons, who broadcast their parents' absence throughout their high school while trying to arrange a party. The third case was staged by an employee, who confessed that he asked a friend to wait outside the gas station, disguise himself, and pretend to rob him. The employee thought that staging it was more believable than outright fabricating the robbery. He wanted to conceal stealing money from the cash register—he needed money to pay a drug debt.

It would have been a mistake to instantly believe that all three of these examples were coincidences. Instead, the initial assumption was that a connection existed. The assumption of a connection has to be explored before an event can be dismissed as a coincidence.

MODUS OPERANDI PARADOX

One specific type of connection is called the **modus operandi (M.O.) paradox**. *Modus operandi* is a Latin phrase meaning "method of operation." A *paradox* refers to a contradiction. The M.O. paradox that occurs early in the theory development process refers to circumstances that cause a concurrent suspicion that either (a) the offence did not happen, resulting in a false report being made, or (b) the offence did actually happen and it was committed by someone who had strong familiarity, either from a long-term relationship or through planning.

Minimizing risks while maximizing benefits is the core of a "natural crime." This low-risk and high-reward M.O. is the fundamental principle that governs the skill of *crime scene analysis*, the process that forms an opinion of whether or not crime scene staging occurred. **Crime scene staging** is defined as intentionally manipulating a crime scene to mislead the police by fabricating an offence or concealing a real offence and diverting suspicion.

In the above three cases, if the circumstances had been "coincidental," concrete evidence would have proved the lack of a connection. In other words, concrete evidence would have dispelled the M.O. paradox suspicion that crime scene staging had occurred.

Anatomy of a Crime

Motive + opportunity + "low risk and high reward" are the general elements of all crimes. These elements form the *natural* way of committing an offence. "Bad character" habits emerge from them.

Every crime is unique to some degree—some specific circumstance differentiates one offence from another. Although the specific circumstances create differences, there are general similarities that form predictable, natural ways of committing certain crimes.

A crime is a task. All tasks have an anatomy, referring to structure and elements that create a certain extent of predictability. There are *four elements* to every task, including crimes. The four elements occur within the three stages of an offence: (a) pre-offence, (b) *actus reus*, and (c) post-offence. The following chart lists the four elements, divided into the three stages:

Elements	Stage
1. goal setting	
2. planning + strategizing	pre-offence
3. execution	*actus reus*
4. outcome + evaluation	post-offence

PRE-OFFENCE ELEMENTS

Two elements occur before the offence: (a) goal setting and (b) planning and strategizing. The time length of the pre-offence stage varies, ranging from only a few minutes to months or even years.

Goal Setting

Like all tasks, every offence starts with some type of *goal*, emerging from a *motive*. A goal is defined as a purpose and objective that results in a reward or benefit. Planning and strategizing create the opportunity to achieve the goal.

Motives emerge from and are driven by a need or unresolved problem that must be solved. Every unresolved conflict is a motivator—it motivates change. It motivates the person to want to do something to change the situation; crime is one solution—it fills the need with the benefit. Therefore, motive and crime represent cause and effect—a naturally occurring process that guides most humans in their daily activities.

Criminals use the same general problem-solving model to commit crimes as the police use to solve the crime. An offender defines his problem—e.g., he needs money. The problem forms the motive, referring to the *mens rea* (intent)—e.g., rob a bank. After the intent is formed, a goal is set; planning and strategizing begin, focusing on achieving maximum reward by being exposed to minimal risk. A "low-risk and high-reward" outcome applies to every imaginable task, legal or illegal, and represents maximum benefit for the criminal.

All crimes are *benefit-oriented*, meaning the offender is seeking a reward, defined as a benefit to the offender. The two general types of reward/benefit are (a) *gratification*, including financial, physical, and emotional, or (b) *avoidance* of pain or consequence.

In other words, the benefit of crime is profit or pleasure. The motivation to acquire the maximum benefit is *need*. The need constitutes the motive, while the reward drives the motive. *Finding the need will prove the motive. Proving the motive can predict the reward.*

Understanding the full concept of need is important for pre-offence investigative strategy. Need brings on unresolved conflict. There are two types of unresolved conflict:

1. Internal conflict, called cognitive dissonance,[25] and
2. External conflict, referring to hatred and rage directed toward others.

Cognitive dissonance is defined as an internal conflict brought on by either unresolved need or unresolved conflict, or by not acting in accordance with one's beliefs. For example, the need for money causes cognitive dissonance. So does doing anything that contradicts a personal belief. Doing something that you believe is wrong causes more cognitive dissonance. Stealing, substance abuse, and hurting others are some examples of acts that cause cognitive dissonance. The wrongdoing does not have to be illegal to cause cognitive dissonance. Smoking, getting drunk, overeating, being out of shape, and being lazy or irresponsible all cause some degree of cognitive dissonance.

Cognitive dissonance is a powerful form of stress and anxiety that grows, sometimes out of control, until reconciliation is reached. Reconciliation is an internal balance and consistency. It refers to a solution to the internal conflict, where the conflict is resolved.[26]

Cognitive dissonance is a motivator, meaning it continuously compels behaviour until reconciliation is reached and the internal conflict stops. If reconciliation is not reached, the unresolved conflict continuously intensifies the need, which intensifies the conflict until chaos and dysfunction result.

If a need is the cause of the cognitive dissonance, filling the need will resolve the internal conflict. If the cause of the cognitive dissonance is guilt brought on from doing something believed to be wrong, there are only two ways to alleviate or resolve the internal conflict: (a) confess or (b) rationalize. "Getting it off your chest" removes the internal stress but so does rationalizing the wrongdoing. *Rationalization* is defined as justification by making excuses (e.g., "every one does it," "I was forced to do it," "it wasn't my fault," "it's not as bad as it seems and it isn't really wrong when you look at it carefully").

Either way, cognitive dissonance creates an investigative advantage because cognitive dissonance causes *unique behaviour*. It forces the person to do and say things that may be memorable to others. The verbal statements and physical acts that are caused by cognitive dissonance constitute incriminating pre-offence conduct. This conduct constitutes *leakage*, referring to acts that reveal intention. Leakage constitutes warning signs or "red flags"; they may be cautionary indicators of future crimes.

Internal and external conflicts interact and are inexorably linked. One causes and perpetuates the other. Stress causes hatred. Hatred increases anxiety, which accelerates rage, back and forth, until personality disorders manifest. These cycles cause a "shattered personality," which reveals itself in dysfunctional behaviour,[27] i.e., more incriminating pre-offence conduct.

The following chart illustrates the relationships between need, unresolved conflict, cognitive dissonance, reconciliation, and crime:

The three concepts of goal, motive, and benefit are inseparable and all have one thing in common—they are *motivators*. They generate structured, well-thought-

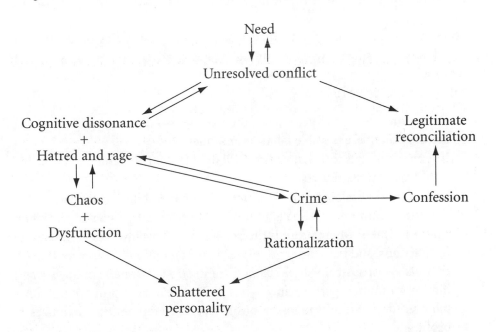

out acts or spontaneous impulsive behaviour that can be identified through investigative strategies.

If a crime has no motive, it is most likely the product of a mental disorder. Section 16 C.C. creates a *defence of mental disorder*, previously called insanity. A crime caused by a mental disorder will likely be committed in an illogical, irrational manner because it will have no purpose.

After the goal is set, a series of decisions occur to achieve the goal by planning and strategizing.

Planning and Strategizing

"The greatest emotion known to mankind is fear. The greatest fear is fear of the unknown."[28] This is the reason we plan: to remove fear of the unknown.

Planning decides *what* to do; strategizing decides *how* to do it. Both require informed decision making. Planning is a *general* decision-making process, while strategizing is a *specific* decision-making process.

PLANNING

The planning stage involves the accumulation of ideas, information, and data for the purpose of acquiring familiarity and devising strategy. Planning is a *change agent*. It changes:

- the unknown to known,
- uncertainty to certainty,
- stress to confidence, and
- the appearance of a pre-offence place that constitutes a secondary crime scene.

All planning includes decision making and physical actions. The extent of planning corresponds to the extent of prior familiarity with the victim: less familiarity results in more planning—more prior familiarity may result in less planning.

After the offender's motive is formed, planning and strategizing occurs to minimize risk and maximize reward. Planning creates opportunity, or allows the offender to seize opportunity.

Offenders fear *three risks*:

1. **Detection** The fear of getting caught is obvious—the consequences of getting caught are possible jail time and fines.
2. **Injury** Criminals fear that victims will fight back. This is one reason why criminals arm themselves.
3. **Failure** One possible result of failure is losing credibility within the criminal community. Crime is a business for criminals: a small business or a large business, where profit is the bottom line. This involves interactions, transactions, and trust. Strength of personal reputation is important to criminals, just as in any legal business transaction. Past performance is an indicator of future performance—it is directly related to profit margin. A poor reputation results in loss of business; a good reputation maximizes profit.

Planning involves thinking of ideas and discussing these ideas with other people. Thinking of a plan to commit a criminal act advances the *intention* (*mens rea*) and is the starting point of forming the *physical act* (*actus reus*).

Planning mobilizes a transfer of physical evidence and a communication transfer. For example:

- **Asking about potential targets** Offenders consult with others, seeking advice about the targeted places and persons.
- **Recruiting accomplices (human resources)** Offenders form a team when one offender chooses not to act alone.
- **Physical resources** Offenders decide what items are needed and acquire them (i.e., weapons, transportation, tools, and disguises). Attempts to acquire are equally as significant as the actual acquisition.
- **Scouting** Offenders visit the place or person the plan to victimize in order to learn layout and habits. Because this type of visit has no legitimate purpose, the offender(s) acts in a manner that others find *suspicious*. Suspicious behaviour draws attention to the offender and it usually is memorable because the behaviour is unique—it is not normal. Attention helps pre-offence witnesses with facial recognition, called *identifying the offender(s)*.
- **Writing** Drawing diagrams and writing notes is a major part of planning. It precedes strategizing.

Forming ideas and communicating them involves interaction with people. Those who saw the planning or heard the offender's plans are *pre-offence witnesses* who may be able to

- identify the offender(s),
- facilitate the discovery of physical evidence, and/or
- prove *mens rea* at the trial.

Extensive planning presents an opportunity to investigators—more items are transferred and more communication occurs, giving investigators more potential evidence. How much planning occurs? The extent of planning depends on two variables: the extent of the offender's (a) prior knowledge and familiarity of the target, and (b) fear of perceived risks.

The amount of planning is proportionate to the amount of prior familiarity, knowledge, and fear of risks (degree of certainty):

- Less prior familiarity and knowledge = more planning.
- Greater prior familiarity and knowledge = less planning.
- Less fear of risks = less planning.
- Greater fear of risks = more planning.

Minimal planning also provides an investigative benefit: it logically suggests *greater prior familiarity* between offender and victim.

What about spontaneous acts? There are two types—*actual* spontaneous acts and those that *appear* to be spontaneous. Actual spontaneity occurs with minimal or no planning; this suggests mental health problems, impulsivity, no control of emotions, limited cognitive ability, or provocation that exceeded limits of restraint.

Acts that appear to be spontaneous are offences that appear to be unexpected because the offender thought and planned silently and alone. The offender may silently think of committing and plan to commit an offence without overt preparation or discussion. The motive existed, but the offender concealed his intent. How can this silent intent be proved? By the offender's confession to any person—police or citizen—or, circumstantially, by the offender's conduct. A confession directly proves what the offender was thinking. Circumstantial conduct may indirectly prove the offender's thoughts.

After sufficient information is acquired and ideas are formed during the planning stage, the next step is to decide on specific strategy.

STRATEGIZING

A **strategy** is a structured scheme that governs *how* to commit the task. It is the cumulative result of several decisions made about tactics.

Strategizing constitutes a *specific* action plan. No strategy can be applied without some extent of *improvisation*, referring to the rapid change needed to adapt to unexpected situations.

Criminal strategy that minimizes risk and maximizes rewards has two general characteristics or features:

- speed, and
- discretion.

Speed

During the interrogation of a violent, repeat offender arrested for multiple house break and enters, he was asked why he chose his specific method of operation. His response explained a simple philosophy: "in and out." That is, minimize the risks and maximize the benefits. He wanted to complete the task as quickly as possible—wasting no time, drawing no attention, and taking portable items.

When analyzing a reported crime to determine validity, determine the duration of the offence. How long did the offence take? The duration should be compatible with the low-risk and high-reward strategy. Offenders prefer speed. Speed is a risk-avoidance strategy. Familiarity facilitates speed.

There are some exceptions to the speed preference:

- **Expectation of presence because of long-term prior familiarity** When an offender is related to or knows the victim, the offender's presence will not draw attention. He belonged there. No one would be suspicious or alarmed to see him at the place.
- **Certainty of privacy** When an offender believes that he has total privacy and is certain no witness will see him, he will not be concerned with speed. This type of certainty also requires substantial knowledge.
- **Carelessness.**

Discretion

This refers to caution used to avoid attracting attention. Examples of discreet strategy include:

- Minimizing noise and damage to enter a place and steal items.
- Entering a place at a location that is not in plain view of witnesses.

Speed and discretion are intended to minimize or eliminate:

- identification by witnesses (facial recognition) during all three stages of the offence.

- being found at the crime scene by police, and
- any connection between the offender and the offence.

The strategy intends to eliminate two types of evidence:

1. **Witness observation** Staying away from *witness sight lines*, referring to places that allow direct observation.
2. **Physical items** Not having possession of incriminating physical evidence if stopped by the police.

Offender's intention *Minimize risk and maximize reward.* Example: strategizing for theft-related offences: the *4 Ps—portability, profit, people, protection*:

1. **Portability** Steal what is easy to carry and leave quickly.
2. **Profit** Sell quickly.
3. **People** Limit exposure to witnesses: pre-offence, during offence, post-offence.
4. **Protection** Minimize risk of injury during all three phases.

Both legitimate crimes and fabricated crimes are recognizable. Both have identifiable elements. Offenders have habits that may develop into incriminating evidence called *similar acts*, referring to a specific rule of evidence that helps prove the offender's identity.

SUPPORTING CASE LAW

The fact that offenders plan and strategize is borne out by countless case law decisions, examples of which can be found on the accompanying website **www.emp.ca/arcaro/criminvestigation5E**. The following two prominent cases are often referenced in court decisions as examples of crime planning.

In *R. v. Klymchuk* (2005)[29] the court found that offenders seek "low-risk" crime. Offenders seek low-risk crime opportunities, defined as places and victims that create minimal or no personal risk to the offender of being detected, injured, or failing. A low-risk crime opportunity is called a *soft target*, defined as a place or victim that an offender prefers and will likely select. Low-risk, soft target characteristics involve the 4 Ps—portability, profit, people, protection.

Regarding property crimes such as break and enter, the following are examples of how offenders apply the 4 Ps during victim selection and planning:

- No witnesses, no occupants (no people).
- Likelihood of portable property (maximum profit).
- Lack of security and absence of plain view point of entry (maximum protection).

No people + portable property = maximum profit

A low-risk, soft target is safe and profitable for the offender. It avoids attracting attention, allows fast execution, and maximizes potential profits.

Offenders avoid high-risk targets, defined as places or victims who pose a risk to the offender. A high-risk target is a *hard target*—these are not preferred victims. The characteristics of a high-risk, hard target are:

- ▸ Ample lighting at points of entry.
- ▸ Presence of security systems—e.g., alarms, dogs, etc.
- ▸ Presence and activity of occupants inside the place.
- ▸ Close proximity to neighbours or traffic.
- ▸ Poor or no likelihood of plain-view valuables.
- ▸ Poor or no likelihood of portable property.

In *R. v. Pilon* (2006)[30] the court listed the preferred strategies and traits of experienced "break and enter" offenders:

1. They move quickly. Speed is preferred.
2. Profit or purpose. The reason for the break and enter is to steal, attempt to steal, or commit some unlawful act that benefits the offender.
3. Portable property is preferred.
4. They try to minimize the transfer of physical evidence by planning.
5. They form habits that become the offender's personal trademark. One habit is often revealed through victim selection. They stick to one type of place. If they start with houses, they stick with houses. If they start with commercial places, they stick with those.

These common elements of property crime are significant to determine (a) whether similar acts are admissible at a trial to help prove identity, and (b) the validity of the offence—whether or not crime scene staging occurred.

SUMMARY

Goal setting, planning, and strategizing build confidence to minimize risk and maximize reward.

Pre-offence decisions and actions create (a) motive and opportunity and (b) habits, referring to M.O. Habits are significant. Habits may fall under two rules of evidence:

1. **"Bad character" evidence** Although generally inadmissible during a trial, it may be used for theory development and forming reasonable grounds during the investigation.
2. **Similar acts** Referring to a rule of evidence that, when admissible as an exception to "bad character" evidence, helps prove offender identity.

DURING THE OFFENCE (ACTUS REUS)

This stage has only one element: execution. It is the central focus of the investigation—the actual crime. It is usually the shortest time period of the three offence stages.

Execute means to carry out the strategy. Execution represents the performance of what was planned. The actual offence is carried out or performed during this stage. This constitutes the *actus reus* (*physical act*) of the offence. This element is the *most important* because:

1. This is the actual crime. It is the only element that must be proved in its entirety.
2. The greatest amount of transfer of physical items usually occurs here.

3. The crime scene is created. The pre-offence appearance changes to the post-offence appearance. The change can be identified and matched to the cause of the change.
4. The planning and strategy are revealed. How an offence was executed shows how it was planned. As soon as the task is executed, an outcome immediately results. The officer can analyze the circumstances to develop theories.

The remainder of the book is devoted to explaining how to reconstruct the *actus reus*.

POST-OFFENCE STAGE

This is the "after the offence" stage. It has two elements: *outcome* and *evaluation*. The outcome focuses on immediate post-offence results. Evaluation refers to short-term and long-term post-offence conduct by the offender(s).

Outcome and Evaluation

Two results occur immediately upon completion of an offence:

1. **The actual consequences of the crime** These includes injuries, stolen property, and damage. The volume of results is directly proportionate to the extent of motive and opportunity. In other words, what results from the act depends on how it was carried out.
2. **Change of crime scene appearance** Every offence has a crime scene—the place where the offence occurred. The crime scene is the place where the greatest volume of transfer usually occurs. All crime scenes have two different appearances: the *pre-offence appearance* differs from the *post-offence appearance*. This change in appearance occurs during the crime. The transition from pre-offence to post-offence appearance can be re-created.

Evaluation means post-offence analysis by the offender of what happened through discussion and conduct. The time length of this stage varies. It involves post-offence transfer of communication and items to maximize the benefit (i.e., sell or dispose of property).

This stage is formally called *post-offence conduct*, and is defined as the offender's incriminating behaviour and statements (verbal or written) that occur between the moment the offence is completed to the close of the investigation. Post-offence conduct is circumstantial evidence that proves offender identity.[31]

During the post-offence stage, the offender will do two things that relate to the offence: (a) he will talk about it and (b) he will move items that were used or stolen during the offence. Two evidence pathways are formed. One for statements and one for physical items.

The two investigative objectives relevant to post-offence conduct are

1. confessions, and
2. item recovery.

CONFESSIONS

The topic of confessions is taught and applied incrementally throughout this book. The following is an introduction: according to the S.C.C., in a series of case law decisions, confessions are the best evidence that proves guilt.[32] A properly obtained, voluntary confession (a) removes all doubt about who committed the crime, (b) prevents the prosecution of innocent people, and (c) is the offender's first step toward rehabilitation and reintegration into society.[33]

Consequently, interrogation is the most important investigative skill for any police officer to master. However, not all confessions are made to police during formal interrogations. Confessions are commonly made to citizens. Offenders make unprompted post-offence confessions, defined as incriminating statements, without any questioning by an authority.

The volume of unprompted confessions corresponds with offender–recipient familiarity. This means that the offender is more likely to tell a familiar person that he committed an offence and less likely to tell a complete stranger.

Every offender makes a conscious decision to confess or not during the post-offence stage. Greater severity of offence often translates into more confessions. Why? Greater severity of crime causes greater cognitive dissonance. This means worse internal conflict and greater stress, along with a stronger need to relieve them. Homicides, for example, are sometimes easier to solve than less severe offences for the simple reason that committing murder generates the worst type of cognitive dissonance. It causes the greatest burden that a person has to resolve internally. Some degree of the internal turmoil is eased each time a murderer tells someone in his inner circle.

Example: In an actual reality investigation explained later in this book, an offender murdered a person whose body was not found until 18 months later. During that time, the offender confessed to at least 22 familiar people in his inner circle, all of whom gave written statements to the police reporting what the offender said. Those 22 incriminating statements were made by the offender to alleviate the strongest cognitive dissonance that a person can suffer.

Interrogation strategies, designed to elicit a confession, emerge from lawful strategies that are governed by case law. Extensive case law research is included in Phase 3 of this book, and continues on the accompanying website **www.emp.ca/arcaro/criminvestigation5E**.

ITEM RECOVERY

Every offence includes the transfer of some amount of physical evidence. Items have greater initial evidentiary value than humans. Consequently, searching for and seizing items is crucial.

The path of post-offence incriminating statements often interacts with the post-offence paths of items. What an offender communicates to others helps the officer find items that the offender used or stole.

Depending of the type of offence committed, the offender's post-offence goals include concealing, disposal, and sale of items used or stolen during the offence. All three require *possession* and *movement* of items. This usually requires conversation between the offender and citizens. In property crimes, offenders use the standard business model during the post-offence stage: advertise, market, and sell.

The *post-offence* stage of one offence often merges with the *pre-offence* stage of a new offence. For example, the theft of an item starts the offence of possession of stolen property. The buyer of stolen property becomes both an offender and a witness to the seller's offence of theft.

Although the blending of offence stages creates some complexities, the investigation may become simplified because more evidence is transferred (items exchanged and words communicated), more witnesses emerge, and stronger habits are revealed. In other words, the volume of incriminating evidence stands to increase exponentially.

TRANSFER OF EVIDENCE

The time length of each stage of an offence varies. The *actus reus* is usually the shortest; pre- and post-offence stages are usually longer. Transfer of evidence occurs at all three stages.

General rule: the volume of evidence transferred generally corresponds to the time periods closest to the crime:

1. The largest volume of evidence transfer occurs *during* the offence.
2. The next largest occurs at the stages immediately before and after the offence (the times closest to the offence). No concrete minute or hour defines these time periods. They are defined by the largest volume of relevant activity—transferred evidence—before or after the actual offence.
3. The least amount of evidence transfer occurs at the longest time away from the offence, both before and after. No concrete time defines this period.

The following diagram illustrates the concept of "blended offence stages" with respect to the transfer of evidence.

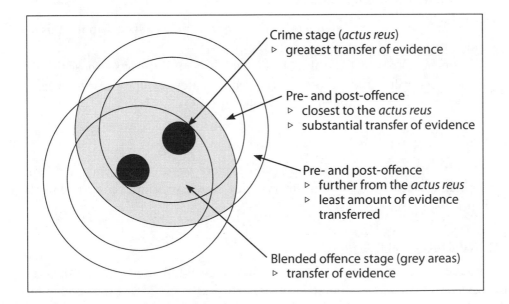

BEST Network Circles

Human networking is complex and extensive. Stanley Milgram is one of many researchers who has demonstrated this. Milgram shows—with his "six degrees of separation" concept—that it's a small world, and we are all connected in some way.[34]

Every person has a unique network of people, a web of relationships. This network can be divided into three "circles" of members, identified by the extent of and type of familiarity they have with the offender. Members of an offender's inner circle are easily identifiable as the people with whom the offender communicates the most and has the strongest familiarity. It is the smallest of the three network levels.

The perimeter of the inner circle is a group of acquaintances with weaker familiarity, but who spend considerable time communicating with the person. Although this is a larger group than the inner circle, it is still possible to identify the members of this group.

The outer circle members have the weakest familiarity and are the least identifiable. Their relationships involve little communication with the person and their contact involves both direct and indirect familiarity. This group learns familiarity from hearsay and "broadcasting" (e.g., media, Internet, and word of mouth—where a person works, lives, and socializes). This group includes four possible types of non-familial relationships called "BEST":

1. **B**usiness: includes any financial transaction relationships—e.g, work (employee–employer), purchases (customer–retailer), rent (tenant–landlord, etc.).
2. **E**ducation: where we learn—e.g., schools, sports, etc.
3. **S**ocial: no formal business or education connection—emotional gratification.
4. **T**emporary: none of the above relationships—minimal or no direct contact; relationship through "broadcasting."

Since both victims and offenders have networks, a police officer can use this to help identify potential suspects and witnesses.

The offender's network can also identify witnesses and suspects—those the offender told about his crime, those who helped the offender, and those who took items from the offender for their own criminal purposes.

INSIDE-OUT RULE

To determine which potential suspects to explore or to obtain an offender's incriminating statements, begin by interviewing the victim's inner circle and work outward—work from the inside out.

POSITIONING RULE

Eventually, an investigation will put the officer in both the offender's and the victim's networks. Positioning oneself in these networks is significant for developing expertise in two vital investigative skills: (a) interrogation and (b) informant development. As an officer gets closer to the centre of an offender's network, he or she will see a dramatic increase in success—more confessions, more informants.

Online broadcasting is a potent form of inadvertently creating familiarity with an offender. "Facebook" is a prime example of an opportunity to position oneself in an offender's network. People divulge incredible amounts of personal information to the whole world—what they own, where they go, when they go there, and with whom.

Learning how to position oneself for success will be explained in subsequent chapters in this book, including witness interviews, informant development, and interrogation strategies.

DEFINING EACH STEP IN THE BASIC INVESTIGATIVE SEQUENCE

Review: The BIS is a theory development model. It is a general step-by-step system that creates exploratory lists of possible suspects by forming sequential "mere suspicions" that eliminate or implicate logical suspects for the purpose of forming reasonable grounds. The sequence prevents (a) haphazard, unstructured investigations and (b) the overlooking or ignoring of logical potential offenders.

Step 1. Validate the complaint.

↓

Step 2. Suspect a relative committed the offence.

↓

Step 3. Suspect an acquaintance committed the offence.

↓

Step 4. Suspect a non-acquaintance committed the offence.

↓

Step 5. Suspect a stranger randomly committed the offence.

Validation

Fabricated complaints are commonly reported to the police for a number of benefit-oriented reasons, including profit and revenge. The frequency of fabricated reports requires verification of every offence and validation of every report before progressing in the sequence. **Validation** is defined as verifying and proving *three facts*:

1. The offence actually occurred and was *not fabricated.*
2. If the offence actually occurred, it *occurred at the reported location.*
3. If the offence actually occurred, it *occurred in the reported manner.*

Validation is complete when these three factors have been proved. Validation requires answering the following questions:

▸ Did the offence actually occur or was it fabricated intentionally? Many reasons motivate people to intentionally fabricate offences. One of the most common reasons is financial gain made by defrauding insurance companies. Recognizing a fabricated offence is necessary to prevent innocent persons from being falsely suspected, implicated, or accused of committing crimes that never happened.

▸ If the offence actually occurred, did it occur at the reported location? A victim may conceal the actual location of an offence and may fabricate a false location to prevent embarrassment. For example, a complainant might have had his car stolen or entered a place that he may not want his spouse or others to know he was visiting. This might cause the complainant to report the actual offence, but may lie about where it happened. If this deception is not detected, three consequences may result:

1. The actual crime scene will never be found. There will be no crime scene analysis and the physical evidence transferred at the real crime scene will not be found.
2. Wrong conclusions and wrong suspicions will be formed.
3. There will be an inability to prove the actual location if a charge is laid—the location is an essential fact-in-issue that must be proved at every criminal trial (failure to prove the actual location may result in an acquittal).

▸ If the offence actually occurred, did it occur in the manner reported? Victims sometimes report real occurrences, but lie about how they happened. Instead, they report partial circumstances; for example: (a) an assault where the victim fails to report that they provoked the assault, and (b) a break and enter where the complainant "pads" the report by inflating the list of stolen or damaged property.

An officer can prove validation or fabrication through *criminal investigation analysis*, which is evaluating the credibility of the report by comparing the reported circumstances with the logical anatomy of the reported offence to identify the presence or absence of inconsistencies. The next chapter explains this analysis procedure.

After the report is validated, progress to step two in the sequence by suspecting relatives.

Suspect a Relative Committed the Offence

After the complaint has been validated, relatives are the first group of suspects for two reasons: (a) it is the most logical group and (b) it is the smallest, easiest group to identify and eliminate.

▸ Relatives are the most logical first group of suspects when no clear suspects exist: they have the most familiarity with the victim. Research shows that relatives frequently commit offences against one another.
▸ Relatives are an easily identifiable group.
▸ The group is small and suspects can be easily eliminated.
▸ Relatives provide a logical starting point and give structure to an investigation when no other evidence exists.

A relative may be intentionally or unintentionally involved. *Unintentional involvement* refers to inadvertent broadcasting of information that helps someone else select a victim and plan the offence; for example, telling people when a house or business is unoccupied, where valuable items are, the layout of a building, and so on.

Starting with this group of potential suspects, identify the presence or absence of three elements of suspicion:

1. bad character,
2. motive, and
3. opportunity.

The presence of any one of these three elements should strengthen suspicion. The absence of all three weakens or eliminates suspicion.

After relatives are eliminated as suspects, proceed to the next stage of assumptions.

Suspect an Acquaintance Committed the Offence

This is the next logical step because this group is reasonably small, can be easily identified, and has strong enough familiarity to create motive and opportunity. Acquaintances include not only "friends," but also those in the BEST network (business, education, social, temporary). Specific examples include:

▸ neighbours,
▸ customers,
▸ work colleagues (employees/employers, etc.), and
▸ close and casual friends.

After this list is eliminated, proceed to the next stage of assumptions.

Suspect a Non-Acquaintance Committed the Offence

This is the most challenging group of offenders to identify—those who gain familiarity through planning. These are not random offenders; they purposely select their victim. The victim will have minimum or no prior knowledge of the non-acquaintance offender. This group usually has no prior relationship with the victim. Usually, the only victim–offender pre-offence contact occurs during the planning stage—for example, the offender enters a business acting as a potential customer.

Consequently, the victim likely cannot help an officer identify this group unless the offender acted suspiciously and memorably during the pre-offence planning. For example, suspicious behaviour is often detected when offenders do not behave the way legitimate customers usually do.

In reality, this group of offenders is not identified *in isolation*, meaning one at a time after a crime is committed. Instead, structured organizational and personal intelligence is constantly learned, recorded, and stored. Intelligence gathering refers to *scouting*—learning the characteristics, traits, habits, and tendencies of individual and organized criminals. In other words, an officer will have the availability of formal intelligence (police records) and informal intelligence (their own memory and notebook recordings) that will allow them to form suspicions based on similar acts. They will know which criminals are *active*, referring to those who are currently committing crimes that go undetected, and their tendencies. The officer will be able to respond to a call, take a report, and recognize a *modus operandi* by simply analyzing the way a crime was committed and recognizing the similar acts.

The size of this group is usually large. Those in it will not be easily eliminated because many will have had *capacity* (motive and opportunity created by planning). Only in cases where an officer can positively eliminate this group of suspects should he or she proceed to the fifth and final assumption.

Suspect a Stranger Randomly Committed the Offence

A *stranger* is a person who is unknown and unfamiliar to the victim and who randomly committed the offence, without any degree of planning. This assumption should be made last because, statistically, a stranger is the least likely person to commit an offence. Cases where a stranger is the offender are rare. Identifying the suspects in this group is challenging for two reasons: (a) the group size is infinite, and (b) no planning means no pre-offence transfer of evidence occurred. A mental disorder is the likely cause of a random criminal act.

It is important to follow the prescribed sequence for the following reasons:

- ▸ The sizes of the groups increase when moving from relatives to acquaintances to strangers, and it is easier to investigate the smaller groups first than to investigate an infinite number of strangers.
- ▸ Relatives, acquaintances, and non-acquaintances who are familiar with the victim are more likely to be offenders.
- ▸ The sequence follows a logical, structured order and is compatible with victim-selection theories.

The sequence should not be used in reverse because (a) the infinite number of possible suspects in the group of strangers cannot be identified or eliminated, and (b) the officer will ignore, and may never consider, the logical suspects from the other groups. In other words, the investigation will likely fail.

Case Study 3.1 Investigation

Minimal information and maximum uncertainty exist. You must form an initial theory and apply the Basic Investigative Sequence.

In Chapter 6, the strategies and investigative theories discussed in Chapters 1–5 are applied to the case study from Chapter 1 to explain how the first officer will begin the investigation. These same principles can be applied to the case study in this chapter.

ENDNOTES

1. Manitoba Justice, *The Inquiry Regarding Thomas Sophonow* (Winnipeg: Manitoba Justice, 2001), http://www.gov.mb.ca/justice/publications/sophonow/.

2. Ontario, *Bernardo Investigation Review: Report of Mr. Justice Archie Campbell* (Toronto: Queen's Printer, June 1996).

3. *R. v. Dalzell*, 2003 CanLII 49355 (Ont. S.C.).

4. *R. v. Nicholas*, 2006 CanLII 52319 (Ont. S.C.).

5. *R. v. Morrison*, [2000] O.J. No. 5733.

6. *R. v. Buchanan*, [2006] O.J. No. 814.

7. *R. v. Michaud*, 2007 CanLII 355 (Ont. C.J.).

8. *R. v. Dalzell*, supra note 3.

9. Ibid.

10. *R. v. Nicholas*, supra note 4.

11. Ibid.

12. L. Wilkins, *Social Deviance* (London: Tavistock, 1964), 75.

13. *Juristat* vol. 16, no. 9 (July 1996).

14. Statistics Canada, 2006, http://www.statcan.ca/english/freepub/85-002-XIE/85-002-XIE2007008.pdf.

15. Ibid.

16. *Juristat* vol. 18, no. 9 (June 1998); *Juristat* vol. 17, no. 11 (November 1997).

17. *Juristat* vol. 18, no. 9 (June 1998).

18. *Juristat* vol. 17, no. 11 (November 1997).

19. Ibid.

20. *Juristat* vol. 18, no. 9 (June 1998).

21. Ibid.

22. *Juristat* vol. 16, no. 6 (June 1996).

23. Ibid.

24. G. Arcaro, "Interrogation Best Practices," Ph.D. research material, University of Regina, 2007.

25. L. Festinger, *A Theory of Cognitive Dissonance* (Stanford, CA: Stanford University Press, 1957).

26. Ibid.

27. C. Rogers, *Client-Centered Therapy: Its Current Practice, Implications and Theory* (London: Constable, 1951).

28. Unknown author.

29. *R. v. Klymchuk* (2005), 203 C.C.C. (3d) 341 (Ont. C.A.).

30. *R. v. Pilon*, 2006 CanLII 16368 (Ont. S.C.).

31. G. Arcaro, "Post-Offence Conduct: Investigative Strategy" (2005) vol. 3, no. 4 *Canadian Journal of Police and Security Services*.

32. *R. v. Smith* (1989), 50 C.C.C. (3d) 308 (S.C.C.).

33. Ibid.

34. S. Milgram, "The Small World Problem" (1967) vol. 2 *Psychology Today*.

CHAPTER 4

First Officer Responsibilities: Emergency Response and Preliminary Investigation

LEARNER SUMMARY

"First officer" is the most demanding and dangerous job in front-line policing, especially when acting as an *emergency responder* for an "in-progress" call.

First officer is a formal role. It involves coordinating a wide range of people and tasks. The first officer has a number of responsibilities governed by laws, from which strategies emerge. *Laws* authorize what an officer may do; *strategies* tell an officer how to do it.

This chapter works in conjunction with the *Basic Police Procedures: Arrest and Search Procedures*, 4th ed. (Toronto: Emond Montgomery, 2009), which explains decision-making models regarding (a) police powers of arrest and investigative detention, and (b) authorities to enter a place with and without a warrant, including Feeney warrants and exceptions during emergencies.

Case Study 4.1

2:05 a.m. You are a uniform officer on patrol. You receive the following radio broadcast: "Break and enter in-progress: house at 1445 Lakeridge Road."

The house is situated in an urban area, near the downtown core. You are nearby, only a few blocks away from the house. While en route, you see no cars and no pedestrians.

2:07 a.m. Arrival. You are the first officer to arrive.

You park in a strategic location (one that does not make you a target—gives you proper protection). You walk toward the house, knowing that these circumstances legally constitute a "common-law exigent circumstance" (CLEC).

A middle-aged woman is at the front door. She informs you, "A man tried to attack my daughter." You ask, "Is he still here, or is he gone?" The woman replies, "He's gone. He ran out the front door." She does not know his direction of travel, and cannot facially recognize the offender.

You identify that there are three people present. The woman at the door is Paula (45). Her two daughters are present: Tammy (17) and Julie (15). No one else lives at this home. Paula is divorced. Her husband moved out of town several years ago.

No one is injured. You search the interior of the house. No suspects are found. You briefly interview all three people separately, obtain the offender's description, and broadcast it to other officers on patrol. You coordinate an exterior search of the perimeter (the surrounding area).

The brief witness interviews result in the following narrative, which summarizes the offence:

At 2:00 a.m., all three women were sleeping in separate bedrooms. The house has three bedrooms, on two floors. Tammy's room is situated on the first floor. Tammy was sleeping alone. Her bedroom door was closed, but not locked.

At that time, Tammy was awakened by noise. She saw the figure of a man in her bedroom. Tammy screamed, and the intruder fled immediately. Paula woke up and saw the intruder run out the front entrance. Paula then phoned the police.

A preliminary investigation revealed the following:

▸ Tool marks (impression evidence) were found on the cut telephone lines situated along the exterior wall of the house, which is parallel with the driveway. The marks appeared to be fresh.

▸ A kitchen window was open, but not damaged. Julie reports that she is "positive" that she closed it before she went to bed, but did not lock it. You believe this is the point of entry (POE).

▸ A length of rope was found on Tammy's bedroom floor. She has never seen the rope before.

▸ No lights were turned on.

▸ Nothing was stolen. No items had been moved.

▸ No one can facially recognize the suspect.

▸ No car was heard.

▸ The search of the surrounding area was negative.

Instructions

1. Without reading further and without any additional information, answer this question: "Was this a random crime?" Explain your opinion.

2. After reading Phase 1 (Chapters 1–6), explain the following:

   a. All your "first officer" responsibilities, beginning immediately after the radio broadcast.

   b. Your investigative strategy.

   c. Your theory, applying the Basic Investigative Sequence.

THE REALITY OF THE "FIRST OFFICER": THE CSI MYTH

The issues of *risk* and *uncertainty* make being the first officer to arrive at a crime in-progress, or at any other emergency, one of the most challenging jobs available.

There are many demanding jobs that require extreme skill under stress, but front-line policing is unique. Regardless of how society and police work changes, one thing will always remain the same—danger to the front-line officer. Police work always has and always will include dealing with violent offenders. Regardless of how technologically sophisticated police work becomes, the job of the first officer will always include significant personal risk.

"First officer" is defined as the first uniform patrol officer to arrive at an "in-progress" or "belated" crime. First officer is both a designation and a role. It is an assignment that includes goals and responsibilities.

First officers are repeatedly exposed to unusual, pressure-filled situations where rapid life and death decisions have to be made under the extreme limitations of minimal time, information, and consultation. First officers are responsible for extremely stressful types of problem solving. A special type of expert thinking is needed in order to rapidly process the volume of observations and information received, and then to make correct decisions within an environment of risk and uncertainty. This is where the "*CSI* myth" conflicts with the reality of front-line policing.

It's great to have long-term career goals—wanting to become a detective, forensic officer, SWAT member, or police chief is admirable. However, recruits must remember that *every* municipal policing career starts in the uniform patrol branch, as a generalist. Officers must work their way up to specialist branches. Regardless of one's level of education, life experience, community service, or fitness ability, recruits cannot bypass the uniform patrol branch—this is where real police work is learned. The uniform patrol branch is where investigative expertise starts; it is the backbone of any police organization. This branch is responsible for immediate public safety. Uniform patrol officers are part of the first responder team that protects and cares for citizens during emergencies. In reality, a specialist is an expert patrol officer. An officer must be an expert generalist before he or she can become a specialist.

The *CSI* myth is a modern version of the endless fallacies that glamorize specialized policing branches such as forensics, but ignore the reality of front-line police work. The entertainment industry does not glamorize front-line policing, despite its role as the core branch of the police profession.

FIRST OFFICER GOALS

The first officer's primary goal is *protection* of both sources of evidence (people and items) for the purpose of forming reasonable grounds. The protection of people is the highest priority; this goal always supersedes the protection of physical evidence. The purpose of forming reasonable grounds is to connect offenders to an offence. This level of belief is needed to prevent innocent persons from being arrested and charged.

The General Rule

The most important rule governing investigative decision making is to *eliminate the worst possible consequence*. This means predicting and forecasting worst-case scenarios and preventing them from happening.

Two general consequences result from failure to follow this rule: (a) harm to people, and (b) loss or destruction of physical items (also called investigative consequence). Harm includes death or injury to anyone, including the officer. The loss or destruction of physical evidence negatively impacts an investigation, but pales in comparison to death or injury to people.

An offender, who may either be present or gone on arrival (GOA), is both a safety risk and an investigative risk. Offenders are at risk to (a) cause harm, (b) commit additional offences, and (c) dispose of or destroy physical evidence.

The first officer's ongoing goal is *risk management*—removing all circumstances that cause risk to persons or items. This involves processing as much information as possible, forecasting worst-case scenarios, and making decisions to prevent them from happening.

The first officer must expect the unexpected. Awareness is key; complacency is dangerous. Experience builds awareness and removes complacency.

Work Coordination

First officers are *coordinators*. They coordinate the wide range of complex work needed to complete the preliminary investigation. Preliminary investigation work is defined by two groups of responsibilities and decisions, called **FOUR + RDM**. This formula refers to the four **F**irst **O**fficer **U**niform **R**esponsibilities that guide investigative strategy, plus **R**apid **D**ecision **M**aking—a model that assists in determining who may be taken into custody and who or what can be searched in order to help prevent the worst-case scenario.

FOUR

The four first officer uniform responsibilities are

1. injuries,
2. interviews,
3. communication with the team, and
4. crime scene protection.

See Table 4.1 for a summary of these responsibilities, and the goals associated with each.

Table 4.1   First Officer Uniform Responsibilities (FOUR)

Injuries	Interviews	Communication with the Team	Crime Scene Protection
prevention + treatment **Goals** public safety + officer safety	blended exploratory questions that combine: witness interviews + front-line interrogation + personal observation **Purpose** identify total number of persons present and their physical condition + classify them as: (a) victims/witnesses, or (b) suspects **Goal** maximum information ASAP	convey information ASAP to platoon and investigative team by: 1. radio, or 2. computer (in cruiser) **Goals** officer safety + form reasonable grounds + maximum information ASAP	identify boundaries + minimize contamination + keep same appearance **Goal** admissibility of seized physical evidence

RDM

Figure 4.1 outlines the rapid decision-making (RDM) model.

Figure 4.1   Rapid Decision-Making (RDM) Model

Application of the RDM model is taught in *Basic Police Powers: Arrest and Search Procedures*, 4th ed. (Toronto: Emond Montgomery, 2009). The RDM model simplifies the complexities of s. 495 C.C. ("police powers of arrest without a warrant") and the investigative detention authority that emerged from case law (*R. v. Mann* (2004)).[1] *Basic Police Powers* teaches the interpretation and application of arrest and custody, as well as search and seizure laws, while this textbook focuses on investigative strategies. The complexity of the first officer role is taught in multiple courses, and more than one textbook is needed.

In reality, FOUR and RDM interact. The tasks and decisions often happen simultaneously, not in sequence. Every investigation is unique; the circumstances differ in each case. Consequently, FOUR and RDM don't always happen in predictable order. The first officer's goal is to *complete the work*. FOUR and RDM represent a workload checklist and guidelines. The highest priority in every investigation is public and officer safety—injury prevention and treatment is key.

In many cases, the first officer cannot possibly perform the entire workload alone. The first officer may delegate the work, do the work himself or herself, or both. The first officer is one of several emergency responders. Injury treatment and prevention will obviously also require the expertise of other emergency responders, including paramedics and firefighters. The police investigation requires teamwork by both generalists (the platoon) and specialists. The first officer is responsible for:

▸ assembling and coordinating the team, and,

▸ ensuring that the preliminary investigation work is completed properly.

In other words, the first officer is responsible for preliminary performance.

Forming the investigative team is challenging. The size of the team and its collective experience will vary, depending on the size of the police organization and when an occurrence takes place. Emergencies do not always happen when an entire platoon and full squad of specialists are available. Investigations overlap. Calls for service happen concurrently. This is why adaptability—the ability to strategize and improvise to respond to rapidly changing circumstances—is vital.

However, the issue of uncertainty places a limit on a first officer's ability to plan. Expecting the unexpected creates the proper cognitive focus to allow a first officer to think defensively and cautiously.

DEFINITION OF PRELIMINARY INVESTIGATION

Every criminal investigation is divided into two stages:

1. a preliminary investigation, and
2. a formal investigation.

The preliminary investigation is defined as the *initial stage* of an investigation. It starts with the notification or report of the offence, and ends with the combined effect of three events:

1. elimination of emergencies and risks,
2. completion of the four first officer tasks, and
3. arrival of specialists (e.g., C.I.B. detectives, forensic officers, etc.).

The preliminary investigation includes the protection of the two sources of evidence (people and physical items). The goal of the preliminary investigation is

$$\text{people protection} + \text{crime scene protection}$$
$$= \text{gain maximum information during minimal time}$$

The formal investigation is defined as the *completion* of the investigation. It takes place after the initial risk is eliminated, the relevant sources of evidence have been identified and protected, and an initial belief has been formed.

The following are the key points of a preliminary investigation:

- There is no concrete time limit that defines the preliminary investigation.
- The preliminary and formal investigations usually blend together. Often, there is no distinct line that separates them.
- The preliminary investigation *structures* the formal investigation by setting goals and the initial direction.
- The preliminary investigation is divided into three time periods: (a) pre-arrival, (b) arrival, and (c) post-arrival.
    - ▷ Pre-arrival includes (a) report/notification, and (b) response (travel) time.
    - ▷ Arrival includes (a) parking, (b) approach, and (c) entry.
    - ▷ Post-arrival includes FOUR + RDM.
- Report/notification refers to how the first officer learns about the offence. There are two ways the first officer may learn about an offence: (a) proactive and (b) reactive.
- Proactive investigations are initiated by a police officer when the officer "finds committing." The officer is an eyewitness, and does not need to be

sent by the dispatcher. Reactive investigations are initiated by a citizen. In a reactive investigation, citizens report, and the police respond. The officer relies on other witnesses to convey information that is often incomplete.

▸ There are three ways that a citizen initiates a reactive investigation: (a) phoning the police dispatcher, (b) physically alerting ("flagging") a patrol officer in public, and (c) attending at the police station.

▸ A reactive investigation involves a *communication path* for reporting the offence; a proactive investigation does not. There are three potential problems with a reactive communication path: (a) it is inaccurate (information is lost in translation), (b) it takes longer to complete, and (c) it involves a limited amount of information.

▸ The most common communication path is citizen → dispatcher → first officer. This path involves a *radio broadcast*. A radio broadcast includes a dispatcher's verbal communication (radio) and written communication (cruiser computer—MDT).

▸ The preliminary investigation may constitute an *emergency* (in-progress circumstances that pose immediate risk to life/health) or a *non-emergency*.

▸ A proactive investigation always constitutes an emergency because of the offender's presence. A reactive investigation may be either an emergency or non-emergency.

▸ A reactive emergency is reported by a "distress call," a case law term defined by the S.C.C. as a "cry for help." Distress calls include:

  ▷ officer needs immediate assistance/backup
  ▷ 911 call accompanied by content
  ▷ disconnected 911 call; no content
  ▷ "unknown problem" call
  ▷ alarm activated
  ▷ specific offence "in-progress."

▸ A non-emergency is communicated by the word "belated" (e.g., "Belated break and enter"). Belated means the offence is not in-progress. The offender is GOA.

▸ The first officer conducts the preliminary investigation. The (a) severity of the offence and (b) a police organization's size, policies, and officer availability will determine the person who conducts the formal investigation. Major crimes are usually investigated by detectives, who lead the formal investigation. Minor crimes are usually investigated either by detectives or the first officer.

RADIO BROADCAST

The radio broadcast is by far the most common way that an investigation is initiated. In relation to belief and strategy, a radio broadcast is the starting point of the decision-making process. The radio broadcast does not merely tell an officer where to go. The contents must be rapidly translated to form an initial belief (such as mere suspicion or reasonable grounds) that corresponds with a specific investigative strategy.

The following are key points regarding radio broadcasts:

▶ **Content** Content is the total volume of information that is communicated to the first officer. This content is divided into two groups of information: (a) nature, and (b) place.

  ▷ *Nature* refers to the type of call for service (what the investigation will be). The volume of information varies significantly, ranging from *uncertainty* (defined as *unknown nature*) to *certainty* (defined as *reasonable grounds*).

  ▷ *Place* refers to the destination (where an officer is being sent). The destination may or may not be the crime scene. The place is usually the location of the (a) offence, (b) complainant, or (c) both. The type of place is a significant factor in officer safety and authorized entry. Experience gained through repeated calls to certain places will give an officer familiarity about the structure and occupancy of a place, which greatly helps in planning officer safety measures. Unfamiliarity with places is a disadvantage; an officer must perform RDM based on his or her immediate observations upon arrival. Additionally, an officer must determine the type of place in order to translate which lawful methods of authorized entry are available. There are three general lawful authorities available for entry: (a) with consent, (b) with a warrant, or (c) without consent or a warrant.

▶ **Hearsay rule** An officer who receives a radio broadcast is the recipient of *hearsay evidence*; the officer did not see the events being reported. Hearsay evidence is generally inadmissible at a trial. This means that the officer cannot testify about the specific contents of the broadcast during trial testimony. The officer cannot say, "I received a radio broadcast of a robbery in-progress" or "of a domestic disturbance" or "of an alarm." Instead, the officer may only testify that he or she received the broadcast, or, simply, "information," and that he or she attended at a specific place in response. Examples of correct testimony are:

  "As a result of a radio broadcast, I attended at 60 Shaftesbury Street."
  "As a result of information received, I attended at 60 Shaftesbury Street."

  Hearsay evidence may be used to form reasonable grounds to arrest without a warrant.[2] Although hearsay evidence is generally inadmissible at a trial, it can contribute to forming reasonable grounds (s. 495 C.C.). This means that the contents of a radio broadcast may contribute either partially (combined with other evidence) or fully (act as sole justification) to forming reasonable grounds.

▶ **Range of certainty** It is possible for the content of a radio broadcast to constitute two types of reasonable grounds: (a) reasonable grounds that an emergency exists and that lives may be at risk, and (b) reasonable grounds that a specific person has committed an indictable offence.

  The degree of certainty corresponds with the type of belief. The volume of information ranges from extreme uncertainty to certainty.

  ▷ Extreme uncertainty (e.g., "911" or "unknown problem") calls are taught separately, in *Basic Police Powers*, supra.

> ▷ Certainty calls (e.g., "Greg Wilson [male, age 40, etc.] punched Kim Wilson") may constitute reasonable grounds if the content identifies one specific person and connects him or her to a specific indictable or dual procedure offence.

Translating the Radio Broadcast Content

Immediately after the radio broadcast is received, a two-step translation starts:

1. place classification, and
2. nature classification.

First, classify the place as one of three types:

1. a dwelling-house,
2. a non-residential building, structure, or motor vehicle (e.g., commercial business, school, all types of motorized conveyances), or
3. a non-structural public place (e.g., public streets, sidewalks).

These three classifications, relating to entry and search, emerge from the combination of ss. 529–529.3 C.C. and case law. Section 348(3) C.C. defines "place," but only in relation to the offence of break and enter.

Second, classify the nature of the broadcast as an emergency or non-emergency.

RULES

1. "Belated" means non-emergency. The equivalent of "belated" is any language that definitely communicates the absence of:

   > ▷ injuries,
   > ▷ risk/threat of harm, or
   > ▷ offenders.

   Non-emergency means:

   > ▷ using normal travel speed during the response time,
   > ▷ upon arrival, reaching a balance between extreme paranoia and extreme complacency, and
   > ▷ that the same post-arrival goals (FOUR + RDM) still apply, except that RDM will likely be delayed.

2. Any language that communicates a "distress call" constitutes an emergency. The *Criminal Code* does not explain the laws relating to distress calls and emergencies; those laws emerge from case law. The leading case is *R. v. Godoy* (1999).[3] Countless derivative cases have emerged and continue to emerge. This textbook's accompanying website (**www.emp.ca/arcaro/criminvestigation5E**) includes an extensive case law literature review that explains several derivative cases that have applied the *Godoy* rules.

3. Translating the content in order to recognize a distress call starts with defining the following language that emerges from the *Godoy* decision. *Godoy* defines six terms, but not the definitive language that constitutes "distress calls."

   a. *Distress call* This is defined as a "cry for help," and may be communicated in a number of different ways.

b. *Officer needs immediate assistance* This is defined as a distress call, made by a police officer, stating that he or she needs immediate back-up. Police officer distress calls are considered to be the highest priority emergencies. Officer distress calls may be communicated by 10-code ("10-78" is the universal officer distress code) or by ordinary language.

c. *911 call* This is defined as:

▷ an "emergency response system to provide whatever assistance required under the circumstances of the call," or

▷ a "distress call" that is intended to solve any crises that occur with or without a crime as the cause.

A 911 call may or may not include the nature of the distress. 911 calls rank second in priority, superseded only by police officer distress calls.

d. *Disconnected 911 call* This is defined as "unknown nature of distress," or "unknown problem." This type of 911 call comes with no accompanying content.

e. *Unknown problem* This is defined as any distress call that does not specify the nature of the call. It is the equivalent of a disconnected 911 call.

f. *Common-law police duties* These are defined as the four duties to:
1. protect life (not limited to crime),
2. prevent death or serious injury,
3. preserve peace, and
4. prevent crime and protect life and property relating to crime prevention.

These four common-law police duties have been codified (legislated into provincial police act statutes). The S.C.C. provided the following example, found in s. 42 *Police Services Act* of Ontario:[4]

(1) The duties of a police officer include,
　(a) preserving the peace;
　(b) preventing crimes and other offences and providing assistance and encouragement to other persons in their prevention;
　(c) assisting victims of crime;
　(d) apprehending criminals and other offenders and others who may lawfully be taken into custody;
　(e) laying charges, prosecuting and participating in prosecutions;
　(f) executing warrants that are to be executed by police officers and performing related duties;
　(g) performing the lawful duties that the chief of police assigns;
　(h) in the case of a municipal police force and in the case of an agreement under section 10 [agreement for provision of police services by O.P.P.], enforcing municipal by-laws;
　(i) completing the prescribed training.
(2) A police officer has authority to act as such throughout Ontario.
(3) A police officer has the powers and duties ascribed to a constable at common law.

Explicit/Implicit Distress Calls

There are two types of distress calls: (a) explicit, and (b) implicit. *Explicit* means that only one possible conclusion is available—distress is clear, unmistakable, and 100 percent positive. *Implicit* means that the distress is implied. It is important to note that (a) both are distress calls of equal value, (b) both are emergencies, and (c) the only difference is the specific content of each, and how it is translated.

Explicit distress calls include, but are not limited, to the following ten calls:

1. **10-78** This is the single most important distress call you will ever hear or use. It means an officer needs immediate backup. Drop everything you are doing and drive to that officer's location. Conversely, you may use 10-78 when you are facing *severe* risk. Do not use 10-78 for non-emergencies such as need a roadside breath unit or more tickets.
2. **911 plus content**
3. **Disconnected 911** (no content)
4. **Specific offence in-progress**
5. **Unknown problem**
6. **Alarm activated**
7. **Shots fired**
8. **Domestic** Countless case law decisions classify the word "domestic" as a distress call that may involve weapons and/or violence.
9. **Disturbance** This call clearly means that a violent act is in-progress. It may mean that two drunks are fighting, but it may also mean that an innocent person is being attacked. Regardless, the word "disturbance" clearly indicates an in-progress offence.
10. **MVC—PI** This is a motor vehicle collision involving personal injuries.

These distress calls are classified as either:

1. a Common-Law Exigent Circumstance (CLEC), involving total uncertainty (no information connecting a specific person to a specific offence), or
2. an *exigent* circumstance (s. 529.3 C.C.), meaning that the distress call information connects a specific person to a specific indictable or dual procedure offence *and* to the inside of a specific dwelling-house.

Both CLEC and s. 529.3 C.C. authorize entry into dwelling-houses without a warrant and without consent.

Implied distress calls include, but are not limited to:

▸ The word "possible," followed by any language that communicates a threat, such as *possible* armed man, *possible* drowning, or *possible* fire ("possible" does not reduce the threat to life; do not use this term as a reason for complacency)
▸ "Noises heard in the basement," or anywhere else in a house
▸ "Suspicious person/car at . . ."
▸ "Yelling heard" from an apartment, a car, or any other place
▸ "Can't understand the caller—too hysterical"
▸ "Unwanted guest"
▸ "Glass breaking"
▸ "Person bleeding at . . ."
▸ "Man running holding a knife . . ."
▸ "Unit to back."

"UNIT TO BACK"

This phrase is used at the end of an explicit or implicit distress call. It is short for: "Is there a unit (officer) who will volunteer to back up the first officer?" The key points of this phrase are:

- "Unit to back" itself constitutes an implied distress call. It is a serious request for volunteers to backup the first officer, not a casual request or frivolous invitation.
- It means that the call is considered dangerous.
- It means that an officer must be in a state of heightened awareness; immediately volunteer to back up the first officer.

Examples of implied distress calls are infinite. They include any language that reasonably and logically implies an immediate need for help. Do not assume that a caller may be wrong; assume that the emergency is legitimate until it can be proven otherwise. Eliminate the worst possible consequence by forecasting worst-case scenarios.

As soon as an officer translates the content of a radio broadcast as an emergency, he or she must:

1. drive in accordance with provincial highway traffic statutes and the *Criminal Code*;
2. make initial entry decisions, in accordance with CLEC, s. 529.3 C.C., or consent;
3. be prepared to apply the *Godoy* rule: a disconnected 911 call or any unknown problem distress call constitutes reasonable grounds to believe that occupants are in distress, and the officer may enter the dwelling-house or any place without a warrant for the purpose of protecting life, preventing death, or preventing serious injury; and
4. know that failure to take lawful measures to solve a legitimate emergency constitutes negligence.

RESPONSE TIME

Response time refers to the travel time during a reactive investigation. It is the time period between receiving the report and the officer's arrival at the scene. While responding to calls, the officer is "en route" ("on the way").

There is no response time for proactive investigations, because the officer's arrival is concurrent with finding the offence being committed.

An officer's driving method is dependent on whether he or she is responding to an emergency or non-emergency. Explicit and implicit distress calls authorize the use of emergency signals and emergency response driving. "Belated" calls require normal driving—no lights, sirens, or speeding.

Emergency response driving rules are governed by the *Criminal Code*, provincial highway traffic statutes, and organizational policies. In order of importance, emergency response goals are:

1. **Prevent negligence** The *Criminal Code* and provincial highway traffic statutes in combination create a *negligence continuum*. The negligence continuum prohibits various degrees of negligence, starting with

unintentional careless driving and progressing in severity to offences ranging from dangerous driving and criminal negligence causing bodily harm or death, to homicide-related offences, including first and second degree murder, manslaughter, and attempted murder (C.C.).

Provincial highway traffic laws limit the number of offences that the police may violate during emergency responses because such laws instruct the public to clear a path for all emergency vehicles (requiring motorists to stop at the side of roadways). For example, the Ontario *Highway Traffic Act* authorizes the police to violate only two sections of the Act: (a) speeding, and (b) "Proceed before green" (an officer cannot ignore red lights and stop signs, but may proceed before the light turns green if it is safe to do so). If an officer drives with negligence, he or she may be liable for:

▷ traffic prosecution (e.g., careless driving),

▷ criminal prosecution (e.g., dangerous driving or criminal negligence causing bodily harm), or

▷ civil prosecution.

2. **Select the best path** The officer must decide on the quickest and most meaningful route to the call (anticipate the offender's exit route).

3. **Conduct the first search** This is the first of three searches that occur during the preliminary investigation of a distress call. The first search is a visual check for suspects (vehicles and pedestrians). The officer must make mental note of the result of this check, and later record the information in his or her notebook.

4. **Form a general strategy based on the information received** Despite limited information, an officer must form some degree of general strategy. "Winging it" is dangerous, and must be avoided. An officer will develop experience and become familiar with (a) the structure and design of places, (b) the habits of people, and (c) specific strategies for successful planning as he or she completes multiple investigations.

Low Response Time

The length of response time is significant for two reasons: (a) protection, and (b) theory development. *Low response time* is defined as four minutes or less. Conversely, high response time is defined as more than four minutes.

Low response time has two benefits. The first is obvious—increased public and crime scene protection. The second is with regard to theory development, when an offender is GOA. The theory development process is:

low response time + three negative searches
- first search: while en route to crime scene
- second search: search of the crime scene for suspects
- third search: search of perimeter

If response time is four minutes or less, and all three searches are negative, an officer's theory is that:

- the offender lives in, or is in, a nearby house/place, or
- the offence did not happen; the report is fabricated.

ARRIVAL: PARKING, APPROACH, AND ENTRY

Arrival includes three strategic decisions relating to parking, approach, and entry. An officer must decide:

1. where to park,
2. how to approach the place, and
3. (a) whether he or she has authority to enter, (b) when to enter, and (c) who enters.

The governing strategic rule for all three decisions is to eliminate the worst possible consequence. This means that an officer must rapidly complete a *risk assessment* by applying the following general problem-solving model:

1. Acquire as much information as possible for all sources, including an officer's own observations. Informed decision making is key.
2. Process the total volume of information and forecast the worst-case scenario.
3. Form alternative strategies using the "risk–benefit" formula (determine all of the negatives and positives associated with each alternative).
4. Consult with experienced officers. Policing is a para-military team environment that includes substantial experience and expertise. A rank structure governs every platoon. Novice officers must understand their experience limitations.

Park and Approach

Every "place" is different. There is no universal, concrete rule that explains exactly where to park and how to approach. Organizational policy provides guidelines. A general practical rule applies: an officer should not make himself or herself a target. He or she should find locations and paths that minimize risk. For example, taking a path past a window is a risk.

Authority to Enter

Does an officer have authority to enter? The answer refers to "entry recognition," defined as analyzing all of the information and matching it with one of the authorized ways of entering. The circumstances of the *Godoy* case constitute the best point of reference; derivatives of this case (found on the accompanying website **www.emp.ca/arcaro/criminvestigation5E**) provide additional points of reference.

Case Law

R. v. Godoy (1999)

CIRCUMSTANCES

At about 1:30 a.m., two officers responded to a disconnected ("unknown problem") 911 call. The nature of the call was unknown because the phone line was disconnected before the caller spoke. The call originated inside of the accused person's dwelling-house (apartment).

Four officers arrived. One officer knocked on the door. A man (later identified as the accused person) partially opened the door. The police asked whether "things were all right inside." The accused person responded, "Sure, there's no problem."

An officer asked if the police could enter in order to investigate whether there was a problem. The accused person responded by trying to close the door. One officer prevented the accused from closing the door by putting his foot in the way. All four officers entered the apartment.

As soon as they entered, the police heard a woman crying. They found her in the bedroom. She was later identified as the accused's common-law spouse. The officers saw "considerable swelling above her left eye" and found her "curled in a fetal position and sobbing." She told the police that the accused "had hit her."

Based on these observations and the victim's brief verbal statement, the police arrested the accused for assaulting his spouse. The accused resisted, and a struggle ensued. One officer suffered a broken finger.

S.C.C.

The S.C.C. ruled that:

- A disconnected 911 call, and all unknown problem distress calls, constitute reasonable grounds of CLEC and authorize immediate entry into any place, including a dwelling-house, without a warrant or consent.

- "The word of the person who answers the door is not enough" to cancel the CLEC. The police still have authority to enter and investigate the potential risk-to-life emergency. The police are entitled to search only for persons (to find and talk to the total number of persons found for protection purposes). In other words, when a person answers the door and reports there is "no problem," the police have authority to enter to confirm that claim.

- The use of force needed to enter was justified.

- The authority to search is not extended to physical evidence.

- If the police had walked away, their failure to investigate would have constituted negligence.

- Police observations and the victim's brief verbal statement were enough to constitute reasonable grounds.

- Police authority to investigate distress calls is defined by three purposes:
    1. find the caller,
    2. identify the reason the call was made, and
    3. provide any assistance that is required.

- The authority to investigate distress calls is *contextual*. This means:
    1. the authority is not automatic, and
    2. the police have to *build context* by justifying their reasons during trial testimony. In other words, the police have to prove the emergency with concrete verbal testimony.

When to Enter and Who Enters: The "Entry Paradox"

In front-line policing, this is one of the most complicated decisions an officer will make. The "entry paradox" refers to emergencies where both risks (negative factors) and benefits (positive factors) exist regarding the decision to either enter now, or delay entry until a SWAT team or larger tactical support unit arrives. The decision-making challenge is to determine who will suffer the greatest risk and who will gain the greatest benefit. An officer may be injured or killed if he or she enters immediately, but the same may happen to the person inside if there is a delay.

In cases where death has occurred inside a place while entry was delayed, extensive public scrutiny happens immediately. The key response to this is *justification*—offering a concrete explanation with specific reasons for the action taken. Justification starts with notebook recording, continues with General Occurrence Report writing, and ends with court testimony.

Organizational policy guides "entry paradox" risk assessment and decision making. The *Godoy* case explains one example of a call that involved 100 percent uncertainty where officers decided to enter without a SWAT team. Other case law articles, available at **www.emp.ca/arcaro/criminvestigation5E**, include SWAT team circumstances.

POST-ARRIVAL

The post-arrival stage begins immediately after entering. Whether the call is an emergency or non-emergency, the post-arrival work goals (FOUR + RDM) are the same. The only difference is urgency. For simplicity, emergencies will be discussed here.

Identify and Classify

Upon entry, the first objective is to sort out who is who—victims, witnesses, and potential suspects. For example, other emergency services personnel may have already arrived and begun assisting injured people. In the process, unsolicited, spontaneous statements may have been made by people who have not yet been classified. The first officer will have to ask the person to repeat the statement, observation, or complaint in order to determine that person's relationship to the offence.

The following strategies will interact, and must be coordinated by the first officer in order to identify and classify the participants:

1. **Build the context** This means creating the "big picture" for the purpose of the ultimate goal—forming reasonable grounds that connect a specific person to a specific offence. An officer must elicit brief narratives from as many people as possible about what happened, and relate this information to his or her own observations. The officer is a *post-offence witness*, and his or her observations are a significant factor in forming a belief.

2. **Conduct the second search** Regardless of what you are told (e.g., the offender is GOA), conduct a search of the crime scene (the interior of the

place). The purpose of this search is to find people. Although the *Godoy* decision restricts the search to people, seize any potential weapons that are found. This search should be standard, automatic practice, because the possibility exists that information about the presence or absence of people may be intentionally or unintentionally wrong. There may be multiple offenders involved, or witnesses may have assumed, rather than witnessed, that the offenders have left. This search is authorized by a series of case law decisions as part of the "duty to investigate distress calls." The search will contaminate the crime scene to some extent; an officer's objective is to minimize contamination, but not at the expense of officer safety. The officer must record in his or her notebook the concrete method of the search in order to justify the crime scene contamination.

3. **Ask each person, individually, "Are you hurt? Do you need to go to the hospital?"**

4. **Conduct the third search** This is a search of the crime scene perimeter (the area surrounding the crime scene). The dimensions are determined by the amount of time elapsed between the time of the offence and the time of arrival.

5. **Classify the people found** The officer must form a belief about who is a complainant/witness, and who may be a suspect.

How to Classify

During and after the care of injured persons, context building continues. Two strategies are needed:

1. officer-specific observations, and
2. exploratory interviews (Phase 1 and Phase 2).

Officer-specific observations are defined as, "making structured observations to 'find committing' offences that constitute a risk." The "find committing" includes:

▸ looking for possession of illegal items,
▸ observing conduct that constitutes an offence, e.g., a threatening act or gesture, or a physical obstruction that impedes your investigation, and
▸ words that constitute an offence (e.g., explicit or implied threat).

An officer is not trying to "trump up" charges; he or she is attempting to assess risk. If an officer finds committing any criminal offence, he or she is authorized to arrest under s. 495 C.C., search under common law, and remove the offender from the crime scene.

An *exploratory interview* is defined as blended questioning that combines the skills of witness interviews and suspect interrogation. The goal of a witness interview is volume of information plus credibility. During an emergency, a formal witness interview is not practical. The goal of an exploratory interview is to ask open-ended questions (questions intended to generate multiple facts without prompting or leading a witness to an implied answer). This witness's initial response is analyzed to determine whether reasonable grounds can be directed to any person. At a crime scene, a simple verbal statement by a victim/witness may constitute reasonable grounds (such as "My husband assaulted me" in the *Godoy* case). It is important to note that:

- ▶ The standard for reasonable grounds at a crime scene is different from that during the formal investigation because the time available to evaluate the credibility of the witness is limited. During the emergency, a brief verbal statement may constitute reasonable grounds; the credibility of the witness can be evaluated later.
- ▶ An officer is obligated to eventually interview every witness in order to form reasonable grounds. However, during an emergency, he or she may form reasonable grounds if he or she honestly believes the information provided by a small sampling of the witnesses.

The above key points are explored in detail in *Basic Police Powers: Arrest and Search Procedures*, supra.

Exploratory interviews are divided into two phases. Phase 1 occurs immediately after entry (identification of the total number of people and classification as witnesses or suspects). Phase 2 occurs after an officer determines that the offender(s) is definitely GOA.

Phase 1 includes open-ended questions; the officer will simply ask each person, "Tell me what happened." Phase 1 will include unsolicited information.

Front-line interrogation is a unique and challenging skill that is developed through experience. The goal is to elicit voluntary incriminating statements from suspects. The S.C.C. has acknowledged that voluntary confessions are the best form of evidence;[5] consequently, incriminating statements are the best types of statements for forming reasonable grounds.

The following are introductory key points for front-line interrogation:

- ▶ The prosecution has the onus to prove that all statements made to persons in authority were voluntarily made. This means that a confession to a police officer is not automatically admissible. However, a confession to a citizen is automatically admissible.
- ▶ Proving voluntariness requires the study of some of the most complicated rules of evidence.
- ▶ Front-line interrogation strategies emerge from the complex rules of evidence. Each strategy must include the absence of inducements, defined as "threats or promises."
- ▶ *Spontaneous utterances* are usually automatically admissible. A spontaneous utterance is defined as "a verbal statement made by a suspect to a police officer without prompting and without any time for the officer to formally caution the suspect."
- ▶ The *caution* is an instruction to an arrested person. The formal caution is, "Do you wish to say anything in answer to the charge? You are not obliged to say anything unless you wish to do so, but whatever you say may be given in evidence." This formal caution is a recommendation that benefits the prosecution in proving that the statement was voluntary.

Section 495 C.C.

If an officer finds committing any offence, or if he or she forms reasonable grounds that any person has committed an indictable or dual procedure offence, the officer may apply the s. 495 RDM model and arrest the person without a warrant. The goals then become:

1. officer safety,
2. preventing Charter violations, and
3. proving voluntariness of statements.

Basic Police Powers: Arrest and Search Procedures, supra, explains in detail how to prevent Charter violations by properly informing the accused of the reason for arrest and the right to counsel. The website for the *Basic Police Powers* textbook (**www.emp.ca/arcaro/policepowers4E**) includes a number of right-to-counsel case law decisions.

Gone on Arrival (GOA): Phase 2 Exploratory Interview

After a definitive conclusion has been made that all offenders left prior to an officer's arrival, the officer will have classified all persons present as "witnesses (including victims)." The exploratory interview should be continued for the purpose of communicating to his or her platoon/investigative team. The goal is to make or designate a radio broadcast as soon as is practical. The exploratory interview strategies correspond with the radio broadcast.

Two general goals of this communication are:

1. officer safety, and
2. forming reasonable grounds.

The Phase 2 exploratory interview strategies are:

1. **Offence recognition** An officer's objective is to determine the specific *actus reus*. If responses to open-ended questions are insufficient, ask closed-ended (intended to generate one fact, without prompting or leading) questions to clarify (e.g., "Did you see a weapon?" or "Was the suspect armed?") The goal of the majority of clarifying questions is to convert abstract language into concrete language. For example, an officer may ask, "How specifically did he assault her?" in order to clarify the meaning of the abstract term "assault."
2. **Identity** An officer must specifically prove who an the offender is. The goal is to achieve *positive recognition*. Positive recognition includes two separate concepts:
   a. determining whether each witness can identify the suspect, and
   b. obtaining a specific description to be communicated to the platoon so that any officer can positively identify the offender if the suspect is stopped by police.

Two questions are mandatory for witness identification:

a. "Do you know the suspect(s)?"

b. "Will you be able to facially recognize him or her in the future, in a formal police lineup?"

The first question determines whether the offender is familiar to the victim. The second question determines the extent of familiarity.

3. **Positive recognition description** When the witness is unfamiliar with the offender, an officer must obtain a specific description that will allow other officers to positively identify the offender. The interview strategy is to simply divide the description into two parts: (a) general characteristics, and (b) specific characteristics.

General characteristics are personal features that are not unique to an individual. Many people have the same types of features, and a general description alone is not sufficient to make a positive identification. In other words, it does not constitute reasonable grounds about recognition; it only constitutes mere suspicion. General characteristics include:

- ▷ gender,
- ▷ ethnicity,
- ▷ age,
- ▷ height,
- ▷ weight,
- ▷ hair colour, style, and length,
- ▷ the presence or absence of facial hair,
- ▷ eye colour,
- ▷ the presence or absence of eyeglasses, and
- ▷ complexion.

Specific characteristics are personal features that are unique to an individual. These features allow for a positive identification, which constitutes reasonable grounds about identity and recognition. Specific characteristics include scars, tattoos, and general items that, when combined with the general description, create a unique description of that person. For example, clothing and shoes are general items. When they are worn by a person who is generally described, those items may become unique to that person. Other factors that are independent from a person's characteristics increase the uniqueness of those general items. Examples of independent factors include proximity to a crime scene, method of travel, and items possessed or being carried. For example, a red T-shirt and blue jeans are obviously not unique. However, when they are worn by a person who matches the general description, who is near a crime scene, and who is in a vehicle similar to one seen leaving the scene, those items may become unique.

4. **Offender's method of travel** Determine conveyance, or if the suspect is on foot.

5. **General/specific description of conveyance** If a conveyance was used, use the same two-part interview strategy to identify the conveyance.

6. **Direction of travel**

7. **Possible destination**

8. **Armed or unarmed** Determine whether the offender(s) were armed, and describe weapons using the same two-part strategy. Never say, "The offender is unarmed." Instead, say, "No weapons seen." This simple technique promotes heightened awareness and prevents complacency.

IDENTIFYING WITNESSES

Witness reluctance to participate in an investigation is commonplace. Often, witnesses want to leave a crime scene for a variety of reasons that will be discussed in the chapter on witnesses. Excessive response time increases the possibility that reluctant witnesses will leave the crime scene.

Accordingly, the first officer should, as soon as is practical, find all the witnesses who have remained and identify each one. Subsequently, the first officer should establish whether witnesses have left. Having conclusive evidence that all witnesses remained prevents the CIB officers from unnecessarily investigating this possibility. Seven methods are available to determine whether witnesses have departed:

1. Upon arrival, note all licence plate numbers of parked cars in the crime scene vicinity.
2. Question the remaining witnesses about who was seen during the crime.
3. Question the suspects, if they are cooperative, about the witnesses who were present.
4. Question informants. They may know people who were present during the crime or the offender may have told them who was there.
5. Canvass the neighbourhood. Witnesses may exist who can provide facts about the crime or about the departure of suspects or other witnesses.
6. Search the area surrounding the crime scene for physical evidence of witnesses who have departed.
7. Observe traffic. Although the first officer has several responsibilities, the traffic in front of the crime scene should be observed when time and available personnel make it possible to do so. The observation should include both vehicular and pedestrian traffic.

The offender or a witness who had departed from the crime scene before police arrival may drive or walk past. This doesn't happen frequently, but offenders have been known to do this. Two reality examples follow.

1. An offender committed an offence with a weapon in an apartment building. He fled in a vehicle and parked one block away from the scene. He entered another apartment building while armed, searching for the person he had threatened. While officers stood in front of the first building, the offender walked past them. Investigation led to the offender's arrest, after which he was asked why he had walked past the officers to get to his vehicle instead of taking an alternate route. He explained that he thought the police would never suspect him if he walked past them and that this would remove any possibility of suspecting him in the future.
2. An offender committed a break and enter. He fled in a stolen car. He was seen by the police and a brief pursuit ensued. The offender parked the car

in a driveway and fled on foot. A search of the area followed. Two officers remained by the car. Ten minutes after the search began, the offender walked past the car. After he was arrested, the offender was asked why he had walked past the car. The accused explained that he had wanted to divert suspicion from himself and simply wanted to know whether the police had sufficient evidence to arrest him.

Certainly every offender reacts and thinks differently after committing an offence. The above scenarios illustrate the possibility that some offenders may travel past a crime scene for a variety of reasons, including

- to divert suspicion,
- a need to know whether the police will arrest them; if they are not apprehended, confidence will develop that they are not suspects, and
- to retrieve items, such as a car.

Brief Informal Interviews

The first officer's goal is to conduct a brief, informal interview (the Phase 1 and Phase 2 exploratory interview) with every witness. A lengthy, formal witness interview will follow during the formal investigation, in order to obtain final written witness statements.

Principles of Law Enforcement Report Writing, 3rd ed. (Toronto: Emond Montgomery, 2008) explains the concept of writing formal written witness statements.

Communication with Platoon

A radio broadcast to other patrol officers must be made as soon as practical. This means making or delegating a radio broadcast as soon as any meaningful information has been obtained. Communication to the investigative team will often be done incrementally until fully complete. In other words, an officer should not delay a radio broadcast for a significant amount of time while building final context.

CRIME SCENE PROTECTION

The crime scene is simply defined as the location where the *actus reus* occurred. A crime scene is the major source of physical evidence transfer. The first officer's goal is to protect the crime scene for forensic officer analysis. The goal of crime scene protection is to keep the appearance of the crime scene the same as the offender left it. There will always be some contamination caused by emergency responders. The objective is to minimize contamination (and, therefore, change). The first officer is responsible for crime scene protection, which starts immediately after the presence or absence of injured persons has been determined.

The next chapter teaches crime scene protection in detail.

Preventing Single Viewing

SCENARIO

Dispatcher reports "Break and enter in-progress." The first officer arrives at the location within two minutes. One occupant is home and reports that the offender left. You are a backup officer conducting the perimeter search. During the search, you hear the first officer make a radio transmission describing the suspect. Six minutes after the offence occurred, you see a man walking on a sidewalk three blocks from the crime scene. The man matches the first officer's description.

Question: Should you drive this suspect to the crime scene so that the complainant can identify by facial recognition?

Answer: No. "Single viewings" do not constitute legitimate identification. Facial recognition/identifying a witness requires a formal lineup.

There are three types of lineups:

1. photo,
2. video, and
3. live.

The same rules govern all three:

1. There must be a sufficient number of *comparison people* in the lineup. Comparison people are defined as individuals who have the same general characteristics as the suspect.
2. There can be no bias present that helps the witness point out the suspect.
3. A single viewing constitutes bias.

Solution: The extent of description will determine whether you can make an investigative detention, apply s. 495 C.C., or use voluntary accompaniment.

Case Study 4.1 Investigation

You are the first officer. Your duties include crime scene protection in order that the forensic analysis of the physical evidence can be carried out.

In Chapter 6, the strategies and investigative theories discussed in Chapters 1–5 are applied to the case study in Chapter 1 to explain how the first officer will begin the investigation. These same principles can be applied to the case study in this chapter.

ENDNOTES

1. *R. v. Mann* (2004), 3 S.C.R. 59, 2004 CanLII 52 (S.C.C.).
2. *R. v. Debot* (1986), 30 C.C.C. (3d) 207 (Ont. C.A.).
3. *R. v. Godoy* (1999), 131 C.C.C. (3d) 129, 1999 CanLII 709 (S.C.C.).
4. R.S.O. 1990, c. P.15.
5. *R. v. Smith* (1989), 50 C.C.C. (3d) 308 (S.C.C.).

CHAPTER 5

Crime Scene Investigation: Protection, Examination, Analysis, Reconstruction

LEARNER SUMMARY

A crime scene is a place that includes *people*, *physical items*, and *events*. People are classified as *offenders* and *non-offenders*; physical items are classified as evidence relevant to an offence and that which is not. The main event is the *actus reus* of the offence; the secondary events are pre- and post-offence conduct by the offender.

Crime scenes start with a pre-offence appearance. The commission of the crime changes that appearance because of transfer of physical evidence. The crime itself is the change agent; it transforms the crime scene's pre-offence appearance to its post-offence appearance. Expert examination and analysis of the post-offence crime scene is called "crime reconstruction." Reconstructing the *actus reus* (the actual offence) means matching the changes by identifying the source of the change to the outcome. This skill allows the expert to form an opinion about what happened, who is responsible, and why the crime occurred.

In addition to protecting human life at the scene of an offence, the job of the first officer is to protect the crime scene's post-offence appearance until the crime reconstruction begins.

Case Study 5.1

7:01 p.m. Radio broadcast: "Alarm, robbery in progress, Brockport Variety Store, 3227 Brockport Road."

The store is situated on an urban street near the downtown core.

7:04 p.m. You are the first officer to arrive.

Tony (44) is the only person in the store. He informs you, "A guy just robbed me with a knife," and he points to a red mark on his neck. Tony reports, "He ran down the sidewalk," and points to a northbound direction on a sidewalk leading to the front of the store.

Tony is not bleeding. You ask him if he needs medical treatment. He replies, "No."

Your preliminary interview reveals the following:

▶ Tony owns the store. At 7 p.m., the store was open for business. Tony was the sole employee. No customers were in the store. The last customer departed at 6:55 p.m.

▶ A male person wearing a ski mask walked into the store. He had possession of a butcher knife. Tony was behind the counter near the cash register. The suspect walked toward Tony, held the knife near Tony's neck, and said, "Give me all your money." The blade of the knife touched Tony's neck.

▶ Tony gave the offender all the cash in the register.

▶ The suspect left prior to your arrival. He ran out the front door, northbound on a sidewalk leading to the front of the store.

▶ Tony cannot facially recognize the suspect and cannot recognize his voice.

You lock the front door to prevent customers from entering. C.I.B. and Forensic/ Ident. officers are notified. They arrive at 7:10 p.m.

Instructions

1. Without reading further and without any additional information, answer this question: "Was this a random crime?" Explain your opinion.

2. After reading Phase 1 (Chapters 1–6), explain the following:

   a. All your "first officer" responsibilities, beginning immediately after the radio broadcast.

   b. Your investigative strategy.

   c. Your theory, applying the Basic Investigative Sequence.

THE INVESTIGATIVE TEAM

Investigations require team work. The core of the investigative team usually consists of patrol officers, forensic/Ident. officers, forensic scientists, and detectives/ C.I.B. officers. Each professional has a distinct role.

1. **Patrol officers** As first responders, patrol officers' priority is *protection* of human life and physical evidence, in that order. Protection of physical evidence requires that the first officer be responsible for the crime scene.

2. **Forensic/Ident. officers** These officers conduct expert examination of a crime scene. This includes:

   ▷ searching for and seizing physical evidence,

   ▷ analyzing certain types of physical evidence such as impressions (e.g., fingerprints, shoe prints), and

   ▷ sending other types of physical evidence to a forensic laboratory for scientific analysis (e.g., bodily substances for DNA analysis).

3. **Forensic scientists** These experts are not police officers. They work in forensic laboratories such as the Centre of Forensic Sciences (CFS) in Toronto. They receive evidence from forensic/Ident. officers and conduct scientific analysis on bodily substances, DNA testing, and some non-bodily-substance testing such as firearm analysis.

4. **Detectives/C.I.B. officers** These officers translate the forensic findings into a belief (e.g., reasonable grounds). Their role includes:

   ▷ leading or coordinating the formal investigation,

   ▷ interviewing witnesses,

> ▷ interrogating suspects,
> ▷ interpreting forensic findings and forming conclusions,
> ▷ crime scene analysis,
> ▷ making arrests,
> ▷ swearing Informations, and
> ▷ writing Crown briefs.

The **Coroner** is not considered part of the "investigative team." However, his or her presence at a crime scene is often required. A Coroner is the only person who can pronounce death—not a police officer or a paramedic. The only time a person can be presumed to be dead is if the body is decapitated or decomposed or if rigor mortis is present. Otherwise, all injured persons are considered alive and must go to the hospital.

This is worth repeating. To prevent negligence, do not let injured persons remain at a crime scene waiting for a Coroner. Assume that people are alive and can be saved. Here is a simple mindset: treat every injured person as if they were a family member. That will ensure that everything humanly possible will be done to save them. Do not be influenced by television and movies where action-hero police officers check a pulse, declare, "He's dead," and leave the body lying there.

In summary, the first officer protects while the forensic/Ident. officers examine the crime scene. Analysis is conducted by both forensic/Ident. officers and forensic scientists. Detectives lead the investigation by translating forensic findings and conducting the investigation. A Coroner is called to the scene to pronounce the death of a person.

The first officer does not conduct forensic examination or forensic analysis. The separation of these duties develops a general rule: a crime scene cannot be properly examined and analyzed for physical evidence until it has been protected.

FIRST OFFICER DUTIES

The first officer to arrive at a crime scene is responsible for guarding and protecting it. If the first officer is a uniform patrol officer, this responsibility should not be transferred unless circumstances occur that would create danger or jeopardize the investigation. However, if a C.I.B. or Ident. officer is the first to arrive, responsibility should be transferred to a uniform officer as soon as is practical. It must be stressed that this transfer can occur only when no chance of crime scene alteration exists. In other words, the initial responsibility to protect the crime scene rests with the first officer to arrive, despite rank or expertise.

The phrase "crime scene protection" sometimes sends a wrong message, giving the impression that protection of the crime scene and items within it is the only security assignment. In fact, the first officer has two protection assignments, each with a different goal.

The first priority or assignment is human protection (including the safety of the officer and emergency responders). This priority corresponds with the general front-line decision-making rule: eliminate the worst possible consequence. The consequence of death or injury is far more severe than an improperly protected crime scene. Therefore, the protection of people always supersedes the protection of items.

The goal of human protection is to prevent death and injury by: (a) ensuring the availability of immediate medical treatment/care, (b) ensuring that emergency service providers attend and assist, and (c) removing all potential risks from the crime scene, including offenders.

Protecting a crime scene means to keep the appearance of the crime scene the same as the offender left. In other words, (a) prevent an unjustified change of appearance of the crime scene between the time the *actus reus* ends and the time the forensic analysis begins; and (b) prevent unjustified contamination.

Contamination is defined as "any post-offence change to a crime scene or item, including change in appearance of the scene or item, relocation of an item, loss of an item, or destruction of an item."[1]

In reality, it is impossible to prevent all contamination during an emergency or an in-progress call.

"In-progress" includes the presumption that offenders are present. Risk to all persons dramatically increases if the offender is present upon the first officer's arrival. The human protection goal during these emergencies includes three objectives that interact concurrently:

1. **Identify and assist injured persons.** Find all involved persons and determine whether any are injured. The officer is responsible for providing emergency services to prevent the condition of injured persons from worsening.

2. **Eliminate risks to uninjured persons.** If no injured persons exist, remove any hazards that may pose a threat to uninjured persons.

3. **Search for offenders.** An offender's presence at a crime scene represents the greatest threat. Search the place immediately for offenders. **Place**, for the purpose of search under s. 487 C.C., includes dwelling-house, building, structure, perimeter of building or house, or conveyance.[2]

   Even if witnesses report that the offender departed before police arrival, the witnesses may:

   ▷ be unintentionally wrong,
   ▷ have intentionally lied to mislead police to help the offender remain undetected, or
   ▷ have legitimately seen only one offender leave, but multiple offenders participated and may be hiding at the crime scene.

Following entry into a crime scene during an emergency, a search of the interior and exterior is mandatory to achieve the three objectives. It is important to search every reasonable place where a person could be concealed in order to prevent negligence of not finding an injured person or an offender. Common-law exigent circumstances authorize a search to achieve that purpose—human protection only, not to examine the crime scene for physical evidence. However, an officer can search for weapons as part of the human protection search.

Whether the call for service is in-progress or belated, an officer must justify entry, search, and seizure of the crime scene. In other words, lawful authority is required to take over a crime scene in order to protect it for analysis. The following are the entry and search authorities.

Lawful Authority to Enter and Search a Crime Scene

There is no general statutory or case law authority specifically called "Crime Scene Protection and Analysis." There is no Canadian criminal law that specifically authorizes entry into and taking ownership of a place because it is a crime scene. In other words, there is no general warrantless entry and search authority specifically for crime scene entry, protection, and examination.

Crime scene protection is actually an informal, slang term. No law directly addresses the procedure of crime scene protection. The authorities are the *search and seizure laws* explained in *Basic Police Powers: Arrest and Search Procedure*, 4th ed. (Toronto: Emond Montgomery, 2009). The authorities are found in both statute and case law. The following is a summary of authorities that allow crime scene entry, protection, and examination. The accompanying website includes ongoing case law literature review (**www.emp.ca/arcaro/criminvestigation5E**).

1. **Consent** The owner or lawful occupier of the place may give the police consent to enter and search the crime scene. Consent guidelines are found in case law.

2. **Section 487 C.C. search warrant** This allows officers to apply for and obtain a search warrant to search any place for specifically named items that are relevant to a criminal offence and to seize those items. The key is proving reasonable grounds that specific items are in a specific place, at the present time. In other words, a belief of strong certainty is needed.

3. **Section 487.11 C.C.** This is a warrantless search authority. It is an exception to the s. 487 C.C. search warrant requirement. The same reasonable grounds belief is needed with the addition of "exigent circumstances," defined as no time to apply for and obtain a search warrant because of a risk of evidence destruction or loss. Section 487.11 C.C. authorizes entry and search of any place, including dwelling-houses, to search for evidence regarding any criminal offence when exigent circumstances make it impracticable to obtain a s. 487 C.C. search warrant. This provision was enacted in response to the S.C.C. decision in *R. v. Silveira* (1995),[3] which authorized the police to enter a house without a warrant to "freeze" the place and prevent the destruction of evidence while waiting for the issuance of a search warrant. These provisions authorize the police to protect a crime scene until a search warrant is obtained. The key to using this authority is proving a *strong certainty* that specific items are in a specific place but that a risk prevents the immediate application for a search warrant.

4. **Common-law exigent circumstances (CLEC)** This type of exigent circumstances applies in emergencies where there is strong uncertainty. Distress calls, such as disconnected 911 calls, allow the entry and search of any place for one purpose—to determine whether injured persons are inside.[4]

5. **General duties of a police officer: common law, case law, and provincial police service statutes** The general investigative powers and duties of a police officer are found in three sources of law: common law, case law, and provincial statutes that regulate police services (e.g., *Police Services Act* of

Ontario). None of these sources specifically refers to crime scene protection and analysis, but all provide general authorities relating to this investigative duty. For example, under s. 42(1) *Police Services Act* the duties of a police officer are:

 ▷ to preserve the peace,
 ▷ to prevent crimes and other offences and provide assistance and encouragement to other persons in their prevention,
 ▷ to assist victims of crime,
 ▷ to apprehend criminals and other offenders and assist others who may have lawfully taken them into custody,
 ▷ to lay charges, prosecute, and participate in prosecutions,
 ▷ to execute warrants that are to be executed by police officers, and
 ▷ to perform related duties.

Additionally, police officers have powers and duties ascribed to a constable at common law. However, the common-law duties of a police officer are not written or listed in any Canadian statute.[5]

The Supreme Court of Canada, in *R. v. Dedman* (1985),[6] stated that the common-law duties of a police officer include the primary duty of preventing crime and a general duty to protect life and property. The S.C.C., in *R. v. Knowlton* (1973),[7] ruled that police officers are in the lawful execution of duties by cordoning off an area if provincial legislation includes principles such as the preservation of peace, the prevention of crime, and the apprehension of offenders, and if reasonable grounds exist that the renewal of an indictable offence may occur.

Crime scene protection may be authorized by common law, based on the case law principle that qualifies police investigative conduct as a common-law authority. Police conduct that interferes with an individual's liberty or freedom is authorized by common law if: (a) the police were acting in the course of their duty, and (b) the police conduct did not involve an unjustifiable use of powers in the circumstances.[8]

Justifiable use of police power during an investigation depends on several factors, including:

 ▷ the duty being performed,
 ▷ the importance of the duty for the public good,
 ▷ the liberty interfered with, and
 ▷ the nature and extent of the interference.

In summary, the intrusiveness of an investigation is reasonable if the police are acting in the course of their common-law duty to protect life and property, and to prevent crime.

6. **Provincial legislation relating to Coroners and medical examiners** If a death is involved, the police may use the authority found in provincial statutes relating to Coroners, such as the *Coroners Act* of Ontario. A police officer has the same authority as a Coroner under this statute,[9] which authorizes: (a) entry and search of any place where a dead body is and any place where reasonable grounds exist to believe the body was removed from, and (b) seizure of anything that the police have reasonable grounds to believe is relevant to the investigation.[10]

Another example is the *Fatality Inquiries Act* of Alberta. It defines the scope and authority of provincial medical examiners to hold crime scenes.[11] No warrant is needed to conduct the entry, search, and seizure.

CRIME SCENE PROTECTION GOAL

The significance or goal of protecting a crime scene, with lawful authority, is admissibility of physical evidence. Specifically, to goal is to prevent a s. 8 Charter violation (unreasonable search or seizure) and possible exclusion (in court) of physical evidence under s. 24(2) Charter. It also ensures that the police are in the lawful execution of their duty, in case any person intentionally interferes with crime scene protection.

Preventing exclusion of physical evidence is accomplished by:

1. minimizing contamination by establishing borders, regulating access into and out of the bordered area, and not disturbing any physical items within the borders; and
2. ensuring continuity of seized items (physical evidence).

Minimizing Contamination

Some causes of intentional and unintentional contamination of a crime scene are beyond a first officer's control. For example:

▸ **Offender's intentional acts** These include "crime scene staging," such as the intentional transfer of physical evidence before, during, or after an offence to confuse the police by diverting suspicion.[12] Such staging might include moving, damaging, and destroying items. The key point is that crime scene staging *still involves transfer of evidence that can be traced back to the offender.*

▸ **Environment** Weather and climate change outdoor physical evidence. Indoor dust reduces the longevity of a fingerprint. The presence or absence of environmental influences must be addressed.

Regardless, first officer duties, if performed properly, will ensure the best possible crime scene protection.

BORDERS

Properly protecting a crime scene depends on establishing its boundaries and then regulating access. There are two parts of crime scenes:

1. the centre, where the actual *actus reus* occurred; and
2. the perimeter, defined as the surrounding area that includes any physical evidence relevant to the pre-offence and post-offence stages.

The first officer establishes the centre by relying on the information received during the preliminary investigation and subsequent observations. After the offence area is determined, the area should be increased simply to compensate for error.

The perimeter is not defined by concrete dimensions, but rather by an opinion of an area that includes the offender's entry and exit routes. The perimeter can be extended beyond this area to include escape routes. Essentially, the perimeter includes all areas surrounding the centre in which officers have determined the presence of the offender.

REGULATING ACCESS

The first officer is responsible for restricting entry to a crime scene. Persons allowed entry are:

- emergency personnel such as ambulance attendants, firefighters, etc.;
- the Coroner, if required;
- additional uniformed officers, if they are required for emergencies or for searching the scene;
- C.I.B. investigators, if they are assigned to the matter; and
- Ident. officers, if they are assigned to examine the scene for evidence.

Some significant aspects of the list must be emphasized:

- No police officers are allowed on a crime scene if they are not performing a function listed above.
- No citizen is allowed to enter, including the victim's family, or the owner of the property. There are two reasons why their entry is prohibited: (a) they will contaminate the crime scene as soon as they enter, and (b) persons with strong familiarity are logical potential suspects.

If these people attend and insist on entering, prevent entry by informing them of the following:

- Their entry will benefit the offender.
- If their concern is for the victim, stress that he or she will be leaving shortly and will likely be attending either at a hospital or police station. A reasonable person will stop persisting.

When the first officer allows authorized personnel to enter the crime scene, contamination occurs on the path they take. The following strategies minimize contamination:

1. **Establish the best route** The *best route* refers to a path ideally not used by the offender—a path that has minimal or no *actus reus* transfer. Therefore, establishing the offender's path is the first challenge. However, if emergency personnel have created a route before your arrival, ensure that the same path continues to be used.

   Record, in your notebook, the following information:
   - the time the route was established,
   - a diagram of the scene, including the route, and
   - a written narrative that describes the appearance of the scene and the route.

2. **Maintain the best route** by ensuring that all persons use it when entering or leaving the scene. In other words, you direct traffic in the crime scene.

Record, in your notebook, the following information:

- ▷ the names and addresses of all persons using the route,
- ▷ all entry and exit times of authorized persons, and
- ▷ any deviation from the route, including the name of the person who left the designated route, a diagram and written description of the deviant route, and observations of any alteration, disturbance, or contamination of the scene.

Obstruct Peace Officer

The offence of "Obstruct peace officer" occurs, in relation to crime scene protection, when any person does one of the following:

- ▸ intentionally alters or contaminates a crime scene while it is being lawfully protected;
- ▸ attempts to enter a cordoned-off crime scene and refuses to heed warnings to the contrary; or
- ▸ refuses to leave a crime scene if he or she is present upon police arrival and is intentionally obstructing protection or examination of it.

Officers may use discretion to arrest and charge. If an arrest may be lawfully made, detention may be extended until *Criminal Code* release provisions are fulfilled. If an Information is laid, the following facts-in-issue (FII) must be proven:

- ▸ a wilful obstruction occurred,
- ▸ the person obstructed was a peace officer, and
- ▸ the peace officer was in lawful execution of his or her duty.

Alternatively, the offender may be released unconditionally, without an Information being laid.

DO NOT DISTURB

At an in-progress call, a thorough search for injured persons or offenders will justifiably disturb the crime scene. Literally, every step an officer takes and every item that is touched transfers some evidence (e.g., shoeprints, fingerprints). Change only the part of the crime scene that is necessary to protect yourself and others— that is, if it is necessary to prevent death or injury. If you have to change the appearance of the crime scene for human protection, you are completely justified and you will never be criticized. However, record any changes made by you and all emergency responders in your notebook.

Non-offenders may change the crime scene immediately before, during, and immediately after the crime for a number of reasons. Examples include self-defence, attempts to escape, phoning emergency responders, cleaning the crime scene out of habit, or trying to preserve the dignity of victim. The fact is that non-offenders legitimately move items before your arrival. Legitimate, unintentional contamination is not an offence. Contamination that intentionally helped the offender escape detection is an offence.

Interview victims or witnesses to determine what contamination of the scene occurred between the conclusion of the offence and your arrival. Any alteration or disturbance must be properly recorded in a notebook. If none occurred, this fact should be recorded.

Do not touch anything. The rule seems simple, but the following are some specific examples:

- Do not close or open any internal or external entrances.
- Do not shut off TVs, stereos, and so on, or lower their volumes.
- Do not shut off appliances unless a risk to life is involved (e.g., gas stove).
- Do not turn on or shut off lights, unless necessary.
- Do not disturb bodies that can be presumed dead.
- Do not clean up any messes.
- Do not deposit cigarette butts anywhere at the scene.
- Do not use bathroom facilities.
- Do not use the telephone unless there is an emergency. Other means of communication are available, such as the police radio.
- Do not lock or unlock doors.

Ensuring Continuity

- **Continuity** is a *chain of possession*—a continuum (a timeline) that proves where the item was from the time of seizure to the time of the trial.[13]
- **Seizure** is defined as "the taking of an item from a person by a public authority without the person's consent."[14]

The following rules apply to continuity:

- **General rule of admissibility** A physical item is admissible if it is relevant evidence and no specific rule of evidence excludes it from the trial.[15]
- **Relevant** means capable of proving at least one FII of the offence alleged on the Information.[16] An item can only be relevant if it is proved to be the *same item* that was seized.

To ensure continuity, every officer who possesses the item must initial the item or a tag attached on the item, and record the time of seizure and time of possession until it is locked in a police property locker. All information must be recorded in the officer's notebook. The officer will be subpoenaed to court to testify about time of possession, and to identify the item introduced by the prosecutor by means of (a) general description, and (b) specific description, referring to unique features (e.g., serial numbers, damage). The officer's initials on the item or tag are considered unique features that the officer is capable of identifying.

Detailed procedures relating to ensuring continuity of a physical item are discussed in Chapter 19.

Consequences of Unsuccessful Crime Scene Protection

Five consequences of unsuccessful crime scene protection may result:

1. **Physical evidence may be lost or destroyed.**
2. **Seized physical evidence may suffer a loss of evidentiary value** if there is any doubt concerning the presence of the item during the actual commission of the offence, or if there is any suspicion that the item has been altered from its condition at the completion of the offence.

3. **False inferences or conclusions may be made by investigators.** For example, if fingerprints are destroyed and not found after an examination, an investigator may falsely conclude that the offender wore gloves. If furniture had been overturned during a fight and the furniture was returned to its original location, the investigator may wrongly conclude that no violence occurred.

4. **Witnesses may not be believed.** A witness may correctly report that an item had been used by the offender as a weapon and that the weapon had been left at a specific location at the crime scene before the offender's departure. If the weapon is lost or destroyed or its location is altered, the witness's claims may be met with skepticism from the investigator. Consequently, the investigator may wrongly conclude that the witness has poor credibility.

5. **Physical evidence may be excluded at the trial.** Physical items have the strongest evidentiary value but no value if they are excluded from court. Their exclusion means that the goal of crime scene protection will not have been met.

Time Length for Crime Scene Protection

There is no statutory authority that imposes time restraints on investigators who have taken control of a crime scene. Essentially, control of the scene extends to whatever time is necessary to lawfully investigate the offence. Three principles govern the duration of police control of a crime scene:

1. If no death is involved and a s. 487 C.C. search warrant was obtained, the time limit specified on the search warrant by the Justice applies.

2. If a death has occurred, provincial Coroners statutes apply: the crime scene is controlled until a post-mortem examination is conducted, if one has been ordered, and expert examination is completed.

3. If consent is the authority used, the crime scene control lasts until the analysis is complete or consent is revoked.

CRIME SCENE RECONSTRUCTION

A properly protected crime scene allows for optimal crime scene investigation. The goal of crime scene investigation is to reconstruct the crime; prove what happened during the crime and how the crime was committed.[17]

The principles of crime reconstruction emerged from over a century of research, starting with the work of three pioneers of crime scene investigation in the 1800s: Alphonse Bertillon, Dr. Hans Gross, and Dr. Edmond Locard.[18] From the work of 20th-century researchers, the following six fundamentals of crime reconstruction emerged:

1. There is a direct relationship between the accuracy of crime reconstruction and examination of the post-offence crime scene. In other words, reconstructing the actual crime depends on accurately examining the post-offence appearance. There are two basic fundamentals of post-offence crime scene examination:

▷ A two-part documentation of the crime scene: (a) photographs and (b) a scale diagram with written narrative.[19]
▷ Strict objectivity, extreme sequential "frame-by-frame" logic, and "viewing witness statements with suspicion."[20]

Two-part documentation

A forensic/Ident. officer will immediately photograph the crime scene and take measurements to concretely recreate the *post-offence* crime scene. The purpose of these two tasks is to create a scale diagram that *preserves* the *exact* post-offence crime scene so that it can be presented in court.

The exact appearance of the crime scene, as a whole, is physical evidence that must be introduced in court to: (a) prove the fundamental FII of location and (b) enable accurate conclusions.

Photographs and scale diagrams are called **secondary evidence**, defined as evidence that is the next best substitution that replaces the original item. Only original items are admissible. Exceptions to the rule that allows secondary evidence to be admissible are: (a) if it is not practicable to bring the original item to court, and (b) if it is allowed by a specific statutory provision.

The original item (the crime scene) generally cannot be introduced at the trial because: (a) the crime scene is perishable—the appearance will change before court, and (b) judges and juries generally do not attend at the crime scene—the crime scene must be brought to court, which is impractical.

Strict objectivity

This means be open-minded, prevent tunnel vision, use reasonable rational thinking, and never give immediate or unjustified *strong credibility* to witnesses and victims. Start with weak suspicion and use a structured process to evaluate the credibility of witness statements. One way to evaluate witness credibility is to examine physical items and the appearance of the crime scene.

2. *The transfer theory provides a trail.* Every offender creates a trail of "trace" evidence, such as impressions (fingerprints, shoe prints, tool marks), hair, blood, glass, paint, soil, and fibres. An expert recreates the crime from "traces" the offender leaves at and takes from the crime scene. It is impossible to commit any crime without making a trail of "trace" evidence.[21]

The purpose of post-offence crime scene investigation is to identify the source of the trace evidence. "Identifying the source" means comparing two items and proving that they have a common origin. It is the principle of cause and effect in reverse. The effect is found first at the crime scene. The cause has to be found afterward. For example, a shoe print (effect) is found at the crime scene of a robbery. You seize a shoe (cause) from a suspect. A comparison is made to determine whether the shoe is the origin of the impression. If a positive match is made, the impression and the shoe have a common origin.[22] Physical evidence that is exchanged between the crime scene, victim, and offender may be connected forensically to prove a link between offender, victim, and the crime scene.[23]

3. Crime reconstruction includes *forming a theory* by interpreting "pattern evidence" (e.g., fingerprints) found at the crime scene in conjunction with laboratory examination of physical evidence.[24]

4. A chain of item possession called "continuity" may be established to help prove "integrity." "Integrity" of physical evidence is crucial for accurate crime reconstruction and admissibility. "Integrity" means *uncontaminated—* untouched, unaltered, unmoved—the same condition as the offender left it.[25]

5. Contamination is a type of evidence transfer that did not occur during the *actus reus*. Contamination constitutes evidence transfer but not the type directly related to the *actus reus*.

   Two researchers have renamed contamination "evidence dynamics"[26] but the word "contamination" still applies.

6. According to Chisum and Turvey (2000), it is wrong to assume that simply "taping off an area, limiting access, and setting out about the task of taking pictures and making measurements ensures the integrity of the evidence found within."[27] This means that post-offence crime scenes are not always 100 percent uncontaminated.

Supporting Case Law

The leading case law that explains crime scene reconstruction is the trilogy of three Ontario Court of Appeal decisions: *R. v. Ranger* (2003), *R. v. Clark* (2004), and *R. v. Klymchuk* (2005).[28]

The following is a summary of the three decisions; an extensive review is found on the accompanying website (**www.emp.ca/arcaro/criminvestigation5E**).

There are three questions that crime scene analysis answers. The court named the questions as the "WHAT question," the "WHY question," and the "WHO question."

▸ The "WHAT question" refers to determining what happened at the crime scene.
▸ The "WHY question" refers to why a crime was committed.
▸ The "WHO question" refers to who committed the crime.

Crime scene analysis is the expert forensic crime scene reconstruction and corresponding expert opinion of what happened, why it happened, and who committed the offence. The "what" opinion is admissible at a trial, if the witness is deemed by the judge to be an expert. The "who" and "why" opinions are inadmissible at a trial. However, they may contribute to forming reasonable grounds during the investigation.

Criminal investigation analysis includes crime scene reconstruction but has a wider scope. According to *R. v. Klymchuk* (2005), *criminal investigation analysis* is "an umbrella designation referring to a number of investigative services offered to police agencies to assist them in their investigations and sometimes offered to the court as expert evidence." These investigative services include crime scene analysis and profiling.[29] One of the crime scene analysis questions includes whether crime scene staging occurred.

Crime scene staging is defined in *R. v. Klymchuk* (2005) as "the intentional alteration of manipulation of the crime scene by the offender to divert attention away from that individual as a logical suspect and/or to divert attention away from the most logical motive."[30] In other words, crime scene staging is a "manipulation to create a misleading impression."

An expert opinion on crime scene staging may be admissible in court, but not automatically. The trial judge has discretion to allow it or exclude it, depending on principles established in *R. v. Mohan* (1994), *R. v. D. (D.)* (2000) and *R. v. J. (J.L.)* (2000).[31] These principles include: (a) focus on crime scene reconstruction, and (b) necessity. This means that if the expert opinion and the justification for the opinion focus exclusively on crime scene reconstruction, then the likelihood of admissibility increases. Although these opinions are not "generally based on any novel science or theory," they are well-accepted practices. The "necessity" principle refers to the trial judge's conclusion about whether the expert's opinion is necessary for a fair trial.

Case Study 5.1 Investigation and Conclusion

Investigation reveals that only one customer entered the store following the robbery. The path of that customer is determined so that no wrong conclusions would be drawn from any physical evidence (i.e., shoe prints and fingerprints) left by the customer.

A search of the interior results in no physical evidence being found. The exit path used by the offender upon departure from the store is determined. You search the path and find a butcher knife stuck in the trunk of a tree situated at the front of the store, approximately 45 feet from the entrance. The knife's position in the tree is six feet above the ground.

The initial facts regarding the discovery and seizure of the knife follow:

1. Corroboration exists to support Tony's otherwise unsubstantiated report that a robbery occurred. Reports of robberies, and of all criminal offences, need to be validated to verify the actual commission of the offence and to eliminate the possibility of a false report. Although the discovery of the knife does not give absolute validation of the offence, it withdraws much of the suspicion of a false report.

2. Following validation of the report, the discovery of the knife shows that Tony's story is highly credible because the knife is similar to the description Tony gave of it during his recollection of a violent, traumatic incident.

Several days later, you arrest Eddie in connection with an unrelated corner store robbery. His mother had given you valuable confidential information because she feared his increasingly violent behaviour and because of her desire for him to end his drug habit. While you are questioning him about other criminal activities, Eddie admits that he had robbed another corner store. His mind had been altered by drugs, preventing him from remembering the name of the store, its location, or the approximate date of the robbery. However, Eddie remembers using a knife and, with his arm stretched overhead, sticking it into a tree outside the store during his departure.

The seizure of the knife during the extended crime scene search provided the only corroboration of Eddie's confession. He picked the store because he was familiar with it and was confident that he could rob it. On the day of the robbery, he had planned by watching the store for several hours to determine when no customer traffic existed.

ENDNOTES

1. W.J. Chisum and B. Turvey, "Evidence Dynamics: Locard's Exchange Principle and Crime Reconstruction" (2000) vol. 1, no. 1 *Journal of Behavorial Profiling.*

2. Section 487 C.C.; *R. v. Grant,* [1993] 3 S.C.R. 223, 1993 CanLII 68 (S.C.C.).

3. *R. v. Silveira* (1985), 97 C.C.C. (3d) 450 (S.C.C.).

4. *R. v. Godoy* (1999), 131 C.C.C. (3d) 129 (S.C.C.).

5. Ibid.

6. *R. v. Dedman* (1985), 20 C.C.C. (3d) 97 (S.C.C.).

7. *R. v. Knowlton* (1973), 10 C.C.C. (2d) 377 (S.C.C.).

8. *R. v. Godoy,* supra note 4.

9. Section 16(1)(b) *Coroners Act.*

10. Ibid.; s. 16(2)(c) *Coroners Act.*

11. R.S.A. 2000, c. F-9.

12. *R. v. Klymchuk* (2005), 203 C.C.C. (3d) 341 (Ont. C.A.).

13. *Morris v. The Queen* (1983), 7 C.C.C. (3d) 97 (S.C.C.).

14. *R. v. Dyment* (1988) 45 C.C.C (3d) 207 (SC.C.).

15. *Cloutier v. The Queen* (1979), 48 C.C.C. (2d) 1 (S.C.C.).

16. Ibid.

17. *R. v. Clark* (2004), 182 C.C.C (3d) 1 (Ont. C.A.).

18. Chisum and Turvey, supra note 1.

19. Ibid.

20. Ibid.

21. Ibid.

22. P.L. Kirk and J.I. Thornton, *Crime Investigation,* 2nd ed. (New York: Wiley & Sons, 1974).

23. Ibid.

24. H. Lee, *Crime Scene Investigation* (Taoyuan, Taiwan: Central Police University Press, 1994).

25. Chisum and Turvey, supra note 1.

26. Ibid.

27. Ibid.

28. *R. v. Clark,* supra note 17; *R. v. Ranger* (2003), 178 C.C.C (3d) 375 (Ont. C.A.); *R. v. Klymchuk,* supra note 12.

29. *R. v. Klymchuk,* supra note 12.

30. Ibid.

31. *R. v. Mohan* (1994), 89 C.C.C. (3d) 402 (S.C.C.); *R. v. D. (D.)* (2000), 148 C.C.C. (3d) 41 (S.C.C.); *R. v. J. (J.L.)* (2000), 148 C.C.C. (3d) 487 (S.C.C.).

CHAPTER 6

Applying Phase 1: Chapters 1–5

LEARNER SUMMARY

Chapters 1–5 each contain a reality investigation whose circumstances are based on (a) anecdotal evidence supporting relevant investigative strategies, or (b) real-life examples that demonstrate how to apply these strategies.

Each reality case study is relevant to the respective chapter. In order to begin the "investigation" of each occurrence (each case study), the strategies and theories learned in Chapters 1–5 must be applied.

In reality, the strategies explained throughout Phase 1 do not work in isolation; they are not mutually exclusive, even though each was taught separately. They apply to every front-line investigation that a police officer completes. It is important to (a) gain a basic familiarity of all strategies, and (b) learn how they apply within the context of a common front-line investigation.

Front-line patrol officers investigate a wide range of occurrences, from simple to complex. One of the most common and most dangerous is an intrusion alarm that calls the police to a potential "in-progress" offence. Phase 1 opens with Case Study 1.1, which replicates this type of common occurrence—an offender commits a break and enter at a commercial premises, but leaves prior to police arrival. Additionally, this investigation illustrates the "mere suspicion bind"—circumstances that create a degree of uncertainty, while compelling the officer to react; again, a common occurrence among front-line officers on patrol.

The case study introduces the concepts that were taught in Chapters 1–5, and serves as a base point of reference. A "base point of reference" is the key to learning how to apply the investigative concepts because it serves as a concrete set of circumstances that forms a contextual learning base—the starting point for learning how to apply complex investigative strategies—and dramatically reduces the investigative learning curve by simplifying some basic investigative concepts and showing how they interact to form a realistic investigative strategy.

The remainder of this chapter demonstrates how the first officer begins the investigation of the offence in Case Study 1.1 by explaining how to make rapid investigative strategy decisions. The first officer duties discussed in Phase 1 are emphasized in this investigation.

These same principles can be used to successfully investigate the offences illustrated in Chapters 2, 3, and 4. The case study in Chapter 5 is based on a true investigation. The conclusion is included in the chapter to demonstrate how following the BIS can lead to a successful investigation.

CASE STUDY 1.1 INVESTIGATION BEGINS

You are a uniform patrol officer assigned to a downtown urban district and working the midnight shift, single-crew (no partner), when you receive this "in-progress" call.

3:00 a.m. Radio broadcast: "Intrusion Alarm, Bravo Electronics, 3227 Brockport St."

The radio broadcast is the starting point of this investigation. Assume that this is a real alarm. Never assume it is a false alarm. The assumption that the alarm is real will align your thought processes and decision-making accordingly. You will make intelligent self-protection decisions. Conversely, an assumption of a false alarm will generate complacent thinking.

Whoever Alleges Must Prove

At the start of each investigation, remind yourself of this rule. This is another way of stating the "burden of proof." The Crown Attorney and the police have the onus to prove that the specific offender(s) committed the specific offence(s) alleged on the Information. The offender does not have the onus to prove innocence. The police have the onus to find evidence. The Crown Attorney has the onus to prosecute. The entire burden of proof is on the Crown and police. The most important general investigative rule to remember is: if you make a formal allegation, you must prove it.

Hearsay Evidence

You are the recipient of hearsay evidence. The contents of the radio broadcast represent hearsay evidence, which is defined as evidence that is not perceived by your own senses. Hearsay evidence is that which you did not witness, but were told about. In this case, you were told that the alarm was activated. The significance is that, legally, rules of evidence generally prohibit hearsay evidence during witness testimony; that is, hearsay evidence is inadmissible. Exceptions exist, but, in general, you cannot testify about what you did not see or hear. You may testify only about what you saw and heard. Consequently, replace the hearsay portion (i.e., any statement about the activated alarm) with the statement, "As a result of information received." If you are subpoenaed to testify at a trial after the offender is charged, your testimony will include the statement, "As a result of information received, I attended at Bravo Electronics, 3227 Brockport St."

Type of Investigation

This is a reactive investigation because you did not initiate the investigation. The alarm company did. There are two types of calls for service, for priority classification: (a) in-progress and (b) belated, meaning not in-progress. An activated intrusion alarm communicates that an offence is "in-progress."

Alarm Paradox

The frequency of false alarms creates the *alarm paradox*. A paradox refers to two sides of a concept or rule that are contradictory or conflicting. It means that there is a positive element and a negative element. An alarm call warns you of potential imminent danger, but the volume of false alarms promotes complacency.

Complacency is a harmful comfort zone. It puts you and the public in danger because complacency adversely affects decision-making. The following rules solve the paradox.

Rule 1: The number one governing general investigative rule—eliminate the worst possible consequence. This is the most important rule that governs investigative decision making. There are two general classifications of consequences: (a) safety and (b) investigative. Safety consequences include death or injury to any person, including yourself. Investigative consequences include loss or destruction of evidence that proves a crime. The offender is both a safety risk and an investigative risk. He may repeat the crime, cause you harm at the time of apprehension, and he may dispose of physical evidence that could have proven his guilt.

"Eliminating the worst consequence" is the golden rule for front-line law enforcement, a rule that is internalized by every novice and remains ingrained throughout every career. With experience, applying this rule develops rapid decision-making (RDM) that allows you to quickly apply a three-step process:

1. rapidly analyze the circumstances of any situation,
2. foresee or predict the worst possible consequences in sequence, and
3. identify concrete solutions to prevent all possible consequences.

Rule 2: Your first belief is that all alarms are "in-progress" offences. This belief remains until you prove otherwise. Believe the alarm is false only after evidence proves there is no "in-progress" offence. Your decision-making will correspond with the belief of an "in-progress" offence and it will protect you. Never assume that an alarm is false no matter how many times you have responded to a false alarm at that place.

Rule 3: The belief that an "in-progress" crime represents an "emergency" and uncertainty. A belated call is not "in-progress" and is not an emergency. This belief governs your thought process with respect to rule 1. Your goal is to reach certainty rapidly.

"En Route"—Search Number One

Your responsibilities on the way to the scene (en route): choose the best route, and arrive safely, while conducting the first of three total searches.

By choosing the "best route," you are anticipating the possible escape path of the offender. Your driving manner is governed by the combined effect of (a) provincial highway laws and (b) police policies.

Sirens and roof lights are authorized during emergencies. However, driving manner is strictly dictated by provincial laws. For example, the *Highway Traffic Act* of Ontario (H.T.A.) allows the police to commit only two H.T.A. offences: (a) exceeding the speed limit (reasonably),[1] and (b) proceeding before green.[2]

This means that you must:

▸ stop at all red lights and stop signs—no exceptions,
▸ not travel at an unreasonable speed that would constitute negligence, and
▸ follow all traffic laws, like all other citizens, to prevent death and injury.

Your travel goal is to avoid negligent driving. You are liable for any negligence while en route to an emergency. Negligence is an abstract term that has wide-ranging interpretation. Your en route travel strategy is governed by negligence avoidance.

While en route, conduct search number one (of three)—a visual observation of motorists and pedestrians. It is possible that you may drive past the offender. Make a mental note of your observations and record them later.

In this case, you see no one. Search number one produces negative results.

Arrival

3:05 a.m. Arrival. You are the "first officer" to arrive at this commercial premise, which is now the "crime scene."

"First officer" is a designation. It signifies a role. As first officer, you are responsible for coordinating a series of tasks that constitute a preliminary investigation. You may perform these jobs yourself, or delegate by assigning them to other officers.

Refer to Chapter 4 to determine your first officer duties relevant to this "in-progress" alarm situation.

Your response time is five minutes. It is only one minute beyond the definition of "low response time," which is four minutes and under.

As soon as you arrive in close proximity to the scene, and before you actually park, your first task is to form a *strategy*, a personal protection plan that includes making four decisions:

1. where to park,
2. how to approach the building,
3. how to search the exterior of the crime scene to determine whether there was forced entry, and
4. when to enter the building to search the interior.

Forming rapid strategy requires implementation of the "strategize and improvise" rule. Determine a general plan and be prepared to adapt to rapidly changing circumstances while you execute it. Every crime scene has different perimeter and interior dimensions. You will have some prior familiarity with some crime scenes and none with others. It is impossible to devise a specific plan prior to entering a crime scene. Only a general plan of action is possible. While you execute it, the key is adapting to new, unexpected circumstances and changes in the environment. Front-line policing involves myriad rapidly changing situations that cannot be predicted with 100 percent certainty. However, experience teaches you to *expect the unexpected*, a cognitive state that allows you to predict worst-case scenarios with some degree of certainty. Adapting to those changes is vital to personal protection. Improvisation is the most challenging form of RDM—rapid decision-making. Practical experience develops RDM expertise.

Apply the "eliminate the worst possible consequence" rule to strategize and improvise effectively, in order to make personal protection decisions:

- Parking, approaching, and searching the exterior for a point of entry are all governed by the "minimum exposure" rule. Prevent yourself from being an open target as much as possible. Minimize your exposure to potential offender sight lines.
- Determine "best paths" that allow you to achieve your goals and stay away from risk sight lines as much as possible.

While en route to the crime scene, search number one was negative. You must complete two additional searches: (a) crime scene interior, and (b) crime scene perimeter. Response time is significant for a number of reasons, including safety— faster response time means faster protection for actual or potential victims, and it gives you a better chance of apprehending the offender at or near the scene. The combination of a low response time and negative results from all three searches combine to form mere suspicion: that (a) the offence was fabricated, or (b) the offender lives or is in a nearby place. Logically, the offender has not gone far.

Response time over four minutes weakens the "low response" theory, incrementally. As each minute passes beyond the four-minute response time, the strength of the suspicion weakens.

In this case, during an exterior search of the building, you find a shattered glass door at the back of the building.

Entry and Search Number Two

The decision to enter the commercial building comes next. Should you enter immediately or delay entry into a crime scene where offenders may be inside? Both decisions represent concurrent risks and risk aversion. Immediate entry protects innocent victims who may be inside with the offender(s), but it exposes you and others to harm.

The correct decision is the one that eliminates the worst possible consequence. A number of factors decide the solution, including the interplay between innocent occupants, the number of offenders, whether the offenders are armed, the dimensions of the place, and the number of officers.

3:06 a.m. A backup officer arrives. The remainder of your platoon is "on the air," waiting for your radio broadcast that will instruct them on the next step.

- ▸ In this case, the decision to enter immediately is made because there are two officers present and a minimum likelihood of innocent occupants inside.
- ▸ Search number two, crime scene interior, begins. The two goals of this search are: (a) the primary goal—to maintain personal safety and apprehend any offenders that are inside, and (b) the secondary goal—to minimize crime scene contamination.
- ▸ The search revealed negative results. The offenders were GOA (Gone on Arrival).
- ▸ Theory development is an ongoing process. Follow the Basic Investigative Sequence, beginning with validating the offence. Fabricated break and enters are not rare. In this case, fabrication is possible.
- ▸ Continue using the BIS to develop a logical list of possible suspects. Your theory development includes interviewing the business manager. Ask the dispatcher to contact management. Do not leave the crime scene unprotected and insecure. Management must attend for two reasons: (a) to determine whether a theft and/or damage occurred and, if so, to provide a concrete list of stolen items and damage, and (b) to secure the building.
- ▸ Your first officer duties include:
  a. interviewing management (there are no other witnesses at this time) to determine (i) validity of the offence and (ii) an "inner circle" list, referring to a list of potential suspects as per the BIS,
  b. radio broadcast to other officers (you advise that the suspects are GOA),
  c. a crime scene perimeter search (search number three), and
  d. crime scene protection.

You either delegate and coordinate, or do it all yourself.

- ▸ You decide to search the perimeter and surrounding area while the second officer protects the crime scene.
- ▸ The second officer identifies the boundaries (centre and perimeter) and records this information in his or her notebook. The second officer also creates the "best route" to be used by authorized persons and begins regulating access to prevent entry by unauthorized persons.
- ▸ Forensics officers are notified so that they can photograph and examine the crime scene for evidence transfer.

Search Number Three

3:28 a.m. Perimeter search. While conducting this search, you see a man walking normally on a sidewalk about 500 metres from the crime scene. He is about 5'11", 200 lbs., stocky build, short brown hair. Although opinions are generally inadmissible in court, distances, height, and weight are examples of non-expert opinions that are exceptions to the "opinion rule of evidence" and are therefore admissible in court.

- You facially recognize the man as Jack Mattone (28). Facial recognition is another admissible non-expert opinion.
- You know he has a criminal record because you have arrested him in the past. Jack was convicted for "Theft under $5,000.00" three years ago. This information constitutes "bad character" evidence. "Bad character" evidence is generally inadmissible *during* the trial. It is typically used *after* a conviction for determining sentencing. "Bad character" evidence includes any past behaviour that proves the capability or potential to commit certain offences. This behaviour includes criminal convictions and any conduct that did not result in convictions or charges (e.g., the offender was given a break and no charges were laid).
- A CPIC check reveals that no warrants are outstanding, which means that Jack is not currently "wanted." He is not awaiting trial on any charges. The CPIC check reveals a "theft under" conviction and two assault charges that were withdrawn three years ago, and a "Threatening" complaint four years ago that resulted in no charges.

Can You Arrest?

- You stop your cruiser next to Jack and note that he is not holding anything. You see that he is sober. You ask him to stop and identify himself. He ignores you and continues walking. A pedestrian's refusal to "stop and identify" is not a criminal offence and does not constitute reasonable grounds to believe that he is connected to the offence being investigated. You may ask a pedestrian to stop and identify himself, but he may legally refuse, or he may consent. Refusing to consent is not a criminal offence and does not constitute reasonable grounds. However, you may use it to form "mere suspicion."
- A number of rapid decisions have to be made to "strike the balance" between protecting the public from a repetition of the offence and preventing taking an innocent person into custody.
- "Striking the balance" means that if Jack did commit the offence, you have to prevent him from repeating the offence or committing another offence. You have to protect the public by stopping him from breaking into other places after you suspected him of having committed this offence. If he commits a home invasion in the next few days and injures or kills someone, you may be criticized as being negligent for having done nothing to explore his possible involvement in this break and enter. However, if he is completely innocent, you have to prevent making a false arrest.

Consequently, you must consider the following questions in making your decision:

- Can you arrest Jack without a warrant under s. 495 C.C.?
- If the answer is no, how can you explore the possibility that he is involved in this offence?

THE RAPID DECISION-MAKING MODEL

The rapid decision-making (RDM) model is explained in detail in *Basic Police Powers: Arrest and Search Procedures*, 4th ed. (Toronto: Emond Montgomery, 2009). The most important step in the model involves a decision to arrest, which is made after determining whether you have s. 495 C.C. authority. The following is a brief explanation of the RDM model as it applies to this "in-progress" call.

Offence Recognition and Classification

You must immediately recognize what offence(s) you are investigating and classify the offence as summary conviction, dual procedure, or indictable.

At this time, three offences are possible:

> ▸ "Break, enter with intent into a place that is not a dwelling-house," until you determine what, if anything, was stolen.
> ▸ "Attempt break and enter," if no entry actually occurred but the damage occurred with prior intent to enter.
> ▸ "Mischief under $5,000.00," if the offence is simply vandalism with no actual or intended entry.

Significantly, all are dual procedure offences, temporarily classified as indictable. (This is relevant to your authority to arrest without warrant if you have reasonable grounds.)

At this time, you may reasonably assume that the offence you are investigating is "Break, enter with intent" at a place that is not a dwelling-house. The offence may change to "Break, enter, and theft" after management searches the interior and discovers that items were stolen.

Belief Classification

You have to decide the strength of certainty that connects Jack to the break and enter. Specifically, you have to classify your belief as either:

> ▸ find committing,
> ▸ reasonable grounds,
> ▸ mere suspicion, or
> ▸ no belief whatsoever.

Belief classification starts with forming the context. List all the available evidence. The relevant evidence in this case study is:

> ▸ 28 minutes have elapsed between the time of the offence and the time the suspect was seen.
> ▸ Close proximity: the suspect is within 500 metres of the crime scene.
> ▸ Bad character evidence exists.
> ▸ The suspect refused to identify himself.
> ▸ You do not see possession of any illegal item; therefore, "find committing" is eliminated as a belief.

In conclusion, your belief is "mere suspicion" that Jack is connected to the break and enter. The reasons are:

- You did not see him commit the break and enter.
- You have not yet received a confession, a credible eyewitness statement, or strong circumstantial evidence that leads to only one conclusion—that Jack committed the offence.

ONE LOGICAL CONCLUSION

Circumstantial evidence does exist but it shows a weak connection because more than one logical conclusion may be made. When your belief stems exclusively from circumstantial evidence, you have to distinguish whether the evidence constitutes "reasonable grounds" or "mere suspicion." This is accomplished by answering the question: "How many logical conclusions do the circumstances lead to—one or multiple?"

- If the answer is only one, reasonable grounds exists.
- If the answer is multiple, mere suspicion exists.

In this case study the answer is multiple conclusions. The conclusions include: (a) he is involved, and (b) he is not involved—he may be legitimately walking to or from home or work or simply visiting someone. He may have committed the crime or he may be innocent. The circumstances do not lead only to the conclusion of guilt. Even though the circumstantial evidence shows only a weak connection, this cannot be immediately dismissed as a coincidence. You have the onus to explore it—you cannot ignore it.

The answer is definitely not "no belief whatsoever." As stated, a connection undeniably exists. The existence of the connection is non-negotiable.

The key point is: although the circumstantial evidence is not strong enough to form reasonable grounds, the goal is to elevate the belief to reasonable grounds. Consequently, remember the definition of reasonable grounds: (a) confession to anyone, (b) at least one credible eyewitness, or (c) circumstantial evidence that shows a strong connection that refers to the existence of only one logical conclusion. All three parts of the definition create your investigative focus. Each one defines a concrete level of evidence that you can easily recognize. You are trying to achieve at least one of them to lawfully form reasonable grounds.

THE "MERE SUSPICION BIND"

When mere suspicion exists, as in this case, you are put in a bind. This *mere suspicion bind* means you have no authority to arrest under s. 495 C.C. based on mere suspicion, but you cannot simply ignore Jack—he is a legitimate suspect. He may be innocent or he may be a dangerous offender. The possibility of his involvement must be explored.

The next step in the RDM model is intended to solve the mere suspicion bind.

Custody Decision

To solve the mere suspicion bind, you must stop Jack and explore his potential involvement. You have to rapidly process four authorities to determine how you can stop him, in the following sequence:

1. Arrest without warrant.
2. Investigative detention.
3. Pedestrian stop.
4. Consent.

The first authority is found in a statute—s. 495 C.C. The other three emerge from case law. The first three authorities are ways to stop the pedestrian without consent—the length and purpose of custody diminish from the first authority to the fourth.

The following is an explanation of the rapid decision-making sequence:

1. Can you arrest without a warrant under c. 495 C.C.? No. Section 495 C.C. includes no authority to arrest without a warrant on "mere suspicion." Additionally, it is impossible to obtain an arrest warrant based on mere suspicion.

2. Can you make an investigative detention? The authority of investigative detention is fully explained in the *Basic Police Powers* textbook, supra. It is a temporary, partial, at-the-scene custody, made without the person's consent, to accomplish three investigative procedures: to (a) ask for identification, (b) conduct brief questioning, and (c) conduct a pat-down search for weapons. The authority to make an investigative detention depends on concrete justification that connects the person to the crime, including time lapse and proximity. The decision in this case was "no," Jack cannot be detained. The reason was the time lapse. Although it was only 28 minutes, that time lapse significantly weakened the connection. If he had been found in close proximity earlier (e.g., en route to the call), an investigative detention and search would have been authorized. Even if an investigative detention was authorized, that type of detention would not force Jack to identify himself or to answer questions. No suspect has to answer police questions about involvement in a crime, at any time, under any circumstances.

3. Can you make a "pedestrian stop"? Yes. A pedestrian stop is the same concept as a motorist stop. It is defined as the brief stop of a pedestrian, without any physical force or physical custody, to ask for identification and conduct a CPIC check to determine: (a) whether he is wanted (e.g., does an arrest warrant exist?), (b) whether he is awaiting trial and bound by the conditions of a release order, and (c) whether he is on probation and bound by conditions. Although the pedestrian is momentarily detained, a pedestrian stop does not automatically constitute a detention by definition for Charter violation purposes. The authority for making a pedestrian stop is found in case law. One of the leading cases is *R. v. L.B.* (2007),[3] which is explained in detail on the accompanying website (**www.emp.ca/arcaro/criminvestigation5E**).

4. Consent is always an alternative strategy. There are two types of consent: express and implied. Express consent is the optimal type; it is the product of all the proper instructions that must be communicated in accordance with the case law requirements.[4] Implied consent is the product of circumstantial evidence. Consent constitutes voluntary accompaniment.

PEDESTRIAN STOP, INVESTIGATIVE DETENTION, AND CONSENT

The differences between a pedestrian stop, investigative detention, and consent are:

▸ Length, purpose, and goal: investigative detentions are longer, more formal and authorize a "pat-down search."

▸ A pedestrian stop is less formal than investigative detention and involves no physical contact.

▸ Investigative detention involves no consent.

▸ Pedestrian stops and consent are differentiated by the extent of prior instructions communicated to the suspect about the issue of *choice*. Pedestrian stops involve no communicated instructions about choices to stay or leave. Consent does involve those instructions.

Two of the above four alternatives apply as the starting point to solve the mere suspicion bind—pedestrian stop and consent. Afterward, short-term (at-the-scene) and long-term strategies are needed to explore the pedestrian's involvement by either eliminating him or forming reasonable grounds.

INVESTIGATIVE STRATEGIES

The following are examples of ten investigative strategies—six are short-term and apply at the scene; four are long-term strategies:

1. **"Are there any warrants out for you?"** This question was actually asked of Jack. He stopped and replied, "No." The key points about this simple question and answer are:

   ▹ Stopping without the use of physical force blends the elements of both "pedestrian stop" and implied consent. There is no detention by definition.

   ▹ The reason Jack stopped is psychological—he knew the answer to the question and he knew that the answer was not incriminating. Anecdotally, this strategy often engages a person into a conversation with the police.

   ▹ The question is within the explorative scope of a pedestrian stop.

2. **Questioning theme.** Interrogation is the most important investigative skill because a properly obtained confession is the best form of reasonable grounds. Although all interrogations are governed by the same "rules of evidence," questioning is classified as: (a) front-line interrogation, or (b) formal interrogation. The differences between the two are the extent of the danger, and time and information limitations. Front-line interrogations are restricted by greater risk and uncertainty. Formal interrogations are

conducted in a controlled environment, with more time and information available.

A general questioning strategy is needed before you start either type of questioning to prevent "winging it." In this case, three questioning strategies were chosen. Jack was asked about:

a. his reason for committing the crime,

b. his reason for being at the crime scene at the time of offence, and

c. his purpose, e.g., pre-offence whereabouts and post-offence destination.

It is not mandatory to inform him of the right to counsel or the "caution" before the questioning starts, because only mere suspicion exists and he is an adult.

Asking for a reason for committing the break and enter is acceptable because:

a. It is not an unlawful inducement. It does not include a threat, promise, or *quid pro quo*, referring to an offer to give a negative or positive in exchange for a confession.[5]

b. There is a concrete suspicion that he is involved. He was not selected randomly and was not targeted.[6]

c. Psychologically and legally, Jack has a choice to refute his participation. An innocent person will emphatically declare and concretely justify his innocence.[7]

d. Asking a legitimate suspect for a reason is far more effective than asking whether he committed the offence: asking "why" is better than asking "did you." "Did you" invites either a lie or an abstract denial, resulting in an unproductive debate.[8]

e. Asking a legitimate suspect for a reason is not "entrapment." Entrapment is inciting or inviting a person to commit an offence that he previously had absolutely no intention of committing.[9]

If no confession occurs, ask why he was outside the crime scene at the time of the offence. If no incriminating statements are made, ask exploratory questions to lock him into answers about where he was, where he was going, and what he was doing. If his denial is true, it should be verifiable. Honest denials are often concrete; dishonesty is often abstract (vague, ambiguous).[10]

The core of interrogation strategy is centered on the concept of voluntariness, which includes the prevention of Charter violations. A wide range of questioning strategies emerge from the endless stream of derivative cases that continue to evolve from the landmark S.C.C. case in *R. v. Oickle* (2000), which can be found on the accompanying website (**www.emp.ca/arcaro/ criminvestigation5E**).

3. **A visual inspection of his clothing.** Look for items relevant to the break and enter (e.g., glass on Jack's clothes) and unrelated items (e.g., weapons and drugs). Glass transfer is unique. Under these circumstances, the presence of glass on his clothes would lead to only one logical conclusion. Glass on his clothes, in conjunction with "bad character" evidence, constitutes reasonable grounds. It would be unreasonable to believe that a

coincidence occurred. His clothes, shoe type, and shoe pattern would be significant for comparison after the crime scene is analyzed. Unrelated possession of illegal items constitutes authority to arrest without a warrant under s. 495 C.C. In this case study, a visual inspection was negative.

4. **Ask for consent to search his clothes.** Same concept as strategy 3.

5. **CPIC check.** In this case, you know Jack's name and age, which allows you to do the CPIC before or while approaching Jack. In reality, the sequence of the CPIC check will vary. The goals of the CPIC check are to determine if he is: (a) wanted, (b) violating a release, or (c) violating a probation order. An outstanding warrant, breach of undertaking, or breach of probation constitutes authority to arrest under s. 495 C.C.

6. **Identify and search possible paths from the crime scene.** Using your analytical thinking, identify all possible paths joining the crime scene to your current location and search them for secondary transfer (e.g., discarded items that were used to commit the offence or that were stolen during the offence). If items are found, they should be examined for additional transfer (e.g., fingerprints).

Because reasonable grounds were not formed at the scene, the following long-term strategies were used:

7. **Crime scene.** A forensics unit or identification officer (more commonly called an Ident. officer) examined the crime scene looking for physical evidence such as fingerprints or shoe prints that may be positively matched to Jack's. The existence of a criminal record indicates that the suspect's fingerprints are on file.

8. **Witness interviews.** Neighbours and inner-circle persons identified through BIS theory development were interviewed.

9. **Informant development.** As you will learn in subsequent chapters, informant development is vital to solving crimes. It is the second most important investigative skill, after that of interrogation. Informants are a unique type of witness. Informant development is a specialized form of network building that is crucial to your career. No relevant information was forthcoming from any informants about Jack's involvement in this crime.

10. **Formal interrogation.** A failed front-line interrogation does not prevent a formal interrogation later. The complex laws relating to voluntariness, right to counsel, and right to silence have transformed during the past decade.

CASE STUDY 1.1 CONCLUSION

In reality, Jack confessed two days later during a formal interrogation after he was arrested for an unrelated break and enter at a commercial business. The three goals of the interrogation were:

- **Obtain a confession for the offence for which he was arrested.** Jack confessed and implicated an accomplice who was a former employee of the commercial business.
- **Obtain a confession for all other unsolved offences that he has committed, including the break and enter in the case study.** An initial confession signifies that Jack's compulsion to confess has been activated, which facilitates additional confessions. Jack's confession for the case study break and enter included reasons for selecting that business:
  - ▷ he was familiar with the premises because he had been inside as a customer,
  - ▷ it was next to a bar that he frequented,
  - ▷ the business sold electronic equipment that was portable, and
  - ▷ there was a strong market for selling stolen electronic equipment.

  Additionally, he implicated two accomplices and three buyers of the stolen electronic equipment, which led to obtaining and executing search warrants.
- **Informant development.** Jack implicated three additional persons in unrelated offences: (a) a convenience store robbery that was committed a week earlier by a person armed with a stolen gun, (b) a person who possessed a large quantity of drugs for the purpose of trafficking, and (c) a person in possession of a quantity of stolen firearms and drugs for personal use.

■ KEY POINTS

1. Jack selected the victims for a reason and planned each offence. Nothing was committed randomly.
2. He was the source of confessions and information that led to derivative investigations. Despite his violent nature and extensive criminal past, he became a long-term major informant. In other words, an experienced criminal cooperated with the police.

The following case law decision is a major point-of-reference that demonstrates the "mere suspicion bind" similar to the one the officer in Case Study 1.1 encountered in dealing with Jack.

CASE LAW

R. v. Young (1997)

ARREST FOR PUBLIC INTOXICATION WHEN MERE SUSPICION EXISTS OF BREAK AND ENTER

> "One might think that there could be no more prosaic event in a constable's night shift on the streets than the investigation of a break and enter and an intoxicated man."—Ontario Court of Appeal

Investigating a break and enter at 4:30 a.m. and finding an intoxicated person near the crime scene is never an ordinary investigation, as the Court suggests in the above quote. The reasons are simple. These circumstances often create the "mere suspicion bind" that requires complex rapid decision-making in a dangerous and stressful environment.

In *R. v. Young* (1997), the Ontario Court of Appeal ruled on making an arrest for public intoxication to solve the "mere suspicion bind" during a break and enter in-progress investigation:

Offence: "Break, enter, and theft."

Circumstances: A police officer found a broken glass door at the front of a business premises at 4:30 a.m. A backup officer responded and, while en route, saw an intoxicated man walking about one block from the crime scene. After assisting the first officer, the backup officer returned to the intoxicated man and asked him for his name, address, and where he had been. The response caused the officer to form a suspicion because the pedestrian was not taking the most direct route home.

The officer asked the pedestrian to empty his pockets after seeing a bulge in one of them. The pedestrian complied and removed $1,151 in cash. The officer questioned him about the amount. Three responses were given: $500, $632, and $832. The officer returned the cash to the pedestrian.

The officer informed the pedestrian about the break and enter, and asked him to accompany him to the crime scene (the verbatim request is not known). The pedestrian complied and was seated in the back of the cruiser. The back doors of the cruiser could not be opened from inside. After returning to the crime scene, the officer was able to determine only that a money box had been tampered with, but could not determine what had been stolen.

The officer believed that reasonable grounds did not exist to believe that the pedestrian had committed the offence. At this time, the officer arrested him for public intoxication under the *Liquor Licence Act* (L.L.A.). The accused was informed of the reason, cautioned, and searched. The money was seized and the accused was lodged in a cell while the break and enter investigation continued.

Hours later, police learned that an amount of money similar to that of the seizure had been stolen. The accused was then arrested for break, enter, and theft. Subsequent examination of the accused's jeans resulted in the seizure of glass particles that were similar to the glass of the broken door.

Trial: The accused was convicted. The trial judge ruled that the arrest for public intoxication was lawful. No Charter violations occurred and no evidence was excluded. The accused emptied his pockets by consent. The accused's voluntary accompaniment to the crime scene did not constitute a detention.

Ontario Court of Appeal: The accused appealed his conviction. The appeal was allowed and a new trial was ordered. The court made the following rulings:

▸ The arrest for public intoxication was lawful; the officer had a bona fide opinion that the accused needed to be arrested for his own protection pursuant to s. 31(4) L.L.A.

▸ A detention occurred before the arrest for public intoxication for which consent was not properly obtained. Detention may have commenced at the time of any one of these events: upon stopping the accused, asking him to empty his pockets, or when he entered the back of the cruiser. The court ruled that valid consent was not obtained in relation to all three events. Consent is the equivalent of a waiver of rights. The Crown has the onus to prove on a balance of probabilities that valid consent was obtained. The procedure for obtaining valid consent is found in *R. v. Wills* (1992). In this case, no evidence existed that proved the accused had knowledge of his relevant rights and the consequences of waiving those rights. Consequently, a s.10(b) Charter violation occurred relating to the detention prior to the arrest for public intoxication.

▸ The accused was not advised of his right to counsel until the arrest for public intoxication, although he was detained without consent before the arrest. In the absence of valid consent, a s. 8 Charter violation occurred relating to the search of the accused's pockets.

▸ The seized money and the accused's statements were both considered to be conscriptive evidence. The discovery of the money would have been inevitable because of a search after the lawful arrest for public intoxication. Consequently, the admission of the money would not affect trial fairness and was not excluded. However, the accused's statement regarding the three different amounts of money was ruled to affect trial fairness and was excluded.

Summary: The conclusions drawn from this case:

▸ A "public intoxication" arrest is legitimate if it is made immediately and not as a solution for the mere suspicion bind. In this case, the accused should have been arrested for public intoxication immediately; if he had been immediately arrested, a subsequent search after the arrest would have been lawful.

▸ Consent is a lawful solution to the mere suspicion bind. Express consent is better than implied consent, and is obtained by strictly applying the consent guidelines established in *R. v. Wills*.

▸ Verbatim conversation is crucial to prove that express consent was obtained. Always record direct quotes in your notebook for future testimony.

ENDNOTES

1. Section 128(113)(b) H.T.A.
2. Section 144(20) H.T.A.
3. *R. v. L.B.*, 2007 ONCA 596.
4. *R. v. Wills* (1992), 70 C.C.C. (3d) 529 (Ont. C.A.).
5. *R. v. Oickle* (2000), 147 C.C.C. (3d) 321 (S.C.C.) and the series of derivative case law, explained in the accompanying website (www.emp.ca/arcaro/criminvestigation5E).
6. Ibid.
7. Ibid., and G. Arcaro, "Interrogation Best Practices," Ph.D. research material, University of Regina, 2007.
8. Ibid.
9. Ibid.
10. Ibid.

PHASE 2
Case Management: Offence Validation and Witness Interviews

While some investigations are conducted by only one officer, most are *team tasks* requiring the skills of both generalists and specialists. One of these tasks is the collection of evidence: witness observations and physical evidence. The admissibility of both types of evidence, in a court trial, is the primary investigative goal. Every team needs a leader, a coordinator who assembles the team, sets goals, plans, devises strategy, directs team members, monitors performance, and reaches a successful outcome. The size of the team varies, depending on the complexity of the investigation. The leader is a case manager. **Case management** refers to the coordination, supervision, and recording of investigative tasks. The case manager is accountable for how and if the outcome is reached.

Following the BIS model, introduced in chapter 3, will assist in the successful outcome of a criminal investigation. The first step in the model is "validate the offence/complaint." In order to do this, proper case management must include an understanding of the indicators of a fabricated offence, such as crime scene staging. How to conduct a witness interview and an understanding of the "Rules of Evidence" that are associated with witness testimony are key to proper case management.

Phase 2 teaches aspects of case management, beginning with a discussion on offence validation.

PHASE 2 LEARNING OUTCOMES

The student will learn

- how to validate an offence
- the "five fundamentals of witness interviews":
  - ▷ *Compellability*: what rules require a witness to appear in court or for an interview during an investigation.
  - ▷ *Competence*: whether or not a witness will be allowed to give testimony in court.
  - ▷ *Rules of evidence*: what a witness can and cannot say in court.
  - ▷ *Witness credibility*: understanding memory recall and memory decay in relation to evaluating witness credibility.
  - ▷ *Interviews*: strategies for questioning witnesses in order to elicit from them the largest volume of accurate information.

CHAPTER 7
Validating the Offence: Criminal Investigation Analysis

LEARNER SUMMARY

The Ontario Court of Appeal has defined "criminal investigation analysis" as a group of investigative processes that includes validating the occurrence, an investigative procedure that determines whether a reported offence is real or fabricated.[1] The first step of the Basic Investigative Sequence (BIS) is validating the offence—proving that the offence actually happened, or if it was simulated to mislead the police.

Offence fabrication, also called "crime scene staging," is a specific type of deception where an occurrence is simulated to conceal what really happened. All crime scene staging conceals another offence. For example, a staged home invasion may conceal a homicide, an insurance fraud, or an obstruction of justice by attempting to wrongfully implicate an innocent person.

Offence fabrication is not rare; it happens often enough to create the need to validate every offence reported. Criminal investigation analysis helps an officer form an opinion about whether a reported offence is valid or not. The analysis involves a comparison of the way the crime was reported with the elements of a logical crime. This comparison identifies the presence or absence of inconsistencies and contradictions. An *opinion* is formed after the comparison about the validity of the report. The formation of the opinion will be simple or complex, depending on the case. Nonetheless, proving validity is the starting point of the BIS in each case.

Offence validation may be extremely simple or complex. As a rule:

▸ The simpler the crime, the harder it is to validate; the more complex the crime, the easier it is to validate.
▸ More witnesses means simpler validation. Fewer witnesses mean more complex validation.

This chapter teaches a validation decision-making model that explains how to validate reported offences.

Case Study 7.1

9:20 a.m. Radio broadcast: "Belated sexual assault. See counsellor at Rutherford High School, 3227 Brockport Road."

9:30 a.m. Attend counsellor's office.

The complainant is a 17-year-old female student. She is in class.

The following is reported by the counsellor.

At 8:30 a.m., the complainant was walking on a sidewalk in front of eight houses. The sidewalk is across from the front entrance of the high school, where school buses usually stop to discharge passengers.

Three men approached the complainant, pulled her into the bushes on the front lawn of one house, and sexually assaulted her. The complainant recognized the men as occupants of a house near the school. These men had been involved in altercations with several students from the school. The complainant reported the assault to the school official when she arrived at school before going to class.

(Refer to the end of Chapter 7 for the conclusion of this case study.)

FABRICATION: THE NEED TO VALIDATE

Research, statistics, case law, and anecdotal evidence shows that fabrication of occurrences is not rare. It is common enough to warrant the need to validate each reported occurrence.[2]

Validation is a specific type of *credibility evaluation*. The credibility of every complainant must be formally evaluated. Strong credibility is not instantly given to a complainant's statement. Strong credibility is an opinion that is formed through a structured process.

This rule applies to all witnesses. An officer is required to evaluate the credibility of every witness statement, including that of the victim. There are three strategies used to evaluate credibility:

1. criminal investigation analysis,
2. forensic analysis of physical evidence, and
3. the ten-point witness credibility evaluation list.

The Ontario Court of Appeal's definition of **criminal investigation analysis** details a number of investigative services, including:

- ▸ profiling,
- ▸ crime scene analysis, and
- ▸ opinion of validity (determining whether a crime scene had been "manipulated to create a misleading impression.")[3]

Forensic analysis of physical evidence can *corroborate* (support) or disprove a witness's statement. Physical evidence interpretation is explained in subsequent chapters.

The **ten-point witness credibility evaluation list** is a structured decision-making model that allows you to justify an opinion of strong or weak credibility. It is a list of ten factors, including motive to lie. This list is explained in subsequent chapters.

EVIDENCE SUPPORTING THE NEED TO VALIDATE

Research

Over a century of research shows that fabrication of occurrences is a common phenomenon that proves the need to validate all reported offences. The following is a sample of this research.

- Hans Gross, one of the pioneers of criminal investigation research, strongly warned about the "eventuality of false reports." His research showed that fabrication is motivated by the desire to profit, get revenge, divert suspicion, or avoid embarrassment. A wide range of offences are fabricated, including assaults, thefts, sexual assaults, break and enters, robberies, and arsons. Sudden death scenes are altered to conceal homicides, suicides, accidents, and "natural" deaths. Some examples include:
  - ▷ a homicide scene altered to appear as a home invasion or suicide
  - ▷ a suicide scene altered to appear as a natural death to avoid embarrassment, or as a homicide to falsely allege negligence
  - ▷ an accident altered to appear as a natural death to divert suspicion of negligence
  - ▷ a natural death altered to appear as a homicide or suicide

  Gross was one of the first researchers to caution against instantly believing a victim's report. Credibility has to be evaluated and every occurrence validated in order to prevent two consequences: (a) suspecting and investigating innocent people based on false allegations, and (b) allowing dangerous offenders to go undetected when a crime (such as a homicide) has occurred but has been concealed.[4]

- Harry O'Connell and John Soderman's[5] research supported the frequency of fabrication, and focused on simulated death crime scenes. Specifically, they emphasized examples of simulated suicide by hanging in order to conceal a homicide by strangulation. Hanging and strangulation produce similar marks, motivating the offender to use this specific method of staging. However, enough differences are present in order to distinguish the marks from each other. Additionally, transfer of trace evidence can help to distinguish strangulation from hanging. For example, examination of the rope will reveal that the fibers of the rope "will lie in the opposite direction of the pulling." If the deceased person slid down the rope during a hanging, the fibers will be directed downward. If a murderer tries to conceal a strangulation by "pulling the body up, the fibers will be directed upwards on the part of the rope which was pulled by the murderer."

  Their research also uncovered additional stagings, including simulated falls from heights to conceal homicide, and simulated break and enters and robberies. They noted that the key to validating an occurrence is exploring the presence or absence of inconsistencies (e.g., how the crime was committed; injury and wound patterns).

- Arne Svensson and Otto Wendel's[6] research focused on simulated break-ins and robberies. Real offences have a "natural" way of being committed, displaying common elements that compose the anatomy of a crime. Creating an imitation crime is not easy, because the simulator may not know the "natural" way and thus create "gaps" or inconsistencies.

Their research included the frequency of sudden-death crime scenes, which complicate classifying the death as homicide, suicide, accident, or natural cause. They noted that the key to all validation is answering the question, "Could the occurrence have logically happened in the way the crime reconstruction shows?"

▸ John Douglas and Corinne Munn's[7] research not only supported the need to validate because of the frequency of simulations, they defined crime scene staging as "intentional alteration of the crime scene prior to the first officer's arrival," and identified only two reasons why it happens: (a) to divert suspicion from the most logical suspect, or (b) to protect the reputation of the victim and his or her family.

These researchers provided their own strategy for validating an occurrence—three questions, and three red flags.

Questions

1. Were illogical items taken from the crime scene?
2. Was the point of entry illogical?
3. Did the crime pose a "high risk" to the offender?

If the answers are "yes" to any or all three, suspect simulation; the offence is invalid.

Red Flags

1. An intruder kills a wife and children, but the husband escapes uninjured.
2. The offender "does not first target the person posing the greatest threat."
3. "The person posing the greatest threat to the offender suffers the least amount of injury."

Any one of these red flags creates suspicion of deception.

Statistical Research

Statistics Canada has published literature regarding "unfounded crimes" in *Juristat*, showing that fabricated offences are not rare.

An **unfounded crime** is defined as a reported offence that did not happen. An unfounded crime includes both intentional fabrication and unintentional error (e.g., report of damage; cause determined to be the environment).

The accompanying website **www.emp.ca/arcaro/criminvestigation5E** includes samples of unfounded crime statistics that support the frequency of fabricated offences, and the awareness needed to explore that possibility.

Case Law

Reporting an intentionally fabricated offence constitutes the dual procedure offence of "public mischief" (s. 140 C.C). The facts-in-issue of this offence are:

- reporting that an offence has been committed,
- knowing that it has not been committed,
- reporting the offence with the intent to mislead a peace officer, and
- causing a peace officer to enter into or continue an investigation.

An *offence* refers to any classification of criminal, provincial, or municipal by-law offence. The *actus reus* is the verbal or written statement made by the complainant that reports the offence and causes an investigation. The *mens rea* is the specific intent to mislead the police.

"Entering into an investigation" includes situations where an officer doesn't immediately believe a complainant, and the complainant confesses that he lied. With experience, officers learn to become experts at detecting deception, and can immediately recognize "Public mischief" in many cases. The offence has occurred even if an officer instantly believed it, because he or she entered into an investigation when the report was received, responded to it, and conducted the complainant interview.

The volume of "public mischief" case law decisions shows the frequency of fabrications and strategies used to investigate this offence. The accompanying web-site **www.emp.ca/arcaro/criminvestigation5E** includes an extensive case law review of "public mischief" decisions.

Anecdotal Evidence

NEED IS A POWERFUL MOTIVATOR

Desperate times motivate desperate measures. "Public mischief" stems from a need. Like all crimes, motives include profit, hatred, and revenge. Common examples include:

- A person needs a new car or a new paint job for his car. He decides to simulate theft, arson, or damage in order to defraud his insurance company. He may drive the car into a canal, burn the car himself and falsely report it as stolen, or simply scratch the car intentionally and falsely report a "mischief" complaint.
- An employee needs money. She goes to work at a gas station or convenience store, steals money from the cash register, and falsely reports a robbery in order to conceal her theft and to divert suspicion from her.
- An impaired driver collides with a parked car or drives into a ditch. He leaves the scene, goes home, and falsely reports his car stolen in order to conceal his "impaired driving" and "fail to remain" offences.
- A broken relationship results in unresolved conflict. Hatred drives one person to harm the other by falsely implicating him or her in a variety of false crimes such as assault and break and enter.

"LOW RISK AND HIGH REWARD" IS A MOTIVATOR

The temptation to fabricate strengthens because of the incorrect belief that it is very easy to do it—low risk, high reward. Some people believe the misconception that it is simple to simulate an offence (such as a break and enter), make a false report to the police, and be rewarded with an automatic, routine outcome.

Common examples include:

▸ making a false claim to an insurance company in order to obtain money, no questions asked,

▸ invoking a counter-charge against a person who has charged an offender in the hopes of forcing a settlement, or

▸ concealing a crime out of desperation by staging another occurrence and assuming the police will believe the simulation.

When the person in need wrongly believes the solution is simple, the likelihood of fabrication increases.

FABRICATORS CONVINCE BY EXAGGERATION

▸ *Deception causes the need to convince others of the lie.* When a person fabricates an offence and crime scene, he or she has a natural strong urge to convince the police of the lie.

▸ *The fabricator is usually inexperienced.* Fabricators often don't know the natural way that a simulated crime is committed. He or she has either never committed such a crime, or is unfamiliar with the "low risk and high reward" strategy that offenders use to select victims.

▸ *Exaggerating the circumstances of the lie is the natural way to convince others of the lie.* People go overboard to convince the police of a lie by means of three "S" diversions: *severity, stress,* and *sympathy* ("Look at how bad it is," "Look at how stressed I am," and "Look at what could have happened to me.").

For example, to convince the police of a false break and enter, the fabricator may exaggerate (a) the force used and the damage caused at the point of entry (exaggerated severity), (b) what was stolen or damaged inside (exaggerated severity), (c) the degree of threat to the victim, such as written death threats on a wall or messages left at the crime scene (exaggerated stress and sympathy).

The three S's are a *product* of exaggeration, with the *intent* to divert suspicion away from the fabricator. They are a self-defence mechanism, protecting the fabricator from the consequences of being detected.

▸ *The exaggeration creates an unnatural occurrence.* Exaggerated circumstances of a fabricated offence are counter-intuitive. They don't make sense because they constitute a "high risk and low benefit" offender strategy. Look at the above break and enter example:

1. Excessive force at the point of entry is not discrete; it draws attention.
2. Excessive stolen items take too long to remove.
3. A thief would not leave death threats for no reason. Written threats represent more transfer of physical evidence, which is what offenders try to avoid.

However, the **modus operandi (M.O.) paradox** (explained in Chapter 3) applies: if the offender has strong familiarity with the victim and if the offender's presence is expected at the crime scene, the method of the crime may be logical.

Investigative Rules

1. An unnatural crime (high risk and low benefit to the offender) may be either: (a) fabricated, or (b) committed by someone with strong familiarity with the victim and an expectation of presence at the crime scene.
2. The M.O. paradox applies to an unnatural crime: the offence may be invalid, or, if it was real, it was committed by a person(s) with strong familiarity who was expected to be there, if he or she was seen at the crime scene.
3. The M.O. paradox is solved by "strongest motive"—determining who had the stronger motive determines an officer's theory.

VALIDATING THE COMPLAINT

The first step of the BIS, in any criminal investigation, is **validating the complaint**. Validation means to verify or prove that the offence:

- actually occurred,
- occurred at the reported location, and
- occurred in the reported manner.

A validation decision-making model allows you to form a justified *opinion* about whether the occurrence was fabricated or not. It eliminates guesswork, tunnel vision, and baseless speculation. Using the model as a validation procedure allows an officer to write justifiable reasons in his or her General Occurrence Report, explaining opinions about whether the complainant has strong or weak credibility and whether the offence is valid or invalid.

If an officer's opinion is invalid, the officer will not investigate other people in order to prevent implicating innocent persons; he or she will continue to investigate the validity of the offence. After validity is proven, the officer can progress to the second step of the BIS.

Validation Decision-Making Model

This model is based on the *presence* or *absence* of **indicators**. The absence of indicators means an opinion of a valid offence. Conversely, the presence of indicators means mere suspicion of invalid offence.

■ KEY POINTS

- **Validation rule** Validation is proved by the absence of indicators of fabrication.
- **Definition of "indicator"** An indicator is (a) circumstantial evidence that causes mere suspicion of fabrication, (b) circumstantial evidence that implies high risk and low reward for the offender, or (c) a contradiction or inconsistency as part of a "low-risk, high-reward" crime.
- **Presence of indicators** Any single indicator or combination of indicators constitutes only mere suspicion of "public mischief." No combination of indicators constitutes reasonable grounds for public mischief.

▸ **Confession of public mischief** A confession to any person (citizen or police) that proves intentional fabrication constitutes reasonable grounds for public mischief.

USING THE MODEL FOR VALIDATION

1. **Evidence** To make an informed decision, obtain the maximum amount of evidence (crime scene investigation and victim/witness statements). Form the context first—create the "big picture."

2. **Elements** Identify each concrete circumstance of the offence in order to form the "anatomy" of the crime you are investigating. Make a list of individual, concrete elements.

3. **Classify** Determine the presence or absence of indicators. Analyze each element of the offence. Identify which one is an indicator of fabrication. Classify each element as either (a) low risk and high reward, or (b) high risk and low reward. The second classification signifies an indicator.

4. **Opinion** Form an opinion of a valid or invalid offence. An absence of indicators means that the offence is valid. Progress to the second step of the BIS.

   A presence of indicators means that the M.O. paradox is present. There is mere suspicion of "public mischief," but a high possibility of a real crime committed by person with strong familiarity.

5. **Motive** Determine whether the complainant had a reason to fabricate. If a motive exists, the paradox is solved: suspect fabrication and continue investigating validity. Stay at the first step of the BIS.

6. **Question the complainant** If mere suspicion of fabrication exists, conduct a series of interviews to reach a final opinion of validity, through:
   ▷ an exploratory interview with the complainant. The goal is to explore inconsistencies. Either obtain a confession, if the offence was fabricated, or justify the inconsistency. If the suspect confesses, reasonable grounds exist to arrest and charge him or her for public mischief.
   ▷ the complainant's inner circle. The goal is to determine whether the complainant made pre-offence or post-offence incriminating statements (such as asking people to help stage the crime, or bragging about it afterward.)

INDICATORS OF INVALID OFFENCES

Any offence may be staged or fabricated. It is impossible to list every offence and every indicator of invalid offences. Four offences have been selected to explain the concept of indicators, because of their frequency and relevance to front-line policing:

1. break and enter,
2. damage to vehicles and vehicle theft,
3. robbery, and
4. sexual assault.

Each offence has a list of common indicators. As stated previously, each indicator constitutes only mere suspicion of public mischief; none is conclusive proof or reasonable grounds.

Break and Enter

This is a common occurrence that happens countless times daily across Canada. Break and enters occur at places classified as dwelling-houses, as well as at places other than residences. Every reported break and enter must be carefully validated because it is incredibly simple to fabricate this offence. One of the reasons why insurance is costly is the frequency of insurance fraud committed.

There is no absolute rule that characterizes all break and enters. Generally, offenders use the "low risk and high reward" strategy: speed, discretion, and benefit. The following are point-of-reference elements for natural, or low risk and high reward, break and enter offences.

- **Point of entry (POE)** The POE will not be in the sight line of witnesses, will have minimal visibility to traffic (cars, pedestrians, and neighbours), and will involve the use of a minimal amount of force in order to avoid attracting attention.
- **Stolen items** Stolen items will be easy to find, and portable (easily carried, transported, and sold). Criminals usually do not park a large truck in front of a location and load many large items onto the vehicle. Televisions, DVD players, stereos, and jewellery are frequently stolen items.
- **Minimal time** A short amount of time spent inside a location reduces the chance of getting caught.

The following ten points are specific indicators of break and enter fabrication and the M.O. paradox.

1. **No forced entry** Most real break and enters have some forced entry. Unlocked doors are possible POEs, but they imply too much of a coincidence. If the offence is valid, the offender likely has strong familiarity.
2. **Excessive force used at the point of entry** An unusual amount of damage at the point of entry attracts attention. This raises a "red flag" of fabrication (attempting to convince by exaggeration). If the use of excessive force is real, this may indicate that the offender has psychological problems.
3. **Daytime entry** Daytime break and enters do occur, but they are conducted discretely. Forced entry via a front door during the day obviously attracts attention (another example of attempting to convince by exaggeration). If the front-door entry was real, familiarity or planning existed.

    The following are two anecdotal examples from actual investigations.

    ▷ A 25-year-old man (a known steroid user) lived with his mother in a quiet, remote subdivision. During a break and enter into his home, the front door was completely knocked off the hinges and only one item was stolen, from a fishing box in the basement. After initial denials, the man told police that he had had a conflict with another man about steroid purchases. It was later proven that this (second) person committed the offence. Why did he commit the offence in an illogical manner, with blatant disregard for the attention that would be drawn? The offender believed that the complainant would not report the incident for fear that his mother would find out about his steroid possession and use. However, the mother found the entry first and reported it to police.

▷ A middle-aged offender did not have the appearance of a criminal. His break-and-enter strategy consisted of dressing in a business suit, carrying a briefcase, knocking on doors and waiting until he found unoccupied homes with unlocked doors. His appearance and conduct drew no suspicion or attention from any person who saw him enter. Additionally, his pride about his ingenuity and success compelled him to brag to police and continue breaking and entering using this method.

4. **Brief absence of the owner** The following complainant statement is a strong indicator of the M.O. paradox: "I was gone for only [concrete time]. When I got back, I found that the break-in had happened."

   A real break and enter during a brief absence is an astoundingly rare coincidence. "I was gone for only…" indicates a fabricated report or strong familiarity.

5. **Stolen property from obscure places without an extensive search** It is illogical that a stranger could directly discover the locations of valuable items without searching for them.

6. **Theft of only one valuable item; nothing else touched**

7. **Theft of an excessive number of large items from multiple locations on the same premises** The following are three anecdotal examples of actual investigations.

   ▷ A married couple left for a one-week vacation. Their two sons, both in high school, remained home. Upon the parents' return, the boys told them that a break and enter had occurred that day, while they were in school. The list of stolen items included a refrigerator, stove, and microwave oven. The extensive quantity required substantial time to remove and a suitable conveyance to transport them. Investigation revealed that the complainants' sons had hosted a party at which the appliances were damaged. Rather than admit this to their parents, they disposed of the items and reported the break and enter to conceal the events of the party. Neighbours witnessed the removal of the property, recognized the complainants' sons, and suspected nothing.

   ▷ A woman left her house during late afternoon to go to church. She returned home one and a half hours later to discover her living-room furniture gone, along with a quantity of other items. She lived with her 21-year-old son. Investigation revealed that her son and nephew stole the property, loaded it on a truck, and paid off a drug debt with it.

   ▷ Management at a large department store discovered that more than $100,000 worth of property had been stolen from a warehouse during two break and enters in one week. The investigation revealed that a transport-truck driver who delivered property for the company had entered the warehouse and loaded other property in addition to his delivery. He then sold it to an established network of customers.

8. **Extensive list of stolen items** After you ask a complainant to write down a list of stolen items, he or she gives you several pages a few days later. "Padding" is a slang term used to describe intentionally adding items to a list of legitimate stolen property. Real break and enters can create the temptation to profit from a real crime by padding the report. This is a specific type of deception, and renders the offence invalid because it did not happen in the manner reported.

9. **Excessive damage to multiple areas inside the premises and no theft** No theft means no monetary benefit. Damaging a place is a non-profit break and enter. It may legitimately be a product of hatred toward the complainant, but spending excessive time committing a non-profit offence constitutes a high risk. This indicates that the offender is trying to falsely incriminate an innocent person because of unresolved conflict. If it is real, this behaviour can indicate psychological problems.

    The following is an anecdotal example of an actual investigation.

    A complainant reported that her house had been entered during a three-hour absence, between 7 and 10 p.m. When she returned, extensive damage was found inside to walls, carpets, and windows. Nothing was stolen. Without being asked, she mentioned her ex-boyfriend as the only suspect she could think of. The complainant later confessed that she staged the offence herself; her intention was incriminating an ex-boyfriend who would not stop harassing her.

10. **Absence of owners during vacation** Break and enters are certainly possible while the owners are on vacation, but the offenders must have learned of the absence. Do not form an immediate opinion that this offence is valid without justification.

    Some people have used vacation absences to stage break and enters in order to defraud insurance companies. If the offence is real, explore the possibility of *familiarity through broadcasting*, defined as unintentionally communicating the absence to others; offenders learn about the absence from the complainant or family (e.g., the complainant tells co-workers; a family's children arrange parties and tell friends).

Damage to Vehicles and Vehicle Theft

Stealing a car is not easy. It requires planning and experience. Damaging a car is a non-profit offence that requires a person to be strongly motivated to commit it. Speed, discretion, and benefit are the characteristics of low risk, high reward strategies. False reports of car damage and car thefts are motivated by need. The following are four indicators of fabrication:

1. **Paint scratched on a car parked in a full parking lot; no other cars damaged** The desire for a insurance-paid paint job is motivation for this offence. The reasons why this is an indicator are that

   ▷ vandalizing a car does not profit an offender,

   ▷ a full parking lot clearly implies several potential witnesses, and

   ▷ scratching only one car is senseless.

Who would risk being caught for a non-profit crime in a crowded area? If mere vandalism were the only motive, why were the other cars left untouched? The suspicion in this case is that the owner scratched the car himself at another location and moved it to a crowded parking lot, believing that the high volume of traffic would convince the police that the damage was authentic—more people means more potential vandals. People who stage this type of offence often have no criminal experience. If the offence is real, it may indicate that the offender has a problem with unchecked impulsive behaviour.

2. **Entry into a car plus theft of stereo, while car parked in a driveway or at the front of the owner's house, in a populated area** This scenario involves too many potential witnesses, or the appearance of the car's owner; removing a stereo takes time. An actual investigation will help explain this indicator.

The owner of a car lived in a populated townhouse complex where the parking lot was situated in the centre of the complex, in plain view of each unit. The complainant parked his car in the complex late in the afternoon. He reported that his car was forcibly entered during the evening hours while the car was parked in front of his house, and a valuable stereo was removed. The removal required substantial time. An unfamiliar person would not logically take these numerous chances of being caught. The suspicion was that the complaint was fabricated or that the offender was so familiar with the complainant that he would have been confident that any potential witnesses would not have been suspicious. In this case, the complainant later confessed that he had fabricated the offence.

3. **Excessive damage to a vehicle to facilitate entry** This scenario attracts attention, and indicates an attempt to convince by exaggeration.

4. **Report of a stolen car after a fail-to-remain collision has occurred** For example, a drunk driver collides with a car or pedestrian, or drives into a ditch. The driver leaves, fearing arrest for impaired driving. To conceal the offences of impaired driving and failing to remain at the scene, he falsely reports his car stolen.

Robbery

Robbery is defined as (a) theft with violence, or (b) assault with intent to steal. The types of robberies are wide-ranging:

▸ pedestrians are assaulted and a purse or wallet stolen,

▸ gas stations and convenience stores are often robbed by a single, armed offender, or

▸ banks are robbed by multiple offenders.

Robberies are not random. Some degree of planning precedes them. The "low risk and high reward" strategy usually involves the following common elements:

▸ Some degree of violence is inherent to all robberies. Offenders are often armed; victims are sometimes assaulted. It is important to note that violence causes stress, which negatively affects memory and recall. A victim's focus is narrowed to the weapon, often making his or her statement justifiably abstract and brief.

▸ Offenders avoid areas of high customer traffic. They may wait outside of the crime scene for considerable time, monitoring customer traffic. Customers may be valuable pre-offence witnesses.

▸ Offenders are often disguised.

▸ The duration of a robbery is usually brief.

▸ Corner stores and gas stations often do not have excessive cash in the register. Regular deposits are made and a float limit is maintained.

Robbery validation ranges from extremely simple to complex. As a rule:

▸ If a robbery is complex, it is simple to validate. Conversely, if a robbery is simple, it is harder to validate.

▸ Validation is simple if many witnesses are present. Fewer witnesses means that validation will be more complex.

SIMPLE VALIDATION: EXAMPLE

Three offenders entered a bank at 2:30 p.m., armed with firearms. A total of 14 people were in the bank. The offenders pointed their firearms at three bank employees, stole over $10,000, and left before the police arrived.

Validation is simple. This type of robbery is too complicated to fabricate, and a number of witnesses verified that the robbery happened. The witnesses will corroborate each other.

COMPLEX VALIDATION: EXAMPLE

A single employee was working at a gas station. At 7 p.m., one offender entered the store wearing a disguise and holding a knife. The offender demanded money, stole $115, and left before the police arrived.

Validation is complicated. This simple robbery is easy to fabricate, and there is no witness other than the victim.

The following are three indicators of fabricated robberies:

1. **Excessive, elaborate description of an armed offender** Victims of violent robberies, especially when weapons are involved, obviously suffer significant stress. Their attention narrows, and is usually focused on the weapon rather than on the offender. A general, brief, vague description of the offender is expected.

   Consequently, legitimate robbery victims often can provide only a general or brief description of an offender. A lengthy, detailed, specific description of the armed offender is an indicator of fabrication because: (a) it contradicts the expected narrow focus of attention and (b) it is an attempt to convince by exaggeration. Exceptions are possible. This is a general rule only.

   The following is an anecdotal example of an actual investigation.

An ice cream store employee reported that a man armed with a large knife held it near the employee's head, and stole all of the money from the cash register. The complainant was specific about every aspect of the offender's description, including jewellery (e.g., the number of rings the offender wore, and descriptions of them). Although it is possible that a robbery victim is calm enough to make these observations, this is unlikely to be the case when his life is being threatened. The complainant later admitted that he had fabricated the robbery and stole the money himself. The interrogation strategy was simple: the complainant was informed of:

▷ the suspicion of fabrication,

▷ the reasons for the suspicion, and

▷ the possibility of implicating innocent persons.

The complainant confessed at the seven-minute mark. The reason for the quick confession—*honesty out, honesty in.* The investigator was honest with the complainant about his suspicions of fabrication and, in return, the complainant felt compelled to be honest about what really happened.

2. **Excessive customer traffic prior to the offence** This indicator applies more to small businesses, such as corner stores and gas stations, than to banks. Many small business robberies are committed when no customers are in the business. This suggests some degree of planning by means of offender surveillance before the offence.

High customer traffic may be a high-risk situation for the offender. The following interview strategies emerge:

▷ Determine the estimated number of customers that entered the store before the robbery. Determine whether it was busy or not, or if it was busier than usual.

▷ Determine (a) time of the last customer before the offence, (b) time of the first customer after the offence, and (c) their names, if possible. This time interval represents the opportunity to commit the robbery. If the robbery occurred with no customers present, the short time interval increases suspicion of fabrication. The last and first customers may be immediate pre-offence and post-offence witnesses or accomplices. If they are witnesses, they are crucial to validation. Interview strategies include (a) recording observations which re-create the pre- and post-offence perimeter, (b) asking witnesses to identify and describe persons they saw in the proximity to the store, and (c) recording descriptions of the vehicles identified by the witnesses.

The credibility paradox occurs if witnesses give an officer meaningful information. What made the observation memorable for the witness? What drew his or her attention to the observation? The paradox stems from the "awareness" rule: if nothing memorable happened, and the witness had no awareness that a crime was about to happen, nothing, or very little information, should be remembered. Conversely, if something memorable draws a witness's attention, and awareness exists, the likelihood of recall increases.

3. **Large thefts: unexplained presence of excessive cash before the offence**

   Excessive amounts of cash stolen is an indicator of fabrication. Most small businesses have a cash float procedure that governs the maximum amount of cash that is permitted in the cash register. Employees are required to make regular deposits in a "lock box" or safe. If the complainant reports that there was excessive cash present because of his or her neglect to make deposits, the coincidence of a robbery occurring during this "high reward" opportunity is unreasonable.

   For example, A gas station/convenience store was robbed. The amount stolen was almost double the amount normally in the cash register. The complainant stated, "I was too busy to make the usual deposit. That never happens." Later, he was questioned about the validity of his complaint. The question strategy included communicating (a) the suspicion of fabrication, (b) the reasons for the suspicion, and (c) that classifying this as an invalid offence would prevent innocent people from being implicated. The complainant confessed that he stole the money, and fabricated the robbery to conceal the theft.

Sexual Assault

"It's her word against his." Never use this phrase at the end of the validation process for a reported sexual assault because the phrase is inaccurate, unfair to the victim, and will diminish your reputation as an investigator. This phrase:

- is a baseless, unjustified *opinion.*
- does not involve a proper evaluation of credibility, and
- does not acknowledge that the offence of sexual assault does not require mandatory corroboration.

Eliminate this phrase from your vocabulary and replace it with a justified opinion of strong credibility or weak credibility.

Believing or disbelieving any complainant requires developing an opinion of credibility based on *concrete* justification. You cannot evaluate the credibility of crime victims based on gut feelings, investigative instinct, a hunch, or road experience. These factors are perfectly acceptable to use in order to *start* the validation process, but not to finish it.

Sometimes, there is a fear of discussing the validity and credibility of sexual assaults because it is a sensitive issue. However, it must be discussed because, like all other crimes, evidence shows that there are both real reports and false reports involved. A balance must be struck in order to both protect the public from sexual offenders and to protect innocent persons from false prosecution. Sexual assault victims must not be held to different credibility standards.

A **sexual assault** is defined as the intentional application of specific type of force, without consent. The specific type of force used is similar to an assault, with the added component of a *violation of the sexual integrity of the complainant.* It is a difficult offence to investigate because (a) similar physical evidence is transferred whether or not the *actus reus* is legal or illegal, and (b) the *actus reus*, with consent, is one of humanity's common acts.

Sexual assault does not require corroboration for a conviction, meaning that there is no mandatory obligation to have supporting evidence beyond that provided by the complainant. However, this causes a paradox. The presence or absence of physical evidence and other witnesses is the key to credibility evaluation, meaning that corroboration is inherent to strong credibility.

An officer's goal is to obtain as much physical and witness evidence as possible in order to make an informed decision about credibility. The only indicator is a *contextual* indicator—the totality of the circumstances. Case Study 7.1 at the beginning of this chapter is the point-of-reference case that explains this indicator, which can be described as "time of offence plus location plus number of offenders." This unscientific formula includes three elements that combine to form a context for the offence: (a) when, (b) where, and (c) who/how many.

a. Day time, in view of potential witnesses, draws too much attention to the offender(s).
b. An open, public place is not the most likely location for an offence.
c. Multiple offenders are certainly possible but, anecdotally, there is less chance of several persons having the same deviant intentions at the same time. Because of prisoner retaliation, sexual assault is not the type of offence that criminals want to go to jail for, and the intent to commit sexual assault is usually specific to one person.

Fabricated Offence—General Indicators

There are three general indicators of a fabricated offence.

1. **No transfer of physical evidence** It is impossible to commit any offence without exchanging physical evidence. When an offender comes into contact with another person or an item, a change occurs because of the transfer of trace evidence. When no transfer is found, the suspicion is that no offence occurred.

2. **Refusal to take a polygraph test** A polygraph test is a lie-detector test. There is no Canadian law that allows the police to compel a person to take the test. Although the test results are inadmissible in court, they are a valuable investigative tool. A person who is requested to take a polygraph test is legally allowed to refuse to give consent to take it. The refusal to give consent is not incriminating evidence, because every person is legally entitled to do so. Additionally, a refusal does not constitute reasonable grounds to arrest a person for "Public mischief." Polygraph test procedures and principles are explained in Phase 3 of this book.

   Although a refusal to consent does not constitute an offence and does not contribute to reasonable grounds, it is one of strongest indicators of public mischief. Refusal is a strong indicator because:

   ▷ When the rationale for and the intended results of the actual polygraph test are properly explained (to ensure that innocent persons will not be implicated), there is no logical reason for the refusal.

> ▷ If the offence really happened, the complainant should readily consent. The complainant should be 100 percent confident that he or she will pass the test, and suffer absolutely no consequences.

Clear explanation of the test will prevent mistrust of the police.

3. **Reporting an offence at the police station** This method of reporting an offence may be an attempt to prevent the police from attending at the alleged crime scene and discovering that no offence occurred there. The complainant hopes that the police will simply write a report and never examine the crime scene. If the report is valid, it is rational to assume that the complainant would want a crime scene examination. Of course, there may be a legitimate reason why the complainant attended at the police station instead of calling the police to attend at the crime scene. An officer is responsible for determining that reason in order to remove this suspicion.

   Some Canadian police agencies have added policies requiring complainants to report property offences at local police stations. These policies may invite false reports because the complainant knows the alleged crime scene will probably never be examined.

Proving Public Mischief: Procedure

None of the previously mentioned indicators constitute reasonable grounds to arrest or charge a complainant with "public mischief." The best evidence to prove public mischief is to obtain a confession from the complainant. After public mischief is suspected, re-interview the complainant. Interview strategies include the following:

- ▸ The only way to conduct questioning is by consent. The complainant cannot be arrested or detained for the sole purpose of questioning.
- ▸ The best place for the interview is the police station. The best method for ensuring voluntary attendance is for an officer to phone the complainant and ask him or her to attend at the police station. Schedule a specific time and date so you will know whether he or she has failed to appear. When scheduling the interview, the complainant should be informed of the reason for the interview ("I have a suspect," or "I'd like to discuss a suspect with you.") This is not a deception; either way, you have a suspect. If suspicion exists that the offence didn't happen, the complainant is the suspect—of public mischief. If the offence did happen, the suspicion is that someone very familiar to the complainant likely committed the offence. Any questions that the complainant has (such as, "Who is the suspect?") must be answered in person during the interview. If the report was fabricated, the complainant will suffer a degree of *cognitive dissonance*— internal conflict. It is a high form of stress caused by guilt over doing something that contradicts personal beliefs. *Cognitive* dissonance is alleviated by one of two responses: (a) confession, or (b) rationalization, defined as a denial justified by lowering personal beliefs.[8]

The complainant will no doubt attend at the interview. Whether the report is real or not, he or she will try to convince you that it really happened.

The officer should inform the complainant of:

- the suspicion of fabrication or the M.O. paradox,
- reasons for the suspicion, and
- the possibility of implicating innocent persons.[9]

The following strategy should be used:

1. The officer should begin the interview by explaining that he or she suspects that a familiar person committed the offence, and the reasons why.
2. The officer should suggest specific family members or relatives as suspects. This logic will be accepted by the complainant.
3. If the complaint is invalid, the victim will likely try to strongly convince the officer that his or her suggestions are wrong; the victim will obviously not want an innocent family member to be a suspect. The officer should ask for concrete reasons why the victim believes that these suspicions are wrong. If the offence is fabricated, the reasons will likely be vague; the complainant will be unprepared to concoct additional deceptions.
4. The officer should then inform the complainant of his or her suspicion of fabrication (the M.O. paradox), and the reasons why.
5. The officer should use a powerful narrative to inform the complainant about the danger of an invalid complaint (the possibility of innocent persons going to jail).
6. If met with silence, the officer should follow the narrative by asking for a reason why the complainant would fabricate the offence. Cognitive dissonance motivates the need to reduce anxiety and stress. If he or she believes that an innocent person will be wrongly jailed, his or her compulsion to confess to the fabrication will be activated. If the complainant believes he or she will suffer the worst consequence, he or she will rationalize, not confess.[10]
7. If the complainant rationalizes, the officer should make a request for a polygraph test. The officer should properly explain the test and the reasons for this request.

Public mischief confessions are not difficult to obtain if the focus of the risk of innocent persons being implicated or suspected is maintained.

BASIC INVESTIGATIVE SEQUENCE PROGRESSION

After a complaint has been validated by the absence of indicators, progress to the next BIS suspicion and explore it. Stay with each suspicion until you eliminate it. The remainder of this book explains specific investigative strategies relating to the application of the sequence. The following is an introduction.

1. **First suspicion: relatives**
   - identify all family members
   - learn personal history and status of each family member, including age, school, employment, habits, associates, and conduct (e.g., violence, thefts)

▷ determine the activity and whereabouts of each person during the offence

▷ analyze the circumstances and determine the presence or absence of motive and opportunity to commit the offence

▷ interview all family members

▷ interview associates to determine whether any family member made any incriminating statement indicating intentional participation

▷ determine whether relevant information that may have assisted in acquisition of familiarity and planning was unintentionally conveyed to other persons

2. **Second suspicion: acquaintances**

▷ identify non-family members who have any degree of familiarity with the victim and his or her surroundings

▷ apply the same general procedures used for relatives

3. **Third suspicion: non-acquaintance who acquired familiarity by planning**

▷ use the most effective investigative method of identifying this type of offender, which is informant development and management (a network of informants is the most vital element)

▷ establish and maintain a list of persons who are criminally active in any type of offence

▷ create a database of information relating to known offenders, including means of transportation, associates, and habits

▷ analyze all daily general occurrence reports that may include relevant information; reading all reports will facilitate connections between events

▷ learn methods of operation through experience (officers will investigate countless offenders—experience permits recognition of how an individual prefers to commit offences)

▷ interview witnesses to determine suspicious conduct of persons before the offence occurred, including unexpected visits to the premises, unusual frequency of visits, visits with no obvious purpose, and behaviour or conversation not consistent with legitimate customers (such as questions asked to acquire knowledge and familiarity)

4. **Final assumption: stranger**

▷ use the same general procedures as for non-acquaintances who acquired familiarity through planning

In summary, eliminate the suspects in each group before progressing to the next stage. This prevents a haphazard, unstructured investigation, and ensures the investigation of likely offenders first.

Case Study 7.1 Conclusion

Two significant decisions were made and carried out:

1. The school official was told about the officer's belief that the details of this offence were fabricated. The suspicion was based on indicators of fabrication.

2. The interview with the complainant was delayed for two hours so that the official could convey the officer's belief and allow the complainant time to consider the consequences of implicating innocent persons and causing them to wrongly go to jail.

The complainant was interviewed two hours later. Her shirt was torn near her shoulder. She had a scrape on her left shoulder blade. She was confronted about two aspects of the validity of her complaint: it hadn't happened, or her boyfriend had done it and she was concealing it.

She confessed that the offence did not happen. She had ripped the shirt herself and rubbed her shoulder against a fence to scrape it. She stated that the reason for fabricating the offence was to gain her father's attention.

COMMENTARY   A very important point must be emphasized. A sexual assault complaint should never be discredited or not believed simply because of the "it's-her-word-against-his-word" reason. Sexual assault does not require corroboration to convict: That requirement was abolished. An offender may be convicted on the word of the complainant without any supporting evidence.

Fabrication should be suspected only when logical indicators exist. If no indicators of fabrication exist, the "her-word-against-his-word" concept should not be a factor in evaluating credibility. If no indicators are present, reasonable grounds exist to arrest. A confession from the offender will be the best form of corroboration.

ENDNOTES

1. *R. v. Klymchuk* (2005), 203 C.C.C. (3d) 341 (Ont. C.A.).
2. H. Gross, *Criminal Investigation* (London: Sweet & Maxwell, 1924); W.J. Chisum and B. Turvey, "Evidence Dynamics: Locard's Exchange Principle and Crime Reconstruction" (2000) vol. 1, no. 3 *Journal of Behavioral Profiling*.
3. *R. v. Klymchuk*, supra note 1.
4. Ibid.
5. Ibid.; O'Connell and Soderman (1936), as in Chisum and Turvey, supra note 2.
6. *R. v. Klymchuk*, supra note 1; Svensson and Wendel (1974), as in Chisum and Turvey, supra note 2.
7. *R. v. Klymchuk*, supra note 1; Douglas and Munn (1992), as in Chisum and Turvey, supra note 2.
8. L. Festinger, *A Theory of Cognitive Dissonance* (Chicago: Stanford University Press, 1957).
9. Ibid.
10. Ibid.

CHAPTER 8
Witness Compellability and Competency

LEARNER SUMMARY

Canadian criminal court is based on five fundamental issues:

1. **Witness compellability** When a witness knows something relevant about a crime, *compellability* laws allow him or her to be subpoenaed to appear at a court trial, whether he or she wants to or not. The police *apply* for a subpoena, prove to a Justice of the Peace (JP) that the witness may have relevant knowledge during a brief *hearing*, and *serve* the subpoena to the witness, leaving him or her compelled to appear at the trial. Witnesses include complainants/victims, independent (or *corroborative*) witnesses, and police officers. The permission or consent of a witness is not needed to obtain a subpoena, which is a simple process. Subpoenas are a vital staple in the proper functioning of the criminal justice system.

2. **Witness competence** After the witness physically appears in court, *competency* laws determine whether the witness will be permitted to testify. The subpoena gets the witness to court, but it does not make the witness competent to testify. There must be proof that the witness has "sufficient intelligence" about the spiritual and legal consequences of lying. All knowledge is proved in one of two ways: (a) a test, or (b) an exemption. Sufficient intelligence regarding the consequences of lying is specific knowledge, but it is considered to be *common* knowledge. This knowledge is so common that both adult and child witnesses generally do not have to pass a test; they are granted exemptions. An exemption is legally called a "rebuttable presumption"—the knowledge is presumed to exist. A test, or competency hearing, only needs to occur if the "other side" objects to the automatic exemption/presumption; this constitutes a challenge to the witness's knowledge. Challenges to adult witness competency are not common. Until January 2006, mandatory competency hearings were required for child witnesses. New legislation has eliminated these

mandatory hearings, making it easier for children to testify. Children and adults are now treated equally in terms of their knowledge of the consequences of lying. This legislation represents significant benefits for the prosecution.

3. **Oath and affirmation** After witness competency is proved, every witness must make a formal promise to tell the truth before testifying. A spiritual promise is call an *oath*. A non-spiritual promise is called an *affirmation*. They have equal value. Both are intended to *bind the witness's conscience* in order to compel him or her to tell the truth. The criminal liability of perjury accompanies both forms of promises.

4. **Trial fairness** The presumption of innocence guarantees the accused person a fair trial. Three laws are included in the "fair trial" concept:

   a. *Open court*: Criminal trials generally cannot be held in private. Trials are open to the public.

   b. *Unobstructed sight line*: Witnesses must testify in the accused's line of sight. This emerges from the common law principle that states that the accused person must be able to "face" his or her accuser.

   c. *Cross-examination*: The first stage of witness testimony is *examination-in-chief*, where the witness communicates a narrative of his or her observations. The second stage is *cross-examination*, where the opposing side is allowed to question the witness for the purpose of raising doubt. If a witness testifies during examination-in-chief, cross-examination cannot be prevented.

5. **"He or she who asserts must prove"** The prosecution always has the burden of proof—the onus to prove the formal allegation set out in the sworn Information. The accused person has no obligation to help the prosecution, and the prosecution cannot force the accused person to testify or incriminate himself in any way.

These five fundamentals form the basis of witness management. The first step is learning the rules of witness compellability and competency. This chapter interprets and applies these rules.

Case Study 8.1

You are a uniform patrol officer. At 11:00 p.m., you and other officers respond to a shooting that occurred in a second-floor apartment situated above a business. Upon arrival, you and the other officers find persons inside the apartment; all four persons suffered gunshot wounds.

Charlie (30) is a known criminal and has a lengthy record for a variety of offences. He is lying on the floor, unconscious. Gunshot wounds on his torso are visible. No vital signs are found.

Jack (32) is Charlie's brother. He is a known criminal with an equally long record. Jack is conscious, suffering a gunshot wound to his shoulder.

Nancy (25) is Jack's wife. She has a past involving extensive criminal activity. Nancy is conscious and has a gunshot wound to her ankle.

Jake (30) is a friend of both Jack's and Charlie's. He also has a criminal record. He is conscious and has a gunshot wound to his thigh.

Jack, Nancy, and Jake inform you that several members of a motorcycle gang had entered the apartment and shot everyone in retaliation for past conflict. All four are transported to the hospital. Charlie is pronounced dead at the hospital by a Coroner.

Further investigation reveals that there is only one entrance to the apartment: a door that opens to a stairway, at the bottom of which is another door. A tenant in another apartment is home.

The tenant's apartment is searched during the preliminary investigation. No gun is found. A few cars are parked in a parking lot next to the building.

Jack, Nancy, and Jake are interviewed at the hospital. All three are uncooperative. Nancy, in particular, is extremely belligerent.

The crime scene is protected and examined by Ident. officers.

(Refer to the end of Chapter 8 for the conclusion of this case study.)

DEFINITIONS

Rules of evidence are the laws that govern admissibility of both witness testimony and physical evidence. These rules include a unique language that will be explained throughout the nine chapters of Phase 2. The following four terms are the fundamentals of this language:

1. **Direct evidence** refers to evidence that proves at least one fact-in-issue (FII) of an offence *without requiring an inference or suggestion.* The best examples of direct evidence are eyewitness testimony or a confession. An eyewitness may directly prove all the FII of an offence.
2. **Main evidence** refers to the *primary* source of evidence that proves most or all of the FII of the offence. The main evidence is the centre, or core, of the prosecution's case. The best examples of main evidence are victim eyewitnesses and confessions.
3. **Corroboration** refers to *supporting* evidence. Corroboration is any evidence that supports and strengthens the credibility of the main evidence.[1]
4. **Circumstantial evidence** refers to a set of circumstances that indirectly proves at least one FII of an offence by means of inference or suggestion. Circumstantial evidence is the opposite of direct evidence. It includes any evidence that does not constitute an *eyewitness account* or *full confession.* Circumstantial evidence alone may form a *prima facie* case. It may be sufficient to convict, if the circumstances lead to only one logical conclusion—connecting the accused person to the crime.[2] If the circumstantial evidence leads to more than one logical conclusion, it will not constitute guilt beyond a reasonable doubt. Circumstantial evidence alone may also provide reasonable grounds to arrest, if the circumstances lead to only one logical conclusion. An example of circumstantial evidence that alone forms reasonable grounds and a *prima facie* case is an accused's fingerprint found on a matchbook cover, near a safe, inside a business premises that has been forcibly entered.[3] The strength of circumstantial evidence is related to the number of logical conclusions it infers.

WITNESS CATEGORIES

Three witness categories exist:

1. eyewitness,
2. corroborative witness, and
3. recipient of a confession.

An **eyewitness** is a person who (a) saw the entire offence being committed (the *actus reus*), and (b) can facially recognize (identify) the offender. Both elements must exist for a person to qualify as an eyewitness. An eyewitness may be the main evidence (i.e., the victim or complainant), or an independent person who corroborates the main evidence. One eyewitness with strong credibility constitutes (a) reasonable grounds, and (b) a *prima facie* case, capable of proving all the FII of an offence.

One credible eyewitness alone is sufficient to convict, *without corroboration*, for nearly all criminal offences, including

- murder,
- attempt murder,
- robbery,
- sexual assault,
- break, enter, and theft,
- assault,
- theft, and
- drug offences.

The following three criminal offences require corroboration by law (mandatory corroboration):

- "Perjury" (s. 131(1) C.C.),
- "Treason" (s. 46(1) C.C.), and
- "Procuring feigned marriage" (s. 292(1) C.C.).

A **corroborative witness** is a supporting witness, referring to a person who can prove some or all of the FII of an offence and who supports the credibility of the main witness. A corroborative witness is also called an *independent witness*—a witness who is not the victim or main witness. Examples include a witness who

- saw the entire offence (*actus reus*) being committed,
- was present at the crime and made a partial observation of the *actus reus*,
- saw the *actus reus*, but cannot facially recognize the offender, or
- saw or heard pre-offence or post-offence circumstances (such as hearing an offender make incriminating statements while planning).

The **recipient of a confession** is a citizen who hears the offender make verbal incriminating statements. This is a *post-offence witness*, who may be either the main witness or a corroborative witness. Confessions to citizens are powerful types of evidence because, generally, they are automatically admissible at a trial. Unlike confessions to the police, a voir dire (admissibility hearing) is not needed to determine the admissibility of a confession made to a **person not in authority**. The prosecution does not have to prove that these types of confessions were voluntarily made. An offender statement that constitutes a full confession represents (a) reasonable grounds, and (b) a *prima facie* case (a conviction may result without corroboration).

CORROBORATION

The quantity of evidence needed to convict is a significant case management issue. The goal is to obtain a maximum amount of evidence from as many sources as possible, including witnesses, physical items, and the offender's confession. However, in some cases, a *minimum* amount of evidence will be obtained. This refers to the minimum amount required to build a *prima facie* case, which includes:

- only one eyewitness or a recipient of a confession, with strong credibility, or
- physical evidence that leads to one logical conclusion.

Although the minimum amount is enough to convict without corroboration regarding all but three offences, the goal is to strengthen the case with as much corroboration as possible. A prosecution based on only one witness is a risk for three reasons. The witness may:

1. fail to appear.
2. recant (change his or her story), or
3. forget (due to memory decay).

Additionally, when the main witness is an accomplice, a child, or has past "bad character," corroboration is:

1. mandatory (relating to the three offences discussed above),
2. legally recommended, relating to these three types of witnesses, and
3. informally recommended, in all cases.

The following is an introductory case law review, outlining the definition of corroboration and the legal recommendation for it.

Common law "Corroboration" was first defined in common law in *R. v. Baskerville* (1916), an appeal decision in England. This decision gave corroboration a technical definition by identifying its three characteristics: (a) independent, (b) relevant, and (c) incriminating. Evidence constitutes corroboration if it is an *independent* source from the main witness; is *relevant*, in that it proves at least one FII of the offence; and *incriminates* the accused in connection with the offence named on the Information.[4]

Case law Two key points emerged from the Supreme Court of Canada decision made in *Vetrovec v. The Queen* (1982):[5]

1. The definition of corroboration was changed, simplifying it to mean *"evidence which confirms a witness's testimony, making the testimony more likely to be true."* In other words, corroboration is any type of evidence (witness or item) that *supports* the main witness.
2. It created a *recommended* corroboration requirement when the main witness is:

> ▷ an accomplice,
> ▷ a child, or
> ▷ a person with "bad" (disreputable) character.

When multiple offenders commit one crime, each **accomplice** is both an offender and an eyewitness (against the others). When multiple offenders commit one offence, the primary objective is to obtain confessions from each one. The secondary objective is to compel each accomplice to testify against the others. Accomplices are excellent eyewitnesses because they saw their partners commit the entire offence and can likely give incriminating pre-offence and post-offence testimony.

There is no statutory requirement that makes corroboration mandatory in relation to accomplices. The testimony of one accomplice is sufficient to convict. However, there are two obvious, but major, problems associated with accomplice testimony:

1. disreputable character: (the accomplice's participation in the crime diminishes credibility), and
2. motive to lie (a desire for leniency in exchange for witness testimony weakens credibility).

Children are victims of horrible crimes, often with no other witnesses present. Section 16.1 *Canada Evidence Act* defines a child witness as any witness under 14 years. No statutory requirement exists for mandatory corroboration of a child's sworn testimony. The testimony of one child, of any age, is sufficient to convict. There is traditional skepticism about child credibility because of the perceived cognitive and memory limitations associated with childhood.

Character and credibility are connected. Many adult crime victims and witnesses have evidence of past **bad character**, referring to a criminal record or any conduct that may infer criminal habits or tendencies. Bad character evidence may weaken witness credibility. There is no mandatory requirement for corroboration of a disreputable witness. The testimony of one bad character witness, regardless of how bad his or her past is, is sufficient to convict. It is possible for a bad character witness to be believed at a trial, his or her disreputable character is a potential credibility problem that must be addressed.

Despite the absence of any mandatory requirement for corroboration relating to these three types of witnesses, there is a *common-law requirement* that *strongly recommends* corroboration in cases that include any of these three witnesses. This common-law rule requires that a trial judge warn a jury about the dangers of convicting an accused person without corroboration when the prosecution's case is based solely on the testimony of either an accomplice, a young child, or a "disreputable" person.[6] It is important to note that this warning serves a dual purpose. The first directly recommends corroboration to a jury. The second indirectly recommends that the police obtain corroboration when the main witness is an accomplice, a child, or has bad character.

What evidence constitutes corroboration? The S.C.C. stated that any witness or item is corroboration if "it strengthens our belief that the witness is telling the truth."[7]

However, the best corroboration in all cases, regardless of who the main witness is, is a *confession* to police or to a citizen. The goal of every investigation is to obtain a voluntary, properly obtained confession. It removes reasonable doubt and satisfies the concern that an innocent person was not arrested. A confession to a citizen is automatically admissible; however, a confession to the police is never automatically admissible, as will be discussed in greater detail later in this book.

In addition to confessions, any evidence that directly implicates the accused, or elevates the *personal* credibility of the main witness, represents corroboration.

WITNESS COMPELLABILITY AND COMPETENCE

There are five fundamental concepts that introduce the topic of witness compellability and competence:

1. "Compel" means to force. "Competent" means permitted to testify.
2. Both offenders and witnesses must be compelled to appear in court. Compelling court appearances are governed by two separate groups of laws, one for offenders and one for witnesses.
3. A summons compels an offender; a subpoena compels a witness.
4. A summons is only one of several documents that are used to compel an accused person to court. A subpoena is one of two documents that compels a witness; an arrest warrant is the second.
5. A "competent and compellable witness" is defined as a witness who may be compelled to appear in court, and who will be permitted to testify.

This chapter relates only to *witnesses*.

Witness compellability and competence are two separate concepts. Compellability refers to the laws governing methods to get a witness to appear in court. Competence refers to the laws that determine whether the witness will be permitted to testify after he or she appears.

Witness Compellability

There are two types of witness *appearances*: (a) at an interview with the police during an investigation, and (b) in court to testify at a trial. Witnesses cannot be forced to appear for interviews during the investigation, but can be forced to appear in court. Witness interviews with the police are conducted by consent only. A subpoena forces a witness to appear in court at a specific place, date, and time.

Witness compellability is defined as the legal authority to demand that a witness appear in court to testify about relevant observations relating to an offence. Once legally compelled, the witness has no choice or alternative but to comply.

WITNESS INTERVIEW

A witness interview is the questioning of a complainant or independent witness during the investigation. It is conducted before the witness appears in court. A witness cannot be compelled to an interview during an investigation. This means that the police cannot:

- arrest or detain a witness, with or without a warrant, exclusively for the purpose of an interview, or
- obtain any document (e.g., subpoena) forcing an appearance with the police for the purpose of an interview.

A witness has no obligation to consent to an interview or comply with a request to be questioned. Consequently, a witness commits no offence by refusing to consent to an interview or failing to comply with a request to be questioned by police.

If a witness gives consent, it is revocable at any time. Where consent is initially given and later revoked during an interview, the officer cannot detain the witness and must either (a) allow the witness to leave or (b) regain consent by employing communication skills. Failure to obtain consent to begin or continue a witness interview does not prevent the issuance of a subpoena, if the officer can prove that the witness is likely to give relevant evidence in court.

Uncooperative witnesses are common. An uncooperative witness is defined as any person who refuses to consent to an interview. Uncooperative witnesses cannot be arrested or charged. The only solution to an uncooperative witness is to compel the witness to the trial by means of a subpoena.

Example

You are a uniform police officer. You arrive at the scene of a disturbance. Bill (50) has been assaulted. Nolan (40) is present. You suspect that Claire saw the offender commit the assault.

1. If you ask Claire to answer questions and she refuses by saying that she doesn't want to get involved, can you arrest or detain her for questioning? *No.* There is no authority in Canada to arrest or detain a witness, with or without a warrant, in order to conduct a witness interview.
2. Can you compel Claire to accompany you to the police station for an interview? *No,* for the same reason as in question 1.
3. Can you charge Claire for being uncooperative and refusing to be interviewed? *No.* It is not an offence to refuse to be interviewed.
4. Under what circumstances can you interview Claire at the scene or take her to the police station? *By consent only.* Claire must voluntarily accompany you.
5. If Claire is initially cooperative and you begin the interview, but she becomes uncooperative at any time during the interview, stating that she is leaving, what procedures are available to you? You have *no authority* to detain her. You must allow her to leave, or regain consent by using effective communication skills.
6. Do the same rules apply to the victim, Bill? *Yes.* Although Bill is the victim/complainant, he is still considered a witness. The same rules apply. Victims are not always cooperative. There are no separate laws dealing with "victim compellability." All witnesses are governed by the same set of rules.

Witness Competence

Witness testimony is defined as a verbal statement made in court under oath or affirmation by a person who is legally competent to testify.[8]

Witness competence is a separate concept from witness compellability. *Competence* is defined as the legal permission to testify in court. *Compellability* forces the court appearance, but it does not make the witness competent to testify. In other words, while a subpoena forces a witness to attend court, the actual document does not make it automatically permissible for the witness to testify. Competency rules determine whether a witness may testify after the witness appears.

COMPELLING DOCUMENTS: WITNESSES

There are two documents used to compel a witness to appear in court: (a) a subpoena, or (b) an arrest warrant.[9]

A subpoena is the most common document used. Neither document may be issued automatically. The issuance of both documents is conditional on proving certain facts or circumstances during a systematic procedure. Before examining the procedure to obtain a subpoena, the concept of a subpoena must be understood.

Subpoena

One of the objectives an officer has in a court case is to ensure that all of the Crown witnesses attend court. To understand the concept of subpoenas and compellability, the following rules explained in the example are important.

You are a uniform police officer. During an investigation, you interview a cooperative complainant of a criminal offence. The complainant undoubtedly will attend court. You have no reason to believe that the witness will fail to appear.

1. Can this witness attend court and testify without a subpoena being issued and served? Theoretically, *yes.* If the witness attends court without a subpoena, the objective has been fulfilled.
2. Can you simply inform the witness verbally to attend court? *Yes.* If the witness complies, the objective has been fulfilled.
3. What is the only consequence of failing to obtain a subpoena? If the witness fails to attend court, *no warrant* may be issued to arrest the witness.
4. If a subpoena is issued and the witness does attend court, does the subpoena permit the witness to testify? *No.* The subpoena only compels or forces the witness to attend court. The subpoena itself does not determine witness competency or whether the witness will be legally allowed to testify.

A **subpoena** is a document signed by a Justice that legally compels a witness to attend court. The subpoena imposes a mandatory obligation on a witness to attend; the witness has no alternative or choice but to comply. Failure to comply with a subpoena may result in the witness's arrest.

However, a subpoena does not make the witness automatically competent to testify. The subpoena itself does not make testimony permissible; the document is not a factor concerning witness competency. A witness could testify if a subpoena were not obtained or served on him or her. For example, a cooperative witness may be verbally asked by a police officer to attend court and testify. If the witness attends court, the Crown may call him or her to the stand and the witness may testify if she or he is competent. In this situation, the objective of introducing the witness's evidence is fulfilled. The absence of a subpoena does not render a witness incompetent to testify and does not prevent the witness from testifying.

However, making a verbal request instead of using a subpoena creates a risk that should be avoided. A witness who ignores a verbal request and fails to attend court cannot have an arrest warrant issued to apprehend him or her. Consequently, the witness cannot be compelled to court and his or her potential evidence will be lost. A subpoena should always be used to compel even a cooperative witness to court, to prevent these consequences if the witness fails to attend court.

A subpoena also solves problems caused by uncooperative witnesses who refuse to be interviewed or refuse to give written statements. A remedy for an uncooperative witness is to have a subpoena issued and served, to compel the witness to testify in court. An uncooperative witness's failure or refusal to be interviewed or to give a written statement does not prevent the issuance of a subpoena.

Whom can the police subpoena to court? Four situational examples follow in which a subpoena can be used. A police officer may encounter any of them during an investigation.

1. A cooperative witness gives a written statement.
2. A witness verbally gives a statement, but refuses to give a written statement.
3. A witness verbally tells another person that he or she has relevant evidence to give about an offence. The other person later informs you about this.
4. A person was present at a crime scene at the time an offence occurred. The person is uncooperative and refuses to give a verbal or written statement.

In each of the situations, a subpoena may be obtained. Obtaining a subpoena is probably the simplest police procedure. The standard of what is needed to be proven is low. A subpoena may be issued to any person who is *likely* to give material evidence in court, according to s. 698(1) C.C.

Material evidence is relevant evidence. **Relevant evidence** has the ability to prove or disprove at least one fact-in-issue of an offence. *Likely* is not defined in the *Criminal Code*, but refers to a probability.[10] Proving **likelihood** requires less evidence than proving reasonable grounds. The likelihood of a witness giving relevant evidence may be proven by means of

‣ a written statement obtained from the witness,
‣ a witness's verbal statement,
‣ a written or verbal statement from another person indicating that the witness has relevant evidence to give, or
‣ circumstances (e.g., presence at a crime scene).

The witness's permission is not needed. If the likelihood of giving material evidence is proven, the subpoena will be issued whether or not the witness consents to testify.

A common misconception is that a complainant or witness decides whether he or she will testify in court and that permission or consent must be obtained to subpoena him or her. For example, when investigating an assault, officers will sometimes ask the complainant, "Are you willing to testify?" The complainant (witness) then believes that he or she controls the decision about whether they will have to appear in court. The officer controls the decision, not the witness. When that question is asked, the officer is simply acquiring information for problem-solving purposes, and for deciding what discretionary action will be taken. If a complainant states his or her intention *not* to testify, this becomes a factor relevant to discretion about whether to charge the offender or solve the problem without charges being laid.

A complainant's reluctance to testify should not deter an officer from charging an offender, if laying a charge is the appropriate method of solving the problem and protecting the complainant and the public from repetition of the offence. In many situations, such as domestics, the complainant who has recently been victimized often cannot decide whether to testify in court. Too many factors, such as fear of the offender, interfere with decision making shortly after an offence. In other words, the officer's obligation is to protect the victim and public from potential future crimes, and the officer should base the decision to subpoena the complainant (witness) on that obligation, not on the witness's reluctance to testify.

PROCEDURE: OBTAINING A SUBPOENA

The procedure used to obtain a subpoena is derived from ss. 698 and 699 C.C., and case law.

1. **An officer who has knowledge of the investigation must appear before a Justice or a provincial division court judge, if the trial is scheduled for provincial division court** If the trial is scheduled for general division court or if the witness lives out of the province, the officer must appear before a general division court judge. This appearance is not in open court; it is usually in the Justice's office. The officer does not have to be the one who investigated the offence or laid the charge. The officer's knowledge of the witness's potential evidence can be acquired by reading the reports and statements, and by being instructed by the investigating officer.

2. **The officer applies for the subpoena by submitting a typed and completed subpoena to the Justice** No independent written application form has to be submitted.

3. **According to** *Foley v. Gares* **(1989),**[11] **the Justice must conduct a hearing, although s. 698 C.C. does not specifically mention this requirement** The purpose of the hearing is to determine whether the witness is likely to give relevant evidence in court. The hearing is mandatory. The Justice has no discretion to waive it and has no authority to issue a subpoena without a hearing. Failure to conduct the hearing may constitute a judicial abuse of power. The consequence may be cancellation of the subpoena.

4. **The Justice has discretion whether or not to have the officer take an oath** The Justice decides whether the officer will give sworn or unsworn testimony.

5. **The officer begins testimony** He or she has the onus to verbally explain the circumstances that prove the witness's likelihood of giving relevant evidence at the trial. The extent of the hearing depends on the circumstances of each case. It is usually brief. There is no requirement that the hearing be thorough or extensive.

6. **The hearing concludes and the Justice exercises discretion whether to issue the subpoena or reject it** The Justice signs it if likelihood of the witness giving relevant evidence has been proven. Otherwise, the subpoena will be rejected and will not be signed. If rejected, the officer may repeat this procedure if additional evidence is obtained in the future. It is possible for an arrest warrant to be issued at this stage instead of a subpoena, if the officer proves that the witness will fail to appear in court even if a subpoena is issued.[12] If the subpoena is signed, it must be *served* by a peace officer, as

defined in s. 2 C.C., by serving it personally or substitutionally by leaving it for the witness at his or her last or usual place of abode with someone who appears to be at least 16 years old, if the witness cannot be conveniently found.[13]

Significance of Subpoena Procedure

A subpoena may be obtained despite the absence of

- a written witness statement (however, the existence of one will facilitate the issuance of a subpoena),
- a witness interview (a witness's refusal to provide information to police during the investigation does not automatically prevent the issuance of a subpoena—the circumstances may prove the witness's likelihood of giving relevant evidence), and
- a witness's consent to testify in court (although witness cooperation is desirable, a witness's consent is not a factor in this procedure; a reluctant witness may be compelled to court despite an unwillingness to testify).

Additionally, officers are not restricted to only one witness interview. Multiple interviews are permitted and desired to obtain as much accurate information as possible.

Arrest with a Warrant

Several methods exist to obtain a warrant to arrest a witness to compel that witness's appearance in court to testify:

1. An officer can appear before a Justice, conduct a hearing, and prove
   - the likelihood that the witness will give relevant evidence
   - that the witness will fail to appear in court if a subpoena is issued.

   Under these conditions, the warrant replaces the subpoena. A subpoena does not have to be issued first. However, the warrant is not automatically issued; the hearing is mandatory and both factors must be proven.[14]

2. An officer may obtain a subpoena properly and attempt to serve it. If the witness is intentionally evading service of the subpoena, the officer can reappear before a Justice and prove
   - proper attempts were made to serve the subpoena (an exact number of attempts is not specified in the *Criminal Code*),
   - intentional evasion of service (a witness's verbal admission to another person may suffice), and
   - the likelihood that the witness will give relevant evidence.[15]

   In this situation, the warrant cannot be issued unless the subpoena is issued first.[16]

3. An officer can obtain a subpoena and serve it properly, but the witness may fail to attend court. In this situation, the prosecutor requests an arrest warrant, called a **bench warrant**. The prosecutor must prove that
   - the subpoena was properly served, and
   - the likelihood exists that the witness will give relevant evidence.[17]

■ KEY POINTS

▸ A bench warrant cannot be automatically issued merely based on the witness's failure to appear in court. The prosecutor must prove the likelihood exists that the witness will give relevant evidence.[18]

▸ Mere production of an unserved subpoena is insufficient to prove the likelihood that a witness will give relevant evidence. The prosecutor must provide additional evidence of likelihood.[19]

▸ Although proof of likelihood is a prerequisite before a subpoena is issued, the first hearing conducted to obtain the subpoena is insufficient to obtain a bench warrant. Another hearing must be conducted after the witness fails to appear in court.[20]

▸ A greater degree of proof of likelihood is necessary to obtain an arrest warrant than for the issuance of a subpoena.[21]

It is important to note that it is not possible to obtain an arrest warrant when a witness has been served with a subpoena and reasonable grounds are formed that the witness will fail to appear in court.[22]

Arrest Without a Warrant

A police officer cannot arrest a witness without a warrant if reasonable grounds exist before or after a subpoena is issued that a witness will fail to appear in court. The s. 495 C.C. arrest warrant authorities are inapplicable because a witness commits no offence by failing to appear in court after a subpoena is served on him or her. The only consequence for the witness after he or she fails to appear in court in response to a subpoena is the issuance of a bench warrant.

For example, if an officer serves a subpoena on a witness and the witness tells the officer that he or she intends to ignore the subpoena, the officer cannot obtain an arrest warrant. If the witness actually fails to appear at the trial, a bench warrant may be issued for his or her arrest.

RELEASE OF AN ARRESTED WITNESS

After a witness is arrested by means of a warrant, the arresting officer and the officer in charge of the police station cannot release the witness. The witness must be brought before a Justice for a hearing to determine whether the witness will be detained in custody or released by means of a recognizance.

The witness cannot be charged for failing to appear at this stage. If detained, the witness remains in custody until the court date. If released by a recognizance, the witness is compelled to court on the specified date.[23] If the witness breaches the recognizance by failing to attend court, he or she may be charged with a dual procedure offence contrary to s. 145(2) C.C.

If a witness is released by means of a recognizance with a condition to appear in court on a scheduled date, a police officer may arrest the witness without a warrant if reasonable grounds exist that the witness is about to or has breached the recognizance by failing to appear.[24]

Compelling Prisoners to Testify

In some cases, a witness will be convicted of an unrelated crime and sentenced to a jail term. While that witness is in custody in a prison, a subpoena cannot be used to compel him or her to court. A different document is needed, called a **court order**. A court order has the same effect as a subpoena (compelling the witness to appear), as well as an additional legal element: this document authorizes the temporary release of the person from prison for the purpose of attending court. No person can leave a prison while serving a sentence; unauthorized absence from a correctional facility is a criminal offence. A court order authorizes a temporary absence.[25]

COMPETENCY

Competency is a separate concept from compellability. *Compellability* brings the witness to the courtroom. *Competency* determines whether the witness may actually testify. Formerly, competency was defined as legal permission for a witness to testify in court at a trial. A subpoena does not make a witness competent; it only ensures attendance in court.

A **competent witness** is defined as a person who is legally allowed to testify in court during a trial.[26] Conversely, an incompetent witness refers to a person who is prohibited from testifying in court during a trial. A witness is competent if two conditions are proven:

- ▸ the witness understands the nature of an oath or solemn affirmation, and
- ▸ he or she has sufficient intelligence to communicate the evidence.[27]

Understanding the nature of an oath refers to knowing the moral and spiritual consequences of lying.[28] Having *sufficient intelligence to communicate the evidence* refers to knowing the legal consequences of lying.[29] In other words, a witness must understand that there are two separate sets of consequences for not telling the truth—spiritual and legal.

Why is an oath required in Canada? A common-law principle, originating in *R. v. Brasier* (1779),[30] required that all witness testimony be under oath because this was the best way to *bind the witness's conscience*, meaning the best way to force the witness to tell the truth.[31]

Some witnesses do not have spiritual beliefs, making the oath meaningless. The solution to this issue is found in s. 14(1) *Canada Evidence Act*, which allows an **affirmation.** An affirmation is a promise to tell the truth that replaces an oath. When a witness is affirmed, the witness says "I *promise* to tell the truth" instead of "I *swear* to tell the truth." Witness testimony under oath and testimony under solemn affirmation have equal value.[32]

Witnesses are classified as *adults* or *children.* Adult witnesses are 14 years old or older; child witnesses are 13 years old or younger. It is important to note that the age definitions that distinguish adult and child witnesses (14 years is the dividing line) are different from those for adult and young offenders (18 years is the dividing line).

In 2005, the C.E.A. was amended by Bill C-2 to create new child witness competency laws. The new laws made child witnesses the "intellectual and spiritual equals" of adult witnesses. The major distinction between the old and new laws is that previous to Bill C-2, no child witness was considered automatically competent to testify. The old laws caused significant obstacles for the police and prosecutors because they made it difficult to prove child competency. There was always a risk of a child witness being prohibited from testifying by the outcome of a mandatory hearing to rule on the child's competency. At the hearing, if the judge ruled that the child understood the nature of the oath and had sufficient intelligence to understand the duty to tell the truth, the child was considered competent. However, if the judge could be convinced that the child failed to understand the nature of the oath and had insufficient intelligence to understand a promise to tell the truth, the child was deemed to be incompetent and not permitted to testify.

The new laws represent a major benefit for the prosecution because the mandatory-hearing obstacle has been removed. Adult and child witnesses alike are presumed competent unless proven otherwise by means of a hearing.

As expressed by Pamela Hurley, Director, Child Witness Project, "We support the changes set out in this section whereby a person under 14 years of age is presumed to have the capacity to testify. We applaud that children under age 14 will not be required to take an oath or make a solemn promise, but instead will be required to promise to tell the truth."[33]

Current Witness Competency Laws

A witness's competency may be challenged by the opposing side. Essentially, the opposing side is challenging the mental capacity of the witness in an attempt to prevent the witness from testifying. If a challenge is made, a competency hearing is conducted. The onus to prove that the witness is incompetent is on the side making the challenge. In other words, the opposing side has the onus to prove that the witness has insufficient mental capacity to understand the nature of an oath and the duty to tell the truth.

Using an *adult* Crown witness as an example, the following procedure occurs when a challenge is made:

1. The Crown calls the witness to the stand.
2. The defence challenges the witness's mental capacity. The challenge may be made only at the trial, not before the trial. Therefore, officers can only predict whether this will occur and may have no knowledge of a challenge before the trial.
3. The trial judge will conduct a hearing at this time. If the trial is before a judge and jury, the jury remains in the courtroom, but it is the judge who determines competency, not the jury. The purpose of the hearing is to determine whether the witness understands the nature of the oath, and has sufficient intelligence to understand the duty to tell the truth.
4. The onus is on the defence to prove that the witness is incompetent.
5. If the witness fulfills both competency conditions, the challenge is defeated and the witness will be allowed to give sworn testimony under oath.
6. If the witness fails to understand the nature of the oath but has sufficient intelligence to understand the duty to tell the truth, the witness will be allowed to give **unsworn testimony**, but the witness must formally **promise to tell the truth** as an oath replacement.

7. The witness is deemed incompetent to testify if the witness does not understand the nature of an oath, and has insufficient intelligence to understand the duty to tell the truth.

The unsworn testimony of a challenged adult witness who testifies under a formal promise to tell the truth has three significant points:

1. No corroboration is required by law to convict an accused. A conviction may occur based on the sole testimony of an unsworn adult.
2. Unsworn adult testimony does not have less value than that of a sworn adult; their testimony has equal value.[34]
3. A promise to tell the truth, an oath, and a solemn affirmation are the same. They equally bind the witness's conscience. A promise to tell the truth does not have less effect than an oath.[35]

An example of a challenged adult witness is found in *R. v. McGovern* (1993).[36] In this case, a 19-year-old sexual-offence complainant was called by the Crown to testify at the trial. She had the mental development of less than a 10-year-old. The accused's lawyer challenged the complainant's mental capacity to testify under oath. The trial judge conducted a hearing and determined that the complainant did not fully understand the nature of an oath or solemn affirmation, but she understood the meaning and importance of telling the truth. Consequently, she was permitted to give unsworn testimony by promising to tell the truth. The Manitoba Court of Appeal ruled that the testimony was the equivalent of sworn testimony and required no corroboration to convict.

The Saskatchewan Court of Appeal made a similar ruling in *R. v. D. (R.R.)* (1993).[37]

Proving Competence

All police officers need a clear interpretation of what is required to prove competence under s. 16(1) *Canada Evidence Act* (C.E.A.) when investigating offences committed against a child victim who is under 14 years and an adult victim whose mental capacity is challenged by the defence.

Three case law decisions, *R. v. Rockey* (1996),[38] *R. v. Marquard* (1993),[39] and *R. v. Ferguson* (1996),[40] provide valuable guidelines about proving that a witness understands the nature of an oath or a solemn affirmation and has the ability to communicate the evidence. These cases date before Bill C-2. Therefore, any reference to there being no presumption that a child is competent to testify should be disregarded. The explanation by the courts regarding adult and child competency hearings is still relevant, however.

Section 16(3) C.E.A. permits unsworn evidence if the witness does not understand the nature of the oath or affirmation but can communicate the evidence. Therefore, the interpretation of "ability to communicate the evidence" has greater importance because the witness can testify on "promising to tell the truth."

In *R. v. Marquard* (1993), the S.C.C. explained several factors relating to competency hearings under s. 16(1) C.E.A.:

1. A child is in the same position as an adult whose competence has been challenged.

2. Witness competence depends on the capacities to observe and interpret, recollect, and communicate.

3. The relevant questions are:

   ▷ Is the witness capable of observing what happened?

   ▷ Is the witness capable of remembering the observation?

   ▷ Can the witness communicate what he or she remembers?

4. The objective of the competency hearing is not to determine whether the witness is credible. That issue is explored during cross-examination. Instead, the issue is whether the witness demonstrates capacity to perceive, recollect, and communicate at the time of the trial.

5. The phrase "communicate the evidence" means more than the verbal ability to communicate. It is necessary for the court to determine in a general way the witness's capability of perceiving, remembering, and recounting events.

In *R. v. Rockey* (1996), the S.C.C. created guidelines about determining whether a child understands a "promise" to tell the truth. It is not necessary that the child define the word promise in some technical sense. Instead, the child has to understand the *obligation* to tell the truth.

The BC Court of Appeal in *R. v. Ferguson* (1996) made five rulings:

1. The court recommends that a child competency hearing be conducted in the presence of the jury to help them evaluate credibility if the child is allowed to testify. However, this court ruled that in some cases conducting the hearing without the jury is acceptable because this court saw nothing in the legislation that made it mandatory in all cases for the jury to be present. The only mandatory requirement is that the hearing be conducted in open court.

2. The failure by the judge to ask a child whether he or she understands the nature of an oath or solemn affirmation does violate s. 16 CEA, but it is "not always an important error." In this case, the child was very young and did not understand "promise." It would have been pointless to ask if she understood the oath.

3. Section 16 CEA states that the court will conduct the competency hearing, meaning that only the judge questions the child. In the Ferguson case, the judge allowed the Crown to question the child. The B.C. C.A. agreed with an Ontario Court of Appeal ruling that the judge does have discretion to allow the Crown to ask questions.

4. The standard of proof for s. 16 CEA is not to prove beyond reasonable doubt that the child can communicate the evidence and understand the nature of a promise. Instead, the standard of proof is lower. It is sufficient for only a "balance of probabilities" to prove these requirements.

5. The child must not only understand the difference between the truth and a lie, he or she must also understand the nature of a promise. There must be evidence that shows that the child understands a moral obligation to tell the truth. The judge has to be satisfied that the child is "committed" to telling the truth and that the promise "gets at the conscience—in a manner intelligible to him or her." A promise given in response to a leading question is meaningless.

Incompetent Child Witness

When a child witness is declared incompetent, an obvious dilemma is created for the Crown and the police because of the loss of the child's evidence. The question then arises whether hearsay evidence is admissible by allowing another person to testify about observations reported to him or her by a child.

Hearsay evidence is testimony about observations made by another person. It is evidence not perceived by one's own senses. The recipient of hearsay evidence did not see the incident occur.

Generally, hearsay evidence is inadmissible. However, the Supreme Court of Canada, in *R. v. Khan* (1990),[41] created flexibility in the hearsay rule and made an exception that significantly benefits the Crown: a trial judge may allow hearsay evidence to be admissible when relevant direct evidence is unavailable. The judge has discretion to permit the admissibility of hearsay evidence when it is "reasonably necessary." However, hearsay evidence is never automatically admissible in cases of incompetent child witnesses.

Reasonably necessary is the evidence that is essential to prove a fact-in-issue.[42] Examples of reasonably necessary circumstances include (a) to replace a child ruled to be incompetent to testify and (b) to corroborate a sworn or unsworn child witness.[43]

The Supreme Court of Canada, in the *Khan* case, summarized this hearsay exception as follows, in the judgment of Justice McLaughlin:

> I conclude that hearsay evidence of a child's statement of crimes committed against the child should be received, provided that the guarantees of necessity and reliability are met, subject to such safeguards as the judge may consider necessary and subject always to the considerations affecting the weight that should be accorded to such evidence. This does not make out-of-court statements by children generally admissible; in particular the requirement of necessity will probably mean that in most cases children will still be called to give viva voce evidence.[44]

The Ontario Court of Appeal, in *R. v. G.N.D.* (1993),[45] established the following factors for judges to consider when determining the admissibility of hearsay evidence in relation to the reliability of a child witness:

- the child's age,
- the child's ability to understand and accurately interpret events,
- the time lapse between the offence and the statement made by the child to another person, and
- the nature of the statement, including whether it was spontaneous, emerged naturally, was obtained by leading questions asked by well-intentioned professionals, or was motivated by parental prompting.

An example of circumstances that resulted in the admissibility of hearsay evidence is found in *R. v. G.N.D.* (1993).[46] A three-year-old child was the victim of a sexual assault. The child made statements to four persons about the offence:

- a child-care worker (two days after the offence)
- a social worker (two days after the offence)
- a police officer (two days after the offence)
- the child's mother (six months after the offence).

At the trial, the child was ruled incompetent. However, all four statements made by the child were admissible by allowing the four persons to give hearsay evidence. Cross-examination of the four persons was allowed. None of the statements was automatically admissible; they were admitted on the basis that all four statements were reasonably necessary in this case and that the child's observations were reliable.

Factors Affecting Competency

Additional factors affect witness competency other than s. 16 *Canada Evidence Act*, including whether the witnesses are

- ▸ accused persons,
- ▸ accomplices,
- ▸ co-accused persons, and
- ▸ spouses.

Accused persons are not competent for and not compellable by the Crown. The Crown and the police cannot subpoena or compel the accused in any manner to testify at his or her own trial. Accused persons are competent for the defence, but are not compellable by the defence. In other words, an accused person chooses whether she or he will testify for the defence. No one may force an accused to testify.[47]

An **accomplice** is a person separately charged along with one or more other persons for the same offence. *Separately* refers to a separate Information. For example, if three persons are charged for committing one robbery, they are accomplices if three separate Informations are laid, as opposed to laying one Information and joining all three offenders on it. Accomplices are competent and compellable Crown witnesses. In other words, the Crown may subpoena one accomplice to testify against another accomplice. No corroboration is required by law to convict; an offender may be convicted solely on the testimony of one accomplice.[48]

A **co-accused person** refers to a person jointly charged with one or more other persons for the same offence. Multiple offenders charged with the same offence may be charged *jointly*, meaning they all may be named on one Information. A co-accused charged jointly on the same Information is not a competent or compellable Crown witness; the Crown cannot subpoena a co-accused to testify against another co-accused.[49]

The Supreme Court of Canada, in *Kowbel v. R.* (1954),[50] stated that a legally married husband and wife are considered one person. Consequently, an accused person's **spouse** is generally not a competent or compellable Crown witness during a legally recognized marriage. For example, if a husband commits an offence and his wife sees it occur or receives a confession from the husband, the wife cannot be subpoenaed by the Crown to testify against her husband, nor can she testify voluntarily for the Crown. This rule applies only to **legally recognized marriages**. A *common-law relationship* is not a legally recognized marriage and the partners are not considered spouses under the *Canada Evidence Act*. Consequently, common-law partners are competent and compellable Crown witnesses.[51]

Exceptions to the spousal incompetence rule exist, creating a significant advantage for the police and the Crown. A spouse is a competent and compellable Crown witness if the other spouse is charged with:

1. **A sex offence, listed under s. 4(2) C.E.A.**

Section 151	Sexual interference
Section 152	Invitation to sexual touching
Section 153	Sexual exploitation
Section 155	Incest
Section 159	Anal intercourse
Section 160(2)	Bestiality
Section 160(3)	Bestiality in presence of person under 14 years
Section 170	Parent or guardian procuring sexual activity
Section 171	Householder permitting sexual activity (under 18 years)
Section 172	Corrupting children
Section 173	Indecent acts
Section 179	Vagrancy
Section 212	Procuring illicit sexual intercourse
Section 215	Failing to provide necessaries
Section 218	Abandoning child under 10 years
Section 271	Sexual assault
Section 272(a)	Sexual assault with a weapon
Section 272(b)	Sexual assault causing bodily harm
Section 273	Aggravated sexual assault
Section 280	Abduction—under 16 years
Section 281	Abduction—under 14 years
Section 282	Abduction—parent/child under 14 years when a custody order exists
Section 283	Abduction—parent/child under 14 years when no custody order exists
Section 291	Bigamy
Section 292	Procuring feigned marriage
Section 293	Polygamy
Section 294	Pretending to solemnize marriage
Section 329	Theft by spouse

2. **Any offence listed under s. 4(4) C.E.A. where the victim is under 14 years of age.**

Section 220	Criminal negligence causing death
Section 221	Criminal negligence causing harm
Section 235	First- or second-degree murder
Section 236	Manslaughter
Section 237	Infanticide
Section 239	Murder
Section 240	Accessory after the fact of murder
Section 266	Assault
Section 267(a)	Assault with a weapon
Section 267(b)	Assault causing bodily harm
Section 268	Aggravated assault
Section 269	Unlawfully causing bodily harm

3. **Inducing a young person to unlawfully leave a place of custody, contrary to s. 136 Y.C.J.A.**

4. **An offence that threatens the health or liberty of the other spouse by means of direct violence or the circumstances surrounding the incident.** This rule is found in s. 4(5) C.E.A., which states that a husband or wife may testify against his or her spouse if the accused spouse is charged with an offence for which common law allows the other spouse to testify. Case law has interpreted the common-law exception as any offence committed by one spouse that affects the health or liberty of the other spouse. The obvious offences are any assaults, threats, or acts of violence by one spouse toward the other.

   The Crown has the onus to prove that the circumstances actually constituted a threat to the other spouse.[52] An example of circumstances that did not constitute a threat is found in *R. v. Sillars* (1978).[53]

   In *Sillars*, a legally married couple separated and lived apart for about one month. The wife moved to a motel. The husband visited her there, where they drank together and discussed their problems. The husband set fire to the motel unit. The wife walked out of the unit when the fire was set. The husband was charged with arson and was acquitted because the wife was ruled to be not competent and not compellable for the Crown. The following reasons were given:

   ▷ Arson is not one of the offences listed in s. 4 C.E.A. that permits the competency and compellability of a spouse.

   ▷ The circumstances did not constitute a threat to the wife because the wife was able to walk out and escape when the fire was set.

CHANGE OF MARITAL STATUS

Marital status changes affect spousal competency and compellability. The determining factor is the marital status at the time of trial. The following rules apply:

▶ If a witness is single at the time of the offence and legally marries the accused after the offence but before the trial, the witness is not a competent and compellable Crown witness; the spouse is legally married at the time of the trial.[54]

▶ If a spouse is legally married at the time of the offence and a legal divorce occurs before the trial, the spouse becomes a competent and compellable Crown witness; the spouse is not legally married at the time of the trial.[55]

▶ The Supreme Court of Canada, in *R. v. Salituro* (1991),[56] stated that an irreconcilable separation is the equivalent of a divorce regarding spousal competency and compellability. If a spouse is legally married at the time of the offence and a separation occurs before the trial, the spouse may be a competent and compellable Crown witness if the Crown proves that no reasonable possibility exists of reconciliation at the time of the trial.

The onus is on the Crown to prove the separation is irreconcilable. The Crown must prove this at the time of the trial when the spouse is called to the witness stand; it cannot be proven before the trial. This matter does not require proof beyond a reasonable doubt; instead, the Crown need only prove it on a balance of probabilities, which requires less evidence. An example of evidence that proves irreconcilable separation is found in *R. v. Jeffrey* (1993).[57]

An accused person was charged with break and enter. His separated wife was called as a Crown witness. During a hearing to determine whether an irreconcilable separation existed, the Crown asked her whether she intended to reunite, under the circumstances that existed at the time of the trial. The wife answered, "No." During cross-examination, she was asked whether she would consider reconciliation if the husband were acquitted. She answered, "I cannot say either yes or no." Additionally, proof existed that she had instituted divorce proceedings.

The Ontario Court of Appeal ruled that irreconcilable separation had been proven on a balance of probabilities. The equivocal response of "yes or no" was an answer to a hypothetical question. However, at the time of trial, the wife believed that the separation was irreconcilable.

In situations where spouses are separated before the trial, investigators should research the circumstances of the separation (i.e., whether divorce proceedings have been instituted and whether a reconciliation is expected).

In summary, legally married spouses are not competent or compellable Crown witnesses when the other spouse is charged with a general, non-exception offence. For example, if a husband commits an offence such as murder, attempted murder, robbery, break and enter, or any type of assault, theft, or fraud where the victim is 14 years or older, and his wife sees it or receives a confession from her husband about one of these offences, the police cannot subpoena the wife and her observations are inadmissible at the trial. However, her observations are significant to the investigator. If she is an eyewitness or the recipient of a confession, her observations constitute reasonable grounds to arrest because inadmissible evidence may be used to form reasonable grounds. After the arrest, it becomes imperative to obtain admissible evidence (e.g., a confession from the husband) to form reasonable grounds to lay an Information and to establish a *prima facie* case.[58]

Conversely, a wife may be subpoenaed to court and her testimony may be admissible for the Crown if her husband is charged with

- a violent offence against the wife,
- a sex offence against a victim of any age, or
- a s. 4(4) C.E.A. offence, such as assault, where the victim is under 14 years.

Case Study 8.1 Conclusion

Investigation revealed that Jack, Nancy, and Jake had intentionally fabricated the story of motorcycle gang members to mislead the officers.

Detectives had searched the exterior of the apartment and found damage to the roof of a car parked beneath the bathroom window of the crime scene. Ident. officers found bullet holes on a wall behind the places where Jack, Nancy, and Jake had been standing.

Jake was released from the hospital. He voluntarily accompanied officers to the police station where he was questioned by consent. During interrogation, he confessed the correct events.

Jake had been visiting Jack and Nancy. Charlie arrived at the apartment shortly before 11 p.m. Charlie was armed with a handgun and wanted revenge regarding a past conflict with his brother Jack. An argument developed; Charlie produced the handgun and fired. Jack and Jake tried to disarm him and a struggle ensued. Charlie, who was debilitated because of a previous injury and disease, was over-powered and disarmed. Jake took the gun and shot Charlie. Jake and Nancy corroborated Jake's statement during a subsequent interview.

Nancy informed CIB officers that she had intentionally shot herself in the ankle and then thrown the gun into the canal so the police would believe the initial fabricated story.

Finally, all were questioned about who left through the bathroom window. They identified another person who had been visiting and witnessed the occurrence. This person was interviewed and gave a witness statement.

ENDNOTES

1. *Vetrovec v. The Queen* (1982), 67 C.C.C. (2d) 1 (S.C.C.).
2. *R. v. Comba* (1938), 70 C.C.C. 205 (S.C.C.).
3. *R. v. Keller* (1970), 1 C.C.C. (2d) 360 (Sask. C.A.).
4. *R. v. Perciballi* (2001), 154 C.C.C. (3d) 481 (Ont. C.A.).
5. *Vetrovec v. The Queen*, supra note 1.
6. *R. v. Perciballi*, supra note 4.
7. *Vetrovec v. The Queen*, supra note 1.
8. P.K. McWilliams, *Canadian Criminal Evidence*, 3rd ed. (Aurora, ON: Canada Law Book, 1991).
9. Section 698 C.C.
10. E. Ehrlich et al., *Oxford American Dictionary* (New York: Oxford University Press, 1980).
11. *Foley v. Gares* (1989), 74 C.R. (3d) 386 (Sask. C.A.).
12. Section 698(2)(a) C.C.
13. Sections 701(1) and 509(2) C.C.
14. Section 698(2)(a) C.C.
15. Section 698(2)(b) C.C.
16. Section 698(3) C.C.
17. Section 705(1) C.C.
18. *R. v. Kinzie* (1956), 25 C.R. 6 (Ont. C.A.).
19. *R. v. Singh* (1990), 57 C.C.C. (3d) 444 (Alta. C.A.).
20. *R. v. Scott* (1990), 2 C.R. (4th) 153 (S.C.C.).
21. Ibid.
22. *R. v. Paul* (1980), 5 W.C.B. 127 (Ont. Prov. Ct.).
23. Sections 706(a) and (b) C.C.
24. Section 495(1)(a) C.C.
25. Section 527(1)(c) C.C.
26. D. Dukelow and B. Nuse, *Pocket Dictionary of Canadian Law* (Toronto: Carswell, 1991).
27. Section 16(2) C.E.A.
28. *R. v. Bannerman* (1966), C.R. 48, at 110 (Man. C.A.), as in *R. v. Khan* (1990), 59 C.C.C. (3d) 92 (S.C.C.).
29. Ibid.

30. *R. v. Brasier* (1779), 1 Leach 199, 168 E.R. 202.

31. *R. v. Bannerman,* supra note 28.

32. Section 14(2) C.E.A.

33. http://www.lfcc.on.ca/Bill_C2_Brief.pdf.

34. *R. v. McGovern* (1993), 82 C.C.C. (3d) 301 (Man. C.A.).

35. *R. v. D. (R.R.)* (1989), 47 C.C.C. (3d) 97 (Sask. C.A.).

36. Ibid.

37. *R. v. D. (R.R.),* supra note 35.

38. *R. v. Rockey* (1996), 110 C.C.C. (3d) 481 (S.C.C.).

39. *R. v. Marquard* (1993), 85 C.C.C. (3d) 193 (S.C.C.).

40. *R. v. Ferguson* (1996), 112 C.C.C. (3d) 342 (B.C.C.A.).

41. *R. v. Khan,* supra note 28.

42. *R. v. G.N.D.* (1993), 81 C.C.C. (3d) 65 (Ont. C.A.).

43. *R. v. Khan,* supra note 28; *R. v. G.N.D.,* supra note 42.

44. *R. v. Khan,* supra note 28, at 105–106.

45. *R. v. G.N.D.,* supra note 42.

46. Ibid.

47. Section 4(1) C.E.A.

48. *R. v. R.J.S.* (1993), 80 C.C.C. (3d) (Ont. C.A.); *R. v. Primeau* (1993), 85 C.C.C. (3d) 188 (Sask. C.A.).

49. Section 4(1) C.E.A.

50. *Kowbel v. R.,* 1954 CanLII 12 (S.C.C.).

51. *Coffin v. The Queen* (1955), 21 C.R. 333 (Que. Ct. Q.B.); *R. v. Jackson* (1981), 61 C.C.C. (2d) 540 (N.S.C.A.).

52. *R. v. Sillars* (1978), 45 C.C.C. (2d) 283 (B.C.C.A.).

53. Ibid.

54. *R. v. Lonsdale* (1973), 15 C.C.C. (2d) 201 (Alta. S.C. App. Div.).

55. *R. v. Marchand* (1980), 55 C.C.C. (2d) 77 (N.S.S.C. App. Div.); *R. v. Bailey* (1983), 4 C.C.C. (3d) 21 (Ont. C.A.).

56. *R. v. Salituro* (1991), 68 C.C.C. (3d) 289 (S.C.C.).

57. *R. v. Jeffrey* (1993), 84 C.C.C. (3d) 31 (Alta. C.A.).

58. *R. v. Debot* (1986), 30 C.C.C. (3d) 207 (Ont. C.A.).

CHAPTER 9

Rules of Evidence, Part 1: Hearsay Evidence

LEARNER SUMMARY

The first thing I saw as I walked into my first police report writing room was a poster of an index finger, pointed at the reader, with one sentence in large bold print beneath it:

"He/she who asserts must prove."

The poster remained there for years as a constant reminder of the concept of "task and rule book." The *task* is the onus to prove an allegation. When an officer lays an Information to formally charge someone, the prosecution has the full "burden of proof." A police officer is fully responsible for proving that the specific person named on the Information committed the specific offence alleged in the wording. The accused person does not have (a) the onus to prove his innocence, or (b) to help the officer, in any way, to prove the allegation against him. The only time that an accused person has to introduce evidence at a trial is after the prosecutor has proved a *prima facie* case. Otherwise, during the entire investigation and at the beginning of every trial, without exception, the officer and the prosecutor have the onus to prove the charge.

As with any other task, an officer has to follow rules. The *rule book* relating to the burden of proof is called the "rules of evidence." These rules govern exactly what evidence the prosecution can present in order to achieve the task of proving a *prima facie* case. These rules of evidence govern both the admissibility of physical items and witness testimony. Witnesses, including the police, may not say whatever they want during trial testimony; there are testimonial limits. The rules of evidence restrict what witnesses may testify about.

Case Study 9.1

Ian owned a house on the outskirts of an urban area. He lived there with his wife and 16-year-old son. Ian's son was killed in a motor vehicle collision. While the family was at the funeral home, the house was entered. Camera equipment owned by the deceased son was stolen.

Reasonable grounds were formed that Craig (28) committed the offence. He was interrogated and gave a written confession. Craig stated that he read about the son's death in the paper and predicted the house would be vacant. In the confession, he stated that he sold the camera equipment to Eric. Craig signed the statement. It was not videotaped.

Eric was later arrested and charged with possession of stolen property under $5,000. Craig was subpoenaed as a Crown witness; at the trial he was called to the witness stand by the Crown.

(Refer to the end of Chapter 9 for the conclusion of this case study.)

INTRODUCTION

A trial judge determines whether verbal testimony and physical evidence are admissible or inadmissible in a trial. Police officers must have the same knowledge as judges and lawyers in order to accurately predict the admissibility of evidence, forecast admissibility problems, and devise strategies as solutions.

Successful case management depends on both the interpretation of and the ability to accurately apply rules of evidence. Both admissible and inadmissible evidence may be used to form reasonable grounds during an investigation, but only the predicted admissible evidence can be used as the foundation of laying an Information and case preparation.

In other words, witness statements inserted in a Crown Brief consist of predicted admissible evidence only (see *Principles of Law Enforcement Report Writing*, 3rd ed. (Toronto: Emond Montgomery, 2008)). Evidence that will likely be inadmissible or excluded should not be included in any citizen's or police officer's statement.

Before learning how to interview a witness and write a statement, the rules of evidence must be learned. Witness interview strategies follow the rules of evidence.

Rules of Evidence—The Reality

There are a number of challenges associated with rules of evidence, including:

1. **The lack of a single rule book** Most tasks have one rule book and a single source of rules. This is not the case with criminal law. There are countless rules of evidence spread throughout statutes, case law, and common law.
2. **Complex language** None of the rules are written in simple, easy-to-apply language.
3. **The negative influence of entertainment** Television shows and movies are the worst influences for students because they show witnesses testifying without limits. Fictional Hollywood witnesses say whatever they want during testimony.

4. **The habits formed by daily, routine communication** The way we talk in everyday life forms habits that are not compatible with communicating in accordance with rules of evidence.

In reality, it is easy to make mistakes during testimony, but there is a cost for those mistakes. The following describes an embarrassing mistake I made while testifying as a novice uniform patrol officer, at a judge and jury trial, where the judge made a public spectacle of what was a simple, honest error.

At 2:00 a.m. during a midnight shift, our platoon received a radio broadcast of an alarm—"Break and enter in progress." The preliminary investigation revealed that forced entry had occurred, that the offenders were GOA, and that a witness statement from a neighbour concretely described the offender's car, containing two male occupants.

A search of the city was coordinated. About 10 minutes later, I stopped a car matching the witness's description. Two men were in the car. Both identified themselves. As I stood by the driver's door, a back-up officer arrived. She told me, "Both these guys are suspects in other break-ins and robberies." Reasonable grounds were formed by circumstantial evidence. The combined effect of eleven concrete circumstances led to only one conclusion—these men committed the break and enter that had just occurred. The statement made by the back-up officer contributed to the reasonable grounds. However, her statement was the eleventh factor, and the least important.

Both men were arrested. Later, at the police station, both men confessed to that night's offence, as well as seven other crimes.

They elected trial by judge and jury. I was called to the stand during the Crown's case. Everything went smoothly up to the point when I said the that the back-up officer had arrived and "*told* me that the two men were suspects in other offences." As I continued, my voice was drowned out by the judge's angry, loud instructions to the jury to disregard what I was saying, and a sarcastic request to the Crown Attorney to ask for a recess in order to "help the officer." A standing-room-only courtroom, including the jury, stared at me as the judge left the room. In addition to my embarrassment, I had no idea what I had done wrong. I knew the definitions of "hearsay evidence" and "bad character evidence." I could recite these rules of evidence at any time or place. However, I forgot how they applied to real-life circumstances. What mattered was not what I knew, but how much of that knowledge I was able to apply.

What I should have said was either (a) "I *received information* from Constable Jones," or (b) "As a result of *information received* from Constable Jones, I arrested both men." A simple solution would have prevented my severe embarrassment.

The Rule Book

In Canada, testimonial evidence is divided into two categories: (a) direct evidence, and (b) indirect evidence. **Direct evidence** refers to knowledge gained from personal observation—what a person knows from what he or she saw or heard. Conversely, **indirect evidence** is knowledge learned from another source, not from personal observation. Based on this concept, at a trial, direct evidence is generally admissible, while indirect evidence is generally inadmissible.

There are three primary examples of indirect evidence that are generally inadmissible at a Canadian trial: (a) hearsay, (b) opinion, and (c) bad character. These are the first three **exclusionary rules of evidence**—those rules that are generally inadmissible at trials. Hearsay, opinions, and bad character all have one thing in common—the person communicating the information does not have first-hand knowledge of what is being said. Instead, the witness is communicating:

- what he or she was told, or
- speculation about what the accused person did or was thinking, beyond the area of the witness's expertise.

Movies and television crime shows are filled with inadmissible evidence. Here are some examples of misleading, unrestricted Hollywood testimony:

- "I just know he did it. I have a gut feeling from my years of experience."
- "He would have killed me if the police had not arrived when they did."
- "Everyone says he has anger-management problems. He's a psychopath."
- "He's anti-social and doesn't get along with people. He's the type of person who could have done this."
- "She told me that he has been abusing her for years."

Seven Key Rules

The following are the seven key "rules of evidence" points that govern witness testimony:

1. **Testimony is not the same as daily, routine communication.** While testimony is unique, formal, "rules of evidence"-oriented communication, daily communication is habitual and informal. Routine, daily communication habits are the biggest detriment to witness testimony because:

   ▷ A strong temptation to say what "he said" or "she said" is developed. We routinely tell others what we were told without actually seeing the event for ourselves.

   ▷ We blur the line between facts available to experts rather than non-experts. For example, we routinely describe people in ways that are reserved for experts (e.g., "She has anger-management problems"; "He's a sociopath"; "She's a compulsive liar"; "He's unstable").

   ▷ Assaults on character, stemming from people's past conduct, are communicated thousands of times daily. Electronic and face-to-face gossip about past behaviour has become a sport. Whether or not the gossip is completely fabricated or embellished, it usually includes sweeping generalizations made in abstract language.

   In other words, we habitually and routinely communicate hearsay evidence, opinion evidence, and bad character evidence.

2. **Say only what you saw and heard with your own senses.** Do not testify about what other people told you. Use the simple phrase "Upon information received from (witness's name)," or "I received information from (witness's name)," to replace what was communicated to you by a witness.

3. **The person who saw or heard the offence is the one who may testify about it.** This key point interacts with the second point. Both relate to the hearsay rule of evidence. Hearsay is generally inadmissible because (a) the police would testify on behalf of the witness, simply reading the witness statement and not subpoenaing the witness, (b) the witness who actually made the observation was not under oath or affirmation at the time he or she reported it to the police, and (c) cross-examination of the witness would be prevented. The absence of an oath/affirmation and the inability to cross-examine the witness violate two of the fundamental laws of trial fairness.

4. **Past conduct is not relevant to current conduct.** An offender's criminal record and past deviant behaviour is allowed *after* the trial ends, for sentencing purposes after a conviction is registered. Generally, it is inadmissible *during* the trial.

5. **Do not provide broad sweeping generalizations; replace abstract language with concrete.** Abstract language is defined as a generalization that has multiple interpretations. It provides a conclusion (e.g., "He assaulted her"; "She has a mental disorder"). The trial judge makes conclusions; witnesses must communicate concrete testimony so that the judge can make a conclusion. Concrete language constitutes evidence, while abstract generalizations do not.

6. **What a witness tells you and what a suspect tells you are two entirely separate concepts.** A suspect's statement must be (a) recorded verbatim and (b) proven to be voluntary. A witness's statement is not recorded verbatim. It has to be constructed, usually beginning with an abstract core and built to a lengthier, concrete version. Voluntariness or reliability only becomes a issue if the witness's testimony conflicts with the original statement.

7. **"Exceptions" are major investigative benefits.** All exclusionary rules of evidence have exceptions. **Exceptions** are defined as circumstances where normally prohibited evidence is admissible. The simplest examples are exceptions to the opinion rule; non-experts may testify about ordinary opinions that require no scientific knowledge, including opinions about a suspect's age, height, weight, and sobriety or intoxication. Exceptions expand the amount of potential admissible evidence available to the prosecution; they provide investigative solutions. For example, a witness gives an officer a statement during an investigation that incriminates the accused person. At the trial, the witness changes his story and says he can't remember or that he lied to the officer. Exceptions to the hearsay rule are the most important investigative benefit because they potentially solve this type of problem. The Khan Rule is the most significant hearsay exception. Created in 1990, this extremely important modern case law decision lifted previously tight restrictions on the prosecution's use of hearsay evidence.

This chapter explains the fundamentals of the exclusionary rules of evidence. The accompanying website **www.emp.ca/arcaro/criminvestigation5E** expands the chapter with continuous rules of evidence case law research.

WITNESS STATEMENTS

There are three types of questioning that need to be defined and differentiated:

1. interview,
2. interrogation, and
3. exploratory questioning.

Theoretically, an *interview* refers to the questioning of a witness, while *interrogation* refers to the questioning of a suspect/accused person. However, political correctness has encouraged the use of "interview" in reference to the questioning of both witnesses and suspects/accused persons, because "interrogation" may suggest unfriendly, pressure-filled questioning. It is recommended that "interview" be used to describe both types of questioning when officers testify in court. However, "interrogation" is still used in case law decisions, and by judges. For teaching purposes, both "interview" and "interrogation" are used in order to prevent confusion, since the strategies and goals of the two types of questioning are different. In this text, "interview" will be used in relation to witnesses, and "interrogation" will be used in relation to suspects/accused persons.

An *exploratory questioning* is a *blended* type of questioning. It is used when the person being questioned may be a witness *or* a suspect. Consequently, the goal of an exploratory interview is to determine whether the interviewee is a witness or a suspect.

A **witness statement** is a written record of a witness's observations obtained from a formal interview. A witness interview includes (a) questioning a witness to obtain facts intended to form reasonable grounds, and (b) evaluating the credibility of the witness.

An interview differs from an **interrogation**, which involves questioning a suspect or an accused person to obtain a confession. Witness statements are usually

▸ dictated by the witness,
▸ recorded by the police officer, and
▸ signed by the witness after the statement is complete.

A witness statement is usually an unsworn document that has six significant functions:

1. **Provides testimonial expectations** Witness statements communicate the anticipated testimony of a witness to the Crown Attorney.
2. **Provides disclosure** Every accused person has a Charter-guaranteed right to know all of the prosecution's evidence in order to design a meaningful defence. All statements obtained from persons by police officers must be disclosed to the accused person before the trial. No statement may be concealed from the accused, including statements of persons whom the Crown will not subpoena to the trial. Failure to provide disclosure of all witness statements to an accused person constitutes a s. 7 Charter violation.[1]
3. **Facilitates issuance of subpoenas** Witness statements prove whether or not a witness is likely to give relevant testimony.
4. **Acts as a solution to problems** This includes refuting hostile or adverse witnesses (witnesses who change their stories).

5. **Acts as record of justification** Witness statements justify an officer's arrest, searches, seizures, use of force, and all other investigative procedures and authorities.

6. **Refreshes memory** A written statement may be used by the witness to refresh his or her memory before the trial begins. Witnesses generally cannot read from the statement during testimony.

Although the written witness statement is important, what ultimately matters is the evidentiary value of a witness's verbal testimony during a trial. There are two key points to consider regarding the evidentiary value of the written witness statement:

1. The police officer who wrote the statement generally cannot read the contents of the statement during testimony to replace a witness's testimony or to corroborate it. Reading the contents constitutes giving hearsay evidence, which is generally inadmissible.

2. The Crown Attorney cannot read the contents of a statement to the court during a trial. The Crown generally cannot introduce the written statement as evidence to replace witness testimony.

GENERAL RULE OF ADMISSIBILITY

The **general rule of admissibility**, found in case law, is the most basic rule that a trial judge uses to determine whether testimony or physical evidence will be admissible or excluded. Evidence is admissible if it is relevant and no exclusionary rule exists.[2]

Relevant means the evidence must prove or disprove at least one fact-in-issue of the offence that the accused is charged with. Conversely, **irrelevant testimony** is inadmissible. It refers to testimony that does not prove or disprove at least one fact-in-issue (FII).

An **exclusionary rule** is a law that specifically states that certain types of testimony are generally inadmissible. Exclusionary rules are also called rules of evidence. Examples of exclusionary rules include (a) hearsay evidence, (b) opinion evidence, and (c) bad character evidence.

The exclusionary rules have exceptions, referring to types of testimony that are admissible. An example of how this rule applies is found in the *R. v. Smith* (1992), a decision discussed later in this chapter.

Hearsay Evidence

Hearsay evidence is evidence that was not perceived by a person's own senses. The person did not actually see the occurrence or hear the statement. Someone else saw or heard it and then informed the person. Hearsay evidence is also informally called **third-person evidence**.

A **recipient** of hearsay evidence refers to a person who was told about an occurrence by another person who actually saw or heard the events. A recipient of hearsay evidence did not perceive it with his or her own senses, meaning that he or she did not see or hear the occurrence.[3] For example, police officers are often the recipients of hearsay evidence. Often, the officer does not see an offence happen. The officer interviews a witness who saw the offence and gives the officer a written statement. The officer is then a recipient of hearsay evidence. He or she receives information about an offence that the officer did not witness. The written statement represents hearsay evidence to the officer.

Hearsay evidence is generally inadmissible. This means that a witness cannot repeat hearsay evidence during testimony. This rule originated in common law and has been confirmed in case law. Witnesses may testify about what they actually saw and heard, not what other people saw or heard. Hearsay evidence should not be included in a citizen's or officer's witness statement. Hearsay evidence may be used during the investigation to form reasonable grounds.

The term *generally inadmissible* means that some exceptions exist. The exceptions to the hearsay exclusionary rule are significant to the police. Exceptions represent an advantage because they expand the type of evidence that may be admissible to prove an offence. Exceptions to the hearsay rule are generally admissible.

Historically, the hearsay rule was very strict. Some limited exceptions included admissions, confessions, *res gestae*, and dying declarations. However, the hearsay rule has been relaxed and undergone changes since 1990. The Supreme Court of Canada, most notably in *R. v. Khan* (1990),[4] created the most profound exception to the hearsay rule, which has benefited prosecutions by expanding the circumstances in which hearsay is admissible.

To understand the significance and benefit of hearsay exceptions, the reasons why hearsay is generally excluded must be understood:

- ▸ The person who actually saw the offence is not under oath. That person would not testify and whomever he or she told would testify.
- ▸ The defence could not cross-examine the person who actually saw the offence, depriving the accused a fundamental right.
- ▸ The trial judge or jury would be unable to evaluate the credibility of the person who actually saw the offence.
- ▸ The judge and jury would be unable to determine whether the person actually saw what he or she told the other person.

If hearsay were always allowed, the police would simply read the witness statement during the trial and conceal the witness.

One of the most basic case management principles is properly applying the hearsay exclusionary rule when writing witness statements and during court testimony. The following are examples of hearsay that are generally excluded, and they demonstrate how to apply the rules during witness statements and testimony.

EXAMPLE 1

You respond to a radio broadcast that states, "Attend 1000 King Street regarding a domestic. Assault in progress." Upon arrival, Emma (30) opens the door and allows you to enter. Her right eye is swollen and bruised. She reports, "Greg punched me 10 minutes ago." Greg is seated in the living room.

1. Do you have reasonable grounds to arrest? Yes. Emma's information exceeds mere suspicion.

2. You arrest and charge Greg. You are called to testify at the trial. Can you say, "I attended at 1000 King Street regarding a domestic. An assault was in progress"?

   To determine the answer, ask yourself, "Did I actually see that event?" If yes, it is not hearsay. If no, then it is hearsay and you cannot say it during testimony. In this case, you did not see the assault being committed. You were told about it by the dispatcher, who learned about it from Emma. The radio broadcast represents hearsay evidence to you. You were the recipient of hearsay evidence.

3. How do you properly testify about why you attended at the address? You may say either "I attended at 1000 King Street as the result of information received," or "I attended at 1000 King Street as the result of a radio broadcast." As a rule, "as a result of information received" is the proper way to substitute hearsay.

4. Can you say, "Emma told me that Greg punched her 10 minutes before my arrival"? No. You did not see the assault. You were told about it. Instead, you should say, "I interviewed Emma. She told me certain information." Another method is, "As the result of information received from Emma, I arrested Greg."

5. Can you say, "Emma's right eye was bruised and swollen"? Yes. You saw these injuries. You perceived them with your own senses.

EXAMPLE 2

You arrive at the scene of a theft. Cindy (30) informs you that she saw a man, 20 years old, 5'10", 180 lbs., with brown hair, enter a car that had a plate number 734 ABDF. You later arrest and charge the offender.

1. At the trial, during your testimony can you say, "Cindy told me that the suspect was male, 20 years old," etc.? No. You did not see these facts. You should say, "I interviewed Cindy. She reported certain information [or, I received information from her]."

2. Can you say, "She gave me the plate number 734 ABDF"? No, for the same reason as question 1.

The following are additional examples of hearsay evidence that are inadmissible and must be avoided during a police officer's testimony:

1. **Owner of property** In trials where the owner of a house or car must be proven, the officer cannot testify that "Aaron is the owner." The actual owner must be subpoenaed and testify that he or she is the owner.

2. **Value of damage or stolen property** The specific value of relevant damage or property is proven by the person who has actual knowledge of the value. The officer cannot testify about a value told to him or her.

3. **Injuries requiring a doctor's opinion** Injuries such as broken bones or internal injuries are not visible to the police. The officer is informed about these injuries by a doctor or the victim who suffered the pain. A doctor's expert opinion during testimony proves injuries. A victim's testimony proves pain suffered, such as a sore neck.

4. **Marital status** Officers are told about marital status. They cannot make statements such as, "The accused is married to the complainant." The person in the relationship must testify about the marital status.

5. **Partner's observations** Uniform officers commonly patrol "double crew." A common error is to testify by using the pronoun "we" relating to observations such as, "We saw the car swerving." The pronoun "I" must be used to explain only what the individual officer saw. One officer cannot testify about what his or her partner saw.

In summary, witness statements and testimony cannot generally include information learned from another person. The phrase "as a result of information received" replaces hearsay evidence in both the statement and testimony.

The Khan Hearsay Exception

The most significant hearsay exception is the **Khan Rule**, also known as the "principled approach," created by the S.C.C. in *R. v. Khan* (1990). Hearsay evidence may be admissible if two conditions are proven: (a) necessity, and (b) reliability.

The Khan Rule has had a profound positive effect on investigations and prosecutions because it significantly expands potential admissible evidence. It has provided solutions to many problems encountered during the investigation of a wide range of offences. The *Khan* case itself solved the problem of child victims of sexual assault who are ruled incompetent to testify. Before the Khan Rule, a child victim, ruled incompetent, likely ruined the Crown's case. The Khan Rule now permits the possible admissibility of the child's statements made to people such as parents, police, and social workers.

Although the *Khan* case related to sexual assaults involving an incompetent child witness, the principles of the *Khan* hearsay exception may be applied to any type of criminal offence, not just sexual assault. The Supreme Court of Canada has used the Khan Rule in two subsequent landmark cases, *R. v. Smith* (1992) and *R. v. K.G.B.* (1993), and solved two other investigative problems:

1. If a victim or witness dies before the trial, the Khan Rule has been used to create a hearsay exception that allows the possible admissibility of the dead witness's statements made to other persons.

2. Witnesses who change their story by giving the police a statement and then contradicting it during court testimony create a significant problem. The Khan Rule has been used to create a hearsay exception that allows the possible admissibility of the original statement given to the police.

To apply the investigative advantages of the *Khan* hearsay exception, necessity and reliability need to be interpreted. The admissibility of hearsay evidence is dependent on proving these two elements.

The S.C.C. defined **necessity** as "reasonably necessary." Necessity does not mean that the Crown needs it for his or her case. Instead, it means that a witness is unable or unavailable to testify. The *Khan* case included the following specific examples of circumstances that prove or establish necessity:

▸ a child incompetent to testify,
▸ a child unable to testify,

- a child unavailable to testify, or
- expert psychological assessments that prove a child's testimony in court might be traumatic or harmful to the child.

The circumstances that prove necessity are not limited to these examples. The S.C.C. left open other possible circumstances by stating, "There may be other examples of circumstances which could establish the requirement of necessity." This means that the *Khan* hearsay exception may be applied to any offence (not just sexual assaults) and to other types of witnesses (not just child witnesses).

The interpretation of necessity is still evolving. It has been addressed in several cases where additional circumstances have been ruled to constitute necessity. For example, the S.C.C. in *R. v. Rockey* (1996)[5] stated that necessity may be proven in cases where a child is competent to testify and hearsay may be admissible to corroborate the child.

Other factors will contribute to the determination of necessity including severity of offence, proper administration of justice, and the fair trial interest for the accused. Additional circumstances that constitute necessity have been established in cases following *Khan* and are explained in this chapter.

Reliability refers to the credibility of the person's observations. Factors that will determine reliability include

- timing, meaning when the child told the other person about the offence,
- the child's demeanour and personality,
- the child's intelligence and understanding, and
- the absence of a reason for fabrication.

The Ontario Court of Appeal in *R. v. G.N.D.* (1993)[6] added other factors:

- the child's age,
- the child's ability to accurately interpret events,
- the time lapse between the offence and the child's statement to another person, and
- whether the child's statement was spontaneous, emerged naturally without prompting, was obtained by leading questions asked by well-intentioned professionals, or was motivated by parental prompting.

The S.C.C., in *Khan*, also commented about another factor that may be the most significant element of proving reliability. The court stated that "special considerations" must be taken because young children are not "adept" and "are unlikely to use their reflective powers to concoct a deliberate untruth, and particularly one about a sexual act which probably is beyond their ken." In other words, a child's young age generally creates a **reasonable presumption** that the child is unfamiliar with sexual acts and, for that reason, should be incapable of fabricating those circumstances.

The S.C.C. emphasized two significant points:

1. There is no strict, complete list of factors that determine reliability.
2. Certain evidence, such as a child's report of sexual assault, should not automatically be considered reliable. (Other case law decisions have added additional rules relating to reliability.)

The Crown must apply during the trial for hearsay evidence to be admissible. The judge then conducts a **voir dire**, referring to an admissibility hearing, to determine whether the hearsay evidence will be allowed or excluded. The jury, if one exists, is absent during the voir dire. The judge determines admissibility, not the jury. A voir dire is conducted during the trial, not before it. The Crown has the onus to prove the necessity and reliability of the hearsay evidence. The trial judge then has discretion to allow or exclude hearsay. The circumstances of the case law decisions that follow illustrate procedures and guidelines relating to the Khan Rule.

CASE LAW

R. v. Khan (1990)

Circumstances A medical doctor was charged with sexually assaulting a three-and-a-half-year-old girl. The complainant made statements to her mother 15 minutes after the offence that incriminated the accused. The mother did not see the offence.

The complainant was four-and-a-half years old at the time of the trial. The trial judge ruled that she was not competent to testify and the accused was acquitted. The Ontario Court of Appeal ordered a new trial. The accused's appeal to the S.C.C. was dismissed and a new trial was ordered. The S.C.C. made the following rulings:

▸ In cases of child sexual abuse, the only evidence is usually a statement made to a third party. If the child is ruled not competent and the third-party statement is excluded, the court will be deprived of all existing evidence.

▸ In this case the mother was allowed to testify about her daughter's statement. This hearsay evidence was allowed because the child's incompetence to testify was sufficient to prove necessity for hearsay evidence, and the reliability was proven because the court found no motive for the child to fabricate the story and her statement to her mother emerged naturally and without prompting. Additionally, the fact that the child could not be expected to have knowledge of the sexual acts that she reported gave her statement to her mother "its own peculiar stamp of reliability."

In this case, her statement was also corroborated by the finding of physical evidence.

CASE LAW

R. v. G.N.D. (1993)

Circumstances The accused was charged with sexually assaulting his five-and-a-half-year-old adopted daughter. The complainant made four out-of-court statements:

1. to a child-care worker, 1–2 days after the offence,

2. to a social worker, 1–2 days after the offence,

3. to a police officer, 1–2 days after the offence, and

4. to her mother, six months after the offence.

The trial judge ruled that the child was not competent to testify. A voir dire was then conducted to determine the admissibility of the four hearsay statements. The trial judge allowed all four statements to be read followed by cross-examination of the recipients of the hearsay evidence. The accused was convicted.

The Ontario Court of Appeal dismissed the accused's appeal and made the following rulings:

- The Khan Rule was applied to this case, which allowed flexibility to the hearsay exclusionary rule. The determining factors regarding the admissibility of the four out-of-court statements were *necessity* and *reliability*.

- Circumstances that prove necessity do not have an exact definition and are still evolving. However, necessity does not mean necessary to the Crown's case. Instead, it means the necessity of the hearsay evidence to prove a fact-in-issue.

- Proving reliability requires that "a circumstantial guarantee of trustworthiness is established." The factors that must be considered to evaluate reliability are the child's age, the child's ability to understand and interpret events accurately, the time lapse between the offence and the statement, and whether the statement was spontaneous, emerged naturally, was elicited by leading questions from well-meaning professionals, or was the result of prompting by parents.

- The three statements made one to two days after the offence were all "part of a reporting sequence closely related in time," and were considered reliable.

- The statement made to the mother six months later was admissible. It was deemed to be reasonably necessary to assist the judge in evaluating the reliability of the previous three statements. The reliability of this statement was not challenged. There was no suggestion that there was any event or conversation that prompted the child to make the statement to her mother.

NEW "RULE OF EVIDENCE" (SMITH)

The Supreme Court of Canada, in *R. v. Smith* (1992),[7] made another prominent ruling regarding hearsay exceptions. In this case, the S.C.C. created another rule of evidence.

Hearsay evidence of statements made by persons who are not available to give evidence at trial should generally be admissible if the trial judge is satisfied that the Khan *principles of necessity and reliability are proven, and no undue prejudice results to the accused and the evidentiary value is slight.*

The court did not formally define "not available" but referred to common law to include unavailable witnesses as persons who died before the trial, or are out of the jurisdiction, or are insane or otherwise unavailable for the purpose of cross-examination.

This rule significantly benefits investigation prosecutions by expanding the offences where the *Khan* hearsay exception rule applies and to the type of witness. The Khan Rule may apply to any criminal offence, not just sexual assault, and to any unavailable witness, not just incompetent child witnesses.

The Crown must apply to have the hearsay evidence admitted. A voir dire must be conducted. The hearsay evidence will never be automatically admissible. The trial judge has discretion to admit or exclude it based on the *Khan* principles.

The *Smith* case provides an example of how this rule of evidence applies.

CASE LAW

R. v. Smith (1992)

Circumstances The accused was charged with second-degree murder. The accused and the victim drove from Detroit to Canada, where they spent two days in a hotel in London, Ontario. The victim's body was found one day later near a service station, lying on a sheet. Fibres found on the sheet matched those from the accused's clothes.

The Crown's theory was that the accused was a drug smuggler who wanted the victim to conceal cocaine in her body when they returned to the United States. The victim refused and was later murdered.

To support this theory, the Crown relied on the evidence of four telephone calls made by the deceased to her mother during a two-hour period on the night before the homicide:

1. The victim said the accused had abandoned her in London and that she needed a ride home.

2. The victim said the accused still had not returned.

3. The victim said the accused had returned and she no longer needed a ride.

4. The victim called from a pay phone near the service station. She told her mother that she was "on her way."

The defence did not object to the mother's testimony regarding the first three statements. The accused was convicted. The Ontario Court of Appeal allowed the accused's appeal and ordered a new trial, ruling that the phone calls were hearsay evidence. The first two were admissible under a hearsay exception to prove only the victim's state of mind at the time of the calls. The third phone call was excluded as being hearsay.

The Crown's appeal to the S.C.C. was dismissed. The Ontario C.A. ruling of a new trial remained intact. The S.C.C.'s reasons were that:

▸ All four phone calls constituted inadmissible hearsay unless an exception existed that allowed their admission.

▸ A common-law exception is the "state of mind" exception, which allows hearsay if it proves the intention of the person who made the statement and it is relevant to a fact-in-issue. The "present intentions" or "state of mind" hearsay exception has been recognized in Canadian case law since 1930. Examples of these exceptions include statements made by a dying person to prove how the death occurred and statements made by an estranged husband about his intention to resume cohabitation with his wife.

▸ The court ruled that the first three phone calls were all inadmissible. They would have been allowed only if the first two statements proved the victim wanted to return home. The first three phone calls did not fall under the "state of mind" exception. The Crown did not appeal the exclusion of the fourth call.

▸ However, the S.C.C. ruled that the non-applicable "state of mind" exception was not fatal to the Crown's appeal because the *Khan* hearsay exceptions had to be considered to determine admissibility of the hearsay evidence. If the hearsay evidence were proved to be necessary and reliable, the statements would be admissible.

- Reliability does not need proof of "absolute certainty." It is proven if a "circumstantial guarantee of trustworthiness" existed, regardless of whether cross-examination is possible. This means that the *Khan* hearsay exception applies to the statements made by a victim before death.

- Necessity does not include "necessary to the Crown's case." However, necessity "must be given a flexible definition, capable of encompassing diverse situations." The court acknowledged that the statements made by a person before death may constitute necessity, but not automatically.

- The S.C.C. did apply the *Khan* principles in this case to determine the admissibility of the hearsay evidence.

- The hearsay evidence in the first two phone calls was ruled to be reasonably necessary and reliable. The necessity was based on the premise that what the victim said to her mother was necessary because the victim died and there was "no possibility" that the person who made the statement could introduce it as evidence. The reliability was proven because the court found no reason for the victim to have lied during the first two calls.

- However, a different conclusion was reached about the third call. It was deemed unreliable and was subsequently excluded. The court ruled that the victim "might have intended" to deceive her mother about the accused having returned to pick her up, or it was "at least possible" that the victim was mistaken.

- The admissibility of the hearsay evidence relating to the fourth call would have to be decided at the new trial, using the *Khan* principles to decide.

In summary, the S.C.C. created the following rule of evidence: Hearsay evidence of statements made by persons who are not available to give evidence at trial should generally be admissible if the trial judge is satisfied that the *Khan* principles of necessity and reliability are proven.

This case also includes an example of how the general rule of admissibility applies. A Crown witness was called at the trial. She testified that she had travelled from Detroit to Canada with the accused in the month before the murder. During this trip, the accused abandoned her at a restaurant after she refused to smuggle drugs from Canada to the United States. The S.C.C. ruled that this evidence was inadmissible because it was irrelevant to the charge of murder in this case. It was evidence that was relevant only to character and implied the accused had the character of a drug smuggler. It was inadmissible because it had no relevance to prove that the accused committed murder.

K.G.B. HEARSAY EXCEPTION

A common problem that occurs during prosecution is having a witness who changes his or her story. This happens when a witness gives the police a written statement implicating the accused person, stating that he or she saw the accused commit the offence or that the accused told the witness that he or she committed the offence. Later, at the trial, the witness contradicts the previous statement during testimony by saying, "I can't remember seeing anything and can't remember making a statement," or "I did not see anything and I did not make a statement," or "I did give the police a statement but the story I told the police wasn't true."

A witness who contradicts a prior statement during testimony at a trial is referred to as a **hostile** or **adverse witness**. Before 1993, the only available method to correct the problem caused by a hostile or adverse witness was a set of procedures found in s. 9 *Canada Evidence Act*, an S.C.C. decision in *R. v. Milgaard* (1971), and common law. The hostile or adverse witness procedure is probably the most confusing trial procedure in Canadian law. If the results are unsuccessful and the witness refuses to acknowledge that he or she saw or heard the relevant evidence, the witness's prior statement given to the police cannot be read by the officer in court and cannot be submitted as evidence. In other words, the witness's evidence is lost. If the procedure is successful and the witness does revert to his original story, his credibility is damaged by the denial in court. In addition to the confusing nature of the procedure, it is not effective. Justice Cory of the Supreme Court of Canada referred to the interpretation of s. 9 C.E.A. as an "irrational and unreasonable obstacle"[8] that should not impede the quest to discover the truth at a trial.

The S.C.C. in *R. v. K.G.B.* (1993) created a new rule of evidence that represents an enormous advantage during prosecutions when a hostile or adverse witness changes his or her story and contradicts the prior statement given to the police during the investigation. The procedure is informally called the K.G.B. interview. Formally, it is another exception to the hearsay rule that allows the witness's original statement, which was given to the police, to be admissible if certain conditions and circumstances are proved.

The **K.G.B. hearsay exception** has simplified the trial procedures and has created investigative procedures that allow the police to conduct a proper interview when they anticipate or suspect that the witness might change his story in court.

To understand and appreciate the K.G.B. hearsay exception and the accompanying investigative procedures, the s. 9 C.E.A. and *Milgaard* procedures will be explained first.

Section 9 C.E.A. and Milgaard

When a Crown witness is called to testify, the prosecutor conducts an inquiry called an **examination-in-chief**, representing the first stage of witness testimony. The purpose of this stage is to bring out the witness's observations by means of questions asked by the Crown. The Crown cannot ask *leading questions* (those that suggest or imply an answer).

After the examination-in-chief concludes, the defence is permitted to **cross-examine**, without exceptions. Cross-examination is the second stage of witness testimony. Its purpose is to raise reasonable doubt, discredit the witness, and bring out favourable evidence for the accused. The third stage, **re-examination**, is permitted by the Crown after cross-examination concludes; the Crown may question the witness about new topics that were raised during cross-examination. Generally, no new topics may be raised by the Crown during re-examination.

The Crown, generally, cannot cross-examine his or her own witness. In other words, the Crown ordinarily cannot discredit his or her own witness. A dilemma occurs when a witness gives the police a verbal or written statement during an investigation that implicates an offender and then contradicts the statement during testimony at the trial. For example, an eyewitness gives the police a written statement, reporting that she saw an offender commit an offence. At the trial, the witness is called by the Crown, changes her story, and fails to testify about what was reported to the police.

A contradiction severely damages the Crown's case because of the doubt created about the accused's guilt. The Crown must correct the contradiction by

- questioning the witness about the previous statement to bring out the truth by the witness testifying about the contents of the statement,
- introducing other evidence to contradict the witness who changed his or her story, and
- discrediting the witness if he or she fails to testify about the actual contents of the statement.

However, as previously mentioned, the Crown cannot automatically cross-examine or discredit its own witness, or submit the statement as evidence so that the contents of the statement may be admissible without the witness testifying about the contents. If a contradiction occurs, the Crown can apply for a voir dire to solve the problem by proving

- hostile witness (common-law principle),
- adverse witness (s. 9(1) C.E.A.), or
- that a contradiction exists between the witness's testimony and his or her previous statement given to police (s. 9(2) C.E.A.).

These common-law and statutory provisions may be considered to be among the most confusing and vague provisions in Canadian law. An examination of these provisions begins with pertinent definitions:

- An **adverse witness** is a witness who gives unfavourable evidence to the side that called him or her. *Unfavourable evidence* is verbal testimony that opposes the side that called the witness.[9]
- A **hostile witness** is a witness who does not testify fairly and with a desire to tell the truth because of a hostile animosity toward the prosecution.[10] A hostile witness may also be defined as an adverse witness who displays animosity or hostility toward the Crown by his or her demeanour and general attitude.[11]

Voir Dire

A **voir dire** is a hearing or inquiry conducted during a trial to determine a specific issue, such as:

- whether a witness is adverse or hostile in order to allow the Crown to cross-examine its own witness,
- the admissibility of evidence (i.e., confessions), or
- the competency of a witness.

A voir dire is referred to as a trial within a trial.[12] The trial essentially is suspended while a voir dire is conducted and resumes when the voir dire concludes. Significantly, a voir dire does not occur before a trial; consequently, the Crown and police can only predict the ruling of the specific issue during the case preparation.

When a Crown witness gives testimony that conflicts with the statement he or she gave to the police, the Crown must apply for permission to cross-examine the witness and to discredit the witness by introducing other evidence. The application is followed by a voir dire, which is conducted in a systematic way, to determine whether the Crown will be given permission to correct the witness's contradiction. Four rulings are possible by the trial judge at the conclusion of the voir dire:

1. **No contradiction exists** The witness's testimony does not conflict with his or her witness statement given to the police. The Crown will be denied permission to cross-examine the witness. The witness's non-implicating evidence stands as is.

2. **A contradiction exists** The witness's testimony differs from the statement given to police (i.e., he or she denies making the statement). The Crown will be given permission to cross-examine the witness only about the contradiction[13] (e.g., how or why the witness gave a statement that differed from the testimony).[14] The Crown cannot cross-examine about any other issue or the witness's character. This cross-examination may be used to prove that the witness is adverse.

3. **Adverse witness** The witness has given unfavourable testimony (e.g., denied the contents of the statement). The Crown may cross-examine specifically, meaning only about the statement inconsistencies, and may now discredit the witness by introducing other evidence. However, the Crown cannot conduct a general cross-examination that includes evidence of the witness's bad character.[15]

4. **Hostile witness** The witness's unfavourable testimony is accompanied by hostile animosity toward the Crown. The Crown will be permitted to conduct a general, unrestricted cross-examination of the witness.[16]

VOIR DIRE PROCEDURE

The following voir dire procedure used to prove a contradiction, an adverse witness, or a hostile witness was established in *R. v. Milgaard* (1971):[17]

1. The Crown calls the witness to the stand.
2. The witness testifies and contradicts a previous written statement (e.g., denies giving the contents of the statement).
3. The Crown makes a verbal application under s. 9(2) C.E.A. to cross-examine the witness. The Crown cannot cross-examine automatically at this stage or introduce or read the contents of the statement.
4. If a jury exists, the judge instructs the jury to leave before the voir dire begins.
5. The voir dire begins for the purpose of determining whether a contradiction exists between the testimony (e.g., denial) and the statement. The Crown has the onus to prove the contradiction.
6. The Crown gives the written statement to the judge to read and compare with the testimony. The contents are not admissible.
7. After the comparison, the judge rules whether a contradiction exists.
    ▷ If none exists, the voir dire ends, no cross-examination occurs, the jury returns, and the witness's denial stands.

▷ If it exists, the Crown now has the onus to prove that the witness actually made the statement. The Crown cannot cross-examine at this stage.

8. The Crown has two methods available to prove that the witness actually made the statement:

▷ The Crown may produce the statement to the witness and ask whether he or she made it. If the witness admits it, the statement is proven to have been made, but the contents are not admissible. If the witness fails to admit it, the Crown may use the second alternative.

▷ The Crown may call the officer who received and wrote the statement, to prove that the witness actually made it. Essentially, the officer must prove that the statement was not fabricated. The witness's signature at the end of the statement and his or her initials at the bottom of each page facilitate proving the statement was actually made. The officer cannot read the contents of the statement to the court. The defence is allowed to oppose the proving of the statements by cross-examining the officer about this issue.

9. If the statement is proven by either method, the Crown will be permitted to conduct specific cross-examination of its own witness, regarding only the inconsistencies but no other issue. The witness's character cannot be discredited. The jury returns and is present during cross-examination.

10. If the witness continues to deny the contents of the statement during cross-examination, the Crown may make further application to have the witness declared adverse or hostile.[18]

11. If the witness is ruled adverse, the Crown may conduct specific cross-examination about the statement only, not the witness's character. The Crown may also introduce other evidence to discredit the witness's denial.

12. If the witness is declared hostile because of the contradiction and the witness's general behaviour, the Crown is permitted to conduct general, unrestricted cross-examination.

During this procedure, the contents of the statements cannot become admissible or be read to the court. The Crown is allowed to ask leading questions during cross-examination while attempting to elicit the truth from the witness. If the witness tells the truth by reverting to the original contents of the statement, the Crown's objective is fulfilled. However, the witness's credibility may have suffered because of the conflicting testimony, which in itself may raise reasonable doubt.

If the witness fails to change his or her testimony and refuses to testify about the contents of the statement or anything that may incriminate the accused, the contents are not admissible in any manner to replace the witness's testimony. The Crown may attempt to discredit this witness, but it is imperative that the Crown introduce other evidence to prove the FII.

In summary, officers should strive to obtain a formal, signed written statement from all witnesses, after interviews are conducted. An informal statement written in an officer's notebook, not signed by the witness, does not constitute a written statement for the purposes of s. 9 C.E.A.[19] Consequently, the absence of a formally signed, written statement may prevent the Crown from correcting a situation where a witness changes his or her story and does not testify as expected.

New "Rule of Evidence" (K.G.B.)

The s. 9 C.E.A. procedure has existed for decades and still exists. It has been a ridiculous, frustrating obstacle in prosecutions, preventing the admissibility of incriminating witness evidence. Section 9 C.E.A. has allowed witnesses the opportunity to change their story with only restrictive measures available to correct the discrepancy. It is encouraging that the Supreme Court of Canada has recognized this. S.C.C. Justice Cory's comment that s. 9 C.E.A. is an "irrational and unreasonable obstacle" is worth repeating.

The *K.G.B.* case established a logical reasonable alternative to s. 9 C.E.A. to remove these obstacles in prosecutions where a witness has given the police a statement that incriminates the accused person.

The S.C.C., in *R. v. K.G.B.* (1993), created the following new rule of evidence: *An unadopted prior inconsistent statement should be admissible for its truth, if a sufficient guarantee of reliability is proven regarding the prior statement.*

This rule of evidence is another hearsay exception that is derived from the *Khan* principles. The K.G.B. Rule now allows the original witness statement to be admissible, if the witness changes his or her story and refuses to adopt the contents of the initial statement given to the police. The prior statement is not automatically admissible. The Crown must first apply for its admissibility during the trial. A voir dire is then conducted to determine whether the initial statement is admissible. The Crown has the onus to prove that the initial statement given by the witness to the police was reliable. The S.C.C. stated that the "best" ways of proving reliability are by:

- ▸ having the statement made under oath, solemn affirmation, or solemn declaration, following an explicit warning that the witness may be prosecuted if he or she lies,
- ▸ videotaping the statement, and
- ▸ having the statement voluntarily made to the police.

These three ways are the "best" proof, but are not the only methods of successfully proving reliability. The oath and videotape are not mandatory requirements. Proving the statement was voluntary is mandatory only if the statement is made to a police officer. It is not a mandatory requirement if it is made to a citizen or a person not in authority.

The S.C.C. explained the alternatives as follows:

- ▸ The oath is not an absolute requirement for proving reliability. Other circumstances may serve to impress upon the witness the importance of telling the truth. "Other circumstances" have not been defined.
- ▸ It is not always necessary that the statement be videotaped. Instead, the mandatory requirement is that the statement must be "fully and accurately transcribed or recorded." A written statement made in the presence of an independent third party may replace the videotape if the third party testifies that the statement as well as the witness's demeanour was observed.

A Justice of the Peace may administer the oath and the warning, and act as the independent third person who observes the statement. An analysis of *R. v. K.G.B.* explains how the relevant principles and procedures apply.

CASE LAW

R. v. K.G.B. (1993)

Circumstances The accused was a young offender who was charged with second-degree murder. The accused and three companions became involved in an altercation with the deceased and his brother. The victim and his brother were unarmed. During the fight, one of the four persons pulled a knife, slashed the victim's face, and stabbed him in the heart.

About two weeks later, the accused's three companions were interviewed separately by the police. Each was accompanied by a parent and one by a lawyer. The police told each witness that they were not charged with any offence, and added "at this time" in two of the three interviews. The witnesses were informed of the right to counsel and that they were under no obligation to answer questions.

All three witnesses consented to have their interview videotaped. None was under oath at the time of the interviews. All three informed the police that the accused had told them he thought he had used the knife to kill the victim.

At the trial, all three witnesses changed their stories. They admitted having made the statements to the police, but said they had lied about what the accused had told them. The three witnesses testified that they had lied to divert possible blame from themselves and claimed to have forgotten or not heard what the accused had said to them.

The Crown applied to cross-examine them on their prior statements pursuant to s. 9 C.E.A. and the judge allowed it. All three witnesses refused to adopt their original statements made to the police.

The judge made the only possible ruling that was available at the time of the trial. The prior inconsistent statements could not be used as proof that the accused actually made the confessions. The witness's statements were inadmissible because the hearsay rule excluded them. The prior inconsistent statements could be used only regarding the witnesses' credibility that they did not hear the accused's confessions.

The accused was acquitted. The Crown's appeal to the Ontario Court of Appeal was dismissed and the acquittal was upheld. The S.C.C. allowed the Crown's appeal and ordered a new trial. The following rulings were made:

▶ Justice Cory stated: "A trial must always be a quest to discover the truth. Irrational and unreasonable obstacles to the admission of evidence should not impede that quest." The irrational and unreasonable obstacle that he was referring to was the interpretation of s. 9 C.E.A. Justice Cory added, "It must be remembered that a young man died as the result of a senseless stabbing. The community has a real and pressing interest in having the guilt or innocence of the respondent established on the basis of the truth. The earlier acquittal was based upon perjured evidence and upon an interpretation of s. 9 C.E.A. that withheld the truth—in the form of prior inconsistent statements—from the consideration of the trial judge."

▶ The lack of cross-examination is the most important danger of hearsay evidence. However, it is the most overrated in relation to prior inconsistent statements because the person who contradicted the original statement is present in court and subject to cross-examination by both the Crown and the defence.

▸ Based on the *Khan* decision, a new rule of evidence was created by the S.C.C.: *The evidence of prior inconsistent statements of a witness other than an accused should be substantively admissible if necessity and reliability are proved.*

▸ A voir dire is mandatory, without the jury present, to determine necessity and reliability.

▸ The requirements of necessity and reliability have to be adopted and refined to suit the specific problems raised by the nature of these statements. The court did not address the method of proving necessity, but gave a general reason as stated in Justice Cory's remarks. The court stated that no "strict interpretation" of necessity exists and will be established in specific cases.

▸ In addition to proving reliability, the court included another requirement that is not part of the *Khan* principles: *Prior inconsistent statements are admissible only if they had been admissible as the witness's sole testimony.*

The S.C.C. explained this requirement as meaning: "If the witness could not have made the statement at trial during his or her examination-in-chief or cross-examination, for whatever reason, it cannot be made admissible through the back door, as it were, under the reformed prior inconsistent rule." The court provided two situations as examples of this requirement.

Example 1 If the contents of the prior inconsistent statement were entirely hearsay (e.g., Simon said he saw Dan fire the gun), this would not normally have been admissible. Therefore, if the witness denies having told the police hearsay evidence, the prior inconsistent statement cannot be used as proof that Dan fired the gun. However, if the contents of the prior inconsistent statement were direct evidence (e.g., I saw Dan fire the gun), this would normally be admissible. If the witness denies making the statement that he or she saw this, then the contents of the prior inconsistent statement will be proof that Dan fired the gun.

Example 2 If the contents of the prior inconsistent statement are a confession by the accused to the witness, the contents will be admissible as proof that the accused did commit the offence if the confession was obtained properly and would have been normally admissible. Confessions made to persons not in authority (i.e., citizens) are automatically admissible. If the contents of the prior inconsistent statement included this type of confession, then the contents would be admissible if the citizen denies it in court.

However, in some cases the police use the services of *informants*, who are formally called **state agents** or **police agents**, and the police arrange for the informant to talk to the suspect specifically for the purpose of obtaining a confession. A police or state agent can be used by putting him or her in a jail cell area with the accused or by arranging for the informant to talk to the suspect when the suspect is not in custody.

The S.C.C. created the following rules governing prior inconsistent statements that include confessions made to a police agent when the agent later contradicts the statement in court:

▸ If the accused was in custody or detention at the time of the confession, the prior statement of the police agent will be admissible only if the confession was made without "elicitation" by the state agent.

▸ If the accused was not in custody at the time of the confession, the prior inconsistent statement will be admissible, regardless of whether it was "elicited" or not.

Determining **elicitation** requires proof of who initiated the conversation. If the accused initiated the conversation and confessed without prompting, no elicitation occurred. If the state agent initiated the conversation and convinced the accused to confess after the accused had shown the intention to remain silent, then elicitation occurred.

Proof of reliability is the primary determining factor regarding the admissibility of a prior inconsistent statement and is more important regarding this type of hearsay than in others. The reason for the higher standard of reliability proof is that a judge has to choose between two statements from the same witness. In other forms of hearsay, only one statement is at issue. Essentially, reliability will determine whether the judge believes the original statement that the witness saw or heard the relevant evidence, or the testimony that claims nothing was seen or heard.

The best proof of reliability is that the witness was under oath or solemn affirmation at the time of the statement given to the police. Each police station usually has a Justice of the Peace present or readily available to administer the oath. The police officer in charge could be made commissioner for taking an oath and is able to administer the oath to witnesses, too.

The oath is the best proof of reliability, but not the only method. The oath is not a mandatory requirement for admissibility of the prior inconsistent statement. Some other fact or circumstance may compensate for or replace the oath.

In addition to the oath, it is preferable (but not mandatory) to warn the witness that a false statement may result in criminal charges such as perjury, obstructing justice, public mischief, or fabricating evidence. A Justice or commissioner should give this warning.

The second important factor in proving reliability is having a judge or jury evaluate the witness's credibility by observing the witness's demeanour, such as reactions to questions, hesitation, and degree of commitment to the statement being made. The best way of providing this opportunity is by videotaping the witness's statement. Videotaped statements are not mandatory for admissibility. An alternative to videotape is "fully and accurately transcribing or recording" the witness interview in the presence of an independent third party, who observes the making of the statement in its entirety and can later testify about demeanour. The third party may be a Justice of the Peace or the witness's lawyer, parent, or adult relative. The third-party alternative should be used in exceptional cases only. The trial judge has discretion to determine whether a specific substitute for videotape is sufficient to prove reliability.

The S.C.C. noted that the police do not have to videotape every witness statement. This procedure should be done when the witness's character suggests that he or she may later contradict the statement during trial, the offence is serious, and the witness's evidence is crucial to the Crown's case.

The videotape may be made at the time of the original interview or after a written statement is taken and the witness will repeat the original statement on videotape.

The final requirement that proves reliability is voluntariness of the witness statement if the statement was made to a person in authority. Proving voluntariness requires evidence that the interview was free from threats, promises, excessively leading questions, or other forms of investigative misconduct.

In the *K.G.B.* case, the S.C.C. ordered a new trial in which the trial judge would be required to apply the new rule of evidence regarding prior inconsistent statements. The absence of an oath administered to the witnesses in this case would not automatically render the prior inconsistent statements inadmissible. An alternative to the oath is whether the witness may be subject to criminal prosecution for some offence if the statement is false.

TRADITIONAL HEARSAY EXCEPTIONS

Spontaneous Utterance

Traditional exceptions to the hearsay exclusionary rule are those that existed before the *Khan* ruling. They originate in a variety of sources of law including common law.

Res gestae is a Latin term that refers to state of mind. The *res gestae* rule has also been called spontaneous utterances made by a crime victim. The *res gestae* rule is this: *A verbal statement made by a victim to another person, after an offence and before or after the arrival of police, is admissible if the statement was made so clearly in circumstances of spontaneity or involvement in the offence that the possibility of concoction can be disregarded.*[20]

The rule originated in common law and has been confirmed in case law. A *res gestae* statement is made by a crime victim either during the offence or shortly after it. Examples include "put the gun down," "stop hitting me," or "he raped me."

If another person hears the victim make these statements, this type of hearsay is admissible if the victim said it during the offence or spontaneously after the offence.

There is no specific interval that constitutes "spontaneous." The following factors contribute to proving whether a victim's statement was spontaneous:

▸ A spontaneous statement must be part of the "actual transaction."[21]
▸ To be part of the actual transaction, there has to be a close and direct nexus, or connection, between the offence and the statement.[22]
▸ The interval between offence and statement has to be minimal enough to prevent the possibility of fabrication.[23]
▸ A spontaneous statement may also be considered a blurted statement made without time for reflection or thought.[24]
▸ If the victim had time to plan or think about what to say, the statement will not be considered spontaneous.

The crucial element of proving spontaneity is the lack of time and opportunity to plan or think about what to say. The following examples show how to apply the *res gestae* hearsay exception.

EXAMPLE 1

A next-door neighbour is interviewed about a crime that occurred at the neighbour's house. The neighbour did not see the crime, but heard the victim say, "Dennis, don't shoot me." The victim made this statement during the offence without any time to think. The victim's remark is then included in the neighbour's statement, despite the fact that the statement is hearsay. At the trial, the Crown applies to have the victim's statement admissible during the neighbour's testimony. If the judge rules that the statement was made spontaneously, the neighbour will be able to testify about what he or she heard. This evidence will help prove the offender's identity.

EXAMPLE 2

This example involves a victim's statement made (1) after the offence to the police who arrive at the crime scene or (2) to a witness who was present. The statement is hearsay and is usually inadmissible. The circumstances of *R. v. Collins* (1997) provide an excellent example and valuable guidelines relating to spontaneous statements made by the victim after an offence.

CASE LAW

R. v. Collins (1997)

Circumstances The accused was charged with sexual assault. A security guard was working at a construction site and heard a woman screaming, "Get away from me, you bastard" several times. He went to investigate and saw the accused having sex with a woman. The security guard phoned the police, who arrived while the sex was occurring. Upon arrival, the complainant said, "He raped me; he raped me." The accused tried to escape, but was immediately apprehended. He told the police that the sexual encounter was consensual. The police charged him with sexual assault. The complainant was intoxicated, highly emotional, and refused to undergo medical examination.

At the preliminary hearing, the complainant was not called to testify because she had consumed alcohol or drugs. The preliminary hearing was adjourned to another date. The complainant was not called when the preliminary hearing resumed because she was under the influence of some substance and could not recall the incident or speaking to the police. The complainant died a few months later, before the trial.

At the trial, a voir dire into the admissibility of the statements that the security guard heard the victim screaming from the alley was held and the trial judge ruled the statements to be admissible. The security guard testified that the sexual assault had included some aggressiveness.

After a voir dire about the statements made by the victim to the police, the trial judge ruled them admissible. The accused was convicted. The accused's appeal to the British Columbia Court of Appeal was dismissed. The court made the following rulings:

- ▸ The repeated statements "Get away from me, you bastard" were admissible in the security guard's testimony. They occurred during the offence and were strong corroboration of the second statements ("he raped me") made to the police. The possibility of fabrication was disregarded.

- ▸ The victim's statements of "he raped me; he raped me," made to the police were admissible as being part of the *res gestae*. These statements were consistent with the security guard's observations. There was no evidence to suggest that the complainant concocted those statements to the police.

Additionally, the statements met the tests of necessity and reliability according to the *Khan* principles. The complainant's intoxication and refusal to undergo medical examination did not cast any doubt on the reliability of her statements.

Dying Declaration

Dying declarations are traditional hearsay exceptions that existed before the *Khan* case. The rule originated in common law and was confirmed by case law.

A **dying declaration** is defined as a statement made by a homicide victim shortly before the victim's death. Dying declarations may be admissible if the following conditions exist and are proven:

- The person who made the statement must be a victim of (a) first- or second-degree murder, (b) manslaughter, or (c) criminal negligence causing death. Dying declarations may be admissible only in trials regarding these charges.
- The victim believed death was imminent. The victim must have had a settled, hopeless expectation of death. This requires proof that the victim believed there was no hope of recovery. This belief is theorized to have the same effect as an oath. It is presumed that a person would not lie when he or she expects to die. The belief may be proven by what the victim says or by the circumstances.
- Death occurred within a reasonable time after the statement was made. No specific period constitutes reasonable time.
- The victim would have been competent to testify had he or she survived. The factors that affect competency apply such as victim's age (e.g., a child), intoxication, and mental condition.[25]

The following procedure applies in cases where the police arrive at a crime scene in which a seriously injured victim is found:

1. One officer is assigned to accompany the victim to the hospital and write all verbal statements made by the victim verbatim. The notes are made beginning at the crime scene, in the ambulance while en route to the hospital, and at the hospital.
2. The officer notes the times that the statements were made and the time when death was pronounced.
3. An officer interviews all persons who may have possibly spoken to the victim between the time of the offence and the time of death. All of the victim's statements are included verbatim in the witness's written statement.

Present Intentions

The Supreme Court of Canada, in *R. v. Starr* (2000),[26] defined the "present intentions" exception to the hearsay rule as: Evidence of a statement made by a person who has since died is admissible to prove the state of mind or present intentions of the deceased person at the time of making the statement.

This rule applies as follows:

- A "present intentions" statement must be made by a person who later dies as the result of an offence. In other words, it applies to a homicide victim.
- Anything that a homicide victim said prior to death to another person is hearsay evidence. For example, if a person is interviewed during a

homicide investigation about any conversation that he or she had with the victim at any time prior to the victim's death, whatever conversation is reported by the person interviewed represents hearsay evidence, which is generally inadmissible.

▶ If the victim had said the statement in a "natural manner and not under circumstances of suspicion," and the statements demonstrated his or her state of mind or present intention at the time the statement was made, the statement will be admissible as an exception to the hearsay rule. In other words, the person who heard the victim say the statement will be able to testify about it in court. The Crown has to prove that these conditions exist. The trial judge has the discretion to admit or exclude the victim's statement.

▶ A statement by a victim prior to death is *inadmissible* if it implies the state of mind, character, or subsequent actions of the accused rather than the victim. In other words, a victim's statement cannot be used to prove the accused person's state of mind; it can only be used to prove the victim's state of mind.

Two examples of "present intentions" were given in *R. v. Starr* (2000):

▶ **Example 1** If the victim had at some time prior to his death told another person "I'm going to Ottawa," that statement would be admissible because it proved the *victim's intention* about where he was going and the statement was made naturally and casually. Additionally, that statement did not imply any other person's state of mind, including the accused person's.

▶ **Example 2** If the victim told a friend that he intended to commit a scam with the person who later was accused of killing him and that statement was considered odd by the friend because the victim usually did not discuss those topics. The statement would be ruled inadmissible for two reasons. First, it implied the accused person's state of mind and intentions. Second, the out-of-character nature of the statement would be deemed to have been "suspicious circumstances."

Procedure: Applying Hearsay Exceptions

The Khan Rule and the case law decisions that have derived from it have significantly changed the content of witness statements of both police officers and citizens. Before the Khan Rule, witness statements consisted generally of what was seen and heard, but not what was said to have happened (as told to the police). Hearsay was generally eliminated from witness statements.

Since the Khan Rule, hearsay should be included in certain witness statements. The following is a summary of circumstances where hearsay may be included in witness statements:

1. **Children** Victims and witnesses under 14 years of age report offences to a number of people, including parents, family members, teachers, doctors, social workers, and the police. Whatever a child reports that he or she heard or saw should be included in the statement of the person who received the hearsay. Additionally, the statement should include

> ▷ the time and place of the statement,
> ▷ the conversation that resulted in the child's report, and
> ▷ any questions and comments made to the child during the child's report.

2. **Deceased person** Investigation that involves the death of a victim or witness should include

> ▷ the victim's statement to any person (police or citizen) immediately before death, and
> ▷ statements made to anyone at any time before death that are relevant to any fact-in-issue, such as offender's identity and possible motives.

3. **Persons who may change their story** Experience, logic, and intuition will create suspicion about witnesses who are candidates to contradict their statement to police by denying it in court. When contradiction is anticipated, have a Justice swear the witness under oath before the interview, warn the witness of the criminal liability of intentionally misleading the police, and videotape the interview. As an alternative to videotape, have a Justice witness the entire interview and record the entire statement, including the witness's demeanour.

   Although anyone is capable of this, the following are groups of people who have a tendency to be uncooperative during a trial:

> ▷ *co-accused persons and accomplices* Many investigations rely on statements provided by co-accuseds who implicate each other regarding the same offence. While awaiting the trial, they may succumb to various sources of pressure to deny their observations.
> ▷ *family members, relatives, and friends* During investigations, the family, including common-law spouses, girlfriends, and boyfriends, give statements implicating the accused to alleviate fear and prevent reoccurrence of crimes they have suffered. As the trial approaches, they change their mind to protect the accused from jail.
> ▷ *uncooperative eyewitnesses* The conduct of certain eyewitnesses, for example, a reluctance to give information or to attend court, will cause obvious suspicion.

4. **Spontaneous utterances** Interview all persons who were in proximity to the offence immediately before, during, and immediately after the offence regardless of whether they saw the actual crime. Include every verbal statement that they heard the victim make in the witnesses' written statements.

Case Study 9.1 Conclusion

During the Crown's examination-in-chief of Craig's testimony, Craig contradicted the original signed, written statement he had given to the police by testifying that he did not sell the stolen property to Eric. The trial was held in provincial court; no jury, therefore, was present. The Crown applied, under s. 9(2) of the *Canada Evidence Act*, to have Craig declared an adverse witness so that he could be cross-examined by the Crown. The statement was presented to the trial judge and a conflict was ruled as existing. The onus fell upon the Crown to prove the statement. Craig admitted making the statement to police. He admitted to the portion of the statement in which he incriminated himself regarding the break, enter, and theft. He did not admit to the portion where he implicated Eric as being the purchaser of stolen property. Craig did not claim that the police officers fabricated that portion of the statement.

Eric was acquitted. The portion of Craig's original statement that he contradicted was inadmissible because of his failure to adopt it at the trial.

COMMENTARY   This trial occurred before the *R. v. Khan* decision. Had it occurred after, the officers may have been able to testify, under the *Khan* hearsay exception, about the contents of the original statement Craig had made.

ENDNOTES

1. *R. v. Stinchcombe* (1991), 68 C.C.C. (3d) 91 (S.C.C.).
2. *R. v. Blackman*, 2008 SCC 37.
3. *R. v. McInroy and Rouse* (1978), 42 C.C.C. (2d) 481 (S.C.C.); *Cloutier v. The Queen* (1979), 48 C.C.C. (2d) 1 (S.C.C.).
4. *R. v. Khan* (1990), 59 C.C.C. (3d) 92 (S.C.C.).
5. *R. v. Rockey* (1996), 110 C.C.C. (3d) 481 (S.C.C.).
6. *R. v. G.N.D.* (1993), 81 C.C.C. (3d) 65 (Ont. C.A.).
7. *R. v. Smith* (1992), 75 C.C.C. (3d) 257 (S.C.C.).
8. *R. v. K.G.B.* (1993), 79 C.C.C. (3d) 257, at 322 (S.C.C.).
9. *Wawanesa Mutual Insurance Co. v. Hanes* (1963), 1 C.C.C. 176 (Ont. C.A.).
10. *R. v. Coffin* (1956), 114 C.C.C. 1, at 22–24 (S.C.C.).
11. *Wawanesa Mutual Insurance Co. v. Hanes*, supra note 9; D. Dukelow and B. Nuse, *Pocket Dictionary of Canadian Law* (Toronto: Carswell, 1991).
12. Dukelow and Nuse, supra note 11.
13. Section 9(2) C.E.A.
14. P.K. McWilliams, *Canadian Criminal Evidence*, 3rd ed. (Aurora, ON: Canada Law Book, 1991).
15. Section 9(1) C.E.A.
16. *R. v. Milgaard* (1971), 2 C.C.C. (2d) 206 (Sask. C.A.).
17. Ibid.
18. *Wawanesa Mutual Insurance Co. v. Hanes*, supra note 9.
19. *R. v. Handy* (1978), 45 C.C.C. (2d) 232 (B.C.C.A.).
20. *R. v. Collins* (1997), 118 C.C.C. (3d) 514 (B.C.C.A.).
21. Ibid.
22. Ibid.
23. Ibid.
24. Ontario Ministry of the Solicitor General, Ontario Police College, *Evidence for Senior Police Officers: Book 2* (Toronto: Queen's Printer, 1984).
25. Ibid.
26. *R. v. Starr* (2000), 147 C.C.C. (3d) 449 (S.C.C.).

CHAPTER 10

Rules of Evidence, Part 2: Character and Communications

LEARNER SUMMARY

The hearsay rule of evidence is the first of three fundamental exclusionary rules, which also include opinion evidence and bad character evidence (such as similar acts and facts).

Additional rules of evidence that affect the admissibility of evidence include "privileged communication," such as

- privilege against self-incrimination,
- lawyer–client privilege, and
- Crown privilege relating to informants.

TV and movies are the worst place to learn the rules of evidence that govern privileged communication. For example, in Hollywood, witnesses give outrageous opinions and refuse to answer questions. Canadian rules of evidence are significantly different from and far more complex than the Hollywood version. This chapter interprets and applies these rules as they relate to investigative strategies.

Case Study 10.1

The Rowing Club is situated at the end of a dead-end street; Jill lives in a house next door to it (see Figure 10.1 on the following page). At 2 a.m., an alarm is activated at the Rowing Club. You are a uniform patrol officer. You are on King Street at the time of the alarm. The following events occur:

2:00 a.m. You hear radio broadcast 1 stating that an alarm was activated. You are not dispatched there. It is not in your patrol district.

2:04 a.m. You hear radio broadcast 2 stating that police officer 1 arrived at the scene.

2:06 a.m. You hear radio broadcast 3 from police officer 1 stating the following:

- a side door was forced open
- an interior search for suspects was negative

Figure 10.1

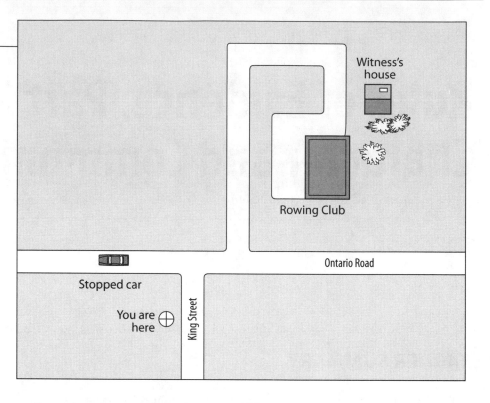

- ▸ the cash register was forced open and 50 cents was in it
- ▸ the parking lot is all mud
- ▸ Jill, the next-door neighbour, is interviewed
- ▸ Jill saw a green Toyota leaving the Rowing Club about 2 a.m. Plate number unknown. Two men were in the car. No identification possible. No description.

2:08 a.m. Dispatcher calls Rowing Club management.

2:15 a.m. Rowing Club owner arrives and informs police officer 1 that

- ▸ an employee had told him that she had locked up at 11 p.m.
- ▸ $100.50 was in the cash register
- ▸ the doors and cash register were not damaged

2:26 a.m. You are stopped at a red light at King Street and Ontario Road. A green Toyota is travelling toward you on Ontario Road. It continues through the intersection. Two men are in the car. You turn left and stop the car on Ontario Road. You approach the driver's door, look inside, and see that both men have mud on their shoes and pants.

(Refer to the end of Chapter 10 for the conclusion of this case study.)

OPINION EVIDENCE

An **opinion** is defined in case law as any inference made from observed facts.[1] An **inference** is a personal belief or conclusion that is not positively known to be an accurate fact.

The rule of opinion evidence is that opinions are generally inadmissible. Witnesses may testify only about what they directly observed, not what they inferred or concluded. The opinion exclusionary rule originated in common law and has been confirmed by case law.[2]

There are three reasons why opinions are generally inadmissible:

1. Opinions are irrelevant, especially when the subject requires expertise.
2. A witness who merely states an opinion cannot be prosecuted for perjury.
3. Opinions would replace the function of a judge and jury.

A jury, in particular, may be "tempted to blindly accept a witness's opinion." The judge and jury are responsible for forming inferences based on facts presented to them by witnesses. This principle forms the basis for the **ultimate issue doctrine**, which states that an opinion can never be admissible when that opinion "touches the very issue before the jury." The following rules summarize these concepts: *the function of the judge and jury is to draw inferences and conclusions; a witness's role is to state facts.*[3]

Exceptions to the Opinion Rule

There are several exceptions to the opinion rule, referring to inferences or conclusions that are admissible. These are investigative advantages because they expand the type of evidence that can be used to prove an offence.

Interpretation of opinion exceptions begins with classifying opinions into two categories:

1. **Non-expert opinion** Inferences based on ordinary daily experience about matters that require no special skill or knowledge, "where it is virtually impossible to separate the witness's inference from the facts on which the inference is based."[4] Most citizens and police officers are non-experts.
2. **Expert opinion** Inferences based on specialized skill and knowledge, made by a witness who is an expert.

NON-EXPERT OPINION

The issue of what constitutes an excluded non-expert opinion and an admissible exception has historically been inconsistent. The two most prominent and frequently quoted decisions that have established guidelines about non-expert opinions are *R. v. Graat* (1982) by the Supreme Court of Canada,[5] and *R. v. German* (1947) by the Ontario Court of Appeal.[6]

Six factors determine whether a non-expert opinion is admissible or excluded:

1. **Ultimate issue doctrine** According to this principle, an opinion is never admissible if the opinion is the "very issue before the jury."[7]
2. **Relevance** An exception to the opinion rule must be relevant to at least one fact-in-issue of the offence that the accused is charged with.[8]
3. **Accuracy** To be admissible, there must be a "virtual impossibility [of separating] the witness's inference from the facts on which the inference is based." This means that there should be no possibility of the person making the opinion to grossly misperceive the facts and arrive at an illogical or unreasonable inference. The facts that need to be analyzed should require no special skill or knowledge. There should be no possibility of making an inaccurate opinion.[9]
4. **Justification** An admissible non-expert opinion must be justified. It must be based on facts that required analysis to form logical reasons that prove

why the opinion was made. An inference that is made without analyzing some facts is a baseless inference. A *baseless inference* is an inference or conclusion made for no reason and with no justification. Baseless inferences actually are not opinions, because the inference was not made on an analysis of facts. Baseless inferences are inadmissible.[10]

5. **Special skill and knowledge** A non-expert's opinion is inadmissible if the opinion is about a matter that requires the special skill and knowledge of an expert.[11]

6. **Ordinary knowledge** A non-expert's opinion is admissible if the matter requires only ordinary knowledge and intelligence based on personal daily experience.

Admissibility of Non-Expert Opinion

Determining the admissibility of a non-expert's opinion is based on the combined effect of the preceding six factors. Examples of non-expert opinions that are inadmissible follow:

1. **The accused person's thoughts** A non-expert cannot state an opinion about what the accused was thinking, especially what he or she was thinking during the offence. In other words, a non-expert cannot give an opinion about the accused's intentions, such as, "It wasn't an accident. He meant to do it."

2. **The accused's person's nature** A non-expert cannot testify about how a person might act or behave because of his or her nature. In other words, opinions such as "She's the type of person who would steal," or "He has a bad temper. He's the type of person who would kill someone,"[12] are inadmissible.

3. **Legal issues such as negligence** A non-expert cannot offer opinions about legal issues such as negligence. That opinion, "would not qualify as an abbreviated version of the witness's factual observations."[13] Paraphrasing, such as saying "She was negligent while driving" is not permitted. Legal issues such as negligence are conclusions reserved for a judge or jury. Instead of paraphrasing, the witness can state only factual observations.

4. **Mental conditions** A non-expert cannot testify about opinions regarding sanity or other psychological problems. For example, a non-expert cannot testify that "He must have been suffering from mental problems." An expert's opinion is required from a psychiatrist or psychologist.

5. **Credibility** A non-expert cannot testify about whether a person is truthful or deceptive. Credibility is an issue decided by a judge or jury. For example, a non-expert cannot say, "I think she was telling the truth."[14]

6. **Scientific matters** Issues such as ballistic, bodily substance, and physical item comparisons require the special skill and knowledge of a scientist.

7. **Injuries** A doctor is required to give expert opinions about medical issues such as injuries.

The Supreme Court of Canada in *R. v. Graat* (1982) stated that "The line between fact and opinion is not clear."[15] The court recognized that exceptions to the opinion rule exist and that non-experts are allowed to give certain opinions during testimony. The S.C.C. adopted the principles created in *R. v. German* (1947), which permit non-expert opinions under the following conditions:

1. "Where the primary facts and the inferences to be drawn from them are so closely associated that the opinion is really a compendious way of giving evidence as to certain facts."[16] *Compendious* means giving information concisely. This means that an opinion is admissible when it summarizes the observed facts. An example is intoxication. A witness describes a person's observed physical symptoms and may summarize the condition as intoxication because the inference and the observed facts are closely related.

2. Matters about which a person of ordinary intelligence has learned through personal knowledge based on daily experience and that do not require specialized skill or knowledge.

Based on these two principles, the following are examples of non-expert opinions that are admissible:

- **Intoxication** Testimony about intoxication is an opinion. The opinion must be preceded by reasons such as specific physical symptoms observed that justify the opinion.[17]

- **Degree of intoxication** An opinion is allowed about whether the intoxication was slight, moderate, or advanced.[18]

- **Ability to drive was impaired** The S.C.C. in *R. v. Graat* ruled that an opinion that a person's ability to drive was impaired is admissible because it represents a degree of intoxication.[19]

- **Sobriety** An opinion of sobriety is admissible and proved by the absence of physical symptoms that imply intoxication. Again, the person's physical condition must be described first before giving the opinion.[20]

- **Identity of a person** A witness identifies an accused in court by means of facial recognition. The witness points to the accused and testifies, "That's her." Proving identity by facial recognition represents an opinion. The credibility and value of this opinion are strengthened if it is justified by the reasons for making the facial recognition. Justification is made by describing the accused's general and specific characteristics during testimony before the actual recognition is made. The opinion's value diminishes significantly if the identification is made without supporting reasons.[21]

- **Voice recognition** When a non-expert witness testifies that a voice heard was a certain person, an opinion is being expressed. Voice recognition is admissible if the witness proves significant familiarity with the accused person's voice. There is no specific method of proving familiarity (i.e., number of times the voice was heard previously or length of time that the accused's was known to the witness). The witness explains how familiarity was obtained. The judge decides case by case.[22]

- **Handwriting** A non-expert opinion about the author of a written document may be admissible if the witness proves familiarity with the person's handwriting through regular or frequent correspondence or exposure to that person's writing. There is no specific method of proving familiarity. It is decided case by case.[23]

- **Apparent age of a person**[24]
- **Estimated speed of a vehicle**[25]
- **Estimated distance, size, and time**[26]

In *R. v. Graat*, the S.C.C. added a general procedural rule about determining the admissibility of a non-expert's opinion: *The trial judge must exercise a large measure of discretion.*[27]

The expanded discretion given to a trial judge represents an investigative advantage by removing restrictions to a limited set of circumstances. Therefore, relevant, justified opinions should be included in witness statements. The Crown will argue for its admissibility based on the *Graat* guidelines.

The S.C.C. created another rule relating to non-expert opinions that should be viewed as an investigative advantage: *The opinions of citizens and police officers have equivalent value.*[28] A citizen's opinion does not have lesser value than a police officer's opinion. The advantage lies in the fact that police rely on citizens as witnesses to prove cases. The police can consider a citizen's opinion to have the same value as an officer's. This expands the available evidence to help prove a case.

Finally, the use of inadmissible non-expert opinions should not be disregarded. Both admissible and inadmissible evidence may be used to form reasonable grounds. Additionally, both types of evidence simply help form suspicions during the early stages of an investigation and create a base from which reasonable grounds develop.

EXPERT WITNESS

An **expert witness** is a person who has acquired special knowledge about a subject through experience derived from scientific work or practical observation. A university degree is not a mandatory prerequisite; it is only a contributory factor that may prove expertise.[29]

Opinions by expert witnesses may be admissible about topics relating to their expertise. A witness must be declared an expert by the trial judge. No witness is automatically granted expert status. The witness must be called to the stand during the trial. A hearing is conducted before the witness testifies, to determine whether he or she is an expert. The side that called the witness attempts to prove the witness's expertise through the witness's verbal testimony regarding his or her qualifications and experience. The judge rules whether or not the witness is an expert afterward. If a witness is declared an expert once, he or she is not automatically granted expert status at future trials; a hearing must be conducted before testimony at every trial.[30]

The Crown and the defence are both allowed five expert witnesses at a criminal trial; both sides may request permission to call additional expert witnesses.[31] Examples of people commonly declared experts include:

1. **Psychiatrists** Psychiatrists typically give admissible opinions about sanity, but other topics may also be addressed. An example of a psychiatrist's admissible opinion is found in *R. v. Lavalee* (1990).[32] In this case, the accused person was charged with murder. She shot her common-law husband in the back of the head after he threatened her and assaulted her. Section 34(2) *Criminal Code* establishes a defence for murder only if the person is under reasonable apprehension of death or grievous bodily harm. The issue in this case was whether an assault and a threat justified the murder. At the trial, a psychiatrist gave an opinion that the accused's history of being assaulted by her common-law husband caused her to suffer *battered wife syndrome*, which was relevant to explain that the accused

> ⊳ perceived the danger posed by the assault and threat as a reasonable apprehension of death, and
> ⊳ remained in the relationship and did not flee from it, despite past assaults upon her.

The Supreme Court of Canada ruled that this opinion was admissible.

2. **Breathalyzer operators** The operator may give expert opinion about an accused person's blood alcohol content at the time of a Breathalyzer test, but not at the time the accused drove.
3. **Identification (Ident.) officers** An Ident. officer may give expert opinions about physical evidence comparison (i.e., fingerprints, shoe prints).
4. **Doctors** Doctors are needed to give expert opinion about injuries.
5. **Forensic scientists** These are persons with the expert knowledge needed to make comparisons regarding physical evidence such as bodily substances, fibres, firearms and ammunition, and impression evidence caused by items such as tools.
6. **Toxicologists** A toxicologist may give an expert opinion about the blood-alcohol level of a motorist at the time the motorist drove.

■ KEY POINTS

1. Expert opinion has significant evidentiary value.
2. When these issues need to be proven during an investigation, an expert is required to conduct the examination or comparison.
3. Expert opinions, such as comparisons, are strong evidence but they are still opinions. This means they are not 100-percent positive and can be refuted. Defence lawyers can diminish the credibility of expert opinions by cross-examination.

BAD CHARACTER EVIDENCE

Bad character evidence is the accused's past behaviour, conduct, and acts that show he or she is the type of person likely to have committed the offence the accused is charged with.[33] Bad character includes a wide range of past behaviour and acts such as convictions of criminal offences, violence, substance abuse, and other relevant misconduct. The Crown and police seek to introduce bad character evidence during the trial to prove that the accused has a tendency or habit toward committing criminal acts and the likelihood that the accused committed the offence that he or she is charged with at a specific trial.

The bad character rule of evidence is as follows:

- ▸ Generally, bad character evidence is inadmissible during the trial.
- ▸ The Crown is generally not permitted to introduce evidence of specific acts for the sole purpose of showing that the accused is the type of person likely to have committed the offence in question.[34]

This rule originated in common law and has been confirmed by the Supreme Court of Canada in case law in two prominent cases: *R. v. B. (F.F.)* (1993)[35] and *Morris v. The Queen* (1983).[36]

The primary use of bad character evidence is to introduce it after the trial and before sentencing as part of the Crown's sentence submission. However, exceptions exist that allow bad character to be introduced by the Crown during the trial.

Bad Character Exceptions

Exceptions to the bad character rule allow bad character evidence to be admissible during the trial. Some specific exceptions are found in statutory provisions in the *Criminal Code* and *Canada Evidence Act*. Additionally, the Supreme Court of Canada created a general case law exception. The most common statutory exceptions are:

- s. 666 C.C.
- s. 12 C.E.A.
- s. 360 C.C.

SECTION 666 C.C.

The Crown may introduce the accused's previous convictions for any offences during a trial if the defence introduces evidence of the accused's good character. The defence may introduce good character evidence in any one of three methods:

1. asking a Crown witness during cross-examination,
2. examination-in-chief of a defence witness, or
3. examination-in-chief of the accused.

The introduction of bad character evidence by the Crown is dependent on the defence introducing good character evidence first. Good character does not include some personal attribute. It does include evidence of the accused's reputation in the community.[37] This section allows the Crown to introduce evidence of previous convictions only, not other past misconduct that did not result in a conviction.[38]

SECTION 12 C.E.A.

Any witness who testifies, including the accused if he or she chooses to do so, may be questioned about past convictions for any offence, including criminal and provincial, and the sentence that was imposed.[39] The arresting officer should do a CPIC check relating to all Crown witnesses and include copies of witnesses' past convictions in the Crown brief to alert the prosecutor and prevent unexpected introduction of past convictions by the defence. The Crown needs prior knowledge of witnesses' convictions to prepare properly. The Crown is allowed to introduce the witness's record during examination-in-chief to show a jury that no attempt is being made to conceal it.[40]

Doing so may diminish the negative effect that the past convictions will have on witness credibility.

SECTION 360 C.C.

If the accused is charged with possession of property obtained by crime, whether over or under $5000, and the Crown successfully proves that the accused had possession of the item, the Crown may introduce the accused's past convictions involving theft or possession of property obtained by crime that occurred during the past five years before proceedings were commenced (charge was laid). The accused must receive notice in writing, at least three days before the trial, that the Crown intends to introduce these previous convictions.

The evidence of prior convictions is considered for the purpose of proving the accused's knowledge that the property he or she possessed was unlawfully obtained. Convictions involving theft include break and enter and robbery. The past convictions cannot be introduced until the Crown has proven possession during the trial.

GENERAL CASE LAW EXCEPTION

The Supreme Court of Canada in *R. v. B. (F.F.)* (1993) created the following general exception to the bad character exclusionary rule: "evidence of bad character is admissible if it is relevant to an issue in a case and if the probative value of such evidence outweighs its prejudicial effect."[41]

This rule gives general discretion to a trial judge to allow bad character evidence if two factors exist:

1. The bad character evidence proves at least one fact-in-issue of a case.
2. The evidentiary value of the bad character evidence is more important than the bias it creates to the fairness of the accused's trial.

This general rule affects the admissibility of another exception called *similar acts and facts*.

Similar Acts and Facts

This exception to the bad character rule originated in common law. **Similar acts and facts** are defined as past conduct and circumstances that show a pattern of conduct, plan, or scheme that is so closely associated to the circumstances of the offence that the accused is charged with that it helps prove identity or intent.

The S.C.C. in *R. v. Guay* (1978) confirmed the similar acts and facts exception and summarized the rule as follows: "similar acts is admissible to show plan, scheme, or pattern of conduct which would rebut a defence of accident, lack of intent, lack of knowledge, innocent association or any other defence that might otherwise be open to the accused, such as good character."[42]

Similar-act evidence may apply to any criminal offence. It is admissible to refute an accused's defence that he lacked the intent to commit the offence or had innocent participation. Similar acts may be introduced during the Crown's case or in response to the defence's case.

Admissibility depends on whether the past acts prove that the accused has done the same thing so often and under such similar circumstances that it would be reasonable to infer the accused did commit the current offence intentionally and that the past conduct was not a coincidence.[43]

Similar acts must be strongly associated with the current offence to show a method of operation that becomes identifiable with the accused. The past conduct must show a repetitive uniqueness associated with the accused.[44]

Although similar-act evidence applies to any criminal offence, it is most commonly used in break and enter, robbery, and sexual assault investigations. Experience has shown that repeat offenders form habits that become an investigative advantage. For example, offenders often commit break and enters in a series of large numbers. One person, or a group, often commit 10, 20, or more over a few weeks. They often form habits and commit these offences in the same manner, including:

- ▸ **Method of entry** Some break-and-enter offenders prefer certain points of entry, tools to force entry, and actual method of entering.
- ▸ **Type of place** Some offenders prefer houses or businesses, and specific types of businesses.
- ▸ **Nature of items stolen** Preferences are formed about what thieves steal. Some prefer electronic equipment while others prefer jewellery. Their preferences are formed by their easiest method of selling the items.
- ▸ **Time of day or night** Some offenders have confessed a preference for a certain time to commit a break and enter.
- ▸ **Accomplices** Some offenders work alone, others with the same accomplices.
- ▸ **Method of transportation** These habits become similar to an offender's signature and significantly help identify the offender.

An example of how the general case law exception is applied relating to similar acts is found in *R. v. B. (F.F.)* (1993), the case where the S.C.C. established the general exception. The accused was charged with sexual assault. The offences occurred during a 10-year period while the accused lived with the complainant and her family. The complainant never made a formal complaint during that time. She formally complained to the police 25 years after the sexual abuse ended. At the trial, the judge admitted evidence of the violence and control the accused exercised over the complainant and her family. This evidence was admitted to explain why the abuse was allowed to continue without police intervention.

The S.C.C. ruled that the bad character evidence was properly admitted because the value of the evidence outweighed the prejudicial effect that the evidence would have on the fairness of the trial. The S.C.C. stated that the bad character evidence showed that the accused had a propensity for violence. It was relevant to several serious issues in the case, such as the defence of innocent association and the system of violent control that the accused exercised over the family.

If an investigation reveals past acts or conduct that show a pattern of repetitive uniqueness, include this evidence in written statements of people who directly observed these acts. The Crown must be informed of the accused's criminal record and any past behaviour that is reasonably relevant to the offence that the accused is charged with. The Crown is then responsible for applying and arguing for its admission at the trial.

In summary, the investigating officer should not make the decision to leave out seemingly irrelevant bad character evidence. The case law general exception gives the trial judge broad discretionary powers that could result in the admission of substantial and significant evidence of past conduct.

APPLYING SIMILAR-ACT EVIDENCE TO PROVE IDENTITY

A ruling made by the BC Court of Appeal in *R. v. Mattie* (2002) illustrates an excellent example of how "similar acts" evidence proves the identity of an offender.

The accused person was charged with two counts of robbery, one count of having his face masked with intent to commit an indictable offence, and one count of possession of a dangerous weapon. The circumstances were as follows:

Two robberies occurred about three hours apart; the first at 7:10 a.m., the second at 10:00 a.m. In the first robbery, the offender was armed with a baseball bat. He used the bat to hit the shop counter several times, demanded money, stole between $200 and $300, and left in a vehicle.

The shopkeeper and a customer described the offender as 5'10" or 5'11"; one said he was skinny, the other said he had a medium build; he wore a mask and a dark jacket; the offender's car was a black Jimmy truck bearing B.C. licence plate FLR 637.

During the second robbery, the offender threw a baseball bat at the shopkeeper, stole the cash register, and fled in a black Jeep 4×4 bearing B.C. licence plate FLR 637. The offender was described as being 5'8" to 5'10" tall, wore a mask, had shoulder-length blond hair, and had white skin.

At 10:20 a.m., the police stopped the offender's vehicle. He was male, white, 5'9" to 5'10" tall, 170 to 180 pounds, had shoulder-length reddish blond hair with a full beard; wore a dark jacket; and had two toques in his car. The offender did not confess.

This was a circumstantial case that focused on identity as the main issue. The trial judge convicted the accused by applying the similar-act rule of evidence to prove the offender's identity in the first robbery. The eight similar circumstances that led to proof of identity and the conviction were:

1. **Type of place** Both robberies occurred in a small grocery store.
2. **Type of vehicle** A black GMC Jimmy bearing B.C. licence plate FLR 637 drove up to each store and parked in front.
3. **Number of offenders** One man entered each store while another man waited in the driver's seat of the parked vehicle.
4. **Type of disguise** The robber wore a mask or toque with eyeholes in it.
5. **Type of weapon** The robber was armed with a baseball bat in both cases.
6. **Skin colour** The robber wore no gloves; he had white skin in both offences.
7. **Height** The offender's description of height was between 5'8" and 5'11" tall.
8. **Build** The robber's build was described as medium or slim.

Additionally, the short time frame between the two robberies and between the second robbery and the time of arrest were both relevant considering the extent of similar elements.

The BC Court of Appeal dismissed the accused's appeal and upheld the convictions. The court ruled that the similar-act evidence in relation to the second conviction was properly admitted at the trial. The determining factor that a court considers when deciding to admit or exclude similar-act evidence is whether the "probative force" (evidentiary value) outweighs the "prejudicial effect" (unfairness to the accused) regarding the interests of the "good administration of justice."

In this case, the BC Court of Appeal ruled that the similar-act evidence did have some "prejudicial effect" against the accused but the "probative value" outweighed the prejudicial effect.

THE SIGNIFICANCE OF INADMISSIBLE EVIDENCE TO REASONABLE GROUNDS

The Ontario Court of Appeal in *R. v. Debot* (1986)[45] stated that inadmissible evidence may be used as a contributory factor to form reasonable grounds, if the evidence exceeds mere suspicion, gossip, or rumour. The court specifically stated that:

> ▸ Hearsay evidence may constitute reasonable grounds.
> ▸ Bad character evidence may be a relevant factor constituting part of the entire circumstances that form reasonable grounds. However, a person's reputation alone constitutes only mere suspicion and is insufficient to form reasonable grounds. As an example, the court ruled that a person's reputation for using and trafficking narcotics does not, by itself, constitute reasonable grounds to believe that the person has possession of narcotics, but it may contribute to reasonable grounds formulation when combined with other evidence.

PRIVILEGED COMMUNICATIONS

A competent and compellable witness generally cannot refuse to answer questions during testimony at a trial. She or he generally must answer all questions that are relevant to any fact-in-issue.

Privileged communication is information that a witness may legally refuse to disclose in court without facing consequences. A **privilege** refers to an option that a witness may exercise to withhold relevant information in court. In other words, it is a legal method of refusing to answer a relevant question, thereby concealing relevant information during a trial.

The Supreme Court of Canada, in *R. v. McClure* (2001),[46] defined "privileged communications" and explained the two categories that they fall into. The court defined privileged communication as legally recognized confidential communications that are protected to serve a public interest.

According to the S.C.C., two categories of privileged communications are recognized:

1. class privilege, and
2. case-by-case privilege.

Class privilege refers to a "blanket" confidentiality afforded by common law to what is communicated about criminal offences within certain types of relationships, including:

> ▸ solicitor (lawyer)–client,
> ▸ spouse–spouse, and
> ▸ police–informant.

A "presumption of admissibility" exists in *criminal court* relating to relevant communications that occur within their relationships. This means that:

- incriminating communication about a criminal offence made by a client to a lawyer or by a spouse to his or her spouse is *generally* protected; the recipient of the incriminating communication cannot *generally* be compelled to testify in criminal court about what was communicated; and
- the identity of an informant who tells the police confidential information pertaining to a criminal offence *generally* is protected and does not have to be revealed in criminal court.

There are exceptions to the blanket protection afforded to these relationships that will be discussed later in this chapter. Consequently, the communication between these people, or the identity of a police informant, is automatically inadmissible unless the other side (Crown or defence) can serve the conditions of an exception that will negate the confidentiality.

Case-by-case privilege refers to a confidentiality that *may* be afforded, but not in all cases. In other words, there is no blanket protection provided; the issue of confidentiality will be decided on a case-by-case basis.

Examples of relationships where incriminating communication about criminal offences is *not automatically protected* and *not automatically inadmissible* include:

- doctor–patient,
- psychiatrist–patient,
- clergy–penitent (religious communication), and
- journalist–informant.

It must be emphasized that the unprotected confidentiality relates to *incriminating communication about criminal offences*, not to other communication.

The S.C.C. in *R. v. McClure* (2001) listed four criteria that must be proved to protect the communication within these relationships:

1. The communications must "originate in a confidence that they will not be disclosed."
2. This "element of confidentiality must be essential to the full and satisfactory maintenance of the relation between the parties."
3. The relation must be "one which in the *opinion of the community* ought to be sedulously fostered."
4. "The injury that would inure to the relation by the disclosure of the communication must be greater than the benefit thereby gained for the correct disposal of litigation."

There is an investigative benefit and significance to the case-by-case privilege: If an offender communicates incriminating statements about a criminal offence to a doctor, psychiatrist, or clergy member, subpoena the recipient of the communication to testify at the criminal trial.

The absence of blanket protection and confidentiality combined with the extent of circumstances that have to be proved to acquire confidentiality results in the probability that the incriminating communication received by the doctor, psychiatrist, or clergy member will be admissible in criminal court. If admissible, the recipient of the communication cannot refuse to disclose the communication and must testify about the contents of the communication.

Self-Incrimination

Occasionally, a witness may be asked a question during testimony at a trial that may require a self-incriminating answer, which refers to an admission or confession of guilt regarding an offence. The witness in this case must answer the question and has no legal privilege or choice to refuse giving an answer; answering is mandatory.[47]

However, witnesses are automatically protected under s. 13 of the Charter in relation to the future use of a self-incriminating answer. A witness's self-incriminating answer given at a proceeding cannot be used as admissible evidence in any other proceedings, except at a trial for perjury. In other words, if a witness admits or confesses to committing an offence while testifying, that response or statement is inadmissible at a future trial if the witness is charged with the offence that the confession related to.

Any other proceeding includes:

▸ A new trial of the same offence that may be ordered by a Court of Appeal.[48]
▸ A voir dire. Any self-incriminating testimony made by a witness or an accused is inadmissible at the trial that the confession related to. A voir dire is another proceeding separate from the trial.[49]

This protection is automatically granted by s. 13 Charter, meaning that the witness need not make an objection or request protection. The creation of the *Charter of Rights* in 1982 essentially made s. 5(2) C.E.A. redundant. Section 5(2) C.E.A. offers similar protection, but the witness must first object to answering the question.

Note that the protection against self-incrimination does not extend to an accused person's admission or confession made during testimony relating to the charge at his or her current trial. If an accused testifies at his or her trial, it is based on free will; no one may compel the accused to testify. If an accused wishes to avoid questioning, the accused may simply choose not to testify. Additionally, the self-incrimination protection extends only to other proceedings, not to the same proceeding.

Spousal Privilege

In cases where a spouse is competent to testify against his or her spouse, the testifying spouse cannot be compelled to disclose any communication made by the accused spouse during a lawful marriage. The testifying spouse has the privilege to refuse to testify about any communication received from the accused spouse during a lawful marriage. The testifying spouse may choose to disclose the communications, but the privilege or choice belongs to the testifying spouse, not to the accused.[50]

If the police lawfully seize a document written by the accused to his or her spouse, the written document may be admissible.[51] The privilege does not extend to communication that occurred between the spouses before a lawful marriage.[52] If the spouses are divorced at the time of trial, the privilege allowed under s. 4(3) C.E.A. no longer exists. The ex-spouse does not have a choice and must disclose all communication when asked.[53]

Lawyer–Client Privilege

The Supreme Court of Canada in *R. v. McClure* (2001)[54] stated that the solicitor–client privilege "commands a unique status within the legal system." The protection for solicitor–client communications is based on the fact that the relationship and the communication between solicitor and client are "essential to the effective operation of the legal system. Social communications are inextricably linked with the very system which desires the disclosure of the communication." This distinctive status with the justice system is the rationale for characterizing the solicitor–client privilege as a "class privilege," meaning that the protection is available to all persons who fall within the class.

The S.C.C. explained the following rules in relation to this privilege:

▸ "No authority should be given carte blanche to search through the files in a solicitor's office in hopes of discovering material prepared for the purpose of advising the client in the normal and legitimate course of professional practice."

▸ "In order for the communication to be privileged, it must arise from communication between a lawyer and the client *where the latter seeks legal advice.*"

▸ "Only communications made for the legitimate purpose of obtaining lawful professional advice or assistance are privileged."

▸ "It is the duty of a solicitor to insist upon this privilege which extends to *all communications* by a client to his solicitor or counsel for the purpose of obtaining professional advice or assistance in a pending action, or in any other proper matter for professional assistance."

▸ "The privilege does not extend to correspondence, memoranda, or documents prepared for the *purpose of assisting a client to commit a crime.*"

▸ The privilege is "that of the client. The privilege may only be *waived* by the client."

▸ "Despite its importance, the solicitor–client privilege is not absolute."

   "Not all communications between a lawyer and client" are privileged. The privilege is subject to *exceptions* in certain circumstances. The S.C.C. explained that "Just as no right is absolute so too the privilege, even that between solicitor–client, is subject to clearly defined *exceptions*. The decision to exclude evidence that would be both relevant and of substantial probative value because it is protected by the solicitor–client privilege represents a policy decision. It is based upon the importance to our legal system in general of the solicitor–client privilege. *In certain circumstances, however, other societal values must prevail.*"

▸ The major exception is called the "innocence at stake test." This exception is allowed rarely, only in "most unusual cases." It is allowed only when there is a *"genuine risk of a wrongful conviction."* The exception applies only when an accused person can prove that his "innocence is at stake" and requires communication between another person (i.e., the real offender) and his or her lawyer to prove his innocence. If the exception is granted, the communications between the actual offender and lawyer may be disclosed to prove the innocence of the person who had been charged with the offence.

There are two stages to the "innocence at stake test" that a trial judge uses to determine the admissibility of a solicitor–client communication, as an exception to the protection afforded by the privilege:

1. During the first stage, there must be production of "material" for the trial judge to review. There has to be some evidentiary basis for the request, to prevent fishing expeditions. In other words, the onus is on the accused to prove that some communication exists between another person and a lawyer that "*could* raise a reasonable doubt" about the accused person's guilt. At this stage, the judge has to decide whether to review the evidence.

2. After the evidence is reviewed, the judge must decide whether the communication is "*likely* to raise a reasonable doubt" about the accused person's guilt. The trial judge does not have to believe that it *definitely* will prove reasonable doubt, only the likelihood. If that likelihood is proved, the communication will be disclosed to the accused and it will become admissible.

The investigative significance of the solicitor–client privilege is outlined below. Verbal or written communication made by an accused person to a lawyer is privileged if:

▸ the lawyer was acting in a bona fide professional relationship with the accused, and
▸ the communication was intended to be confidential.[55]

Consequently, a lawyer cannot be compelled by the Crown to testify about conversation or written communication with an accused (i.e., a confession). This privilege belongs to the accused person; a lawyer cannot waive the privilege; only the accused may waive the privilege.[56] The privilege continues even if the accused changes lawyers.[57] Generally, documents seized by the police that were written by the accused to a lawyer are inadmissible.[58] An exception to this privilege is communication that amounts to a consultation about how to commit an offence.[59]

Upon arrest, an accused is afforded an automatic right to privacy when speaking to a lawyer.[60] Consequently, a police officer who overhears conversation between an accused and a lawyer (i.e., a confession) cannot repeat the statement during testimony at a trial. If the conversation were intended to be private, statements made by the accused to a lawyer are inadmissible.

Police–Informant (Crown) Privilege

According to the S.C.C. in *R. v. McClure* (2001), the police–informant privilege, like the solicitor–client privilege, is an "ancient and hallowed protection."

An **informant**, essentially, is a person who provides evidence to the police and whom the police choose not to subpoena to the trial. Police officers are heavily dependent upon confidential evidence received from informants to form reasonable grounds in relation to arrests and searches. The courts have recognized the need to maintain confidentiality between police and informants for society's best interests.[61]

The privilege of concealing the identity of an informant belongs to the Crown, not to the Crown witness (i.e., police officer). Theoretically, a police officer does not have to divulge the name of the person who supplied confidential information, but the Crown has the exclusive right to invoke the privilege. Neither the police officer nor the informant has the privilege.[62]

The officer cannot testify about the informant's observations because doing so would constitute hearsay evidence. However, this information is usually only used in the formulation of reasonable grounds for a search or an arrest—i.e., it is not intended to be used at a trial.

The only exception to this privilege is in cases where the disclosure of the informant's identity is necessary to demonstrate the accused's innocence. For the necessity to exist, evidence must be introduced at the trial to indicate that the informant (a) could not or did not actually make the observations that he or she reported or (b) participated in the offence in a manner that might demonstrate the accused's innocence,[63] meaning he or she wrongly implicated or framed the accused. In other words, evidence at the trial must exist that the informant obstructed justice by falsely implicating the accused.

This exception is called the "innocence at stake" test, the same name as the exception for solicitor–client. This test details the circumstances under which an informant's identity "might have to be revealed." According to the S.C.C. in *R. v. McClure* (2001), "the value of reliable informers to the administration of justice has been recognized for a long time, so much so that it too is a class privilege. This explains why the high standard of showing that the innocence of the accused is at stake before permitting invasion of the privilege is necessary. Should the privilege be invaded, the State then generally provides for the protection of the informer through various safety programs, again illustrating the public importance of that privilege."

Case-by-Case Privilege

Essentially, no other witnesses have a blanket privilege to conceal conversation or information received from an accused person. The significance to police officers is that persons having no blanket privilege may be subpoenaed by the police and cannot automatically refuse to answer questions in relation to communication (i.e., a confession) received from an accused person. Essentially, persons with no blanket privilege are competent and compellable Crown witnesses, including:

- clergy–penitent,
- doctor–patient, and
- psychiatrist–patient.

The confidentiality of communications in these relationships commonly causes confusion in the study of criminal investigation. Most people expect confidentiality when they communicate with clergy members and medical professionals. The confusion arises from the *nature* of the communication. Non-criminal communication is protected. However, communication that incriminates a person relating to a *criminal* offence has no blanket protection. If a person confesses a criminal offence in any of these "case-by-case" relationships, the confession will be disclosed by the recipient during court testimony unless the four criteria as stated by the S.C.C. are proved.

The S.C.C. in *R. v. McClure* (2001) explained the *reasons* for not granting these relationships blanket protection. Medical and religious communication "do NOT occupy the unique position of solicitor–client privilege or *resonate the same concerns*." The class privileges protect relationships that are "integral to the workings of the legal system itself." Those relationships are "part of the system, not ancillary to it." Conversely, medical and religious communications, *"notwithstanding their social importance*, are not inextricably linked with the justice system" in the same way as solicitor–client and police–informant.

CLERGY

The Supreme Court of Canada in *R. v. Gruenke* (1991)[64] ruled that clergy members do not have a blanket privilege in relation to confessions received from accused persons. In the *Gruenke* case, the accused made confessions to a pastor regarding a murder. The pastor testified at the trial about the confessions, which were ruled admissible. The court stated, however, that clergy members may be allowed a case-by-case privilege if the following conditions exist:

▸ The confession was made in full confidence that it would not be disclosed.
▸ Confidentiality is essential to fully and satisfactorily maintain the relationship between the clergy member and the accused.
▸ The harm to the clergy–accused relationship must be greater than the benefit gained to the administration of justice.

In summary, a clergy member may possibly be allowed a privilege in relation to a confession received by an accused if the accused has established a prior relationship of confidentiality with the clergy member and the offence is not severe enough to harm or disrupt the relationship. The offence in the *Gruenke* case was murder and the expectation of maintaining confidentiality was not clearly demonstrated. The Supreme Court stated that no common-law privilege exists for clergy members because a communication between clergy and offender does not have the same importance to the justice system as does a lawyer–client privilege.

INVESTIGATIVE SIGNIFICANCE

Psychiatrists, doctors, counsellors, teachers, family members, and media personnel do not have a blanket privilege to conceal information that they received from an accused person, relevant to a criminal offence. Consequently, they are competent and compellable Crown witnesses for criminal offences. Officers should *subpoena* these people if interviews reveal that an accused person made inculpatory remarks about a criminal offence to them.

Case Study 10.1 Conclusion

Do reasonable grounds exist to arrest? Yes. Break, enter, and theft into a place other than a dwelling-house is dual procedure (which is temporarily classified as indictable). Circumstances that exceed mere suspicion are

- same colour and type of car,
- same number of occupants (and same gender),
- close proximity (about 1 km from offence scene),
- 26-minute time lapse, and
- mud on shoes and pants of both men.

You arrest the suspects and interrogate them separately. Both confess. They are charged separately. They are subpoenaed to testify against each other. You testify about the verbatim conversation that composed the interrogation.

The witness list will be composed of

- the owner of the Rowing Club,
- the Rowing Club employee,
- Jill,
- police officer 1, and
- you, the arresting officer.

All five statements must include the anticipated evidence of each witness. They must not include inadmissible evidence, only admissible evidence. The following is a table of what should be included and excluded in the statements and testimony:

Witness	Can Say	Cannot Say
Rowing Club Owner	- owned the place - received a phone call - attended at 2:15 a.m. - saw 50 cents in register - description of damage to register and door	- what employee told him - who called about the break and enter and what was said
Rowing Club Employee	- locked up at 11 p.m. - $100.50 in register - no damage to door or register - set alarm	- anything told to her about the offence
Jill	- lives next door - looked outside at 2 a.m. - saw green Toyota leaving Rowing Club - saw two men in the car	- no reference to alarm or break and enter
Police Officer 1	- as a result of radio broadcast, arrive at 2:05 a.m. - door open, describe damage - searched interior (negative) - 50 cents in register - describe damage to register - mud-covered parking lot - interviewed Jill - made radio broadcast	- contents of radio broadcast - no reference to "forced entry" or "break and enter" - no opinions about what suspects did - what owner reported - what employee reported - what Jill reported

(Continued)

Witness	Can Say	Cannot Say

You, arresting officer	▸ heard three radio broadcasts
	▸ where you stopped suspects
	▸ details about suspect car and occupants
	▸ verbatim conversation re:
	  ▹ arrest
	  ▹ reason
	  ▹ right to counsel
	  ▹ caution
	  ▹ search of suspects
		▸ contents of radio broadcasts
		▸ opinions
		▸ no reference to past dealings with suspects

SUMMARY

Applying rules of evidence requires extensive and intense practice. This skill develops from writing statements, including your own, and testifying (at trial and at any type of hearing, such as a bail hearing). Extensive, intense practice helps break the habits of daily, routine communication while developing the expertise of communicating in accordance with rules of evidence. There is no other magic formula.

ENDNOTES

1. *R. v. Graat* (1982), 2 C.C.C. (3d) 365 (S.C.C.).
2. Ibid.
3. Ibid., at 369–370.
4. Ibid.
5. Ibid.
6. *R. v. German* (1947), 89 C.C.C. 90 (Ont. C.A.).
7. *R. v. Graat*, supra note 1.
8. Ibid.
9. Ibid.
10. Ibid.
11. Ibid.
12. H.J. Cox, *Criminal Evidence Handbook* (Aurora, ON: Canada Law Book, 1991).
13. *R. v. Graat*, supra note 1, at 381.
14. *R. v. Marquard* (1993), 85 C.C.C. (3d) 193 (S.C.C.).
15. *R. v. Graat*, supra note 1.
16. *R. v. German*, supra note 6, at 442.
17. *R: ex rel Neely v. Tait* (1965), as in Cox, supra note 12.
18. *R. v. Graat*, supra note 1.
19. Ibid.
20. Ibid.
21. *R. v. Browne and Angus* (1951), 99 C.C.C. 141 (B.C.C.A.).
22. *R. v. Rowbotham* (1988), as in Cox, supra note 12.
23. *R. v. Pitre* (1932), 59 C.C.C. 148 (S.C.C.).
24. *R. v. German*, supra note 6; *R. v. Graat*, supra note 1.

25. *R. v. Graat*, supra note 1.

26. *R: ex rel Neely v. Tait*, supra note 17.

27. *R. v. Graat*, supra note 1, at 381.

28. Ibid.

29. *R. v. Sockett* (1952), as in Salhany, supra note 21.

30. Cox, supra note 12; Salhany, supra note 21.

31. Section 7 C.E.A.

32. *R. v. Lavalee* (1990), 55 C.C.C. (3d) 97 (S.C.C.).

33. *R. v. B. (F.F.)* (1993), 79 C.C.C. (3d) 112, at 136 (S.C.C.).

34. Ibid.

35. Ibid.

36. *Morris v. The Queen* (1983), 7 C.C.C. (3d) 97 (S.C.C.).

37. *R. v. Demyen* (1976), 31 C.C.C. (2d) 303 (Sask. C.A.).

38. *R. v. Drysdale* (1969), 2 C.C.C. 141 (Man. C.A.).

39. *R. v. Boyce* (1975), 23 C.C.C. (2d) 16 (Ont. C.A.).

40. *R. v. Boyko* (1975), 28 C.C.C. (2d) 193 (B.C.C.A.).

41. *R. v. B. (F.F.)*, supra note 33.

42. *R. v. Guay* (1978), 42 C.C.C. (2d) 536, at 547 (S.C.C.).

43. Ontario Ministry of the Solicitor General, Ontario Police College, *Evidence for Senior Police Officers: Book 1* (Toronto: Queen's Printer, 1984).

44. Ibid.

45. *R. v. Debot* (1986), 30 C.C.C. (3d) 207 (Ont. C.A.).

46. *R. v. McClure* (2001), 151 C.C.C. (3d) 321 (S.C.C.).

47. Section 5(1) C.E.A.

48. *R. v. Dubois* (1985), 22 C.C.C. (3d) 513 (S.C.C.).

49. *R. v. Tarafa* (1989), 53 C.C.C. (3d) 472 (Que. S.C.); *R. v. Erven* (1978), 44 C.C.C. (2d) 76 (S.C.C.).

50. Section 4(3) C.E.A.

51. *R. v. Kotapske* (1981), 66 C.C.C. (2d) 78 (Que. S.C.), aff'd. 13 C.C.C. (3d) 85 (Que. C.A.).

52. *R. v. Andres* (1986), 26 C.C.C. (3d) 111 (B.C.S.C.).

53. *R. v. Marchand* (1980), 55 C.C.C. (2d) 77 (N.S.S.C.)

54. *R. v. McClure*, supra note 46.

55. *R. v. Solosky* (1980), 50 C.C.C. (2d) 495 (S.C.C.).

56. *Bell et al. v. Smith et al.* (1968), as in Cox, supra note 12.

57. Ibid.

58. *R. v. Solosky*, supra note 55.

59. Salhany, supra note 21.

60. *R. v. McKane* (1987), 35 C.C.C. (3d) 481 (Ont. C.A.).

61. Salhany, supra note 21; T.G. Cooper, *Crown Privilege* (Aurora, ON: Canada Law Book, 1990).

62. Cooper, supra note 61.

63. *R. v. Collins* (1989), 48 C.C.C. (3d) 343 (Ont. C.A.).

64. *R. v. Gruenke* (1991), 67 C.C.C. (3d) 289 (S.C.C.).

CHAPTER 11

Understanding Witness Credibility

LEARNER SUMMARY

Rules of evidence are the starting point of witness interviews. Chapters 11–15 focus on (a) objectives for witness interviews, (b) problems that arise from them, and (c) solutions to these problems.

OBJECTIVES Every witness interview has two objectives: (a) volume, and (b) credibility. *Volume* means obtaining the maximum amount of information from the witness. *Credibility* means that the witness, and his or her information, is honest, accurate, and believable.

The primary aim for every witness interview is for the witness to remember and recall as much information as possible, and to ensure that the witness achieves the strongest level of credibility possible.

Obtaining volume and evaluating credibility are investigative skills. Both require strategies that involve knowledge of how the memory functions.

PROBLEM The "frailties" of eyewitness testimony represent the greatest investigative challenge.

The weakness of eyewitness testimony is a case law principle. It cautions judges and police officers that eyewitness testimony is weak by nature, and that efforts should be made to evaluate credibility instead of automatically believing witnesses.

More than a century of memory research has shown that human memory is still a mystery. The complex memory path and decay process complicates the evaluation of witness credibility. There is no consensus on how humans process observations, remember, or forget. Despite the countless studies that have explored memory, and witness accuracy in particular, no universal conclusions have been reached that provide perfect witness interview strategies.

Additionally, there is no exact, concrete formula that will accurately evaluate a witness's credibility. There is no specific statutory or case law strategy that guides the police in determining whether a witness has strong or weak credibility. Consequently, the investigative objective is to strengthen witness testimony by achieving the objectives of volume and credibility.

SOLUTION Obtaining the maximum volume of information requires interview strategies. Interview strategies are based on psychological concepts relating to memory research, and are guided by case law decisions that help front-line officers justify a witness credibility decision.

This chapter will examine these objectives, problems, and solutions.

Case Study 11.1

The First National Bank is situated at 38 Main Street in a business district. An alleyway runs along one side of the bank. A municipal parking lot is at the back of the bank. On April 25 the bank opened for business at 10 a.m. A manager and 13 employees worked inside that day.

At 2:30 p.m. Jane (15) was a passenger in the front seat of a car driven by her mother. Jane's mother drove to the bank and parked along the curb near the front entrance. She left the car running and entered the bank. Jane remained seated in the front passenger seat. She was situated approximately 5 metres from the bank's front entrance. Her view was unobstructed.

Three men walked beside the bank in the alleyway. They stopped on the sidewalk of Main Street near the bank's front entrance and visually searched the area. Jane saw one of them holding nylon stockings. As she looked at his face, she saw that he was looking directly at her.

Jane became frightened and realized that they intended to rob the bank. She feared that the men had noticed that the car she was in was running and would decide to use it to escape.

Jane saw all three men place nylons over their heads. They entered the bank; all were armed with firearms. About three minutes later, they left the bank through the front entrance. Jane saw the offenders leave and run alongside the bank, down the alleyway from where they had come.

Jane was first interviewed 15 minutes after the offence. She provided a formal, written statement in which she gave lengthy descriptions of the offenders. She described two of the three suspects as follows:

Suspect 1: 6'1", 180 lbs., long, straight, brown hair, brown moustache, wearing a cross earring. He looked directly at Jane before putting the nylon over his head. Jane made eye contact with him. She saw his face for about 10 seconds.

Suspect 2: 5'8", 160 lbs., short blond hair, "baby face," freckles. Jane saw his face for about 10 seconds before he put the nylon over his head.

Jane confidently informed police that she could identify two offenders by means of facial recognition. Several hours later, she attended at the police station where she assisted an Ident. officer in creating two facial composite drawings of the offenders whom she could identify. Both composite drawings were meticulous. Jane had no doubt about the facial appearance of both offenders. All of the offenders were unfamiliar to her.

(Refer to the end of Chapter 12 for the conclusion of this two-part case study, which continues at the beginning of the next chapter.)

FUNDAMENTAL RULES: OBJECTIVES, PROBLEMS, AND SOLUTIONS

Objectives: Volume and Credibility

A police officer's job includes (a) obtaining the largest volume and most detailed written statement possible from each witness, and (b) making a legitimate decision about the witness's credibility.

Witnesses make a wide range of observations, but the two most important are:

1. eyewitness identification, and
2. hearing a suspect's incriminating statement.

Obtaining the maximum volume requires expert witness interview strategies that start with two basic rules:

1. officers cannot rely on the "base narrative," and
2. witnesses cannot be allowed to write their own statements.

Base narratives and self-written witness statements fail to achieve the "volume" objective. Neither will result in the necessary maximum amount of information.

The **base narrative** is the first response to an open-ended, exploratory question that asks the witness, "What did you observe?" or "What happened?" An open-ended question is defined as a question intended to generate multiple facts. The goal of this initial question is to obtain the base narrative. This core observation is obtained without any additional interview techniques, and is the starting point of the witness statement, not the final product. Additional interview skills will expand the volume of the base narrative.

Self-written witness statements are vague and unstructured because witnesses do not know what information is expected to be included in a professional statement. Statement analysis will not work because witnesses are not suspects. It is impossible to achieve the necessary volume and to evaluate credibility if witnesses are allowed to write their own statements.

Witness statements are the product of a three-part process where (a) the *officer questions*, (b) the *witness dictates*, and (c) the *officer records* the response. Allowing witnesses to write their own statements is a poor strategy that must be avoided because:

- Witnesses do not know what is relevant. They do not know the facts-in-issue (FII) that compose the offence being investigated. Consequently, they will likely neglect relevant information in their statements.
- Witnesses are not experts in the rules of evidence. They do not know what is admissible and inadmissible in court.
- Witnesses are not experts in statement writing. They will write unstructured, out-of-sequence statements.
- Witnesses often use abstract language. They usually do not explain observations using concrete language.
- Witnesses lie, or are unintentionally wrong.
- Evaluating witness credibility is almost impossible. When a witness writes his or her own statement, an officer will not be able to accurately determine whether the witness's observations are true or accurate.

Allowing a witness to write his or her own statement will result is an *amateur statement* that will be criticized by the Crown Attorney. People who work in law enforcement—public police, private security, and border protection personal—are professional writers. The only witnesses who should write their own statement are professionals. For example:

▸ store security investigators—are usually the only eyewitnesses to shoplifting.
▸ border officers—are the primary eyewitness in border arrests for possession offences.

Both the security investigator and the border officer are expected to be professional statement writers. They can write their own statements because the product will be a *professional statement.*

Credibility

Credibility is earned, not given. The phrase "strong credibility" means "I believe what I was told." A witness may report a lengthy, multiple-page statement, or may say, "I didn't see anything" or "I can't remember."

RULE Do not make an automatic decision that a witness has "strong" credibility. There are two possible credibility decisions or ratings: (a) strong, or (b) weak/none. An officer either believes what a witness reports, or does not. Do not start with "strong credibility" without a reason for this decision. According to volumes of case law, start with healthy skepticism—an assumption of weak credibility. Use a decision-making process that reaches and justifies a final conclusion. An exception is an emergency or in-progress investigation where a witness may temporarily be given strong credibility because of an exigent circumstance. Afterward, a formal witness interview determines the final credibility rating—did the witness in fact tell you the truth?

EXAMPLE

You respond to a domestic involving a possible stabbing. Upon arrival, you see a woman, approximately 30 years old, at the front door. She is bleeding from a wound on her forearm. The woman is holding an infant. A man of approximately the same age is standing in the room, about five metres from the woman. He is unarmed, and says nothing. The woman points to him with her uninjured hand and says, "He stabbed me." This one-sentence verbal statement constitutes an *opinion.* You are not familiar with the woman. You recognize the man as a person you have arrested twice in the past—once for assault and once for causing a disturbance. However, you have no other information. You have no time to formally evaluate credibility. You can give the woman temporary strong credibility, which is sufficient to form reasonable grounds. Justification for this temporary credibility rating includes the following:

1. An emergency exists. There is no time to conduct formal interviews.
2. She has a wound that is bleeding.
3. An immediate risk to life exists. A weapon was used. It has to be found and seized.
4. There is no reason not to believe her at this time, under these circumstances.

The definition of "reasonable grounds" does not require 100 percent certainty.

You have authority under s. 495 C.C. to arrest the man for two counts of attempted murder. Afterward, the woman will be formally interviewed. You will make and justify a final credibility conclusion. If you believe her statement, she is considered to have strong credibility. If you later do not believe her because she lied, she is considered to have weak or no credibility, and may be charged with public mischief. You will have been justified in making the arrest because of the legitimate, temporary strong credibility you gave her.

Problems: The "Inherent Frailties" of Witness Testimony

The biggest investigative problem is the potential for witness unreliability. There are only two sources of evidence: (a) humans, and (b) items. Humans pose the greatest problems because humans may fail to:

- cooperate during the investigation; they fabricate or withhold information,
- accurately remember information,
- appear in court, or
- testify honestly.

Fear is a major cause of each failure. Reluctance to report or testify is caused by fear. Memory decay occurs in every human, and is accelerated by stress. Removing fear helps remove witness failures.

There are inherent frailties in eyewitness identification. Canadian case law and formal research overwhelmingly acknowledge that eyewitness observation is weak by nature. Weakness is a characteristic of eyewitness testimony.

The following quotes, by the Supreme Court of Canada, makes the "inherent frailties of eyewitness identification" a case law principle, and a warning to all trial judges and police officers:

> By reason of the many instances in which identification has proved erroneous, the trier of fact must be cognizant of the inherent frailties of identification evidence arising from the psychological fact of the unreliability of human observation and recollection.[1]

> Errors of recognition have a long documented history. Identification experiments have underlined the frailty of memory and the fallibility of powers of observation. Studies have shown the progressive assurance that builds upon an original identification that may be erroneous.... The very question of admissibility of identification evidence in some of its aspects has caused sufficient apprehension in some jurisdictions to give *pause to uncritical reliance* on such evidence, when admitted, as the basis of conviction....[2]

Another quote, by the Supreme Court of Canada in *R. v. Nikolovski* (1996), not only reiterates the warning about these inherent frailties, but also includes six practical guidelines for assessing the strength of a witness's credibility:

> The courts have long recognized the frailties of identification evidence given by independent, honest, and well-meaning eyewitnesses. This recognized frailty served to emphasize the essential need to cross-examine eyewitnesses. So many factors come into play with the human identification witness. As a minimum, it

must be determined whether the witness was physically in a *position* to see the accused and, if so, whether that witness had *sound vision, good hearing, intelligence*, and the ability to communicate what was seen and heard. Did the witness have the *ability to understand* and recount what had been perceived? Did the witness have a *sound memory*? What was the *effect of fear or excitement* on the ability of the witness to perceive clearly and to later recount the events accurately? Did the witness have a *bias* or at least a biased perception of the event or the parties involved?[3]

Numerous case law decisions impose a duty on a trial judge to warn a jury about the potential weakness of eyewitness identification in cases where identification of an accused person (facial recognition) is made by only one eyewitness. When the Crown's case consists of only one eyewitness, the trial judge has a mandatory duty to instruct the jury that there have been several past cases in which witnesses with undisputed honesty and adequate opportunities for observation made positive identifications that were later proven wrong.[4]

RESEARCH

Eyewitness research has grown considerably during the past 30 years. More than 85 percent of all eyewitness research has been published since 1978. Eyewitness researchers have found that eyewitness testimony may be unreliable in some circumstances but the most important finding is that a wide range of variables may affect eyewitness accuracy. The complexity of evaluating eyewitness credibility stems from the number of influences that may negatively affect witness accuracy. There is no single cause or simple list of all-encompassing causes for witness inaccuracy.[5]

The following rules emerge from formal research.

Do Not Give Immediate "Strong Credibility"

A Rand Corporation report found that, although successful criminal investigations rely heavily on eyewitness accuracy, eyewitness information has been determined to be largely inaccurate and, in many cases, partially manufactured. Psychologists have argued that rigid dependence on eyewitness information may result in false inferences and conclusions. Caution must be exercised to properly evaluate witness credibility.[6]

Follow the 12–32 Percent Rule

Research shows that only one-third of witnesses have "initial accuracy," referring to a credible base narrative. In many investigations, there will be multiple witnesses. The 12–32 percent rule alerts an officer to an *expectation*—he or she can expect the possibility that 66 percent or a group of witnesses may be initially inaccurate in their base narrative (initial response).

The following are actual studies.

STUDY 1 Researchers studied a case involving a simple theft. Five students sat in a classroom. Only one knew about the experiment (he was to be the thief). A bag with a calculator in it was on a table. The researcher was in the room and asked whether anyone had seen the bag and calculator. The intended thief pointed to it in the presence of the other four persons. The researcher left the room. The thief then took the bag and left. Shortly afterward, the four witnesses were asked to facially recognize the offender and were shown a photo lineup of six mug shots. The experiment was repeated 25 times to test 100 students. Only 12.5 percent correctly identified the offender.[7]

STUDY 2 Two researchers went to various convenience stores posing as customers. They were in the stores for an average of four to five minutes. They intentionally drew attention to themselves and had lengthy conversations with each store clerk. Two hours after the researchers left, two persons entered each store posing as law enforcement personnel searching for the two customers. A photo lineup of six mug shots was presented to each store employee. Only 32 percent of the witnesses accurately identified either customer.[8]

In summary, empirical research shows that more than two-thirds of the witnesses who gave significant attention to the offender and who had a lengthy duration of observation and a short interval between observation and recall inaccurately identified offenders. Conversely, only 12 to 32 percent, less than one-third, accurately recognized an offender under excellent conditions for their observations.

Anecdotal evidence corroborates these findings. Case Studies 11.1 and 12.1 are excellent examples of two witnesses who saw a robbery under favourable conditions, yet made incorrect observations and identification. Many investigations involve well-intentioned citizens who are unintentionally wrong, even though they appeared initially to have strong credibility. Additionally, in reality, witnesses will often intentionally lie by withholding observations or fabricating information. Deceptive witnesses are a significant, common problem in the world of front-line policing.

Follow the 66 Percent Conformity Rule

Conformity (also known as "group pressure" or "peer pressure") is defined as adopting the behaviour and thinking of others, even if the adopter does not fully believe in it. Witness conformity is the adoption of observations made by another witness that were not actually made by the reporting witness.

Many people do not want to differ from a group. They are not willing to report details that deviate from what others report. Instead of relying on inner fortitude in order to stand by their beliefs, conformists relinquish independent thought and adopt the thinking of others.

Research shows compelling evidence that the majority of humans have a strong tendency to be conformists. Specifically, studies have found that two-thirds (66 percent) of people are easily influenced, meaning that they have strong potential to be followers.

The following are two classic conformity studies.

ASCH'S LINE EXPERIMENT
Solomon Asch (1956) conducted an experiment by assembling 10 subjects and presenting two cards to each subject. The first card had three black lines of varied lengths: 6¼ inches, 6⅜ inches, and 8 inches. The second card had one line measuring 8 inches. Each subject was asked to announce, in the presence of all subjects, which line on the first card equalled the length of the line on the second card. Nine subjects had been instructed to intentionally lie by choosing a shorter line. The

tenth subject was the real subject and was seated in a position to answer last. Asch discovered that more than 66 percent of the real subjects conformed to the false judgments despite their obvious knowledge of the correct answer. Subjects explained their conformity by expressing concern about their vision and sanity and by saying they were embarrassed to deviate from the majority opinion.[9]

MILGRAM'S SHOCK EXPERIMENT

Stanley Milgram (1963) performed an experiment that illustrates people's tendencies to comply with authority even when the resulting behaviours conflict with their principles.[10] The experiment paired subjects in a teacher–learner relationship. The teacher was a real subject who administered a test of memory. The learner was a mild-mannered, middle-aged man whose role for Milgram was to answer and act in a predetermined fashion. The teacher had access to the controls on a shock generator, which he or she believed to be real. The teacher was told to administer electrical shocks to the learner as punishment for incorrect answers. The experimenter urged the teacher to increase the voltage for incorrect answers. Sixty-five percent of the teachers complied, despite cries of anguish by the learner and despite their own serious internal conflict over their actions.[11]

These studies show that two-thirds of people have a tendency to

▸ conform with the wrong observations of others even though they know themselves to be right,
▸ conform with authority even if they know it is wrong to do so,
▸ change their actual observations to reflect what the majority of a group believe happened, and
▸ adopt the opinion of a stronger-willed person regardless of whether it is right or wrong to do so.[12]

Conformity must be suspected and explored when a group of witnesses is found at a crime scene. When an officer arrives at a crime scene and finds a group of witnesses, there are two sources of conformity influences: (a) witness discussion during the officer's response time (e.g., one witness insisting, "I'm telling you, the guy was over six feet tall"), and (b) the officer's questions during the interview (e.g., "You didn't see a gun, right?"). Both sources of conformity try to imply, suggest, or pressure a certain response. A majority of witnesses will likely conform to an influence, and simply report the answer that was suggested or implied.

The following are strategies that both prevent and correct the negative effects of conformity.

▸ Follow the "no huddle" rule—do not bring the entire group together and interview the members simultaneously. Separate members as soon as possible. There are two reasons for this:
  1. to prevent discussion, and
  2. to fulfill the case law requirement that an officer form reasonable grounds based on the totality of the circumstances. This means that information must be obtained from multiple sources—in this case, each person individually. A group interview results in "single source" information.
▸ Once separated, ask each witness whether any group discussion occurred.

- If discussion occurred, ask
    - ▷ the time discussion started and ended,
    - ▷ the topics discussed,
    - ▷ who actually stated the observations during the discussion, and
    - ▷ if the observations heard from others affected what was actually seen or heard.
- Emphasize that each witness can report only what was actually seen or heard and must disregard the observations of others.
- Emphasize that the officer did not witness the offence and is relying on the witness; avoid leading questions that include or suggest answers.

The following are examples of simple instructions to give to witnesses:

"You may have discussed what you saw with the other witnesses before we arrived. You're not in trouble if you did. If you heard others say anything, disregard it. I want to know only what you yourself honestly saw and heard."

"I will be asking you several questions about what you saw. I wasn't there. I didn't see it. I'm relying on you."

These two strategies incorporate the following important concepts that prevent and correct conformity:

- **Fear removal** Fear is always a negative motivator. Tell the witness that prior discussion with witnesses before your arrival will not cause legal problems, if it was unintentional (with no intent to mislead witnesses in order to help the accused escape detection).
- **Officer's objective** Tell the witness that the objective is simple: report honestly.
- **Accountability of information** Witnesses often have the erroneous belief that an officer will know everything about every crime that happened. This turns the interview into a perceived test, where the witness believes that the officer already knows the correct answers and that he or she had better know them, too. By telling the witness that an officer was not an eyewitness, "accountability of information" is transferred to the witness. This removes witness fear, promotes honesty, and removes the officer as a source of negative influence if he or she makes a strategic mistake and asks a leading question.

Follow the 40/126 Processing Rule

Research shows that *understanding* what is seen or heard is not simple; a complex processing of information takes place. To understand an observation, a person must process an average of 40 "bits" of information per second. The highest processing capacity is 126 bits of information per second. Not every person reaches this. The 40-bit average shows that the average witness processes only about one-third (33 percent) of his or her upper-limit capacity.

The implications of this finding include:

- There is a limit to what can be processed. The average witness cannot process every bit of information that is seen and heard. This means that the average witness will not achieve anywhere near 100 percent recall.

▸ If the average number of information bits is not processed, the observation is not fully understood. This will result in faulty recall.

▸ When the offence involves two or more people talking simultaneously (e.g., arguing), it is unlikely that that verbatim quotes will be 100 percent accurate.

▸ Complex incidents are very difficult to process with 100 percent precision. Simple incidents are easier to process.

Understand Memory Path and Decay

Witness observation follows a complex path of acquisition, storage, and retrieval. Witness observations are *acquired* through the senses. The two most common senses used to acquire an observation are (a) vision and (b) hearing. The observation will be a *stored* memory. It then must be *retrieved* from storage.

Acquisition is the time of the offence (time of observation). Storage is the time between the offence and the police interview. Retrieval (or recall) is the time of the interview.

The path corresponds with three memory systems: (a) sensory register, (b) short-term memory, and (c) long-term memory. Each system has a time and information capacity associated with it.

An observation starts with the **sensory register**. It holds information for only a fraction of a second. The 40/126 processing rule happens here. About 50 percent of information is lost. The observation is then transferred to the **short-term memory**. It holds information for about one minute (30–60 seconds). Short-term memory capacity is 5–9 items. The final step for an observation is transfer to **long-term memory**, which is an unlimited storage system, in terms of both capacity and time.

Decay occurs at each step; not all observed information reaches the final system.

Figure 11.1 summarizes the path and decay of memory.

EBBINGHAUS'S FORGETTING CURVE

Hermann Ebbinghaus, a pioneer of scientific memory research, published the first significant memory study in 1885, focusing on memory retention and the rate of forgetting. (See Figure 11.2.)

Ebbinghaus concluded that conscious review, through studying, rehearsing, or thinking about the new information, dramatically slows the rate of forgetting and increases retention, causing an incline toward 100 percent recall.[13] Afterward, forgetting again occurs but conscious review will reverse the decline.

The significance of the Ebbinghaus study, relative to witness credibility, is in determining whether a witness practised "conscious repetition" (also known as

**Figure 11.1
Memory Path and Decay**

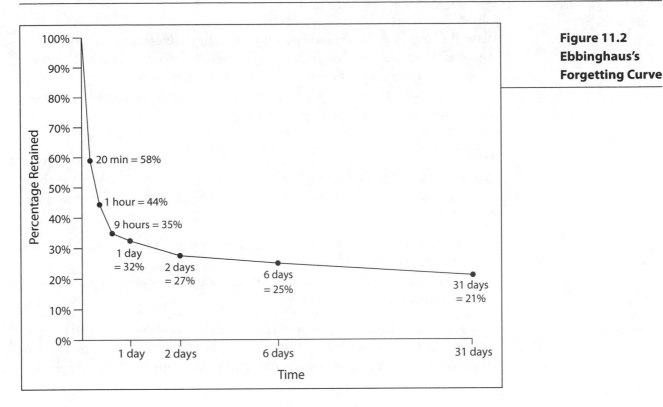

**Figure 11.2
Ebbinghaus's
Forgetting Curve**

"mental reps"), defined as thinking about or studying the observation in order to make a conscious effort to memorize the information. If no conscious repetition has occurred, decay has happened. People forget what they don't think about.

Solution: Statement Analysis

Despite the research that supports the weakness of witness testimony, not every witness is completely wrong or inaccurate. Researchers at the University of British Columbia have argued that the problem with eyewitness testimony is not as significant as others suggest. A 1992 study showed that the memories of crime victims tend to be more accurate because the victim is involved and "invested" in the incident, unlike participants in laboratory research.[14] Being invested involves:

▸ more attention and mental repetition, two key factors that help transfer observation along the memory path to long-term memory, and

▸ more meaning attached to the observation, because of the combined effects of severity and uniqueness of the offence. These factors make the event more memorable.

In *R. v. Fliss* (2002),[15] the S.C.C. stated that "common sense would say" that some observations may remain in one's memory forever, if the circumstances are unique or distinct.

An important rule emerges from these findings, called **SUMM**:

Severity + Uniqueness + Meaningful = Memorable

SUMM helps an officer to evaluate witness credibility. Witnessing a crime constitutes a *unique observation*. It doesn't happen often in a person's life. The greater the severity of an observation, the greater the uniqueness. Uniqueness is a significant factor that makes an observation meaningful to the witness. The extent of meaningfulness of an event determines how memorable an experience is. If an experience is meaningful to us, we remember it. If it is not meaningful, we forget it.

SUMM helps transfer an observation from short-term to long-term memory, which has limitless storage and recall capacity.

STRATEGY

Determine the extent of meaningfulness of a witness's observation. Was the observation unique for the witness? Was the offence severe? The answers create *expectations*:

- ▸ If the observation was unique, it was meaningful. Expect greater recall and a lengthy statement.
- ▸ Conversely, if an event was not unique, it was meaningless. Expect a poor statement, with few or no facts.

An officer's job is to determine whether a witness is believable. The first step in statement analysis is applying SUMM. Analyze the statement for compatibility or contradictions in order to determine strong or weak credibility. The four possible credibility conclusions follow.

1. Unique, severe circumstances + "can't remember" = **weak credibility**. Contradictions exist. Suspect deception; the witness may be withholding information. The uniqueness and severity of the observation should have been memorable.
2. Unique, severe circumstances + lengthy statement = **strong credibility**. Compatible analysis.
3. Meaningless event + "can't remember" = **strong credibility**. Compatible analysis. If an event is meaningless to a witness, it is logical to believe that the witness cannot remember.
4. Meaningless event + lengthy statement = **weak credibility**. Contradictions exist. Suspect deception.

HOW THE MEMORY WORKS

A witness's ability to accurately remember relies on success in three memory stages: (a) acquisition, (b) retention, and (c) retrieval.

Acquisition is the learning and observing stage. Once information is acquired, a record, called the **memory trace**, is deposited in the nervous system. This stage has also been called the **encoding stage**. Encoding involves noticing information and transforming it into a form that can be stored in memory. Sometimes, information is encoded automatically, without effort. In other cases, something has to be done with the information, such as making an association, that significantly improves recall. Optimum encoding requires focusing attention on the information being observed and learned.[16]

Retention is the storage of the observation for future use. **Retrieval** is the remembering stage. For witnesses to remember the memory trace or the retained information, they must use **recall** or **recognition**. An example of a recall question is

"What was the suspect wearing?" An example of a recognition test is a photo line-up. The interview techniques used will affect the amount of retrieval.

REMEMBERING

Remembering an observation requires successful completion of acquisition, storage, and retrieval. **Forgetting** may result from failure of any one of these stages.[17] In many instances, a witness's inability to remember is attributed to a retrieval failure rather than a retention (storage) failure.[18] A major cause of forgetting is **interference**, referring to new or old information that interferes with what is now being learned or recalled. There are two types of interference: proactive and retroactive. **Retroactive** is old information already stored in memory. **Proactive** is new information that interferes with remembering previously acquired information.[19] As discussed earlier in this chapter, psychologists commonly theorize that the following memory systems are involved in retrieving memories, or remembering:

- ▸ sensory register,
- ▸ short-term memory, and
- ▸ long-term memory.

A sensory register system permits a witness to hold information that has been observed for only a fraction of a second. Existence of this system is supported by studies conducted by George Sperling, who showed subjects nine letters arranged in three rows of three. The presentation lasted 50 milliseconds. Immediately afterward, the subjects were asked to recall the letters. Recall scores were about 50 percent, but Sperling theorized that the subjects saw more letters than were reported. In the next experiment he had the subjects recall only one of the three rows of letters rather than all three. Under these conditions, the subjects could almost always report the line of letters correctly no matter if they were from the top, middle, or bottom rows. This led Sperling to believe that the subjects saw the whole array of letters and stored them in their sensory registers as an icon, meaning a replica. However, the icon lasts for only one-half second; by the time the subjects reported the fourth or fifth letter, in the original study, the icon was gone.

For example, if a witness sees something that lasts less than one second, about 50 percent of the observation may be remembered for only seconds afterward. The observation erodes rapidly if the witness does not mentally repeat the information.

Consciously rehearsing or repeating information, such as repeating a telephone number, can transfer the information from the sensory register to the short-term memory. This system allows a witness to hold information for about one minute; the storage capacity is limited. Research indicates that an average adult person can recall about seven items, give or take two, after observing an event. This short-term memory span appears to be consistent regardless of whether the items are digits, letters, or words, or whether they are learned visually or aurally. The majority of items entering short-term memory are forgotten because of (a) **decay**: the memory trace is eroded by the passage of time, or (b) **interference**: the items from short-term memory are removed by existing, competing items in short-term memory or by items that enter afterward. If a witness does not mentally repeat the information, the majority of the information will be lost after about one minute.

The long-term memory system permits a witness to hold a large amount of information for a lifetime. The storage capacity of long-term memory is enormous; data indicate the size of an average college student's reading vocabulary is about 50,000 words.[20]

The transfer of information from short-term to long-term memory depends on mental repetition of the information. Consequently, the transfer process can be hindered by events occurring during the **retention interval**, the time lapse between acquisition (the offence) and retrieval (the police interview).

Mental activity during the retention interval, such as learning new information or concentrating on other thoughts, may obstruct the repetition necessary to transfer information from short-term to long-term memory.[21]

For example, a witness may see a licence plate number, made up of seven digits, for a brief period. Transference could occur if the witness is permitted to concentrate on the plate number without thinking about something else or being interrupted from the time the plate number was seen until the witness is asked to recall it.

Determining the memory system from which a witness's observation is originating benefits the officer's evaluation of the witness's credibility. If a witness is interviewed within one minute of an observation, the number of items recalled will likely exceed the 5–9 range.

If the interview occurs more than one minute after an observation, a witness may recall a large amount of detail if the information has been transferred to long-term memory. Conversely, the witness will recall few details accurately if no transfer occurred from short-term to long-term memory. Determining whether information has been transferred to long-term memory cannot be positively done. It requires a logical evaluation based on whether the witness had sufficient uninterrupted time to rehearse or repeat the information. Otherwise, it is an inexact procedure.

Officers can make an initial credibility evaluation by assessing the compatibility of the number of details recalled and the memory system that the witness is using. For example:

- Few details from long-term memory means the witness may be withholding information.
- Many details from short-term memory means the witness may be fabricating intentionally or unintentionally.
- Few details (5–7) from short-term memory is credible.
- Many details from long-term memory is credible.

Many factors affect the transfer of information from short-term to long-term memory, thereby affecting recall and retrieval. Determining the presence or absence of these factors assists officers in evaluating witness credibility.

FACTORS AFFECTING RECALL AND RETRIEVAL

Intent to Learn

The **intent to learn** involves

- an awareness that an incident is about to occur,
- the focus of attention or concentration to an area before an incident occurs, and
- a belief that recall will be required (i.e., police will interview).

The intent to learn is one of the most important factors in evaluating witness credibility. The ability to memorize observations increases if the intent to learn exists before an incident. Research data indicate that intentional learners possess superior recall compared to the limited recall ability of the incidental learners. An **incidental learner** is a person who did not intend to learn an incident (e.g., no awareness existed before the incident) or one who did not expect to be asked to recall the event. Intentional learners have better recall of an incident because they likely repeat the observation, increasing the chance of transfer from short-term to long-term memory.[22]

For example, if a man were arguing with an acquaintance and the acquaintance assaulted him, the victim would be considered an *intentional learner*. His attention was focused on the acquaintance and he may have anticipated a police interview. These factors likely would cause him to mentally repeat the observations, transfer the observation from short-term to long-term memory, and have high recall. An *incidental learner* usually sees a partial incident or the aftermath because of the incident's unexpectedness. For example, a man may be sitting in a bar watching a television and have no awareness that an assault is about to occur. A sound may alert him to the incident, but he will probably see the aftermath and observe nothing relative to the actual assault. Another example of an incidental learner is one who sees a crime but believes it is too insignificant for the police to become involved and that he or she will never be questioned about it; this will likely prevent this witness from mentally repeating the observation.

The existence or absence of the intent to learn is a crucial factor in evaluating a witness's credibility. To establish whether or not the intent existed, every witness should be asked

- What he or she was doing before the offence. Determine whether the circumstances indicate the witness's awareness that the offence was about to occur. Ask the witness what he or she was looking at before the offence occurred and, more important, why. The reasons may indicate whether the witness did or did not direct attention toward the offence location. If a witness reports that an entire offence was seen, ask what caused his or her attention to be focused there.
- Whether an offence was expected.
- Whether he or she thought that a police interview would occur.

A witness who expects an offence to occur and to be asked to recall it should likely recall more details. A witness who has no awareness should report a small number of details. The witness's credibility is dependent on the compatibility of the existence or absence of the intent to learn with the number of details reported. For example:

- ▸ A witness who reports lengthy details and had the intent to learn is compatible with credibility.
- ▸ A witness who reports minimal details and had no intent to learn is compatible with credibility.
- ▸ A witness who reports lengthy details and had no intent to learn is incompatible with credibility and may be intentionally or unintentionally inaccurate.
- ▸ A witness who reports minimal details and had the intent to learn is incompatible with credibility and may be intentionally withholding or unintentionally unable to recall.

Memory Reconstruction

Witnesses commonly recall the core of an event but use inferences to fill voids in their observations.[23] Retrieval may be inaccurate if the past is reconstructed from partial knowledge and inferences.

Memory reconstruction experiments have concluded that original stories retold over time may develop discrepancies through the elimination, elaboration, or manufacture of details. **Reconstruction** occurs because the person cannot remember the original story.[24]

Memory reconstruction and testimony accuracy are significantly related. Witnesses may testify confidently about circumstances that do not reflect fact, but do reflect their own inferred assumptions. For example, witnesses of vehicle collisions commonly see the aftermath of the impact that occurred a few seconds earlier. Inaccuracies about the accident may result if the witness attempts to retrieve observations of the incident by knowingly filling the voids/gaps in their memory of the collision with inferences made from seeing the aftermath.[25] If an officer suspects that a witness has used inferences to fill the voids in his or her memory, the officer should simply ask whether the observation is fact or an inference. Quite often, asking a witness, "Are you sure you actually saw it?" may generate an honest, accurate response.

CONFIDENCE

A **confident** witness is one who reports observations without reluctance or hesitation. Approximately 75 percent of police officers and prosecutors agree with the assumption that a confident witness has accurately recalled memories.[26] However, research data on eyewitness recall accuracy have resulted in conflicting conclusions: 13 studies found that eyewitness confidence has a significant positive relation to accuracy, and 18 studies found no relationship or a negative relationship to accuracy.[27]

Bothwell, Brigham, and Deffenbacher (1987) tested the hypothesis that the relationship between eyewitness confidence and accuracy increases when the eyewitness is given more time to see the offender's face during an offence. Their finding supported the hypothesis by indicating that the confidence witnesses gained from increased exposure to an offender's face resulted in an increase in recognition.

Smith, Ellsworth, and Kassin (1989) examined two specific questions:

1. Are confident witnesses more accurate than hesitant witnesses?
2. Are witnesses' confident statements more accurate than their hesitant statements?

The answer was the same for both questions: an eyewitness's confidence is not a good predictor of accuracy.

Despite conflicting research, experts suggest that evaluating eyewitness credibility solely on the basis of eyewitness confidence is a dangerous, misleading practice. Their conclusion is that confidence does not indicate the accuracy of the witness, and does not indicate the accuracy of specific statements made by that witness.

Personal Characteristics and Conditions

The individual characteristics and conditions of a witness may result in inaccurate facts reported to an investigator. Consider the following witness characteristics when evaluating witness credibility.

AGE

Children under 14 years old and persons over 50 may give inaccurate eyewitness facts because of physiological factors such as underdeveloped memory or loss of memory. Additionally, very young people and senior citizens are more likely to simply identify an offender as opposed to giving a description.[28]

SENSORY CAPABILITIES

Vision, hearing, and the ability to judge height, weight, and distance vary among witnesses. An investigator must determine whether witnesses have any sensory defects and the degree of the defects. A witness's judgmental ability can be assessed by asking for his or her perception of a detail to which the answer is known to the investigator. For example, the witness can be asked to judge the investigator's height and weight and to judge a predetermined distance. If the witness's perception is poor, a description of an offender or of an event can be translated in relation to the witness's capabilities.

Another method is to ask the witness to compare the offender's height and weight to your own. Simply stand before the witness and ask how much taller or shorter, heavier or lighter the offender was in comparison.

STRESS

Stress has three classifications:

- ▸ Low stress results from little or no perception of danger to life.
- ▸ Medium stress results from perceived danger to life or close proximity to offence.
- ▸ High stress results from perceived extreme, immediate danger to life and is usually suffered by the actual victim.

Witnessing an offence may cause stress from fright or excitement; perception may be affected. A low level of stress does not tend to cause any distortion of perceptions. A medium stress level can potentially interfere with a witness's alertness and interest at the time of the observation. Empirical evidence exists that a high stress level may increase recall due to heightened awareness. However, if the offender is holding a unique item, such as a weapon, the witness may direct attention from the offender's face and body to the item.[29]

The Supreme Court of Canada in *R. v. Nikolovski* (1996) added the following perspective to witness stress caused by a violent crime: "It cannot be forgotten that a robbery can be a terrifyingly traumatic event for the victim and witnesses. Not every witness can have the fictional James Bond's cool and unflinching ability to act and observe in the face of flying bullets and flashing knives. Even Bond might have difficulty accurately describing his would-be assassin."[30]

ALCOHOL OR DRUGS

Extensive literature exists about alcohol's effect on memory, although virtually none relates to witness memory. However, police reports indicate that alcohol consumption is a common factor among witnesses. Witnesses who have been drinking are more common than sober witnesses in most investigations.[31] Research indicates that alcohol disturbs the storage of information in short-term memory and that alcohol's effects are greater on storage than on retrieval of information. The researchers concluded that (a) alcohol consumption before learning erodes or obstructs memory, and (b) alcohol consumption after acquisition of information or at the time of retrieval does not hinder memory.[32]

Heavy alcohol consumption has a strong effect on memory; multiple studies conclude that it may cause severe amnesia.[33] Moderate alcohol consumption causes less information acquisition about an event, but its effect on recall is undetermined. Yuille and Tollestrup (1990) studied the effects of moderate consumption on storage and retrieval. Strong empirical evidence supported their hypothesis that alcohol affects witness memory. Sober witnesses consistently recalled 20.5 percent more information than did impaired witnesses.[34]

In addition, this study by Yuille and Tollestrup recommends that police officers interview moderately impaired witnesses immediately after the offence, while the amount and accuracy of recall is still intact. Supporting evidence was found in data indicating that impaired witnesses recalled almost 25 percent more information when interviewed immediately after an offence than when interviews were delayed. In other words, delaying the interview until the witness is sober may result in the loss of 25 percent of the witness's observation. The accuracy of an impaired witness's information is unaffected by an immediate interview. Yuille and Tollestrup caution that this recommended practice is applicable only to moderate alcohol consumption; it is not applicable to heavy alcohol consumption.

The abilities to identify a suspect or recall facts are hindered by the use of narcotics or medication.[35] A witness under the influence of a hallucinogenic drug (e.g., marijuana, LSD) may inaccurately perceive the duration of an event to be longer than the actual time;[36] similar misperceptions are caused by caffeine and nicotine. Sedatives produce the opposite effect, a misperception of shorter periods.[37]

The condition of every witness must be determined and accurately described in the witness statement to alert the Crown attorney. If alcohol consumption is suspected, your visual observation of physical symptoms must be noted, including

- the smell of alcohol on the breath,
- bloodshot eyes,
- slurred speech, and
- lack of balance.

Ask the witness: "How much did you have to drink? What did you drink?" Note the type of conversation you are having with the witness, whether it is coherent and logical or not.

If drug consumption is suspected, the witness may be reluctant to admit it because of the obvious fear of being charged. An effective method is telling the witness, "I need to know what drugs you did and how much. I don't care what you did. It's important to my investigation and the victim." Emphasizing your investigation and lack of concern about the drug use should result in an admission. Determining drug consumption is important for your assessment of the witness's credibility and to inform the Crown Attorney rather than letting the drug-use issue be raised unexpectedly at the trial.

In addition to personal characteristics, external factors affect the accuracy and capability of witness observation.

POSITION

Establishing a witness's position can verify that he or she was actually present and is capable of making the reported observation. It will also determine

- the distance between witness and offender,
- the level of lighting at the crime scene during the commission of the offence, and
- any item or situation that may have interfered with, obstructed, or distracted the witness.

Afterward, the investigator can corroborate that the witness could see and hear at that specific distance. This can be tested by observing what the witness perceives at the same distance and location in the presence of the investigator, and asking the witness to see or hear something at the same distance.

Assessing the level of lighting at the time of the offence not only ensures a degree of accuracy but also allows the observation test to be conducted at the crime scene under similar conditions. Subsequently, the investigator should occupy the reported position of the witness and note the presence or absence of obstructions. Proper notebook recordings should be made of the results to corroborate the witness's observations at the trial. Determining the sources and levels of noise at the crime scene may establish the accuracy with which the witness later reported hearing the offender's conversations.

DURATION OF OBSERVATION

Witnesses who facially describe and recognize an offender must be questioned about their opinion regarding the duration of their observations. The credibility of facial identification increases with the duration of the observation.[38] The duration of observation can be verified by the opinions of other witnesses, confessions made by the offender, and the circumstances of the offence. No specific amount of time constitutes sufficient duration. A good indicator of sufficient duration to verify facial recognition is whether the witness spoke to the accused. Often, a conversation creates the necessary time and attention to remember facial features.

Although no specific time constitutes sufficient duration of observation, the Supreme Court of Canada in *R. v. Reitsma* (1998)[39] ruled that an eyewitness's 15-second observation of an offender who was inside a house during a break and enter was a brief, limited time of observation and was used to rule that a positive identification during the trial had no evidentiary value.

PROCEDURE

To summarize the factors that affect witness observation, the following questions should be asked and procedures followed to determine the relevant details:

1. Where were you when you saw the offence?
2. Did the distance between you and the offender change (e.g., if driving a car)?
3. Was anyone else there?
4. Describe the lighting.
5. Describe the noise.
6. Did anyone or anything obstruct your sight?
7. Have the witness occupy the position occupied at the time of the offence and ask the witness to report what can be seen from that distance.
8. You occupy the witness's position at the time of observation to determine whether anything obstructed his or her sight.
9. Where were you looking before the offence? Why (reasons)?
10. What brought your attention to a certain location before the offence?
11. Did you think an offence was going to happen?
12. Did you think that the police would attend?
13. For how long did you observe the offender?
14. Did you talk to the offender?
15. Did you actually see this or are you assuming it happened?
16. Did you talk to other witnesses before the police arrived?
17. What did other witnesses tell you?
18. What time did your discussion with other witnesses start? What time did it end?
19. Disregard what other witnesses saw. Tell me only what you remember seeing.
20. I wasn't there. I didn't see it happen. I'm relying on you.
21. Do you wear contact lenses?
22. Have you ever had vision or hearing problems?
23. (Test perception of distance) How far is that object from us? Or, How wide is this room?
24. (Test perception of height and weight) How tall am I? How much do you think I weigh? How much taller or shorter was the offender compared to me? How much heavier or lighter was the offender compared to me?
25. Were you afraid for your life?

26. How much have you had to drink?
27. I need to know whether you did any drugs before you saw the offence. I don't care whether you did.

HYPNOSIS

Does hypnosis improve eyewitness memory? Research suggests it does not. Under controlled laboratory conditions, people did not show improved memory under hypnosis.[40] Hypnotized subjects gave more information and showed more confidence, but they gave more inaccurate information.[41] The confidence shown makes hypnotized people more convincing, but they are not more accurate.

REPRESSED MEMORY

Repressed memory is the removal of an unpleasant memory from consciousness. A form of motivated forgetting is used to block the event from one's memory.[42] It is a suppressed memory that can be recovered later in life. The repressed memory issue has been controversial. Since the late 1980s a number of adults have reported being sexual assault victims as children. Psychologists have been divided about the existence of recovered repressed memories.[43]

Some psychologists are skeptical of recovered repressed memories that occurred in the first few years of life. One researcher concluded that no empirical evidence exists to support the idea that adults have memories of events that occurred in the first few years of life.[44]

Connie Kristiansen at Carleton University argues that the issue is not whether repressed memory occurs, but how often it happens. In her research, she reports that **false memory syndrome** does not occur in "epidemic proportions." She calls repressed memory "dissociated memory," which refers to trauma that leads a person to dissociate himself or herself from an occurrence. Researchers who oppose the repressed memory theory have reported finding some people with these memories.[45]

The repressed memory theory poses the obvious problem of trying to distinguish fabrication from actual recall of a memory that had been blocked for a substantial time and recently recalled.

What positions have Canadian courts taken about recovered repressed memory? The Supreme Court of Canada has indirectly recognized the existence of recovered repressed memory in three cases (two criminal, one civil):

- ► *R. v. François* (1994),[46]
- ► *R. v. L. (W.K.)* (1991),[47] and
- ► *M.(K.) v. M.(H.)* (1992).[48]

The most profound decision was made in the *François* case. The jury was allowed to consider recovered repressed memories as a factor in evaluating the complainant's credibility. The accused in that case was convicted for raping the complainant 10 years before the offences were reported. The jury believed that the complainant blocked out the offences for years until a flashback recovered the memory. The circumstances and decision follow.

The accused was charged with raping the complainant, who was 13 years old at the time, during the early 1980s. The complainant reported the offences 10 years later because she feared the offender. There were contradictions about the number of offences. The complainant reported three offences to the police. At the preliminary hearing, she testified that five to six offences had occurred. At the trial, she testified to 10 to 20 occurrences. Additionally, she swore during child-support proceedings a few years earlier that she had never been sexually abused.

During cross-examination, the complainant explained the contradictions by testifying that she had blocked out the rapes until 1990, when her memory returned during a flashback. A jury convicted the accused. The Ontario Court of Appeal upheld the conviction. The S.C.C. dismissed the accused's appeal and upheld the conviction in a four to three decision. The S.C.C. made the following binding rulings:

▸ The controversy about recovered repressed memories among experts was acknowledged by the court, who resolved it by ruling that, "it is sufficient for the purposes of this appeal that the jury's acceptance of the complainant's evidence on what happened to her was not, on the basis of the record, unreasonable."

▸ The defence had the opportunity to cross-examine the complainant about the possibility of fabrication. She denied the defence lawyer's suggestion that her recovered memory was the product of pressure she was suffering.

▸ The S.C.C. concluded that "it was open to the jury, with the knowledge of human nature that it is presumed to possess, to determine on the basis of common sense and experience whether they believed the complainant's story of repressed and recovered memory, and whether the recollection she experienced in 1990 was the truth. To do so cannot be characterized as unreasonable."

▸ The jury's verdict of guilty was not "illogical or speculative or inconsistent with the main body of evidence."

In summary, the *François* case showed that recovered repressed memory is a factor to consider in the evaluation of witness credibility. The "trier," in this case the jury, is responsible for evaluating each witness's credibility. The S.C.C. placed the onus on the jury about whether or not to believe a recovered repressed memory. The jury's decision must be based on the specific evidence introduced at a particular trial. This means that a recovered repressed memory is one factor that must be considered within the total evidence introduced to determine the complainant's credibility. It must be emphasized that the S.C.C. stated that the decision to believe a recovered repressed memory requires a non-expert's "knowledge of human nature" based on logic and experience. In this case, the jury believed the complainant. Surprisingly, the S.C.C. did not give its opinion about the validity of a repressed memory and minimized the controversy surrounding repressed memory by stating that the issue of believing it requires a non-expert's knowledge of human nature. It would have been better had the S.C.C. stated more specific guidelines.

The S.C.C. in *M. (K.) v. M. (H.)* (1992) again recognized repressed memory in a civil suit where an incest victim was awarded tort damages. The S.C.C. made the following rulings relating to repressed memories:

- Researchers have uncovered behavioural patterns suffered by adult survivors of incest, referred to as **accommodation syndrome** or **post-incest syndrome**.
- The classic psychological responses to incest trauma are numbing, denial, and amnesia.
- During the assaults, the incest victim typically learns to shut off pain by *dissociating*, achieving "altered states of consciousness … as if looking on from a distance at the child suffering the abuse."
- The victim may partially or fully repress her memory of the assaults and the suffering associated with them. "Many, if not most, survivors of child sexual abuse develop amnesia that is so complete that they simply do not remember that they were abused at all; or … they minimize or deny the effects of the abuse so completely that they cannot associate it with any later consequences."
- Many abuse victims show signs of **post-traumatic stress disorder (PTSD)**, a condition characterized by avoidance and denial that is associated with survivors of traumatic events, for example, prisoners of war and concentration camp victims.
- PTSD victims frequently experience flashbacks as adults.
- Those suffering from post-incest syndrome will "persistently avoid any situation, such as initiating a lawsuit, that is likely to force them to recall and, therefore, to re-experience traumas."
- The syndrome impedes recognition of the nature and extent of injuries suffered, either because the victim completely represses the memory or because the memories, if not lost, are too painful to confront directly. The syndrome prevents the victim from starting court proceedings until the victim can realize that the abuser's behaviour caused psychological harm.
- A triggering mechanism such as psychotherapy enables the victim to overcome the psychological blocks.
- In this case, the evidence showed that the victim was a typical incest survivor. The victim's therapy triggered her cause of action. The S.C.C. ruled that the statute of limitations did not begin until that time.

In summary, although considerable controversy exists about recovered repressed memory, the S.C.C. has recognized and accepted it as a legitimate cause of victims' delay in reporting sex offences. Additionally, the S.C.C. has allowed trial judges and juries to consider it as a factor while determining credibility. The skepticism of the majority of the police community and courts has caused repressed memory incidents to be largely rejected. It is considered unreliable by most people in the criminal justice system; the major reason is that psychotherapy is needed to trigger the memory.

Case Study 11.1 Conclusion

Refer to the end of Chapter 12 for the conclusion of this two-part case study, which continues at the beginning of the next chapter.

ENDNOTES

1. *R. v. Burke* (1996), 105 C.C.C. (3d) 205, at 224–225 (S.C.C.).
2. *R. v. Sutton* (1970), 3 C.C.C. 152, at 162–163 (Ont. C.A.).
3. *R. v. Nikolovski* (1996), 111 C.C.C. (3d) 403, at 411–412 (S.C.C.).
4. *R. v. Sutton*, supra note 2, as in P.K. McWilliams, *Canadian Criminal Evidence*, 3rd ed. (Aurora, ON: Canada Law Book, 1991).
5. G.L. Wells and E.F. Loftus, *Eyewitness Testimony* (Cambridge: Cambridge University Press, 1984).
6. Brigham et al., 1982; Lortus (1979), as in S. Wood et al., *The World of Psychology*, 2nd Cdn ed. (Scarborough, ON: Prentice-Hall, 1999), at 198.
7. Wells and Loftus, supra note 5.
8. Ibid.
9. H. Gleitman, *Basic Psychology* (Toronto: George J. MacLeod Ltd., 1983).
10. D.R. Buchanan, "Enhancing Eyewitness Identification: Applied Psychology for Police Officers" (1985) vol. 13, no. 4 *Journal of Police Science and Administration.*
11. Gleitman, supra note 9.
12. Hollin and Clifford, as in D.R. Buchanan, "Enhancing Eyewitness Identification: Applied Psychology for Police Officers (1985) vol. 13, no. 4 *Journal of Police Science and Administration.*
13. H. Ebbinghaus, *Memory: A Contribution to Experimental Psychology* (1885) (New York: Dover, 1963, reprint).
14. Yuille and Tollestrup (1992), as in Wood et al., supra note 5, at 198.
15. *R. v. Fliss* (2002), 161 C.C.C. (3d) 225 (S.C.C.).
16. Wood et al., supra note 5, at 181.
17. Ibid.
18. Gleitman, supra note 9.
19. Ibid., at 192–194.
20. Ibid.
21. Ibid.
22. Ibid.
23. Bransford, Barclay, and Franks (1972), in E. Scrivner and M.A. Safer, "Eyewitnesses Show Hypermnesia for Details About a Violent Event" (1988) vol. 73, no. 3 *Journal of Applied Psychology.*
24. Gleitman, supra note 9.
25. Ibid.
26. Brigham and Wolfskid (1983), as in V.L. Smith, P.C. Ellsworth, and S.M. Kassin, "Eyewitness Accuracy and Confidence: Within- Versus Between-Subject's Correlations" (1989) vol. 74, no. 2 *Journal of Applied Psychology.*
27. G.L. Wells and R.C.L. Lindsay, "Methodological Notes on the Accuracy–Confidence Relation in Eyewitness Identifications" (1985) vol. 70, no. 2 *Journal of Applied Psychology.*
28. Buchanan, supra note 10.
29. Johnson and Scott (1976), as in Buchanan, supra note 10.
30. Ibid.

31. J.C. Yuille and P.A. Tollestrup, "Some Effects of Alcohol on Eyewitness Memory" (1990) vol. 74, no. 3 *Journal of Applied Psychology*.

32. Ibid.

33. Lisman (1974), as in Yuille and Tollestrup, supra note 31.

34. Supra note 27.

35. Supra note 10.

36. Fischer (1967), as in G.L. Wells, *Eyewitness Identification* (Toronto: Carswell, 1988).

37. Yarmey (1979), as in Wells, supra note 37.

38. Ellis (1981), as in Buchanan, supra note 10.

39. *R. v. Reitsma* (1998), 125 C.C.C. (3d) 1 (S.C.C.).

40. Buckhout et al. (1981), as in Wood et al., supra note 5, at 199.

41. Dywan and Bower, 1983; Nogrady et al., 1985, as in Wood et al., supra note 5, at 199.

42. Gleitman, supra note 9.

43. Ibid., at 199.

44. Ibid.

45. Ibid.

46. *R. v. François* (1994), 91 C.C.C. (3d) 289 (S.C.C.).

47. *R. v. L. (W.K.)* (1991), 64 C.C.C. (3d) 321 (S.C.C.).

48. *M. (K.) v. M. (H.)*, [1992] 3 S.C.R. 6.

CHAPTER 12

Witness Interviews: Strategies and Procedures

LEARNER SUMMARY

The ultimate purpose of witness interviews is to *elicit information*. The information elicited from a witness has enormous significance; it affects the strategy that will be used to continue an investigation and influences decision making, including whether to conduct searches, make arrests, and lay charges.

There are some problems associated with eliciting information from witnesses. Some witnesses may be reluctant to divulge observations. Others may lack the communication skills to provide *specific* details pertaining to observations made. Consequently, simply asking witnesses "What happened?" and recording the first response to that question is not only inadequate, it often invites *general* or *vague* responses. A witness's response equates to *telling a story*. Many witnesses are poor storytellers simply because of the inexperience of being a witness and the human nature to tell stories in general terms.

The extent of *specific* information elicited from a witness determines the quality of decisions made during an investigation. The extent of the interviewer's skills determines the extent of specific information elicited.

A witness interview is an interaction between two people who often are unfamiliar with each other. It is a *conversation with a purpose*, a unique dialogue that must be coordinated and structured with logic and skill to produce meaningful outcomes.

Consequently, *mastery of communication* is the prominent skill that contributes to interviewing excellence. How we communicate determines the quality of any conversation and the extent of meaning that is achieved. Master communicators elicit the maximum amount of credible, specific information from witnesses.

Communication, like any other skill, is mastered through *repeated experience* of applying effective principles. Studying interviewing principles provides a fundamental basis and a blueprint. Experience, however, develops expertise. Through experience we learn how to communicate effectively in a wide range of situations. All conversations and dialogue are situational. There is no proven formula that works in every conceivable situation. Principles, therefore, are simply general guidelines. Myriad factors, learned through experience, will develop communication expertise.

The primary goal of an investigation is to prove who committed the offence. Evidence has to be obtained that proves beyond a reasonable doubt that a specific person committed the offence. Secondary goals include proving what was committed, how it was committed, and where and when the offence occurred.

Ideally, an investigator wants many eyewitnesses, several physical items, and a confession to achieve these goals. The ideal investigation rarely occurs and there is often a strong reliance on only one or a few witnesses. The actual reliance is on the witness's memory.

An investigator will ask the witness's memory to do two things: (a) recognize the offender and (b) recall the event of the offence. Facial recognition may be perceived as being strong or weak evidence, depending on the manner in which it occurred. The strength of recall is affected by several factors, including the types of interview questions.

This chapter explains witness interview principles that help achieve these investigative goals, including (a) lineup identification and (b) specific interview techniques that affect recall.

Case Study 12.1 (Continuation of Case Study 11.1)

At 7 p.m., Mark attended at the police station. He asked to speak to the officer in charge of the bank robbery investigation. He stated that he had seen the suspects leave the bank. The first assumption was that he was involved in the robbery. He was interviewed at the police station. He reported the following.

He (Mark, 21) was operating a motorcycle on Main Street while returning home from work. He lived two blocks from the bank, less than two minutes away from it. As he drove past the bank, he saw three men leaving through the front entrance. They ran down an alley adjacent to the bank toward the municipal parking lot situated at the rear of the bank. Mark drove around the block and saw a white van leaving the parking lot. While driving behind the van, at a distance of about two car lengths, he had an unobstructed view of the rear licence plate. He memorized the plate and drove along the right side of the van, which had stopped for a red light. He saw two men in the van, but could not describe them. The van continued forward. Mark turned right and drove home. He arrived at his home, which was situated two blocks from the bank. He immediately wrote the plate number on paper. The elapsed time from observation was about four minutes. He gave the paper to the police. The recorded number was REVL 466. Mark was confident of each digit and letter except the L. Extensive record checks were made. None produced positive results. Investigators assumed the possibility of error and checked the plate number by reversing the letters and digits to 466 REVL. The plate was registered to a silver van owned by Bill. Investigation revealed that this plate had been implicated in robberies that occurred in other cities. Reasonable grounds did not exist at this stage about Bill's involvement with the robbery.

The investigation continued. During surveillance, officers observed a male person entering Bill's van. This person was later identified by police as Justin. Justin's facial features bore a remarkable resemblance to the composite drawing of Suspect 2, the blond "baby-face" suspect. Afterward, Bill had been seen by police buying cigarettes in a variety store. Later, an officer seized a $20 bill that was part of the stolen bait money.

(Refer to the end of Chapter 12 for the conclusion of this case study.)

PROVING IDENTITY OF OFFENDER

Proving identity simply means proving who specifically committed the offence. Evidence must prove beyond reasonable doubt that the person named on the Information committed the particular offence that the accused is charged with on that same Information.

An offender's identity is the most important fact-in-issue in every trial. Various types of evidence may prove identity in court or form reasonable grounds during an investigation, including:

- confessions,
- fingerprints,
- identification of the accused in the dock at the trial (i.e., witness pointing at the accused), and
- lineup identification.

LINEUP

Witness or **lineup identification** is one method of proving identity using facial recognition of an accused person. When a witness facially recognizes an offender during a lineup or in court, the witness is giving an opinion. The opinion has high evidentiary value only if it is credible. Several factors affect the credibility of an identification opinion, including the following two rules:

1. Witness or lineup identification may have diminished credibility if the witness is unable to explain facts that form the basis of the opinion.
2. An opinion must be justified to be admissible and to have strong value. This means that reasons for making the opinion should always be determined from the witness and stated during the witness's testimony in court.

A **baseless opinion** is one that has no reasons that justify the opinion. A baseless, unjustified opinion has little value or credibility and may be inadmissible. A **justified opinion** obviously has stronger evidentiary value than a baseless opinion. For example, when a witness points out the accused in court or in a lineup, the witness may strengthen his or her credibility by explaining which of the accused's physical features formed the basis of the opinion.

There are two occasions when an eyewitness may be required to identify an offender:

1. **During the investigation** The purpose of this identification is to form reasonable grounds to arrest and charge. However, this identification will

not suffice for the trial. The eyewitness will have to identify the offender again in court.

2. **In court, at the trial** Even if the offender was identified during the investigation, the accused must be identified during the trial. The purpose of this identification is to prove identity beyond reasonable doubt and convict the accused. Although both identifications are important, the identification at the trial in court is the one that matters. Without it, the accused cannot be convicted if no other evidence exists to identify the accused.

The major problem with in-court identification is the lengthy interval that usually separates the offence date and the trial date. An eyewitness sees the offender on the offence date, and then is asked to recognize him or her several months or years later. Memory decay and changes in the accused's appearance may prevent a positive identification in court. The interval itself may create sufficient reasonable doubt if a positive in-court identification is made.

Another problem with in-court identification is bias. The accused is seated "in the dock." There are no other persons around the accused for the witness to compare him or her with and to select the accused from. These two reasons create a degree of doubt and bias. Lineup identification solves these problems.

Lineup Definition

A lineup can verify an eyewitness's identification of an accused person.[1] It is a means of preserving the credibility of facial recognition for use as evidence in court. Otherwise, the witness's ability to facially recognize the offender at the trial may deteriorate with the passage of time.[2]

Lineup identification is a procedure in which an eyewitness may recognize the offender during the investigation, before the trial. It may be conducted anytime between the offence date and the trial date, but the closer it is conducted to the time of offence the better. A minimal time between the observation and the lineup prevents forgetting and will benefit the witness's credibility.

A lineup identification is then saved and literally brought to court as physical evidence. It condenses the time between observation and recognition to increase credibility. Without a lineup, several months or years may elapse before the trial in which the eyewitness would have to identify the accused in court.

Significance of Lineup Identification

The Supreme Court of Canada, in *R. v. Reitsma* (1998), confirmed the following rule: The identification of an accused person for the first time while the accused is "in the dock" during a trial is generally regarded as having little, if any, weight.[3]

This means that if no lineup identification is made before the trial, the recognition of an accused person during the trial will have almost no evidentiary value. In other words, it will likely not be considered an identification. A lineup identification during an investigation is necessary to add value to the in-court identification.

A positive lineup identification constitutes reasonable grounds that the person recognized was the offender and that he or she should be arrested.

One of the most important questions to ask a witness during an interview is, "Can you recognize the suspect if you see him or her again?" If the answer is yes, a lineup should be presented to the witness as soon as possible.

If the witness states that he or she cannot recognize the suspect, it is possible that the witness is lying and is reluctant to identify the offender and testify. A lineup should still be considered. No lineup is needed if the witness has longtime familiarity with the offender.

Factors Affecting Witness Credibility

In many cases where lineups are used, the witness has little or no familiarity with the suspect. If the witness knows the offender (e.g., the accused is a relative), a lineup is not needed. Seeing a person only once and being asked to recognize that person later is not as simple as it appears. Numerous factors affect the credibility of an identification opinion:

- duration of observation,[4]
- distance of observation,[5]
- time between observation and identification,[6]
- existence or absence of previous familiarity,[7] and
- number of specific physical features that a witness recognizes or describes.[8]

Eyewitnesses may remember only a limited number of an offender's identifying features.[9] A danger exists that they may fill voids in their memory with lineup observations resulting in inaccurate memory reconstruction about an offender's appearance.[10]

There are other potential problems with witness identification. Some crime victims may perceive a lineup as a test to evaluate their honesty and may feel compelled to pick someone. They may, unfortunately, believe that their credibility is dependent on a positive identification and select someone without being positive, because of fear of failure to select an offender. They may identify any person who has similar physical characteristics to those they reported earlier to the police.[11] A victim's bias caused by an intense desire to apprehend the suspect may also contribute to inaccurate identification.

Principles of Lineup

No statutory guidelines exist regarding lineups. Guidelines are found in case law. The principles of lineup identification started in *R. v. Smierciak* (1946)[12] and continue to evolve in derivative decisions following the "lineup recommendations" created by the Sophonow Inquiry, released in Manitoba in 2001.

If a witness has no previous knowledge of or familiarity with an accused person, the witness's facial recognition must be independent and based on the witness's free judgment. This means that the witness's recognition should not be assisted by suggestion, assistance, or bias.

If the witness's recognition is affected by any bias, the credibility of the recognition is reduced or destroyed totally. To maintain high credibility of a witness's identification, an unbiased lineup is required. The features of an unbiased lineup include:

▸ **Preventing a single viewing of the accused by the witness after the accused's arrest**   The witness should not be shown the accused alone in person or by a single photo between the time of the arrest and the time of the lineup presentation.[13] A single viewing before a lineup causes the risk of the face seen in the single viewing becoming stamped on the witness's mind rather than the face seen during the offence. Clinical studies have supported this.[14]

▸ **Providing a sufficient number of selections with the suspect to reduce the possibility of error**   These selections are referred to as *comparison persons*. The purpose is to ensure that the witness is able to compare the suspect with other persons to prevent the bias of a single viewing. No specific number of comparison persons has been specified by case law.

▸ **Ensuring the accused is not distinctive from the comparison persons**   The accused should not stand out from the others in any way. All comparison persons in a lineup should have appearances similar to the accused.[15]

The Sophonow Inquiry: Recommendations

The Sophonow Inquiry, which examined a wrongful conviction, made recommendations for lineups. These recommendations are not law. Their value is best described by the Ontario Court of Appeal in *R. v. Goulart-Nelson* (2004): the Sophonow lineup recommendations are "*persuasive tools to avoid wrongful convictions arising from faulty eyewitness identification.*"[16] There are "no rigid rules" about how a judge will apply these recommendations. At this point, they are considered "strong recommendations," but are not law.

The following are the recommendations from the Inquiry.

EYEWITNESS IDENTIFICATION PROCEDURES

LIVE LINEUP

▸ The third officer who is present with the prospective eyewitness should have no knowledge of the case or whether the suspect is contained in the lineup.

▸ The officer in the room should advise the witness that he does not know if the suspect is in the lineup or, if he is, who he is. The officer should emphasize to the witness that the suspect may not be in the lineup.

▸ All proceedings in the witness room while the lineup is being watched should be recorded, preferably by videotape but, if not, by audiotape.

▸ All statements of the witness on reviewing the lineup must be both noted and recorded verbatim and signed by the witness.

▸ When the lineup is completed, the witness should be escorted from the police premises. This will eliminate any possibility of contamination of that witness by other officers, particularly those involved in the investigation of the crime itself.

▸ The fillers in the lineup should match as closely as possible the descriptions given by the eyewitnesses at the time of the event. It is only if that is impossible, that the fillers should resemble the suspect as closely as possible.

At the conclusion of the lineup, if there has been any identification, there should be a question posed to the witness as to the degree of certainty of identification. The question and answer must be both noted and recorded verbatim and signed by the witness. It is important to have this report on record before there is any possibility of contamination or reinforcement of the witness.

The lineup should contain a minimum of 10 persons. The greater the number of persons in the lineup, the less likelihood there is of a wrong identification.

PHOTO PACK LINEUP

▸ The photo pack should contain at least 10 subjects.

▸ The photos should resemble as closely as possible the eyewitnesses' description. If that is not possible, the photos should be as close as possible to the suspect.

▸ Everything should be recorded on video or audiotape from the time that the officer meets the witness, before the photographs are shown through until the completion of the interview. Once again, it is essential that an officer who does not know who the suspect is and who is not involved in the investigation conducts the photo pack lineup.

▸ Before the showing of the photo pack, the officer conducting the lineup should confirm that he does not know who the suspect is or whether his photo is contained in the lineup. In addition, before showing the photo pack to a witness, the officer should advise the witness that it is just as important to clear the innocent as it is to identify the suspect. The photo pack should be presented by the officer to each witness separately.

▸ The photo pack must be presented sequentially and not as a package.

▸ In addition to the videotape, if possible, or, as a minimum alternative, the audiotape, there should be a form provided for setting out in writing and for signature the comments of both the officer conducting the lineup and the witness. All comments of each witness must be noted and recorded verbatim and signed by the witness.

▸ Police officers should not speak to eyewitnesses after the lineups regarding their identification or their inability to identify anyone. This can only cast suspicion on any identification made and raise concerns that it was reinforced.

It was suggested that, because of the importance of eyewitness evidence and the high risk of contaminating it, a police force other than the one conducting the investigation of the crime should conduct the interviews and the lineups with the eyewitnesses. Ideal as that procedure might be, I think that it would unduly complicate the investigation, add to its cost and increase the time required. At some point, there must be a reasonable degree of trust placed in the police. The interviews of eyewitnesses and the lineup may be conducted by the same force as that investigating the crime, provided that the officers dealing with the eyewitnesses are not involved in the investigation of the crime and do not know the suspect or whether his photo forms part of the lineup. If this were done and the other recommendations complied with, that would provide adequate protection of the process.[17]

In *R. v. Friesen* (2005), the court included an excellent review of how to apply the Sophonow recommendations:

SEQUENTIAL (ONE AT A TIME) PROCEDURES

False identifications may be the result of the relative judgment (all at once) process. When this "one at a time" procedure is compared to simultaneous (all at once) procedures, the sequential procedure is superior. Trial scientists found that the traditional procedure (viewing all photos at once) permits the relative judgment process to reduce accuracy. In the sequential procedure, each photo is examined individually and the witness decides whether or not that person is the culprit, before viewing subsequent photos. This superior absolute judgment process increases accuracy.

SEQUENTIAL (ONE AT A TIME) PRESENTATIONS

In a sequential (one at a time) procedure, an eyewitness views the photos individually and makes a decision (that the photo is/is not the perpetrator) before viewing the next lineup photo. Compared to the usual simultaneous procedure, it is clear that the sequential procedure produces a lower rate of false identifications in perpetrator-absent photo-lineups. Therefore the fifth recommendation, if added, would be that the photo-lineup would be sequentially rather than simultaneously (all at once) presented. . . .[18]

SEQUENTIAL LINEUPS

The traditional lineup approach of police authorities has been to simultaneously show an eyewitness a suspect and foils or distractors. For example, an eyewitness might be asked to view a lay-out of 12 photographs.

In sequential lineup procedure, on the other hand, the witness is shown one photo at a time and has no idea how many images he or she will be shown where no positive identification is made.

Because of a witness's desire to make an identification and the natural belief that the person responsible for the crime will be in a photo array, eyewitnesses examining a simultaneous lineup have been shown to engage in relative or comparative judgment strategies—comparing the photos in pursuit of identification of the individual who looks most like the witness's imprinted memory.

The photo pack must be presented sequentially and not as a package.[19]

SEQUENTIAL PHOTO LINEUP

When presenting a sequential photo lineup, the lineup administrator or investigator should:

2. Provide the following additional viewing instructions to the witness:

    a. Individual photographs will be viewed one at a time.
    b. The photos are in random order.
    c. Take as much time as needed in making a decision about each photo before moving to the next one.
    d. All photos will be shown, even if an identification is made prior to viewing all photos; or the procedure will be stopped at the point of an identification (consistent with jurisdictional/departmental procedures).

3. Confirm that the witness understands the nature of the sequential procedure.
4. Present each photo to the witness separately, in a previously determined order, removing those previously shown.
5. Avoid saying anything to the witness that may influence the witness's selection.
6. If an identification is made, avoid reporting to the witness any information regarding the individual he or she has selected prior to obtaining the witness's statement of certainty.[20]

Three types of lineups are available:

1. live,
2. photo, and
3. video.

The principles outlined above apply to all types of lineups. The following are summaries of how to compose them.

FORMING A LIVE LINEUP

Live lineups are not the most common type of lineup. An accused person has no legal obligation to participate in a lineup and cannot be compelled to do so. There is no document that can be served to a suspect to force participation in a live lineup. Participation in a lineup can occur only with the accused's consent.[21] Accused persons who agree to participate in a lineup must be informed of the right to counsel and have the right to consult a lawyer before the lineup begins.[22] Identification evidence has been excluded from court when an accused agreed to participate in a lineup without being given an opportunity to obtain legal advice.[23]

A person who refuses to participate cannot be charged. The evidence that a person refused to participate is generally inadmissible because there is no obligation for a person to participate in a live lineup.[24]

A live lineup needs a sufficient number of comparison persons. The other problems with a live lineup are that no one can be compelled by any means to participate in the lineup and the comparison persons cannot have different appearances than the suspect. Only people who have similar physical features, including age and height, may be used.

FORMING A PHOTO LINEUP

A proper **photo lineup** is an unbiased and organized set of facial photographs presented to a witness for the purpose of identifying an accused by facial recognition.

An **unbiased** photo lineup has been accepted as one that is in accordance with the findings of the Sophonow Inquiry. The accompanying website **www.emp.ca/arcaro/criminvestigation5E** includes ongoing reviews of derivative case law decisions which further explain the evolution of applying photo lineup procedures.

The photo lineup is real evidence. The witness and officer must be subpoenaed to the trial, and the lineup must be introduced through testimony.

Photos may be obtained (a) by consent, or (b) on arrest or an Information being sworn for dual procedure or indictable offence, under authority of the *Identification of Criminals Act*.

FORMING AND PRESENTING A VIDEO LINEUP

The Ontario Court of Appeal, in *R. v. Parsons* (1993),[25] ruled that video lineups are better than photo lineups because they afford witnesses the opportunity to view the entire body and movements.

In *R. v. Parsons* (1993) the accused and three accomplices were arrested for robbery. Afterward, the accused refused to consent to participate in a live lineup, on the advice of counsel. Subsequently, the police videotaped the accused, without his knowledge and consent, while he walked down a hallway. The police later video-taped 12 other people separately, including the three accomplices and nine other comparison people unrelated to the offence. One 45-minute tape was made, composed of the consecutive individual tapes.

Witnesses viewed the tape and the accused was identified by facial recognition. The tape was ruled to be fair and admissible. The accused was convicted and later appealed to the Ontario Court of Appeal, seeking exclusion of the tape on the grounds that the filming occurred without consent, which constituted a s. 7 Charter violation. The court dismissed the appeal and confirmed the videotape's admissibility for the following reasons:

- An accused's refusal to participate in a live lineup does not prevent the police from using alternative means to identify, such as a video lineup.
- An accused may be videotaped without consent.
- Videotapes are better than photo lineups because they afford witnesses the opportunity to view body movements.
- Recording facial or bodily features does not violate self-incrimination rules.

The use of video is legal and is an acceptable investigative aid.

Positive Identifications

To prevent diminished or destroyed witness credibility and a reduction of the identification's evidentiary value, avoid the practices that will cause lineup bias. The following rules should be followed:

1. Often, the police arrest offenders in the vicinity of a crime scene shortly after the offender's departure from the crime scene. If the witness has lost sight of the offender, do not return to the crime scene with the offender who is in custody in the cruiser to allow the eyewitness to view the offender for identification purposes. This process constitutes a single viewing. Instead, transport the accused to the police station and conduct a lineup. The Supreme Court of Canada in *R. v. Reitsma* (1998) stated that when the police show only the suspect to a witness and the witness positively identifies the suspect, the identification will have little, if any, weight. The S.C.C. ruled that this type of identification is the same as a first-time identification during a trial, which also has little or no value. If the police arrive at a crime scene and the witness is present, no lineup is necessary if the witness had uninterrupted sight of the offender from the time of offence until the time the witness identifies the offender to police.[26]

2. If no suspicion exists about who the offender is, do not give a random stack of mug shots to eyewitnesses. Previous exposure to mug shots interferes with the witness's ability to recognize faces that were seen before viewing the mug shots.[27] Research indicates that witnesses who view stacks of 100 mug shots tend to err more often in a subsequent lineup than those who avoided random mug shot viewing.[28] If a suspicion exists about an offender's identity, insert his or her mug shot into a formal photo lineup and present it to the witness.

3. Eyewitnesses should not be presented a single photo of the offender without comparative mug shots or before a lineup. A single photo viewing, before a lineup, could create a bias and may adversely affect the credibility of a positive identification.

The Supreme Court of Canada in *R. v. Reitsma* (1998) created the following general rule that should guide the police in the avoidance of improper identification procedures: "Generally, anything which tends to convey to a witness that a person is suspected by the police or is charged with the offence has the effect of reducing or destroying the value of the identification evidence."[29]

In summary, if an investigator intends to present a lineup to an eyewitness:

1. Present as soon as possible after the offence.
2. Prevent the eyewitness from taking part in a single viewing of the accused or of photos before the lineup is conducted.
3. Do not convey that any person is suspected or charged by the police.

SIGNIFICANCE OF POSITIVE IDENTIFICATION

A witness's positive identification by facial recognition during a lineup constitutes reasonable grounds to arrest and charge. What if the witness positively identifies the suspect during the lineup but fails to identify the suspect in court at the trial? In *R. v. Swanston* (1982)[30] it was established that if a witness fails to identify an accused person at a trial, evidence of a photo lineup positive identification may be used as proof of identification.

QUALIFIED IDENTIFICATION

A **qualified identification** is an identification that is not positive, but the witness states that the photo recognized is similar to the offender. An example of a qualified identification is found in *R. v. Reitsma* (1998). An eyewitness selected a photo in a lineup and stated that it was "similar to the suspect although I cannot be 100 percent sure from the photo. I feel I could identify the individual in person."[31]

What is the significance of this type of qualified identification? The circumstances of the *Reitsma* case are as follows.

The complainant entered his house and found a suspect inside. The complainant saw the offender for about 15 seconds from a distance of approximately eight feet. The complainant later made the qualified identification during a photo lineup. The police arrested and charged the suspect with break, enter, and theft. At the trial, the complainant made a positive in-court identification. The trial judge convicted the accused. The British Columbia Court of Appeal dismissed the accused's appeal and upheld the conviction.

The S.C.C. allowed the accused's appeal and acquitted the accused. The following rulings were made:

▸ The qualified identification did not constitute a positive identification.
▸ The in-court identification occurred 11 months after the offence.
▸ The frailties of eyewitness identification may be most pronounced when the complainant is unfamiliar with the offender and observation was limited to a brief, stressful encounter.

▸ The 15-second observation was considered brief.

▸ The identification during the trial was the first identification made.

▸ A first-time in-court identification without a prior positive lineup identification is generally regarded as having little if any weight, because (a) the accused is not surrounded by similar persons for comparison, (b) the witness anticipates the offender will be present, and (b) the accused is readily identifiable in the courtroom.

NO LINEUP

Remember that a photo lineup identification is only one method of proving the identity of an accused. Despite the advantages that a lineup presents, there is no requirement to conduct one.[32] For example, if a witness knows the offender (i.e., is a friend or relative), a lineup is not necessary to preserve identification; despite the time lapse until trial, the witness should be able to identify the accused at the trial without difficulty.

Finally, a failed lineup does not mean that identity cannot be proved at all. Other means such as a confession or fingerprint or DNA comparison will prove identity.

IN-COURT VIDEOTAPE IDENTIFICATION (NO WITNESS)

Generally, for an identification to be valid in court, a witness must make it under oath. He or she may be cross-examined. The Crown has the burden of proof, which means that he or she must introduce evidence to prove a *prima facie* case.

A judge or jury are the "triers" of the case. They analyze and examine evidence that is introduced to them. They cannot produce or introduce evidence.

The growing use of video cameras in premises has raised an issue regarding identification of offenders. Videotapes of offenders have become prevalent evidence, especially during robbery investigations.

Some videotapes permit clear facial recognition of offenders and allow comparisons of other physical features. A videotape is physical evidence that has unquestioned relevance at a trial, which permits its admissibility. If a witness, such as the victim, facially recognizes the accused person as being the offender seen in a videotape, identity is proven.

However, in some cases a videotape may show an accused committing an offence, but no witness is capable of positively identifying an accused as being the offender. A controversy exists about whether a trial judge or jury may compare a person depicted in a videotape with an accused person and identify the accused person without any witness identifying the accused or without any other corroboration.

The Supreme Court of Canada answered this controversy in *R. v. Nikolovski* (1996),[33] which provides a significant advantage during prosecutions involving videotape evidence.

CASE LAW

R. v. Nikolovski (1996)

Issue Can a trial judge or jury identify an accused person on the basis of viewing a videotape alone, without any Crown witness identifying the accused or without any other corroboration?

Offence "Robbery."

Circumstances A robbery occurred at a convenience store at 2 a.m. One employee was working. A security video camera was operating and recorded the entire robbery. One offender, armed with a knife, entered the store and stole $230. The employee gave the police a physical description of the suspect, but was unable to describe his clothing.

Two days later, the employee was shown a photo lineup consisting of 12 photos. He suspected three men shown in the lineup, one who was the accused. However, he suspected one man who was not the offender and stated that he was only "25 to 30 percent" sure that he was the offender.

The officers who presented the lineup later testified that the employee looked at the accused's photo and said, "That's him" or "He looks just like him." However, the employee looked at another photo and said, "He looks a bit like him also."

A detective was present, who was familiar with the offender having known him for several years. As the result of investigation, the accused was arrested, but denied committing the offence.

Trial At the trial, the Crown introduced the videotape as evidence. The employee reviewed the videotape during his testimony. Afterward, he was asked if the man who robbed the store was in the courtroom. The employee stated that he did not think so and could not identify the accused.

A detective testified that he had been familiar with the offender for several years and was present at the time of the arrest. He testified that the accused had a sparse moustache that was absent on the day of the trial. However, the Crown did not ask this detective to identify the accused by means of videotape comparison. The detective testified that the accused denied committing the offence by informing the police that he had been at home with his mother and brother. The defence introduced no evidence.

The trial judge viewed the videotape and concluded that the accused committed the offence, stating, "I'm satisfied on looking at the tape that that's him and he's convicted." The accused appealed the conviction to the Ontario Court of Appeal on the grounds that the only evidence of identity was the trial judge's opinion without any Crown witness's identification or without another corroboration.

Ontario Court of Appeal The appeal was allowed and the conviction was quashed. The reason for the acquittal was that an identification made exclusively by a trial judge without corroboration by a witness is insufficient to convict.

The Crown appealed to the Supreme Court of Canada.

Supreme Court of Canada The S.C.C., in a 7–2 decision, allowed the Crown's appeal and restored the conviction. The following reasons were given:

▸ A videotape becomes relevant and admissible evidence after it is proven that the tape has not been altered or changed and that it depicts the scene of the crime.

▸ A videotape can and should be used by a trial judge to identify an accused. Identification may be based exclusively on a trial judge's opinion without any Crown witness supporting the identification. No other corroboration is required.

▸ Courts have long recognized the weakness of identification made by honest witnesses because of various factors that contribute to unintentional human error. Witness credibility is dependent on whether the witness

▹ was in a physical position to make the observation,

▹ has sound vision, hearing, intelligence, and the ability to communicate the observation,

▹ has a sound memory,

▹ was adversely affected by fear to observe and recall, or

▹ is biased.

▸ Robberies are traumatic events causing stress that may affect the ability to accurately describe an offender. Bias may arise resulting from a victim's strong desire to convict. Videotape does not suffer stress.

▸ In some cases, videotape may be the only evidence available. For example, the witnesses may be murdered during the robbery. Common sense dictates that a trial judge should not be denied the ability to use videotape to identify an accused person.

▸ A conviction may be based on a single witness. Therefore, a single videotape may be the sole evidence capable of convicting an offender.

▸ If a jury tries an accused, the same rules apply. A jury may identify an accused by viewing a videotape and comparing the offender depicted in the video with the accused in the courtroom. No witness or corroboration is required to convict. However, the jury must be instructed to consider whether (a) the video has sufficient clarity and (b) the duration of observation of the offender is sufficient.

Summary This ruling gives officers an advantage during investigations. If a videotape clearly shows an offender for a sufficient time, a witness is no longer needed to positively identify the offender. The judge or jury now can simply view the videotape and form their own opinion of identity. The only issue is the admissibility of the videotape, which is physical evidence.

Admissibility of Videotape

To ensure admissibility of the videotape, follow this procedure:

1. **Seize the videotape lawfully.** The owner of the premises likely owns the videotape. Lawful seizure may be made in one of two ways:

   a. by consent, following the case-law procedural guidelines. Obtaining valid consent in these cases should be done without difficulty.
   b. by a s. 487 *Criminal Code* search warrant.

2. **Prove continuity.** The seizing officer initials the videotape to help identify the tape in court as being the same one seized. The tape is stored in a police property locker at the trial. Any officer who had possession of the tape from the time of seizure until the trial must be subpoenaed to prove

continuity. The purpose is to prove that the tape has not been altered. The number of officers who take possession of the tape during that interval should be minimized.

GENERAL INTERVIEW PRINCIPLES

There are no exact scientific methods of ensuring that a witness recalls an entire event accurately. One of the objectives of an effective interview is to help a witness to remember while preventing retrieval failures. The type of questioning may affect a witness's memory favourably or adversely.

There are general principles that create practices to follow and to avoid during the interview that may help recall while preventing retrieval interference. These are discussed below.

Leading Questions

Leading questions are those that imply, suggest, or contain an answer. During a study on the effect of question format on recall and retrieval, subjects viewed a video-tape of a car collision. There was no broken headlight on the film. One group was asked, "Did you see *the* broken headlight?" The other group was asked, "Did you see *a* broken headlight?" Those who were asked about "the" headlight were more likely to report incorrectly seeing one than the group asked about "a" headlight.

Using "the" implies that an object or event actually did exist, which constitutes a leading question. The only issue then becomes whether the witness saw it, not whether it existed or occurred. The danger of using "the" is that a witness may adopt the suggestion and say yes because the witness may conform to what he or she believes the officer knows as fact. The use of "a" creates no suggestion and may likely prevent the witness from incorrectly reporting seeing it.[34]

The premise that forgetting is the result of a failure to retrieve and not a failure to store suggests that leading questions cannot facilitate accurate retrieval.[35] Eliminating leading questions that include "the," which suggest positively that something existed, may prevent inaccurate or insufficient answers.

In the previous scenario, the best way to determine what the witness saw is to say "Describe the damage on the car." No answer is suggested.

An issue that must be determined in every case is whether the offender was armed. The best method is to ask, "Was the suspect holding or carrying anything?" An acceptable method is to ask, "Did you see a weapon?" Avoid asking, "Did you see the weapon?"

Misleading Questions

In some cases involving multiple witnesses or when the officer has knowledge of a fact before interviewing the witnesses, some officers test a witness by asking **misleading questions**. These are questions about a fact or circumstance that the investigator knows to be false. For example, if a suspect is already known to be 20 years old, have brown hair, be 6'3", 230 lbs., and clean shaven, an officer might test the witness—by asking, for example:

- ▸ Was he 40 years old?
- ▸ Was he about 5'8", 150 lbs.?
- ▸ Did he have blond hair?
- ▸ Did he have a beard?

Misleading questions must be avoided. They interfere with memory and recall. Research consistently shows that misleading questions cause witnesses to adopt the suggested wrong information and report it as fact. Researchers have theorized that the reason for this is that the false information is inserted into the witness's memory of the observation.[36]

Conformity is another reason. Witnesses may perceive the police to be correct and simply conform to wrong information. Conversely, research shows that witnesses who are not asked misleading questions are more accurate.[37]

In some instances, an officer may ask an unintentionally misleading question because of inexperience. This type of question may be asked because the officer speculates or makes conjectures before obtaining accurate facts. One research study indicates that misleading questions do not affect memory accuracy if the witness is certain about his or her observations.[38] Witness certainty is related to and can be affected by perceived expertise of the interviewing officer. Research has examined the relationship between misleading questions and perceived officer's expertise:

1. The adverse effect of a misleading question is not caused by the question. Instead, it is caused by the witness's perception of the officer's knowledge of the investigation. Misleading questions cause inaccuracy when the witness believes that the officer has a considerable amount of information relating to the investigation.
2. Witnesses who are certain about their observations may not be easily swayed by misleading questions. However, a witness's certainty can be diminished if the witness believes the officer knows a lot of facts about the offence.[39]

In summary, this research indicates that misleading questions may adversely affect memory if the witness (a) perceives the officer as being knowledgeable and having considerable expertise, and (b) is uncertain about his or her observations. The following procedures will prevent possible witness inaccuracy and interference with memory recall:

- ▸ Do not intentionally ask misleading questions to test a witness.
- ▸ To avoid the adverse effects of inadvertent misleading questions, do not convey to the witness that you already know a great deal of information about the offence and investigation. Instead, ensure that the witness perceives you as being ignorant of the circumstances relating to the offence. A recommended comment that should be made to witnesses before the actual interview begins is: "I didn't see the offence happen. I'm relying on you to tell me about it." Emphasizing the reliance on the witness may prevent the witness from conforming to suggestions and adopting observations inferred by misleading questions. The witness will not feel compelled to agree with any inadvertent suggested observations about what may have happened.

Excessive Closed-Ended Questions

There are two types of questions: (a) open-ended and (b) closed-ended. **Open-ended questions** are intended to generate several facts. Examples include: "What did the offender look like?" and "What happened?"

Closed-ended questions are intended to generate only one fact. Examples include: "How tall was the offender?" "What colour was his T-shirt?" and "Can you facially recognize him?"

Excessive closed-ended questions should be avoided. They have a purpose and should be used only when needed. Research shows that police interviews may include too many closed-ended questions and at inappropriate times.

Data collected from the examination of 11 tape-recorded interviews by police officers concluded that a typical witness interview consisted of three open-ended questions and 26 closed-ended questions, a ratio of almost 1:9. An open-ended question started the interviews. Seconds later, the format altered and a multitude of closed-ended questions followed.

Closed-ended questions have advantages and disadvantages. The advantages are that they:

- prevent haphazard descriptions,
- add structure to the interview,
- clarify general or vague answers, and
- generate relevant facts.

The use of excessive closed-ended questions causes disadvantages that outweigh the advantages. The disadvantages include the following:

- **A less concentrated form of retrieval is used.** The memory uses only a narrow focus instead of the broader focus used to answer open-ended questions. Closed-ended answers are brief, usually one word.
- **Mental passivity develops.** The witness becomes accustomed to waiting for the next question, rather than trying to remember. Passive thinking is caused by the narrow focus required to answer a closed-ended question and may prevent an efficient return to a broader focus if the witness becomes used to narrowly focused, closed-ended questions. Retrieval increases only in mentally active witnesses. It may become impossible in mentally passive witnesses.
- **Responses and facts are limited only to the request made.** The witness usually offers no more information than has been asked. Excessive closed-ended and insufficient open-ended questions may cause the witness to forget or neglect to give other relevant information.[40]

There is no scientific, foolproof ratio of open- and closed-ended questions that should be asked. Each interview is different. The following guidelines prevent asking excessive closed-ended questions and at wrong times during an interview:

1. Start each interview with an open-ended question. This creates a mentally active memory.
2. Avoid starting with a closed-ended question. Interviews should not start with a narrow focus.

3. Avoid interrupting an open-ended response with a closed-ended question. Let the witness complete the open-ended answer.

4. Ask an open-ended question to begin questioning of a separate issue. For example, "Describe the suspect" is better than asking a series of closed-ended questions to obtain a physical description.

5. Use closed-ended questions to obtain facts that the witness has neglected during the open-ended response. Some witnesses give thoroughly structured answers. Others give brief, haphazard answers. Closed-ended questions are needed to structure the answer and to expand poorly structured answers.

Order of Questions

Research has shown that the order of questions affects recall. If the order of questions conflicts with the witness's mental image of the observation, recall may be obstructed. A study revealed three common problems in the order of questions asked during an interview. The three problems serve as a procedural guideline, explaining the interview method that should be avoided and the consequence of using the method.

1. **Asking questions in a rigid, systematic manner** This prevents the flexibility to adjust to a witness's memory. An example is a witness's response to a particular question that leads to another issue. The witness's memory has now focused on that part of the observation. A potential mistake would be to return to the original issue or proceed to another one that had been predetermined. A rigid, systematic order of questions is effective if the witness's mental image stays compatible with that structure. Some flexibility is necessary when the witness's memory is focused on a specific image.

2. **Interrupting answers to open-ended questions with a related closed-ended question** For example, an officer asks, "What was the suspect wearing?" The answer may include only a general description such as, "a T-shirt, blue jeans. . . ." The temptation may occur to interrupt at the point to ask closed-ended questions to specifically describe the shirt, such as, "What colour was the T-shirt?" The order of the question is incorrect. It interrupts the reporting of an entire general description. The question narrows the witness's focus and mental imagery, which may prevent a full broadening of the mental image and complete, accurate description of the person. The clarifying question should be asked after the open-ended response is complete to maintain compatibility with the witness's focus and mental image.

3. **Asking questions that are unrelated to or not relevant to the witness's response, before completion of that topic** Haphazard, closed-ended questioning prevents accurate optimum recall. One topic should be finished before moving to the next topic. An example of improper order of questions is:

> Q: "Did the suspect have a weapon?"
> A: "Yes."

Q: "Can you recognize him if you see him again?"

A: "Yes."

After the witness said that a weapon was seen, the next series of questions should have been intended to obtain a description of the weapon. The topic of the weapon was not finished before asking about identification capability.

Asking questions out of sequence is usually the product of inexperience, impatience, or inattention. Sometimes focus is lost during an interview and the officer may remember something that he or she forgot to ask earlier, or may suddenly think of a question that is believed to be important. If the witness is talking about another topic when this occurs, let the witness finish and ask unrelated questions afterward.

In summary, improperly alternating unrelated questions may interrupt recall.[41]

Negative Questions

"You didn't see a weapon, right?" is an example of a negative question. These questions imply that the officer believes that

- the witness does not know the answer,
- the fact or circumstance did not exist, or
- the witness merely did not observe it, although the fact or circumstance existed.

Negative questions should be avoided because they may result in the same consequences as leading or misleading questions. If the witness perceives the officer as being an expert on the subject, he or she may agree with the officer.[42] Negative questions may produce inaccurate responses and prevent accurate recall.[43]

Incompatible Language

Witnesses have varied levels of intelligence. An evaluation must be made quickly about each individual's intellect. Communication must be compatible with the intelligence level to prevent the misinterpretation of questions or the formation of psychological barriers.[44]

Incompatible language may be in the form of words that exceed the witness's intelligence or unprofessional language that causes a witness to unnecessarily focus on it. Both types may affect witness accuracy.

Interruptions (Distractions)

"What did you see?" or "What happened?" These are two examples of simple initial open-ended questions that begin a witness interview. Research indicates a significant statistic: 35 percent of all correct facts given by a witness occur during an uninterrupted response to an initial open-ended question. This means that more than one-third of all accurate facts will likely be received if the witness is not interrupted while answering the initial question.

The same research shows that

▸ Officers interrupt the initial response an average of four times.
▸ The first interruption usually occurs only 7.5 seconds after the initial question is asked.

None of the witnesses who were involved in the study was allowed to answer initial open-ended questions without interruption by the officer. Other distractions existed during the interviews, including police radios and other officers entering the room.

Experience shows that these data reflect common distractions and interruptions that occur during witness interviews. The study concludes that interruptions and distractions during an open-ended response are likely to result in the following two consequences:

1. If the witness is recalling from a vivid mental image, the concentration is lost and the witness may not be able to reacquire the same vivid clarity of the initial mental image.
2. If interruptions become frequent and the witness begins to expect them, the witness may

   ▷ believe that he or she has only a short time to answer and may rush recall or the answer, or
   ▷ use less effort to recall from a vivid mental image, which may result in inaccuracies.[45]

Eliminating interruptions and distractions will allow the witness to maintain a vivid mental image and may result in optimum recall of accurate facts. The following simple procedures will eliminate consequences of interruptions and distractions:

1. Let the witness answer open-ended questions uninterrupted. The responses may not be thorough. Quite frequently, the answer will be brief or unstructured. The temptation arises to interrupt and ask clarifying closed-ended questions. These questions should not be asked during the response.
2. Make rough notes of closed-ended questions that are needed to clarify and structure the answer. Ask them after the witness has finished the open-ended response.
3. Avoid interviewing a witness in open areas. A police station is a busy place with limited interview rooms. Find a room away from high-traffic areas. Notify others that an interview is in progress to prevent disruptions. Lock the door if possible.
4. Shut off police radios and phones. There should be no need to keep a portable police radio on during an interview. People are fascinated by police radios. They will concentrate on the radio instead of the question. Police radios are probably the biggest distraction possible during an interview.

Multiple Interviews and Hypermnesia

Commonly, a witness is interviewed once. However, no statute law prevents more than one interview, and the admissibility of a witness's testimony will not be adversely affected if repeated interviews by the police precede it. The ultimate test of a witness's credibility will occur during testimony under oath at a court trial. Multiple interviews of a witness are recommended because they enhance recall.

Laboratory experiments indicate that multiple recall attempts do not increase memory errors, but may produce **hypermnesia**, which means net gains in the amount of information recalled. Hypermnesia refers to "increased recall levels associated with longer retention intervals."[46] Hypermnesia occurs during a second or subsequent interview when a person recalls information that was left out or forgotten in a first, or previous, interview.

The sequence of the hypermnesia process begins when the witness recalls information during an initial police interview or during the recording of a statement. The second stage commences in any subsequent interview when the witness remembers more information than in the first or in a previous interview. Hypermnesia can be produced only by multiple interviews when the witness is encouraged to make repeated attempts to recall.

Scrivner and Safer (1988) conducted experiments on the relationship between hypermnesia and the observation of a violent event. Ninety subjects watched a videotape of an offender committing a house break and enter and shooting three people. The duration of the offence was two minutes. The offence was composed of 47 details. After viewing the tape, the subjects were given initial interviews. Subsequently, in four successive interviews, they recalled increasingly more details on each attempt.

Researchers concluded that recalling the details of a violent event increased in completeness and accuracy with multiple interviews. This contradicts the theory that honest witnesses inform police of all they know during the initial interview.

Case Study 12.1 Conclusion

An unbiased photo lineup was prepared. It included Justin's mug shot. The lineup was presented to Jane two days after the robbery. Jane immediately and confidently identified Justin as being one of the suspects she saw enter the bank. This circumstance, combined with other facts discovered in the investigation, constituted reasonable grounds to arrest Justin for the indictable offence of robbery.

Justin was subsequently arrested, informed of his right to counsel, and was cautioned. He was interrogated at the police station. Investigation revealed that Justin definitely was not involved in the robbery. He looked exactly like the composite drawing of Suspect 2 and Jane had identified him in the photo lineup, but she had been wrong.

Additionally, another remarkable coincidence resulted from the positive identification in the lineup. Justin knew the three offenders very well and was a friend of theirs! During interrogation, he denied participating in the robbery. However, he had met with the three friends the previous night and they informed him about the planned robbery and asked him to participate. He refused. It was proven that he was nowhere near the crime scene when the robbery occurred. As a result of the mistaken identification by Jane, Justin gave a written witness statement that provided reasonable grounds to arrest Bill, Owen, and Rick for the indictable offence of robbery. All three were subsequently arrested, informed of their right to counsel, and cautioned. All three were interrogated. Each admitted participating in the robbery and gave investigators a written confession.

COMMENTARY Jane was proven to have no credibility. Her descriptions and lineup identification were completely wrong. Mark incorrectly wrote down a licence plate that he had seen four minutes previously. Both these examples show the frailties of witness observations even when optimum conditions exist to make the observations.

Finally, all three offenders confessed. They were charged separately so they would be competent and compellable to testify against each other. The confessions and accomplice testimony were the crucial evidence, not the witnesses' observations, which proved to cast considerable doubt on their respective accuracy.

ENDNOTES

1. *R. v. Parsons* (1993), 84 C.C.C. (3d) 226 (Ont. C.A.).
2. *R. v. Horsefall* (1991), 70 C.C.C. (3d) 569 (B.C.C.A.).
3. *R. v. Reitsma* (1998), 125 C.C.C. (3d) 1 (S.C.C.).
4. *R. v. Browne and Angus* (1951), 99 C.C.C. 141 (B.C.C.A.).
5. Ibid.
6. *R. v. Mezzo* (1986), 27 C.C.C. (3d) 97 (S.C.C.).
7. *R. v. Leaney* (1987), 38 C.C.C. (3d) 263 (S.C.C.).
8. *R. v. Cosgrove* (1977), 34 C.C.C. (2d) 100 (Ont. C.A.).
9. Doob and Kirshenbaum (1992), as in T.E. Reed, "Eyewitness Identifications of an Armed Robber Within a Biased Police Lineup" (1984) vol. 12, no. 3 *Journal of Police Science and Administration*.
10. Ibid.
11. Ibid.
12. *R. v. Smierciak* (1946), 87 C.C.C. 175 (Ont. C.A.).
13. Ibid.
14. *R. v. Goldhar* (1941), 76 C.C.C. 270 (Ont. C.A.).
15. Molpass and Devine (1983), as in D.R. Buchanan, "Enhancing Eyewitness Identification: Applied Psychology for Police Officers" (1985) vol. 13, no. 4 *Journal of Police Science and Administration*.
16. *R. v. Goulart-Nelson*, [2004] O.J. No. 4010 (QL), at paragraph 11.
17. *The Inquiry Regarding Thomas Sophonow: The Investigation, Prosecution and Consideration of Entitlement to Compensation* (Winnipeg: Manitoba Justice, 2001), as in *R. v. Friesen*, 2005 SKPC 68.
18. Larry Gist and Curtis E. Wills, "Useful Advice on Photo Lineups," October 4, 1999; "Research and Valid Photo-Lineups: Recommendations from 130 Years of Memory Research," reprinted in (July/August 1999) vol. 12, no. 4 *Mouthpiece*; New York State Association of Criminal Defence Lawyers from

"The Voice" by permission of the Texas Association of Criminal Defense Lawyers, as in *R. v. Friesen*, supra note 17.

19. Justice Casey Hill (Ont. Sup. Ct. J.), *Eyewitness Identification Evidence: Emerging Issues* (December 2004), as in *R. v. Friesen*, supra note 17.

20. *R. v. Friesen*, supra note 17.

21. *R. v. Dilling* (1993), 84 C.C.C. (3d) 235 (B.C.C.A.).

22. *R. v. Ross* (1989), 46 C.C.C. (3d) 129 (S.C.C.).

23. Ibid.

24. *R. v. Marcoux* (1976), 24 C.C.C. (2d) 1 (S.C.C.).

25. *R. v. Parsons*, supra note 1.

26. *R. v. Horsefall*, supra note 2.

27. Brown, Deffenbacker, and Sturgill (1977), as in Buchanan, supra note 15.

28. Davies, Shepard, and Ellis (1979), as in Buchanan, supra note 15.

29. *R. v. Reitsma*, supra note 3.

30. *R. v. Swanston* (1982), 65 C.C.C. (2d) 453 (B.C.C.A.), as in *R. v. Foster* (1994), File No. CC921248 (B.C.S.C.).

31. *R. v. Reitsma*, supra note 3.

32. *R. v. Horsefall*, supra note 2.

33. *R. v. Nikolovski* (1996), 111 C.C.C. (3d) 403 (S.C.C.).

34. Loftus and Zanni (1975), as in H. Gleitman, *Basic Psychology* (Toronto: George J. MacLeod Ltd., 1983).

35. R.P. Fisher, E.R. Geiselman, and D.R. Raymond, "Critical Analysis of Police Interview Techniques" (1987) vol. 15, no. 3 *Journal of Police Science and Administration*.

36. V.L. Smith and P.C. Ellsworth, "The Social Psychology of Eyewitness Accuracy: Misleading Questions and Communicator Expertise" (1987) vol. 72, no. 2 *Journal of Applied Psychology*.

37. Ibid.

38. Ibid.

39. Ibid.

40. *R. v. Swanston*, supra note 30.

41. Ibid.

42. Smith and Ellsworth, supra note 36.

43. *R. v. Swanston*, supra note 30.

44. Ibid.

45. Ibid.

46. Payne (1987), as in E. Scrivner and M.A. Safer, "Eyewitnesses Show Hypermnesia for Details About a Violent Event" (1988) vol. 73, no. 3 *Journal of Applied Psychology*.

CHAPTER 13

Applying Witness Interviews and Statements

LEARNER SUMMARY

Upon arrival at a crime scene where an offence has recently occurred, only brief, informal witness statements are taken to fulfill the objectives of the preliminary investigation. In all other circumstances, either after the preliminary investigation, or when a belated offence is reported, formal interviews are conducted to obtain a written witness statement that will be included in the Crown brief after a charge has been laid.

A variety of circumstances affect the time available to conduct formal witness interviews. In this chapter, specific interview procedures will be explained. These procedures have been derived largely from experience; they will show what has and has not achieved optimal results, and include

- systematic, specific witness interview procedures,
- methods used to detect witness deception, and
- the format used to write a formal witness statement.

Case Study 13.1

COMMENTARY   All forms of report writing, including written statements, are vital methods of communication. Mediocre statements cause miscommunication and may convey insufficient justification for certain procedures, such as making an arrest. Mistakes are learning experiences. The following witness statement was dictated by a complainant to an officer who had less than two years of policing experience. The statement was the basis for charging the offender with attempted break and enter.

Statement—June Lee will say

I am 45 years of age. I live at 10 King Street, Apartment 6, with my husband Edward. I am employed as a court clerk for Provincial Court—Family Division.

On November 6, I was at home with my husband. We were watching TV. At about 9 p.m., I heard people screaming in the hallway of our floor. I heard a voice say, "Move out of here. Go back to where you came from." Then someone started banging on the door. I heard more yelling, such as, "Did you hear me? Move out, go back to your own country." I heard him turning the doorknob, trying to get into the apartment. I feared for my safety as well as my husband's. We had been living in fear for about one month. We've been threatened to move and we've had damage caused to our car. The people in the apartment across the hall have been harassing and threatening us for the past month. I called the police and officers arrived within minutes. I spoke to an officer in the doorway of my apartment and I reported this incident to him. The other officer was speaking to the people in the apartment across from ours. The tenant started threatening us and the officer arrested him.

Signed, June Lee

November 6

(Refer to the end of Chapter 13 for the conclusion of this case study.)

PURPOSE

The objective of a formal interview is to obtain the maximum amount of honest, accurate information in writing. Before learning how to interview a witness and write a statement, the general purpose of a written witness statement must be understood.

The primary purpose of a written witness statement is to include it in the Crown brief, to inform the Crown Attorney of the evidence that the witness is expected to testify about in court during the trial. In other words, it is the **predicted testimony**. The statement also serves as

- ▸ a written record for reference during the investigation,
- ▸ a method of communication,
- ▸ justification for conducting a specific procedure in case a complaint is made against the investigating officer,
- ▸ a method of refreshing the witness's memory before the trial, and
- ▸ proof that facilitates the issuance of a subpoena.

A witness statement represents hearsay evidence to the officer who was the recipient of it.

Generally, the statement cannot be used for the following purposes:

- ▸ it cannot be read by the interviewing officer during his or her testimony, and
- ▸ it cannot be submitted by the Crown Attorney to the judge or jury to replace the witness's testimony.

Exceptions to these rules do exist and were explained in previous chapters.

In summary, the witness interview helps form reasonable grounds during the investigation. However, the witness must generally testify about the reported observations at the trial. Ultimately, what the witness testifies about in court is what really matters.

GENERAL RULES

Two general rules are relevant to every witness interview:

1. **A witness cannot be arrested, detained, or compelled to be interviewed**
   Attitudes of witnesses vary considerably. Some are cooperative, but some
   are not. Witnesses may be interviewed by consent only. There is no
   authority to arrest or detain a witness specifically for questioning. No
   document can be served to a witness to compel him or her to attend at a
   police station to be questioned. The subpoena is the answer to any witness
   problems. A subpoena may be issued to compel the witness to court,
   whether he or she is cooperative. Obtaining a written statement is not the
   only method of proving the required conditions to have a subpoena issued.
   A witness's refusal to be interviewed or to give a witness statement does not
   automatically prevent the possibility of obtaining a subpoena.

2. **The witness dictates, the officer writes** Although there are divided
   opinions on this issue, for optimum results never let a witness write his or
   her own statement, because

   ▷ Deception cannot be easily detected.
   ▷ Witnesses do not know (a) rules of evidence, (b) what is relevant to
      the prosecution of the offence, (c) how to structure their observations
      in chronological order, or (d) how to be specific and avoid
      paraphrasing.
   ▷ A statement written by a witness is likely to be haphazard and
      unstructured, vague and lacking specific details, and filled with
      inadmissible comments.

The witness should always dictate the statement while the officer writes it.
Those who advocate having a witness write his or her own initial statement may do
so because expert statement analysis may be needed. If so, an initial statement written
by the witness is acceptable. Afterward, a formal statement should be dictated
to ensure proper structure and to elicit all observations and information. A skilled
officer can probably use this format to form opinions about credibility.

PRELIMINARY CONCEPTS

Establishing the Interview Environment

The place chosen to conduct the interview should fulfill four objectives:

1. It should allow the investigator to gain the witness's trust.
2. It should allow the investigator to detect deception.
3. It should allow the investigator to evaluate the witness's credibility.
4. It should allow the witness to recall as much as possible.

The following factors must be considered when choosing a suitable interview
location:

▸ **Minimize distractions** The investigator requires control over this process.
   Distractions cannot be eliminated if interviews are conducted in bars,

houses, workplaces, parking lots, or police cruisers. These are usually inappropriate interview locations and do not generate optimum results.

▸ **Remove the witness from familiar surroundings** Familiar surroundings increase the witness's tendency to be deceptive and decrease the investigator's ability to recognize witness deception.

▸ **Choose an environment that reflects a professional atmosphere** Honesty requires trust and sincerity between investigator and witness. An investigator can create this relationship by acting with professionalism. Using public places or houses for an interview reduces the environment to an amateurish level.

▸ **Establish and maintain privacy** Witnesses are more cooperative if they believe that their status as witnesses and the content of their information will be treated with confidentiality. To ensure privacy, an investigator should not allow a witness's relatives or friends to be present. Besides destroying the private nature of the interview, these people may disrupt the proceedings by attempting to correct the witness's observations or by filling voids in the witness's information with their own opinions or inferences. Privacy can also be destroyed if there are too many officers at the interview. Generally, one investigator is sufficient to conduct an interview, but a second officer may be acceptable in certain circumstances.

Fulfilling these objectives can be accomplished by following three rules. Deviation from these rules should not occur unless there is no other alternative.

1. The best location for a witness interview is in a police station because
   ▹ the officer can control and minimize distractions,
   ▹ it is a professional atmosphere,
   ▹ the witness will not be in familiar surroundings, and
   ▹ privacy can be ensured.

   What type of room is best for interviewing? If available, a spacious, contemporary office is advantageous. First, it is the most professional place to bring a victim or independent witness. Second, it allows the officer to view the witness's entire body, which will help detect deception (discussed later in the chapter).

2. The witness should not be accompanied by anyone during the interview. There is no need to have anyone else present. The presence of relatives and friends serves no purpose but to interrupt and distract the witness. Experience has shown that they tend to answer questions for the witness. The witness is not the accused and needs no help from anyone for the interview, except from the officer. Privacy is another reason why no one should be present during a witness interview. The witness may be the victim who must divulge intimate details or a bystander who initially wants to maintain confidentiality between the officer and himself or herself. The lack of privacy may interfere with the witness's willingness to divulge personal facts relevant to the investigation.

3. Only one officer should be present to conduct the interview. A witness is not a suspect. An effective witness interview is not dependent on having two officers in the room. The presence of an additional officer is acceptable

only if he or she has total knowledge of the offence and if a primary interviewer has been chosen before the interview. If the witness is uncooperative and may become adverse in court, a two-officer interview should be conducted to corroborate the fact that the witness actually gave the statement. A primary interviewer is needed to prevent unstructured questioning and interruptions by either officer. Experienced partners work well together to prevent haphazard questioning.

Establishing Trust

The trust between the witness and officer may be the most important factor that determines honesty and cooperation. One of the officer's objectives is to obtain honesty from witnesses. A fact of reality is that witnesses are frequently dishonest. It would be naive or gullible to believe that all witnesses have the desire to be honest. Some witnesses, including the actual victim, have a variety of reasons that motivate dishonesty. Some want to conceal facts, while others want to fabricate.

Honesty is largely a product of trust between two people. Trust requires a degree of familiarity. Other factors are involved, such as the witness's immediate impression about the officer's level of professionalism and expertise. The problem with witness interviews is that the officer and witness are likely unfamiliar with each other. They are often strangers. A successful witness interview is strongly dependent on acquiring the witness's trust in a short time. This requires gaining familiarity as soon as possible, which may be done by using simple procedures. What impresses a witness immediately? Experience has shown that they want to perceive the officer as being a competent professional who can solve their problems. The following procedures help build trust.

First, the officer must ensure that the witness knows he or she is a police officer. Proper identification of a police officer to a witness serves two purposes. The first concerns legal implications. A witness must have no doubt that the interviewer is a police officer. If the witness is charged with public mischief, the term *police officer* becomes a fact-in-issue. During a subsequent trial, the Crown must prove beyond reasonable doubt that the witness knew he or she was misleading a peace officer. Section 2 C.C. includes police officer in the definition of peace officer.

Even if the officer is wearing a uniform, the witness should be informed of the officer's occupation and of the police force of which that officer is a member. For example: "I'm Constable Lynn. I'm a police officer with the Niagara Regional Police Force." Informing the witness only of rank and name may cause reasonable doubt in the mind of a witness about the officer's occupation; not all people associate the rank of constable with the occupation of police officer. All identification, regardless of rank, should be accompanied by a badge presentation, for corroboration purposes.

The second purpose of an identification is to form a base of trust and sincerity. Identification acts as a social introduction between two strangers. People talk more easily and openly if they feel some social connection, however small, between themselves and the other person. It also helps to explain unfamiliar terms or duties. For example, a CIB officer must describe his or her duties. The term *CIB* is usually meaningless to a witness. Clarifying this issue can be achieved by explaining, "I'm a detective in the criminal investigation branch." If the investigator has been designated as the officer-in-charge, this fact should also be conveyed to the witness.

The manner in which a witness is addressed may adversely or positively affect trust. The terms *ma'am* and *sir* are appropriate when the witness's age exceeds that of the investigators. A first-name basis may annoy some witnesses if they are older than the officer is. Conversely, if the witness is younger than the officer, the witness may think the use of ma'am and sir is insincere and hypocritical. An officer has to judge each situation and use the address he or she thinks is most appropriate at the time.

Informing witnesses honestly of their legal status may make the witness less apprehensive about facing the legal system, and thus more likely to answer questions honestly. If the investigator knows that the witness's evidence will be required for the trial, the witness should be told that a subpoena will be issued. Any deception by the investigator at the interview can result in problems later. Deceiving the witness about a court appearance may result in adverse testimony at the trial. Additionally, the witness should be informed that a Crown Attorney will be prosecuting the case; some witnesses are unfamiliar with the operation of the criminal justice system and may erroneously believe that they must obtain legal counsel.

Finally, casual conversation unrelated to the offence is effective. It allows the witness to gain familiarity with the investigator and for the investigator to determine the witness's honest conduct by observing physical symptoms and demeanour during honest answers. The witness should be asked about his or her personal history (e.g., occupation, recreational activities). The witness has, generally, no reason to lie. His or her conduct can later be compared with responses and behaviours to questions asked during the interview. This assists in the determination of intentional deception.

Unrelated conversation provides time for a witness to form opinions and judgments about the officer's professionalism and expertise. Casual conversation has a profound impact on trust development. An effective simple technique that accelerates trust development is having the witness answer a personal question, no matter how intrusive it is, such as, "Do you like where you work?" Any type of personal opinion is a major step toward building trust.

Consequently, immediately starting the formal questioning without some unrelated conversation may be a disadvantage and may not achieve the best results.

Conducting the Interview

The questions asked during an interview are intended to prove beyond reasonable doubt:

- the identity of the offender and the witness's capability of recognizing the offender in the future,
- that the offender committed the *actus reus*,
- the existence of *mens rea*, and
- the existence or absence of the witness's intent to learn and other factors affecting observation.

The intended result of the interview is to produce a formal written statement. The primary purpose of this statement is to instruct the Crown Attorney about the evidence that a witness will testify about during a court trial. The statement should alert the Crown Attorney to all factors that may cause reasonable doubt about the evidence.

The optimal interview consists of two stages, if time permits: (a) questioning —rough notes stage, and (b) statement stage.

Rough notes should be made during the interview and the formal statement should be written after. Ideally, when the witness dictates the formal statement, the interviewer should not be asking major open-ended questions. They should be asked during the questioning stage and the answers should be recorded in rough notes. The actual statement stage is a repeat of the first stage, but only clarifying closed-ended questions should be asked. The rough notes stage is a method of

- organizing the facts in a structured sequence,
- analyzing the contents and determining what areas are vague and need expanding, and
- evaluating the witness's credibility.

Before starting the interview, the investigator, and any other officer present, should become familiar with the offence by reviewing the existing evidence and information, including

- names of involved persons,
- addresses and personal information,
- times of relevant events,
- location of offences and appearance of crime scene, including the surrounding area, and
- physical evidence related to the offences.

Knowing as much information as possible will allow the formation of specific questions for thoroughness and the evaluation of credibility. Conversely, if all relevant facts are not known, it will be difficult to create specific questions and detect deception.

Finally, an interview is premised on three time periods that composed the incident:

1. **Before:** an indefinite period preceding the commission of the offence.
2. **During:** the period in which the actual commission of the offence took place, bordered by and including the beginning and end of the *actus reus*.
3. **After:** an indefinite period following the commission of an offence.

These three periods will dictate the structure and arrangement of the questions.

SYSTEMATIC QUESTIONING PROCEDURES

To ensure systematic questioning, an interview should be divided into four stages of questioning:

1. entire incident,
2. before the offence,
3. during the offence, and
4. after the offence.

Several reasons make this the best system. Recalling an incident entirely allows the witness to give a base or foundation of information. It may or may not be organized but it provides a general explanation of the event. Experience has shown that the general description usually lacks the specificity that the witness is capable of explaining. The vagueness must be corrected by additional questioning.

After the general description is provided, the entire event is then subdivided in chronological order. The witness can focus attention and recall from a vivid mental image if the entire event is divided into three smaller components: before, during, and after.

Each stage starts with an open-ended question with an uninterrupted response. Closed-ended questions are then asked to fill voids and clarify details. Rough notes are written first, before the formal statement is written. The rough notes include

- the reported facts and circumstances,
- the voids or vagueness for later reference, and
- any contradictions and inconsistencies.

Should the statement be the witness's verbatim response? No. The formal written statement will be the final complete version of the witness's observations, structured and specifically explained as the result of effective questioning. A witness's initial verbatim answer to the first open-ended question should never be the final statement because it will be vague and likely unstructured.

Procedure: Stage 1

Ask an open-ended question to obtain general observations of the entire incident (e.g., "What did you see?" "Tell me only what you saw and heard, not what you were told"). Allow an uninterrupted answer. Most of the answer will likely describe events during the crime only. Events that occurred before and after the offence are usually absent or poorly explained.

Procedure: Stage 2

Ask an open-ended question for general facts relating to the time before the crime. Generally, this period includes the entire day beginning from the time the witness woke up. If the crime involves a history of events that led to it, the period is expanded. Start with a question such as, "What did you do all day leading up to the offence?" Closed-ended questions will follow to (a) clarify vagueness and fill voids or omissions and (b) prove the identity of the offender. Questions should be asked during this stage about

- prior familiarity with the suspect (Was the offender known? If so, for how long? Has the suspect ever been seen before? When was the suspect first seen on the offence day?),
- approximate direction of observation,
- whether the witness could identify (facially recognize) the suspect,
- what the offender looked like, if applicable,
- the offender's method of travel to the crime scene,
- the vehicle, if one was involved, and
- the times of all relevant observations.

During Stage 2, obtain information that will prove any facts-in-issue of the offence. The most relevant evidence during this stage relates to the suspect's verbal intentions and any other planning.

Be sure to ask about

- all verbatim conversations with or heard from the suspect,
- the witness's alcohol or drug use,
- the reasons for the witness being present at the crime scene, to verify his or her actual presence,
- a precise description of the crime scene appearance, and
- the existence or absence of the intent to learn.

Ask what the witness was doing immediately before the offence to determine whether his or her attention was directed to the offence location. Questions that require answers include

- Where were you looking before the offence happened?
- Why was your attention there?
- Did you think (the offence) was going to happen?
- How long was your attention focused there before the offence?
- Were any other persons present?
- Did you see any weapons? (If yes) Can you describe them?

In summary, the important elements to determine are

- the witness's condition and factors affecting observation,
- the witness's intent to learn and awareness,
- the suspect's identity,
- the suspect's verbatim comments (intent),
- the suspect's conduct (planning), and
- descriptions (suspect, vehicles, crime scene, weapons).

Procedure: Stage 3

Ask open-ended questions to obtain general observations about events during the offence. Allow uninterrupted answers. Then, ask closed-ended questions to determine the details in eight categories:

1. **Physical acts** Obtain precise explanations of what the suspect did. The most important technique to use is avoiding paraphrasing. Paraphrasing means condensing and includes words such as threatened, damaged, stole, and assaulted. These are general terms that are names of offences, and are conclusions that the judge or jury must make. Instead of using paraphrases that name the offence, precisely describe the act. Examples include:

   - She said, "I'm going to kill you."
   - He clenched his right hand and punched her, striking her jaw.
   - She picked up the cassette tape from the counter and put it in her pocket.
   - She walked to the store entrance and left. She did not pay for it.

   The paraphrasing rule is the most important element to determine the efficiency of the interview. The absence of paraphrased observations will ensure accuracy of the witness's observations. Closed-ended questions will guide the process of precisely describing the act or conduct performed by the suspect. Explaining a specific procedure to follow is not possible. Each case dictates the type of questions that will be asked. Experience is the most critical factor in the development of this skill.

2. **Verbatim conversation** Ask for direct quotes and avoid general terms.

3. **Witness's position during the observation** Where was the witness during the crime? What was the distance? Did the distance change? Did anything obstruct his or her sight?

4. **Witness's stress level** Ask the witness whether he or she felt threatened or believed his or her life or health was in danger.

5. **Any other factors that affected observation** If none, include this later in the statement.

6. **Descriptions of relevant persons, vehicles, and places** A systematic way of acquiring a description of a person or item is to obtain a general description first, followed by the specific description. A general description refers to characteristics and features that are not unique and shared by many. Examples for a person include gender, height, weight, and hair colour. Examples for an item include type, make, model, and colour. It is not possible to provide a positive identification using general descriptions.

   Once this questioning is complete, continue with a specific description, referring to unique characteristics or features exclusive to that person or item. Examples for a person include scars or tattoos. Examples for an item include serial numbers and damage or wear and tear. Specific descriptions allow for positive identification. This method of questioning and describing arranges the description in a structured manner and helps the witness recall by starting with a wide mental image and progressing to a narrow one.

7. **Prove the facts-in-issue of the offence** The events during the crime must be directly relevant to the elements that compose the offence. Offence recognition is the first skill needed. After the correct offence is recognized, the correct facts-in-issue must be identified because the evidence must prove each beyond reasonable doubt. The facts-in-issue of the offence committed will provide the strategy for questions asked during the interview.

8. **Distinguish what the witness actually did and did not see** Throughout the questioning, witnesses should be asked repeatedly whether they actually saw a reported observation or are merely assuming that it happened. This technique is extremely effective to distinguish fact from assumption. Witnesses have a tendency to fill gaps with generalizations that include acts that were not actually seen.

In summary, the important elements of Stage 3 are:

▸ exactly what the accused did, said, possessed, and used
▸ the witness's (a) position during the observation, (b) duration of observation, (c) perception of risk to him or herself, and (d) descriptions of people, items, and places.

Procedure: Stage 4

Ask an open-ended question to obtain general observations relating to the period after the offence. The interval starts at the conclusion of the offence, but the length of time varies. It may include only a few minutes after the offence or events that occurred days or weeks afterward.

What occurs after an offence that becomes relevant evidence? The following are the important events to determine:

1. **Statements by the offender** After the offence, suspects make verbal statements relating to the offence to a variety of people at various places. No type of evidence is more valuable than a suspect's confession. Confessions made to citizens are usually automatically admissible, whereas confessions made to police officers are not. A strong emphasis must be placed on determining what the suspect said anytime after the offence. Witnesses present at the crime scene have to be asked about what the suspect said, verbatim, between the time the offence ended until the time he or she departed or until the police arrived. In other cases, a person familiar with the suspect may be interviewed about conversations with the suspect that occurred days, weeks, or months after the offence. Besides the verbatim statements made by the suspect, witnesses must be asked:

   ▷ when the statement was made (date and time),
   ▷ where the statement was made (location), and
   ▷ who was present, if anyone.

   These facts will add to the witness's credibility during the investigation and during the court testimony.

   Finally, the investigation does not end once an arrest is made. The accused person may make statements to people after the arrest and release. Witnesses should be asked about all conversations with the accused at any time before the trial.

   The entire content of a suspect's conversation must be recorded, not just the direct confession. Denials, alibis, and unrelated conversations should be recorded in the witness statement for the Crown Attorney to examine and predict whether the defence will argue that the witness was a person in authority, which may affect admissibility of the statement.

2. **Physical evidence** After the offence, the suspect's conduct will affect the possible search for and seizure of physical evidence relevant to the offence, including the removal and disposal of items. Pertinent information that witnesses should be asked about includes the following:

   ▷ Whether the suspect possessed a weapon.
   ▷ Whether the suspect took any item from the crime scene
   ▷ Whether the suspect left any item at the crime scene (e.g., weapon, clothes such as hat or jacket).
   ▷ Whether the suspect concealed any item in his clothing.
   ▷ If the suspect left the crime scene with any items, what specifically was taken.
   ▷ Whether, after departure from the crime scene, any item was sold, disposed of, or destroyed. These events may occur at any time after the offence, so the time shortly after the offence should not be the only focus of attention.
   ▷ Whether the suspect had any visible injuries. If the suspect was cut, blood may have been transferred to other places. Other visible injuries may be seen that may give a conclusion that the suspect will

seek medical attention. The transfer of bodily substances could result in significant recovery of physical evidence.

3. **Direction and method of travel** Witnesses must be questioned about

   ▷ how the suspect left, whether on foot or vehicle,
   ▷ what the vehicle looked like,
   ▷ who was seen accompanying the suspect,
   ▷ the direction of departure, and
   ▷ possible whereabouts, if the suspect is known to the witness.

In summary, witnesses must be questioned about (a) what the suspect said, (b) what the suspect did with property or items, and (c) how the suspect left the crime scene.

Rough Notes

After the fourth stage, the witness's observations are written in rough notes when time permits. Rough notes are not the formal statement. Instead, they are informal statements that the officer writes from the explanation dictated by the witness.

The rough notes should include notations to remind the officer of voids in the story that need to be filled, vague responses that need clarification, and any discrepancies or contradictions. Appropriate questions are then formed to correct these problems.

Time restrictions are a reality in daily policing and may prevent the rough-note stage. If time is limited, a formal statement may have to be written without rough notes preceding it. However, for optimum results, rough notes should be written first, before the formal statement. Rough notes provide the following advantages:

▸ They are a first draft that may not have the best structure and specificity. They serve as a basis for a higher-quality formal statement.

▸ They prevent the statement from being recorded verbatim. Witness statements are different from accused-person statements regarding the format of the content. Witness statements should not be recorded word for word as dictated by the witness, because the observations will likely be incomplete and unstructured, and because the witness does not know what is relevant for a thorough statement. The rough-note stage guides the witness.

▸ They allow the witness another recall attempt. The witness has to remember during the writing of the rough-note stage. A second recall occurs during the writing of the formal statement. Multiple recall attempts may result in a net gain of information.

▸ The rough-note stage provides a suitable opportunity to evaluate witness credibility before the final statement is written. Usually, the final statement is accepted as the version believed to be accurate and true. It will form part of or the entire justification to conduct various procedures such as arrest, search, and laying charges. The credibility of every witness must be evaluated to ensure that beliefs are properly based and formed.

If deception is detected during or at the end of the rough-note stage, it can be corrected before the formal statement is written.

In summary, the witness's credibility should be evaluated before the final statement is written. The principles and procedures of credibility evaluation will be explained in the next chapter.

CONCEPTS OF SPECIFIC ELICITATION

The problems with general observations or information elicited from witnesses have been emphasized throughout this chapter. *General* witness statements contribute to uninformed decisions, conclusions, and opinions. Eliciting *precise* information is a vital skill, one that is crucial to making informed decisions, conclusions, and opinions.

The following list includes general principles that provide a framework to help elicit precise information. These principles apply to how a written witness statement should be recorded, how a witness should respond, and how you should communicate to witnesses:

1. **Avoid using only non-descriptive language.** Many phrases and words that we routinely use have little or no specific meaning. For example, "The suspect *looked* angry or hostile." Even worse is the phrase "The suspect *was* angry or hostile." "Looked" and "was" suggest a degree of guessing by the person making the statement and require guesswork by the recipient of the statement. These types of phrases are suitable as an *introduction* to that particular topic. The interviewer is then responsible for eliciting specific descriptions and conduct through the witness's observations that will justify the opinion and permit others to form a logical conclusion. This rule is also applicable to police officers during their report writing and court testimony.

2. **Avoid using unspecified nouns.** A dangerous type of generalization is the use of "they," such as, "They were becoming hostile." The obvious question is "Who are *they*?" Nameless references may implicate innocent people or divert suspicion from the guilty.

3. **Avoid using terms of evaluation or judgment.** "The situation was *chaotic*," "He was getting *worse*," and "It got *bad*" are vague evaluations and judgments of events and people. Again, they serve only as an introduction to a topic and require precise descriptions and explanations to remove guesswork and to justify the judgment.

4. **Avoid mind reading.** Witness reports of "I *just knew* it was going to happen," or "I *felt* it," or "I *just know* he did it" are intuition-based speculations that require the interviewer to fill in the gaps through guessing —or mind reading. Intuition-based responses not only have no evidentiary value, but also they suggest that the witness *knows* the circumstances that caused the intuition and is concealing or withholding that information.

5. **Avoid using "outcomes" to describe an act.** Quite often, when a witness is asked to recall and explain observations, they report the *outcome*, or the result, of the incident instead of *how* the outcome was reached. For example, "I was assaulted by him," "He stole my money," and "He damaged my car" all report outcomes without explaining how that outcome was

reached. A paraphrased outcome has little or no evidentiary value. An outcome is a conclusion that has to be made by the *interviewing* officer during the investigation, and by a judge during a trial. An outcome only introduces the topic; a witness has to be questioned about how the outcome was reached to explain precisely the *actus reus* of an offence.

6. **Avoid gap filling.** When a generality is reported to an interviewer, there is a tendency to "fill in the gaps" of the story. Human nature sometimes causes interviewers to clarify vagueness by *assuming* certain acts occurred because of logical deduction. Witness generalities and vagueness must serve only as a broad picture of an event and *create clarifying questions* to ask the witness. The clarifying questions will fill gaps by witness observation instead of interview assumption.

7. **Identify clarifying questions.** The key skill that develops communication and witness interviewing expertise is the ability to form all possible clarifying questions that will fully complete the explanation of an incident with all *relevant precise information*. This skill is developed by the interviewer's *mental re-enactment* of the occurrence. When a witness reports observations, the interviewer should be forming a vivid mental image of the incident. With practice, the interviewer must learn to not accept an incomplete mental re-enactment of the incident. A method that will accomplish this objective is *compartmentalizing* the incident, meaning breaking down or dividing the incident with structured units chronologically. The extent of the image clarity and vividness will determine the quality of clarifying questions. By compartmentalizing the image, the interviewer will be able to identify vagueness and ambiguity, conditions that will allow clarifying questions to emerge. Complete mental re-enactment not only requires precise descriptions of people and items, their positions in the image, and precise conduct, but it also includes knowing what *did not occur*. Quite often, the emphasis on what happened causes us to ignore what did *not* happen. Some common topics that require clarification include:

   ▷ Who were all the people present? What are their descriptions?
   ▷ Where were they positioned?
   ▷ What did they say precisely (verbatim)?
   ▷ Are there specific acts relevant to the offence?
   ▷ What acts caused specific conduct?
   ▷ Describe any items and their position.

8. **Develop rapport with the witness.** In any relationship, the extent of communication success is largely dependent on and greatly influenced by the level of *rapport*. Arguably, rapport is the essence of all successful communication. Rapport is a unifying bond of varying strength that develops during the interaction between people, when the participants connect on some type of understanding of shared or common interests. Depending on a number of variables, rapport develops at varying speeds; it may develop quickly or after a prolonged time. Rapport is not constant—it is a fluctuating concept; it can diminish as quickly as it can develop, depending on a number of situational factors.

Rapport is developed through a series of responses and reactions during communication, where opinions and judgments are formed, shaped, and accumulated. In other words, rapport is an *outcome*, or result, of accumulated thoughts. In a narrow view, rapport emerges from a degree of trust predicated on a number of variables including appearance, conduct, and words. A broader view of rapport includes a stronger bond that emerges from a deeper understanding of what the participants share in common.

There are two kinds of rapport: (a) short-term rapport and (b) long-term rapport. Short-term rapport is a temporary bond that is not as strong as a long-term rapport bond. Short-term rapport has a more tenuous and fragile connection, which can be diminished far more easily than a long-term rapport connection. Conversely, long-term rapport features a stronger bond that is not easily diminished; a sinister act is needed to injure long-term rapport. Both types, however, will elicit information to some degree.

How is rapport developed, especially in a short-term relationship such as police–witness? Every human being has experienced the development of short-term and long-term rapport. We all have an individualized method of developing rapport based on our personal systems of *beliefs and values*. We use our personal beliefs and values every time we develop rapport and then internalize our criteria and methodology. This process explains why we buy from certain businesses but not others, why we seek advice from some people but not others, how we select service providers, and how we select whom to confide in.

There are countless reasons that explain why we develop rapport with some people and not others but, as mentioned, they emerge from our personal beliefs and values. Consequently, there is no concise list of methods and reasons that, when neatly packaged, guarantees rapport with another person. Yet there is one constant that may be a universal criterion that we all consider to some extent. Whether we have consciously thought of it or not, our short-term rapport often emerges from our perception of a person's **professionalism**.

Despite a wide range of interpretations about what constitutes professionalism, it is an evaluation made based on a comparison between preconceived expectations and observations made of words and behaviours. Every person has preconceived expectations of service providers such as police officers, business owners, doctors, and teachers. We expect a certain level of conduct and performance. When we meet these people on a "professional" basis, we instinctively begin a process of judging their appearance, actions, and words. We then accumulate these judgments, often quickly, and form an opinion—either they are professionals (persons whose competence we trust) or they are inexperienced amateurs (persons whose competence is suspect).

Generally, those who we judge as professional are people who meet our performance expectations. Conversely, those who do not meet our performance expectations are deemed to be inexperienced amateurs.

Those who we deem professional act and perform as expected—they do nothing to distract our evaluation. Those who we judge as amateurs often do something to distract our evaluation. For example, if you visit your doctor and her dialogue includes vulgar language, or he has food stains on his clothing, these *distractions* certainly will contribute to a negative opinion.

Distractions are words, conduct, or performance that create a negative perception and divert attention from the task at hand. Conversely, professionalism is the absence of distractions and meeting the performance expectations of others.

Case Study 13.1 Conclusion

The witness statement proved to be awful. Supervisors questioned the validity of the arrest because the statement lacked significant information, including

▸ identity and recognition of the offender

▸ proof of the facts-in-issue of the offence (attempted break and enter)

▸ specificity of certain acts relative to *mens rea*

▸ the order of events before, during, and after the offence

June was re-interviewed and the following second statement was obtained:

Statement—June Lee will say:

> I am 45 years of age. My husband Edward and I have been legally married for 20 years. We have no children. We immigrated to Canada from Asia 20 years ago. We are the tenants of 10 King Street, Apartment 6, in [city]. I am employed by Provincial Court—Family Division, where I hold the position of court clerk.

> Edward and I moved to our current apartment on October 1. A man named Luke Ray lives in Apartment 5 with his wife. Their apartment is across the hall from ours. Luke is a white male, 25 years old, 6'1", average build, shoulder-length dark hair parted in the middle, dark moustache. I know his name because I checked his mailbox. I have seen him on numerous occasions during the past month.

> Sometime during the first week of October, I parked my car in the back parking lot at about 6 p.m. Luke was in the parking lot, standing about 30 feet from me. He made a racist remark and said "Go back to your own country." About three or four days later, in the evening, Edward and I were in our apartment. A loud party was in progress in Luke's apartment. I heard a man yelling racist remarks about our Asian descent. The man was in the hallway. I opened our door slightly and saw Luke in the hallway. He said, "Move out of here or we'll burn your car with you in it." Sometime during the middle of October, I found a racist remark scratched on the side of my car.

> About one week ago, at 10 p.m., I heard banging on the door. I heard a man's voice, which I believed to be Luke's, yelling racist remarks.

> On November 6, I worked the 9 a.m. to 5 p.m. shift. Edward worked similar hours. We arrived home at about 5:30 p.m. We ate supper at 6 p.m. We consumed no alcohol. At 7 p.m., we sat in our living room and watched TV. The entrance to our apartment is about 10 feet from the living room. I locked the door at that time.

> At about 9 p.m. I heard people screaming in the hallway. Edward and I were watching TV. I heard a man's voice, which I recognized as Luke's, yelling, "Move out of here. Go back to where you came from." I heard banging on our door shortly afterward. I heard the same voice yelling, "Did you hear me? Move out; go back to your own country." I heard the doorknob being moved. I saw it moving back and forth repeatedly. I looked out the peephole on the door. I

saw Luke standing alone in the hallway. I heard more banging on the door. I immediately phoned the police.

Officers arrived a few minutes later. As I reported this incident to one officer with our door open, I saw the other officer speaking to Luke in his apartment. Luke was seated at a table. His wife and two other men were also seated there. I was about 20 feet from them. Luke got up and walked toward me saying, "You want trouble?" The officer arrested him and removed him from the building.

Signed, June Lee

November 6

COMMENTARY This experience demonstrates the consequences of writing poor witness statements, one being that the validity of an arrest would be questioned.

CHAPTER 14

Evaluating Witness Credibility: Deception

LEARNER SUMMARY

In previous chapters, the procedure of validating a complaint was explained. It represents one example of applying the complex skill of evaluating witness credibility. That procedure is a specific, narrow method of evaluating credibility by analyzing circumstances and recognizing indicators of intentional fabrication.

The complete process of making a final evaluation of credibility is a broader, wide-ranging procedure that must be used to make a final assessment about whether to believe what a witness has reported. This includes detecting unintentional inaccuracies, which are common.

This chapter explains a systematic procedure for making logical conclusions about witness honesty and accuracy. Typically, intuition and common sense are used to form an opinion of credibility. This chapter establishes formal step-by-step guidelines to help justify the decisions about credibility that officers make every day. **Evaluating credibility** means forming an opinion about whether a person has been honest and told the truth. It involves analyzing the reported circumstances and making a conclusion about their reliability.

Whether we are aware of it or not, we all evaluate credibility every day. We receive information and judge its truthfulness and form an opinion about the person who gave it. Credibility evaluation may be perceived as a skill formed by life experience. In law enforcement, that skill has to be developed to an advanced level. If deception is not detected, innocent persons may be wrongly charged and actual offenders will not be apprehended or prosecuted.

A witness's credibility is evaluated twice within the criminal justice system:

1. by the police during the investigation, and
2. by a judge or jury during the trial.

Despite the significance of the procedure to evaluate credibility, there are major problems associated with it:

▸ Evaluating credibility is not a scientific procedure; officers rely on their opinions. Opinions can easily be wrong.

▸ Acquiring an advanced skill level requires a combination of experience and logic. Inexperience is a problem that every novice officer will have. Nothing can accelerate the process except repeated practice, which may take considerable time.

▸ Finding guidelines in Canadian law about credibility evaluation is difficult. The subject is largely ignored in statute law. Specific procedures are not established by any law.

Case Study 14.1

Shane and Marie owned a house on the outskirts of a city. Their 16-year-old son was killed in a motor vehicle collision. While the family was at the funeral home, their house was entered. Camera equipment and a high-school blazer that the son was to be buried in were stolen. There were no immediate suspects.

Several days later, officers attended at the detention centre to interview Chris (28). He had been incarcerated after being convicted of break and enter. Chris had been a valuable informant in the past and was questioned about this break and enter.

Chris implicated a friend, Adam (28). Chris stated that Adam told him:

▸ he had committed the break and enter,

▸ he had tried to enter a ground-level window,

▸ he had changed his mind and forced open a door,

▸ he had searched the house and found the camera equipment, and

▸ he had decided to take all the equipment after initially choosing only a few items.

Chris was asked for the date and location of the conversation. He casually said that he couldn't remember and changed the conversation to how Adam was trying to sell the stolen camera equipment. Chris's credibility was rated as strong, constituting reasonable grounds to arrest Adam.

(Refer to the end of Chapter 14 for the conclusion of this case study.)

WITNESS DECEPTION

Witnesses, including victims, often lie to the police. **Witness deception** is a prevalent problem and can impede an investigation or wrongly implicate an innocent person. There are two types of witness deception: (a) intentionally withholding or concealing evidence and (b) intentionally fabricating evidence.

The most common type of witness deception is **withholding information**. The reluctant, uncooperative witness is a daily reality during investigations. Any person can be deceptive. The type and character of witnesses vary significantly. Some have extensive criminal records, while others are law-abiding citizens. Both types can be deceptive. Experience in policing with deceptive people will inevitably create a skepticism that is vital to detect lies, which are detrimental to an investigation.

Uncooperative Witness or Victim

"I didn't see anything" is a witness response that officers hear countless times. Learning to detect and correct intentional withholding of evidence requires an understanding of the most common reasons that motivate this type of deception. The reasons include:

> ▸ **Fear of the offender** Victims and independent witnesses likely will have been influenced by TV shows, movies, and the media to believe that the offender will retaliate.

> ▸ **An attempt to conceal their own wrongdoing** Uncooperative victims may have committed or participated in an illegal act that resulted in their victimization. For example, an uncooperative assault victim may have participated in a drug transaction with the offender. Refusing to inform the police about the assault is the victim's attempt to conceal his or her illegal drug activity.

> ▸ **Financial loss** Appearing in court may result in lost wages.

> ▸ **Moral deficiency** Some people simply do not care that a crime occurred and have no desire to correct a wrong conduct.

> ▸ **Unfavourable opinion of the police or criminal justice system** Victims and witnesses who have a criminal record often blame the police and the criminal justice system for consequences suffered because of the crime. They may have no desire to assist the police in any manner, including reporting what they saw regarding the offence currently being investigated.

> ▸ **Favourable attitude toward the offender** A witness may know the offender or may not want the offender to suffer consequences. This attitude results in a desire to help the offender escape detection and prosecution.

Fabrication or Exaggeration

Some victims and witnesses intentionally mislead the police by reporting a false offence or by fabricating observations regarding an offence that actually occurred. Several reasons motivate fabrication, including:

> ▸ **Financial gain** Property crimes, such as theft, mischief, and break and enter, are fabricated to defraud insurance companies.

> ▸ **Retaliation** Personal crimes, such as assault, are fabricated to countercharge or force the charge against the person to be withdrawn as part of a mutual deal. Retaliation also occurs when a person intensely dislikes another person and believes that a false report will cause substantial inconvenience for the disliked person.

> ▸ **Hostility toward the offender** A victim of an actual crime may have an overwhelming desire to convict the offender. This may be the impetus for fabricated observations.

> ▸ **Attention** Personality or mental problems may create a need for attention or sympathy that may be fulfilled by police officers who investigate the false report. Some people like the attention given by investigating officers.

HONEST PERSON PROFILE

To detect a deceptive witness, the general characteristics of an honest person need to be examined for comparison. No precise list of characteristics positively associated with an honest person exist. No one characteristic that positively shows honesty exists. Some witnesses can hide deception and be convincing.

The following informal profile of an honest witness has been created from personal experience. It includes general characteristics that help recognize honesty and form a justifiable initial opinion, but will usually not give a conclusion about credibility. A step-by-step procedure will be explained later in the book, which will guide the final evaluation about credibility.

1. **Calmness** Lying causes stress that is revealed in some way. If a person is being honest, stress would, logically, be absent. Without stress, the witness should not show hostility toward the officer because the witness is not the bad guy.

2. **Patience** Honest witnesses do not want any part of their story misunderstood. When someone is telling the truth, he or she will likely be patient with any series of specific questions asked to clarify certain points. They do not try to rush through the interview.

3. **Logical answers** A series of honest answers usually are logical. Deceptive answers usually are illogical and are not sensible because of vagueness.

4. **Direct answers** Honest people answer the question asked. They have no reason to avoid answering.

5. **No hesitation** When a person knows something with certainty, there should be no reason for hesitation or indecision while answering. Some hesitation is expected in response to specific closed-ended questions that require the witness to recall something that was not immediately remembered.

In summary, honest witnesses generally do not

▸ complain or get annoyed about being interviewed,
▸ avoid answering the questions asked,
▸ give vague answers,
▸ hesitate excessively before answering, or
▸ try to rush the interview.

DETECTING DECEPTION: VERBAL INDICATORS

Although investigators should view all witness reports with skepticism, detecting deliberate deception is an inexact science. However, a witness may give physiological and verbal indicators during deception that an investigator can recognize. Physiological indicators will be explored in Phase 3. This section will concentrate on the verbal indicators, listed below, that have been proven (through experience) to signal witness deception.

1. **Diversion** Constant subtle diversions to unrelated topics in response to specific answers reveal the witness's desire to avoid answering. If the

witness has reported seeing very little or nothing, constant diversions are an attempt to convince the officer that he or she really has no meaningful evidence to offer.

2. **Anger** Illogical fits of rage by a witness toward the police are stress induced. The stress is likely caused by lying. The officer's questions create an internal conflict that manifests itself in anger.

3. **Insincere politeness** Some victims and witnesses have extensive criminal records and do not have a favourable attitude toward the police. Insincere politeness may indicate their desire to prevent suspicion of deception. In other cases, uncooperative witnesses may begin interviews with some degree of belligerence. An unexpected change of behaviour, such as politeness, may indicate an attempt to convince the officer of deception.

4. **Sudden silence** A common response to questions asked after a witness reports seeing nothing is silence. The questions are intended to determine reasons why the witness saw nothing. The answers should be simple if nothing was really seen. Sudden silence is an indicator that the witness is trying to fabricate an answer.

5. **Contrasting conduct** Based on personal observations, not scientific evidence, some people behave one way while being honest, and another while being deceptive. The contrasting conduct may be subtle, but it may be discernible. It is important to observe a witness's conduct during introductory questions where honesty is expected (e.g., name, address, employment, etc.). Then, during actual questioning, the witness's conduct should be observed for subtle or blatant changes that may indicate deception.

6. **Vague, illogical answers** When a witness is reluctant to report everything that he or she observed or all the events that occurred, answers may be vague and illogical. Unrehearsed deception often includes circumstances and explanations that are not sensible. If an explanation leaves you confused, it may mean that it is a lie.

In summary, these indicators are not conclusive proof of deception. They are general observations that should cause suspicion about the witness's truthfulness.

Procedure: Evaluating Credibility

Forming reasonable grounds depends strongly on evaluating witness credibility. This is a procedure and skill that requires forming an opinion about the honesty of a witness's observations, whether the witness reports a small or large amount of fact. There are only two types of opinions formed about witness credibility:

1. **strong** (the witness's report is believed), or
2. **weak or no credibility** (what the witness reported is not believed).

Two examples apply.

1. A witness reports seeing an entire offence and can facially recognize the offender. If the witness has strong credibility, the report is believed. If weak credibility is detected, the report is not believed.

2. A witness reports that he was present but saw nothing during an incident. If the witness has strong credibility, the witness is believed. If weak credibility is detected, the witness is not believed and the opinion is formed that the witness is withholding evidence.

One credible eyewitness, who saw the entire offence and can facially recognize the offender, is sufficient to form reasonable grounds. Conversely, reasonable grounds cannot be formed if the only eyewitness's credibility is evaluated as weak.

The time that an officer has to evaluate a witness's credibility varies. Two basic situations occur: (a) the offender is present or has recently departed from a crime scene or (b) a belated report is made of an offence and the offender has departed a considerable time ago.

Arrival at a crime scene where an eyewitness is present and the offender is also present or nearby does not allow for a formal witness interview. The eyewitness will usually make a brief, verbal statement such as, "That's the guy who hit me." An instant decision is needed. The witness reasonably may be believed under the circumstances. If no other evidence exists, the eyewitness's brief verbal statement constitutes reasonable grounds to arrest. In this situation, it is reasonable to assume that the report is not false. After the arrest is made, the eyewitness is formally interviewed and suitable time will be afforded to evaluate credibility. If it is later proven that the witness has weak or no credibility and the report was fabricated, the arrested person will be released unconditionally and the witness may be charged with public mischief, if the fabrication was an intentional attempt to mislead the police.

When the offender is not present at a crime scene and a formal interview can be conducted, there is ample time to make a suitable evaluation.

Finally, two additional subdivisions of witnesses—informants and children—must be interviewed and evaluated in the same manner as other traditional witnesses. However, additional factors affect the accurate evaluation of their credibility. These factors, and the legal aspects relating to informants and children, do not require different interview techniques; they merely add to the existing format.

CREDIBILITY AND REASONABLE GROUNDS

Reasonable grounds exist if there is strong credibility regarding the observations of

- one eyewitness, including hearing a confession, or
- one accomplice, if the accomplice's observation constitutes eyewitness evidence or the accomplice receives a confession.

Reasonable grounds do not exist if

- an eyewitness or an accomplice has been evaluated as having weak or no credibility, or
- a corroborative witness reports facts that constitute only mere suspicion that the offender committed the offence, despite the credibility rating.

A *prima facie* case can be established based on one eyewitness, either an independent person or an accomplice, but reasonable doubt can easily be created.

Therefore, despite the existence of reasonable grounds to arrest an offender, the investigator should strive to corroborate the testimony of only one eyewitness or accomplice to remove all reasonable doubt. Corroboration can be obtained through

- confession by the offender,
- observations of other witnesses, and
- physical evidence.

However, reasonable grounds to arrest may exist if one corroborative witness has been evaluated as having strong credibility. The determining factor will be if the corroborative witness is almost an eyewitness (e.g., if all of the facts-in-issue are proven directly or circumstantially).

Below are some examples of corroborative witnesses who would almost qualify as eyewitnesses.

- A person who sees an offender running from the scene of a bank robbery when the offender is carrying physical evidence (e.g., a weapon or a canvas bag). Although the person does not qualify as an eyewitness, reasonable grounds exist if the witness is evaluated as having strong credibility.
- A police officer responding to a house break and enter in progress who sees a person in the backyard running from the house is not an eyewitness to the offence. Yet reasonable grounds exist to arrest the offender. The officer in this situation qualifies as a corroborative witness.

Procedure

There are no formal guidelines and no specific procedures about how to evaluate credibility. No Canadian statute explains how to do it. This section explains case law guidelines and an informal procedure derived from experience that help provide a systematic method of evaluating credibility.

The Supreme Court of Canada has established three general principles regarding credibility evaluation. By listing only three general qualities, the court is obviously recognizing that credibility evaluation is an inexact science:

1. In *R. v. Marquard* (1993),[1] the S.C.C. stated that credibility is an opinion that may be formed by an ordinary, non-expert person. Evaluating credibility does not require a special skill or the knowledge of an expert. Ordinary people judge honesty or deception daily.
2. In *R. v. Marquard* (1993),[2] the S.C.C. stated that three personal qualities are needed to evaluate credibility:
   ▷ experience,
   ▷ logic, and
   ▷ intuitive sense.

Experience is the key element. Repeated exposure to deceptive people will advance the ability to analyze facts and circumstances logically. It will heighten the intuitive sense that officers rely on routinely. Experience cannot be taught. Inexperienced officers should strive to practise this skill by participating in as many investigations as possible.

3. In *R. v. Nikolovski* (1996),[3] the S.C.C. listed factors considered during the evaluation of credibility. The evaluator must determine:

   ▷ whether the witness was physically able to make the observation,
   ▷ whether the witness had (a) sound vision, (b) good hearing, (c) intelligence, and (d) the ability to communicate what was seen and heard,
   ▷ whether the witness could understand and recall what had been perceived,
   ▷ whether the witness had a sound memory,
   ▷ whether fear or excitement had affected the witness's ability to perceive clearly (acquire) and later recall the events accurately,
   ▷ whether the witness had a bias or at least a biased perception of the events or persons involved, and
   ▷ whether the stress caused by a traumatic event such as a robbery had any effect.

THE TEN-POINT LIST

Experience has shown that taking into account certain factors, including those listed by the S.C.C., will adequately justify a logical opinion about credibility.

The following ten-point list is a procedural guideline that can be used to justify an opinion about credibility. It is an informal procedure only. It is not a law. The list includes 10 factors that should be considered when evaluating credibility. The factors are derived from a combination of the case law decisions previously noted, and personal experience.

The first objective of this list is to determine the presence or absence of each factor. Afterward, the 10-point list is applied to the information reported to determine compatibility, which helps justify an opinion of strong or weak credibility.

1. **Acquisition position** Determine whether the witness was actually present during the offence and, if so, whether the witness's position allowed acquisition of the observation. Questions that need to be answered include:

   ▷ What was the witness's exact position (e.g., was he or she standing, sitting, in a car, etc.)?
   ▷ Was the view unobstructed?
   ▷ If obstructions existed, what type and what degree of obstruction existed?
   ▷ Was there any noise that affected hearing and, if so, what volume level?
   ▷ Did the distance and position change (e.g., as a result of driving in a car while making the observation)?

2. **Intent to learn** This refers to prior attention focused on the crime area and to an awareness that a crime was about to occur. Determine where the witness's attention was before the offence happened and the reasons why. Relevant questions include:

   ▷ What happened just before the incident?
   ▷ Where was the witness looking?
   ▷ Was the witness attentive to the offence location or the offender?

> ▷ What caused the witness to focus his or her attention?
> ▷ Was the witness aware that some type of incident was about to occur?

For example, a pedestrian may be standing on a sidewalk at an intersection waiting to cross. Two cars collide in the intersection. Commonly, the sound of the collision causes the witness to look. The witness sees the aftermath, if the noise created the attention. In this case, nothing happened before the collision that drew his or her attention to either car. Consequently, no intent to learn existed. No awareness of the incident means that the witness likely did not see the event happen but saw only the result. In the same case, awareness of one of the cars may have been caused by squealing tires, excessive speed, or some other unusual act. The attention to the cars created the intent to learn the event by raising an awareness that some incident may be about to occur. The existence of the intent to learn suggests that the witness likely saw the entire incident occur and should be able to recall and report a substantial number of details about the event. Focused attention ensures optimum acquisition of the observation.

The existence or absence of the intent to learn is compatible with the amount of information reported:

> ▷ The existence of the intent to learn and a lengthy, detailed statement are compatible, indicating strong credibility.
> ▷ The absence of the intent to learn and few or no details are compatible, indicating strong credibility. It is logical that nothing was seen if no prior awareness existed.
> ▷ The existence of the intent to learn and a brief statement are not compatible, indicating weak credibility. The witness may be withholding information. If prior awareness existed, the witness logically should have observed more than is being reported.
> ▷ The absence of the intent to learn and a lengthy, detailed statement are not compatible, indicating weak credibility. If no prior awareness existed, the witness likely would not have seen the entire incident. It is logical to suspect that some details may be intentionally fabricated or simply assumed as opposed to actual observations.

3. **Duration of observation** The length of time a witness observed a person or an occurrence may substantially increase the witness's accuracy.[4] There is no specific time that constitutes sufficient duration of observation. It is difficult to accurately determine whether a witness had enough time to acquire an observation, particularly the facial features of an offender. One method that helps is asking whether the witness had any conversation with the offender. Dialogue tends to focus attention facially. If a conversation did occur, you have a strong indication that sufficient duration existed. Otherwise, there needs to be some element that drew attention, such as an offender's possession of a weapon, which will suggest the witness had enough time to make optimum acquisition.

4. **Retention period** This refers to the interval between the time of observation (offence) and time of recall (interview). The time that elapses may affect the accuracy of recall. Which is better for accuracy, a short or

long retention period? It depends on a process called **rehearsal**. If an observation is repeated continually, it transfers from short-term memory to long-term memory. If no rehearsal or repetition occurs, the observation stays in short-term memory. Observations in short-term memory are lost quickly, usually in less than 30 seconds.[5] If repetition occurs, the observation may transfer to long-term memory, becoming a permanent memory that lasts a lifetime.[6] Therefore, a longer retention period may afford the witness the time to rehearse or repeat the observation and transfer it to long-term memory. The problems with longer retention, however, outweigh the advantages:

▷ Short-term memory is easily disrupted. An interruption or distraction may result in the loss of information within a few seconds.[7]

▷ There is no specific number of repetitions or specific time of rehearsal that will always result in a transfer to long-term memory. It is a vague concept that cannot be measured or determined accurately. The interviewing officer will not be able to positively determine that the witness has transferred the observation to long-term memory.

▷ **Ebbinghaus's curve of forgetting** measures retention at various time intervals. This experiment shows that forgetting begins very quickly after acquiring information and then gradually tapers off. A significant amount of forgetting can occur within the first 24 hours of acquiring information. The forgetting curve indicates that only 58 percent of information is retained after 20 minutes. This means that almost half of the information acquired may be forgotten during a 20-minute retention time.

▷ 44 percent of retention occurs after one hour, meaning more than one-half of information is forgotten after one hour.

▷ the forgetting rate tapers off to a 25 percent retention rate after six days and drops to 21 percent after 31 days.

▷ 100 percent recall is achieved only within seconds of acquiring the information.[8]

In summary, a longer time between the offence and the interview will likely result in substantial forgetting. A short interval will enhance recall and prevent a significant loss of information.

5. **Interference with mental repetition during the retention period** Repeating information mentally is essential for transferring observations from short-term to long-term memory. After a witness sees an offence, distractions and interruptions will likely occur, causing a loss of information within seconds. Witnesses acquire other information after the offence from other people, or by seeing something, or by having to think of other things, such as dialing a telephone. These events disrupt short-term memory. In other words, the less a witness has to think about or is distracted by after the offence and before the interview, the more information that may be accurately recalled. Witnesses should be asked about what they did during the time between the offence and interview to determine whether mental repetition was disrupted.

6. **Sensory problems** This refers to vision or hearing problems and also includes inaccurate perception of details such as height, weight, age, and distances.

7. **Alcohol or drug consumption** The effects of these two substances were explained in Chapter 11.

8. **Excessive stress** Refer to Chapter 11 for discussion about the three categories of stress. Excessive or high stress levels may affect observation by narrowing focus on a weapon, for example.

9. **Conformity** Discussion among witnesses after an offence may cause a witness to adopt incorrect observations, simply to conform with the observations of others.

10. **Motive to lie** The common reasons for witness deception were explained in Chapter 11.

Applying the Ten-Point List

The content of a witness statement can be compared to the presence or absence of the 10 factors of credibility to determine compatibility. This is an informal, unscientific procedure that helps form a logical opinion about credibility.

Factors 1 through 4 are positive factors, while 5 through 10 are negative factors. The presence of the first four factors, combined with the absence of the last six factors, represents fulfillment of the 10-point list. If the list is fulfilled, ideal circumstances exist for optimum recall. This type of witness should be able to give a lengthy, detailed statement.

If any one of the first four positive factors are absent or any one of the final six factors are present, the 10-point list is not fulfilled. This means that optimum recall may not occur. This type of witness will likely not be able to report lengthy, detailed observations; instead, their observations will be brief or contain no details.

The following four formulas for compatibility should help form an accurate opinion of credibility:

1. **Lengthy, detailed statement and the 10-point list fulfilled are compatible.** Credibility should be rated as strong, meaning that the observations are believable.

2. **Brief or no observations and the 10-point list fulfilled are incompatible.** Credibility should be rated as weak. Deception should be suspected. Optimum conditions existed, which suggests that the witness should have reported more details. The witness is likely withholding evidence.

3. **Brief or no observations and the 10-point list unfulfilled are compatible.** Strong credibility should be given. It is believable that the witness saw nothing because less than optimum conditions existed. The witness is likely not deceptive. He or she honestly saw nothing.

4. **Lengthy, detailed statement and the 10-point list unfulfilled are incompatible.** Credibility should be rated as weak. It is not believable that the witness saw a substantial amount if less than optimum conditions existed. The witness may be fabricating or simply assuming the details.

METHODS OF CORRECTING INTENTIONAL DECEPTION

A witness who deliberately distorts the truth or who is reluctant to disclose observations is suffering from an internal conflict. The conflict could stem from a fear that the offender will retaliate if the witness gives honest answers or from a desire to protect the offender. Most witnesses feel they are incapable of resolving the conflict because they have probably never had to resolve this type of conflict before. Thus, they rely on the investigator for a solution. The witness views the investigator as an expert and assumes that he or she will propose a solution to alleviate the conflict.

Obtaining the truth from a deceptive witness is dependent on the witness admitting the reason for the fabrications. These reasons may be obvious to the investigator, but it is important for the witness to admit that a conflict exists because then the need for deception no longer exists. The witness will then be aware that the investigator knows that information is being withheld or fabricated because of the internal conflict. The witness will believe that honesty is the only resolution to his or her internal conflict.

Obtaining the admission is not difficult:

1. Demonstrate clearly that the witness's reason for deception will not be recorded in writing. This can be conveyed to the witness by:
   ▷ emphasizing this promise verbally, and
   ▷ distinctly dropping the pen used to record any notes onto the table.

2. Ask for the reasons for the deception, emphasizing that the response is for the benefit of the investigator's curiosity only. The reasons commonly admitted are:
   ▷ fear of offender's retaliation,
   ▷ fear of speaking publicly in court, or
   ▷ favourable attitude toward this offender.

Regardless of the reason established, the investigator can effectively negate the witness's fears addressing the admitted reason for deception.

▶ **Fear of offender retaliation** Assure the witness that offender retaliation will not occur. Most investigators can honestly inform the witness that witnesses are very rarely harmed by offenders. Additional reassurance can be given if the investigator knows the offender and can give reasons as to why he or she is sure the offender will not harm the witness.

▶ **Fear of speaking publicly in court** Give a precise explanation of court procedure. If multiple witnesses exist, explain that he or she will not be alone. If multiple witnesses do not exist, explain that police officers will be present assisting the Crown Attorney in case preparation. Additionally, describe a typical situation in court to alleviate concerns about intense cross-examination, presence of media, and so on.

▶ **Favourable attitude toward the offender** Emphasize the emotional burden that the witness will suffer should the offender repeat the offence on another innocent victim. Regardless of the type of attitude the witness has toward the offender, the investigator should emphasize the need to deter the offender rather than to punish.

Usually, these three proposals offer acceptable resolutions to the witness's internal conflict. Most witness conflicts are of a nature that can be resolved with virtually no consequences to the witness.

THE FORMAL STATEMENT

At the conclusion of the interview, two objectives are fulfilled: (a) the witness's first recall attempt is complete and (b) observations have been recorded in rough notes. Recording the formal statement can now begin. The witness should always dictate it while the investigator records it. A statement written by the witness will

- not be in proper statement format,
- be unstructured and haphazard,
- be severely lacking in sufficient detail regarding the facts-in-issue of the offence,
- prevent the investigator from evaluating the witness's credibility, and
- provide temptation to fabricate or withhold observations.

For these reasons, an officer should never allow a witness to write the statement. When recording a witness statement, officers should remember the purposes of a witness statement. Listed in order of significance, the purpose of a witness statement is to provide the following:

1. instructions to the Crown Attorney conveying the potential evidence of the witness,
2. legal remedy for a hostile witness,
3. a documented record to aid the investigator's memory, and
4. written grounds justifying an investigator's actions.

The investigator must remain aware of these purposes during the statement process.

Format of a Formal Statement

To record the statement, the investigator again takes the witness through the periods before, during, and after the offence, and asks closed-ended questions based on the rough notes taken in the interview. This format, which may appear repetitive to the witness, serves two purposes:

1. It allows the witness to make a second recall attempt in which additional information may be recalled.
2. It allows the investigator to confirm the initial observations.

What follows are the five areas into which a statement is divided, with the information that is needed in each area:

1. **Heading** The witness's name followed by "will say" is the accepted heading (e.g., "Marcia Smith will say"). The statement then follows in the first person (i.e., as though the witness is telling the story).

2. **Introduction** The witness is introduced by means of a current personal résumé where such facts as address, marital status, number of children, and occupation (including position and employer) are recorded. If there is no occupation, state the witness's specific status (e.g., welfare recipient, disability pension, etc.) for factual information only, not for judgmental purposes or as reasons to form opinions about credibility.

3. **Events before the offence** The witness's activities preceding his or her observations of the offence are recorded here. Facts may include:

   ▷ day and date,
   ▷ work hours,
   ▷ visits or socializing,
   ▷ relevant contact with offender, including verbatim conversation, which may corroborate *mens rea*,
   ▷ witness's physical and mental condition (for example, whether he or she consumed alcohol or drugs), and
   ▷ offender's identity or description (witness's capability of recognizing the offender in the future).

4. **Events during the offence** Observations relating to the *actus reus* of the offence are recorded here. Requirements include:

   ▷ time,
   ▷ description of each act relating to the facts-in-issue. This description should avoid paraphrasing by using offence words such as "assault" or "threaten,"
   ▷ verbatim statements of the offender's conversation, and
   ▷ identity of the offender, or a description if the identity is not known (capability of recognizing offender later).

5. **Events after the offence** Observations relating to the witness's activities after the offence are recorded here. Requirements include:

   ▷ relevant acts by the offender corroborating *mens rea* and the facts-in-issue, and
   ▷ verbatim record or statements made by the offender.

After taking the statement, have the witness read it. If mistakes exist, have the witness delete errors by drawing a single line through them and initialling the change, or you may make any corrections and have the witness initial them. Ensure that the witness signs or initials each page, following the last word on each page, and signs the last page with his or her usual signature, after the last word.

Watch the witness sign or initial each page. An investigator should also record in a notebook:

▸ the time the interview commenced,
▸ the exact description of the interview's location,
▸ the presence or relevant absence of other persons, and
▸ the time of the interview's conclusion.

If, at any time during the recording of the statement or in the interview, the investigator believes the witness may be adverse or hostile, he or she should ask another officer to be present during the interview and the signing of the statement. If the witness refuses to give a signed written statement, record all oral statements, verbatim, and record the information noted above in a notebook. If verbal statements are made without a written statement, prepare a written report of these statements for the purpose of instructing the Crown Attorney of these circumstances.

Case Study 14.1 Conclusion

Adam was arrested and interrogated. He gave a written confession. In it, he implicated Chris as an accomplice. Chris was later arrested. He confessed that he had participated in the offence.

Chris had been honest about his statement implicating Adam; Adam did commit the offence. Chris's deception was about how he knew. Adam did not tell him about it. That was the reason why Chris could not remember the date and location of the fictitious conversation.

ENDNOTES

1. *R. v. Marquard* (1993), 85 C.C.C. (3d) 193 (S.C.C.).
2. Ibid.
3. *R. v. Nikolovski* (1996), 111 C.C.C. (3d) 403 (S.C.C.).
4. D.R. Buchanan, "Enhancing Eyewitness Identification: Applied Psychology for Police Officers" (1985) vol. 13, no. 4 *Journal of Police Science and Administration.*
5. S. Wood et al., *The World of Psychology*, 2nd Cdn ed. (Scarborough, ON: Prentice Hall, 1999), at 192–194.
6. Ibid.
7. Ibid.
8. Ibid.

CHAPTER 15

Informants and Children

LEARNER SUMMARY

Informants and children are two types of witnesses for whom procedural concepts need additional explanation. First, it must be emphasized that both groups are witnesses. This means that the procedures and principles explained previously apply substantively to both informants and children. However, there are unique aspects to their observations that add to the interview procedures used for conventional witnesses.

This chapter includes the relevant laws and procedures relating to informants and children.

Case Study 15.1

Leeann, six years old, was a Grade 1 student at an elementary school situated one-half mile from her residence. She walked home from school on a sidewalk across from the playground of a neighbouring school at 12 p.m. each day.

On October 15, Leeann reported the following. At 12 p.m. the previous day, she was walking home alone from school. While walking past the playground, she noticed a lone man seated in the driver's seat of a blue parked car.

The man called to her and asked her to come to the car. Leeann continued walking. She heard him ask, "Do you know where the Centennial Pool is?" Leeann ignored him and ran home, arriving within one minute. She reported nothing then.

She was questioned about the man and the car. The following descriptions were obtained:

Suspect: male, white, dark complexion, dark hair, dark beard, early twenties (determined by comparisons with known persons).

Vehicle: blue in colour, similar to a Dodge Dart (based on her perception of similarity to her grandfather's car), a shiny column separated the driver's and passenger's windows.

She had never seen the man or the car before. She was not certain she could recognize either if seen again.

Based on her age and the delayed report, the validity of this incident report was met with doubt.

(Refer to the end of Chapter 15 for the conclusion of this case study.)

INFORMANTS

An **informant** is a witness who provides confidential evidence to the police and whom the police choose not to compel to court by means of a subpoena. The officer who receives the information chooses not to divulge the informant's identity in order to maintain confidentiality. An informant can be classified as:

- an **eyewitness**, which means he or she saw the offence being committed by the offender (e.g., as an accomplice),
- a **corroborative witness**, which means he or she saw or heard facts that incriminate the offender (commonly, these facts relate to the disposal of physical evidence such as weapons or stolen property, and to confessions or inculpatory statements made by the offender in the presence of the informant), or
- a **hearsay witness**, which means he or she has knowledge of facts, but did not obtain them firsthand with his or her own senses (usually, these facts are told to the informant by an eyewitness or a corroborative witness).

Significance of Informants

Based on personal experience, confidential informants are the most important element in criminal investigations because

- Offenders tell others about crimes they have committed.
- Information about crimes travels rapidly within the criminal community.
- A wide range of people expose offenders, including repeat offenders with extensive criminal records and the accused's family members and acquaintances.
- A variety of motives create the impetus for people to give confidential information to the police.
- Informant evidence is the best way to solve a large number of offences in a short amount of time, accelerate the successful solution of a major crime, and prevent major crimes before they happen.

Informant networks are crucial partnerships that add to the effectiveness of police organizations. Some informants have short-term value, while others are long-term partners who help solve crime faster than any other investigative procedures.

Developing a network of informants is also vital to individual police careers. A common misconception is that only detectives develop networks of informants. Uniform patrol officers can obtain confidential information in the same manner as detectives.

Finally, what a veteran officer once said is worth repeating: "You know you're a *good* investigator when you can pick up a phone, call an informant, and find out who committed a crime. But the *best* investigator knows about a crime before it happens."

RULES OF EVIDENCE

The admissibility of an informant's evidence is governed by the investigator. If the investigator decides not to issue a subpoena to an informant, then he or she has decided to maintain confidentiality about the informant's identity. Confidentiality becomes an issue if the investigator believes that (a) the informant's safety will be jeopardized by court testimony or (b) the informant will be of use in this role in the future.

It is the investigator alone who decides whether an informant becomes a compellable witness based on the criterion of confidentiality. However, the decision is revocable; the informant may be compelled to testify at the trial if confidentiality is no longer required.

An informant's evidence is useful only in the formulation of reasonable grounds for arrest. It is of no use in developing the reasonable grounds necessary to lay an Information or to form a *prima facie* case. An investigator cannot testify about the informant's evidence in court because of the hearsay nature of the testimony. In summary, only the informant can introduce his or her evidence in a trial; if the informant is not compelled to court, the informant's evidence will be excluded from the Crown's case.

EVALUATING INFORMANT CREDIBILITY

Evaluating an informant's credibility as strong can be accomplished in the following manner:

1. Grade the informant according to the 10-point witness credibility evaluation process discussed in Chapter 14.
2. If the credibility is graded as strong, determine the informant's motive.
3. The motive must be compatible with a strong rating.

Informant Motives

An informant's motives for reporting information to the police are usually apparent without the need for extensive questioning. Usually the motive can be determined by combining a logical analysis of the circumstances with experience and intuitiveness, without asking the informant what the motive is.

Questioning the informant specifically about a motive is not recommended unless there is no other alternative; it may make the informant lose confidence in the officer's experience. Informants are more likely to be honest and give more information if they think the investigator is experienced, because most informants usually believe that an experienced investigator will not violate confidentiality by allowing the informant's identity to be divulged. Informants frequently believe that their motives are abundantly clear; questioning an informant about an obvious topic makes the investigator appear inexperienced, decreasing the informant's confidence that the investigator will protect the informant's anonymity.

The following are common informant motives. Each has a suggested credibility rating.

1. **Fear** This motive is the fear that an offender's behaviour has deteriorated to a level that poses a threat to the public. The intention of an informant motivated by fear is to deter the offender's dangerous conduct. Usually, this belief is founded on strong evidence that the informant has received, such as a confession. Fearing an offender's behaviour is usually well founded. Wives, common-law wives, girlfriends, and mothers of offenders often are the best examples of informants motivated by fear. (Credibility is strong.)

2. **Bargaining** Offenders frequently provide information intended to "make a patch," or bargain for the reduction of charges or sentences, or to obtain release from custody after an arrest. (Credibility is usually strong, especially if the bargaining relates to a release after an arrest.)

3. **Need to express knowledge** Everybody likes to appear knowledgeable about something. People living within a criminal subculture may become experts on criminal activity. Showing their vast knowledge of this subject may satisfy a desire to impress others. In addition, many informants enjoy opportunities to demonstrate greater knowledge of criminal activity than the officer has. (Credibility is usually strong.)

4. **Eliminate competition or accomplices** Criminally active informants may financially benefit if criminals competing in the same crimes are convicted. Sometimes included in this motive is the informant's desire to implicate his or her accomplices in an offence they committed together so that suspicion is moved away from the informant. The informant speculates that the accomplices will not implicate him or her, the police will end the investigation, and he or she will never be detected or arrested. (Credibility is usually strong.)

5. **Morals** Informants often are criminally inclined. Thus, officers often think they have no sense of right or wrong. However, despite the informant's apparent lack of scruples when it comes to his or her own criminal behaviour, criminal informants do inform on others simply because they believe the offender's condut to be wrong. (Credibility is strong.)

6. **"Playing cop"** Some informants, whether criminally active or not, provide information because they enjoy being part of the police investigation. In addition, they find fraternizing with investigators appealing because they receive attention. (Credibility is strong.)

7. **Financial reward** Greed may be a motivation to fabricate information. If an informant knows that he or she will be rewarded with money, the temptation to lie may increase. Paying informants should be avoided for this reason and because proper interview techniques will usually elicit the desired information. (Money as the sole motivation usually represents weak credibility.)

8. **Combination** In most situations, an informant's credibility and motives are a combination of the above. (Credibility is usually strong.)

An eyewitness informant or the recipient of a confession with strong credibility constitutes reasonable grounds.

INTERVIEWING INFORMANTS

The interview process for informants does not differ from the format used for other witnesses. The first objective is to determine whether the informant is an eyewitness, a corroborative witness, or a hearsay witness.

A variety of reasons may motivate an informant to falsely implicate a person. Additionally, informants participate in crimes and implicate their accomplices, attempting to conceal their own guilt. Consequently, other factors must be determined not only to evaluate credibility, but also to determine whether the informant participated in the crime:

1. Why was the informant present when the observations were made? Officers should ask why the informant was present during the observation or conversation.
2. If a confession was received from the offender, where and when did the conversation occur, what composed the conversation, and how did the conversation lead to a confession by the offender?
3. Do the date, time, and location lead to the conclusion that the informant:
   ▷ was innocently present at the crime and saw what happened, but did not actually participate?
   ▷ participated in the crime?
   ▷ actually spoke with the accused after the offence?
4. Who else saw the observations or heard the confession? These people not only may corroborate the informant, but also may act as witnesses for the trial.
5. If the information is hearsay evidence, from whom did he or she receive it? The person who told the informant could provide direct evidence and give testimony in court that constitutes a *prima facie* case.
6. How specific is the information? If the informant's evidence contains an unusual number of precise details, or if the informant cannot remember exactly where and when he or she received a confession, there is a high probability that the informant participated in the crime. If the investigator develops this suspicion, it should not be conveyed to the informant until all the information has been received from him or her.

DEVELOPING INFORMANTS

Developing informants is not an intricate science. It simply involves constant communication with persons believed to be knowledgeable about criminal activity. The best method is to discuss crime openly with any person detected in any offence. For example, this can take place when a known criminal is stopped by a uniform patrol officer for a provincial statute violation.

Also, criminal activity should be discussed with every offender arrested for committing any criminal offence, after the investigation has ended. Although this practice is especially effective after an accused person has confessed to a crime, it is often ignored because investigating the offender's wrongdoing takes priority. Casual talk about crime develops informants.

MANAGING INFORMANTS

After an informant has been developed, proper informant management is necessary to fulfill two objectives:

- to ensure officer safety and the informant's safety, and
- to prevent the commission of offences by the informant.

These objectives can be fulfilled if these guidelines are followed:

1. Never permit informants to remain undetected for crimes proven to have been committed by them as a bargain or patch for information received. An officer's discretionary authority allows charges to be laid or to resolve the crime without charges. If no charges are laid, proper documentation must exist in a police report. For example, if an informant is released unconditionally, a formal police report must state this and the reasons justifying it.
2. An informant may suggest that he or she accompany the targets of an investigation (during the commission of an offence) so they can help make the detection and arrest easier. Do not grant permission. The investigator must persuade the informant to avoid such conduct because all participants will qualify as parties to the offence.
3. Never withdraw a charge against an informant without the Crown Attorney's consent. The Crown has exclusive ownership of all Informations. Withdrawal of an Information without the Crown's consent constitutes the offence of "Obstruct justice."
4. Never make promises in advance without absolute knowledge that the agreement or arrangement will be honoured.
5. Never pay money to an informant unless there are no other alternatives. Most informants will incriminate others without being paid. If proper interview techniques are used, there is usually no need to pay a person for evidence.
6. Never divulge the identity of an informant if confidentiality is requested. There are two consequences that come from violating confidentiality:
    a. the informant's safety may be jeopardized, and
    b. the criminal community will likely become aware that an officer is incapable of maintaining informant confidentiality, making it difficult for that officer to develop other informants.
7. Never name the informant in police reports or court documents.
8. Do not act upon an informant's evidence if the informant's identity can be determined from the officer's actions (e.g., executing a search warrant under circumstances that clearly indicate who the informant was).

9. If conversation occurs between a person and an officer and the officer knows that person is another officer's informant, the officer should never let the informant know this. This reinforces the informant's confidence in the other officer's ability to maintain confidentiality.

10. Meetings between officers and informants should follow these guidelines:

   ▷ The officer should select and decide locations and times.

   ▷ Knowledge of meetings should be given to other officers.

   ▷ If the informant adamantly prefers a specific location and time, the officer should intentionally change them; if the change is met with opposition, do not attend.

   ▷ Avoid setting patterns of locations and times.

   ▷ If a meeting requires the attendance of other officers, the officer who developed the informant should always be present.

   ▷ The informant should be instructed about how to behave if he or she inadvertently meets officers in public places so as not to arouse any suspicion of his or her informer status (for example, if the informant usually displays rude and annoying behaviour toward police officers while in the company of others, he or she should not change that behaviour during inadvertent meetings).

CHILD WITNESSES

The Supreme Court of Canada has created several procedural guidelines by the following rulings made in various case law decisions.

1. "Negative stereotypes should not be applied to the evidence of children."[1]

2. "The notion that the evidence of children is inherently unreliable has now been totally rejected."[2]

3. "This is part of a larger trend in the evolution of evidence law in which courts have moved away from the tendency to view the evidence of certain classes of witnesses as inherently untrustworthy."[3]

4. "We now recognize that, in general, juries are competent to assess the evidence and credibility of all witnesses, including that of children."[4]

5. "We now accept that while children may not be able to recount precise details and communicate the when and where of an event with exactitude, this does not mean that they have misconceived what happened to them and who did it."[5]

6. "The law affecting the evidence of children has undergone two major changes in recent years. The first is the removal of the notion, found at common law and codified in legislation, that the evidence of children was inherently unreliable and therefore to be treated with special caution. The repeal of provisions creating a legal requirement that children's evidence be corroborated does not prevent the judge and jury from treating a child's evidence with caution where such caution is merited in the circumstances of the case. But it does revoke the assumption formerly applied to all evidence of children, often unjustly, that children's evidence is always less reliable than the evidence of adults."[6]

7. "On the basis of research which made it clear that conventional assumptions about the veracity and powers of articulation and recall of young children are largely unfounded, the [Badgley Report] committee recommended that children's evidence be heard and weighed in the same manner as any other testimony."[7]
8. "[Y]oung children are generally not adept at reasoned reflection or at fabricating tales of sexual perversion. They, manifestly, are unlikely to use their reflective powers to concoct a deliberate untruth, and particularly one about a sexual act which in all probability is beyond their ken."[8]

The last quote is the most profound one for police officers to remember. Children, generally, should be incapable of fabricating sexual offences because they should not have prior awareness of the nature of the act. This principle formed the basis of the hearsay exception known as the Khan Rule (explained in Chapter 8), which allows people who receive a report of an offence from a child to testify about what the child told them, if the evidence is necessary and reliable.

Although children may lack the same memory capacity as adults, a child's credibility and accuracy should not be rejected merely because of the child's age. Empirical research indicates that young children's memory reports are highly incomplete, but their reported observations are quite accurate.[9] A child's memory performance may be poorer than an adult's because of inefficient encoding abilities.

Observations made by independent child witnesses (i.e., non-victims or bystanders) of brief events are less accurate than those made by child victims of crime, such as sexual abuse. Studies indicate that young children have strong memories for prominent events involving themselves. Children may easily make facial recognition if they have an extended duration of observation.[10]

Often children's observations are wrongly perceived as being inaccurate because of their

- underdeveloped sense of time,
- tendency to omit events that connect an entire offence,
- inability to understand adult use of language, and
- underdeveloped speech abilities.[11]

The differences in accuracy between children and adults were empirically tested. Three age groups of students—five and six year olds, nine and ten year olds, and college-aged students—participated in touching activities. A male experimenter administered skin sensitivity tests requiring repeated touching of hands, arms, and face. The experiment also included the removal of the students' jackets and coats, and a brief intrusion by another adult. Afterward, the subjects were asked to identify the experimenter and the other adult by means of photo lineups. The results indicated that young children lack adult skills of recall and that they give relatively lengthy accounts of events in which they participated. Kindergarten and elementary-school children had poorer memories than older children and adults; underdeveloped recollective skill was identified as the cause. The conclusion did not support the exclusion of child testimony; instead, it mitigated negative factors concerning child witness credibility.[12]

Evaluating Children's Credibility

In *R. v. Marquard* (1993),[13] the Supreme Court of Canada stated: "Negative stereotypes should not be applied to the evidence of children." In *R. v. B. (G.)* (1990),[14] the Supreme Court of Canada stated that a "commonsense approach" should be used when evaluating the credibility of young children; adult standards of accuracy should not be applied to children. However, the standard of proof cannot be lowered when dealing with children; the same standards of proof apply to both children and adults. The court explained that a flaw in a child's testimony, such as a contradiction, should not have the same negative effect on credibility as would a similar flaw or contradiction made by an adult. The reasons given by the court were:

1. Young children probably cannot recount precise details and communicate the when and where of an event with exactitude. However, this does not mean that they have misconceived what happened to them or who did it.[15]

2. No formal or specific legal guidelines have been established for officers to evaluate child credibility to form reasonable grounds. Child credibility may be evaluated by using the same 10-point list used for adults. Additional factors to consider during investigations involving child victims and witnesses are:

   ▷ Child complainants and victims are more accurate than child independent witnesses.

   ▷ Elementary-school students lack the memory skills of older children and adults.

   ▷ Children should not be evaluated as being inaccurate merely because of age.

   ▷ Child credibility should not suffer because their communication skills are below adult levels.

   ▷ Contradictions or flaws in a child's observations should not immediately diminish credibility.

At a trial, the judge or jury, if one exists, are responsible for evaluating child witness credibility. In cases involving child victims, the Crown and police obviously strive to elevate the child's credibility by means of corroboration. One much-debated method of doing this is by relying on "expert" testimony.

Expert testimony about the credibility of a witness is inadmissible. However, expert testimony is admissible relating to human conduct and psychological and physical factors that may result in behaviour relevant to credibility. An example of how these rules apply is found in *R. v. Marquard* (1993).[16]

An accused was charged with aggravated assault upon her three-and-a-half-year-old granddaughter for burns caused by putting the child's face against a hot stove door. Upon arrival at the hospital, the child initially told the medical staff that she had burned herself with a lighter. At the trial, a doctor testified after being declared an expert in child abuse and pediatrics. The doctor gave the following opinions during testimony:

▸ The child was lying when she told the hospital staff that she had burned herself with a lighter, but was telling the truth when she testified that she had been assaulted.

▸ Children commonly explain injuries caused by assault as being accidental.

▸ A reason why children initially conceal an assault and lie by saying that it was an accident is that abused children feel responsibility for the behaviour and injury. They are not willing to tell the hospital staff about a perceived wrongdoing because they worry about what strangers might do to them for the same behaviour that caused the injury by a relative.

The Supreme Court of Canada excluded the opinion that the child lied to the hospital but told the truth about the assault in court. The judge or jury are responsible for credibility evaluation, not expert witnesses. However, the doctor was justified in the opinions about why children may lie about the cause of injuries.

The court gave another example of admissible expert testimony that benefits the Crown and police in sexual assault prosecutions in which young victims fail to promptly report the offence. Delayed sexual assault reports often create the inference that the story was fabricated. Expert testimony is admissible to explain reasons why young sexual assault victims delay the report and do not complain immediately.

Criminal Code

The *Criminal Code* has two provisions that are advantageous to the Crown in sexual offence cases involving young victims: (a) s. 486(2.1) C.C. and (b) s. 715.1 C.C.

An accepted common-law tradition is that an accused has the right to be in the sight of witnesses who testify against him or her; in other words, the accused must face the accuser.[17] However, young victims may be allowed to give their examination-in-chief out of the sight of an accused person (e.g., outside the courtroom or behind a screen) if all of the following conditions exist:

▸ the charge is sexual assault, sexual interference, or sexual exploitation,

▸ the witness is the complainant,

▸ he or she is under 18 years of age at the time of the trial or preliminary hearing, and

▸ the judge forms an opinion that the witness's "exclusion is necessary to obtain a full and candid account of the acts" from the witness.[18]

For this section to apply, the Crown must make a motion during the trial. The judge conducts a hearing to determine whether a screen or testimony outside the courtroom is necessary to obtain candid testimony. The Crown must introduce evidence; the judge cannot form an opinion without evidentiary basis.[19] The Crown may call witnesses, such as an expert witness (e.g., psychologist). For example, a psychologist may examine the witness before a trial and then give an opinion about whether a screen is necessary for the witness to testify candidly. Mere testimony by the complainant stating that he or she is uncomfortable about testifying usually is insufficient evidence.[20] The defence is allowed to cross-examine the expert. Afterward, the judge makes a final decision. If the witness is allowed to testify outside the courtroom, arrangements must be made for the accused, the judge, and the jury to watch the complainant's testimony by means of closed-circuit television.[21] After the victim's examination-in-chief is complete, the defence is allowed to cross-examine the witness; s. 486(2.1) does not protect the victim from cross-examination.

Additionally, a videotape of the complainant's examination-in-chief may be admissible if the following conditions are fulfilled according to s. 715.1 C.C.:

▸ the complainant is under 18 years of age at the time of the offence;

▸ the accused person is charged with an offence relating to sexual assault, sexual interference, or sexual exploitation;

▸ the videotape is made within a reasonable time after the offence;

▸ it contains a description of the acts reported; and

▸ it is adopted, relating to its content, during testimony.[22]

Videotape adoption is complete if the witness believes the discussed events to be true, no matter whether he or she recalls them.[23] Reasonable time has not been specified, but it depends on the circumstances of each case. The Supreme Court of Canada, in *R. v. L. (D.O.)* (1993),[24] ruled that five months was reasonable relating to the circumstances of that case. If the videotape is admissible, the victim may be cross-examined. Section 715.1 C.C. does not protect the victim from cross-examination.

The constitutional validity of both sections has been challenged, but neither has been ruled to be a Charter violation.[25]

Case Study 15.1 Conclusion

The validity of Leeann's report was investigated in the following manner.

A search of recent police reports revealed a complaint made by a nine-year-old girl on October 14. The girl reported that she was walking home from school at 3 p.m. on a street about one mile from the location of Leeann's incident. A blue car stopped near the girl. A male driver was the lone occupant. He asked the girl for directions to the Centennial Pool. She ignored him and continued walking. She described the driver as being male, white, dark complexion, dark hair, dark beard. The vehicle was blue in colour and a silver piece separated the driver's window and the rear passenger's window. Officers canvassed the neighbourhood of Leeann's incident and two young girls reported that a man in a blue car had called to them while they were walking alone during daylight hours.

A records check revealed that more than 20 complaints had been reported by young girls in the area during the past five years. The complaints consisted of (a) a suspicious male stopping near the young girl and asking for directions to the Centennial Pool or (b) the young girl approaching the car to look at a map and the driver exposing himself to her.

Investigation resulted in the identification of the car. A chrome (silver) column separated the driver's and passenger's windows. The owner of the vehicle matched the description of the suspect. The owner had a twin brother. Investigators attended at the owner's home, but he was absent. A message was left with the suspect's mother requesting that he attend at the police station.

Six hours later, the owner of the car voluntarily attended at the station. He consented to an interrogation. He confessed to being responsible for Leeann's incident and all others during the preceding five years. His conduct in Leeann's incident did not constitute a criminal offence. Exposing himself to the young girls did, however, constitute the summary conviction offence of "Indecent act." None of the indecent acts was committed within the preceding six months, thereby preventing arrest and prosecution. The offender's conduct qualified as behaviour governed by the *Mental Health Act* (M.H.A.). The arrest provision under the M.H.A. was not applicable because the officers did not find the offender committing the inappropriate conduct. This matter was resolved with the offender's voluntary admission to a psychiatric facility.

COMMENTARY   All witnesses were children. Their observations all lacked sufficiency for reasonable grounds formulation. None appeared able to accurately identify the offender. However, all descriptions of the offender and vehicle were accurate and sufficient to create a suspicion. The suspicions became reasonable grounds by means of a confession obtained from a consent interrogation.

ENDNOTES

1. *R. v. Marquard* (1993), 85 C.C.C. (3d) 193 (S.C.C.).
2. Ibid., at 201.
3. Ibid.
4. Ibid.
5. Ibid., at 201.
6. *R. v. W. (R.)* (1992), 74 C.C.C. (3d) 134, at 142–143 (S.C.C.).
7. *R. v. Marquard*, supra note 1, at 202.
8. *R. v. Khan* (1990), 59 C.C.C. (3d) 92 (S.C.C.).
9. Chance and Goldstein (1984), as in M.R. Leippe, A.P. Manion, and A. Romanczyk, "Eyewitness Memory for a Touching Experience: Accuracy Differences Between Child and Adult Witnesses" (1991) vol. 76, no. 3 *Journal of Applied Psychology.*
10. Leippe, Manion, and Romanczyk, supra note 9.
11. Ibid.
12. Ibid.
13. *R. v. Marquard*, supra note 1.
14. *R. v. B. (G.)* (1990), 56 C.C.C. (3d) 219 (S.C.C.).
15. Ibid.
16. *R. v. Marquard*, supra note 1.
17. *R. v. L. (D.O.)* (1993), 85 C.C.C. (3d) 289 (S.C.C.); *R. v. Levogiannis* (1990), 62 C.C.C. (3d) 75 (Ont. C.A.).
18. Section 486(2.1) C.C.
19. *R. v. M. (P.)* (1990), 1 O.R. (3d) 341 (C.A.).
20. Ibid.
21. Section 486(2.2) C.C.
22. E.L. Greenspan and M. Rosenberg, *Martin's Annual Criminal Code* (Aurora, ON: Canada Law Book, 2008).
23. *R. v. Meddoui* (1990), 61 C.C.C. (3d) 345 (Alta. C.A.) as in *Martin's Annual Criminal Code*, supra note 22.
24. *R. v. L. (D.O.)*, supra note 17.
25. Ibid.

PHASE 3
Interrogations and Confessions

A confession is the best type of evidence that can be obtained in an investigation. There is no stronger or more valuable evidence than an offender saying he or she committed an offence and explaining how it was committed.

A confession is the best form of reasonable grounds. It is proof beyond reasonable doubt that the accused person committed the offence. However, there are two problems associated with a confession:

1. Confessions are usually the product of an interrogation. Interrogation is an inexact science. It is a skill that requires substantial experience to develop.

2. Confessions to the police are not automatically admissible. Extensive, complex rules of evidence govern the admissibility of a confession. Interrogation techniques are premised on those rules of evidence.

All police officers, including uniform patrol officers, require interrogation skills. Confessions are vital evidence in major cases and routine ones, including shoplifting and impaired driving.

Phase 3 first explains the rules of evidence that govern the admissibility of confessions, followed by an explanation of interrogation principles and procedures.

PHASE 3 LEARNING OUTCOMES

The student will learn to interpret and apply:

- rules of evidence regarding the admissibility of confessions, including the Contemporary Confession Rule emerging from *R. v. Oickle*
- right to counsel procedures to prevent s. 10(b) Charter violations
- the contemporary "right to silence" rules to prevent s. 7 Charter violations
- the contemporary "caution" rules
- Y.C.J.A. rules regarding young offender interrogations
- a model based on the psychological concept of cognitive dissonance, in both front-line interrogations and formal interrogations

LEARNER SUMMARY

The Supreme Court of Canada has stated, "Confessions are among the most useful types of evidence. Where freely and voluntarily given, an admission of guilt provides a reliable tool in the elucidation of crime, thereby furthering the judicial search for the truth and serving the societal interest in repressing crime through the conviction of the guilty."[1]

Confessions are the best way to establish reasonable grounds and are crucial to proving a *prima facie* case. Additionally, confessions and admissions remove any doubt during an investigation about whether the correct offender has been arrested and charged.

A common misconception is that only detectives interrogate suspects. All officers, including uniform patrol officers, need to know how to obtain a confession and the rules of evidence governing admissibility. Confessions and admissions are valuable regardless of the severity of the offence in question.

Before a confession can be used by the prosecution, it must be ruled admissible. Confessions made to a police officer are not automatically admissible. Numerous rules of evidence affect admissibility and govern interrogation techniques. The rules must be learned before the methods used to interrogate are learned.

This chapter discusses the rules of evidence that govern the admissibility of confessions.

Case Study 16.1

John was arrested on November 22 in relation to the break and enter at Dave's house while the family was at the funeral home. He was cautioned and informed of his right to counsel.

He was questioned by two investigators in a spacious, contemporary office at the police station. An interrogation occurred, during which John confessed. What would make a repeat offender want to confess his crime?

(Refer to the end of Chapter 16 for the conclusion of this case study.)

DEFINITIONS

A **suspect** is a person not formally charged by means of a sworn Information. Reasonable grounds do not exist to formally accuse; only mere suspicion exists. An **accused person** is a person formally charged with a criminal offence. Reasonable grounds exist to accuse and a sworn Information has been laid.

A **statement** is anything written or verbally made by a suspect or accused person out of court (e.g., during the investigation, before the trial), including the suspect's conduct. **Conduct** refers to non-verbal acts such as nodding the head and shrugging the shoulders. An **inculpatory statement** is a self-incriminating statement made by a suspect or accused person out of court.[2] An **exculpatory statement** is a denial or alibi made by a suspect or accused person out of court.[3]

An **admission** is an inculpatory statement made by a suspect or accused person out of court that proves at least one fact-in-issue of the offence.[4] A **confession** is an admission made by a suspect or accused person out of court that proves all facts-in-issue of the offence.[5]

A **person in authority** is usually someone the accused believes can influence his or her prosecution. A **person not in authority** is usually someone the accused does not believe can influence his or her prosecution.

A **voir dire** is a hearing or inquiry conducted during a trial to determine the admissibility of confessions. A voir dire is also referred to as a *trial within a trial*.[6]

As stated in Chapter 8, *interview* and *interrogation* describe types of questioning. For the purpose of teaching, interview refers to witness questioning while interrogation refers to suspect/accused person questioning. This will prevent confusion while studying these topics. However, the word "interrogation" has some inherent intimidation associated with it. It is recommended that "interview" be used to describe *all* questioning, including that of suspects/accused persons, particularly when testifying in court. It should be noted that there is no legal authority upon which this is based; there is no statutory definition of interview or interrogation and no statutory requirement about what to call them.

THE PURPOSE OF A CONFESSION

An effective police investigation may include obtaining a confession from a suspect as one of its aims (S.C.C.).[7] Confessions have the strongest evidentiary value of any evidence because they remove any doubt about guilt. There is no investigation where the amount of evidence is so great or overwhelming that a confession would not benefit or strengthen the case. Therefore, officers should always try to obtain confessions from every suspect charged or arrested, regardless of the amount of evidence accumulated during an investigation. When admissible, a confession is the best proof of guilt[8] because:

- ▸ It corroborates existing evidence and establishes proof beyond a reasonable doubt.
- ▸ It is often the only method of solving a crime, thereby acting as the main evidence.
- ▸ It proves all the facts-in-issue.

In addition, every arrested person should be interrogated with the intention of obtaining unrelated confessions for the purpose of solving other crimes. Officers should assume that every offender is a *recidivist* (a person who repeats undesirable behaviour). Interrogation eliminates or confirms this assumption. Often, a recidivist uses an arrest as an opportunity to clear past undetected offences, rather than gamble with possible re-arrest for past crimes after release.

However, despite the evidentiary significance of a confession, there are problems that may be encountered during a trial. First, not all confessions are automatically admissible. Some may be excluded during the trial. Second, admissions and confessions must be introduced through witness testimony. The person who heard the accused's statement must repeat it during testimony. As explained in previous chapters, there are potential problems with all witness testimony (e.g., credibility and failure to appear in court).

SIGNIFICANCE OF CONFESSIONS AND ADMISSIONS

A confession made by an offender during an investigation constitutes reasonable grounds. It exceeds mere suspicion on the basis that "a person in his right mind, and of his own will, is unlikely to confess to a crime unless he did in fact commit it."[9]

The significance of confessions to formulating reasonable grounds is as follows:

1. Verbal inculpatory statements made during a consent interrogation constitute reasonable grounds.
2. A verbal statement is considered the main evidence. It is capable of proving all the facts-in-issue. A written confession following a verbal statement corroborates the main evidence.
3. An admissible confession to a person in authority establishes a *prima facie* case.
4. An inculpatory statement or confession made to a person not in authority constitutes reasonable grounds.
5. A confession made to a person not in authority establishes a *prima facie* case.
6. Inculpatory statements and confessions made by an accused that implicate an accomplice constitute
    ▷ reasonable grounds, relative to the accomplice,
    ▷ grounds to prove the "likelihood of giving material evidence" for the purpose of issuing a subpoena for the suspect to act as a Crown witness, and
    ▷ a *prima facie* case, without the need of "corroboration by law."

RULES OF EVIDENCE: THE TRADITIONAL "CONFESSION RULE"

Confessions made to persons not in authority are automatically **admissible**; no voir dire is required to determine admissibility. Confessions made to a police officer are not automatically admissible evidence. A voir dire must be conducted to determine whether the confession was obtained legally. A legally obtained confession must not violate (a) the Confession Rule and (b) s. 24(2) Charter. Therefore, the judge, either during the voir dire or before, must first decide whether the confession was made to a person in authority or to a person not in authority.

Person in Authority

"Person in authority" was defined by the S.C.C. in *R. v. Hodgson* (1998)[10] as follows:

- Persons engaged in the arrest, detention, and prosecution of the accused.
- Police officers and prison officials or guards who are readily identified to the accused.
- Persons whom the accused reasonably believes are acting on behalf of the state and could influence or control the proceedings against him or her.

There is no absolute list of persons who qualify as persons in authority. Police officers and jail guards are "automatically considered a person in authority solely by virtue of their status."[11] Other persons may be considered persons in authority including parents, doctors, teachers, or employers. The issue of who is a person in authority is decided from the "viewpoint of the accused." There must be a reasonable basis for the accused's belief that these other persons could influence or control proceedings, or are acting on behalf of the state. By itself, the status of parents of the accused, parents of the complainant, doctors, teachers, psychiatrists, and employers, or the mere fact that they may have some personal authority over the accused, is not sufficient to qualify them as persons in authority for the purposes of the Confession Rule. Undercover police officers are usually considered to not be persons in authority. The determination of who is a person in authority is made case by case.

In *R. v. A.B.* (1986),[12] the Ontario Court of Appeal created some guidelines. A 13-year-old accused person was charged with sexual assaults upon his 5- and 8-year-old stepsisters. The accused confessed to his mother and two psychiatrists; all of the confessions were ruled admissible. The Ontario Court of Appeal concluded the following to be persons in authority:

- The complainant may qualify, depending on the circumstances.
- The parent of an infant victim or complainant may qualify, depending on the "factual background."
- A person who makes an inducement to an accused person in the presence of a person in authority. Accordingly, the person making the inducement becomes "an agent of the person in authority."
- A person whom the accused person believes had "some degree of power" over him or her at the time the statement was made.

Other examples of "persons in authority" include social workers. In *R. v. Sweryda* (1987),[13] the accused was charged with assault on his daughter. He made a statement to a social worker after the social worker told the accused that she had to determine whether to remove the child from the home. The Alberta Court of Appeal ruled that the social worker had a peace officer's authority under the *Child Welfare Act* (1984) and was capable of initiating prosecution. In addition, the accused perceived her as such.

Person Not in Authority

A "person not in authority" may be defined as a person who the accused person reasonably believes cannot influence his or her prosecution, favourably or otherwise, and who is not acting on behalf of the state.

In *R. v. A.B* (1986),[14] the court concluded the following to be persons not in authority:

- A Crown witness, generally.
- In this case, the accused's mother because the statement was made at a time when the mother had no intention of calling the police. A report was made almost one year later.
- A psychiatrist, even when examining an accused person to determine his status as a dangerous sexual offender.
- A doctor who examines the accused person.

Other examples of those who may qualify as persons not in authority are:

- Clergy members and counsellors, if the accused's fundamental right to freedom of religion, guaranteed in s. 2(a) Charter, is not violated.[15]
- Undercover police officers, if the accused's fundamental right to remain silent, as guaranteed in s. 7 of the Charter, is not violated.

The status of an undercover officer, pursuant to the Confession Rule, was examined in *Rothman v. The Queen* (1981).[16] The accused person was charged with possession of narcotics for the purpose of trafficking. After being cautioned and informed of his right to counsel, the accused refused to make a statement during interrogation. After he was detained in a police cell, an undercover officer (posing as a truck driver under arrest for a traffic violation) was lodged in the same cellblock. The accused told the officer that he "looked like a narc." The officer convinced him otherwise. Subsequently, the accused made inculpatory statements to the officer. The Supreme Court of Canada ruled that the officer was a person not in authority, based on the accused person's belief. The officer's conduct was deemed to have not brought the administration of justice into disrepute. A voir dire to test voluntariness was not required.

In *R. v. Hebert* (1990),[17] the Supreme Court addressed the relevance of a s. 7 Charter violation regarding undercover officers. This will be examined later in this chapter.

The final determination of who is considered a person in authority or not in authority is made by a judge during a trial. The decision is made after a voir dire is conducted.

Generally, the accused and defence must make a motion during the trial to request that the judge decide whether the person who received a confession is a person in authority or not. The defence has the onus to prove that there is a valid issue of consideration. The judge then conducts a voir dire to allow the defence to introduce evidence to prove that the accused reasonably believed that the person acted on behalf of the state or could influence or control proceedings.

The benefit for the defence to prove that the person was a person in authority is to force the Crown to prove that the confession was voluntarily made. Otherwise, the confession is automatically admissible if it was made to a person not in authority.

The Confession Rule and the Charter

An investigator may be confident of the admissibility of an accused person's confession made to a person not in authority. Its relevance is abundantly clear and no rule excludes it. Admissions and confessions constitute exceptions to the Hearsay Rule; when made to a person not in authority, statements are admitted automatically without a voir dire.[18]

However, confessions made to a person in authority will not automatically be admissible. A voir dire must first be conducted. Confessions can be rendered inadmissible if they violate the Confession Rule or s. 24(2) Charter or a combination of those two. The Crown has the onus in regard to the Confession Rule; the defence has the onus in regard to Charter violations, although evidence of a s. 10(b) right to counsel Charter violation during the Crown's case may result in exclusion of the evidence.[19] Discussions of the Confession Rule and the Charter follow.

CONFESSION RULE

The evolution of self-incrimination laws are traced to the sixteenth century, when judicial examination of accused persons was permitted prior to and during a trial. Reform occurred between the seventeenth and nineteenth centuries. An English court decision ended judicially precipitated self-incrimination, allowing only voluntary statements made by an accused person to be tendered as evidence during a trial. Eventually, the courts adopted a skeptical attitude toward all interrogation. Clarity of confession admissibility in English courts did not exist in the nineteenth century because of conflicting self-incrimination laws.

A 1914 English decision in *Ibrahim v. The King*[20] created the following **Confession Rule**: no statement made by an accused person to a person in authority is admissible evidence unless the prosecution proves that the statement was voluntarily made.

The Supreme Court of Canada adopted the Ibrahim Rule in *Prosko v. Regina* (1922).[21] In *Boudreau v. The King* (1949),[22] the court confirmed the rule concerning inculpatory statements and defined **voluntary** as meaning free from inducement of persons in authority.[23]

In *Erven v. The Queen* (1978)[24] and *Piche v. The Queen* (1969),[25] the Supreme Court of Canada expanded the Confession Rule to include inculpatory and exculpatory statements made by the accused person to a person in authority before, during, or after the offence.[26]

The significance of the Confession Rule is as follows:

1. It applies to statements made by an accused person, before, during, or after the offence.
2. It applies to both inculpatory and exculpatory statements.
3. The recipient of the statement must be a person in authority.
4. The Crown has the burden of proving voluntariness beyond a reasonable doubt.
5. The rule does not apply to statements made by an accused to a person not in authority.

Voluntariness

The term *voluntary* can be defined as free from inducement.[27] An **inducement** is any threat of violence and direct or implied promises.[28] The definition of an inducement can be expanded to include words or acts that cause an accused person to believe that his or her status will improve or worsen, relating to the charge, depending on whether or not he or she makes a statement.[29] An act or words can constitute an inducement despite the absence of intent for the person in authority to commit the inducement. Proof that a police officer did not intend for the remarks to imply a threat or promise is insignificant;[30] it does not cancel the inducement.

Inducements can be categorized as major or minor. **Major inducements** will result in exclusion of the confession.[31] **Minor inducements** are a temporary classification. This type of inducement may be ruled to be a major inducement or no inducement. A trial judge uses discretion to decide how a minor inducement is eventually ruled. If the minor inducement reasonably creates a threat or promise, it will be considered a major inducement that will cause the confession to be excluded. If a minor inducement does not reasonably constitute a threat or promise, it will be considered to be no inducement, meaning the confession was voluntarily made.

The primary determining factor used to decide whether a minor inducement will exclude a confession is the caution. A **caution** is a formal warning to the suspect that he has no obligation to speak to or answer questions. The formal caution that is usually read to a suspect is as follows:

> "Do you wish to say anything in answer to the charge? You are not obliged to say anything unless you wish to do so, but whatever you say may be given in evidence."

When this warning is read to a suspect, he or she has been cautioned. The caution is not a mandatory statutory requirement. This means

- The caution does not originate from a statute. It is not in the *Criminal Code*, Charter, or any other statute.
- There is no law that obliges the police to caution a suspect. Failure to caution is not a statutory violation.

The caution is a recommended guideline only. Its purpose is to help prove that a confession was voluntarily made. Cautioning a suspect before questioning works as an advantage for the police because the caution generally removes minor inducements. If the caution is read to the suspect and a minor inducement occurs afterward, the minor inducement will likely be negated and considered to be no inducement by the trial judge.

Three general rules apply from this:

1. Cautioning a suspect before questioning will not automatically make a confession to the police admissible. It will only help remove minor inducements.
2. Failure to caution will not automatically exclude a confession.
3. Failure to caution is not a Charter violation. Failure to caution simply means that the police failed to take advantage of a beneficial procedure that helps prove the voluntariness of a confession.

MAJOR INDUCEMENTS

Major inducements include (a) violence or (b) promises or threats relating to the nature and quantity of charges, the length of a sentence, and interim release after an arrest. Examples of what actually constitutes violence include the following.

▶ **Actual violence** This is self-explanatory and includes any degree of actual physical force applied during questioning.
▶ **Threats or suggestions of violence** This includes any verbal statement or conduct that reasonably causes the suspect to believe that he or she may be assaulted during questioning. Whether the officer intends to actually use violence is irrelevant. For example, during the questioning of a suspect in a heinous crime, the temptation may exist to state an opinion about what the suspect should suffer. Statements such as, "People like you deserve a beating for hurting people, you're lucky that nothing will happen" or, "I'd like to punch you in the head for what you did, but I won't," do not directly state the intention to use violence, but these constitute a major inducement because the officer's intention to not use force is irrelevant to the issue. The suggestion has been made that violence may occur.

Examples of promises or threats include those relating to the following:

▶ **Charges** For example, "If you confess, I'll only charge you with assault instead of assault causing bodily harm," or "I'll only charge you with one count instead of several."
▶ **Sentence** For example, "If you confess, I'll try to get a lesser sentence," or "If you don't confess, you'll likely get a longer sentence."
▶ **Interim release after an arrest** Offenders are usually very concerned about whether or not they will be released after an arrest. Therefore, a statement causing the offender to believe that release is dependent upon a confession is unacceptable.

Any promise or threat relating to charges, sentence, or release constitutes a major inducement.

MINOR INDUCEMENTS

Minor inducements include

▶ The *environment* of custody and the presence of an excessive number of officers during interrogation.[32]
▶ Despite the lack of a general rule forbidding use of specific questions or phrases, the inclusion of *"better"* in certain sentences has created a

presumption of an inducement (e.g., "you had better," "it would be better"). In *R. v. Oickle* (2000), the S.C.C. acknowledged that the word "better" sometimes implies a threat, but not automatically.[33] It depends on the context—how the word is used. It cannot be used to imply a real threat or promise.

- In *R. v. Bird* (1989), the accused made an inculpatory statement to police after an officer told him that he wanted to help the accused and that the accused could help himself. The type of help was not expressed. The court ruled the comment to be an inducement even though there was no doubt that the officer intended to act properly and may have genuinely desired to help the accused with a perceived problem.[34]

- Excessive cross-examination by a police officer during the interrogation becomes an inducement only when it is so excessive that it may reasonably be construed as threatening to the suspect. In reality, excessive cross-examination needs to be accompanied by some type of hostile conduct to be an inducement. There are no specific guidelines that always apply. Each interrogation will be judged case by case.

- Prolonged interrogation under certain circumstances. No specific time constitutes prolonged interrogation. Time lengths vary depending on the circumstances. Examples have included a three-hour questioning and interrogation conducted over several days.[35] Excessive questioning is considered an inducement only if it prevents voluntariness.[36]

- Repeated questioning after an accused person has refused to make a statement. This circumstance is not absolute. It is not an inducement if proof exists that a statement was made after the accused voluntarily changed his or her mind about making a statement.[37]

- Repeated accusations of lying.[38]

- Circumstances that affect human dignity, known as *oppression*. Examples have included the questioning of an accused wearing only a blanket after his clothes were seized, or the denial of food, beverages, or sleep.[39]

- Certain lies and tricks. Intentionally misleading an accused about non-existent evidence will exclude a statement, if the statement is a result of the deception.[40] Justice Lamer, Supreme Court of Canada, in *Rothman v. The Queen* (1981), justified the need for certain "tricks" or "other forms of deceit" during police investigations. Prohibited lies and tricks were defined as conduct that "shocks the community." Examples cited were police officers posing as chaplains and lawyers to elicit confessions.[41]

ACTS NOT CONSTITUTING AN INDUCEMENT

- **Lies or tricks** In *R. v. Green* (1988),[42] officers intentionally lied about the existence of a witness. It occurred early in the interrogation. The accused later confessed to a murder. The court ruled the statement to be admissible. The lie was not an inducement because it was separated in time and not instrumental in the emergence of the proof of his guilt.

- **Off-the-record statements** These statements refer to those made by an accused to a person in authority under the assurance that the statement will be treated confidentially. The Supreme Court of Canada, in *R. v. Smith* (1989),[43] upheld a conviction of robbery where the Crown relied on an off-the-record confession made by the accused to the police. The actual issue was whether the accused's right to counsel was violated regarding the confession. In this case, the off-the-record confession was admissible because no right to counsel violation had occurred. In *R. v. Moran* (1987),[44] the accused appealed a murder conviction on grounds including that the trial judge erred by ruling that an off-the-record inculpatory statement, made to police officers, was irrelevant to voluntariness. The Ontario Court of Appeal dismissed the appeal and did not exclude the off-the-record statement. In other words, the court agreed with the trial judge that the voluntariness of a statement is the factor that determines admissibility, and not whether the statement was made on or off the record. An off-the-record statement will be admissible if a sincere assurance is made by a person in authority that an accused's statement will be confidential. However, if an officer insincerely promises confidentiality, knowing that he or she will reveal it later to trap or trick the accused into confessing, the statement could be rendered involuntary.

▸ **Invoking spiritual, religious, or moral beliefs** Urging a person to confess on this basis is not an inducement.[45]

▸ **Specific phrases and words** Examples are "I can tell you that you won't be mistreated," "This looks bad," "You should get it off your chest and ease your mind," and a police officer's statement that he or she could help the accused through the court, made after the accused acknowledged committing the act that he required help for.[46]

▸ **Accusations of lying** A police officer's statement to an accused that he or she does not believe the accused or that the accused is lying is not a threat.[47]

▸ **Factual statements** A factual statement made by a police officer usually is not an inducement unless it implies that a confession would improve or worsen the accused's position relating to the charge. A police officer's response to an accused person's question will not be an inducement if the answer represents a fact that does not imply that a confession will favour the accused's status.[48] For example, an accused often asks whether he or she will be released from custody. Explaining the bail hearing release procedure is factual; giving an opinion about whether the accused will be released is not factual.

▸ **Prolonged interrogation** A lengthy time period of questioning has not always excluded confessions as evidence in court. A statement made after a series of interrogations over a five-day period was admitted because no evidence existed of threats or promises. Prolonged interrogation does not always adversely affect admissibility of statements providing there is no mistreatment or oppression involved.[49]

Based on the author's personal experience in provincial court trials, the following are significant interrogative statements that have not constituted an inducement:

▸ **Victim's suffering** Informing the offender that the victim "can't sleep at night" or "is worried that [the offender] will return" or "is receiving medical or psychological treatment" have not been considered inducements because they are not threats or promises and they are factual statements.

- ▸ **Possible future conduct** Telling an offender that his or her pattern of crimes may progress to more serious offences has been considered acceptable. Statements such as "If you don't stop this, you might kill someone some day" have been ruled to not be inducements because they are not threats or promises.
- ▸ **Opinion about mental health** Stating an opinion to an offender that committing a break and enter, robbery, or sexual assault is "not normal" and shows that the offender may need psychological help has not been an inducement. They are not threats or promises. Telling an offender that he may need professional treatment or assistance to correct a harmful behaviour is a strong solution to the problem and may be crucial to prevent future crimes and protect the public.

HELP FOR THE ACCUSED

A popular type of comment made by officers during interrogations is a suggestion that the accused seek help for his or her behaviour. This topic is effective and relevant; however, the manner in which this suggestion is made is significant regarding whether it will constitute an inducement.

A valuable example and analysis was made by the Alberta Court of Appeal in *R. v. S. (S.L.)* (1999).[50] The circumstances of the case follow.

The accused was charged with sexually assaulting a seven-year-old child. During an interrogation, a police officer told the accused, "The only way you can get help is if you can admit to what you've done and you're not (admitting it)." The accused later confessed. The trial judge ruled that no inducements were made and that the confession was voluntary. The Alberta Court of Appeal allowed the accused's appeal and entered an acquittal. The following analysis and reasons were given:

- ▸ The Supreme Court of Canada stated that "voluntariness is determined by a careful investigation of the circumstances surrounding the statement of the accused, and involves a consideration of both objective and subjective factors."
- ▸ In *R. v. Bellieau* (1985),[51] the Alberta Court of Appeal ruled that the following comment was not an inducement: "One of the best ways to deal with these situations is to talk about it to share your feelings with someone." The reason that this was not an inducement was that it was not an offer of help contingent upon a confession.
- ▸ In *R. v. Bird* (1989),[52] the Manitoba Court of Appeal created a specific rule: "the suggestion that an accused should make a statement in order that the police officer might help the accused with a perceived problem is an inducement which negates the voluntary nature of the statement."
- ▸ An invitation to tell the truth is not an inducement.
- ▸ A suggestion that the accused seek help for aberrant behaviour is not an inducement. However, in this case, the officer went further. The officer made it clear that the "only way" he could get better was to tell the truth. The officer planted in the accused's mind the notion that the path to rehabilitation (getting better) had to begin with a confession. The offer of help was contingent upon a confession. The officer's comment was ruled to be an inducement. The confession was not voluntary and was excluded.

In summary, suggesting that an accused seek help for his or her behaviour is not an inducement. Suggesting or offering help contingent upon confessing is an inducement.

MENTAL CAPACITY

Although not explicitly stated in the Ibrahim Rule, the Crown not only has the onus to prove that the confession was voluntarily made by an accused to a person in authority, the Crown must also prove that the accused had sufficient mental capacity when the statement was made, meaning that the accused had an operating mind at the time he or she confessed.[53] **Sufficient mental capacity** refers to the cognitive ability to voluntarily confess. It includes several factors, such as shock, intoxication, and mental disorders, which may affect the voluntariness of a confession.

Operating Mind

Operating mind is a case law term that refers to a mental capacity that permits a person to voluntarily confess and that is free from conditions that may cause an involuntary statement. Shock is one condition that may cause an involuntary statement despite the absence of inducements.

In *R. v. Ward* (1979),[54] the accused was arrested for criminal negligence resulting from a motor vehicle collision. The accused was questioned shortly after regaining consciousness, while still in shock. Despite the absence of inducements, the accused's statements were excluded because a reasonable doubt existed of whether the statement originated from an "operating mind."[55]

In cases where the suspect has been involved in an event where a physical impact or trauma occurred, precise notes must be recorded to describe the suspect's condition and verbatim conversation preceding the actual inculpatory statement. The suspect's behaviour and responses to unrelated questions (e.g., name, address, place of employment) are crucial evidence that a judge will consider to determine whether shock existed.

INTOXICATION

Offenders are commonly intoxicated at the time of arrest. There are different degrees of intoxication that affect the mental capacity of a suspect. A confession from an intoxicated person is not automatically inadmissible. The issue is whether the confession was voluntarily made and whether the accused had an operating mind despite the intoxication.

In *McKenna v. The Queen* (1961),[56] the statement of an intoxicated person was ruled admissible because the degree of intoxication did not negate an "operating mind."[57] The court in *R. v. Yensen* (1961)[58] clearly stated that liquor consumption does not always prevent voluntariness and added, "Many men make very compelling speeches, both privately and publicly, when they are under the influence of liquor."[59] This statement is profound because it simply explains a commonsense principle that some intoxicated people are capable of having coherent conversation. **Coherency** is the key factor when determining whether intoxication interferes with an operating mind. The above case law rulings show that confessions made from coherent intoxicated persons will pass the operating-mind test. Again, precise notes are needed to describe the suspect's condition and responses to unrelated questions.

It is important to remember that intoxication is a temporary condition. The suspect should be re-interviewed when sober.

An **incoherent** intoxicated person refers to one who is incapable of maintaining a meaningful conversation. No special skill is needed to identify this condition. A statement from this type of offender may likely be excluded because of the absence of an operating mind. Interrogation should be conducted again when the suspect is sober.

In summary, officers should question all intoxicated persons at the time of arrest because there are no specific laws that define a degree of intoxication that will always cause a confession to be excluded.

MENTAL DISORDERS

In some cases, suspects display behaviour that causes suspicion of a mental disorder. One in particular, **schizophrenia**, is associated with symptoms of auditory hallucination that may cause an inner compulsion to confess. The issue of whether an offender who suffers from a mental disorder has an operating mind was decided by the S.C.C. in *R. v. Whittle* (1994).[60] The court ruled that *a confession originating from an inner compulsion caused solely by a mental disorder is not inadmissible unless it is combined with improper police conduct.* Compulsion to confess motivated by inner voices does not constitute involuntariness.

The accused does not have to possess analytical ability to prove an operating mind. If the accused does not have this ability, the confession will be considered voluntary despite evidence of a mental disorder. The operating-mind test requires that the accused possess a limited degree of cognitive ability to understand what he or she is saying and to comprehend that the evidence may be used in proceedings against the accused. It also refers to the capability of making an active choice, meaning a good or wise choice or one that is in the accused's interests.

SECTION 24(2) CHARTER

The Confession Rule is only one of two rules of evidence that determine the admissibility of a confession. The second rule of evidence is s. 24(2) Charter. It is the most prominent exclusionary rule and applies to all types of evidence including confessions.

Section 24(2) Charter is a general rule that lacks specific guidelines; they were created by the Supreme Court of Canada in two case law decisions: (a) *R. v. Collins* (1987) and (b) *R. v. Stillman* (1997).

A complete interpretation of s. 24(2) Charter, *R. v. Collins* and *R. v. Stillman*, is provided on the website **www.emp.ca./arcaro/crimInvestigation5E**. The following is a summary of the relevant principles.

General Rule

Evidence, including confessions obtained in a manner that violates a Charter right, are excluded if the admission of the evidence would bring the administration of justice into disrepute. At a trial, proof must first exist that a Charter violation actually occurred. Common Charter violations include

- ▸ s. 8 Charter (unreasonable search and seizure),
- ▸ s. 9 Charter (arbitrary detention or arrest),

- ▶ s. 10(a) Charter (reason for arrest not disclosed),
- ▶ s. 10(b) Charter (right to counsel not given), and
- ▶ s. 7 Charter (principles of fundamental justice).

If no Charter violation occurred, s. 24(2) Charter does not apply. The onus is on the accused to prove that a Charter violation occurred.[61] The Charter violation must be proven to have occurred before the confession was obtained or during the course of obtaining it.[62] If the Charter violation occurred after the confession was obtained, s. 24(2) Charter does not apply.

The trial judge has discretion to admit or exclude a confession obtained after the commission of a Charter violation. The determining factor is whether the admission of the confession at the trial would bring the administration of justice into disrepute.

Procedural Rules

Section 24(2) Charter is applied by the trial judge during the trial, not before it. In other words, the admissibility of a confession is determined by a judge during the trial. It cannot be determined before the trial. A confession obtained after the commission of a Charter violation is not automatically inadmissible. A confession obtained after a Charter violation may be admissible if its admission does not adversely affect the reputation of the administration of justice.

R. v. COLLINS (1987)

Three groups of factors affecting the reputation of the administration of justice are:

1. trial fairness,
2. severity of the Charter violation, and
3. the possibility that exclusion of the confession would bring it into disrepute.

Specific factors affecting the reputation of the administration of justice are:

- ▶ the type of evidence obtained,
- ▶ what specific Charter right was violated,
- ▶ the severity of the Charter violation,
- ▶ whether the Charter violation was deliberate or inadvertent or committed in good faith,
- ▶ whether the violation occurred because of urgency or necessity,
- ▶ whether other investigative methods were available,
- ▶ whether the evidence would have been obtained without the violation,
- ▶ the severity of the offence, and
- ▶ whether the evidence was essential to prove the charge.

General Procedural Rules

If trial fairness is in some way adversely affected by the admission of evidence obtained after a Charter violation, the evidence should be excluded. The admission of physical evidence rarely creates an unfair trial. Physical evidence is usually admissible despite the commission of a Charter violation.

The admission of self-incriminating evidence that originates or emerges from the accused person (e.g., a confession) after a Charter violation tends to create an unfair trial. Confessions obtained after a Charter violation are usually inadmissible, but not automatically excluded.

R. v. STILLMAN (1997)

This case adds guidelines relating to trial fairness, which is Group 1 of the *Collins* case. It does not determine Groups 2 and 3 of the *Collins* case and does not replace the *Collins* decision.

The primary objective of trial fairness in this case is to prevent an accused person from being compelled, forced, or conscripted to provide evidence in the form of statements or bodily samples.

If an accused is compelled as the result of a Charter violation to participate in the creation or discovery of self-incriminating evidence, such as a confession or giving bodily samples, the admission of this type of evidence would generally tend to render a trial unfair.

Three-Step Procedure

1. Classify the evidence as conscriptive or non-conscriptive. Conscriptive evidence is defined as evidence with which an accused is compelled to incriminate himself or herself. A confession is conscriptive evidence.
2. If the evidence is classified as conscriptive evidence, the Crown has the onus to prove on a balance of probabilities that the evidence would have been discovered by alternative non-conscriptive means. If the Crown fails to prove this, the judge will generally exclude the conscriptive evidence at this stage. Confessions are often excluded at this stage.
3. If the Crown successfully proves Step 2, then the trial judge considers Group 2 and Group 3 factors from the Collins case.

Derivative Evidence

Derivative evidence is defined as a physical item that is discovered as a result of conscriptive evidence after a Charter violation has occurred. Derivative evidence is considered to be conscriptive or self-incriminating. The admission of derivative evidence generally renders a trial unfair. Derivative evidence is usually excluded.

The commission of a Charter violation before a confession is obtained will usually result in exclusion of the confession under s. 24(2) Charter. Consequently, the prevention of Charter violations is vital to ensure the admissibility of a voluntary confession.[63]

THE CONTEMPORARY CONFESSION RULE: A REVIEW BY THE S.C.C.

The Confession (Ibrahim) Rule has evolved for almost a century and remains the cornerstone of the rules of evidence governing the admissibility of confession. Since its inception, however, the social world, technology, and the justice system have changed to some extent.

Similarly, the Confession Rule has transformed. Myriad case law decisions represent an ongoing dialogue that continuously shapes and moulds the Confession Rule. Although its fundamental premise remains the same, the Confession Rule has been redefined and modified through case law interpretation. The expanded version has been called the **Contemporary Confession Rule.**

The Supreme Court of Canada, in *R. v. Oickle* (2000),[64] wrote a lengthy judgment that discussed the Contemporary Confession Rule and summarized the evolution of the traditional Confession Rule with a unique perspective that provides valuable insights for students to comprehend the importance of the contemporary rule.

This section explains the S.C.C. interpretation and perspectives in two parts. The first part reviews the development of the traditional Confession Rule. The second part explains the elements and features of the contemporary version.

The Traditional Confession Rule: An S.C.C. Review

The following is a summary of the Confession Rule's development as explained by the S.C.C. in *R. v. Oickle* (2000):

- There are two approaches to the application of the Confession Rule: (a) narrow approach, and (b) broader approach.
- The Confession Rule, or Ibrahim Rule as it was initially called, emerged from English criminal law. The Confession Rule was defined in *Ibrahim v. The King* (1914)[65] as follows:

    No statement by an accused is admissible in evidence against him unless it is shown by the prosecution to have been a voluntary statement, in the sense that it has not been obtained from him either by fear or prejudice or hope of advantage exercised or held out by a person in authority.

This rule created the "narrow approach," meaning that confessions were excluded only "where the police held out explicit threats or promises to the accused."

- The S.C.C. adopted the Ibrahim Rule in *Prosko v. The King* (1922), and applied the narrow approach in landmark cases including *Boudreau v. The King* (1949), *R. v. Wray* (1971), and *Rothman v. The Queen* (1981).
- The Ibrahim Rule gives an accused only a "negative right," that being "the right *not* to be tortured or coerced into making a statement by threats or promises held out by a person who is and whom he subjectively believes to be a person in authority." In other words, the narrow approach said that if the police committed no inducements, the confession was voluntary and, therefore, admissible.
- The S.C.C. in *R. v. Hebert* (1990) recognized a "broader approach" to the Ibrahim Rule. This approach modified and expanded the Ibrahim Rule, stating the following:

    The absence of violence, threats, and promises by the authorities does not necessarily mean that the resulting statement is voluntary, if the necessary mental element of deciding between alternatives is absent.[66]

This "broader approach" emerged from the "operating mind" doctrine developed by the S.C.C. in cases such as *Ward* (1979), *Horvath* (1979), and *Whittle* (1994). These cases focused on "voluntariness conceived more broadly." Inducements were not the issue in these cases. Instead, other factors that affect voluntariness were explored, including:

- shock,
- hypnosis,
- "complete emotional disintegration," and
- "atmosphere of oppression."

Although these four elements have nothing to do with violence, threats, or promises, they affect an accused's "operating" mind, which in turn influences voluntariness.

- The Charter constitutionalized a new set of protections for accused persons in ss. 7 to 14, creating a second exclusionary method independent of the Ibrahim Rule. This meant that even if a confession were voluntary, it could be excluded if a Charter violation occurred.[67]
- The Ibrahim Rule has a wider scope than the Charter. For example:
    1. **The s. 10(b) Charter right to counsel applies only "upon arrest or detention."** Not all interrogations occur after an arrest; they often are conducted when a person is merely suspected and has not been arrested. The Ibrahim Rule, by contrast, applies to any questioning by the police both before and after an arrest.
    2. **They have different standards of proof.** Regarding the Charter, *the accused has the onus to prove* that a Charter violation occurred; the standard of proof is a "balance of probabilities," which is a lower standard than "beyond a reasonable doubt." Regarding the Ibrahim Rule, *the Crown has the onus to prove* that the confession was voluntary; however, the Crown has a higher standard of proof by being required to prove voluntary "beyond a reasonable doubt."
    3. **The remedies are different.** A Charter violation *may* exclude a confession; however, an Ibrahim Rule violation *will always* exclude a confession.

The S.C.C. acknowledged that although it has *not* recently addressed the *precise* scope of the Ibrahim Rule, it has refined several elements of the rule, without ever integrating them into a coherent whole. Consequently, the S.C.C. deemed it important to restate the rule, for two reasons. First is the "continuing diversity of approaches as evidenced by the courts below in this appeal." This statement acknowledges that a wide range of interpretations and rulings have been made by lower courts. An inference can be made, then, that inconsistencies have been recognized throughout various levels of court.

The second reason is the "growing understanding of the problem of *false confessions*." The concern about false confessions is consistent with the justice system's primary objective of preventing wrongful conviction of the innocent. Consequently, to review and define the Confession Rule (Ibrahim), the S.C.C. emphasized two items for consideration: first, it is imperative to recognize which interrogative techniques commonly produce false confessions. Second, they stressed the importance of keeping in mind the "twin goals"[68] of the Confession Rule:

1. protecting the rights of the accused
2. without unduly limiting society's need to investigate and solve crimes.

Maintaining a healthy balance between these two goals is the very essence of the Confession Rule. The S.C.C. clearly does not favour the accused over the investigative process, or vice-versa. The S.C.C. recognizes that "the police are unable to investigate crime without putting questions to persons, whether or not such persons are suspected of having committed the crime being investigated." They acknowledge that "Properly conducted police questioning is a legitimate and effective aid to criminal investigation," but warn us of the risks of improper questioning. The S.C.C. issued a caveat to all members of the justice system to "never lose sight of either of these two objectives."

FALSE CONFESSIONS

Research conducted with mock juries indicates that people find it difficult to believe that someone would falsely confess to a crime. Most people believe that it is counterintuitive that an innocent person would confess to a crime he did not commit. Yet, a large body of literature documents hundreds of cases where confessions have proven false (refer to *R. v. Oickle* (2000) for a reference list of relevant literature).

The literature theorizes that there are five basic kinds of false confessions that help us understand why they occur. The S.C.C. cautions that any of these five elements will *not* automatically exclude a confession; instead, they provide only a useful taxonomy of false confessions. The five types are:

1. **Voluntary** These are *not* the product of police interrogation. They are choices made by the person to falsely confess. The S.C.C. is concerned with the other four types.
2. **Stress-compliant** These occur "when the aversive interpersonal pressures of interrogation become so intolerable that suspects comply in order to terminate questioning." They are elicited by "exceptionally strong use of aversive stressors typically present in interrogation and are given knowingly in order to escape the punishing experience of interrogation." Another feature of this type is confronting the suspect with fabricated evidence to convince the suspect that his claims of innocence are futile.
3. **Coerced-compliant** These are the product of coercive influence techniques (i.e., threat and promises). The majority of false confessions are of this type.
4. **Non-coerced-persuaded** These are produced by tactics that cause an innocent person to become "confused, doubt his memory, be temporarily persuaded of his guilt and confess to a crime he did not commit." Again, the use of fabricated evidence can convince an innocent person of false guilt.
5. **Coerced-persuaded** This type combines the features of the above two types.[69]

The S.C.C. concluded that:

1. Compliant personalities combined with personal histories and special characteristics or situations can trigger false confessions when persuaded by interrogative suggestions.
2. "The strength of mind and will of the accused, the influence of custody or its surroundings, [and] the effects of questions or of conversations" are all factors that must be considered when a court endeavours to determine voluntariness of a confession.
3. Non-existent evidence poses risks. Presenting fabricated evidence to a suspect is dangerous; it has the *potential* either to persuade a susceptible person or convince him that his claims of innocence are wrong.
4. False confessions are rarely the product of *proper* interrogations. Instead, they "almost always involve shoddy police practice and/or police criminality."
5. Eliciting a false confession requires "strong incentive, intense pressure, and prolonged questioning." The S.C.C. then made an important acknowledgment that favours the investigative process: "Only under the *rarest* of circumstances do an interrogator's ploys persuade an innocent suspect that he is in fact guilty." This proclamation gives the prosecution an advantage. It clearly reminds all courts that false confessions are uncommon and extraordinary circumstances have to be proved to convince a reasonable person that an innocent person falsely confessed to a crime.

Videotape

Since the Crown has the onus to prove voluntariness, how an interrogation is reconstructed during a trial determines admissibility of a confession. Traditionally, prior to technological advances, officers' notes read during testimony represented the sole source of evidence. Officers' notes were usually written after questioning concluded; memory, then, became a prominent issue regarding credibility. Trying to remember a conversation of modest duration can be a daunting task. The S.C.C. identified two other problems. Even if the content were accurate, notes do not reflect the tone of the conversation and the body language used. Both are essential elements for a court to determine voluntariness.

The S.C.C. favours videotaped interrogations because videotaping permits informed judgments and deters improper police techniques. However, the S.C.C. has not made videotaping a mandatory requirement to prove voluntariness. The court emphasized that notes alone, without video recording, are *not inherently suspect*. The current position of the S.C.C. is that videotape "greatly assists" a trial judge in assessing a confession.

These issues led to a redefining and modification of the traditional Confession Rule. What has emerged is a new concept called the Contemporary Confession Rule.[70]

THE CONTEMPORARY CONFESSION RULE

The contemporary version of the Confession Rule essentially adds "reliability" of a confession to "voluntariness." Reliability and voluntariness are two separate concepts.

Voluntariness refers to *how* a confession was elicited. It asks the question, "Did the suspect freely say it?" **Reliability** refers to the credibility of the final product. It asks the question, "Is this confession the truth? Can it be believed, or is it a false confession?"

Although the primary issue is voluntariness, the S.C.C. stated that it "overlaps with reliability." A confession that is not voluntary will often be unreliable, but not always.

The contemporary rule will still be applied "contextually," meaning on a case-by-case basis within the context of the specific circumstances of each case. The S.C.C. recognized that "hard and fast rules" cannot be rigidly set because they would not be able to account for the wide range of circumstances associated with each confession.

The traditional rule narrowly considered voluntariness exclusively. The contemporary rule now includes four *general* factors that trial judges must consider when determining admissibility of a confession.

1. Threats or Promises

This remains the core of the rule. Obvious violence or threats will exclude confessions but, as the S.C.C. noted, the majority of cases will *not* be so clear.

Offering leniency from the courts in exchange for a confession is "clearly a very strong inducement and will warrant exclusion in all but exceptional cases." Examples include suggesting that a reduced charge or sentence will be given if the suspect confesses. The offer by the police has to be "explicit" for the inducement to occur. The court left a window open for admission of an induced confession but did not define the "exceptional circumstances" that allow it.

Another type of inducement is an offer by police to ensure psychiatric assistance or other counselling for the suspect in exchange for a confession. The court stated that while this is clearly an inducement, it is *not as strong* as an offer for leniency; this type of inducement has to be factored with the entirety of the circumstances. This rule has two significant elements:

- An offer to give psychiatric assistance in exchange for a confession will *not* always exclude a confession. An example is found in *R. v. Ewert* (1991), where the police made a "bold offer" to help the accused receive psychiatric help *if* the accused confessed.[71] Although the bold offer was an inducement, it was *not* a factor in the suspect's decision to confess and the confession was admitted. This example illustrates the *contextual* application of the rule.
- Offering psychiatric assistance but *not* in exchange for a confession apparently is not an inducement. The psychiatric assistance has to be reliant on the confession for an inducement to occur.

Threats or promises do not have to be aimed directly at the suspect for an inducement to occur; this includes promising leniency to another person if the suspect confesses. The following rule applies that determines whether an inducement was committed: For a promised benefit to a person other than the accused to exclude a confession, the "benefit must be of such a nature that when considered in light of the relationship between the person and the accused" it would motivate the accused to make an untrue confession. In other words, the strength of the relationship has to be confined with the extent of the benefit. An example of an improper inducement is telling a mother that her daughter would not be charged with shoplifting if the mother confessed to the offence she was being questioned for. By contrast, a one-year relationship that occurred in prison was insufficient to exclude a confession.

According to the S.C.C., "Threats come in all shapes and sizes." The most common phrase that suggests a threat is "it would be better" to confess, thereby implying that dire consequences may emerge from a refusal to talk. Myriad confessions have been excluded in documented cases.

Conversely, phrases such as "it would be better if you *told the truth*" will not automatically exclude a confession. As stated previously, these types of phrases have to be considered within the context of the circumstances and the entire conversation. The governing rule, then, is this: "it would be better" comments exclude confessions only where the circumstances reveal an "implicit threat or promise."

The final type of threat or promise relevant to *R. v. Oickle* was the use of *moral or spiritual inducements*. The rule created by the S.C.C. is that although these are inducements they will "generally not produce an involuntary confession, for the very simple reason that the inducement offered is not in the control of the police officers."[72]

Additionally, the S.C.C. ruled that:

> Confessions which result from spiritual exhortations or appeals to conscience and morality, are *admissible* in evidence, whether urged by a person in authority or by someone else.

The Court summarized several salient rules that directly influence investigative procedures:

- "Courts must remember that the police may often offer some kind of inducement to the suspect to obtain a confession." Few suspects spontaneously confess. In the vast majority of cases, the police must convince the suspect that it is in his best interests to confess. This becomes improper only when the inducement, either alone or combined with other factors, is *strong* enough to raise reasonable doubt about voluntariness.
- "Very few confessions are inspired solely by remorse." The accused's motives for confessing are "mixed" and include *his hope of leniency*. A self-generated hope by the accused is not an inducement, even if it is the accused's dominant motive for confessing.

However, in most cases this type of hope for leniency "will, in part, at least, owe its origins to something said or done" by a person in authority. It would be rare for a suspect who is being "firmly but fairly questioned" to reduce their detection time by confessing. The court's rule, then, is as follows:

> The most important consideration for trial judges in all cases is to determine whether an explicit offer was made by the police, regardless of whether the offer resembles a threat or a promise.

2. Oppression

After considerable debate among lower courts about whether oppression is part of the Confession Rule, the S.C.C. found that it "clearly has the potential to produce false confessions," thereby ending the debate. Oppression is part of the Confession Rule and is a relevant consideration when determining voluntariness of confession. Oppression is described as "inhumane conditions" that would motivate a person to falsely confess "purely out of desire to *escape those conditions*."

The S.C.C. pointed to an Ontario Court of Appeal decision in *R. v. Hoillet* (1999)[73] as one of the best examples of oppression. The accused was arrested and charged with sexual assault. He was under the influence of crack cocaine and alcohol at the time of his arrest. After two hours in a cell, his clothes were seized for forensic testing and he was left naked for one-and-a-half hours. He was given some light clothes, no underwear, and poor-fitting shoes. Questioning started shortly after. He fell asleep five times during the interrogation. He was denied requests for warmer clothes and tissue to wipe his nose. Despite admitting that he clearly understood his right to remain silent and the fact that the police made *no* explicit threats or promises, the Court accepted the accused's testimony that he confessed with the hope of getting warm clothes and ending the interrogation. The Ontario Court of Appeal concluded that the statement was involuntary.

The S.C.C. listed some factors, but not all, that *may* create an atmosphere of oppression:

- deprivation of food, clothing, water, sleep, or medical attention,
- excessively aggressive, intimidating questioning for a prolonged period of time,
- denying access to counsel, and
- use of non-existent evidence.

The S.C.C. stated the following rules relating to the use of fabricated evidence:

- It is a "dangerous" practice.
- The use of fabricated evidence by itself is not automatic grounds for exclusion; it is a relevant factor when combined with other circumstances.

3. Operating Mind

The S.C.C. considers this doctrine to be a part of the Confession Rule process but it should be considered to be a separate entity that requires a distinct hearing. The operating mind doctrine refers to circumstances other than threats, promises, and oppression that induce a confession including a *mental capacity that permits a person to decide freely whether to confess voluntarily or not.* The S.C.C. states that this doctrine "does *not* imply a higher degree of awareness than *knowledge of what the accused is saying and that he is saying it to police officers.*"[74] In other words, the accused suffered from no condition that compelled him to confess or to fail to recognize or understand that the police were his interrogators.

4. Other Police Trickery

Unlike the first elements, this doctrine is a "distinct inquiry." Although it is still relevant to voluntariness, its specific objective is to maintain the integrity of the criminal justice system.[75] The procedure for the inquiry was established by the S.C.C. in *Rothman v. The Queen* (1981). A voir dire is conducted to determine whether the police said or did anything that could have induced a false confession. The issue at the voir dire is the *police conduct* as it relates to the confession's reliability, but not the reliability itself.

Yet, the S.C.C. emphasized that the courts should be wary not to unduly limit police discretion. This led to a poignant quote made by the S.C.C. that established a general rule:

> The investigation of crime and the detection of criminals is not a game to be governed by the Marquess of Queensbury Rules. The authorities, in dealing with shrewd and often sophisticated criminals, must sometimes of necessity resort to tricks or other forms of deceit and should not through the rule be hampered in their work. *What should be repressed vigorously is conduct on their part that shocks the community.*[76]

Consequently, deceptive practices are not totally prohibited; only those that "shock the community" are totally prohibited. Examples of what might shock the community include:

- a police officer posing as a lawyer or clergy member, or
- injecting truth serum into a diabetic under the pretense that it was insulin.

Summary

The S.C.C. provided a commonsense summary of general guidelines. In the past, courts have been drastically inconsistent by excluding a confession because of relatively minor inducements while in other cases ignoring "intolerable" police conduct and admitting confessions. The S.C.C. directed lower courts to end these inconsistencies and provided the following guidelines:

- A relatively minor inducement, such as tissue to wipe a nose and warmer clothes, *may* become an "impermissible inducement" serious enough to exclude a confession *if it is combined with other acts such as deprivation of sleep, heat, and clothes for several hours in the middle of the night.*
- Conversely, when proper treatment is given, "*it will take a* stronger *inducement to render the confession involuntary.*"

CASE LAW

R. v. Oickle (2000)

Specific circumstances and factors were evaluated by the S.C.C. in *R. v. Oickle* (2000)[77] to determine whether they constituted inducements and how they affected voluntariness.

Offence Seven counts of arson

Facts The police investigated a series of eight fires during a 14-month period. Four buildings were situated in close proximity to the accused's home. One vehicle was owned by the accused's fiancée and one by his father. All fires occurred between 1:00 and 4:00 a.m. Each fire was deliberately set.

The accused was a volunteer firefighter and responded to each fire.

A list of eight suspects was compiled. Each was asked to submit to a polygraph test. The first six passed, narrowing the list. The accused had initial doubts about the test but eventually consented.

The accused's test was conducted by police at 3 p.m. in a motel room. The accused, although he was not under arrest, was informed of:

1. his right to silence,

2. his right to counsel,

3. his right to leave at any time, and

4. the fact that the polygraph officer's interpretation of the polygraph results was not admissible but anything said by the accused would be admissible.

A pamphlet explaining the polygraph procedure was given to the accused and he signed a consent form. The polygraph officer conducted a lengthy pre-test interview before conducting the test itself. It consisted of wide-ranging questions, including personal ones. The pre-test interview was designed to build trust and to compose control questions. At the conclusion, an exculpatory statement was taken, forming the basis of the polygraph test.

The actual polygraph test followed, lasting only a matter of minutes. The officer did not ask about any specific fire; instead, he asked only if the previous exculpatory statement was true. At the conclusion of the test and analysis, the officer informed the accused that he had failed the test, reminded him of his rights (although he wasn't under arrest), and questioned him for one hour. During this time, the accused asked, "What if I admit to the car? Then I can walk out of here and it's over?" The officer responded "You can walk out at any time," but the accused remained.

Another officer relieved the polygraph examiner. After 30 to 40 minutes, the accused confessed to setting fire to his fiancée's car. He was emotionally distraught, acknowledged his rights again, and gave a written confession to that incident but denied the rest.

The accused was transported to the police station, three hours and 15 minutes after the test concluded. En route, he was still upset and crying. He was taken to an interview room with videotaping equipment that recorded the subsequent interrogation about the other fires. Twice he asked to go home to bed because he was tired. He was denied this request because he was under arrest; questioning continued.

Another officer took over and questioned the accused for more than an hour. At 11:00 p.m., six hours after the polygraph test ended, the accused confessed to seven of the eight fires, denying he set fire to his father's van. The accused gave a written confession.

At 6:00 a.m., the accused consented to a re-enactment. The police drove him to each crime scene, where he described how he had set each fire.

At the trial, a voir dire was conducted regarding the confessions and the re-enactment. The trial judge ruled that they all were voluntary and admissible, resulting in convictions on all counts.

The accused appealed to the Nova Scotia Court of Appeal. That court ruled that all statements were involuntary and were excluded, resulting in acquittals.

The Crown appealed to the S.C.C. This court found all statements to be voluntary and admissible, thus restoring the convictions.

Nine specific issues, *each concerning common interrogation practices*, were raised regarding the voluntariness of the confessions. The S.C.C. ruled that each circumstance was *not* an inducement. The following is a review of all nine circumstances and the ruling that showed how the Contemporary Confession Rule was applied. Each represents a valuable study about interrogations and their relevant rules of evidence:

1. **Minimizing the severity of the crime** As will be explained in subsequent chapters, minimizing the severity of the crime is an effective interrogation technique. The issue in this case was a common statement made by police during interrogations: "there is little difference between being convicted of one fire compared to 10." In cases of multiple offences, officers use their experience in court and state their opinion that the actual number of convictions is irrelevant to sentencing. As was the case in this interrogation, the police consider the multiple offences to be a "one package type of thing."

    Additionally, the officers in this case said the accused was not really a criminal and that the police did not want to treat him as one; this also is a common approach that actually displays civility.

    The S.C.C. ruled that these were not inducements. Although the police did minimize the *moral significance* of the crimes, there was never any suggestion by the police that a confession would minimize the *legal consequences* of the crimes.

    The Court stated the following rule that guides these particular techniques:

    > Minimizing the moral significance of an offence is a common and usually unobjectionable feature of police interrogation. The real concern is whether the police suggested that a confession will result in the *legal consequences being minimal*.

2. **Offers of psychiatric help** The police used a common phrase during this interrogation: "I think you need help. Maybe you need professional help." However, at no time did they suggest that this help would be received only in exchange for a confession. There is a distinction between explaining the potential benefits of receiving help and making offers of help that are conditional on a confession. The first one is proper; the second is not.

3. **"It would be better. . ."** This particular interrogation included several such comments, including the suggestion that a confession would:

    ▷ make him feel better,

    ▷ generate respect from his fiancée and members of the community, and

    ▷ better address his apparent pyromania.

However, none of these included an *implied* threat or promise. Instead, they were "moral inducements." The general rule that emerged was that:

▷ Suggesting possible benefits of a confession is acceptable if no insinuation exists of an implied threat or promise.

▷ These amount to "moral inducements" that lack the element of implied threat or promise. Moral inducements do not exclude confessions.

4. **Alleged threats against the accused's fiancée** The police told the accused that if he confessed, it would be unnecessary to the investigation to subject his fiancée to extensive interrogation. The court noted that their relationship had the required strength—it was strong enough to induce a false confession

if she were in fact threatened. However, *no threat* was made toward her. Thus, the two elements of third-party inducement were not fulfilled. The court created the following rules:

▷ If the police had offered to drop pending charges against the fiancée or if they had threatened to charge her, the accused's confession would have been involuntary because of the inducements that would have existed.

▷ Merely promising *not to polygraph* the fiancée in exchange for the confession was *not* a strong enough inducement to raise reasonable doubt about voluntariness.

▷ The confession occurred two hours after the police made these remarks. The timing shows *no connection* between the police inducement and the confession.

5. **Abuse of trust** Building trust, as will be discussed in subsequent chapters, is essential to elicit confessions. The police gained trust in a reassuring manner. The S.C.C. found no act by the police that abused the trust and that was intentionally built. The Court made a bold statement about this issue:

Excluding a confession because the police caused the accused to trust them would send a *"perverse message"* that they should engage only in "adversarial, aggressive questioning to ensure they never gain the suspect's trust."

6. **Atmosphere of oppression** Quite simply, the S.C.C. ruled that the police never deprived the accused of food, water, or sleep. No evidence was fabricated. Although the re-enactment was done when the accused had had little sleep, he was already awake and was clearly told that he could stop at any time. The court found "at best mild inducements" that did not create an oppressive environment.

7. **Informing the suspect of the uses to which the polygraph test can be put** The issue in this case was the failure to inform the accused clearly that the polygraph test was inadmissible in court to show whether the accused was lying or telling the truth. The S.C.C. ruled that this failure is insufficient to exclude a confession. The general rule created was:

Failure to inform a suspect about the inadmissibility of a polygraph test *will not automatically produce an involuntary confession*. By itself, this circumstance will not exclude a confession. Instead, the "most it can do is be a factor in the overall voluntariness analysis."

8. **Exaggerating the polygraph's validity** The police repeatedly told the accused that the polygraph was an "infallible determiner of the truth." The S.C.C. agreed that these are exaggerated claims, considering the existing literature that shows that they are "far from infallible." The court referred to a Quebec Court of Appeal decision in *R. v. Amyot* (1990), which concluded that the representation of the polygraph as infallible renders a confession inadmissible. The S.C.C. found that this case was different. In the *Amyot* case, the confession followed the polygraph test results "almost immediately." In this case, the accused was "not overwhelmed" by the polygraph results.[78]

The issue is whether the polygraph test creates an oppressive atmosphere. Various lower courts have taken varied approaches to determine this. The prominent factor seemingly is whether the test causes *"emotional disintegration."* In this case the accused cried, but this did not constitute emotional disintegration. As a rule, the S.C.C. stated the following:

▷ The mere fact that a suspect cries upon confessing is *not* evidence of "complete emotional disintegration."

▷ "*Tears are to be expected* when someone finally divulges they committed a crime—particularly when the suspect is generally a law-abiding and upstanding citizen."

▷ "Simply confronting the suspect with adverse evidence, like a polygraph test, is *not* grounds for exclusion."

▷ Police exaggeration of the reliability or importance of any evidence does not, by itself, render a confession involuntary. "Eyewitness accounts are by no means infallible." The S.C.C. has previously ruled admissible a confession made after the police told a suspect they did not believe his denials because several eyewitnesses reported that they saw him commit the offence.

9. **Misleading the accused regarding the duration of the interview** The issues here were misleading the accused about the expected duration of the polygraph test and the length of interrogation that follows a failed test. Additionally, the Criminal Lawyers' Association argued that the police should clearly separate post-test interrogation from the test itself instead of conducting immediate intense questioning. The S.C.C. rejected these arguments, ruling that none of these circumstances render a confession involuntary.

Conclusion The importance of this case cannot be overstated. Had the S.C.C. not reversed the Nova Scotia Court of Appeal rulings, the essence of police interrogation would have been dramatically altered. Immeasurable limitations would have been imposed on the investigative process.

The S.C.C. validated and confirmed nine common interrogation practices. That, by itself, represents valuable investigation benefits and advantages.

Students should view this case as a landmark decision and an excellent example of how the criminal justice system operates and how case law decisions emerge. Excellent police work was recognized by the trial judge and the S.C.C. However, the frightening aspect is that the court of appeal of a province tore apart investigative excellence. Fortunately, the S.C.C. noted the errors in the appeal court decision and restored the trial judge's decisions.

In conclusion, the police now have clear guidelines concerning common interrogative practices that have been proven to succeed.

Case Study 16.1 Conclusion

The Interrogation

Police Officer 1: "We want to talk to you about a break-in we know you've done. You know where [city] is, don't you?"

John: "Yeah."

Police Officer 1: "You know where Dave _____ lives? You've heard of him?"

John: (pause) "Yeah. I think he works for the paper."

Police Officer 1: "You broke into the house when they were arranging their kid's funeral. You walked into his bedroom and stole his camera equipment."

John: (No response.)

Police Officer 1: "Dave wants the camera equipment back. It means a lot to him. It was his son's pride and joy. Under the circumstances, we think he should get it back. We intend to get it back, because you know where it is and you could tell us."

John: (No response—eyes turned red and glassy.) "I didn't know about that till I read it in the paper. I want you to know that house was picked at random."

Police Officer 1: "You're going to be charged with this break and enter and we're going to take a statement, if you want. You still have the same right as before about calling a lawyer."

John: "No. I don't need one."

John gave a written confession and implicated Ben, the informant who had implicated John, as an accomplice. He also provided information about the purchaser of the stolen camera equipment.

On November 27, Ben was arrested for the same break and enter. He was cautioned and informed of his right to counsel. The interrogation was conducted by the same investigators in the same office. The questioning was as follows:

Ben: "Come on, [officer's given name]. Can't we make a deal here? Can't we work something out?"

Police Officer 1: "No, we can't."

Ben: "Are you going to listen to some speeder? I can't believe this. [Officer's given name], you have to listen to me. I didn't have anything to do with this."

Police Officer 1: "You sold the cameras and VCR. You and John split the money. You broke in there and stole it. Here, read his statement."

Ben: (Reads John's statement.) "The guy's juiced all the time. Can't we work something out?"

Police Officer 1: "Does any of this bother you?"

Ben: "Sure it does."

Police Officer 1: "John says it was your idea to break into Dave's house. He said he didn't know it was his house until he read it in the paper."

Ben: (Shook his head, indicating no.)

Police Officer 1: "Was it your idea?"

Ben: (Shook his head.) "No."

Police Officer 1: "Does it bother you to do this?"

Ben: (No response.)

Police Officer 1: "We'd really like to know why you did this. Do you read the obituaries and plan these?"

Ben: "No."

Police Officer 1: "Then, really, what's the reason? There's got to be a reason for this."

Ben: "Drugs." (Placed right hand to left forearm and simulated the injection of a needle.) "You don't know what it's like. You get your mind all ——ed up."

Police Officer 1: "How bad were you? What kind of habit did you have?"

Ben: "A $300 habit."

Police Officer 1: "A day or a week?"

Ben: "A day."

Police Officer 1: "Three hundred dollars a day. Where did you get $300 a day? That's $2100 a week."

Ben: "All kinds of wheeling and dealing."

Police Officer 1: "Isn't it hard to live with, doing things like this? Does it bother you to break into people's houses?"

Ben: "Yeah. Sometimes during the day I think about it and it bothers me."

ENDNOTES

1. *R. v. Smith* (1989), 50 C.C.C. (3d) 308, at 324 (S.C.C.).
2. Lecture, Ontario Police College, 1984.
3. Ibid.
4. P.K. McWilliams, *Canadian Criminal Evidence*, 3rd ed. (Aurora, ON: Canada Law Book, 1991).
5. Ibid.
6. D.A. Dukelow, and B. Nuse, *Pocket Dictionary of Canadian Law* (Toronto: Carswell, 1991).
7. *R. v. Smith*, supra note 1, at 324.
8. International Association of Chiefs of Police, *Criminal Investigation* (Arlington, VA: IACP, 1989).
9. McWilliams, supra note 4, at 14–18.
10. *R. v. Hodgson* (1998), 127 C.C.C. (3d) 449 (S.C.C.).
11. Ibid.
12. *R. v. A.B.* (1986), 26 C.C.C. (3d) 17 (Ont. C.A.).
13. *R. v. Sweryda* (1987), 34 C.C.C. (3d) 325 (Alta. C.A.).
14. *R. v. A.B.*, supra note 12.
15. *R. v. Gruenke* (1991), 67 C.C.C. (3d) 289 (S.C.C.).
16. *Rothman v. The Queen* (1981), 59 C.C.C. (2d) 30 (S.C.C.).
17. *R. v. Hebert* (1990), 57 C.C.C. (3d) 1 (S.C.C.).
18. McWilliams, supra note 4.
19. Ibid.
20. *Ibrahim v. The King* (1914), (1919) 24 Cox C.C. 174.
21. *Prosko v. Regina* (1922), 38 C.C.C. 199 (S.C.C.).
22. *Boudreau v. The King* (1949), 94 C.C.C. 1 (S.C.C.).
23. K. Roach, P. Healy, and G. Trotter, *Criminal Law and Procedure: Cases and Materials*, 9th ed. (Toronto: Emond Montgomery, 2004).
24. Ibid.
25. *Erven v. The Queen* (1978), 44 C.C.C. (2d) 76 (S.C.C.).
26. *Piche v. The Queen* (1969), C.C.C. 1979 1 257 (Man. C.A.).
27. R.J. Marin, *Admissibility of Statements* (Aurora, ON: Canada Law Book, 1989).
28. *Boudreau v. The King*, supra note 22.
29. *R. v. Fennell* (1881), 7 Q.B.D. 147 (C.C.R.).
30. Lecture, Ontario Police College, 1984.
31. McWilliams, supra note 4.
32. Lecture, Ontario Police College, 1984.

33. *R. v. Oickle* (2000), 147 C.C.C. (3d) 321 (S.C.C.).
34. *R. v. Bird* (1989), 50 C.C.C. (3d) 90 (Man. C.A.).
35. McWilliams, supra note 4.
36. Ibid.
37. H.J. Cox, *Criminal Evidence Handbook* (Aurora, ON: Canada Law Book, 1991).
38. Lecture, Ontario Police College, 1984.
39. McWilliams, supra note 4.
40. *Rothman v. The Queen*, supra note 16.
41. Cox, supra note 37.
42. *R. v. Gree* (1988), 36 C.C.C. (3d) 137 (Alta. C.A.).
43. *R. v. Smith* (1989), 50 C.C.C. (3d) 308 (S.C.C.).
44. *R. v. Moran* (1987), 36 C.C.C. (3d) 225 (Ont. C.A.).
45. Roach, Healy, and Trotter, supra note 23.
46. McWilliams, supra note 4.
47. Ibid.
48. Lecture, Ontario Police College, 1984.
49. McWilliams, supra note 4.
50. *R. v. S. (S.L.)* (1999), 132 C.C.C. (3d) 146. (Alta. C.A.).
51. *R. v. Bellieau* (1985), 58 A.R. 334 (Alta. C.A.).
52. *R. v. Bird*, supra note 34.
53. *R. v. Ward* (1979), 44 C.C.C. (2d) 498 (S.C.C.); *R. v. Whittle* (1994), 92 C.C.C. (3d) 11 (S.C.C.).
54. Ibid.
55. Ibid.
56. *McKenna v. The Queen*, [1961] S.C.R. 660.
57. Ibid.
58. *R. v. Yensen* (1961), 130 C.C.C. 353 (Ont. H.C.J.).
59. Ibid.
60. *R. v. Whittle*, supra note 53.
61. *R. v. Stillman* (1997), 113 C.C.C. (3d) 321 (S.C.C.).
62. Ibid.
63. Ibid.
64. *R. v. Oickle*, supra note 33.
65. *Ibrahim v. The King*, supra note 20, at 609.
66. *R. v. Hebert*, supra note 17.
67. *R. v. Ward*, supra note 53; *Horvath v. The Queen*, 1979 CanLII 16 (S.C.C.); *R. v. Whittle*, supra note 53.
68. *R. v. Oickle*, supra note 33.
69. Ibid.
70. Ibid.
71. *R. v. Ewert* (1991), 68 C.C.C. (3d) 207 (B.C.C.A.)
72. *R. v. Oickle*, supra note 33.
73. *R. v. Hoillet* (1999), 136 C.C.C. (3d) 449 (Ont. C.A.).
74. *R. v. Whittle*, supra note 53.
75. *Rothman v. The Queen*, supra note 16.
76. Ibid.
77. *R. v. Oickle*, supra note 33.
78. *R. v. Amyot* (1990), 58 C.C.C. (3d) 312 (Que. C.A.).

CHAPTER 17

Preventing Charter Violations

LEARNER SUMMARY

At a trial, the admissibility of a confession made to a police officer depends on its voluntariness and the absence of a Charter violation. Preventing Charter violations requires interpretation and procedural application of several Charter provisions, including

1. s. 10(a) Charter (reason for arrest),
2. s. 10(b) Charter (right to counsel), and
3. s. 7 Charter (principles of fundamental justice).

The explanation follows this order, reflecting the actual procedural sequence.

Case Study 17.1

Mike and Sarah owned a house on an urban street. In addition, they owned a business. On Friday, November 22, Mike put $5000 cash and several thousand dollars worth of payroll cheques into a canvas bag. He brought it home and hid it in their bedroom. Mike and Sarah went away for the weekend; their only child, a 16-year-old daughter named Alicia, stayed home alone.

Alicia was occasionally absent from the house during the weekend. When Mike and Sarah returned Sunday night, they discovered that the canvas bag with the payroll money was missing.

Police were called. An initial investigation revealed no signs of forced entry. Few items in the house had been disturbed. No other property had been stolen.

(Refer to the end of Chapter 17 for the conclusion of this case study.)

SECTION 10(a) CHARTER: REASON FOR ARREST

A statutory requirement set out in s. 10(a) of the Charter guarantees that a person, after an arrest or detention, will be informed promptly of the reasons for the arrest. Section 29(2)(b) of the *Criminal Code* repeats the requirement. The **reason for arrest** can take the form of

- a description of the act if a specific offence has not been decided, such as when the arrest is made at the scene of the offence, or
- the specific charge(s), as soon as it has been decided to charge a person with a specific offence.

Procedure

The procedure for informing an offender of the reason of the arrest is divided into two categories based on location: (a) at the scene of the arrest and (b) at the police station.

At the scene of the offence, where an offender is arrested then or shortly afterward, an officer has two alternatives about how to inform the accused about the reason for the arrest.

1. Explain a *general* reason that is sensible considering the circumstances, such as being under arrest for:
   - punching that person,
   - stealing that car,
   - stabbing that person, or
   - shooting at that person.

   Although a general reason does not state a specific offence, it provides a reasonable explanation.

2. If the officer quickly analyzes the circumstances at or near the crime scene and accurately recognizes the offence committed, a *specific* offence may be given as a reason, such as:
   - "Assault,"
   - "Theft under $5,000.00,"
   - "Impaired driving,"
   - "Attempt murder," or
   - "Mischief under $5,000.00."

If a specific offence is given as a reason, the officer has the onus to prove that the accused reasonably understood. If doubt exists whether the accused reasonably understands, an additional explanation providing more information may be required. For example, the name of some offences, such as mischief, may not be understood and would require an explanation.

After the accused is informed of the reason, ask the accused whether he or she understands and, if necessary, to explain to you, the officer, what it means. Record the accused's responses in a notebook for reference during court testimony at a trial.

After the accused has been transported to *the police station* and a decision about specific charges has been made, inform the accused about each specific offence that he or she will be charged with, as soon as practical. Failure to properly inform an arrested person of the proper reason for an arrest constitutes a s. 10(a) Charter violation that may result in the exclusion of evidence obtained after the violation.[1]

SECTION 10(b) CHARTER: RIGHT TO COUNSEL

General Principles

A police officer must inform the arrested person of the right to counsel without delay on arrest or detention.[2] This is a statutory requirement created by s. 10(b) Charter. This section creates only the general base component of the right to counsel. Since the enactment of the Charter in 1982, additional components have been created by case law decisions. These components constitute the entire right-to-counsel package, although only the base component is contained in s. 10(b) Charter.

The right to counsel consists of four distinct components that apply to both adult and young offenders (ages 12 to 17 years):

1. base component,
2. *Brydges* component (legal aid existence and availability),
3. *Bartle* component (toll-free number), and
4. privacy component.

Additional rules apply to young offenders.

When does an accused have to be informed of the right to counsel? The Supreme Court of Canada, in *R. v. Schmautz* 1990),[3] says "at the moment when he or she is arrested or detained."

Adult offenders must be informed of the right to counsel only upon arrest. This means that an adult offender (18 years or older) does not have to be informed of the right to counsel when mere suspicion exists and the offender voluntarily accompanies the officer for any purpose, such as questioning. For example, if mere suspicion exists that Dominic (19) has committed a robbery and Dominic consents to be questioned by a police officer, the officer does not have to inform Dominic of the right to counsel because Dominic has not been arrested or detained.

The rule for young offenders differs. A young offender must be informed of the right to counsel at any time during an investigation, including during voluntary accompaniment when no arrest or detention occurs. Essentially, a young offender must be informed of the right to counsel any time an officer has contact with, deals with, or speaks to him or her, including during voluntary accompaniment when only mere suspicion exists.[4]

BASE COMPONENT: ADULT

The right to counsel must be clearly communicated to an arrested person.[5] The base component used to inform an adult offender of the right to counsel is: "It is my duty to inform you that you have the right to retain and instruct counsel without delay. Do you understand?"

The officer has the onus of proving that the accused understood the right. Usually, the question "Do you understand?" and an affirmative answer of "Yes" by the accused are sufficient to prove knowledge. The offender's verbatim response should be recorded in a notebook, rather than simply recording that the accused understood. If circumstances exist that suggest the accused does not understand, then the officer must provide an additional explanation such as, "This means you have the right to call a lawyer of your choice." Record the explanation and the offender's response verbatim. Avoid paraphrasing, such as "I explained it further and then the accused understood."[6]

BASE COMPONENT: YOUNG OFFENDER

The base component used to inform a young offender of the right to counsel includes the same information used for adults and additional information. Besides a lawyer, a young offender must be informed of the right to call three other types of people:

1. a parent,
2. any adult relative, or
3. any other appropriate adult chosen by the young offender.[7]

A young offender must be informed of the right to have any number of these four persons present.[8]

All information told to a young offender must be said in language compatible with that particular young person's intelligence.[9] Consequently, an officer may have to inform a young person about the right to counsel in simple language that the young person understands.

Afterward, the young person must be asked whether he or she understands. If the young person acknowledges by stating "yes," he or she should be asked to explain the right to counsel. The answer must reflect the correct meaning of the right to counsel. If the young person answers incorrectly, inform the young person about the correct explanation and ask him or her again to explain it. Write the entire conversation verbatim in a notebook, including the right to counsel and all responses made by the young offender. Court testimony should reflect the recorded verbatim conversation. Do not paraphrase the conversation by simply stating, "I informed the accused of the right to counsel and he or she understood." This phrase will be insufficient during court testimony because it is a conclusion that only the trial judge may make.

This base component represents only the first component and is not the total right-to-counsel information. Case law has added additional requirements, or components. If an officer informs an adult or young offender about only the base component, a s. 10(b) Charter violation will have occurred because the base component by itself is insufficient.

BRYDGES COMPONENT

The Supreme Court of Canada, in *R. v. Brydges* (1990),[10] added a second mandatory component to the right to counsel. An officer must inform both adult and young offenders about the existence and availability of legal aid, regardless of the accused person's financial status.

Legal aid is legal advice and service provided to an accused person who is eligible for it. The service extends during the course of the prosecution and court proceedings.[11] Additionally, temporary, free legal advice is available immediately after an arrest. The police are required to inform an accused person of two elements that comprise the *Brydges* component:

1. the availability of temporary, free, and immediate legal service, and
2. that the accused may be eligible for permanent legal aid, meaning until the completion of court proceedings.

The specific content of the **Brydges component** is printed on right-to-counsel cards that police officers are given. The *Brydges* component must be read to all arrested persons, regardless of whether the accused can afford a lawyer. Failure to inform an accused person of the *Brydges* component constitutes a s. 10(b) Charter violation, which may result in the exclusion of evidence that the police obtain after the violation is committed.[12]

BARTLE COMPONENT

The Supreme Court of Canada, in *R. v. Bartle* (1994),[13] added a third mandatory component to the right to counsel. Police officers must inform both adult and young offenders of a toll-free telephone number to reach duty counsel. This telephone number provides an accused person with a specific method of obtaining temporary, free, and immediate legal advice. This telephone number must be given to all arrested persons, in all cases, whether the accused can afford a lawyer or has a lawyer that he or she uses or calls regularly. In other words, no exceptions exist; it is a mandatory obligation.

Failure to inform an arrested person of the toll-free number constitutes a s. 10(b) Charter violation and may result in the exclusion of evidence obtained by police after the violation occurs.[14] Again, the trial judge considers various factors in determining whether to admit or exclude the evidence.

PRIVACY COMPONENT

The Ontario Court of Appeal, in *R. v. Jackson* (1993),[15] added both a mandatory and recommended procedure about informing an arrested person about the right to exercise the right to counsel in private. Whether mandatory or recommended depends on certain circumstances.

A police officer has a *mandatory* obligation to inform all adult and young offenders of the right to privacy if any of the following conditions exist:

▸ The accused says something to, or in the presence of, the officer who informed the accused of the right to counsel that indicates to the officer that the accused either (a) does not understand that he or she has the right to counsel in private or (b) is concerned about whether such a right exists.
▸ The accused knows that the right to privacy exists but is concerned about whether privacy will be given.
▸ The circumstances surrounding the information of the right to counsel cause the accused to reasonably believe that he or she will have no privacy to exercise that right and must telephone a lawyer in police presence.

An example of circumstances that caused the accused to reasonably believe that no privacy would be given is found in the *Jackson* case. The accused was arrested for "Over 80" and was informed of his right to counsel upon arrest. A

Breathalyzer demand was made and the accused was transported to a police station.

The accused was seated in an interview room; a police officer sat across from the accused, pointed to a phone book and a telephone on a desk, and asked him whether he wanted to call a lawyer. The officer made no move to leave and the accused said no. During a half-hour interval when they remained together in the room, the officer repeated the right to counsel and the accused again refused.

At the trial, the accused testified that he would have called his lawyer, but chose not to because he believed he would not have been afforded privacy. The court ruled that a s. 10(b) Charter violation occurred because of the following reasons:

▸ These circumstances would sufficiently cause a reasonable person to believe that the right to phone a lawyer had to occur in the officer's presence and that no privacy would be given.
▸ These circumstances sufficiently caused the officer to have a reasonable apprehension that the accused believed that no privacy would be given.

It is not mandatory for an officer to inform an accused person of the right to privacy if no circumstances exist that would cause the accused to reasonably believe that privacy will not be given. However, the Court added a *recommended* procedure for officers to use in all cases by stating that it is a "simple matter" for police offenders to add the words "in privacy" to the right-to-counsel information content. Additionally, the Court stated that "it is desirable that this be done."[16]

Proving Knowledge

The Supreme Court of Canada, in *R. v. Evans* (1991),[17] stated that an accused person cannot be expected to exercise the right to counsel if the accused fails to understand it.[18] Consequently, officers have the onus to clearly communicate the right and prove that the accused understood it.

In most cases, the question "Do you understand?" with a response of "yes" implies that the accused understood what was said.[19] It is recommended that this response always be followed with a question such as "What does this mean?" The purpose of this question is to elicit a correct explanation from the accused person that accurately reflects the meaning of the right to counsel and proves that the accused had sufficient intelligence to understand it. A correct explanation should include a reference to the right to call a lawyer. Record the response verbatim. During court testimony, state the question asked and the response made instead of paraphrasing by saying "the accused understood." Paraphrasing must be avoided during court testimony because it represents a conclusion that only a trial judge may make.

However, if a positive indication exists that the accused does not understand the right, the Supreme Court added the following: "The police cannot rely on their mechanical recitation of the right to the accused; they must take steps to facilitate that understanding."[20]

An example of a positive indication is a response made by the accused that indicates no understanding or doubt about the ability to understand. An accused's limited capacity is another example of a positive indication. In the *Evans* case, the police were aware of the accused's limited mental capacity and the accused said he did not understand the right to counsel. If the accused indicates that the right to counsel is not understood, the right to counsel must be explained in simple language, such as:

- It means you can call a lawyer and talk to him or her.
- You can talk to a free legal aid lawyer right now.
- This is the toll-free telephone number that you can call to talk to a lawyer for free.
- You can apply to legal aid and you might receive a free lawyer for the trial if you are eligible.

Record the additional explanation verbatim and the accused's response in a notebook. After receiving the response, ask the accused to explain the right. Record the explanation verbatim. The accused's explanation should accurately reflect the officer's simpler explanation. Whenever the accused's knowledge of an issue requires proof, the best proof is the accused's verbatim response, including the correct additional explanation learned from the officer's instructions.

Another example of possible indication of failure to understand is an accused's intoxication. A slightly or moderately intoxicated person (meaning a person who is coherent and capable of having a conversation) may be capable of understanding what is told to him or her. However, in these cases, the following procedure may remove doubt about the accused's knowledge:

- Explain the right to counsel in simpler language, whether the intoxicated accused says that the right is understood.
- Ask the accused to explain it.
- Repeat the procedure after the accused is sober.

Young offenders must have all the right-to-counsel information told to them in language compatible with the specific young person's intelligence. This procedure is a preventive measure to avoid the potential exclusion of evidence, such as a confession or physical evidence obtained afterward.

Caution

The **caution** is a warning to the accused that he or she does not have to say anything to the police, but that if he or she does say anything, it may be used in evidence at the trial. An example of a formal caution is "Do you wish to say anything in answer to the charge? You are not obliged to say anything unless you wish to do so, but whatever you say may be given in evidence."

After the formal caution is read to the accused, translate it into ordinary language. An effective translation is, "You don't have to talk to me. It's *your choice*. But if you do, I may be able to report what you tell me when I testify in court. Do you understand?" Ask the accused to tell you what this means and record the response verbatim.

The caution is not a statutory requirement. No statute, such as the Charter or the *Criminal Code*, creates a mandatory requirement to inform an accused person of the formal caution. Consequently, failure to caution the accused is not a Charter violation. The caution is a guideline, or a recommended practice, included in the Judges' Rules as established in England in 1912. The purpose of the caution is to assist officers with the onus of proving that confessions made by accused persons are voluntarily made. Voluntariness of a confession is a prominent factor that must be proven to ensure the admissibility of the confession. Reading the caution to an offender after an arrest does not automatically result in admissibility of a confession. The entire circumstances of the conversation during an interrogation determines voluntariness and the admissibility of a confession. The caution is an advantage available to police officers to help prove the voluntariness of a confession.

In summary, failure to caution an accused simply represents the failure to use an advantage that facilitates admissibility of a confession.[21] Failure to caution an accused person will not result in automatic exclusion of a confession or any other evidence obtained as a result of interrogation.

INVOKING RIGHT OR WAIVER

After the accused is informed of the right to counsel, he or she has two choices or options regarding the right to counsel:

1. Invoke the right to counsel for the purpose of exercising it (ask to call and speak to a lawyer).
2. Waive the right to counsel (decline the right to call a lawyer).

The police have a duty to provide the accused with a reasonable time to decide whether to exercise the right to counsel. An exact number of minutes is not specified. Instead, the amount of time must be reasonable and is dependent upon the circumstances of each case.

The British Columbia Court of Appeal, in *R. v. Hollis* (1992),[22] created two rules that are relevant to the accused's decision by stating: "If the accused understands the right, the decision by the accused is expected to be made quickly." Again, no specific amount of time that applies in every case was included.

The accused's decision about calling a lawyer must be the product of free choice. This means that the police cannot persuade or influence the accused in any manner or use any inducements to force the accused to make a specific decision.

The Supreme Court of Canada, in *R. v. Burlingham* (1995),[23] addressed the issue of police persuasion or influence regarding the accused's decision to call a lawyer. The court ruled that s. 10(b) Charter specifically prohibits the police from "belittling" an accused's lawyer with the "express goal or effect of undermining the accused's confidence in and relationship with defence counsel." This prohibition is a component of s. 10(b) Charter. In the *Burlingham* case, the police denigrated the role of the defence lawyer by making disparaging remarks about the lawyer's loyalty, commitment, availability, and legal fees. Additionally, the police suggested that they were more trustworthy than the accused's lawyer. These comments constituted a s. 10(b) Charter violation, and significant evidence that was obtained afterward, including a confession, was excluded under s. 24(2) Charter.

In some cases, the accused makes no decision and gives no response about exercising the right to counsel. When the accused does not say whether he or she wants to invoke or waive the right to counsel, the question arises whether the police should assume that the accused has invoked the right to counsel? The BC Court of Appeal answered that question in the *Hollis* case with the following rule: "If the accused does not state a decision, the police have no obligation to assume or guess that the accused will decide to call a lawyer and may continue the investigation as if the right to counsel has been waived."[24]

In summary, the accused may

- ask to call and speak to a lawyer (invoke and exercise the right),
- decline to call a lawyer (waive the right), or
- make no decision (the right is waived).

Procedure: After Right Invoked

Invoking the right to counsel means to ask for any opportunity to call and speak to a lawyer. An accused person may invoke the right to counsel at any time while he or she is in police custody, from the time after an arrest is made until the time of release. The accused is not limited or restricted to a period (e.g., having to invoke the right immediately after being informed of it).

The Supreme Court of Canada, in *R. v. Manninen* (1987),[25] imposed two mandatory obligations upon police officers when the accused asks to invoke the right to counsel:

1. give the accused person a reasonable opportunity to exercise the right to counsel, after the right is invoked, and
2. cease questioning, delay the investigation, and do not attempt to obtain evidence from the accused until he or she has had a reasonable opportunity to call and speak to a lawyer.

The following rules and procedures must be followed after the accused invokes the right to counsel by asking to call a lawyer:

RULE 1
Provide the accused with an opportunity to call a lawyer without unnecessary delay.[26] The opportunity is not defined by a specific number of minutes or hours.

RULE 2
Delay the investigation and do not attempt to elicit evidence from the accused until the accused has exercised the right by actually speaking to a lawyer and receiving legal advice. This rule prohibits the questioning of an accused person between the time the accused asks for the opportunity to call a lawyer (invoked) and the time the accused actually speaks to a lawyer (exercised). If the police initiate questioning during that time and the accused confesses, a s. 10(b) Charter violation will have occurred and the confession will likely be excluded under s. 24(2) Charter.

RULE 3
How much time constitutes a reasonable opportunity? How long must the police delay their investigation until the accused calls and speaks to a lawyer? The Supreme Court of Canada answered these questions in *R. v. Smith* (1989) by ruling that an accused must be reasonably diligent in attempting to call a lawyer.[27] This imposes a time limit on the accused to call a lawyer, but the time limit is not in specific minutes. Instead, it prevents the accused from causing unnecessary delays in an investigation. Without this limit, it would be possible to intentionally hinder an investigation and cause evidence to be destroyed or lost.

Consequently, the police obligation to cease questioning and delay the investigation is cancelled if the accused is not reasonably diligent in exercising the right to counsel. The accused person does not lose the right to counsel; the police simply do not have to delay the investigation unreasonably until the right is exercised. Visit the accompanying website **www.emp.ca/arcaro/criminvestigation5E** for a more detailed analysis of the *Smith* case.

RULE 4

Where should the accused be given the opportunity to call a lawyer? Ensuring personal safety and preventing escape are primary concerns after an arrest is made. It is recommended that the opportunity to call a lawyer be given at the police station, if the accused is transported there justifiably. Permitting the accused to phone in public or from a home poses a risk. Any arrested person is capable of using violence toward the arresting officer and is capable of attempting an escape.

The accused's movement in public or in a house should be restricted after an arrest. The accused should be placed in the police car as soon as possible. If an accused makes a phone call before being transported to the police station, he or she may be calling someone other than a lawyer to seek assistance in escaping while en route to the police station. Additionally, too many consequences are possible during the time it takes an accused to make a call in public or in a house because of the accused's ability to move freely. For example, the accused may know of and easily remove a weapon stored near the phone. Giving the accused the opportunity to call a lawyer from the police station minimizes unnecessary risks.

It must be emphasized that the only possible consequence of delaying the opportunity to call a lawyer until arrival at the police station is the possible exclusion of a confession that the accused may give during the delay, while en route to the police station.

If the circumstances do not justify continued detention and transportation to the police station, then the accused may call from the location of the arrest.

RULE 5

Some time will elapse between the time the right to counsel is invoked and the time it is exercised. If the accused initiates conversation during this time, record the accused's remarks verbatim in your notebook. The police cannot initiate conversation or questioning during this time. However, if the accused initiates conversation and confesses or makes incriminating verbal statements, that evidence should likely be admissible.[28]

RULE 6

Do not limit the accused person to only one phone call.[29] Informing an accused that only one phone call will be allowed or limiting the accused to only one phone call constitutes a s. 10(b) Charter violation, according to the Ontario Court of Appeal in *R. v. Pavel* (1989). A reasonable opportunity to exercise the right to counsel does not limit the accused to any specific number of phone calls. Instead, the accused must be allowed to make reasonable attempts to contact a lawyer.

The Alberta Court of Appeal, in *R. v. Whitford* (1997),[30] reiterated that an accused cannot be limited to a single phone call. The court stated the following valuable procedural guidelines:

- ▸ If an accused wants to make two or three successive phone calls to pursue and exercise the right, he or she must be permitted to do so while not being obstructed by police questioning.
- ▸ If an accused wants to call both a lawyer and Legal Aid, he or she must be allowed to do so. The accused cannot be restricted to choosing only one. Additionally, if the accused manages to contact a lawyer and still wants to call Legal Aid, he or she must be allowed to do so. The court stated, "The accused is not required to play 'Let's Make a Deal' with his [or her] Charter rights."

Both the Ontario and Alberta courts clearly show that the accused has a right to make successive calls to lawyers. There is no restriction to only one phone call regarding a lawyer. This extends only for the purpose of obtaining legal advice, not for any other purpose such as calling family and friends.

Caution must be used to answer common questions asked by accused persons, such as "How many calls can I make?" To prevent a Charter violation,

- ▸ never include a specific number in the answer, and
- ▸ inform the accused that he or she can make a reasonable number for the purpose of getting satisfactory legal advice.

It must be emphasized that a young offender's right to counsel includes the right to contact and speak to parents or other appropriate adults whom the young offender believes may provide assistance or give advice. Consequently, a young offender may require several phone calls to contact a lawyer, parents, or adults for the entire right to counsel to be exercised.

An adult's right to counsel guarantees the right to receive advice from a lawyer only. Section 10(b) Charter does not specifically include the right for an adult offender to contact other adults, such as parents or spouses. Consequently, a problem may arise when an offender who is 18 years old or older requests to call a parent, spouse, or other adult. The solution is to determine whether such a phone call is reasonably necessary to contact a lawyer. Most lawyers have answering services after business hours. Phone books and lists of lawyers' phone numbers are provided to an accused at most police stations. The need to call another adult to help contact a lawyer is usually unnecessary. Unnecessary phone calls to other adults have potential consequences, such as the destruction or loss of evidence. This consequence must be prevented to ensure a successful investigation.

RULE 7

Allow the accused to make phone calls and speak to a lawyer in private.[31] The right to counsel includes in it the right to privacy, according to case law decisions. Accused persons must be allowed to make phone calls and speak to lawyers in private and do not have to ask for privacy. The right to privacy is automatically allowed. Officers cannot remain in the room when the accused makes phone calls or while an accused speaks to a lawyer in person, nor can the conversation be monitored or overheard by any means. Any confessions or incriminating evidence obtained as the result of this privacy violation will likely be excluded.

RULE 8

After the accused person makes a phone call, determine the result of the phone call. The right to counsel is exercised only after the accused has spoken to and received advice from a lawyer. Then the officer is permitted to question the accused. In many cases, particularly after business hours, an accused person must leave a message with an answering service to contact a lawyer. A message left by the accused for a lawyer to call the police station does not constitute the exercising of the right.

When the accused makes a phone call, the officer will not be in the room and will not be listening to the conversation. The officer must determine the result of the phone call to begin the questioning of the accused. The officer must obviously rely on the response of the accused. The accused may give the officer one of three responses: (a) he or she spoke to a lawyer, (b) a message was left, or (c) no response (the accused does not say whether he or she spoke to a lawyer).

If the accused says that he or she spoke to a lawyer, questioning may begin at this stage. If a message was left, the officer cannot initiate questioning while waiting for the lawyer to call. However, if the accused initiates conversation and makes incriminating statements, record them.

The Nova Scotia Court of Appeal in *R. v. MacKenzie* (1991)[32] ruled that an accused's confession to police while waiting for a lawyer to call after a message was left are admissible if the accused initiates the conversation. Although the accused's conviction was later overturned, the reasons were not related to this circumstance. The Supreme Court of Canada in *R. v. Hebert* (1990)[33] stated that, "in the absence of eliciting behaviour on the part of the police, there is no violation of the accused's right to choose whether or not to speak to the police" if the accused initiates conversation and confesses.

If the accused makes no response and does not tell the officer whether or not a lawyer was spoken to, two questions, which are answered in case law, arise:

1. Does the officer have to ask the accused about the result of the phone call?
2. Does the accused have an onus to tell the officer that a message was left?

The British Columbia Court of Appeal in *R. v. Ferron* (1989)[34] ruled that the police are not obliged to "ask again and again" if the accused has spoken to a lawyer after the accused makes phone calls. The Alberta Court of Appeal in *R. v. Top* (1989)[35] ruled that the accused should inform the police about the results of the phone calls, particularly if messages are left.

Consequently, if the accused makes no response after making a phone call, the officer may assume that the accused exercised the right and may question the accused.

In summary, if an accused person invokes his right to counsel, then exercises it by calling a lawyer and leaving a message, use the following procedure:

1. If the accused does not state that a message was left, question the accused.
2. If the accused states that a message was left,

   ▷ do not initiate conversation with the accused; but
   ▷ if the accused initiates conversation, allow him or her to continue.

RULE 9

The Alberta Court of Appeal in *R. v. Whitford* (1997)[36] provided a valuable procedural guideline about what the issue is after an accused calls a law office. The court stated:

> The relevant inquiry after an initial phone call to a law office is not simply whether the accused did or did not speak to a lawyer. After all, the lawyer might tell the accused that he is too busy, too expensive, or simply not interested in acting for and advising the accused. He might even recommend that the accused contact Legal Aid. An accused is entitled to a reasonable opportunity to have meaningful contact with and advice from counsel.

This rule applies if the accused is not intentionally trying to impede or frustrate the investigation.

These rules address the following problem: What if the accused completes a first phone call to a law office and immediately says that he or she does not want to speak to the police until speaking with Legal Aid? Can the police begin questioning after the first phone call? Do the police have to let the accused call both a lawyer and Legal Aid? The Alberta Court of appeal stated:

- The only reasonable interpretation of the accused's request to also call Legal Aid is that he or she did not receive meaningful legal advice during the first call to a lawyer.
- The police cannot question the accused after the accused completes the first call and immediately says he or she does not want to speak to police until also speaking to Legal Aid. Starting questioning after the first phone call and before the second one constitutes a s. 10(b) Charter violation.

If the accused is a young offender and speaks to parents or other adults, allow an additional reasonable opportunity to call a lawyer. The Supreme Court of Canada in *R. v. T. (E.)* (1993) stated that a parent is not an alternative to a lawyer.[37] Consequently, a young offender who speaks to a parent or adult is entitled the additional right to speak with a lawyer. Do not prevent the right to counsel from being exercised because the young offender has received advice from a parent or adult.

Interrogation is a crucial investigative technique that may yield substantial evidence. After an **adult accused** exercises the right to counsel by speaking to a lawyer, no rule prohibits the police from questioning the adult in the absence of counsel. When a lawyer speaks to an accused, the advice likely will be to remain silent. The right to remain silent is a fundamental principle that is included in s. 7 Charter.

However, the Supreme Court of Canada in *R. v. Hebert* (1990)[38] stated that no rule prohibits the police from questioning an adult accused in the absence of a lawyer, after the accused has spoken to the lawyer. The police must allow the accused an opportunity to decide whether to remain silent or not, but if the accused volunteers information then no Charter violation will have occurred.

Additionally, the police are permitted to persuade the accused to answer questions provided that the police persuasion does not "deny the suspect of the right to choose" to remain silent.

In summary, questioning is allowed after an adult accused speaks to a lawyer, if the accused chooses not to remain silent or volunteers information and initiates conversation.

After a **young offender** exercises the right to counsel, questioning is allowed, but the lawyer or adult with whom the young offender consulted must be present, unless the young offender waives this in writing.[39] Section 146 Y.C.J.A. creates the following rule: a young offender may be questioned after a lawyer or adult is consulted with, but the young offender decides who will be present during the questioning.

The young offender may have a lawyer, parent, or adult present, if he or she chooses. If the young offender chooses otherwise, the young offender must sign a written waiver. The police do not decide who will be present during a young offender's questioning.

Waiver

Choosing not to invoke the right to counsel means declining an opportunity to call a lawyer. If an accused person chooses not to invoke the right to counsel after being informed of it, the right to counsel is then waived and the investigation and questioning may continue immediately.[40] A **waiver** of the right to counsel means that the person relinquishes or gives up the s. 10(b) Charter right to retain a lawyer and receive legal advice.

After a valid waiver has been made by an accused person, the police have no other obligation regarding the right to counsel and may question the accused person. The onus is on the prosecution to prove that the accused made a valid waiver of the right to counsel. The Supreme Court of Canada in *R. v. Prosper* (1994)[41] stated that the standard of proof required for a valid waiver must be "very high" and that "courts must ensure that the right to counsel is not too easily waived."

Several elements comprise a valid waiver and must be proven by the police:

▸ **The waiver must be clear and unequivocal.** This means it must be unmistakable and not vague. The accused's words must specifically indicate that he or she does not want to call or speak with a lawyer. If any other inference may be made by the reader, reasonable doubt will exist about the waiver's validity.

▸ **The waiver must be voluntarily made.** It must be free from inducements, meaning direct or indirect compulsions, such as threats or promises that may force an accused to waive the right to counsel.

▸ **The accused must understand the entire nature of the right to counsel**, referring to the meaning of all the components.

▸ **The accused must understand what is being given up**, which refers to legal advice.[42]

An officer's testimony relating to a waiver must meticulously include the verbatim conversation that comprises the waiver. A simple phrase such as "The accused waived his right to counsel" would be insufficient to prove a clear, unequivocal waiver. Consequently, the verbatim conversation should be recorded rather than paraphrased in a notebook. A young offender's waiver must be in writing.[43] A verbal waiver is sufficient only with regard to an adult offender's waiver.

Failure to prove any of the elements that compose a waiver constitutes a s. 10(b) Charter violation.

An effective practice, after a waiver, has been to contact a lawyer on behalf of the accused, even if the accused does not want to call a lawyer. A lawyer's instructions to an accused are not fatal to an ensuing interrogation. This practice removes the possibility of a s. 10(b) Charter violation and will elevate officer credibility.

WAIVER BY AN INTOXICATED PERSON

Accused persons at the time of an arrest are often intoxicated, posing a potential problem to the police if the accused waives the right to counsel. If an intoxicated accused person waives the right to counsel, the officer must prove that the accused was aware of the consequences of waiving the right.[44]

The Supreme Court of Canada in *R. v. Clarkson* (1986) stated that the prosecution has the onus of proving that an intoxicated accused person who waives the right to counsel was aware of the consequences of the waiver. Therefore, the officer must prove:

- the elements that comprise the waiver, and
- the accused had knowledge that (a) legal advice will be given up and (b) information obtained afterward, such as a confession, may be used as evidence at the trial.

The following 10-step procedure may fulfill this onus.

1. Read all the components of the right to counsel.
2. Ask the accused if each component is understood.
3. Record the response verbatim.
4. State additional explanation in ordinary language and record the explanation verbatim.
5. Ask if the explanation is understood and record the response.
6. Ask the accused to explain the right to counsel to you and record it verbatim.
7. Record the waiver verbatim.
8. Explain that the consequences of the waiver are that legal advice will be given up and that evidence obtained may be used at the trial. Record the explanation verbatim.
9. Ask if the explanation is understood. Record the response verbatim.
10. Ask the accused to explain the consequences of the waiver. Record the explanation verbatim.

Various degrees of intoxication exist ranging from slight to moderate to advanced. Slightly or moderately intoxicated offenders are often coherent and may converse rationally, with an operating mind. Consequently, if the officer believes that the accused has understood all aspects of the waiver, questioning may occur immediately after.

If the intoxication is advanced causing incoherence that prevents comprehension of the required elements, questioning should be delayed until the accused is sober. Then, the right-to-counsel procedure should be repeated.

WAIVER BY A MENTALLY ILL PERSON

Finally, the S.C.C. in *R. v. Whittle* (1994),[45] addressed the issue of a waiver made by a mentally ill person who suffered from schizophrenia and heard inner voices. The court stated that a valid right-to-counsel waiver requires the following elements:

- an accused's limited cognitive ability, the same degree that is required to prove fitness to stand trial,

- the accused's understanding of the function of counsel, and
- the accused's knowledge that counsel can be dispensed with, despite the fact that doing so would be contrary to the accused's best interest.

In the *Whittle* case, the accused waived his right to counsel before confessing. Evidence was introduced that the accused was mentally unstable, suffered from schizophrenia, and showed symptoms of auditory hallucinations. The S.C.C. ruled that the accused's waiver was valid because it included all of the above elements.

CHANGE OF MIND

If the accused person invokes the right to counsel, then changes his or her mind and waives it, inform the accused that a reasonable opportunity will be given to contact a lawyer.[46] The Supreme Court of Canada in *R. v. Prosper* (1994) created a mandatory obligation for police officers when an accused person initially invokes the right to counsel, changes his or her mind, and later waives the right. Under these circumstances, the police must inform the accused of

- the right to a reasonable opportunity to call a lawyer, and
- the police obligation to hold off questioning and their investigation during the reasonable opportunity.

Failure to inform an accused of both elements constitutes a s. 10(b) Charter violation.

Change in Focus of an Investigation

A common occurrence during investigations is that the nature of the offence changes while the accused is in custody and is being questioned. This also means that the reason for the arrest may change during the accused's custody and interrogation. This is formally called **change in focus** during an investigation.

There are many examples of when the focus changes, such as an injured victim who is alive at the time of the accused's arrest but dies while the accused is in custody. The relevant issue is whether the police have a mandatory obligation to re-inform the accused of the right to counsel after the focus changes.

The S.C.C. in *R. v. Black* (1989)[47] answered the question. In that case, the accused was arrested for attempted murder. She was informed of the right to counsel and exercised that right by consulting with a lawyer. Afterward, the victim died and the police told the accused the charge had changed to second-degree murder. She immediately asked to speak to her lawyer again, but was unable to contact him. She then gave a confession without having successfully contacted the lawyer, after the reasons for the arrest changed.

The S.C.C. excluded the confession under s. 24(2) Charter. The court ruled that

- a s. 10(b) Charter violation had occurred,
- when the reason for an arrest changes, the police must inform the accused of the new reason and the right to counsel again, and
- an accused must be re-informed of the right to counsel after the reason for arrest changes, and the accused is entitled to another reasonable opportunity to call a lawyer.

The second opportunity is necessary for the accused to exercise the s. 10(b) right to counsel in a meaningful way. In this case, the accused had not fully exercised her right to counsel when she spoke to her lawyer about the first charge.

If the accused waives the right to counsel relating to the original reason for the arrest, the waiver does not extend to a request for a lawyer in relation to a second reason, if the focus of the investigation changes.

The *Black* decision created significant interrogation procedures. The reason for the arrest must be sufficient to exercise the right to counsel in a meaningful way. When the reason for an arrest or the focus of an investigation changes, officers must re-inform the accused of the right to counsel and provide a reasonable opportunity to exercise it. The result of the first right to counsel is not relevant to the second reason for arrest.

What follows are actual case law decisions relating to this issue. The effect of s. 10(a) Charter upon the s. 24(2) Charter exclusionary rule is illustrated in *Smith v. The Queen* (1991).[48]

CASE LAW

Smith v. The Queen (1991)

The accused was charged with first-degree murder after shooting a friend with a shotgun at the friend's residence. The accused was arrested several hours later. The reason given by the police was for "a shooting incident at the residence of [the deceased]." The accused was cautioned and was informed of his right to counsel; he stated that both were understood.

Subsequently, the accused made an inculpatory statement to police. The accused was not informed that the victim had died. During the interrogation, the police officer became aware that the accused had no knowledge of the death. The accused was informed of the death two and one-half hours after the arrest.

At the trial, the accused sought exclusion of the statement on the basis of a ss. 10(a) and 10(b) Charter violation. The trial judge admitted the statement and the accused was convicted of second-degree murder. An appeal to the Nova Scotia Court of Appeal was dismissed. A further appeal to the Supreme Court of Canada was also dismissed. The first question concerned whether failure to inform the accused that his friend had died "deprived him of the power to appreciate his need for a lawyer." The court concluded that a s. 10(b) violation occurred.

The second question concerned whether s. 10(a) was violated. The Crown concluded that it was, because of failure of the police to inform the accused that the death resulted from the shooting. The court concluded that the s. 10(a) violation lacked severity to bring the administration of justice into disrepute. Therefore, the s. 24(2) Charter exclusionary rule did not apply.

CASE LAW

R. v. Evans (1991)

In *R. v. Evans* (1991),[49] the accused person was arrested for a *Narcotic Control Act* offence. The police also suspected that his brother had committed two murders and had hoped the accused would implicate his brother.

The accused was informed of his right to counsel, but stated he did not understand it. The officers had prior knowledge that the accused had below-average mental capacity. The officers made no attempt to explain the meaning of his right. Interrogation ensued and the accused became the prime suspect in the murders.

The officers failed

▸ to advise the accused that he was being detained on suspicion of committing murder, and

▸ to reiterate his right to counsel.

Interrogation included a lie concerning the finding of the accused's fingerprint at one of the crime scenes. The accused subsequently made inculpatory statements in relation to the murders, which formed the entire basis for the murder charges, and was convicted. The Supreme Court of Canada allowed the accused's appeal and acquitted the accused. The court's judgment included the following:

▸ Section 10(b) Charter was not complied with at the time of the initial arrest. The Court stated, "The police cannot rely on their mechanical recitation of the right to the accused; they must take steps to facilitate that understanding."

▸ Section 10(a) Charter must be complied with by sufficiently stating the reason for detention to permit the accused the opportunity to make a reasonable decision regarding the s. 10(b) Charter right to counsel.

▸ The police failed to explain the caution after the accused stated that he did not understand it.

▸ The accused's confession was unreliable because of his deficient mental state combined with the circumstances in which the statements were taken. The unreliability of the confession was based on the accused's emotional immaturity, his tendency to be subject to suggestion, and the officer's lie that his fingerprints had been found at the crime scene.

▸ The police have a duty to inform an accused of the right to counsel a second time when the accused is arrested for a minor offence and new evidence indicates that the accused is a suspect for a "different, more serious offence." The police must repeat the right to counsel when there is a "fundamental and discrete change in the purpose of the investigation, when involving a different and unrelated offence or a significantly more serious offence than that contemplated at the time" of the first right to counsel.

▸ However, police do not have to reiterate the right to counsel every time "that the investigation touches on a different offence," during an "exploratory investigation."

▸ An arrest made in relation to one charge with the intention of interrogating on another charge may constitute an abuse of detention and violations of ss. 10(a) and 10(b) of the Charter.

▸ In situations where a detained accused voluntarily incriminates himself or herself in relation to other charges without prior police knowledge, it is not a violation of s. 10(a) or 10(b) Charter.

CASE LAW

R. v. Sawatsky (1997)
R. v. Witts (1998)

The Ontario Court of Appeal in *R. v. Sawatsky* (1997)[50] established valuable procedural guidelines that are relevant to common situations that occur during interrogations.

- The police will not be required to immediately restate the right to counsel in relation to other offences if the arrested person brings up other unrelated offences during questioning.

- The right to counsel must be restated before questioning about those offences if the police embark on an investigation of the offences brought up by the arrested person.

- The link between an arrested person's need to understand the extent of his or her jeopardy and the effective exercise of the right to counsel determines when the police must re-inform the person of the right to counsel.

- Once the police have a realistic indication that an arrested person may incriminate himself or herself in an unrelated offence, the police should reiterate the right to counsel and connect the right to the new offences if the police wish to investigate those offences.

- In some cases, the mere statement of the accused will be insufficient to constitute a realistic indication of self-incrimination. The court used the example in *R. v. Whittle* in which a mentally ill arrested person was in custody for minor charges and announced that he had committed a murder. The police had no knowledge of that crime. There was no obligation to restate the right to counsel until the police could verify the information so they could "determine that the statements should be taken seriously."

- If the accused's information is specific and credible so as to constitute reasonable grounds to take it seriously, the police must restate the right to counsel because questioning will go beyond the exploratory stage.

- During the exploratory stage of a new, unrelated offence, the right to counsel does not have to be restated.

In the *Sawatsky* case, an arrested person was asked exploratory questions about an unrelated arson. Once the accused had identified the house and the motive for the arson, the officer could take the statement seriously because of specificity and credibility. The exploratory stage ended there. The officer was obliged at this point to restate the right to counsel.

Another common occurrence is to arrest a person for one offence during a time when the same person is suspected of having committed other (multiple) offences. The procedure is to inform the accused of the right to counsel in relation to the original offence and question him or her for the purpose of obtaining a confession for that offence. Afterward, questioning can continue regarding the other offences; however, the questions should be directed to one offence at a time. The issue is whether the right to counsel has to be restated before questioning about each offence that the arrested person is suspected of having committed.

The Manitoba Court of Appeal in *R. v. Witts* (1998)[51] settled that issue. In that case, officers arrested the accused for assault with a weapon. After questioning about that offence, the investigating officers questioned the accused about a specific break and enter. The accused confessed. The right to counsel was restated after the confession. Interrogation continued regarding other break and enters. The accused confessed to one additional break-in at a specific place and an attempted break and enter at another. Officers took the accused for a ride to identify a third place. The accused did so.

After returning to the police station, the accused was told he would be charged with these three additional offences. The right to counsel was read to him again after the confessions. One hour later, he was interrogated about two other break and enters. He confessed to both. The right to counsel was restated after the confession. The accused gave six written confessions.

The trial judge excluded the first confession, but allowed the five remaining ones. The accused's appeal to the Manitoba Court of Appeal was allowed and he was acquitted on all counts. The following reasons were given:

▸ The police were backward in restating the right to counsel. The pattern used was to question, receive verbal inculpatory statements, and then read the right to counsel. The officers had grounds for suspecting the accused's involvement. There was no reason why the right to counsel should not have been stated before the break and enter questioning because this investigation was unrelated to the original reason for his arrest.

▸ Although the nature of the offence did not change (they were all break and enters), the severity significantly increased when the number of offences jumped from one to four. Each offence involved a house, which has a maximum penalty of life imprisonment. A s. 10(b) Charter violation occurred when the interrogation continued without reminding the accused of the right to counsel.

▸ It is not necessary to read the right to counsel in a "rote-like" manner. "It is sufficient to simply remind the accused that the rights previously extended to him are still available to him with respect to possible new charges."

▸ The confessions were excluded under s. 24(2) Charter in accordance with the principles created in *R. v. Stillman* (1997). The confessions were deemed to be conscriptive evidence and no suggestion existed that the accused's involvement would have been discovered by alternative means.

SECTION 7 CHARTER: PRINCIPLES OF FUNDAMENTAL JUSTICE

Right to Remain Silent

If you read s. 7 Charter, you will not see the phrase "right to remain silent." It is not printed in the Charter, but it is a right that does exist. The S.C.C. in *R. v. Hebert* (1990)[52] confirmed that s. 7 Charter incorporates the right to remain silent as a measure to prevent compelled self-incrimination. This right gives the choice to the accused to decide whether to speak to the police or remain silent. If an accused chooses freely to answer questions, the right to silence is waived.

If the right to remain silent is deprived, then a s. 7 Charter violation has occurred.

The S.C.C. created the following three procedural guidelines relating to the right to remain silent:

1. In the absence of eliciting behaviour, no s. 7 Charter violation occurs. **Eliciting behaviour** is any conduct that forces the accused to answer questions after he or she has invoked the right to remain silent.
2. The right to remain silent applies only to detainees.
3. The right to remain silent does not affect the use of undercover police officers prior to detention.

After a person is arrested or detained, he or she has a choice about answering questions. If the right to remain silent is invoked, a confession cannot be elicited by asking questions afterward. The accused must initiate conversation about the offence after the right is invoked, thereby waiving the right to remain silent. This means that when an arrested person says, "I don't want to answer questions" or "I won't talk to you," the right to silence is invoked and questioning must end. The police cannot initiate conversation about the offence after the right is invoked.

However, the right may be waived by the accused by either answering relevant questions about the offence or initiating conversation about it. Once the accused chooses to speak to the police the right has been waived, which eliminates the possibility of a s. 7 Charter violation occurring.

These rules do not apply to persons who are not detained or under arrest. Persons who are questioned by consent and are not under arrest may choose initially to remain silent and not answer questions. However, if the police continue questioning and the accused later confesses, no s. 7 Charter violation will have occurred. If the suspect is not under arrest, the police may initiate conversation or continue questioning if the accused initially chooses to remain silent. This rule was established by the S.C.C. in *R. v. Hicks* (1990).[53]

The final issue is whether the police have a mandatory obligation to use the phrase "right to remain silent" when warning or cautioning an accused. The police in Canada do not have to inform an arrested person specifically of the right to remain silent; that is done in the United States. In Canada, the formal caution is read to the accused, which has the same effect because it informs the suspect that he has no obligation to speak to the police. The phrase "right to remain silent" is not included in the formal caution used by Canadian officers. The British Columbia Court of Appeal in *R. v. Van Den Meerssche* (1989)[54] ruled that failure to inform an accused of the right to remain silent is not a s. 7 Charter violation. The following S.C.C. case law decision is an example of how s. 7 Charter was applied in a significant case.

The fundamental right to remain silent was used to exclude confessions made by an accused person to an undercover police officer in *R. v. Hebert* (1990).[55] The accused person was arrested for robbery. He was informed of his right to counsel and he was cautioned. After consulting with counsel, he chose not to make a statement, thereby invoking his right to remain silent. He was placed in a police cell-block with an undercover police officer, who initiated a conversation. The accused made inculpatory remarks to the officer. The Supreme Court of Canada ruled that s. 7 was violated and excluded the confession under s. 24(2) Charter.

The court concluded that "tricking" the accused person into confessing after the accused had exercised his right to counsel and declined to make a statement violated s. 7, despite the fact that the police were relying on the pre-Charter decision of *Rothman v. The Queen* (1981)[56] regarding the status of an undercover police officer being a person not in authority. Section 7 was deemed to be broader than the Confession Rule.

The admissibility of confessions made to undercover police officers includes the following rule: if an accused person invokes his or her right to remain silent he or she waives it if he or she decides voluntarily to speak to police (i.e., initiates a conversation), having full knowledge and appreciation of the consequences.

Judges' Rules

The **Judges' Rules** are guidelines established in England in 1912 for judges and police officers. They are not statutory requirements in Canada, meaning they are not law, but they have been adopted by Canadian courts to assist in determining the admissibility of accused persons' statements. Application of the Judges' Rules does not guarantee admissibility. Conversely, failure to adhere to the Rules does not result in automatic exclusion.[57] By adhering to the Judges' Rules, officers may facilitate proving that a confession was voluntarily made; in other words, using these rules is an advantage to the police.

The Supreme Court of Canada in *R. v. Fitton* (1956) stated that the ultimate test of statement admissibility remains the issue of voluntariness, not compliance with the Judges' Rules.[58] The Judges' Rules are paraphrased as follows.

1. The suspect should be cautioned before questioning if intention or reasonable grounds exist to arrest or charge. The time chosen to caution is not proven merely by the officer's decision. The court will determine at what stage a reasonable officer should have formulated reasonable grounds, after examination of the circumstances. The accepted formal caution is:

   > Do you wish to say anything in answer to the charge? You are not obliged to say anything unless you wish to do so, but whatever you say may be given in evidence.

2. Questioning is proper without cautioning the suspect if no intention or reasonable grounds exist to arrest or charge the suspect.
3. Persons in custody should not be questioned without a caution.
4. An accused should be cautioned before volunteering a statement, even if he or she has been previously cautioned.
5. The caution should be used in its formal manner.
6. Spontaneous utterances, referring to statements made by an accused to an officer before there is time to caution, are admissible. The caution should be administered as soon as possible after the spontaneous utterance.
7. Cross-examination and leading questions are prohibited when the accused is making a voluntary statement. Clarifying questions are permitted (e.g., What time? To whom are you referring?).
8. If there are two or more accomplices and one gives a separate statement, allow all of them to read the statement. Do not invite a reply; if a response is made, caution the person who makes it. The reader's immediate reaction,

conduct, and verbal response should be noted; it may signify adoption of the statement's contents as being true. The adopted statement may become admissible.

9. Strive to obtain any accused person's statement in writing, which has been read by the accused and signed by him or her at the end. Failure to obtain a written statement or the accused's refusal to sign it does not negate admissibility; the determining factor about the admissibility of a confession remains the confession's voluntariness.[59]

Significance of the Caution

- ▸ A caution is not a statutory requirement.
- ▸ Questioning a suspect under circumstances that equate to mere suspicion does not require a caution.
- ▸ A caution is required if reasonable grounds exist that the person being interrogated committed the offence.
- ▸ The caution may remove minor inducements.[60]
- ▸ A secondary caution may remove minor inducements made by any officers during any interrogation, prior to a statement being given by the accused. The formal secondary caution is the following: "If you have spoken to any police officer or anyone with authority or if such person has spoken to you in connection with this case, I want it clearly understood that I do not want it to influence you in making any statement." The secondary caution is not a statutory requirement.[61]
- ▸ The final phrase "may be given in evidence" should not be altered to include "used against you." It may be construed as an inducement despite the admissibility of statements in the past when the altered version has been used.[62]
- ▸ In *R. v. Guerin* (1987),[63] the court ruled that "repeated cautions" are not necessary "at every step" of the examination. Repeated cautions should be used only when excessive time has elapsed between interrogations to render the initial caution ineffective. Regardless, the Ibrahim Rule (the Confession Rule) remains the primary determinant.

Youth Criminal Justice Act and Admissibility

The relevant right-to-counsel rules pertaining to adults also apply to young offenders. However, additional rules pertaining to admissibility of statements made by accused persons or suspects aged 12 to 17 years, inclusive, are established by the *Youth Criminal Justice Act* (Y.C.J.A.).

Sections 25 Y.C.J.A. requires that every young offender be informed of the right to counsel not only upon arrest or detention, but also at any stage of the proceedings against a young offender, including before or during a decision whether to institute alternative measures. In other words, a young offender must be informed of the right to counsel any time the police speak to him or her, whether or not the young offender is under arrest or the young offender is being interrogated by consent when mere suspicion exists.

Section 146 Y.C.J.A. extends a young offender's rights. No statement, oral or written, made by a young offender to a person in authority is admissible unless the young offender is informed of the right to consult with (a) counsel, (b) a parent, (c) an adult relative, or (d) any other appropriate adult chosen by the young person, and is given a reasonable opportunity to consult with them. The reference to the admissibility of any statements requires compliance with s. 146 Y.C.J.A. when an officer questions a young offender with the young person's consent, if only mere suspicion exists.

A young offender may waive the rights, but the waiver must be in writing. No such requirement exists for adults.

Section 146 Y.C.J.A. raises two questions regarding non-compliance with its provisions:

1. Does a s. 146 Y.C.J.A. infringement constitute a s. 10(b) Charter violation?
2. Does a s. 146 Y.C.J.A. infringement affect the admissibility of confessions? Confessions are not mentioned in the section.

Appeal courts have ruled that non-compliance with s. 146 Y.C.J.A. constitutes a s. 10(b) Charter violation.[64] In relation to confessions, s. 24(2) Charter will apply to determine admissibility.[65] Generally, self-incriminating evidence is usually inadmissible when obtained after a s. 10(b) Charter violation.[66]

The Supreme Court of Canada established additional significant guidelines relating to young offender confessions in *R. v. T. (E.)* (1993).[67]

▸ The opportunity to consult with an adult is not an alternative to the right to counsel unless the right to counsel is waived. Section 146 Y.C.J.A. has the appearance of allowing a parent to be an alternative to counsel; a parent is not an alternative to counsel unless the young offender waives the right to counsel in writing. To lawfully waive the right to counsel, a young offender must be aware of the consequences of waiving this right.

▸ In situations where a young offender makes two confessions and the first is inadmissible because of a right-to-counsel Charter violation, the second statement may also be inadmissible even if the young offender speaks to a lawyer before the second confession.

Common-law guidelines have been created to assist the courts in the determination of a young offender's statement. Included are the following:

▸ An adult relative should accompany the young person to the questioning site.
▸ The young offender will decide who is present during an interrogation (e.g., counsel, parent, adult relative, or any adult).
▸ Questioning must occur as soon as possible after arrival at a police station.
▸ The young offender must be cautioned in a manner understandable to him or her. Emphasis must be added to an explanation of the consequences of making a statement.
▸ Any charge must be explained sufficiently to ensure the young person's comprehension of it.
▸ If the young person is 14 years of age or older and is charged with a "presumptive offence"[68]—for example, first or second degree murder, manslaughter, or aggravated sexual assault—the youth must understand that he or she may be sentenced as an adult.

In summary, the basis of admissibility of a young offender's statement is contingent upon:

- the age and intelligence of the young person,[69]
- the compatibility of the investigator's language with the young person's intelligence to explain the provisions of s. 146 Y.C.J.A., and
- proof beyond a reasonable doubt that the young person understood all that was explained.

The following three decisions reflect these principles when the young person invokes s. 146(4) Y.C.J.A. by waiving his or her rights. A court's acceptance of a young person's waiver is dependent on the following:

1. A police officer has not complied with s. 146(2) Y.C.J.A. by merely reading the rights from a form and not explaining them.[70]
2. The explanation of the rights must be in language appropriate to the young person's age and intelligence.
3. The young person must
   - understand what is being waived,
   - understand the consequences of waiving his or her rights, and
   - waive his or her rights in writing.[71]

Voir Dire

The admissibility of a confession made to a person in authority is decided at the trial during a hearing called a voir dire. A **voir dire** is a judicial proceeding conducted during the trial. The purpose of a voir dire is to determine whether evidence, such as confessions, will be admissible or excluded. A voir dire may be referred to as an admissibility hearing. It has also been called a trial within a trial. A voir dire is never conducted before a trial.

During a voir dire, the trial judge will decide whether

- the confession was voluntarily made,
- a Charter violation occurred before the confession,
- s. 24(2) Charter applies, or
- the confession will be admitted or excluded.

Additionally, a voir dire may be used to determine the status of the person who received the confession regarding whether he or she was a person in authority or not in authority.

The Crown has the onus during the voir dire to prove that a confession was voluntarily made. This means that the officer in charge of the case should subpoena all officers who had any contact or conversation with the accused between the time of arrest and the time the confession was obtained. These officers should be added to the witness list in the Crown brief.

The accused has the onus to prove whether a Charter violation occurred.

A jury will never be present during a voir dire. The trial judge is exclusively responsible for the decision about admissibility, not a jury.

The defence may admit admissibility by waiving the voir dire.[72] During the Crown's case at a voir dire, the following four questions are relevant regarding voluntariness:

1. Did anyone threaten the accused person or promise him or her anything?
2. Did the accused believe the person could make good the promise or threat?
3. Did the accused make the statement because of the promise or threat?
4. Were the statements the product of an operating mind?[73]

PROCEDURE

1. The trial must be under way. A voir dire cannot be conducted before the trial. Consequently, officers can only predict the admissibility of a confession before the trial.
2. The officer who received the confession is called to the stand. The officer testifies about the circumstances and the conversation prior to any inculpatory statement made by the accused. However, the officer cannot read the statement; a voir dire must be conducted first.
3. The judge declares that a voir dire is commencing.
4. If a jury exists, they leave the courtroom. A voir dire is conducted in the absence of a jury. The trial judge is solely responsible for determining admissibility.
5. The Crown has the onus to prove voluntariness. The Crown calls witnesses, usually beginning with the officer who took the confession, who is already on the stand. All other officers who conversed with or came in contact with the accused are also subpoenaed and called to testify. The Crown examines each witness about the circumstances leading to the confession. The relevant issues are whether promises or threats were made. The confession itself is not read during the voir dire.
6. The defence is allowed to cross-examine all Crown witnesses.
7. The defence is allowed to call witnesses, usually the accused, to raise a reasonable doubt about the voluntariness of the statement. Additionally, the defence may seek exclusion of the confession under s. 24(2) Charter; however, the defence has the onus to prove whether any Charter violations occurred.
8. The judge decides whether the confession is admissible or not and the jury returns. If inadmissible, the confession will never be read during testimony. If admissible, the officer who received the confession reads it in the presence of the judge and jury.

DETERMINING PERSON IN AUTHORITY

Another purpose of a voir dire is to determine whether the person who received a confession is a person in authority. The reason that a defence lawyer will try to change the status of a citizen from a person not in authority to one who is, is to force the Crown to prove voluntariness of the confession during a voir dire. A confession to a person not in authority is automatically admissible. If the defence can successfully change that status to a person in authority, then the confession is not automatically admissible. The Crown will have the onus to prove voluntariness. A voir dire is then required where Charter violations and s. 24(2) Charter may exclude the confession.

The principles and procedures relating to this type of voir dire were created by the S.C.C. in *R. v. Hodgson* (1998).[74]

▸ "The defence must raise the person-in-authority issue with the trial judge." This means that the defence must make a motion in the form of a verbal application to challenge the status of a person not in authority. In other words, the defence has the onus to ask for a voir dire.

▸ During the voir dire, the defence has the burden of proof, or onus, to prove that the person who received the confession actually is a person in authority. This means the defence has the onus to prove that the accused reasonably believed that the person to whom he or she confessed acted on behalf of the state or could influence or control the proceedings against him or her.

▸ If the defence is successful, the Crown then has the **persuasive burden** of proving beyond a reasonable doubt that the receiver of the confession was not a person in authority. If the Crown fails to do so, then the Crown has the onus to prove the voluntariness of the confession.

▸ In extremely rare cases, the judge may direct that a voir dire be conducted solely on his or her decision, without a motion by the defence requesting it. This is possible only if the evidence introduced at the trial suggests the need for a voir dire to determine the status of the receiver of the confession. These cases are extremely rare because of the obligation on the defence to request a voir dire.

In summary, officers must be prepared to prove that citizens who receive confessions did not act as state agents and do not control or influence the accused's proceedings in court. Officers can only predict whether the defence will make a motion to challenge the status of a person not in authority.

The best procedure to be prepared for a voir dire regarding the status of the receiver of a confession is to include all the circumstances and verbatim conversation relating to the accused's confession to the citizen. Precise details of the events surrounding the confession will allow the Crown to make an effective argument in the event that a voir dire is conducted.

Case Study 17.1 Conclusion

The first assumption by investigators was that the report had been fabricated. The report was validated after investigation eliminated any logical motive to falsely report the stolen payroll.

Subsequently, the daughter, Alicia was suspected of participating in the offence and was questioned. She denied being involved. She told officers that she told only her boyfriend Dylan about the payroll. Dylan was questioned; he denied committing the offence. During the interview, Dylan provided confidential information about several incidents. Included in his information were incriminating facts about Seth. He informed police that he had told Seth about the payroll. Seth was familiar with the house, having delivered food there previously. Seth later told Dylan that he had entered the house through unlocked patio doors and had stolen the payroll.

Dylan's information provided reasonable grounds. Investigators intended to preserve his informant status and chose not to subpoena him to court.

Seth was arrested at his house on December 10 at 6:20 p.m. He was cautioned and informed of his right to counsel. He stated that he understood both. En route to the police station, Seth invoked his right by asking to call his lawyer. He phoned his lawyer from the police station at 6:25 p.m., two minutes after arriving there. The lawyer was not available. Seth left a message with the lawyer's answering service. The call concluded at 6:32 p.m. Seth remained in an interview room. No conversation occurred between 6:32 p.m. and 6:36 p.m.

At 6:37 p.m., the police officer initiated the following conversation while waiting for Seth to exercise his right to counsel:

Police Officer: "I've got this list of the stolen cheques. Do you still have them?"

Seth: (No response.)

Police Officer: "Did you destroy them? These are all payroll cheques. Did you cash them?"

Seth: (Shook his head, indicating no.)

Police Officer: "Then did you destroy them?"

Seth: "Let's put it this way, I haven't got them."

Police Officer: "Are they still around or not?"

Seth: (pause) "They're destroyed."

Police Officer: "Did you destroy them yourself?"

Seth: "They're destroyed, honest."

Police Officer: "Okay. Where are they? Did you burn them?"

Seth: "They're at the bottom of the canal."

Police Officer: "You threw them in yourself?"

Seth: (Nodded his head, indicating yes.)

Police Officer: "Whereabouts in the canal?"

Seth: "Train bridge."

Police Officer: "What are the cheques in?"

Seth: "This leather thing." (Showed size with his hands.)

Police Officer: "What colour is it?"

Seth: "Brown, I think."

Police Officer: "And you didn't cash any of them in?"

Seth: "No, they didn't interest me."

Police Officer: "Do you have any of the cash to give back to the owner?"

Seth: "No, not a cent."

Police Officer: "You spent everything?"

Seth: "Everything. I gave lots away."

Police Officer: "That reminds me. Why did you give Doug Smith money?"

Seth: "For dope. Then the jerk stiffed me."

Police Officer: "How much did you give him?"

Seth: "Fifteen hundred dollars."

Police Officer: "And how much dope could you buy for that?"

Seth: "Oh, about two pounds."

Police Officer: "And he stiffed you for the whole thing?"

Seth: "The jerk never gave me an ounce."

Police Officer: "How did you know exactly where the money was?"

Seth: "Well, I didn't. I went in to look for DVD players and things like that. Then I found the money and took it instead. I didn't want the cheques on me."

Police Officer: "So you spent the rest?"

Seth: "I only spent about $800. I gave the rest away, bought beer for people. I went out a lot."

Police Officer: "How much money did you steal?"

Seth: "There was $4800."

Police Officer: "But you went right to the cash. How did you know it was there?"

Seth: "I heard about it, that it was there."

Police Officer: "There was another guy with you?"

Seth: (Shook his head.) "I went in alone."

Police Officer: "Do you know anyone else on this list?" (referring to the cheques)

Seth: "No. I can't really remember the names."

Police Officer: "Did you ask Smith to get rid of them [the cheques]?"

Seth: "No way. Cheques don't interest me. I didn't want to keep them long."

Police Officer: "Did you talk to Smith about the cheques?"

Seth: "I know he's into that. But I'm not."

Police Officer: "Do you want to give a statement?"

Seth: "I'll tell you what I just said. Sure. The cheques are gone, really."

Seth subsequently gave a written confession. At 7:05 p.m. Seth's lawyer phoned the police station and spoke to Seth.

During the trial, a voir dire was conducted. The trial judge ruled that the statement was voluntarily made. However, Seth's s. 10(b) Charter right to counsel was violated and the confession was excluded under s. 24(2) Charter, on the basis that its admission would bring the administration of justice into disrepute. In spite of this, the trial judge commended the officer's honesty and lack of malice.

ENDNOTES

1. Section 24(2) Charter.
2. Section 10(b) Charter.
3. *R. v. Schmautz* (1990), 53 C.C.C. (3d) 556 (S.C.C.).
4. Section 25(2) Y.C.J.A.
5. *R. v. Anderson* (1984), 10 C.C.C. (3d) 204 (Ont. C.A.).
6. Ibid.
7. Section 25 Y.C.J.A.
8. Ibid.
9. Ibid.
10. *R. v. Brydges* (1990), 53 C.C.C. (3d) 380 (S.C.C.).
11. *R. v. Hermanus* (1993) (B.C. Prov. Ct.), as in (1993) vol. 12, no. 35 *The Lawyers Weekly*.
12. Section 24(2) Charter.
13. *R. v. Bartle* (1994), 92 C.C.C. (3d) 289 (S.C.C.)
14. Section 24(2) Charter.
15. *R. v. Jackson* (1993), 15 O.R. (3d) 709 (Ont. C.A.).
16. Ibid.
17. *R. v. Evans* (1991), 63 C.C.C. (3d) 289 (S.C.C.).
18. Ibid.
19. Ibid.
20. Ibid., at 305.
21. Canadian Criminal Justice System, Ontario Police College précis (1986).
22. *R. v. Hollis* (1992), 76 C.C.C. (3d) 421 (B.C.C.A.).
23. *R. v. Burlingham* (1995), 97 C.C.C. (3d) 385 (S.C.C.).
24. *R. v. Hollis*, supra note 22.
25. *R. v. Manninen* (1987), 34 C.C.C. (3d) 385 (S.C.C.).
26. *R. v. Hollis*, supra note 22.
27. *R. v. Smith* (1989), 50 C.C.C. (3d) 308 (S.C.C.).
28. *R. v. Hebert* (1990), 57 C.C.C. (3d) 1 (S.C.C.).
29. *R. v. Pavel* (1989), 53 C.C.C. (3d) 296 (Ont. C.A.).
30. *R. v. Whitford* (1997), 115 C.C.C. (3d) 52 (Alta C.A.).
31. *R. v. McKane* (1987), 35 C.C.C. (3d) 481 (Ont. C.A.); *R. v. LePage* (1986), 32 C.C.C. (3d) 171 (N.S.C.A.).
32. *R. v. MacKenzie* (1991), 64 C.C.C. (3d) 336 (N.S.C.A.).
33. *R. v. Pavel*, supra note 29.
34. *R. v. Ferron* (1989), 49 C.C.C. (3d) 432 (B.C.C.A.).
35. *R. v. Top* (1989), 48 C.C.C. (3d) 493 (Alta. C.A.).
36. *R. v. Whitford*, supra note 30.
37. *R. v. T. (E.)* (1993), 86 C.C.C. (3d) 289 (S.C.C.).
38. *R. v. Hebert*, supra note 28.
39. Section 146 Y.C.J.A.
40. *R. v. Hermanus*, supra note 11.
41. *R. v. Prosper* (1994), 92 C.C.C. (3d) 353 (S.C.C.).
42. Ibid.; *R. v. Clarkson* (1986), 25 C.C.C. (3d) 207 (S.C.C.).
43. Section 146(4)(b) Y.C.J.A.

44. *R. v. Clarkson*, supra note 42.

45. *R. v. Whittle* (1994), 92 C.C.C. (3d) 11 (S.C.C.).

46. *R. v. Prosper*, supra note 41.

47. *R. v. Smith*, supra note 27.

48. *Smith v. The Queen* (1991), 63 C.C.C. (3d) 313 (S.C.C.).

49. *R. v. Evans*, supra note 17.

50. *R. v. Sawatsky* (1997), 118 C.C.C. (3d) 17 (Ont. C.A.).

51. *R. v. Witts* (1998), 124 C.C.C. (3d) 410 (Man. C.A.).

52. *R. v. Hebert*, supra note 28.

53. *R. v. Hicks* (1990), 54 C.C.C. (3d) 575 (S.C.C.).

54. *R. v. Van Den Meerssche* (1989), 53 C.C.C. (3d) 449 (B.C.C.A.).

55. *R. v. Hebert*, supra note 28.

56. *Rothman v. The Queen* (1981), 59 C.C.C. (2d) 30 (S.C.C.).

57. *R. v. Fitton* (1956), 116 C.C.C. 1 (S.C.C.).

58. Ibid.

59. Lecture, Ontario Police College, 1984.

60. Ibid.

61. Ibid.

62. P.K. McWilliams, *Canadian Criminal Evidence*, 3rd ed. (Aurora, ON: Canada Law Book, 1991).

63. *R. v. Guerin* (1987), 78 C.C.C. (3d) 380 (Que. C.A.).

64. *R. v. P.R.C.* (1993), 78 C.C.C. (3d) 442 (Sask. C.A.).

65. Ibid.

66. *R. v. Elshaw* (1991), 67 C.C.C. (3d) 97 (S.C.C.).

67. *R. v. T. (E.)*, supra note 37.

68. Section 2(1)(a) Y.C.J.A.; R.J. Marin, *Admissibility of Statements* (Aurora, ON: Canada Law Book, 1989).

69. Ibid.

70. *R. v. M. (M.A.)* (1986), 32 C.C.C. (3d) 566 (B.C.C.A.).

71. *R. v. W. (B.C.)* (1986), 27 C.C.C. (3d) 481 (Man. C.A.), as in E.L. Greenspan and M. Rosenberg, *Martin's Annual Criminal Code* (Aurora, ON: Canada Law Book, 2008).

72. Marin, supra note 68, at 214.

73. *R. v. Sweryda* (1987), 34 C.C.C. (3d) 325 (Alta. C.A.).

74. *R. v. Hodgson* (1998), 127 C.C.C. (3d) 449 (S.C.C.).

CHAPTER 18

Interrogation Principles and Procedures

LEARNER SUMMARY

Some people will have you believe that **interrogation** is a coercive or even barbaric procedure. Lawyers, for example, get paid to try to exclude confessions by attempting to prove they are the product of unethical methods. Anyone who believes that interrogation is some sort of heinous procedure is not thinking of the victim. Interrogation is a vital skill for all police officers, both uniform patrol officers and detectives, to prove a wide range of offences.

Confessions are the best type of evidence to form reasonable grounds and prove guilt beyond reasonable doubt. In many cases, interrogations accelerate an investigation, resulting in a quick solution and the resolution of a large number of crimes in a relatively short time.

Some offenders confess with minimal questioning. Others require more extensive questioning. Why do people confess their crimes? We all have some degree of compulsion to confess. Various theories and opinions exist about why people confess, but there is no solid foundation of empirical data.

Interrogation is an inexact science. There is no one method that works in every case. Successful interrogation requires a combination of procedures and methods to suit the circumstances and the offender. Officers develop and use a wide range of techniques in the absence of studies that suggest or prove that any one single procedure is more effective than the next.

However, three factors contribute significantly to successful interrogation:

1. **Verbal communication skills** The ability to verbally communicate to all types of offenders is critical to success. Interrogation is essentially an extremely focused, advanced form of verbal communication. It cannot be emphasized enough to those who want a police career that this verbal communication is a vital skill in many aspects of policing, especially interrogation.

2. **Analytical thinking and instinct** During interrogations, instant decisions are made about what to ask or say. Decisions are made based on the responses and behaviours displayed by the suspect, combined with the interrogator's logical analysis of the responses.
3. **Experience** As with any skill, repeated practice is necessary to develop effective interrogation skills.

This chapter discusses theories relating to why people confess, general interrogation principles, and specific interrogation procedures for optimum results.

Case Study 18.1

Joe: "Ah my friends. I have a guilty conscience."

Police Officer 1: "That's terrible. It's not a nice thing to have."

Joe: "This thing's been bothering me. I want to get it off my chest."

Police Officer 1: "Oh really? What's that?"

Joe: "I want to clear a few B & Es up. From a few years ago."

Police Officer 1: "Oh yeah? How long ago? You want to start in '75?"

Joe: (laughs) "Hey, not that long ago. There's just one that's been bothering me. I've had a guilty conscience."

(Refer to the end of Chapter 18 for the conclusion of this case study.)

AUTHORITY TO INTERROGATE

The Ontario Court of Appeal in *R. v. Moran* (1987) stated that "A police officer is entitled to question any person whether reasonable grounds or mere suspicion exist, to determine whether an offence has been committed and who committed it."[1]

The point of this quotation is that the police may ask questions of a person who is under arrest for an offence and one who is not. The person being questioned has the right to remain silent and refuse to answer. Additionally, the police have no authority to

- arrest or detain a person specifically for the purpose of questioning, or
- compel any person to answer questions.[2]

There are two circumstances in which interrogations occur:

1. when reasonable grounds exist and the accused has lawfully been arrested, and
2. when mere suspicion exists. No arrest can be made. The suspect may be interrogated by consent only. The suspect must voluntarily accompany the officer.

Procedural rules apply to both situations.

Finally, when multiple suspects are involved in one offence, a decision must be made about whom to question first.

CONSENT INTERROGATION: MERE SUSPICION

If only mere suspicion exists that a suspect committed an offence, the investigator can choose to interrogate the suspect at the end of an investigation, when all other methods of formulating reasonable grounds have been exhausted, or at the beginning of an investigation, when the investigator is confident that a confession will be elicited from the suspect. Confidence can be attributed to the suspect's propensity to confess to crimes, based on

- past confessions given to police, or
- opinions of persons known to the suspect.

However, regardless of when the interrogation occurs, in the absence of reasonable grounds it must be conducted with the accused person's consent. No lawful authority exists in Canada to arrest or detain a person for the sole purpose of questioning. Consent can be obtained in two ways:

1. The best method is to telephone the suspect and ask him or her to be at the police station at a scheduled time. The reasons why this is the best method are that:
    ▷ The police are not involved in transporting the suspect, which helps prove consent and voluntary accompaniment.
    ▷ The suspect knows he is not under arrest. Many suspects believe that cooperation will help direct suspicion from themselves and they are confident that their denial will suffice to eliminate suspicion.

    This method has been proven to ensure voluntary attendance. Do not fabricate a reason for the request. State the precise reason for this request. For psychological reasons that will be explored later in this chapter, informing a person that the police wish to question him or her regarding, for example, "break and enters you have committed," "a store you have robbed," or "a woman you have sexually assaulted," usually creates sufficient internal conflict to cause the suspect to resolve it by attending the scheduled questioning session.
2. Personally find the suspect and ask him or her to accompany you voluntarily to the police station.

The officer has the onus to prove that the consent was valid. This requires proof of an absence of a psychological compulsion to confess. Valid consent comprises several components:

- The accused's consent must be unequivocal, meaning it must be clear, unmistakable, and not ambiguous.
- Consent must be voluntary, meaning free from coercion or any other external conduct that prevents the accused the freedom to choose whether to give consent.
- The accused must be aware of the specific act to be conducted by the police (e.g., an interrogation).
- The accused must be aware of the consequences of giving consent (e.g., criminal charges may be laid and the confession may be used in court).

- ▸ The accused must be aware that consent may be refused. No obligation exists to give consent and no one may be charged for refusing to consent.
- ▸ The accused must be aware that consent may be revoked at any time, after it is given.
- ▸ If the accused gives consent, for that consent to be valid, the onus is on the officer to show that the accused never revoked it at any time after.[3]

If an adult suspect attends the interrogation, the caution and right to counsel are not necessary, but the investigator must be confident and accurate that the facts obtained during the investigation do not constitute reasonable grounds before the interrogation starts.

A consent interrogation involving a young offender does require a right to counsel because s. 25(1) Y.C.J.A. requires one to be given at every stage of the proceedings. A waiver of a young person's rights must be in writing and must be signed by the young person.

If the suspect revokes his or her consent at any time during the interrogation, he or she cannot be detained. In this situation, the investigator has two alternatives:

1. Terminate the interrogation and allow the suspect to leave.
2. Regain consent and record verbatim the conversation that regained consent.

What follows are relevant factors that may serve as guidelines to prove that a suspect was never detained at any time during a consent interrogation. The officer should note:

- ▸ the precise language used by the officer to request the suspect to attend at the police station. When recording notes or testifying in court, officers should not paraphrase by stating, "the accused gave consent." Instead, verbatim conversation (i.e., a direct quote) should be recorded in notes and stated during testimony. The trial judge will decide whether consent was valid and, if given, it was not revoked.
- ▸ whether the officer escorted the suspect to the police station or whether the suspect provided his or her own transportation. The latter method is preferred to help prove consent.
- ▸ why the circumstances actually constituted mere suspicion and not reasonable grounds. The onus is on the officer to prove only mere suspicion existed and that an arrest was not justified. However, a trial judge will determine whether mere suspicion or reasonable grounds existed.
- ▸ the suspect's belief. This is the determining factor. The suspect must believe that he or she was not detained.[4]

PROCEDURE: UNSUCCESSFUL CONSENT

Should the interrogation not elicit a confession, or if the suspect fails to attend a consent interrogation, the following alternatives exist:

1. **The suspect can be the target of surveillance before arranging the interview and before he or she attends at the police station.** The suspect will know the investigator is suspicious. Surveillance may result in witnessing the suspect disposing of evidence, or speaking to other persons.

Subsequently, these persons can be interviewed to determine if inculpatory statements were made to them by the suspect. These recipients will likely be classified as persons not in authority.

2. **The police can use an informant.** They can send an informant to the suspect's house to be present when the investigator phones to request a consent interrogation, for the purpose of noting statements or reactions by the suspect. If the suspect attends a consent interrogation and it fails, an informant can be sent to speak to the suspect afterward for the same purpose.

3. **The final alternative is to make additional requests to obtain consent at a later date.** Initial failure should not prevent future attempts to conduct a consent interrogation. Significant internal conflict may cause the suspect to change his or her mind later.

REASONABLE GROUNDS TO ARREST

If reasonable grounds exist and an arrest is made, specific procedures should precede an interrogation. These procedures will ensure that any confessions obtained by officers will be admissible.

1. The police officer should identify himself or herself as such regardless of whether the officer is wearing a uniform or plain clothes. This identification should include the officer's rank and name. The officer should clearly state that his or her occupation is that of police officer. Production of a police badge should accompany the verbal identification.

2. Tell the suspect that he or she is under arrest.

3. Take physical custody of the accused. Usually, touching or holding the accused's arm suffices.[5] (The above three steps are not statutory requirements. They are performed for the purposes of a voir dire, to prove that the accused was speaking to a person in authority, and proving the facts-in-issue should the accused escape custody, resist arrest, or assault the officer.)

4. Caution the accused in accordance with the Judges' Rules. However, the standard version is not a statutory requirement. An informal caution may be acceptable and desirable to facilitate understanding, if it includes the essential elements of the standard version. ("You don't have to tell me anything about this charge. You're not being forced to say anything. If you want to say anything or give a statement, it's entirely up to you. But if you say anything, it can be used in court.")

5. Inform the accused of the reasons for the arrest, in compliance with the statutory requirement found in s. 10(a) Charter and s. 29(2) *Criminal Code*. A description of the offence will suffice at the scene of an offence, if the specific charges are not known. The accused must be informed of the specific charges as soon as is practical.

6. Inform the accused of his or her right to counsel, in compliance with the statutory requirement found in s. 10(b) of the Charter. The standard version is, "It is my duty to inform you that you have the right to retain and instruct counsel without delay. Do you understand?" If the accused does

not understand, explain the right by using the term "lawyer." If the accused does understand, ask him or her to explain it to prove that he or she does understand.

7. Inform the accused of the existence and availability of Legal Aid, in compliance with the Supreme Court of Canada ruling in *R. v. Brydges* (1990).[6] Ask whether this is understood; repeat the procedure used for right to counsel. Do not inform the accused that a lawyer or Legal Aid will be appointed to him or her. This may constitute an inducement because it is misleading. Legal aid must be applied for; rejection is a possibility. Inform the accused of a toll-free telephone number for Legal Aid to comply with the S.C.C. *Bartle* decision.

8. If the accused invokes his or her right to counsel, allow appropriate phone calls to be made as soon as is practical. A suggested practice is to ensure that the calls are made at a police station. Allowing calls at the scene of an arrest can result in consequences detrimental to the officer and to public safety. An arrested person may suffer from internal conflict that might be resolved in escape or violence toward the officer. Allowing the freedom to use telephones at the scene of the arrest increases these possibilities. The admissibility of statements should not supersede the prevention of behaviour detrimental to safety. All statements made during the interval between invoking the right to counsel and speaking with a lawyer will likely be inadmissible in court. The officer has one alternative: have the accused repeat the statements after he or she has spoken to a lawyer.

9. If the accused does not invoke his or her right to counsel, commence interrogation. The accused's waiver should be recorded verbatim.

10. If the accused person is a young offender, the preceding steps must be made in language that can be proven to be comprehensible to the young offender. The right to counsel must be accompanied by asking the accused whether he or she wishes the presence of parents, adult relatives, and any adult who may assist the young person. A waiver of these rights must be in writing and must be signed by the young person. Ask the young person to explain the information given in each step.

11. The onus is on the arresting officer to prove beyond a reasonable doubt that this format has been complied with. To remove doubt, the precise verbatim conversation should be recorded in the officer's notebook as soon as is practical afterward, ensuring that the notes are contemporaneous. General comments and paraphrasing should be avoided. (For example, avoid saying, "The accused was told the reason for arrest, cautioned, and informed of his right to counsel. He understood all of it.")

Initial Assessment

Once a suspect is arrested, an officer can decide whether an interrogation is needed because the suspect may intend to confess. This discussion can be made simply by asking the suspect, "What happened?" This question, which is not considered an inducement, usually causes one of three reactions:

1. **Immediate confession** Some suspects immediately volunteer confessions without questions. An interrogation under these circumstances is not only unnecessary, it may needlessly jeopardize the voluntariness of the confession. Admissibility is virtually certain.

2. **Denial or alibi** The suspect may make exculpatory statements. If disproved, the statements may become inculpatory. In addition, the inference can be made that the suspect has waived his or her right to remain silent.

3. **Remain silent** This circumstance indicates that questioning may have to be preceded by a waiver of the right. Two alternatives exist:

   ▷ Ask questions not directly related to the offence (e.g., activities before the offence, personal status, etc.). Voluntary answers may imply a waiver.

   ▷ Delay the interrogation after a commentary has been made to the suspect summarizing the offence and the evidence obtained during the investigation. A delay may afford time for the suspect's conscience to be sufficiently activated, causing the suspect to converse, thereby reversing the right to remain silent when the interrogation resumes.

   Questioning a suspect who has chosen to remain silent does not violate the right if the suspect is not denied the right to choose whether to remain silent or not.[7]

Multiple Accused Persons

Investigations commonly result in the simultaneous arrest of multiple accomplices. A decision is required to determine the first person to be interrogated. The purpose of correctly deciding is to obtain a confession from the first accomplice for the others to read and adopt.

The decision can be confidently made by

- researching past arrests of the suspects and learning which ones have confessed,
- questioning the arresting officers about who was talkative and cooperative, and
- considering opinions learned from informants prior to the arrest about who is likely to confess first.

After the decision has been made, the first accomplice should be informed that he or she has been chosen because of the belief that he or she is not the most dangerous offender and his or her conscience better understands the moral wrong of the offence.

If a written confession is obtained implicating other accomplices, begin the second and subsequent interrogations by allowing the accomplices to read the written confession. Do not invite a response immediately; instead, note any verbal statement or physical conduct (e.g., nodding head), which may be inculpatory. If the statement is accepted, the accomplice has adopted it. Regardless of this adoption, obtain a written confession to corroborate the first inculpatory statement.

If the accomplice denies the truth of the first accomplice's confession statement, interrogate him or her about it. Ask the accomplice whether the statement is entirely fabricated. If the accomplice claims total fabrication, ask whether he or she would give a witness statement to that effect for the purpose of charging the first accomplice with public mischief and obstructing justice. If the suspect denies that the statement is fabricated, record the denial verbatim; it may be inculpatory. Continue the interrogation.

INTERROGATION PREPARATION

Successful interrogations are the result of knowing all the evidence and circumstances and knowing how to activate a person's conscience.

Case Knowledge

A successful interrogation cannot be conducted in the absence of complete knowledge of all the evidence and circumstances of the investigation preceding the interrogation. Commonly, a CIB officer is required to interrogate a person who has been arrested by a uniform officer. The CIB officer may not have participated in the preliminary investigation. The following actions should precede the interrogation:

1. Speak to the arresting officer personally. Do not rely on written reports. Thorough and accurate reports may be lacking because of the experience required to master this skill.
2. Determine the following:
    ▷ the reported observations of all witnesses,
    ▷ the existence or absence of physical evidence, and
    ▷ the precise conversation between the uniform officer and the suspect, including the verbatim dialogue of location and time of arrest, reason for arrest, right to counsel, caution, all statements made by the accused, both inculpatory and exculpatory.
3. If necessary, visit the crime scene to acquire the necessary familiarity with that environment.
4. Determine the existence or absence of the suspect's criminal history.
5. Learn the suspect's personal history (e.g., age, marital status, occupation or employment, and relationship to victim, if applicable).

Failure to prepare thoroughly results in the inability to detect deception and ask effective questions to elicit honesty.

Interrogation Location

All formal interrogations should be conducted at a police station, never anywhere else. This environment removes familiarity from the suspect. Removal of familiarity is essential because (a) detection of deception is greatly facilitated and (b) the accused will not consider his or her use of deception to be a viable alternative to the resolution of internal conflict. People tend to feel more comfortable about lying in familiar surroundings.

Interrogations conducted in an environment familiar to the accused, therefore, have two disadvantages: (a) deception will not be easily detected and (b) the suspect's propensity to be deceptive increases.

Two types of rooms are available for interrogation:

1. a standard, small, interrogation room, composed of cement block walls, no window, a table, and three chairs, or
2. a spacious, contemporary office constructed and furnished unlike the standard type.

The spacious office is the preferred room because

- it exemplifies professionalism, an essential element to elicit a confession,
- detection of deception is easier, and
- its evidentiary value for the purpose of a voir dire is higher.

Diagrammed in the officer's notebook should be a description of the room, including the precise seating arrangement, all furniture and items in the room, and entrances and windows.

To prevent any disruptions, notify all office staff that an interrogation is being conducted and disconnect telephone service to the chosen room to further prevent office staff from mistakenly disturbing the interrogation.

Number of Officers

A confession of an offence is essentially an act of confidential honesty. It is common for people to confide in others such as clergy, doctors, psychologists, teachers, coaches, family members, and friends. Some common elements are associated with confidential honesty, including (a) telling one person privately, (b) familiarity, and (c) trust.

Confidential honesty is disclosed usually to one person, in private, who is trusted and familiar. It is not usually disclosed to a group. This concept is the same in relation to confession to the police. The only difference is that the suspect and the officer are often unfamiliar with each other and the trust that is associated with familiarity is sometimes absent.

A one-officer interrogation has proven to be beneficial and usually is the best method to obtain a confession. The reasons are that the suspect only has one officer to judge in relation to trust and to gain familiarity with, and it is compatible with the theory that confessions are more easily made to one person privately rather than to a group. There is limited time during an interrogation to develop the necessary familiarity and trust. It is much easier to develop it when only one officer is questioning the suspect. If two officers interrogate, the time and effort increase.

Familiarity and trust do not necessarily mean kindness and friendship. Acquiring familiarity and trust means gaining knowledge about the officer's expertise, competence, and professionalism. A strong determinant regarding confessions is the suspect's perception of the officer's level of expertise.

Another advantage of a one-officer interrogation is the communication style and procedure. Interrogation is a communication skill that is developed in stages. No one masters it in a short time or becomes an immediate expert. There are distinct varying degrees of expertise, as with any other skill. Therefore, it is likely that two officers may have different levels of expertise. Inexperience tends to cause communication mistakes. A two-officer interrogation is most effective when:

- The officers have experience working together. This means they have experience communicating to one person, which is a skill itself.
- The communication method resembles a one-on-one conversation.

Effective communication often is premised on a one-on-one basis, rather than in a group, especially when it involves the elicitation of confidential honesty. This technique will be explained later in this chapter.

It is common to have a two-officer interrogation simply to have another officer witness the questioning. This practice has been the product of pressure and paranoia created by courts and society that police have minimal credibility about what happens inside an interrogation room. A witness should not be necessary to corroborate a police officer. One officer alone should be capable of recording notes and establishing his or her own credibility. It is common for police officers to be conditioned to believe that everything they do needs a witness for it to be believed. It is a sad commentary about the perception of policing if a two-officer interrogation is needed simply for corroboration. The use of videotape, explained later in this chapter, will help eliminate the need for a witness to be in the interrogation room.

In summary:

1. One-officer interrogations are highly effective because they are compatible with the principles of why people confide honest disclosures.
2. Two-officer interrogations are effective when the officers have experience in questioning a suspect together and use a communication style that resembles a one-on-one conversation.
3. Two officers should be the maximum number of officers present during an interrogation. More than two officers is ineffective because their presence may constitute an inducement that may exclude a confession. Also, the method of communication will not be compatible with the reasons why people confess.

Other People Present During an Interrogation

Sometimes relatives, friends, or the lawyer of the suspect will want to attend the interrogation; sometimes the suspect will ask that they be allowed to attend. However, the presence of a lawyer, relatives, or friends deters honesty. People need privacy to confess to a crime and are more likely to confess if they are talking to only one person. Persons seeking emotional and spiritual comfort after violating moral laws do not confess their sins before two or more priests or a congregation of people; religious confession is predicated on the privacy afforded by the priest–penitent relationship. Interrogation is not unlike that concept. Interrogation should be conducted on a one-on-one basis.

There are methods to solve an adult offender's request for extra people to be present during an interrogation. If the accused asks that relatives or friends attend, simply ask for the reason. If the suspect has no intention of immediately confessing, delay the interrogation. Afterward, inform the suspect that the presence of these people will interfere with honesty. Tell him or her that the absence of relatives or friends will neither benefit the investigators nor worsen his or her situation.

If s. 10(b) of the Charter is invoked, allow consultation with a lawyer. Consultation with a lawyer does not prevent the suspect from confessing afterward. If the accused invokes his or her right to remain silent, comply with the decision. At an appropriate time after the lawyer–client consultation, begin a conversation with the accused about an unrelated topic and then direct the conversation to the offence. The accused may withdraw his or her right to remain silent by voluntarily denying the offence. Ask the accused to explain his or her denial. The accused's continued denial of the offence may be construed as implied withdrawal or waiver of the right to remain silent.

The Supreme Court of Canada in *R. v. Smith* (1989) quoted K. Jull: "There is nothing inherently wrong with the taking of a statement from a person who feels the need to relieve guilt pressures and who therefore waives his right to counsel."[8]

A second alternative to dealing with the right to remain silent is to simply regain consent from the accused. Many suspects do not make their right to remain silent absolute. In reality, officers should be aware that suspects do revoke their right to remain silent and confess to the offence even after having consulted with their lawyer. Often they voluntarily withdraw their right when asked to discuss the offence. An effective method is to ask the accused to listen to a different perspective of the offence, and tell the accused that he or she is not required to answer any questions. If consent is given, the different perspective should involve a discussion about the moral wrong of the offence.

If the interrogation involves a young offender, the rule is simple: the young person will decide who will be present. Conduct the interrogation in compliance with the young offender's desire for whom he or she wants present.

Theoretical Concepts

Interrogation is a unique conversation that emerges during the interaction between people, consisting of *situational dialogue and conduct* intended to elicit information. The challenge of interrogation is that the information sought:

1. is self-incriminating, and
2. provides no tangible benefit to the person who confesses.

Naturally, there is some resistance by the offender. A strategy is needed to persuade the offender to agree to self-incrimination that gives him or her no tangible benefit.

Interrogation expertise exclusively depends on communication mastery. It is a science that involves a complex interaction of *stimulating an offender's conscience while building rapport.*

Conscience and *rapport* are concepts that when linked together form a potent, legally acceptable method of persuasion that will elicit confessions.

COMPULSION TO CONFESS THEORY

Think of a time when you did something that you believed was wrong—something that contradicted your personal values:

1. Did you experience an unpleasant feeling?
2. How was that unpleasant feeling eliminated?

Now, think of a time when you did something wrong but it did *not* bother you. Can you think of a reason why a wrongful act did not create a very unpleasant feeling? Think about these two scenarios during the discussion relating to conscience.

A successful interrogation requires two general elements:

1. A belief that the suspect is capable of confession regardless of the nature of the crime and the suspect's history. Negativity often surrounds confession. "He won't confess. He's been through this before" is an example of a negative attitude that will interfere with or prevent an effective interrogation.
2. A willingness to devote the time necessary to elicit a confession. Some offenders confess with little or no questioning. Others need extensive questioning. A commitment is needed to invest adequate time.

These two elements create a proper attitude and confidence that an accused will confess.

Before learning how to obtain a confession, it is important to understand the reasons why people confess. An interrogator often has an advantage over the suspect simply by knowing the reasons why people confess. The primary reason that people confess is the **compulsion to confess**, which is an internal urge, caused by the conscience, to alleviate internal conflict. We often hear that some person has "no conscience." Theorists claim that this is not true. Every person has a conscience. The degree to which the conscience is developed varies. Some people have a poorly developed conscience, while others have a strongly developed one. Numerous factors are involved in the development of a conscience. One of the primary factors is the degree of moral values, which simply refers to the ability to distinguish between right and wrong.

Committing a wrongdoing causes a degree of **internal conflict**. The feeling of guilt creates a degree of pressure. Every person has some level of a compulsion to confess, which is a mechanism to relieve guilt pressures and remove the internal conflict. The compulsion to confess is a trait that gives an advantage to the interrogator. The desire to relieve guilt pressures and conflict is a significant benefit that has to be used fully.

Theoretical evidence that supports the compulsion to confess generated by the conscience is found in (a) Theodore Reik's conscience theory, and (b) Leon Festinger's cognitive dissonance theory.

Conscience Theory

Sigmund Freud theorized that human personality is composed of three subsystems: the id, the ego, and the superego.[9]

The **id** is the primitive system governed by the pleasure principle. It seeks instant gratification and avoids pain. Urges created by the id are not in harmony with reality. An infant is governed solely by the id.

The **ego** is the part of the personality that is in closest touch with social reality. Unlike the id, the ego is governed by the reality principle. Gratification is not abandoned; it is merely postponed. As the infant grows older, he or she learns that realities may interfere with immediate gratification, but gratification is not prohibited. Once the ego is developed, strategies are learned to achieve the desired gratification by socially accepted means.

The **superego** develops with maturity. This part of the personality judges whether the ego's performance was good or bad. Superego development signifies the formation of a **conscience**. The superego represents the internalization of socially and culturally accepted rules. The superego rewards acceptable ego behaviour with feelings of pride and punishes the ego's deviant conduct with feelings of remorse and guilt.[10]

Struggles with the id, ego, and superego create unconscious internal conflict. Internal conflict is initially activated by **anxiety**, an intensely unpleasant emotional state similar to fear. A person tends to alleviate anxiety in any way possible.[11]

Theodore Reik, a Freudian theorist and psychiatrist, hypothesized that a compulsion to confess exists within every person. The compulsion is derived from internal conflict created by the id's desire for immediate gratification and the ego's challenge to the id's desires.

A strong compulsion to confess is dependent on several factors:

▸ If the id's need to express impulses is condemned by external realities, a weaker ego can only express them by means of a confession.

▸ If the stress generated by the ego to repress the id's impulses is sufficiently intense, a confession is a way of returning the repression. "Repression starts from the ego and confession returns to the ego."

▸ A confession is the superego's attempt to reconcile a conflict between the id and ego.

▸ A confession is the superego's (conscience's) attempt to punish an act perceived as wrong.[12]

In summary, Reik theorized that every person not only has a compulsion to confess, but also that the compulsion can be strengthened or weakened because it is a fluctuating concept, not a constant one. Interrogation questions and comments are intended to activate or strengthen the compulsion to confess and prevent weakening it.

Cognitive Dissonance Theory

According to Leon Festinger, **cognitive dissonance** is an uncomfortable, unpleasant, internal conflict caused by the individual's perceived inconsistencies between his or her (a) beliefs and knowledge and (b) behaviour. In other words, cognitive dissonance develops within a person when that person commits an act he or she believes is wrong.

Every person strives to attain consistency within himself or herself. Consistency depends on behaviour that is harmonious and compatible with his or her beliefs and knowledge. It may be considered a feeling of knowing that what he or she is doing is right, not wrong.

Festinger hypothesized that cognitive dissonance is a psychological tension that has **motivational characteristics**, meaning it will motivate the person to attempt to reduce dissonance by doing something to achieve consistency.[13]

A confession may be the conduct designed to reduce internal conflict if the suspect recognizes that his or her conduct was incompatible with his or her beliefs, not the beliefs of others.

Questions and comments made during interrogation are intended to allow the accused person to recognize

1. the incompatibility between his or her beliefs and conduct or, in other words, to emphasize to the offender that what he or she did was actually wrong.
2. that the internal conflict can be alleviated. The offender may be instructed that the guilt feeling or internal conflict may be eliminated by confessing.

Evaluating and Activating the Compulsion to Confess

An individual's compulsion to confess can be categorized as either strong or weak. A strong compulsion will result in a confession. The compulsion to confess is not constant within a person; it is a fluctuating urge. A person's compulsion will activate during an interrogation. Continual evaluation of the individual's compulsion is necessary to avoid questions and comments that weaken or fail to strengthen it.

A person with a **weak compulsion** to confess is characterized as being:

▸ id-oriented, having an underdeveloped superego (conscience) or an undersocialized ego that has not successfully internalized social rules. Under these circumstances, the superego may not easily punish the act by confession if the act is not perceived to be sufficiently wrong.
▸ morally deficient, which prevents the person's immediate perception that his or her conduct is inconsistent with his or her beliefs. The person does not believe that the act committed was wrong. Under these circumstances, the individual's weak cognitive dissonance may not provide sufficient motivation to confess.

Therefore, the primary determinant of a strong or weak compulsion is how the suspect perceives his or her actions or behaviour. There are two general perceptions that an offender has about his or her crime. The accused may perceive the offence as either *morally wrong* or *selfishly wrong*.

Morally wrong refers to an offender's belief that someone other than himself or herself has or will suffer the worst consequence for the crime. These consequences include

▸ victim's injuries, fear, or loss of property,
▸ adverse effect on the accused's family, or
▸ potential harm to future victims if the crimes are repeated.

A morally wrong belief causes more pressure from guilt and internal conflict than a selfishly wrong belief. It strengthens the compulsion to confess and results in a confession.

Selfishly wrong refers to an offender's belief that he or she will suffer the worst consequence for the crimes. The consequences include

- prison or other sentence,
- loss of job and income, or
- poor reputation because of bad publicity.

A selfishly wrong belief causes minimal internal conflict and weakens the compulsion to confess. A confession will not likely occur.

The objective of interrogation is to strengthen the compulsion to confess to a sufficient degree for a confession to be required to relieve the internal conflict. Generally, this involves the following objectives:

- causing the offender's conscience to perceive the crime as being morally wrong instead of selfishly wrong, and
- motivating the offender to reduce cognitive dissonance and achieve cognitive consistency.

EVALUATING DEGREE OF COMPULSION

Before choosing an interrogation plan, the offender's degree of compulsion to confess should be evaluated; this will determine the nature of questioning. It can be done by simply asking, "What do you think is wrong with (type of offence)?" and "What do you think is the worst consequence of (type of offence)?" The accused's answers will fall into one of the two perceptions of the offence. He or she will indicate whether he or she believes the crime was morally or selfishly wrong by the response. Afterward, a decision can be made about the degree of strengthening needed to activate the offender's compulsion to confess.

There is no one specific method or procedure that will motivate the offender's conscience or strengthen the compulsion to confess. Instead, it requires a combination of methods and techniques that must be compatible with the specific circumstances of the interrogation.

CONCEPT OF RAPPORT

At first glance, the concept of rapport pertaining to a police–offender relationship seems to be a contradiction because of the inherent tension, distrust, or animosity that is associated with it. Despite those environmental elements that are incongruent with rapport, a degree of rapport must exist to elicit a confession; it is the essence of all successful communication.

Rapport should not be confused with meaning a warm, friendly relationship. Instead, there is a much broader meaning that includes a complex unifying bond that develops and manifests in a variety of ways.

The following are general principles that are critical to interrogation rapport building:

- Rapport will be stifled unless the involved persons clearly understand their *roles*. Although it may appear obvious, the offender must know that the officer is not the judge or jury. Instead, the officer has a legal obligation to investigate the offence, not to decide on or administer punishment. How is this conveyed? The police do not have to apologize to the offender for having to investigate or interrogate him or her. Instead, it is conveyed through an *absence of animosity* toward the offender. In other words, we don't have to like what harm offenders bring to others, but we don't have to vocalize our dislike. The offender's role is simple—he or she has a *problem* that needs to be solved. When both sides understand these salient points, the critical rapport foundation has been built.

▸ Rapport is not possible unless the involved parties agree on some common beliefs. A difference of beliefs, especially when conveyed emphatically during conversation, produces *conflict* to some extent. Confessions or admissions of confidentiality are unlikely to emerge when communication is surrounded by hostility or acrimony. Rapport, conversely, develops when *agreement* occurs, referring to the sharing of common beliefs. Agreements generate understanding of each other's roles to an extent where distrust starts to disappear. Agreements should not be confined with needless or insincere sympathy. Instead, they are acknowledgments that both parties understand that one has a problem and the other has to solve it.

▸ Agreements do not have to be *announced* to exist. More often, there is a mental, or *cognitive*, acceptance of what has been communicated where the agreement is not actually verbally acknowledged.

▸ Agreements can be reached on a number of topics during an interrogation:

   ▹ **Causes** Every act, including criminal ones, has a cause. Accurate identification of the cause by the officer will result in the offender's agreement mentally. It is human nature to provide an excuse for an act first before actually admitting to it. Understanding, not sympathizing with, the cause once it is agreed upon is a major rapport builder.

   ▹ **What is important to the offender** Every person has a clear set of priorities that can be identified and agreed on during communication.

   ▹ **The victim's suffering** Victims suffer impact from crime in different ways. Offenders are more than capable of agreeing with this fact during discussion.

   ▹ **Offender's desire to change** Regardless of long-term habits, offenders usually have some desire to change this life, particularly when the *benefits* of the change are clearly articulated.

   ▹ **The act was wrong** If the offender removes himself from the crime, he should agree with you that the act itself was wrong and not socially acceptable.

   ▹ **The existence of a problem** Human nature prevents us from responding favourably to hard criticism. However, when strategically linked to *causes*, the interviewer's suggestion that the offender has a problem will be listened to and accepted, if the offender perceives that the interviewer understands the *connection between cause and crime*.

   ▹ **The offender's rational conflict** An emphatic, articulate communication about the features and consequences of cognitive dissonance will be believed and agreed on by the offender because, to some extent, he or she will be suffering the effects of it.

> ▷ **The benefits of a confession** Conveying to an offender that a confession removes cognitive dissonance and is an integral element of behavioural change will be at least considered by the offender and, depending on the interviewer's skill, it will then be agreed on. This agreement is the most potent one—which, when fully accepted by an offender, will not only strengthen rapport, it should sufficiently persuade the offender to take that course of action.

- The number of agreements made is directly proportionate to the strength of the rapport.
- Communication occurs in three ways: words, tone of voice, and body language. Research shows that:
  - ▷ 55 percent of communication results from *body language.*
  - ▷ 35 percent of communication results from *tone of voice.*
  - ▷ only 7 percent of communication results from *words.*

  This means that the majority of rapport is developed through body language including facial expressions, gestures, and the quality of countless subtle movements. Words represent the factor that contributes least to rapport.[14] Unfortunately, body language is not a science learned through formal study. It is learned through experience and formed by habit.
- Rapport is enhanced by revealing your competence. A potent rapport builder is revealing yourself as a competent, trustworthy professional (see Chapter 3).

Finally, we all have experienced rapport building and confession elicitation in non–law enforcement relationships. For example, some parents are outstanding interviewers capable of eliciting a multitude of confessions from their children. Spouse–spouse, girlfriend–boyfriend, teacher–student, coach–athlete, and employer–employee are other relationships where we have been both interviewer and offender. The experiences learned in these relationships are invaluable. We internalize many of the behaviours that have succeeded. The only difference between these relationships and police–offender is that some of them have created long-term rapport, whereas police–offender relationships often begin with no rapport. Otherwise, rapport building can be guided by a blueprint of general guidelines but our successes will depend on the totality of life experiences.

INTERROGATION TECHNIQUES

Several interrogation techniques will be explained in this section. All are based on personal experience and have been proven to be effective during actual interrogations. Before explaining them, the following points must be emphasized:

- Every interrogation is unique. Each one is composed of certain dialogue suited to the circumstances of the case and to the suspect.
- The uniqueness of every interrogation means that there is no specific technique or set method that will positively work in every case. Also, there is no specific order in which the techniques must be used. For example, there is no one method or order of questions that will always work to get a confession for a break and enter or any other specific offence.

- ▸ The listed techniques are suggested methods that may be used in any interrogation. They are not exclusive to a certain type of offender.
- ▸ There is no scientific research or evidence that proves that any one set method will always work. Interrogative techniques are largely opinions based on personal experience. If experienced officers were asked about what techniques work, there would be many different responses.
- ▸ The techniques should be used in combination to suit the type of offender and nature of the offence.

The most important fact to remember is that the success of any interrogation technique is dependent on advanced verbal communication skills. The manner in which questions and comments are conveyed determines the success or failure of an interrogation.

Skeptics also fear false confessions as a consequence of interrogation. Yet what would motivate a rational person to admit criminal responsibility for an act, despite his or her innocence? In *Hardy's Trial* (1794),[15] L.C.J. Eyre said, "The presumption upon which declarations are evidence (against a defendant) is that no man would declare anything against himself, unless it were true."[16] B. Parke in *Slatterie v. Pooley* (1840)[17] said, "What a party himself admits to be true, may reasonably be presumed to be so."[18]

Additionally, the Supreme Court of Canada in *R. v. Smith* (1989) stated that confessions "may contribute to the person's rehabilitation and reintegration into society as a responsible individual."[19]

List of Techniques

What follows are the most common and effective methods for eliciting a confession. Each technique will be explained in greater detail after this list.

- ▸ Focusing on the reason.
- ▸ Determining the accused's role.
- ▸ Determining the accused's perception of the offence.
- ▸ Using subcultural deviance theory.
- ▸ Eliciting a partial confession
- ▸ Conveying informant information.
- ▸ Explaining existing evidence.
- ▸ Eliciting personal admissions.
- ▸ Calling the accused a liar.
- ▸ Identifying the accused's goals and priorities.
- ▸ Convincing the accused of the need to change.
- ▸ Playing on internal conflict.
- ▸ Explaining the benefits of a confession.
- ▸ Conveying an accomplice's confession.

These are the general categories from which specific methods are established. All may be used in one-officer or two-officer interrogations. If two-officer interrogations are used, a specific proven procedure that involves a cycle of one-on-one dialogue (as explained) should be used.

Finally, two other techniques that have proven effective will be explained. They are (a) unrelated conversation and (b) monologue.

FOCUSING ON THE REASON

Probably the most effective method is to ask *why* a person committed an offence, instead of asking *whether he did* commit the offence. Never ask a suspect, "Did you do it?" Instead, ask, "*Why* did you do it?" Asking for a reason is the best way of eliciting an inculpatory statement because

- ▸ It emphasizes to the offender that there is no need for a confession.
- ▸ It removes the debatable issue of whether the suspect committed the offence. The issue is not whether he or she committed it, but rather why he or she did it.
- ▸ Asking the suspect whether he or she did commit the offence increases his or her confidence that little or no evidence exists to support a conviction.
- ▸ It causes the offender to perceive that the officer is confident that sufficient evidence exists.
- ▸ Offenders often make up a reason that they believe is a suitable defence or excuse for the officer not to charge them. Any reason given proves the identity of the offender, which at least satisfies the officer that an innocent person has not been accused.
- ▸ It tends to remove deception as a choice. Lying usually increases when a person is given an option that includes a denial.

If a denial is given, be persistent. Continue asking for a reason. Emphasize that, "There has to be a reason why you did this." Another effective statement to make is, "I need to know the reason." Although neither of these statements are inducements, care has to be taken not to imply that a certain reason will favour or worsen the suspect's prosecution or sentencing.

If denials continue, it is acceptable and effective to suggest reasons, such as, "Were you broke? Did you need money? Did you do it for drugs?" These are leading questions but they are not threats or promises.

In some cases, the suspect asks, "Why do you need to know a reason?" or, "Why is the reason important?" The answer that has been acceptable and effective is a factual response: "I need to know so I can make decisions to make sure you don't do this again." The reason is needed to help prevent future repetition of the offence.

All responses, including denials, must be recorded verbatim in notebook entries.

Additionally, a response may include conduct, such as shrugging shoulders or simulating the injection of a needle into the forearm. These responses are inculpatory statements. Notebook entries and testimony must include explanation of the act without paraphrasing or making conclusions. An example of how to explain conduct is "He placed his right hand near his left forearm and moved his right thumb up and down."

An additional benefit of asking why the accused committed the offence rather than whether he or she did commit it is that it emphasizes that the investigator has no evidentiary need for a confession. Offenders may give obviously deceptive reasons. Do not debate the reason; extend questioning from it. The deceptive reason is inculpatory.

DETERMINING THE ACCUSED'S ROLE

Sometimes, when only one person is suspected or arrested, it is easy to forget that he or she may not have acted alone and may have committed the offence with accomplices. The suspect being interrogated may have simply played a role in the offence. Determining the suspect's role is another way to remove the issue of whether he or she did it. The issues become what role the accused had and who he or she did it with.

Instead of asking "Did you do it?" ask any of the following:

▸ "Who helped you?"
▸ "Who did it with you?"
▸ "How many people were involved?"
▸ "Did you do it alone?"
▸ "What did you do, drive?"
▸ "What did the others do?"

Asking "Did you do it alone?" may be the initial question. It removes the issue of whether the accused committed the offence. The response may be inculpatory.

When determining the suspect's role, leading questions that suggest answers are effective. For example:

▸ "Did you keep six [watch out]?"
▸ "You didn't actually break in [or rob, etc.], did you?"

These suggestions imply a lesser role, one that the accused may admit to. Finally, after the accused admits his or her role, the accomplices' identities need to be established.

DETERMINING THE ACCUSED'S PERCEPTION OF THE OFFENCE

The accused must be convinced that the offence is morally wrong, not selfishly wrong. However, some offenders have underdeveloped moral character and do not perceive right from wrong appropriately, resulting in a weak compulsion to confess.

In these cases, the accused's perception of the offence has to be altered. Questions and statements must be made to convince the accused of the moral wrong that was committed, to strengthen his compulsion to confess.

▸ Emphasize the victim's suffering and need for peace by having the accused identified. This can be conveyed by explaining the "TV syndrome" from which victims commonly suffer. They fear repetition of the offence and that the accused is psychotic. Example: "I just want to be able to tell the victim that we know who did this and that he's not a deranged maniac who'll harm her again."
▸ Compare the victim with a member of the accused's family. Ask the accused to imagine his or her mother or grandmother suffering from the effects of the crime.
▸ Inform the accused that his or her family is suffering because of the criminal activity. Remind the accused that family members love and care for him or her, emphasizing their intense desire for the accused to cease criminal behaviour.

- Stress the greater consequences that could have resulted from the act; that is, whatever the offence was, emphasize that someone may have been killed or injured.

- Emphasize the hurt that potential victims may suffer in the future by the accused's repetition of criminal acts, unless that behaviour terminates; that is, other victims will suffer loss of property or may be injured if the crimes continue.

- Avoid passing negative judgment. Instead, inspire the accused by reinforcing methods of correcting deviant conduct, such as making decisions and a commitment to change. Challenge the accused to decide upon an altered lifestyle. After a true decision is made, a confession may relieve guilt pressures and facilitate the accused person's rehabilitation and reintegration into society.[20]

- Inform the accused about the severity of the offence and simply emphasize that what he or she did was very wrong and that he or she is failing to understand that it is wrong. Many offenders simply have never been told that what they do is morally wrong. It is possible to change an offender's perception of right from wrong in a relatively short time by emphatic, convincing communication that the specific crime committed is not socially acceptable. A multitude of statements can be used to convince the offender. It's also effective to explain why moral deficiency develops. Summarize social rules that the accused may have failed to internalize. That is, the accused's upbringing may not have taught him or her proper values. Consequently, the accused may rationalize justification for his or her conduct.

- Ask the accused what bothers him or her. A common misconception is that criminals are heartless and have no feelings of guilt. Experience has shown otherwise. Repeat offenders who appear to be cold and ruthless do express feelings of remorse. Eliciting this feeling from a suspect requires the suspect to alter his or her perception of the behaviour by asking him or her simply:

  - "Does this bother you?"
  - "Does it bother you to hurt people? It has to bother you."
  - "I know it must bother you."
  - "It probably bothers you so much that it eats you up. You try to hide it, but you really want to stop and change so that doing this won't bother you anymore."

These questions and statements will have a profound impact. They force the suspect to think of others and to reflect on the behaviour. The suspect likely has never had to do this before. He or she may appear to be disinterested but surely will be resurrecting some feelings of guilt, remorse, and internal conflict. The key factor is to persist with this technique until some response is given. It is a mistake to abandon this technique if it is met with silence.

USING SUBCULTURAL DEVIANCE THEORY

The subcultural deviance theory suggests that association or exposure to delinquency causes the adoption of criminal values.[21] A number of interrogative techniques derive from this theory. A desire is correlated to establish and maintain a compatible status with peers from the subculture. The internalization of aberrant morals and values, combined with an effort to attain acceptance and loyalty of other subculture members, is an impetus for deviance.

In other words, the theory implies that criminals are the product of their environment. Some begin to understand the severity of their deviance. Their awareness becomes advantageous during interrogation. An offender's repeated exposure to the criminal community is the basis for a number of effective interrogation techniques:

1. **Discuss psychological and sociological explanations of deviant conduct**
   This discussion may allow the accused to recognize the causes of his or her behaviour. Essentially, blame is transferred from the accused to other sources. For example:

   ▷ alcohol or drug abuse,

   ▷ personality or mental disorders, which can be corrected by treatment, or

   ▷ failure to internalize acceptable social rules due to parental neglect, parental abuse, familiarization of deviant behaviour by excessive exposure to member(s) of criminal subcultures, and society's inability to provide means to achieve goals.

2. **Explore the need for psychological help** Committing a break and enter, robbery, or sexual assault is not normal behaviour. Those acts clearly suggest that the offender may have psychological problems.

3. **Tell the accused what he or she did or continues to do is not normal** He or she will not argue with that. Ask the accused, "Have you ever thought of getting a psychologist's help?" or, "Have you ever thought that you need psychological help?" The effectiveness is based on persistence and not being malicious or insulting. There has to be a sincerity about these questions. If the questions are not perceived by the suspect as being insulting, he or she may continue the dialogue and agree that he or she has in fact thought of it, and may choose to accept this as an explanation for repeated criminal acts. It has been proven that questions directed at the need for psychological help do have an impact on offenders. These types of questions are not inducements. They are not threats or promises. Avoid telling the suspect that you will help him or her "get help" if he confesses because, as explained in the previous chapter, this constitutes an inducement.

4. **Appeal to the accused's need for recognition** Many criminals have either failed at or been unable to achieve socially accepted goals. Their need for achievement is translated to criminal activity instead. When they succeed at it, a sense of pride and a desire for recognition result. This manifests in an urge to brag. Boasting about crimes is an advantage because of the obvious inculpatory statements that may compose the bragging. A boastful criminal may be condescending, annoying, or insulting, so it requires patience to promote and encourage this behaviour. If the suspect shows a

need to express knowledge, encourage it by acting dumb. Some criminals enjoy believing that they are smarter than the police about criminal activity. For example, some criminals will brag about large numbers of break and enters, and gloat about not being caught. They do not think that verbal statements are incriminating and they omit specific information about the places believing that the confession cannot be matched to the occurrences. In one case, an offender bragged about how many daytime break and enters he had committed. Although he never admitted the locations, the circumstances were easily matched to the occurrences.

5. **Allow the boastful criminal to express knowledge about other people who are criminally active** It often starts with a statement such as, "You guys don't even know who robbed that gas station last night." This means that he or she is bragging that he or she knows and you don't.

6. **Listen without interruption** Often a boastful criminal needs no special encouragement to continue the dialogue. Others may be encouraged by complimentary remarks about the offence, such as "I know you did this. No one else could think this up (or have planned it this well)." In some interrogations, compare the offender's work with other known criminals and give compliments, such as "Brendan and Sean couldn't have done this. They're too stupid."

7. **Blame accomplices** Some criminals are followers who conform to the behaviour of their associates. Blaming accomplices is effective because the suspect may diminish his or her participation and perceive his or her role in an offence as being less severe. Blaming others may be suggested by saying, "I know this wasn't your idea. I know you didn't think of the plan. It was someone else's idea. You just went along. The guy who thought this up is the real dangerous one." There is no direct promise in any of these statements.

ELICITING A PARTIAL CONFESSION

Complete confessions are the result of activating an accused's strong compulsion to confess. The process may involve a gradual strengthening of a weak compulsion. This can be facilitated by employing strategies intended to obtain a partial confession, which essentially is made up of fragmented inculpatory statements.

A partial confession derives from questions intended directly or indirectly to prove intention, opportunity, any single fact-in-issue, or extensions of these elements. In other words, these responses are intended to connect the accused to the *crime scene*, the *victim*, a relevant *item*, or an *intention*. The following examples may accomplish this, by establishing the accused's

1. knowledge of the victim

    ▹ "Do you know him?"
    ▹ "Do you know where he lives?"
    ▹ "You've known her for a long time, haven't you?"
    ▹ "How long have you been a friend of his?"

2. animosity toward the victim

    ▹ "Do you hate him?"
    ▹ "How long have you disliked him?"
    ▹ "You probably can't stand her, right?"

3. knowledge of the location of a property crime or crime scene
   ▷ "Do you know where the store is or what street it's on?"
   ▷ "The store is on King Street, right?"

4. presence at the crime scene or in its vicinity before, during, or after the offence
   ▷ "When was the last time you were there?"
   ▷ "Have you been there since it happened?"
   ▷ "How often have you been there?"
   ▷ "You get gas there, right?"
   ▷ "You were there yesterday, right?"
   ▷ "Why were you there today?"

5. needs, which may have been fulfilled by the commission of the offence
   ▷ "Were you broke?"
   ▷ "Did you need drugs?"
   ▷ "Have you tried to date her before?"

6. intention of wanting to have committed the offence or of wanting to have had it occur
   ▷ "Have you ever thought of doing something like this?"
   ▷ "Do you think he deserved it?"
   ▷ "Did you ever wish this would happen to him?"

7. possession of means or capability to commit the offence
   ▷ "Have you ever owned a gun?"
   ▷ "Have you ever fired a gun?"
   ▷ "Can you unlock a door without a key?"

The answers to these questions alone do not constitute reasonable grounds. They strengthen the compulsion to confess and may be considered inculpatory statements. A combination of several of these statements may constitute reasonable grounds and may form sufficient circumstantial evidence to convict.

CONVEYING INFORMANT INFORMATION

It is common to hear gossip or seemingly irrelevant information from criminals about other associates or known criminals, including

- relationships,
- places criminals frequent,
- substance abuse, and
- altercations.

The gossip heard about other criminals becomes useful when a person is interrogated who has been the subject of the gossip. Conveying the gossip to the suspect makes him believe that people have been giving information to the police about his or her activities.

An accused's compulsion to confess can often be strengthened if the interrogator implies that there is evidence to prove guilt, even if only mere suspicion exists. One way to do this is to imply that informers have given information about the offence. An accused is often strongly affected when told by the investigator that police informants are in abundance. "Everyone rats on everyone. That's a fact. Happens every day," is an effective technique that is commonly met with an accused's acknowledgment (e.g., "I know, I can't trust anyone"). After the accused acknowledges this fact, ask him or her to think of whom he or she has told about the offence or who has knowledge of some aspect of it. The suspect then is aware of the possibility that an informant implicated him or her.

An investigator can emphasize this fact by casually making the person aware of some unrelated, personal activity of which the investigator has knowledge. This shows the need to acquire gossip from as many sources as possible during daily tours of duty and recording all information learned about active criminals, whether significantly related to criminal activity or not.

Fabrication of the existence of evidence should be avoided. This may prevent exclusion of the statement and the accused may detect the deception if he or she can easily conclude that such evidence could not be available. However, instructing or teaching the accused about available forensic investigation information and procedures (e.g., fingerprints, DNA) should be acceptable, because facts are being related, not lies.

EXPLAINING EXISTING EVIDENCE

When overwhelming evidence exists about a suspect's guilt, the evidence should be explained to the suspect. He will learn about it legally through disclosure. It cannot be concealed after he is charged, so it should be conveyed during the interrogation. Knowledge of the evidence will likely create internal conflict in most suspects and increase the pressure being felt.

ELICITING PERSONAL ADMISSIONS

An extremely effective method to strengthen the compulsion to confess is to elicit personal admissions. This refers to the disclosure of personal facts or opinions that are not directly related to the offence. When a person discloses intimate details of his or her life, a form of confidential honesty is conveyed. This is communicated only when trust has been developed or an internal conflict is being eased. People will disclose very personal details frequently. It is seemingly part of human nature to talk about oneself and to want to talk to someone about a problem or feeling.

The significance of doing so is that the person's urge or compulsion to communicate personal issues is very strong. This is an excellent indicator that the same compulsion will result in a confession.

At any stage of an interrogation, especially during the denial period, the conversation should turn to personal issues. A number of topics may be explored, including relationships, work, financial status, and family. The more intimate the admission, the better. Essentially, this line of questioning is similar to being nosy. No topics are out of bounds. Any personal question should be asked.

CALLING THE ACCUSED A LIAR

Offenders commonly lie when making denials. Many are habitual liars and have been allowed to lie during most of their lives. People who are lied to often allow it without comment. When a deceptive person is told that he or she is a liar, significant internal conflict and pressure occurs. Many offenders who lie by denying an offence do not know how to react to being told that they are lying because they have probably never been called a liar.

For this reason, deceptive answers cannot be overlooked. If you believe that a suspect's response is deceptive, telling him or her that you believe he or she is a liar is extremely effective. It is not an inducement if it is not accompanied with threatening conduct and if it is not repeatedly said in a cross-examination style. After the suspect knows your belief, he or she has choices to make that are foreign because the accused likely will be unfamiliar with the honesty displayed. There is nothing unethical or unlawful about being honest with a suspect pertaining to his or her deceit.

Finally, if the suspect is a repeat offender who has been interrogated before and has been deceitful in the past, convey to him or her that habitual deceit is a serious character flaw that will prevent a successful life. This is a logical statement that has a positive impact on some offenders because they know the truth about the statement. There should be no hesitation to challenge a suspect to end the habitual deception and begin practising honesty.

IDENTIFYING THE ACCUSED'S GOALS AND PRIORITIES

Everyone likely has one or several unfulfilled goals that he or she secretly thinks about. Ask the offender for his or her goals or where he or she wants to be 5 or 10 years from now. If met by silence, suggest as many socially acceptable goals as possible to create a vision of a productive life and person. Additionally, ask the offender to list priorities or, in other words, state what is important to him or her.

CONVINCING THE ACCUSED OF THE NEED TO CHANGE

After his or her goals and priorities are identified, state succinctly the obvious need for behavioural changes. This discussion requires no scientific knowledge. Simply emphasize that behavioural change is conducive to goal fulfillment and create a plan with or without his assistance.

PLAYING ON INTERNAL CONFLICT

The offender's conscience will have created a degree of uncomfortable internal conflict. Explain graphically the consequences of *stress* caused by internal conflict. Stress has severe negative effects on physical and mental health. The explanation should cause the offender to evaluate these consequences seriously.

EXPLAINING THE BENEFITS OF A CONFESSION

Legal benefits cannot be explained to an offender; they constitute an inducement. Instead, explain two major benefits of a confession:

1. relief of stress caused by internal conflict, and
2. the foundation for behavioural change.

CONVEYING AN ACCOMPLICE'S CONFESSION

If an accomplice has confessed in writing or electronically, show it to the person being questioned. At the conclusion, note any uninvited response. If he acknowledges the accomplice's confession as being true, he has actually adopted it as his own confession.

Types of Dialogue

When a suspect does not immediately confess, the type or nature of the dialogue is crucial. There are two types that have been effective: (a) unrelated conversation and (b) monologue.

Unrelated conversation is conversation that is unrelated to the offence. It includes no questions or statements directly related to the offence being investigated. There are two purposes of unrelated conversation:

1. It provides the suspect an opportunity to gain familiarity and develop trust. When two strangers meet and talk, it is rational to pass judgment. The officer wants the suspect to form a favourable opinion of him or her during this stage.
2. It allows the officer to observe subtle conduct. During unrelated conversation, questions should be asked to which the answers are already known or where honesty is expected. The suspect's responses and conduct should be noted to determine his or her honest conduct. This includes the suspect's mannerisms, seated position, eye contact, hand gestures, and other subtle relevant gestures. Some people display contrasting conduct when they lie.

There is no specific amount of time that makes this dialogue effective. It is a case-by-case decision.

An interrogation is not a straight question-and-answer session. It is composed largely of **monologues**, referring to lengthy speeches, directly relevant to the offence, spoken by the officer with little or no response from the suspect. The purpose of a monologue is to introduce as many interrogation techniques as possible to alter the accused's perception of the offence and strengthen the compulsion to confess. A monologue is similar to a lecture in which a combination of questions, comments, and opinions are stated. One of the objectives is for the accused to think about what is being said and begin the cognitive process of making choices.

A monologue is the officer's opportunity to expose the suspect to a different perspective about the offence and the victim and to the interrogation process. Officers are encouraged to use as many techniques as possible during a monologue. Exposing the suspect to a broad range of interrogation techniques is logical because one of them may trigger the desired response. Restricting the number of techniques used may limit the investigator to those that do not work under the specific circumstances.

This interrogation technique is extremely effective for both uniform officers and detectives. Uniform patrol officers may have less time available, but they still need to obtain confessions while investigating a wide range of offences.

Monologues must be uniquely constructed with instant decisions about what to ask or say next. There is no one specific procedure that can always be used. A large part of this skill is the ability to compose a monologue that is suitable and compatible to each specific case. The following is an example of a monologue that includes various interrogation techniques; this monologue is effective and contains no inducements.

Why do you do these things?

There has to be a reason.

You know the reason.

Are you ever going to stop?

Do you ever think about the harm you're causing?

Do you ever think about the people you hurt?

You know you're hurting people.

The victim is suffering. Your family is suffering.

There has to be a reason why you do this.

Is it drugs? Money?

Don't you want to stop getting arrested?

Is this a habit now?

I'm sure you want to change.

This isn't normal. Have you ever thought of getting help?

Don't you think you need help?

It has to bother you to hurt people.

What kind of help will make you change? Tell me. Just ask for it.

Do you care about hurting others?

Do you care about anything? Anyone? What do you care about most?

You have to stop doing this. You really have no choice because you might hurt someone badly someday. Have you ever thought about that?

This wasn't right. It's wrong. You know it's wrong.

You probably have a lot of legitimate reasons for doing these things.

It's not your fault that you didn't learn right from wrong, but now you know. I'm sure it bothers you to do wrong and you know you can't go on.

Did you do this alone? No, you didn't. What did you do?

Who was with you?

The following are examples of inducements that must be avoided during monologues:

Do you know what jail is like?

Do you know what happens to guys like you in jail?

You need an attitude adjustment.

You're going to lose everything.

Who will hire you with a criminal record?

Have you ever been to jail before?

If you don't confess, a judge will think you don't care about what you did.

Do you know how old you'll be when you get out of jail?

Expressive Cop–Silent Cop Cycle

A one-on-one dialogue is the best procedure to ensure optimum communication. In some situations, two officers interrogate. What procedure is most effective? A cycle of dialogue where a one-on-one dialogue is conducted is usually best. This method has proven to be more effective than simultaneous or alternate dialogue that involves a three-way dialogue. The good cop–bad cop method is an example of a three-way dialogue that is personally not recommended. The reasons for avoiding it follow.

Imagine having committed a crime. Two strangers are asking you to confess. One is enraged, displaying venomous malice toward you. The other person is calm, friendly, and unusually supportive of your predicament. Will you feel a desire to confess your misdeed by divulging this innermost secret, which you have in all likelihood not shared with loved ones and cherished companions, to this bizarre pair? Or will your mind be occupied by questions like these?

1. What is the hostile person capable of doing?
2. Why is the other person, an obvious colleague who shares similar intentions, being polite?
3. Are they being sincere? Or are they acting? The dubious authenticity of the traditionally accepted good cop–bad cop interrogation technique may not only be abundantly clear to the offender, but it may

   ▷ insult his or her intelligence, or
   ▷ evoke reciprocating hostility, which will act as the means to alleviate the offender's internal conflict, instead of eliciting a confession.

Also, two interrogators are not able to create the same atmosphere of trust and sincerity that one officer alone can achieve. Therefore, the good cop–bad cop method serves no useful function during a two-officer interrogation; avoid using it.

This does not mean that two officers should never conduct an interrogation together. If two officers know each other well and work well together, they may use a method called the **expressive cop–silent cop cycle**. This method is based on the same principles as the one-officer interrogation. Singular conversation is the fundamental premise of this technique. In this method, each officer takes turns trying to establish a relationship of trust and sincerity while strengthening the accused's compulsion to confess. While one talks to the accused, the other remains silent and takes notes.

PROCEDURE

1. Officer 1 assumes the expressive cop role. He or she begins the interrogation with a lengthy monologue, using comments designed to:
   ▹ alter the accused's beliefs about a wrongful act,
   ▹ cause the accused to perceive the act as being morally wrong instead of selfishly wrong, and
   ▹ permit the accused to judge the officer's sincerity for the purpose of trusting the officer.

   Writing during this monologue eliminates any effectiveness. The expressive cop cannot write notes.

2. Officer 2 remains silent and writes notes.

3. Roles are reversed and a new cycle begins. Role reversal occurs only when Officer 1 has
   ▹ exhausted all means to strengthen the accused's compulsion to confess, or
   ▹ failed to establish trust.

4. Cycles of role reversals continue until trust is established between the accused and one officer. This is signified by the development of meaningful conversation with the accused. The effectiveness of the role reversal will terminate if the accused is aware of the reasons. The officer must, therefore, never verbally signify the role reversal. The effectiveness of the role reversal will end if:
   ▹ the accused is aware of the technique, or
   ▹ the silent cop begins a new cycle by reversing roles during the expressive cop's successful conversation.

Accordingly, the officers must never verbally signify the need for a new cycle. Success of this method is contingent on the officers' instinctive knowledge of the necessity for a new cycle, by means of unspoken mannerisms, acquired through the experience of conducting interrogations together.

GUILT: CERTAINTY OR UNCERTAINTY

An investigator has two possible perceptions before and during an interrogation: an investigator is either certain or uncertain about the accused's guilt. The investigator's inclination is predicated on the existence or absence of reasonable grounds.

Certainty or uncertainty about guilt creates distinct formats of interrogation that are not drastically different and are contrasted only by subtleties of the questions and comments.

Certainty of Guilt

The conclusive formulation of reasonable grounds confidently permits an investigator to develop certainty of the accused's guilt and to maintain that belief during the interrogation despite any deception by the offender that may occur. A diminished belief of certainty when reasonable grounds exist reduces the effectiveness of questions and comments, creates an improper format, and results in unsuccessful interrogation.

The following format has a specific purpose. The order and the avoidance of detrimental questions and comments are significant to activate the person's compulsion to confess when guilt is certain.

PROCEDURE

1. **Never let your belief or the accused's belief about certainty of guilt waver** Constant reminders of the existing evidence will maintain the certainty.

2. **The expressive cop summarizes the investigation by stating a synopsis of the existing evidence** Do not be reluctant to divulge the strength of the evidence. Emphasis will create awareness in the accused that guilt is certain. An internal conflict is, consequently, fortified.

3. **Immediately after concluding the synopsis, ask the accused for reasons contributing to the crime** Never ask whether he or she committed the offence; only ask why. The person's culpability or guilt should never be the issue.

4. **Begin the process of altering the accused's beliefs and perceptions of wrong** Use the techniques to convince him or her that the offence was morally wrong rather than selfishly wrong.

5. **Challenge the accused to make a conscious decision and commitment to end criminal behaviour** Stress the urgency of this decision to avoid additional hurt to his or her family members and potential victims. A confession may facilitate rehabilitation and reintegration into society.

6. **Do not ignore the possibility of accomplices to the offence, despite a lack of evidence** Explore the possibilities offered by the subcultural deviance theory and suggest that the accused may simply have followed a leader. Note the response. If the accused rejects the insinuations that an accomplice planned the offence, the denial may become inculpatory if it is proven that he or she acted alone.

7. **Answer the accused's questions honestly, but do not allow him or her to interrogate** Inducements may be created by responding or not responding to an accused person's questions. Common questions asked include the following:

   ▷ *Am I going to be released if I confess?*

   Answering definitely "yes" or "no" will obviously be an inducement. Avoiding the question and making no response can be an inducement if proof exists that a qualified opinion could have been made. An honest opinion should be given based on the officer's past experience. Most CIB officers have acted as prosecutors during bail hearings. The CIB officer should explain the approximate number of bail hearings prosecuted and the procedure that has to be followed. A lengthy monologue is suggested, during which the officer explains the difficult task that the prosecutor faces to prove the necessary elements (i.e., primary grounds: failure to attend court; secondary grounds: danger to the public resulting from potential repetition of the offence) to detain the accused in custody until trial.

Emphasis must be placed on the fact that bail hearing decisions are predicated primarily on the presumption that the accused is innocent of the charge during the bail hearing. The inference drawn from an accurate explanation is that the accused person should be released. This should not constitute an inducement because the legal philosophy of judicial interim release does favour the accused.

> ▷ *What will I get if I confess?*

A response to this question that may avoid an inducement should include an explanation that the result of a trial cannot be accurately predicted. Each trial is different depending on the human behaviour involved. Explain the section and maximum penalty. These are facts.

8. **Minimize the investigator's desire to elicit a confession** A recommended way of achieving this desire without jeopardizing the voluntariness of a statement is to say the following: "It doesn't matter whether you confess to this, whether you give a statement or not. That's totally up to you." Using this method partially reinforces the caution and helps prove voluntariness. Afterward, comments should be directed toward the prevention of future criminal behaviour, which explains to the accused why the interrogation is continuing despite the investigator's indifferent attitude toward the confession.

Uncertainty About Guilt

Uncertainty about a suspect's guilt exists in the absence of reasonable grounds, when only mere suspicion exists. Interrogation under these circumstances must be conducted by consent. The caution and right to counsel are not necessary if the suspect is an adult; they are required for young offenders. Verbal inculpatory statements made during the interrogation usually lead to reasonable-grounds formulation. Afterward, an arrest may be justified, creating the necessity for the caution and right to counsel.

Despite any verbal inculpatory statements, a request should be made for a written statement, for corroborative purposes.

PROCEDURE

1. The suspect should never know the status of the investigation and that mere suspicion exists. Display confidence that guilt is certain.
2. Construct reasonable grounds by means of partial confessions.
3. Never act surprised by any inculpatory responses. Create the illusion that the facts were previously known.
4. Direct the interrogation away from the offence. Ask personal questions. People have a tendency to speak freely about their personal lives, when asked. This causes the suspect to divulge unrelated secrets, and thus establishes trust, which usually leads to a confession.
5. Ask the suspect whether he or she is willing to take a polygraph test.
6. Let the suspect speak without interruption. More responses increase avenues of questioning.
7. Use any of the interrogation techniques (e.g., reasons).

PROCEDURES AFTER CONFESSIONS ARE OBTAINED

Written Statement

A verbal confession will be documented verbatim in the officer's notebook. The accused should be asked to give a written statement. Refusal will not exclude the verbal confession. The admissibility tests are the Confession Rule and s. 24(2) Charter. A written statement is documented on an approved form. The statement requires

1. the date,
2. the time started,
3. the time ended, and
4. the accused person's full name, date of birth, and address.

In addition, the statement must include sufficient details of the charge to which the statement pertains. Each statement should contain only one charge.

The formal wording required on a sworn Information is not necessary. Sufficient details follow:

> You are charged with: Robbery. To Wit: On April 25, 2008, at the Bank of Nova Scotia situated at 38 East Main Street City of _____, contrary to the provisions of s. 334 of the *Criminal Code* of Canada.
>
> Q: Do you understand the charge?
> A: _____.

The caution and the secondary caution are printed on the form. Both are read to the accused and the accused is asked whether he or she understands.

The written statement follows the question, "What, if anything, do you wish to say?" Usually, the accused dictates the statement while the investigator records it. At the conclusion, the accused is asked to read it and sign it. The response is recorded. The accused should be asked to read the first line of the statement aloud to prove that he or she is literate. The accused signs after the last word and at the bottom of each page and initials any corrections if he or she chooses to do so. Refusal to sign it does not affect admissibility.

Each interrogation must determine whether the accused acted alone or with an accomplice. If one or more accomplices exists, the accused may incriminate them in the written statement. Should the accused choose not to divulge their identities, take the statement and continue the interrogation afterward to determine identification of accomplices.

Additional Interrogation

Once a confession is given, the police officer has activated the compulsion to confess. If the accused has committed other crimes, confession to those should be imminent. Every suspect should be questioned afterward for the purpose of solving other crimes. Assume that the suspect has committed multiple offences based on the premise that recidivism occurs frequently if the suspect is not detected. Property-crime offenders commonly repeat their crimes until they are detected.

Interrogation should continue by explaining this premise to the accused person. The same techniques and format used during interrogation regarding the principal, or original, offence are applicable. If additional confessions are made, request written statements. A separate written statement is required for each confession.

Recording the Interrogation

Each officer must make personal notes in a formal notebook. The Ontario Court of Appeal in *R. v. Barrett* (1993)[22] stated that every officer present during an interrogation should make independent notes, meaning individual notes. For example, an unsatisfactory procedure is having one officer record notes and the second officer simply signing the first officer's notebook.

The precise conversation that occurs during interrogation must be recorded verbatim in the officer's notebook, referring to direct quotes or word for word. Verbatim notes undoubtedly will not be perfectly accurate; they can only reflect the officer's best attempt at recollection. The purpose of verbatim notes is to recreate the precise conversation for a voir dire. Silence, pauses, and conduct must be included in the notes. Rough notes are usually made during an interrogation. These, combined with the officer's memory, will assist the writing of verbatim notes in the formal notebook. The rough notes are retained for court; they may be stapled to the respective page of the notebook or kept in a file. They should be brought to court and kept by the officer during testimony.

During an interrogation, the officer asking the questions usually is not the officer writing rough notes. This officer's verbatim notes are not expected to be complete. The Ontario Court of Appeal in *R. v. Barrett* (1993)[23] stated that complete notes are not expected from the officer conducting the interrogation. In the *Barrett* case, the interrogating officer recorded every question and answer while the second officer merely witnessed the interrogation and took no notes. The second officer simply signed the first officer's notebook and copied the notes into his own notebook. The court noted surprise that the interrogating officer's notes were purporting to be verbatim and were the only set of notes in existence.

Each officer should not only make his or her own notes, but also the individual notes must reflect the individual officer's own personal observations and memory, not those of the other officer. Some discussion between partners is inevitable and acceptable if each officer's respective notes reflect only what the individual officer can remember as true. The most significant aspect is the officer's testimony in court. Each officer must testify only about what he or she can honestly remember, not what another officer remembered. In *Archibald v. The Queen* (1956),[24] the Quebec Superior Court stated that a police officer may discuss observations with another officer as long as he or she can swear under oath and testify that the personal observations are nothing but the truth.

Additionally, the officer's notes should be **contemporaneous**, meaning made at the time of the observation or shortly afterward. Consequently, unreasonable delays between the interrogation and the recording of the notes may prevent the use of the notes by the officer during court to refresh his or her memory.

PROCEDURE

1. Write rough notes during an interrogation. Retain all rough notes for court by stapling them to the formal notebook or keeping them in a separate file.

2. Enter the time when the verbatim conversation was recorded in a notebook to prove the notes were contemporaneous (i.e., made shortly after the interrogation). Contemporaneous notes are those that were made by the officer, shortly after the observations. Use of notes during testimony must be preceded by permission from the trial judge; this requires proof that the notes are contemporaneous.

3. Each officer must make independent, personal notes in a formal notebook. One set of combined notes is insufficient, and simply copying a partner's notes is inappropriate. Use rough notes and recollection to record verbatim conversation. Avoid paraphrasing the entire conversation or portions of it. The format of the conversation may be written by printing the person's initials followed by the verbatim statement. Examples are found in this chapter's case studies. If collaboration occurred with a partner, record this fact and admit it when asked in court, during testimony.

4. Interrogations conducted by one officer may not have the benefit of extensive rough notes. Writing during conversation diminishes the effects of questioning and comments. A lone officer must rely on memory to record verbatim conversation. The interrogating officer's notes likely will not be precise and are not expected to be perfect.

5. Draw a rough diagram of the room in the formal notebook, including

   ▷ seating arrangement, and
   ▷ doors, windows, and furniture.

In summary, do not write notes or testify about a conversation that is not clearly remembered from one's own memory.

VIDEOTAPED CONFESSIONS

Videotaping interrogations has become a relevant factor in determining the admissibility of confessions. In *R. v. Lim* (1990),[25] the trial judge drew an inference that the failure of the police to provide a video or audio record of an interrogation suggested that the police did not want an electronic independent record because it would not have supported the officer's oral testimony. Additionally, the trial judge stated: "The police appear to have set the stage for a battle of credibility on the voir dire and excluded any independent source of information which could have supported one side or the other."

The Ontario Court of Appeal in *R. v. Barrett* (1993)[26] strongly recommended the use of videotapes during interrogations and the taking of confessions to prove voluntariness by stating:

> Universal use of videotapes would obviously be of assistance to judges in weighing evidence and reaching a just conclusion but, beyond that, there is the potential to benefit the entire administration of justice.

Videotape has "immensely superior" evidentiary value in comparison with witness recollection, according to the court. When officers choose not to videotape confessions, as in this case, the court stated: "[T]he police force has, by its own choice in this case, denied the court the opportunity of an undeniable record of what led to the conviction. Given the modest cost of videotape equipment such critical evidence should not, in fairness, be restricted to sworn recollection of two contesting individuals as to what occurred in stressful conditions months or years ago."

The court recognized that interrogation techniques are not offensive and that the police may be reluctant to publicize these techniques, but it stated that exposure of these methods would be a detriment. Regardless, the basis of admissibility remains voluntariness. The Supreme Court of Canada reversed the Ontario Court of Appeal's decision in *R. v. Barrett*, but on unrelated grounds.

An electronically recorded interrogation constitutes a *search without a warrant.* Attempt to obtain the accused's consent pertaining to the recording. In the absence of consent, the recording should be admissible because there should be "no reasonable expectation of privacy" in a police interrogation room.

Commentary

It is incomprehensible and inexcusable *not* to try to get a confession from every arrested person. Failing to try to question every arrested person makes no sense. There is no conceivable excuse that would justify not questioning an arrested person. Imagine any other professional not trying to achieve the best possible results. An opportunity to interrogate is an opportunity to establish the strongest possible case and to develop expertise through accumulated practice and repetition.

Case Study 18.1 Conclusion

On Saturday, June 29, Joe contacted two investigators. He was serving an 18-month jail sentence in a provincial reformatory as a result of his break-and-enter convictions. Joe requested their presence. He initiated the conversation. It concluded as follows:

Police Officer 1: "What are you trying to get at? How many have you done? You want to clear up all you've done for your whole life?"

Joe: "No, just one. Look. I don't want no lawyer, nothing. I'll plead guilty. I just want to clear my conscience."

Police Officer 2: "About what?"

Joe: "About a year and a half ago. A welding shop."

Police Officer 2: "What welding shop?"

Joe: "The _____ Welding Shop."

Joe was informed of the charge, cautioned, and informed of his right to counsel. He gave a written confession for the break and enter.

ENDNOTES

1. *R. v. Moran* (1987), 36 C.C.C. (3d) 225 (Ont. C.A.).
2. Ibid.
3. *R. v. Wills* (1992), 70 C.C.C. (3d) 529 (Ont. C.A.).
4. *R. v. Moran*, supra note 1.
5. Lecture, Ontario Police College, 1984.
6. *R. v. Brydges* (1990), 53 C.C.C. 380 (S.C.C.).
7. *R. v. Hebert* (1990), 57 C.C.C. (3d) 1 (S.C.C.).
8. *R. v. Smith* (1989), 50 C.C.C. (3d) 308, at 324 (S.C.C.).
9. H. Gleitman, *Basic Psychology* (Toronto: George J. MacLeod Ltd., 1983).
10. Ibid.; E. Boyanowsky, "Psychological Bases of Criminal and Deviant Behaviour," study guide, School of Criminology, Centre for Distance Education—Continuing Studies, Simon Fraser University, Burnaby, B.C. (1990).
11. Gleitman, supra note 9.
12. T. Reik, *The Compulsion to Confess* (New York: Grove Press, 1959); R.S.M. Woods, *Police Interrogation* (Toronto: Carswell, 1990).
13. L. Festinger, *A Theory of Cognitive Dissonance* (Stanford, CA: Stanford University Press, 1957).
14. Anthony Robbins, *Unlimited Power* (New York: Ballantine, 1986).
15. *Hardy's Trial* (1794), 24 St. Tr. 199 (U.K.).
16. P.K. McWilliams, *Canadian Criminal Evidence*, 3rd ed. (Aurora, ON: Canada Law Book, 1991), at 14–18.
17. *Slatterie v. Pooley* (1840), 151 E.R. 579 (U.K.).
18. Ibid.; McWilliams, supra note 16.
19. *R. v. Smith*, supra note 8.
20. Ibid.
21. R. Agnew, "The Origins of Delinquent Events: An Examination of Offender Accounts" (1990) vol. 27, no. 3 *Journal of Research in Crime and Delinquency*.
22. *R. v. Barrett* (1993), 82 C.C.C. (3d) 266 (Ont. C.A.).
23. Ibid.
24. *Archibald v. The Queen* (1956), 116 C.C.C. 62 (Que. S.C.), as in D. Bellemare, *How to Testify in Court* (Montreal: Les Éditions Yvon Blais, 1985).
25. *R. v. Lim (No. 2)* (1990), 1 C.R.R. (2d) (Ont. H.C.J.) 148, as in *R. v. Barrett*, supra note 22.
26. *R. v. Barrett*, supra note 22.

CHAPTER 19
Detecting Deception

LEARNER SUMMARY

"We do everything either out of our need to avoid pain or our desire to gain pleasure."[1] An individual learns by experience that honesty may be painful. Admitting to wrongdoing is not often positively reinforced by reward. It frequently results in some form of punishment or embarrassment. Lying becomes a means of avoiding the pain of such consequences.

Everyone has been confronted with a situation that requires a judgment about a person's honesty. Conduct is seen and inconsistencies are heard that create suspicions about dishonesty, but making a conclusive judgment commonly involves a mystifying process.

Scientific and unscientific means exist to facilitate a confident conclusion. The subject of this chapter will be the detection of deception by verbal and non-verbal communication, physiological changes, and polygraph examination.

Case Study 19.1

During an investigation of numerous break and enters, reasonable grounds were formulated implicating Henry (16) with break and enters at two variety stores. In addition, mere suspicion existed that he had committed two other break and enters at business premises.

Henry was arrested for the first two incidents. He was cautioned and informed of his right to counsel and his right to have an adult present. He waived his rights in writing and an interrogation followed at the police station.

The initial phase of the investigation consisted of honest answers to personal questions and confessions to the two break and enters. These responses were immediate. Henry never asked investigators to repeat any questions.

Afterward, he was questioned about the suspicion that he had committed the other two break and enters.

(Refer to the end of Chapter 19 for the conclusion of this case study.)

OBSERVING CONTRASTING CONDUCT

Some people may have distinct behaviour during honesty, or deception, or both. A person's conduct and appearance during honesty likely alter, to some degree, during deception. In addition, verbal and non-verbal manifestations during an individual's deceptive period may imply a uniqueness or a deceptive behavioural signature. At the beginning of an interview, an officer should establish what normal, honest behaviour is for a suspect so that he or she can then watch for behaviour that differs and that may indicate deception.

The best place to observe a suspect's behaviour is in a spacious, contemporary office at a police station. This has previously been mentioned as a desirable interrogation setting for its evidentiary value during a voir dire, but it also serves a second function. The suspect can be seated in an open position, allowing for visibility of the entire body and for observing conduct or physiological changes that may indicate deception.

Observing Normal Conduct

Normal conduct, or conduct during honesty, must be judged to detect contrasting conduct, which may later identify deceptive responses.

Unfamiliarity with the suspect and insufficient time may prevent a comprehensive assessment of normal conduct. Pre-interrogation questions can be used to evaluate normal conduct. During that time, questions should be asked to obtain answers that are already known to the investigator (e.g., name, date of birth, address, marital status, occupation or employment, and personal history).

This process should not be accelerated. Extension of a restricted period can be accomplished by expanding questions although the topics do not change (i.e., ask the same thing in a different manner).

While the suspect answers honestly, mentally note his or her vocabulary, speech pattern, demeanour, posture, mannerisms, and general physical appearance. Contrasting future conduct may indicate deception.

Observing Deceptive Conduct

In addition to watching for conduct that contrasts with normal behaviour, there are other verbal and non-verbal indicators that may mean that a person is trying to deceive the interrogator.

SOME COMMON INDICATORS OF DECEPTION

People who are telling the truth have a desire to express innocence in such a manner that it will be believed and that no possibility exists that it might be disbelieved. During interrogation, honest people commonly do not

- complain,
- avoid answering questions,
- question the officer's motives, or
- attempt to accelerate the process.

Common indicators of deception were researched by Reid and Arthur. This research, based on polygraph examination sheet analysis, resulted in the following composite of a typical deceptive person:

- displayed non-genuine friendliness,
- provided evasive answers,
- was uncooperative,
- was fearful,
- displayed nervous facial and bodily movement, and
- was untalkative.[2]

PERSONAL HISTORY

Lying may be considered an attempt to portray a desired role or to give a desired impression. Research indicates that an inverse relationship exists between birth order and lying. Firstborns are usually the product of inexperienced and inconsistent parenting. A firstborn likely will have higher self-esteem due to the amount of attention received during the time of being the only child. This also results in higher achievement, motivation, and internal control. Consequently, lying manufactures excessive guilt and internal conflict in firstborns. Empirical data suggest that firstborns are less likely to lie during an investigation than are persons further down in the birth order. Conversely, it is suggested that a person lower in the birth order has a higher propensity for lying during interrogation.

A suspect's criminal history may also be relevant to deception. Recidivists possibly have a weaker social conscience. Consequently, a recidivist may perceive lying as having little consequence. Empirical study also indicates that a person has a higher tendency to lie when questioned for a serious offence (e.g., indictable) as opposed to a minor office (e.g., summary conviction).[3]

Verbal Indicators of Deception

No single response by a suspect can conclusively prove deception. The following responses, or combinations, may indicate deception. None constitutes reasonable grounds if made during a consent interrogation.

- **"I'll tell you what you want, but I didn't do it."** A rational, innocent person would not suggest making a confession to a crime of which he or she is innocent.
- **"I didn't do it but I know who did."** This usually indicates that the suspect participated in the offence. Ask for the offender's identity and an explanation for this knowledge. Allow an uninterrupted response even if the suspect declines to divulge an identity. An excessively detailed and accurate account of the crime indicates that the suspect being questioned was present during the crime. An innocent person who may have received knowledge of the crime from the actual offender would not have been the recipient of an excessively detailed confession. Hearsay evidence usually lacks specificity.
- **"I didn't do it, but I can help you about other things."** Unprovoked willingness to incriminate offenders of unrelated crimes indicates a desire to prepare a bargain before he or she confesses or is charged. Pause the interrogation. Accept the information. Resume the interrogation afterward.

- **An excessively detailed alibi** An innocent person would not remember insignificant activities that coincide with the time of an offence of which he or she purports to be ignorant. This type of answer probably has been rehearsed. An additional test of the suspect's honesty should be conducted by intentionally asking the suspect about his or her whereabouts and activities on an unrelated date in the distant past. A detailed response may indicate a propensity to deceive. The suspect should not have intended to learn and remember events at a time when no need to remember existed.

- **"If I did do it, what would I get?"** Inquiries about sentences are odd requests from innocent persons.

- **Detailed cross-examination by accused** Unexpected and thorough cross-examination of the investigator by the suspect represents a rehearsal of questions intended to create reasonable doubt in the investigator's mind and to divert suspicion. Preparation occurred because of the suspect's anticipation of an interrogation. Preparation and anticipation would not have been thought of by an innocent person.

- **Refusal to take a polygraph test** An innocent person welcomes the opportunity to conclusively prove innocence. Rejection or reluctance to undergo a polygraph examination is an extremely strong indicator of deception, but does not constitute reasonable grounds.

- **Answers not related to the question** Innocent persons are attentive and embrace chances to refute questions related to an offence. Unrelated answers indicate an attempt to divert suspicion.

- **Duration of response** Long, vague answers indicate deception. The excessive duration of a response demonstrates an attempt to convince the officer of the authenticity of a deceptive answer. Vagueness represents a fabricated explanation.

- **No response or hesitation before responding** An honest response is not usually preceded by hesitation. Lengthy pauses or no response to a question directly related to the offence strongly indicate that an alibi or denial is in the process of being fabricated. Hesitation may be the product of indecision with regard to resolution of an internal conflict. An innocent person knows the response and does not require time to think. Failure to respond frequently is a precursor to a confession. It may signify that a strong compulsion to confess has been activated and that a strong internal conflict exists that requires resolution.

Non-Verbal Indicators of Deception

Non-verbal indicators are conduct, acts, or gestures displayed by a suspect that may indicate deception. The accused may be covering up a failure to control a subconscious attempt at self-incrimination. An interrogator should be cautious about interpreting non-verbal indicators as indicators of deception. It is here that the evaluation of a suspect's normal conduct is crucial. Non-verbal indicators have increased meaning if they contrast normal conduct.

Caution must also be exercised to avoid interpreting a meaningless act as a manifestation of guilt. This caution holds true especially if only a single occurrence of an indicator occurs. A single occurrence does not necessarily represent deception.

However, the interrogator should note when several types of indicators frequently combine.

As a final caution, be aware that non-verbal indicators are usually insignificant when made by an intoxicated suspect.

The following are non-verbal gestures that may indicate deception:

- **Hand to face movements** Covering the mouth, talking through fingers, and constant nose touching may be an attempt to prevent words from escaping. Stroking the chin, rubbing a cheek, scratching an eyebrow, pulling an ear, and grooming hair are common during deception.
- **Self-manipulation** Rapid arm, hand, and foot activity may occur during deception. Gross trunk movement, shifting of hips, and looking at a watch may indicate an unwillingness to cooperate.
- **Nervous gestures** Buttoning a dress or zippering a coat, tugging at pants, straightening a collar, smoothing a tie, and attention to lint indicate attempts to purge oneself of guilt and to divert attention.
- **Altering environment** Moving a chair away from the officer or leaning back may indicate unwillingness to cooperate and an attempt to increase the distance from the officer.
- **Tendency to close up** Crossing arms or legs may indicate a desire to occupy less space during a feeling of discomfort and a fear of having deception discovered.
- **Voice pitch** Research indicates that voice pitch rises during deception.[4]

EYE CONTACT

A suspect's inability to look an officer in the eye has traditionally been accepted as conclusive evidence of deception. Lack of eye contact, however, is not a strong indicator of deception. An individual's personality may prevent eye contact at any time.[5] No eye contact may be a meaningful indicator if it differs from the suspect's normal conduct. Additionally, eye contact can be maintained during deception if the suspect is consciously repressing non-verbal indicators.[6]

PHYSIOLOGICAL CHANGES

Physiological changes refer to body changes. No single, specific physiological response exists that is unique to or exclusively indicates lying. For example, arousal generated by lying is not distinguishable from other types of arousal.

The human nervous system is composed of the **central nervous system (CNS)** and **peripheral nervous systems (PNS)**. The CNS comprises the brain and spinal cord. The PNS comprises all nervous systems outside the CNS.

The PNS has two divisions: the **somatic nervous system (SNS)** and the **autonomic nervous system (ANS)**. The ANS serves the heart, blood vessels, respiratory system, and digestive system. The ANS has a predominantly involuntary character: thinking is not required for this system. Two branches compose the ANS:

1. The **sympathetic system** prepares the body to release energy and accelerates the heart and respiratory function; prepares the body for flight as a response to fear.[7]
2. The **parasympathetic system** saves energy and slows the heart and respiratory function; relaxes the body after a fearful situation.

In response to fear, the sympathetic system causes increased heartbeat, rapid breathing, and sweaty palms. ANS responses are often indicators of emotional arousal.[8]

The most commonly used physiological indicator of emotional arousal is the **skin conductance response (SCR)**, also known as the *galvanic skin response*—a measure of skin resistance to conducting electrical current.

Sweating closely corresponds to changes in emotional state and is a highly sensitive indicator of slight ANS changes. Perspiration rate increases are proportionate to emotional arousal increases. An increase of perspiration lowers skin resistance to electrical conductance. Therefore, skin conductance increases as emotional arousal (e.g., fear, anxiety) increases. Slight perspiration changes can be recorded by polygraph examination.[9]

Examples of physiological changes that may be physically manifested during deception are:

▸ **Sweating** Indicates elevated nervousness and tension generated by increased activity of normal body function. It could indicate deception, but it does not represent conclusive proof. It could indicate high emotionality, instead. The suspect can be informed of these details to enhance internal conflict.

▸ **Skin-colour change** Normal skin colour is the result of a potassium and sodium chloride balance in skin cells. Lying may disrupt the balance causing paleness or flushing. Flushing usually occurs in the latter part of an interrogation as a reaction to an officer's successful lie detection.

▸ **Pulse increases** Lying generates excessive adrenaline secretion from the kidneys into the bloodstream, resulting in accelerated heart action. However, pulse increases will not occur if the suspect is suffering from diabetes, kidney disease, severe cold, or flu. Lying sometimes produces a discernible pulse in the veins of the neck, head, and face due to a temporary pressure imbalance between the right and left side of the heart.

▸ **Dry mouth, lips, and tongue** One cause may be lying, but other strong emotions cause similar reactions. Excessive swallowing is a consequence of this dryness.

▸ **Respiration changes** Deception may accelerate or decrease breathing. Changes occur 30 percent of the time when lying. When a breathing change is caused by lying, it is usually in the form of a decrease (70 percent of the time). Therefore, an acceleration of breathing is possible, but less likely.

▸ **Stammering and stuttering** This reaction is the result of muscle tension caused by initial breath holding followed by a surge of words. Characteristically, stammering and stuttering are followed by normal speech. In addition, tension of speech organs may cause the subject to forget words.

▸ **Inability to sit still** Deception may result in involuntary movements caused by a temporary loss of control, balance, and coordination, which can prevent the suspect from sitting still.[10]

POLYGRAPH EXAMINATION

A polygraph examination does not detect lies. It records physiological changes during an emotional reaction caused by lying. A polygraph detects autonomic arousal to specific critical questions relevant to the offence (e.g., "Did you stab Will with a knife on February 1, 2007?").

These responses are compared with those to control questions—questions intended to generate emotional reaction, but which are irrelevant to the offence being investigated. The fundamental premise of a polygraph test is that innocent persons will have greater concern for control questions than for critical questions, thus resulting in a greater autonomic arousal to the control question.[11]

For the purposes of detecting deception, a polygraph examination records changes in heartbeat, respiratory rate, blood pressure, and sweat activity in the fingerprints. The recordings are interpreted by a polygraph examiner to determine an opinion of honesty or deception. The polygraph examiner is a police officer. The accuracy of the polygraph examination depends on the examiner's skill in interpreting recordings.

Legal Aspects of Polygraph Examination and Test Results

Officers should be aware of some of the legalities surrounding the use of the polygraph:

- "The polygraph has no place in the judicial process where it is employed as a tool to determine or to test the credibility of witnesses." The Supreme Court of Canada rendered this judgment in *R. v. Beland* (1987).[12] The basis for this decision was not doubt about the polygraph accuracy; instead, the use of polygraphs was found to conflict with "the well-established rules of evidence,"[13] meaning that a judge and jury exclusively will determine credibility of witnesses. Polygraph test results cannot replace the judge's or jury's opinion of credibility.
- A polygraph examiner's opinion of test results is inadmissible in court for the Crown and defence.[14]
- Revoking an offer to undergo a polygraph examination is admissible evidence. In *R. v. Smith (1985)*,[15] the accused offered to take a polygraph test regarding the issue of knowledge of property being stolen. The accused later refused to take the test. The revocation was admitted as evidence.[16]
- A polygraph examination is not automatically considered an inducement. Commonly, a properly conducted polygraph test does not affect the admissibility of a confession obtained during or after the test. However, a polygraph examination may be an inducement; an example is illustrated in *R. v. Amyot* (1990).[17]

The accused was charged with arson of a building he owned. After several months of investigation, police requested that he take a polygraph test and he gave both verbal and written consent. At the conclusion of a 45-minute test, the examiner told the suspect that test results indicated he was not telling the truth. The examiner told the suspect that disclosure of the truth could rectify matters. The accused asked what would happen now and the examiner informed him that he could not say as long as he did not know the truth. The suspect, in tears, confessed. The examiner asked the accused to repeat the confession to investigators. The accused agreed and verbally repeated it to investigators. The accused was cautioned and gave a written confession. No right to counsel was given after the test concluded. The trial judge ruled the confessions to be voluntary and the accused was convicted.

On appeal, the Quebec Court of Appeal reversed the trial judge's decision and entered an acquittal on the following basis: The police hoped to use the polygraph test to confuse the accused, thus rendering it an instrument of inducement. Telling him that he had lied was designed to disrupt his confidence and induce a confession. The examiner's conduct constituted intimidation and coercion, causing doubt about the confession's voluntariness.

The repetition of the confession to the investigators was also involuntary. The caution did not remove the inducement. In addition, a s. 10(b) Charter violation occurred when no right to counsel was deemed necessary in this situation because the confession to the examiner was made in a "climate of constraint." The court ruled that these circumstances constituted a detention as in the definition rendered by the Supreme Court of Canada in *R. v. Thomsen* (1988).[18] In addition to deprivation of liberty by physical custody, detention occurs when a police officer assumes control by "demand or direction." The necessary element of compulsion may arise from a "reasonable belief that one does not have a choice as to whether or not to comply."

▸ No person may be compelled to take a polygraph examination. Valid consent must be obtained from the person to be tested before the polygraph examination.

THE RELEVANCE OF THE POLYGRAPH RESULTS TO REASONABLE GROUNDS

Even a highly skilled examiner may not be 100 percent accurate. Canadian courts have not accepted polygraph results as being sufficiently accurate to warrant admissibility.

Based on these facts, a conclusion of deception does not formulate reasonable grounds. Rather, the deceptive result equates to suspicion. Consequently, the following procedure applies to interrogation after a deceptive test result:

1. The suspect may volunteer a verbal confession or make one in response to an examiner's questions. The verbal confession constitutes reasonable grounds. Custody of the suspect is given to the CIB officer. The CIB officer arrests the suspect, states the reason for the arrest, cautions the suspect, and informs him or her of the right to counsel. A written statement is obtained by the CIB officer.
2. Without a verbal confession to the examiner, a consent interrogation will be conducted by the CIB officer. If a verbal confession is made, reasonable grounds exist. The CIB officer arrests the suspect, states the reason for the arrest, cautions the suspect, and informs him or her of the right to counsel. Subsequently, a written statement is obtained.

3. The examiner must be subpoenaed to court to testify during a voir dire.
4. Note that refusal to consent to a polygraph examination does not constitute reasonable grounds to arrest. It represents suspicion of deception or guilt.

Who Can Be Tested?

The following people can be tested only if they give consent. No legal compulsion exists.

- A suspect of an offence when no reasonable grounds exist.
- A victim or witness for the purpose of validating the commission of an offence or the observations reported.

In rare circumstances, an accused person may be tested when reasonable grounds exist. The test, after an Information has been sworn, is required only if suspicion is created that crucial evidence has been fabricated.

If sufficient evidence exists to swear an Information, a polygraph test usually will not be conducted. In summary, most polygraph tests of suspects are conducted before an Information is sworn.

Who Cannot Be Tested?

People who have not given their consent cannot be tested. In addition, an examiner usually will not test the following persons:

- a person claiming to have consented involuntarily,
- a person previously tested by an examiner from another police force,
- a young offender, unless parental consent is obtained,
- a physically or psychologically abused person,
- a person suffering from heart disease, unless a physician's approval is obtained, or
- a pregnant woman.

Procedure: Polygraph

What follows are accepted polygraph procedures:

1. A CIB officer interrogates the suspect. The suspect denies committing the offence. Only mere suspicion must exist at this stage. If reasonable grounds exist, there is no need for a polygraph test.
2. The CIB officer must obtain the suspect's consent to undergo the polygraph.
3. The CIB officer calls the polygraph examiner and schedules an examination. They review the facts of the investigation and determine specific issues that require examination.
4. The examiner and the CIB officer formulate their critical questions, relative to the offence, which require a "yes" or "no" answer.

Example 1

▷ Did you kill Paul on April 4, 2008?

▷ Were you there when Paul was killed on April 4, 2008?

▷ Do you know for a fact who killed Paul on April 4, 2008?

Example 2

▷ Did you see who killed Thomas on August 4, 2007?

▷ Did you see Kevin hit Thomas with a rock on August 4, 2007?

▷ Did you see Thomas being killed on August 4, 2007?

Usually, only one series of three questions is asked during an examination. A second series is possible. Multiple offences cannot be tested in one test. One test per crime is conducted.

5. The method of transportation used by the suspect is critical. The officer may drive the suspect or the suspect may provide other transportation. The crucial issue is that the suspect must believe that he or she is not under arrest or being detained.

6. The CIB officer takes the suspect to the examination office and introduces the suspect to the examiner.

7. The examiner discusses the investigation with the suspect, in private, before the examination begins. The examiner will require written consent from the suspect before conducting the examination.

8. For test purposes, the suspect has:

▷ pneumatic tubes across the chest and shoulders,

▷ finger pads on the hands, and

▷ a cardio cuff on the arm.

The equipment records physiological changes on paper by drawing linear formations similar to a graph.

9. A normal response pattern is established. The suspect is asked to answer truthfully in response to a **card test**, which constitutes control questions.

10. A deceptive response pattern is established. The suspect is asked to intentionally lie to questions. No unique physiological pattern is associated with lying. Consequently, every person will react differently and a deceptive response pattern is created that is associated with the suspect.

11. The critical questions are rehearsed by the examiner and the suspect.

12. The actual examination is conducted by asking the critical questions.

13. The examiner analyzes the readings.

14. One of the following conclusions is made:

▷ truthful

▷ deceptive

▷ inconclusive—reactions were the same to control and critical questions. Changes are not noticed. Significance: treat the suspect as if the test never occurred.

Validity and Reliability

Faith in polygraph results has caused controversy. Judging the credibility of a polygraph examination requires examination of its (a) reliability and (b) validity.

Reliability denotes the consistency of the examination's results; **validity** represents the accuracy. Accuracy is contingent upon the examiner's ability to interpret readings. Accurate interpretation may increase if the suspect is afraid of severe consequences if he or she lies. In this case, the suspect's emotions during deception will contrast to a greater degree with his or her normal response, as opposed to a lack of fear of consequences from lying. The control questions chosen significantly affect the validity of the test.

Empirical evidence supports polygraph validity and reliability as being consistently and highly accurate. Hunter and Ash (1973) conducted a study to determine accuracy and consistency of polygraph examiners in judgment of real-life cases. Results clearly indicated that polygraph examiners' accuracy is high. The average accuracy was 86 percent in correctly identifying honesty and deception, ranging from 82.5 to 90 percent. Figures were obtained by examination of the same polygraph results at two different times sufficiently separated by time for memory not to be a factor.

ACCURACY OF EXAMINER DIAGNOSIS

Twenty-six physiological characteristics may be used in deception detection. Laboratory studies have suggested that **galvanic skin response (GSR)** is the most reliable indicator. The majority of professional examiners believe that respiration is the best indicator. Slowik and Buckley (1975) studied the accuracy of individual physiological indicators. Seven examiners, averaging 3.8 years of experience, interpreted 30 cases (15 truthful, 15 deceptive) involving 141 questions. The results were:

- respiration alone was 80.5 percent accurate,
- GSR alone was 80.0 percent accurate, and
- blood pressure alone was 77.1 percent accurate.

When errors were made, the most common, by a two-to-one margin, involved liars being judged as truthful as opposed to truthful persons being judged as liars.

Interpretation of the 141 questions individually attained an overall accuracy of 81.0 percent. Accuracy of the indicators were:

- respiration alone was 77.5 percent accurate,
- GSR alone was 73.5 percent accurate, and
- blood pressure alone was 72.9 percent accurate.

When errors were made, deceptive persons again were inaccurately judged to be honest, by a three-to-one margin.

Optimum accuracy occurs when all three indicators are used; deceptive response patterns may occur in only one or two indicators. Respiration was judged to be the most accurate indicator when used alone.

ACCURACY FOR PSYCHOPATHS

"The psychopath shows a remarkable disregard for the truth. Typically, he is at ease and unpretentious in making a serious promise or in falsely exculpating himself from accusations, whether grave or trivial. His simplest statement in such matters carries special powers of conviction. Overemphasis, obvious glibness, and other traditional signs of the clever liar do not usually show in his word or in his manner."[19]

Psychopaths are continually being redefined. Definitions have included:

- a morally irresponsible person who repeatedly commits crimes,
- one who has an apparent sound mind, but is dominated by a criminal instinct,
- a person having an antisocial personality and personality disorder, and
- a sociopath.[20]

Characteristics of a psychopathic personality include

- superficial charm and average to above-average intelligence,
- absence of delusions, irrational thinking symptoms, and nervousness,
- dishonesty and insincerity,
- lack of remorse or guilt,
- ability to maintain composure under stressful conditions,
- impulsivity, preventing a professional criminal career because of a propensity for committing major errors, and
- ability to receive pleasure from the reaction of shock from others when guilt is confessed.[21]

Psychopaths are generally underaroused. They maintain poise and serenity in tense situations. Nervous reactions are typically absent. Lykken (1955) empirically found that psychopaths emitted similar skin conductance during honesty and deception, while non-psychopaths had significant differences. However, these results were set aside because of the dissimilar atmosphere of the laboratory and real life. Polygraphs are not expected to detect deception in psychopaths, considering this analysis.

However, this assumption has been refuted by empirical research. Ruskin and Hare (1978) tested 24 psychopaths and 24 non-psychopaths in a mock crime involving a $20 theft. They were tested for lie detection using sophisticated equipment. Results indicated that deception was detected in psychopaths as easily as in non-psychopaths.[22]

Because of criticism of the above results over the absence of real-life pressure, Patrick and Iacono (1989) tested the accuracy of polygraph examinations of psychopaths under stressful circumstances. The subjects were prisoners who were tested for an offence that would result in the deprivation of money for other inmates and the exposure of the offender's identity to that group. Despite the stress of the threat, these results supported the Ruskin and Hare experiment. Psychopaths are no more likely to beat polygraph examination than non-psychopaths. Therefore, psychopathy with regard to suspects is generally not a factor during polygraph tests.

ACCURACY FOR CHILDREN

Abrams (1975) tested polygraph accuracy with regard to children. The results indicated that the accurate detection of deception begins at age 11. No implication exists that tests of younger children will be inaccurate; the probability of inaccuracy merely increases.

ACCURACY FOR ADULTS WITH LOW IQ

Results of tests conducted by Abrams and Weinstein (1974) indicated that adults having an IQ of below 70 to 75 cannot be accurately evaluated by polygraph. Test results of adults with an IQ of 69 or lower were rendered meaningless. Honesty was detected in adults having an IQ of 65 to 75, but deception could not be detected.

Case Study 19.1 Conclusion

Henry initially denied being responsible for the other two break and enters that he was suspected of committing. However, his responses deviated from his normal, honest responses. His denials were preceded with the question, "What?" Thirteen responses began with Henry asking, "What?" After the denials, he also confessed to those break and enters.

ENDNOTES

1. A. Robbins, *Awaken the Giant Within* (New York: Summit Books, 1991), at 55.
2. F.S. Horvath, "Verbal and Non-Verbal Clues to Truth and Deception During Polygraph Examinations" (1973) vol. 1, no. 3 *Journal of Police Science and Administration*.
3. J. Budnick, K.G. Love, and L. Wisniewski Jr., "Predictors of Liar/Nonliar Status: Birth Order, Age, Reason for Polygraph Investigation, and Previous Arrest" (1983) vol. 11, no. 4 *Journal of Police Science and Administration*.
4. J.L. Waltman, "Nonverbal Communication in Interrogation: Some Applications" (1983) vol. 11, no. 2 *Journal of Police Science and Administration*.
5. A.S. Aubry Jr. and R.R. Caputo, *Criminal Investigation* (Springfield, IL: Charles C. Thomas, 1965).
6. Waltman, supra note 4.
7. C.R. Bartol, *Criminal Behavior: A Psychological Approach* (Englewood Cliffs, NJ: Prentice Hall, 1980).
8. H. Gleitman, *Basic Psychology* (Toronto: George J. MacLeod Ltd., 1983).
9. Bartol, supra note 7.
10. Aubry and Caputo, supra note 5.
11. Gleitman, supra note 8.
12. *R. v. Beland* (1987), 36 C.C.C. (3d) 481 (S.C.C.).
13. J.L. Gibson, *Canadian Criminal Code Offences*, rev. ed. (Toronto: Carswell, 1991).
14. *R. v. Phillion* (1978), 33 C.C.C. (2d) 535 (S.C.C.).
15. *R. v. Smith* (1985), 16 C.C.C. (3d) 10 (Ont. H.C.J.).
16. Gibson, supra note 13.
17. *R. v. Amyot* (1990), 58 C.C.C. (3d) 312 (Que. C.A.).
18. *R. v. Thomsen* (1988), 40 C.C.C. (3d) 341 (S.C.C.).
19. H. Cleckley, *The Mask of Sanity* (St. Louis: C.V. Mosby Company, 1976), at 341.
20. Ibid.
21. Ibid.
22. Bartol, supra note 7.

PHASE 4
Physical Evidence

Physical evidence is recognized as having higher evidentiary value than evidence derived from people. A real object cannot be discredited to the same extent as a witness if the object is properly seized, examined, and protected until its presentation in court.

Forensic science includes expert analysis of physical evidence and the opinion formed from that analysis. The nature of the opinion determines the ultimate evidentiary value in court, but is also important to the formulation of reasonable grounds during an investigation.

The theory of transfer suggests that physical evidence is transferred during the commission of every criminal offence. The possibility therefore exists in every investigation to find physical evidence to prove or corroborate one or all of the facts-in-issue (FII) of an offence.

The chapters concerning evidence will examine types of physical evidence, information derived from opinions formed after the analysis of items, procedures for collecting physical evidence and proving continuity, and the significance of findings relative to the formulation of reasonable grounds.

PHASE 4 LEARNING OUTCOMES

The student will learn

- ▸ to interpret and apply rules of evidence regarding the admissibility of physical evidence, including the general rule of admissibility
- ▸ to interpret and apply continuity procedures in the seizure and collection of physical evidence
- ▸ to interpret and apply forensic evidence analysis to front-line investigations
- ▸ interpret and apply findings regarding forensic analysis of non-bodily substances, including impression evidence, glass, and firearm discharges
- ▸ to interpret and apply findings regarding forensic analysis of bodily substances, including DNA testing
- ▸ to interpret and apply a sudden death investigative model to reach a proper conclusion in every sudden death investigation

CHAPTER 20

Admissibility: Rules of Evidence

LEARNER SUMMARY

Physical evidence is items or objects that prove at least one fact-in-issue of an offence. Examples include:

- weapons,
- appliances,
- drugs,
- documents,
- money,
- vehicles,
- tools,
- impressions,
- clothing fibres, and
- bodily substances.

The list is endless and includes any tangible item.

Physical evidence has substantial evidentiary value and is significant in forming reasonable grounds and a *prima facie* case. However, the conclusions drawn from physical evidence are useless if the evidence cannot be found and collected properly. The police must search for and seize items following lawful authorities. Rules of evidence then govern the admissibility of each item.

The following steps and procedures are relevant to ensure the evidentiary value of physical items:

- search and seizure,
- collection,
- analysis,
- opinion,
- interpretation and significance to reasonable grounds,
- introduction as a court exhibit, and
- admissibility.

Case Study 20.1

Tom's decomposed body was found on a rural canal bank, 18 months after he had been reported missing. The body was positively identified by means of dental record comparisons.

The initial suspicion was that Tom had been murdered because of a drug deal. However, investigation revealed facts that created suspicion that Ryan had committed the homicide because of a domestic problem; Ryan's sister had been living with Tom.

Information was received that Jeff was Ryan's close friend; officers suspected that Ryan had made numerous inculpatory comments to Jeff during the past 18 months.

(Refer to the end of Chapter 20 for the conclusion of this case study.)

SEARCH AND SEIZURE AUTHORITIES

Search is defined as looking for things, including spoken words, to be used as evidence of a crime.[1] **Seizure** is defined as the taking of a thing from a person, by a public authority, without that person's consent.[2] Both definitions are found in case law.

Many sources of search and seizure authorities exist. There is no one specific rulebook. This results in the search and seizure process being perceived as complex and confusing. The sources of specific search and seizure rules include the *Criminal Code* of Canada (C.C.), case law, and common law. The Charter states general rules governing search and seizure.

Despite these complexities, police officers should not view these rules as being restrictive or a hindrance to investigations. Instead, they should be considered as authorities that provide advantages because of the many alternatives available to police officers. Close examination of search and seizure authorities will reveal that police officers have a variety of lawful means to search for and seize physical evidence.

There are three methods under which officers may search persons and places and seize evidence:

1. by consent,
2. with a warrant, and
3. without a warrant.

Section 8 Charter guarantees citizens the right to be secure against unreasonable search and seizure. Section 24(2) Charter will exclude evidence from a court trial obtained in a manner that infringes s. 8, if the admission of the evidence would bring the administration of justice into disrepute. Consequently, a Charter violation does not automatically exclude physical evidence from a trial.

A complete explanation of procedures pertaining to search authorities is found in the companion text, *Basic Police Powers: Arrest and Search Procedures*, 4th ed. (Toronto: Emond Montgomery, 2009).

GENERAL RULE OF ADMISSIBILITY

The general rule of admissibility is created in case law.[3] The rule states that physical evidence is admissible if (a) it is relevant and (b) no exclusionary rule exists to prevent its admissibility.

Relevant evidence is defined in case law as evidence that proves at least one fact-in-issue concerning the offence with which the accused is charged.[4] Additionally, for an item to be relevant it must be proven that the item introduced in court is the same item that was seized during the investigation. Proving that the evidence is the same item requires proof of continuity of the item, a procedure explained later in this chapter. If the item is proven to be the same one seized, then it is relevant. If the item is not proven to be the same one seized, then it is not relevant and will be excluded because it may be one of several thousands that exist.

An **exclusionary rule** is a law that specifically renders evidence inadmissible. The primary exclusionary rule is s. 24(2) Charter. This provision states that any type of evidence will be excluded if (a) it was obtained during or after the commission of a Charter violation, and (b) its admission would bring the administration of justice into disrepute.

Two S.C.C. decisions create procedural guidelines that determine admissibility under s. 24(2) Charter: *R. v. Collins* (1987) and *R. v. Stillman* (1997). These two cases and s. 24(2) Charter have been explained and interpreted in previous chapters. The most important rule to emphasize is that physical evidence seized after the commission of a Charter violation is not automatically excluded. It could be admissible despite the commission of the Charter violation. The trial judge, not a jury, determines admissibility of evidence.

COLLECTION: CONTINUITY

Physical evidence is seized at a number of places and intervals during an investigation, including:

- ► crime scene analysis conducted by an Ident. officer, and
- ► during searches (buildings, vehicles, places, and persons) by uniform patrol officers or detectives.

The seized item must be properly collected and stored for court. A decision is needed regarding forensic analysis. This refers to an examination of the item by an Ident. officer or an expert scientist at a forensics laboratory for comparison or to find additional physical evidence on the item such as fingerprints, fibres, and blood.

If forensic analysis is not required, the seizing officer collects the evidence and stores it in a police storage room until court. If forensic analysis is required, the item is usually given to an Ident. officer to conduct certain analysis, such as impressions, or to send it to a forensic lab for analysis.

The admissibility of the seized item depends on its relevance, which is determined by proving continuity. Continuity is a procedure that is intended to prove:

- the item presented in court is the same item that was seized, thereby proving relevance,
- the item was not altered between the time of seizure and time of trial,
- the whereabouts of the item between the time of seizure and time of trial is known, and
- positive identification of the item by the seizing officer can be made.

Physical evidence is introduced at a trial through a witness. This means that the seizing officer is called to the stand, sworn in, and testifies about

- the date, time, and place of seizure,
- a general and specific description of the item seized,
- a visual examination of the item after it is presented to him or her by the Crown, and
- a justified opinion that it is the same item by means of positive identification.

The Crown Attorney cannot simply submit the item as an exhibit without the witness. Positively identifying an item during testimony requires recognition of specific, unique characteristics of the item. Unique features include (a) serial number, (b) damage, (c) wear and tear, and (d) officer's initials.

The seizing officer initials items for the purpose of placing a unique identifying feature that will allow positive recognition during testimony.

Procedures: Seizing and Continuity

An Ident. officer usually seizes evidence and items at major crime scenes that will require forensic examination. In other circumstances, any officer is responsible for evidence seizure. Continuity procedure begins at the time of seizure, ends at the time of the trial, and includes the following methods:

1. On discovery of the item, establish its location by measuring its proximity to two fixed objects at the crime scene.
2. Have the item photographed by the Ident. officer.
3. If the item requires forensic analysis, package it in a container. Never combine items in one container—one item per container. If examination is not necessary, a container may not be required.
4. Seized items must never be placed, for the purpose of visual comparison, near another item where possible transfer may occur. For example, a tool must never be positioned near a tool mark to make a visual comparison. This practice will create the inference that transfer occurred during comparison, not during the offence.
5. The officer's initials and the date and time of seizure are written on the container. If a container is not required and any evidence on the item will not be disturbed, initial the item's surface. If the surface is inappropriate, tape paper to it and initial the paper. All officers taking possession of an item during a transfer must initial the item.
6. Never leave the item unattended at the crime scene or in the police cruiser while en route to the police station. Storing it in the cruiser's trunk while returning to the station is beneficial in case an emergency arises that demands a quick exit from the cruiser.

7. Upon arrival at the police station, store the item in an approved property locker. Secure the locker; a property officer should be the only person with a key for the lock.

8. If forensic analysis is required, an Ident. officer will deliver it to a laboratory and return it after completion of testing.

9. If forensic analysis is not required, the property officer becomes the sole possessor of the item until court.

10. On the trial date, the officer-in-charge takes possession of the item and takes it to court.

11. All officers having had possession of the item must be subpoenaed and attend court.

12. The item is introduced during the examination-in-chief of the seizing officer. First, the seizing officer explains the seizure and states a general and specific description of the seized item. The Crown then gives the item to the officer for visual examination. The seizing officer gives an opinion about positive identification by recognizing unique features, including his or her initials. All other officers who had possession of the item testify in the same manner to prove no alteration of the item occurred and that it is the same item.

Notebook Entries Relating to Continuity

Several facts relating to the continuity procedure are recorded in a notebook:

- the time of seizure and precise description and condition of the item (all identifying features),
- the location of the item—by written measurements and a sketch of the crime scene,
- the method of collection—packaging or how manually lifted,
- the time of initialling,
- the location of the initials,
- the time of departure from the crime scene,
- the location of the item in the cruiser,
- any stops while en route to the police station—if none occurred, record that fact,
- the time of arrival at the police station,
- the time of storage,
- the locker number, the fact that the door was locked, and by whom (seizing officer),
- any witnesses to the above events,
- any times of transfer of possession to or from other officers,
- the condition of the item and location of initials made during any possession transfer, and
- any contamination or alteration of the item that may have occurred.

Forensic Comparison

Once the evidence has been properly collected, the forensic lab analyzes it. This analysis consists of a comparison process known as forensic comparison. The purpose of forensic comparison is to determine whether a known sample and an unknown sample have the same origin. Officers should always deliver both the known (control) sample and the unknown sample to a forensic laboratory and ensure that continuity procedures are applied to both. They must also ensure that the two samples are always packaged separately.

The known sample may be seized physical evidence or a control sample—a sample whose origin is known. For example, a break and enter occurs at a house and a shoe print is found in a flower bed. A suspect is found a short time later. The suspect has soil on his or her shoes. The soil on the shoes will be the unknown sample. The soil at the house will be the control or known sample.

A forensics lab analyst compares the known and unknown samples and forms an opinion about how closely they match. In the case of the known soil sample, the lab would compare it with the unknown soil sample found on the suspect's shoes. In the case of fingerprints, the suspect's prints and the unknown prints would be compared.

COMPARISON RESULTS

Forensic analysis of known and unknown samples results in one of four conclusions:

1. **certainty** (The samples have the same origin. Identification is positive. No reasonable doubt exists.)
2. **probability** (The samples probably have the same origin. Identification is not possible. Reasonable doubt exists.)
3. **possibility** (The samples possibly have the same origin. Considerable reasonable doubt exists.)
4. **negative or uncertainty** (The samples do not have the same origin.)

These conclusions are opinions, which may only be introduced as evidence at a trial by an expert. Section 12 *Canada Evidence Act* (C.E.A.) allows five expert witnesses for the Crown and the defence. Permission may be granted for additional expert witnesses.[5] Expert testimony is an exception to the opinion rule (a rule of evidence that prohibits opinions from being stated during testimony), and elevates the probative value of the opinion. Expert status is not automatically granted. After the witness is called to testify, he or she recites, under oath, his or her practical experience, research conducted, or education received in the field in which expert status is requested. The trial judge determines whether expert status will be granted. Examples of people who can be classified as experts include (a) Ident. officers and (b) forensic laboratory analysts.

BEST EVIDENCE RULE

After an item is seized, analyzed, and determined to be admissible, the next question is, what has to be introduced in court—the original item or a substitute such as a photograph? The **best evidence rule** answers the question. It states that the original item must be introduced, but exceptions exist where a substitution, such as a photo or drawing, is allowed. The exceptions to the best evidence rule are for

- **size** (when the item is too large to be brought to court, such as a car),
- **perishable items** (evidence that is temporary and can vanish may be substituted, such as tire impressions), and
- **items not practical to introduce** (such as an entire crime scene).

A statutory provision allows substitute evidence. An example is s. 491.2 C.C., which allows photographs to be introduced in certain circumstances. Substitute evidence includes:

- photographs and videotape,
- scale diagrams, and
- certificates of analysis.

Photographs

Photographs of an original item are allowed as substitution evidence when one of the exceptions to the best evidence rule exists. Photographs require the expertise of Ident. officers. Their presence is dictated by a request from the first officer or a CIB officer when verbal evidence insufficiently describes a crime scene and it is not possible to take primary evidence to the trial. Scenes of major crimes require photographing (e.g., homicides, sudden deaths, robberies, sexual assaults, and break and enters).

Section 491.2 Criminal Code

Photos, by definition, include still photos, videotapes, and motion pictures. The Ident. officer must be subpoenaed to court to introduce photographs taken by him or her. Excessively insulting or grotesque homicide photos may be excluded to prevent shocking a jury. If photos are unusually grotesque, one photo is commonly allowed as evidence. The trial judge determines the photos that the jury will view.

Section 491.2 C.C. creates significant advantages to investigators; the photographs can be submitted as secondary evidence

1. without subpoenaing the Ident. officer who photographed the evidence and the officer who seized the item, or
2. instead of the original item
   - if the property was seized under federal statute authority, or
   - if the offence committed is theft, robbery, break and enter, possession of stolen property, or fraud or false pretences. Consequently, this section is inapplicable if the seizure was made under common-law authority to search after an arrest or non-statute, case law authority, or if the offence is other than the property offences listed (e.g., murder, assault, etc.).

Section 491.2 also allows the property to be returned immediately to the owner rather than detained until trial. Section 491.2 now allows the Ident. officer to complete a certificate, declaring that he or she was the photographer and the photo is a true photo.

Section 491.2 C.C. creates another advantage. The seizing officer does not have to attend court to introduce the seized item. Instead, the officer is permitted to swear an affidavit, declaring that he or she seized the item, detained the item until a photo was taken, and knows that the item was not altered from the time of seizure until the time of the photo. The affidavit may then be admitted at the trial as documentary evidence to replace the officer's testimony. The advantage created by these provisions is that continuity can be proven by means of a certificate and affidavit, thereby preventing cross-examination of the officers. The trial judge does, however, have the discretion to exclude the provisions of s. 491.2 C.C. and to order the attendance of the officers and the original evidence in court.

This section applies only to the listed offences and to evidence seized by federal statute authority (e.g., by search warrant and search-without-warrant authorities). It does not apply to evidence seized by consent or by the common-law search of an arrested person.

Section 652 Criminal Code

Section 652 C.C. allows a judge discretion to permit a jury to leave the courtroom for the purpose of viewing any place such as a crime scene. When a viewing is ordered, the judge and accused must accompany the jury.

Scale Diagrams

Crime scene photographs (including motor vehicle collision fatalities) may require supplementation with scale diagrams. These are prepared by an Ident. officer. Scale diagrams

- provide accurate measurements, which photos cannot display,
- assist witness testimony to illustrate the relationship of observations, and
- are admissible as an exception to the best evidence rule.

A scale diagram should be constructed in the following manner:

1. North should face the top.
2. The diagram should be readable in one direction.
3. The diagram should include all items present at the crime scene (e.g., furniture, doors, physical evidence, and bodies). All items require two measurements to fixed-object reference points. Body locations are measured from the head and foot to two reference points each. Two officers usually are required to measure. The Ident. officer holds the tape end requiring a reading. This ensures that he or she can testify about the distances under oath. The assistant holds the zero end of the tape. Both are subpoenaed to court.
4. The diagram should include a legend in one corner to identify items, thus avoiding a cluttered diagram.

INTRODUCING PHYSICAL EVIDENCE AT A TRIAL

Any physical item that the Crown intends to use as evidence must be introduced or admitted at the trial through a witness, during testimony in the witness box.[6] In other words, the Crown cannot simply submit physical evidence directly to a judge. The witness called to introduce the item is usually the person who seized it. Additionally, all other persons who handled or came in contact with the item before or after the seizure should be subpoenaed by the investigator to prove continuity. The same rule applies to substitution evidence.

TYPES OF PHYSICAL EVIDENCE

Although physical evidence is anything that is a tangible object or real item, it can be categorized as bodily substances and non-bodily substances. The significance of this division is that **bodily substances** are self-incriminating evidence when they are seized from the suspect and are more likely to be excluded if they are obtained after the commission of a Charter violation.

Non-bodily substances have a different relationship to admissibility. These items existed before a Charter violation occurred and are more likely to be admitted under s. 24(2) Charter.

Finally, all types of physical evidence lead to a conclusion that needs interpretation about reasonable grounds.

Impressions

Impressions are imprints or patterns or marks found on surfaces caused by various objects such as

- fingerprints,
- gloves,
- shoes,
- tires, and
- tools.

When impression evidence is found, the object that caused the impression must be identified and seized to compare the pattern of the impression and the item that left it. The problem is that some objects that leave impressions have patterns that change with additional use after the offence is committed. For example, tires, shoes, and tools all have patterns that leave impressions. Continued use of these items causes the patterns to change because of wear and tear. Consequently, the object leaving the impression must be identified and seized as soon as possible after the commission of the offence to prevent pattern alteration caused by further use.

Fingerprints are the best type of impression for two reasons:

1. The pattern that caused the impression is not likely to change after the offence, unless the offender cuts the area of the hand that caused the fingerprint impression.
2. A record of fingerprints may be kept for comparison.

Impressions have two characteristics:

1. **Class characteristics** These refer to general characteristics such as type, make, model, style, size, right, or left. These cannot form certainty opinions or positive comparisons because they lack specific comparison traits.
2. **Individual characteristics** These refer to specific, unique features, such as wear and tear caused by use. A quantity of individual characteristics may form a certainty opinion and positive identification.

Impression comparisons are made by an Ident. officer or a forensic analyst. The results of the comparison are an expert opinion. A certainty opinion, or positive identification, requires comparison of class and individual characteristics. Certainty opinions, under certain circumstances, constitute reasonable grounds or may create mere suspicion.

Comparisons based only on class characteristics and no individual characteristics cannot result in a positive identification. Only probable or possible opinions may be formed. Reasonable grounds cannot be formed by these opinions; they constitute mere suspicion.

Fingerprints

Fingerprints are one of the most valuable types of physical evidence. The uniqueness of fingerprints can create conclusive opinions critical to the formulation of reasonable grounds and can prove the facts-in-issue beyond a reasonable doubt.

Fingerprints are among the most positive means of personal identification. No two people have been found to have the same fingerprint pattern and no two fingerprints of any one person are the same. Identical twins have different patterns.

Fingerprint patterns do not change from birth to death and are often the last surface to decompose after death. Superficial injuries (surface cuts that are not deep or penetrating) heal properly without scars forming; the ridge patterns maintain their original shape. Permanent scars result only if the inner skin (the dermis) has been damaged; however, the resulting pattern and the scar compose a unique, identifiable pattern.

FINGERPRINT CLASSIFICATION AND CHARACTERISTICS

Fingerprints consist of intricate patterns that form ridges. Sweat pores are arranged in regular rows along the crests of these ridges. Ridge patterns have three class characteristics or types (see Figures 20.1, 20.2, and 20.3).

Figure 20.1   Loop Pattern Fingerprint

Loop: This pattern is composed of ridges that enter on one side, flow upward, curve, and exit on the same side, plus a delta (triangular) formation. Loops represent about 60 percent of all patterns.

Figure 20.2   Whorl Pattern Fingerprint

Whorl: This pattern consists of two or more delta or triangular formations. Whorls represent about 25 percent of all patterns.

Figure 20.3   Arch Pattern Fingerprint

Arch: This pattern is characterized by a slight rise at the centre, creating a distinct angular formation. Arches represent about 5 percent of all patterns.

Each classification has subdivisions, which represent the remaining 10 percent of patterns. In addition to ridge patterns, fingerprints are composed of ridge characteristics representing the individual characteristics (see Figure 20.4). Ridge characteristics are the basis by which an Ident. officer examines and compares fingerprints to form an expert opinion. Examples include:

- **islands** (shore ridges or dots): 9.5 percent frequency of appearance
- **lakes** (ridges forming enclosures): 2.5 percent frequency of appearance
- **bifurcation** (ridges forming forks): 14.5 percent frequency of appearance
- **ridge endings:** 47 percent frequency of appearance
- **short ridge:** 10 percent frequency of appearance
- **bridge:** 7 percent frequency of appearance
- **spur:** 6.5 percent frequency of appearance.

FINGERPRINT IMPRESSIONS

Fingerprint impressions are created by the deposit of perspiration from the pores onto a surface when a finger touches the surface. Water composes 98.5 percent of perspiration. The remainder consists of organic acids, including salts. The types of impressions are:

- **latent** (usually, the impression is not visible and must be developed by dusting or chemical means)
- **visible** (formed by a finger covered with a substance such as blood, oil, grease, or dirt)
- **moulded** (formed when fingers come in contact with a soft, pliable surface)

Figure 20.4
Ridge Characteristics

Ridge characteristics are the basis by which an Ident. officer examines and compares fingerprints to form an expert opinion.

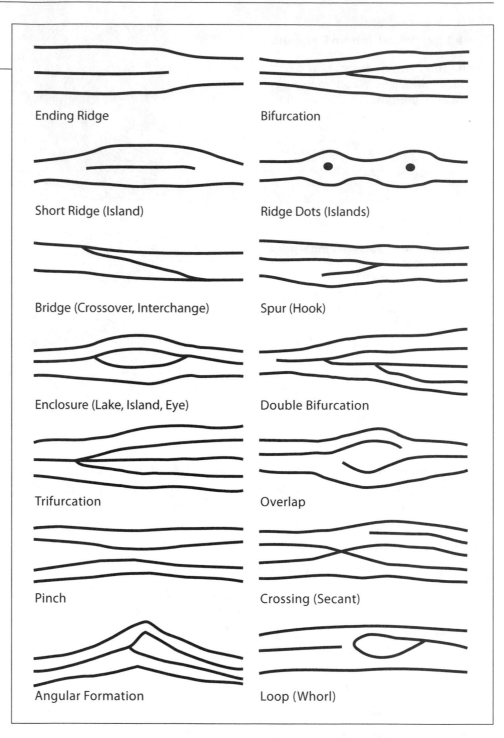

The best type of surface for successful impression development depends on two factors:

1. **Smoothness of surface** (e.g., glass, metal, paper). Coarse, porous surfaces may be unsuitable (e.g., wood, cloth, leather, vinyl).
2. **Size of surface** The surface must be sufficiently large and continuous for an identifiable impression to be made on it. Insufficient surfaces may include keys, steering wheels, doorknobs, cash register keys.

Impression development is, however, possible on some unsuitable surfaces (e.g., some types of cloth, coarse paper towels, and human skin). From an investigative perspective, unsuitable surfaces should never be dismissed or rejected without examination.

Fingerprint impressions should be developed as soon as possible after an offence has occurred. This is true despite the fact that the life span of the impression can be several days or considerably longer under extremely optimum conditions that protect it from deterioration. An impression's life span depends on:

- **The quality of the impression** Coarse skin leaves deep, distant impressions, thereby slowing the deterioration of the impression. Coarseness depends on a person's age, size, physical characteristics, and employment. Persons with sweaty hands tend to leave impressions with increased longevity because of increased salt residue from the quantity of perspiration; however, excessive perspiration may smear the print because of the inability to maintain proper contact with the surface. Conversely, persons with excessively dry skin may reduce the quality and longevity of the impression. Non-physical factors, such as insufficient pressure and short duration of contact, may also reduce longevity due to poor impression quality.
- **Environmental conditions** Exposure to certain climate conditions drastically reduces longevity of the impression. Most notable are rain, direct sunlight, and dust accumulation.

The development of fingerprint impressions takes place as follows:

1. Latent prints can be made visible or visible prints can be enhanced by dusting the impression with **graphite powder** that adheres to the ridges. The print is then photographed. Subsequently, the print is covered with cellophane adhesive tape. The tape is lifted and placed on white cardboard. The cardboard is initialled by the identifying officer who lifted the print and the print is protected until its presentation in court.
2. **Iodine fuming** can be used for paper, porous surfaces, and skin to develop deposited impressions. Within two weeks, oil deposits of the print absorb iodine fumes. Examination on skin must be conducted immediately. Examination of a living person's skin after two hours of deposit will likely be unsuccessful. The skin of a deceased person can be successfully examined up to 24 hours after deposit. Iodine fumes are poisonous and corrosive. The procedure should be conducted only in well-ventilated areas.
3. **Laser light** can be absorbed by sweat compounds deposited on a surface. The print becomes visible and is photographed. Laser light is useful on unsuitable surfaces such as cloth, wood, and skin. Laser detection does not destroy other evidence on the surface such as hair, blood, and fibre. It is also a useful way of developing prints on surfaces that have undergone extreme environmental temperature changes and when the print is old.

Identifying an offender by means of a developed fingerprint impression is contingent upon the following factors:

1. A record of the offender's fingerprints must exist for comparison purposes. The *Identification of Criminals Act*[7] authorizes police officers to fingerprint and photograph offenders without consent if the offender is arrested or charged with an indictable offence. This procedure extends to dual procedure offences, by virtue of the *Interpretation Act*.[8] Therefore, existence of fingerprints is not dependent on a conviction of those offences. However, a record will not exist if a person has been arrested or charged only with summary conviction offences or has never been arrested or charged. If a record of fingerprints does not exist for a suspected offender, no law authorizes the authorities to compel him or her to give a record without consent. Thus, the available course of action is to obtain the offender's consent.

2. The expert opinion of an identifying officer that the offender's fingerprint pattern is the same as the pattern found on the developed impression. The opinion can only be one of absolute certainty or uncertainty. Probability cannot be the conclusion. The opinion is predicated on the following rule: *Identity is established through the continuous agreement of ridge characteristics in sequence.*[9]

The comparison is based on examination of ridge characteristics (i.e., lakes, bifurcation, etc.). The characteristics must be identical in size and in relative location to other characteristics, also known as points. No Canadian law exists that establishes a minimum number of characteristics or points that conclusively signify a positive or certain identification. The accepted minimum by Canadian courts is 10 to 12 points of comparison.[10]

Evidentiary Value and the Relevance to Reasonable Grounds

Fingerprint evidence alone does not always constitute a *prima facie* case, but it may in certain circumstances. This evidence can be useful in several ways.

▶ **Positive fingerprint evidence represents circumstantial evidence and proves that the suspect was present at the crime scene at some time.** However, because the age of a fingerprint impression cannot be determined, the fingerprints cannot prove or corroborate the time of the suspect's presence. Also, fingerprint evidence does not directly prove the *actus reus* or *mens rea*. Therefore, the Crown must:

  ▷ prove by means of witnesses that the suspect did not have legitimate or lawful access if the prints were found on a fixed object, and
  ▷ prove that the object and the print were not legitimately placed or made at an unrelated time (i.e., before or after the offence) if found on a movable object.

  If the Crown can prove that the suspect did not have legitimate access, reasonable grounds exist to arrest (e.g., fingerprints found at the scene of a break and enter).

  An example is found in *R. v. Keller* (1970).[11] In this case, police investigated a break and enter at a business premises, where a safe had been opened by means of a cutting torch. A paper matchbook cover was found on the floor inside the premises, near the safe. The matchbook cover was examined by an Ident. officer and a latent fingerprint impression was found. No other fingerprints were found on the matchbook cover.

The fingerprint on the matchbook cover was positively identified as having been made by the accused person's right thumb. No other evidence existed. The accused was arrested and was convicted. The Saskatchewan Court of Appeal stated that this circumstantial evidence was consistent with only the conclusion that the accused committed the break and enter; no other rational conclusion could be made.

In summary, the circumstantial evidence of only one fingerprint may be sufficient to establish a *prima facie* case and convict if the only rational conclusion that can be made is the accused person's guilt. If any other rational conclusion exists, reasonable doubt is sufficient to result in an acquittal.[12]

In cases involving possession offences, such as stolen property and narcotics, fingerprints can show that the accused handled the item, but additional evidence should be obtained to prove control and knowledge beyond a reasonable doubt.

In *R. v. O'Keefe* (1958),[13] the Ontario Court of Appeal stated: "The mere fact that a person has handled stolen goods and left his fingerprints on them is not conclusive proof that he had possession in law of them. That fact alone does not raise any presumption that they came into his possession in a dishonest or unlawful manner. The inference cannot be drawn from that fact alone that he had any control whatsoever in respect of the stolen goods."

In *R. v. Lepage* (1993),[14] the accused was charged with possession of a restricted drug (LSD) for the purpose of trafficking. The accused's fingerprints were found on a baggie that contained blotter papers with hits of LSD on them. The baggie was found under a couch inside the accused's house, which had two other occupants. The Ontario Court of Appeal ruled that the accused's fingerprints on the bag were insufficient to conclude that he had possession of the blotter paper containing the drugs. The bag itself could have been innocently handled prior to the drugs being placed inside it and his fingerprints were not found on the blotter paper.

▸ **Positive fingerprint identification usually corroborates other FII.** For example, the identification of the victim's fingerprints corroborates the victim's evidence by supporting his or her presence.

▸ **Positive fingerprint identification can establish identity.** In cases involving property offence crimes (e.g., break and enter), the identity of an accused can be proven beyond a reasonable doubt by means of fingerprint evidence alone.[15] Even if no comparison can be made because of the absence of an offender's fingerprints record, a list of known, active criminals can be eliminated to assist an investigation.

Fingerprints of the owner found on stolen property can prove ownership.

▸ **Positive fingerprint identification may cause a suspect to fabricate an alibi that can then be disproved during interrogation or in court.**

Impressions Left by Gloves, Shoes, Tires, and Tools

Fingerprints are the best type of impression to identify an offender because the pattern does not change and the causes (offender's prints) can be recorded and filed by police forces.

Other types of impressions can be identified, but with greater difficulty. Gloves, shoes, tires, and tools do not have permanent, unchanging patterns and, obviously, no records exist of the owner of the items. The finding of an impression caused by one of the above items requires seizure of the item from which the impression originated as soon as possible after the offence, for the purpose of a comparison. Immediate seizure is essential to ensure that the pattern of the item is the same as when the impression was created. If seizure is not immediately made, continued use of the object will result in a pattern different from that which created the impression at the time of the offence.

GLOVES

Leather glove impressions may allow class characteristic comparisons of creases, pores, and hair follicles to the piece of skin from which the glove is made. Vinyl glove impressions can be compared to class characteristics such as placement of patterns and spacing of stitches.[16]

SHOE PRINTS

Footwear impressions can be found on tiled or polished floors, chairs, desks, papers where an offender stood, or in snow or mud and entry or exit paths to a crime scene. One of the advantages of finding shoe prints is that most shoe companies (e.g., Nike, Adidas) have distinct patterns to determine certain class characteristics.

Shoe prints may not be visible inside a building. Shoe prints on floors may be detected by turning off lights and laying a flashlight on the floor to allow the light beam to skim the floor surface. A trail may be found, for example, at the point of entry—the most likely place when considering these should be the first steps after leaving the external environment. Markers can be used to protect the prints until an Ident. officer can photograph them. Photos cannot be used if the item (e.g., paper) can be brought to court, in accordance with the best evidence rule. Shoe prints can be enhanced with fingerprint powder. Photographs should be taken of the original print, without powder, and of the enhanced version, in case admissibility of the enhanced version violates the best evidence rule.

Finding at least four shoe prints, two of each shoe, may provide the following information about the suspect:

- ▸ approximate height,
- ▸ possible wounds,
- ▸ whether he or she was carrying any items, and
- ▸ whether he or she was walking rapidly or running.

Normal walking creates steps 20 to 40 inches apart. Step length increases with height and speed. An excessive distance may indicate above-average height or running. Noticeably shorter steps indicate that the suspect walked hesitantly due to the unfamiliarity of the surroundings.

Impressions on soft surfaces such as grass or dirt can determine the following:

▸ If the suspect walked, his or her heel contacted the ground first. Weight was then shifted to the sole and finally to the ball of the foot. The toe of the shoe leaves the surface as the heel of the opposite foot contacts the surface, creating a weight transfer. The greatest pressure applied to the surface will have occurred at the heel and toe area. In addition, the majority of people apply pressure to the outside of the foot when walking. A shoe print impression that has similar depth at the heel, toe, and outside and lesser depth at the instep may indicate walking.

▸ Running, walking rapidly, and carrying items will increase the depth of shoe print impressions. Rapid running creates deeper heel impressions; slower jogging creates deeper toe impressions.[17]

TIRES

Tire impressions can reveal the direction of travel and indicate which tires on a vehicle created the impression. A vehicle moving forward in a straight line leaves an impression of rear tires. Conversely, a reversing vehicle leaves impressions of front tires. A vehicle making a turn can leave impressions of all four tires.

The tire manufacturer can be determined by examining (a) the tread formed by a series of parallel designs and (b) the width between ridges (holes designed to grip the roadway).[18]

TOOLS

Most tools used in offences (e.g., screwdrivers, crowbars, and hammers) have identifiable individual characteristics on the tool surfaces and edges, which can be detected by laboratory examination. The individual characteristics, exclusive to each tool, are created (a) during manufacture or (b) through wear caused by use (which is usually more significant).

Tool marks are generally divided into two categories:

1. **Impressions** (indents made in surfaces softer than the tool), and
2. **Striations** (scratch marks on a surface caused by sliding a tool on a hard surface (e.g., metal).[19]

Individual characteristics may be visible in both or may require laboratory examination. In addition, evidence may be transferred from the surface to the tool and vice versa.

When seizing the tool, never fit it into the impression. This act will create reasonable doubt that the tool created the impression at the time of the offence. Comparisons are made by expert examination.

The items creating impressions can be searched for and seized under the following circumstances:

1. If the person has actual possession, on lawful arrest only (common-law authority).
2. If the items are situated in a place by means of a *Criminal Code* search warrant, after the items have been adequately described and named in an Information to obtain a search warrant, and a Justice is satisfied that

reasonable grounds exist that the items are in the place and will afford evidence to a specific *Criminal Code* offence.

3. When lawfully on any premises or place by any means (search warrant or invitation) and the item is in plain view. *R. v. Shea* (1982)[20] defined plain view as being inadvertently found.

4. With the possessor's consent.

Evidentiary Value and Relevance to Reasonable Grounds

The comparison of glove, shoe, tire, or tool impression with the item allows the Ident. officer or lab analyst four levels of expert opinion:

1. certainty or positive identification,
2. probable,
3. possible, or
4. negative or uncertain.

The significance of these findings is as follows:

1. Certainty or positive identification is based on comparisons involving both class and individual characteristics. If evidence exists that the suspect had possession of the object, reasonable grounds may exist to arrest. A *prima facie* case may be established, but a confession will obviously remove any reasonable doubt.

2. Comparisons based only on class characteristics and without individual characteristics may result in a probable or possible opinion. Neither is sufficient to formulate reasonable grounds; they constitute mere suspicion only. This evidence, at best, may provide corroboration.

3. The object creating the impression must be seized as soon as possible after the offence to ensure that individual characteristics do not alter from additional use.

4. Broken pieces of the object found at the crime scene may result in an opinion of certainty or positive identification when compared with the seized object. Under some circumstances of Point 1, reasonable grounds have been formulated.

Body Elements

The commission of offences against persons or property may result in the transfer of **body element evidence** from the accused person's body to the victim's body (i.e., blood, semen, hair). These elements may undergo DNA testing for comparison. Forensic analysis of body elements can

- ▸ validate the report of a complainant,
- ▸ formulate reasonable grounds, and
- ▸ elevate mere suspicion to the status of reasonable grounds by corroborating existing evidence.

BLOOD

Blood is the most common bodily substance found during an investigation. The finding of a suspected blood sample requires initial forensic analysis to determine that the sample is, in fact, blood.

Moist blood samples can be microscopically examined to reveal the presence of red blood cells, which will prove beyond a doubt that the substance is blood. Commonly, blood will be in the form of a dried stain when received by a forensics lab. Red blood cells will have disintegrated. Consequently, the nature of the sample must be determined by forensic examination, such as by a phenolphthalein test.

Subsequently, the blood sample must be determined to be human blood. The presence of human proteins forms the basis of this conclusion. A successful test, therefore, is contingent upon the preservation of human proteins. They can be preserved for a long time if drying occurred at room temperature. Protein destruction results from high temperatures and bacterial contamination. Therefore, blood from burned or decomposed bodies may not be accurately concluded to be of human origin.[21]

Adult blood may possibly be distinguished from infant blood (under six months). The age of a blood stain cannot be accurately determined.[22]

Blood is classified as belonging to one of four groups, based on the presence or absence of **A** and **B antigens**. **Type O** is representative of 46 percent of the population. This type indicates zero, or the absence of A and B antigens. **Type A** (40 percent), **type B** (10 percent), and **type AB** (4 percent) are the remaining blood classifications, as a percentage of population.[23]

Evidentiary Value and the Relevance to Reasonable Grounds

Blood grouping is not specific to one individual. Consequently, blood samples cannot positively identify a suspect without DNA testing.

The racial origin of an individual may be determined if a large number of specimens exist. A single specimen does not permit this opinion.

The forensic analysis of a blood sample as the sole source of evidence does not constitute reasonable grounds. The results are corroborative only. For example, blood found on a weapon, the accused's clothing, or a victim's clothing may result in the finding of one blood type (accused's or victim's) or two different types that match to the accused and victim. Although the latter has obviously higher evidentiary value, it does not exceed mere suspicion.

An offender's blood samples to determine blood type for comparison can be obtained only by consent or from medical records.

SEMEN

The primary evidentiary value of **semen** is the validating significance that it affords during the investigation of a sexual assault. Although the offender's *mens rea* cannot be established to prove or disprove the issue of consent, the finding of semen samples during a medical examination can remove any doubt about the validity of the *actus reus* concerning a sexual assault complaint.

Semen is composed of cells called **spermatozoa**, which are live, actively motile organisms. Millions may be present. The density of spermatozoa often varies in the same person, as well as in different individuals. Motile (capable of motion) spermatozoa allow a fluid or stain to be identified as containing semen. Semen is identified more easily when the sample is fresh.

Spermatozoa do not die quickly. Destruction can occur because of cold, heat, or lack of moisture.[24] Forensic analysis of a fluid or stain may result in the following opinions:

1. The finding of living or dead spermatozoa positively identifies a substance as being semen.
2. Spermatozoa may remain motile in the vagina of a living person for an average of three to four hours.
3. Non-motile spermatozoa remain identifiable in a vagina for about 24 to 48 hours and possibly for several days.
4. Semen examination may reveal the male person's blood group if he is a secretor (capable of producing spermatozoa in the semen). For comparison purposes, the blood types should be established of (a) the suspect, (b) the victim, and (c) any person with whom the complainant had sexual intercourse within 48 hours of the examination.
5. The absence of spermatozoa does not prevent the identification of a substance as being semen, but it presents greater difficulty. Spermatozoa absence can be attributable to

   ▷ a vasectomy,
   ▷ a congenital disease,
   ▷ a venereal disease, or
   ▷ damaged spermatozoa on a dry stain.

6. The age of a dried stain cannot be determined.
7. The time of intercourse cannot be accurately determined. However, an opinion may be made that the elapsed time between intercourse and collection of the sample is consistent or inconsistent with the finding.

The examination of a sexual assault victim is conducted by a physician. An Ident. officer may be present. The samples are turned over to him or her to be forwarded to a forensic laboratory.

Evidentiary Value and the Relevance to Reasonable Grounds

In summary, forensic analysis of fluids or stains can determine whether the substance is semen, whether spermatozoa are present, the blood type of the offender, and whether the suspect is a secretor. Positive identification—an opinion of certainty about a specific individual—is not possible without DNA testing. Therefore, this evidence alone does not constitute reasonable grounds. It validates or corroborates a victim's complaint.

HAIR

Hair and **fibres** are categorized as **trace evidence** (minute or small). Hair can be easily transferred from an accused person to a victim or surroundings and from a victim to an offender. The nature of trace evidence may prevent the offender's knowledge of its presence and disposal of the evidence.

Hair has three major components: (a) root end, (b) shaft, and (c) tip end. The forensic analysis of scalp hair permits the most meaningful analysis; however, a single hair sample can determine the following information:

- the hair length, if the root and tip exist,
- whether the hair is human or animal,
- the racial origin,
- the region of the body where the hair originated (e.g., scalp, beard, pubic, limb),
- whether the hair was forcibly removed or fell out naturally,
- whether the hair was shattered by a blunt or sharp instrument,
- blood type, if the root exists,
- whether the hair was artificially coloured,
- whether the hair was permanently waved,
- the presence of hair spray,
- the texture,
- an estimate of the time since the last cutting, and
- the presence of grease, oil, or paint, suggesting an occupation.

The age of a person cannot be determined accurately, but infant hair can be distinguished from adult hair. The gender of a person cannot be accurately determined; however, presence of other evidence (e.g., colouring or spray) may suggest an opinion.[25]

Evidentiary Value and the Relevance to Reasonable Grounds

A suspect cannot be compelled to give hair samples for comparison. Hair samples can be obtained by:

- consent,
- search warrant of suspect's home (e.g., seizing a hairbrush, accompanied by an admission by the suspect that the samples belong to him or her), or
- common-law search of the arrested person—hair may be on his or her clothing.

In *R. v. Alderton* (1985),[26] the Ontario Court of Appeal stated that hair samples cannot be taken by violence or threats. Hair sample seizures made in this manner may constitute a s. 8 Charter violation. In *R. v. Williams* (1992),[27] the British Columbia Supreme Court stated that while a s. 8 Charter violation would be serious, "the taking of head hair is among the least intrusive trespasses on personal privacy and dignity." In circumstances such as in the *Williams* case, where the offence was murder, this evidence would not be automatically excluded, even if the accused's valid consent was absent, unless the accused showed that the admission of the evidence would likely bring the administration of justice into disrepute. In other words, the onus is upon the accused to prove that unreasonably seized hair samples should be excluded under s. 24(2) Charter.

The Supreme Court of Canada in *R. v. Dyment* (1988)[28] stated that "the use of a person's body without his consent to obtain information about him, invades an area of personal privacy essential to the maintenance of his human dignity."

The following two cases illustrate how hair samples seized from accused persons were excluded as evidence under s. 24(2) Charter.

In *R. v. Hodge* (1993),[29] the accused person was arrested for an attempted robbery. Thirty-six hours later, the police told the accused that if he did not provide hair samples, the samples would be forcibly removed. The accused complied. The New Brunswick Court of Appeal ruled that taking hair from an accused without consent constituted a Charter violation. The seizure could not be justified as a search after an arrest because the arrest had been completed when the seizure occurred. The samples were excluded under s. 24(2) Charter.

In *R. v. Foster* (1994),[30] the British Columbia Supreme Court excluded hair samples that were taken from an accused by means of threats of force for the purpose of DNA testing. Four officers confronted the accused in a small room; one officer told the accused they wanted to take hair and would use force to take it. The accused refused and the threat was repeated. The accused agreed under protest and allowed the officer to pluck 25 hairs from his head. The officers believed they were acting lawfully, relying on the Ontario *Alderton* case. At the trial the officer testified openly and honestly about the circumstances. The court excluded the hair samples and DNA test results under s. 24(2) Charter.

A comparison of hair samples cannot result in a positive identification or an opinion of certainty about a specific individual. However, an opinion can be formed that hair did not originate from a specific person. Consequently, the analysis of hair, as sole evidence, does not constitute reasonable grounds; it is corroboration to existing evidence.

DNA TESTING

DNA (deoxyribonucleic acid) is a chemical; it is a large molecule found in all life forms, from viruses to human beings, that creates a genetic blueprint or a biological code. DNA is found in the nucleus of each of the body's cells and is the essential building block of the human cell. DNA is formed at the time of conception from genetic materials contributed by both parents, and it makes each individual unique.

DNA is the means by which characteristics are passed from generation to generation (e.g., blood type, eye and hair colour, and certain diseases such as cystic fibrosis and muscular dystrophy).

Four chemical building blocks compose DNA: thymine, cytosine, adenine, and guanine. These bases are joined in a fashion similar to a string of beads. The first letter of each forms DNA language. Many sequence possibilities can exist in a single DNA strand.

The genetic code in a DNA molecule is repeated in each cell of one person. Therefore, each person does not have numerous DNA codes; each person has only one DNA code, found in every cell. For example, a blood cell, a piece of skin, spermatozoa, and a hair root cell from one person will have the identical genetic code. Therefore, DNA from one type of cell (e.g., spermatozoa) can be directly compared with the DNA of another type of cell (e.g., blood).

Every person has a different DNA code. The odds are billions to one against any two individuals having the same DNA code. Only identical twins have the same DNA code.

DNA testing is the comparison of the DNA code of body elements seized at a crime scene or from a victim and the DNA code of a suspect or accused person. DNA from one type of body element (e.g., spermatozoa) can be compared with the DNA of another type of body element (e.g., hair or blood), representing an advantage to the police. If the police seize some body element at a crime scene and determine the DNA code, the same body element does not have to be used from the accused to compare DNA codes. For example, if the offender's blood is found at the crime scene, the offender's hair may be used for DNA comparison.

Results of sample comparisons are the same as for fingerprints—either no match is made or a positive identification (opinion of certainty) is made. This is consistent with the premise that the samples originated from the same person.

The advantages of DNA testing are as follows:

1. Testing requires only small samples.
2. Successful analysis of very old samples can be made, even if a degree of contamination has occurred (five-year-old blood stain, three-year-old semen stain).
3. In sexual assault investigations, a seminal fluid sample of a suspect can be a mixture of semen and the victim's blood and vaginal secretions. The victim's blood type may mask the suspect's blood type. The condition of a seminal fluid sample in this situation does not prevent successful DNA testing.

Admissibility of Body Elements Seized for DNA Testing

The Supreme Court of Canada in *R. v. Dyment* (1988)[31] did not directly address the issue of DNA testing, but stated that using body elements to obtain information about a person without the person's consent is an invasion of privacy and that the Charter prevents a police officer from taking a substance, such as blood, for this purpose. An unreasonable seizure constitutes a s. 8 Charter violation and may result in the exclusion of the evidence under s. 24(2) Charter.

In *R. v. Williams* (1992),[32] the *Dyment* decision was applied in relation to the seizure of body elements for the purpose of DNA testing. Justice Melnick wrote that DNA analysis can be as strong as any other single item of evidence. Consequently, an accused's consent to give hair samples for DNA testing must be of a "high level" and of the "clearest order." Additionally, he stated that the seizure of living body parts for the purpose of DNA testing cannot be justified by means of a common-law search after an arrest because of the factors in the *Dyment* ruling.

Seizure of blood, saliva, and hair without an accused's consent for DNA testing is unreasonable and constitutes a s. 8 Charter violation. Justice Melnick stated that the taking of living body-part samples without an accused's consent should be either expressly authorized by statute or by the Supreme Court; clearly no statutory provision currently exists and he was not convinced that a ruling from the highest court existed.

He added that while such a Charter violation would be serious, the taking of hair samples would be the least intrusive. In circumstances such as murder, this evidence would not be automatically excluded, even without the accused's consent, unless the accused showed that the admission of the evidence would likely bring the administration of justice into disrepute.

However, the same court, in *R. v. Foster* (1994),[33] excluded hair and saliva samples taken from an accused by means of threats of force, for the purpose of DNA testing, regarding the offences of robbery, sexual assault, unlawful confinement, and break and enter.

CASE LAW

R. v. Borden (1993)

In *R. v. Borden* (1993),[34] police investigated a sexual assault of a 69-year-old woman. A semen stain was left by the accused on a blanket. The DNA code was determined, but no suspect existed. A few weeks later, the same offender committed another sexual assault. The second victim identified him and the accused was arrested only for the second sexual assault. Afterward, the police merely suspected the accused for the first sexual assault of the senior citizen, but no incriminating evidence existed. The police decided to obtain a blood sample for the purpose of DNA testing for comparison with the seminal stain found in the first sexual assault. An officer asked the accused for a blood sample, but did not mention the first sexual assault. The accused verbally consented. After consultation with the Crown Attorney, a consent form was drafted stating the following:

> I [name] do hereby give my consent to the [name of police department] to take a sample of my blood for the purposes relating to their investigations.

After consulting with a lawyer, the accused signed the consent form and provided a blood sample. DNA testing resulted in a positive match with the semen stain and the accused was charged for the first sexual assault. The accused was convicted at his trial, but the Nova Scotia Court of Appeal allowed the accused's appeal and entered an acquittal. The reasons given were:

▸ Valid consent requires that the accused must be aware of the potential consequences of giving consent.

▸ The accused's consent was not an informed one. It did not constitute a waiver of s. 8 Charter.

▸ The taking of the blood sample constituted a s. 8 Charter violation.

▸ Section 10(a) and 10(b) Charter violations also occurred because the police should have informed the accused that he was a suspect for the first offence. After the emphasis of the second offence ended, the accused should have been informed of the change in the purpose of the investigation.

▸ The Charter violations were serious enough to exclude the blood sample under s. 24(2) Charter.

Forensic DNA Analysis Warrant

A new search warrant, the **forensic DNA analysis warrant**, came into force in July 1995 and is found in s. 487.04 C.C. It authorizes the seizure of certain bodily substances in restrictive circumstances for the purpose of forensic DNA analysis. This warrant represents a significant, advantageous investigative procedure for the police. Prior to this warrant, no specific authority existed to seize bodily substances for forensic DNA analysis. Police had relied on indirect authorities such as consent and search of a person after an arrest, as illustrated in the previously mentioned cases.

An application must be made by completing an Information to obtain a warrant. The applying officer must prove reasonable grounds to believe that a bodily substance has been found relevant to the offence and that the suspect was a party to the offence. Only a provincial court judge can issue the warrant. The warrant authorizes the seizure of (a) hair, (b) saliva, and (c) blood.

EVIDENTIARY VALUE AND THE RELEVANCE TO REASONABLE GROUNDS

> [T]he analysis of DNA can have as forceful and significant an effect as any other singular item of evidence in a criminal investigation.
>
> —Justice Melnick, B.C.S.C., *R. v. Williams* (1992)[35]

> When an individual's known DNA profile is found to match with the DNA profile of cells of formerly unknown origin, the fact that both cell samples came from the same individual can be stated with a degree of certainty rarely encountered in the law. A good DNA match, theoretically, is evidence of the highest probative quality.
>
> —Justice Freeman, N.S.C.A., *R. v. Borden* (1993)[36]

A positive identification, or opinion of certainty, relating to DNA comparison constitutes reasonable grounds and, often, a *prima facie* case. The evidentiary value of a DNA match is "virtually conclusive of guilt." Conversely, a DNA mismatch is "conclusive of innocence."[37]

It has been assumed that inaccuracy of DNA testing is virtually impossible if proper scientific procedures have been adhered to. The reliability of DNA testing may be explained by drawing an analogy: "[T]he reliability of a fingerprint analysis depends upon the skill of the fingerprint analyst, while a DNA analysis is a biochemical procedure in which the human factor plays a smaller role."[38] The high degree of DNA testing reliability virtually eliminates the possibility of convicting an innocent person.[39]

OTHER PHYSICAL EVIDENCE

Glass

"The single most important characteristic of glass as evidence is the simple fact that it breaks."[40] This simple fact helps officers at a crime scene in the following ways:

1. The side of the glass that received the impact can be determined.
2. Evidence such as fingerprints, blood, hair, or fibres may be left on the broken pieces.
3. Broken glass may be found on an offender.
4. A sequence of bullet holes can be determined.

DETERMINING THE SIDE WHERE FORCE ORIGINATED

Force applied to glass causes bending in the direction of the force. A projectile that penetrates glass without shattering it creates two types of fracture lines (see Figure 20.5).

Figure 20.5
Radial and Concentric Lines

Two types of fracture lines, radial and concentric, are created when force is applied to glass.

Source: Adapted from International Association of Chiefs of Police, *Criminal Investigation* (Arlington, VA: I.A.C.P., 1989).

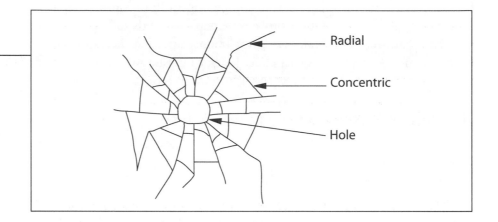

Radial lines are patterns of lines formed in an outward direction from the point of impact caused by the projectile. Radial lines occur on the opposite side from the force. They are the first fracture lines to occur.

Concentric lines form widening circles around the point of impact. They intersect and stop at radial lines. Concentric lines occur first on the same side as the force and occur second after the radial lines form.

A shell-like formation occurs along the fracture edges of glass when it breaks. The shell-like formation is characterized by elevations and depressions. This condition is referred to as **conchoidal fractures**.

The shell-like formations of a conchoidal fracture are shaped by curved lines. The direction of the curve indicates the direction of the force causing the break, and this can be determined by examining the edges of radial and concentric lines. On the edge of a radial line, conchoidal fractures curve perpendicularly toward the direction of the force. On the edge of a concentric line, conchoidal fractures curve perpendicularly away from the direction of force.[41] The procedure used by an Ident. officer to determine the side of the force is as follows:

1. Examine the glass for transfer of evidence (e.g., fingerprints).
2. Select and remove a piece of glass near the point of impact.
3. Mark the interior and exterior sides.
4. Identify the radial and concentric lines.
5. A radial break is illustrated in Figure 20.6a. The direction of the force occurred on the same side as the curve and opposite the straight-line portion of the conchoidal fracture.
6. A concentric break is illustrated in Figure 20.6b. The direction of the force occurred on the same side as the straight lines and opposite the curves of the conchoidal fracture.

Determining the side of the force can (a) validate or disprove the reported offence (e.g., break and enter) and (b) corroborate an observation or claim made by a complainant or victim.

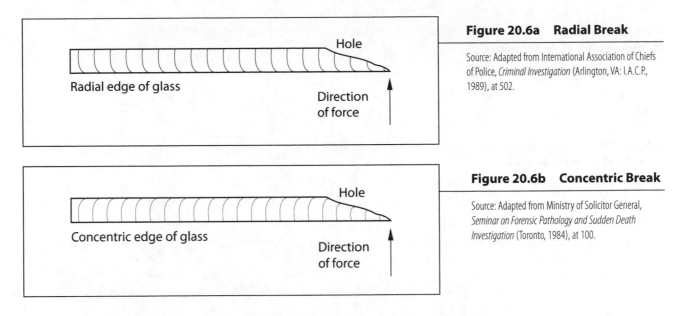

Figure 20.6a   Radial Break

Source: Adapted from International Association of Chiefs of Police, *Criminal Investigation* (Arlington, VA: I.A.C.P., 1989), at 502.

Figure 20.6b   Concentric Break

Source: Adapted from Ministry of Solicitor General, *Seminar on Forensic Pathology and Sudden Death Investigation* (Toronto, 1984), at 100.

The majority of broken glass travels in the direction of the force. However, some fragments, up to about one-third, can fall backward, toward the direction of the force. Two significant factors result:

1. Glass fragments may be found on both sides of a broken window; for example, at the scene of a break and enter. This may not immediately indicate suspicion of a fabricated report. The conchoidal fracture examination is essential in this situation to determine whether the force originated from inside or outside the building.
2. A transfer of glass onto the offender may occur because of the reverse direction of some fragments. The offender may not be aware of the presence of these particles, preventing their disposal. Finding this evidence may contribute to formulation of reasonable grounds.

As shown in Figure 20.7, the direction from which a bullet penetrates glass usually can be established by examining the shape of the entry hole. Perpendicular penetration causes glass fragments to be pushed ahead, causing a saucer-shaped hole in the exit side of the glass. A bullet striking at an angle from the right causes a saucer shape to occur to the left side. The opposite occurs from a bullet striking from the left.

The sequence of multiple bullet holes can be established. This concept is predicated on the fact that a radial line will stop when it meets a previously made radial line. Therefore, if radial lines from one bullet hole are stopped by those of another, it may be concluded that the latter were made first (see Figure 20.8).

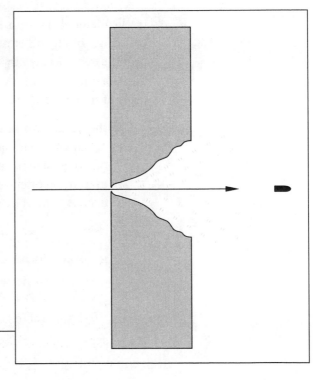

Figure 20.7   Perpendicular Penetration

Source: Adapted from Ministry of Solicitor General, *Seminar on Forensic Pathology and Sudden Death Investigation* (Toronto, 1984), at 101.

Figure 20.8
Multiple Bullet-Hole Sequence

1. Radial lines of first bullet hole are complete.

2. Radial lines of second hole stop at those of the first.

3. Radial lines of third hole (last) meet those of the first and second.

Source: Adapted from Ministry of Solicitor General, *Seminar on Forensic Pathology and Sudden Death Investigation* (Toronto, 1984) and International Association of Chiefs of Police, *Criminal Investigation* (Arlington, VA: I.A.C.P., 1989).

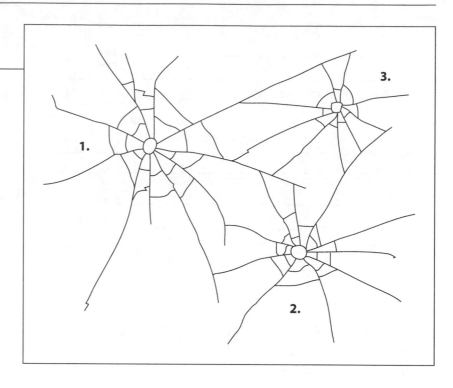

Evidentiary Value and the Relevance to Reasonable Grounds

The presence of glass on an offender as the sole evidence does not constitute reasonable grounds. Without other evidence, it creates mere suspicion. Transfer usually constitutes corroboration.

Fibres

Like hair, fibres are classified as a trace evidence. A **fibre** is the smallest unit of a textile material. Therefore, fibres may be transferred from clothes, carpets, furniture coverings, or any other material to either the victim or offender and, if found, may provide evidence to support a case. For example, if fibres found on a victim match those of an offender's coat, this is incriminating evidence for the Crown. The advantages of fibres are:

▸ their size permits ease of transfer,

▸ offenders are not aware that they have transferred fibres to the crime scene or taken them from the scene, and

▸ even if the offender was aware of the transfer, disposal of fibre evidence usually cannot be accomplished because of a fibre's size.

Fibres are divided into two categories:

1. **natural**, which include

  ▷ animal-derived fibres (e.g., wool, silk, and fur),

  ▷ vegetable (e.g., cotton, linen, and hemp), and

  ▷ mineral (e.g., asbestos); and

2. **synthetics**, which are manufactured fibres that include nylon, polyester, and rayon.

Manufactured fibres represent about 75 percent of the total American textile fibre production; thus, the majority of fibres examined by laboratories are manufactured. Vegetable fibres represent 24 percent, animal fibres 1 percent, and mineral fibres are rarely found either in the fabric of material or at crime scenes.[42]

EVIDENTIARY VALUE AND THE RELEVANCE TO REASONABLE GROUNDS

Fibres from an unknown source—those found and seized at a crime scene—can be compared with a known source with varying degrees of significance.

- A single fibre or several loose fibres can be compared with a larger item resulting in an opinion that they are similar. This does not constitute a positive identification or an opinion of certainty. Reasonable grounds cannot be formulated on this basis.
- An opinion that the seized fibre is similar to the known item is predicated on no significant differences that relate to colour, size, cross-sectional shape, and surface appearance being detected by a forensic laboratory examiner.
- An opinion of similarity can be elevated to the status of high probability if the fibre type is uncommon.
- Judging a fibre type as being uncommon is based on the opinion of a forensic laboratory examiner.
- Examples of uncommon fibre types include (a) coloured fibre types used in the manufacture of a relatively small number of items, (b) objects that were manufactured in the distant past and become rare as time passes, and (c) items that people do not commonly come in contact with. Consequently, fibre types from such items would be uncommonly found on an individual's clothing.
- An opinion of high probability can corroborate such evidence as (a) a victim's complaint of sexual assault, (b) a murder victim's surroundings at the time of the homicide, and (c) a victim's and an accused person's presence at a crime scene and their contact with objects.
- A degree of reasonable doubt accompanies an opinion of high probability. Based on the comparison of one object, reasonable grounds or a *prima facie* case do not exist. Fibre evidence rarely is the main evidence; rather, it usually corroborates the main evidence.

A notable exception was illustrated by an investigation conducted in Atlanta, Georgia, that involved the deaths or disappearances of 30 children and young men over a 22-month period, beginning in July 1979. In February 1982, an accused person was convicted of the murders relating to two of the victims. During the trial, fibre evidence comparisons were sufficiently significant to link the victims to the accused person's residence and automobiles. Fibre evidence represented the main evidence; it was corroborated by other evidence and circumstances. The accused's bedroom carpet had been manufactured in small quantities for a short time. Carpet in the accused's station wagon was similar to carpet last installed by the car manufacturer in 1973. Trunk liners in two other cars, which the accused had access to, were constructed with fibre that was not commonly seen by forensic lab examiners. The above sources of fibres were all judged to be uncommon.[43]

Firearms

The seizure and forensic analysis of bullets and cartridge cases can determine the following information:

- Bullet
  - type and make of firearm from which it was fired
  - whether it was fired from a specific firearm
  - if multiple bullets, whether they were fired from the same firearm.
- Fired cartridge case
  - type and make of firearm from which it was fired
  - whether fired from a specific firearm
  - if multiple cases, whether fired from the same firearm.

Firearm identification principles can be simplified as follows. Identifying a firearm by means of comparing the projectile and casing is the same concept as identifying the author of a signature or the originating typewriter of typed material. Class and individual characteristics of a firearm may create a recognizable signature on the bullet and cartridge cases, upon firing of the weapon.[44] A positive identification or an opinion of certainty can result from forensic examination and comparison in the following circumstances:

1. **A bullet fired from a specific rifle or handgun** Their barrels have interior spiral grooves, created by the edge of a cutting tool. The grooves (individual characteristics) are engraved into a bullet when it passes through the barrel, thereby creating its signature. Repeated firing may alter the grooves—the individual characteristics—but positive comparisons have been made of grooves cut into bullets fired from a firearm immediately after assembly. Therefore, positive identification of bullet to firearm is actually a tool mark comparison.
2. **A cartridge case fired in a specific weapon** An impression caused by a firing pin onto a cartridge creates a signature—an individual characteristic. Similarly, a fired cartridge ejected from a semiautomatic weapon will have an identifiable impression created by the ejection mechanism.
3. **Live (unfired) ammunition** Can be identified as having been in a chamber, if it was mechanically ejected.

A positive identification or an opinion of certainty usually cannot be made in relation to a projectile (e.g., slugs or pellets) and a shotgun. A shotgun barrel is smooth-bored, free of grooves or individual characteristics. However, the Centre of Forensic Sciences in Toronto reported a positive identification of a slug fired from a sawed-off shotgun. The opinion was based on individual characteristics formed by jagged edges on the barrel opening, created by cutting off the barrel. Signature grooves were engraved on the projectile as it left the barrel.[45]

EVIDENTIARY VALUE AND THE RELEVANCE TO REASONABLE GROUNDS

A positive identification in any of the above-mentioned situations constitutes reasonable grounds, if possession of the firearm is proven.

A lesser opinion (probability or possibility) does not constitute reasonable grounds in the absence of other evidence. A probable or possible opinion acts as corroborative evidence. Reasonable doubt accompanies such opinions and thus prevents the establishment of a *prima facie* case.

Gunshot Residue

Gas escapes from the cylinder and barrel of a firearm upon its discharge. This leakage causes lead, barium, and antimony to be deposited on the hand holding the weapon. Examination of a suspect's hand can be conducted to detect gunshot residue. Discovery of such evidence can corroborate proof that the suspect (a) had possession of a firearm, and (b) discharged a firearm.

The traditional paraffin test, to examine nitrate residue, is no longer practised.[46] It has been replaced with gunshot residue handwashing. The procedure is intended to detect the presence and levels of lead, barium, and antimony. Gunshot residue handwashing is accomplished by having a suspect submerge his or her hand in a bag containing 5 percent nitric acid and 95 percent distilled water. The solution is forwarded to a forensic laboratory for analysis. A gunshot residue conclusion is predicated on elevated levels of the three components. The possibility exists that traces of one or more components may be normally present on a person's hands (e.g., auto mechanic) according to his or her occupation.[47]

Elevated levels must be proven by an analyst's testimony in court. Secondary evidence, in the form of a certificate, is not permitted. Gunshot residue handwashings must be conducted only with the accused person's consent. No law compels the accused to submit to this test.

EVIDENTIARY VALUE AND THE RELEVANCE TO REASONABLE GROUNDS

The presence of elevated gunshot residue levels does not positively prove that a person fired a firearm. In addition to a normal trace presence, reasonable doubt exists because of the possibilities that the suspect handled a recently fired firearm or was present in an area where a firearm had been fired. Therefore, elevated gunshot residue levels alone do not constitute reasonable grounds. They primarily function as corroboration.

Additional factors contribute to the presence or absence of gunshot residue:

1. An excessive amount of elapsed time between the offence and the test increases the possibility that gunshot residue will be absent. Gunshot residue can be eliminated by rapid hand washing or manual contact with other objects or surfaces. The preferable time of the test is within four hours of the offence. Other North American theories vary the time to up to 12 hours.
2. The design of a firearm can affect the level of gunshot residue deposited on the hands. Handguns usually produce greater levels of gunshot residue than shotguns or rifles. A person shooting a rifle or shotgun will have little or no gunshot residue on his or her shooting hand; elevated levels may, however, exist on the back of the hand holding the barrel. This becomes significant if an offender's dominant hand shows a gunshot residue absence, but elevated levels are discovered on the non-dominant hand.

3. Modern ammunition may not be composed of lead, barium, and antimony. For example, Remington 22 rimfire cartridges, commonly used in Canada, contain only lead. Antimony is absent in Winchester and CCl 22 rimfire cartridges.[48]

Case Study 20.1 Conclusion

Based on the speculation that Jeff was the recipient of hearsay information, he was interviewed. During the initial conversation about Jeff's personal history, he responded clearly, without hesitation, and looked at the officers. When questioned about receiving confessions from Ryan, Jeff remained silent and stared blankly and aimlessly away from the officers. After the questions were repeated, he denied hearing such remarks.

Subsequently, he was questioned about whether he was present during the disposal of Tom's body. Jeff began trembling and his responses were incoherent. He was asked to take a polygraph test regarding his knowledge of the homicide and he consented. Officers arranged to meet him at his home the next day at 8:30 a.m. to take him to the police station. Officers attended as scheduled. Jeff was absent. A search was conducted. Jeff was found dead.

ENDNOTES

1. *R. v. Sandhu* (1993), 82 C.C.C. (3d) 236, at 247 (B.C.C.A.).
2. *R. v. Dyment* (1988), 45 C.C.C. (3d) 207 (S.C.C.).
3. *Morris v. The Queen* (1983), 7 C.C.C. (3d) 97 (S.C.C.), as in J.L. Gibson, *Canadian Criminal Code Offences*, rev. ed. (Toronto: Carswell, 1991).
4. Ibid.
5. E.L. Greenspan and M. Rosenberg, *Martin's Annual Criminal Code* (Aurora, ON: Canada Law Book, 2008).
6. *R. v. McInroy and Rouse* (1978), 42 C.C.C. (2d) 481 (S.C.C.).
7. R.S.C. 1985, c. I-1, s. 2(1).
8. Ibid., s. 34(1)(a).
9. G.M. Chayko, E.D. Gulliver, and D.V. MacDougall, *Forensic Evidence in Canada* (Aurora, ON: Canada Law Book, 1991).
10. Sources for the fingerprint section include an Ontario Police College précis entitled "Physical Evidence" (1984), lecture notes from criminal investigation course at O.P.C., and interviews with Niagara Regional Police Service Ident. officers.
11. *R. v. Keller* (1970), 1 C.C.C. (2d) 360 (Sask. C.A.).
12. Ibid.
13. *R. v. O'Keefe* (1958), 121 C.C.C. 273 (Ont. C.A.).
14. *R. v. Lepage* (1993), 87 C.C.C. (3d) 43 (Ont. C.A.)
15. *R. v. Keller*, supra note 11.
16. International Association of Chiefs of Police, *Criminal Investigation* (Arlington, VA: I.A.C.P., 1989).
17. Ibid.
18. Ibid.

19. Ibid.

20. *R. v. Shea* (1982), 1 C.C.C. (3d) 316 (Ont. H.C.).

21. F.A. Jaffe, *A Guide to Pathological Evidence* (Toronto: Carswell, 1991).

22. Ontario Ministry of the Solicitor General, Public Safety Division, Centre for Forensic Sciences, *Laboratory Aids for the Investigator* (Toronto: Queen's Printer, 1984).

23. Jaffe, supra note 21.

24. International Association of Chiefs of Police, supra note 16.

25. Ibid.; Chayko, Gulliver, and MacDougall, supra note 9.

26. *R. v. Alderton* (1985), 17 C.C.C. (3d) 204 (Ont. C.A.).

27. *R. v. Williams* (1992), 76 C.C.C. (3d) 385 (B.C.S.C.).

28. *R. v. Dyment*, supra note 2.

29. *R. v. Hodge* (1993), 80 C.C.C. (3d) 189 (N.B.C.A.).

30. *R. v. Foster* (1994), File No. CC921248 (B.C.S.C.).

31. *R. v. Dyment*, supra note 2.

32. *R. v. Williams*, supra note 27.

33. *R. v. Foster*, supra note 30.

34. *R. v. Borden* (1993), 84 C.C.C. (3d) 380 (N.S.C.A.).

35. *R. v. Williams*, supra note 27.

36. *R. v. Borden*, supra note 34.

37. Ibid.

38. Ibid.

39. Ibid.

40. Chayko, Gulliver, and MacDougall, supra note 9, at 687.

41. International Association of Chiefs of Police, supra note 16.

42. H.A. Deadman, "Fibre Evidence and the Wayne Williams Trial" (March 1984), *F.B.I. Law Enforcement Bulletin.*

43. Ibid.

44. Chayko, Gulliver, and MacDougall, supra note 9.

45. Interview with Centre of Forensic Science analyst (Toronto, Ontario, 1991).

46. Jaffe, supra note 21.

47. Ibid.

48. Chayko, Gulliver, and MacDougall, supra note 9.

CHAPTER 21

Sudden-Death Investigation

LEARNER SUMMARY

When a sudden death occurs in unnatural circumstances, the police, with the Coroner or medical examiner and pathologists, must investigate and determine the reason for the death. Even if the reason seems obvious, such as a suicide or an accidental drowning, the death must still be investigated to prove that it is not a homicide.

To correctly resolve a sudden-death investigation, the police and medical team work together to gather the evidence and analyze it while following investigative objectives and sequences.

"No sudden death can be looked at strictly from a medical point of view, any more than it can be looked at strictly from a legal point of view. The investigation of sudden death is a team effort."[1] A unified effort involving the first officer, CIB officer, Ident. officer, Coroner, and pathologist can successfully fulfill the objectives of a sudden-death investigation by answering:

- ▸ Who died?
- ▸ Where?
- ▸ When?
- ▸ How?
- ▸ By what means?

Case Study 21.1

At 11 p.m., officers responded to a call from a second-floor apartment regarding a shooting. Upon their arrival, the following observations were made.

Jim was lying on his back on the living room floor. A bullet wound was visible on his chest. He was unconscious, but was not decapitated, not decomposed, and not in a rigor mortis state. He was transported to the hospital, where he was pronounced dead by a Coroner.

Matt, Jennifer, and Andrew were also in the living room. All three had suffered non-fatal gunshot wounds; all were conscious. Before being taken to the hospital, Matt told the first officer that members of a motorcycle gang had entered the apartment and opened fire. No firearm was present.

(Refer to the end of Chapter 21 for the conclusion of this case study.)

ARRIVAL AT A SUDDEN DEATH

In most cases of sudden death, the police are the first to arrive. One of their first decisions is to determine whether a Coroner or medical examiner should be notified. If a Coroner is contacted, the police must then conduct the rest of the investigation for him or her. Section 9(1) *Coroners Act* in Ontario states that the police force having jurisdiction must make available as many officers as are necessary to carry out the Coroner's duties.

A **Coroner** is a practising doctor whose job it is to inquire into deaths that do not appear to have occurred naturally. He or she is appointed by an order-in-council for a term that does not allow the Coroner to exceed 70 years of age or until a voluntary or requested resignation is tendered. Approximately 385 Coroners in Ontario work part time on a fee-for-service basis. Each has provincial jurisdiction and usually serves an appointed area.

Coroners become involved in about 27,000 of an estimated 62,000 deaths each year in Ontario. Deciding whether to report a death to the Coroner is governed by s. 10 *Coroners Act*, which states that every person who has reason to believe that a deceased person died

1. as a result of

    ▷ violence (including homicides, suicides, accidents),
    ▷ misadventure (reaction to medically induced drugs),
    ▷ negligence (medical or custodial neglect, such as child or elder abuse),
    ▷ misconduct (medical or surgical problems, including religious or ethical circumstances), or
    ▷ malpractice (obvious medical negligence),

2. by unfair means (varied interpretation),
3. during pregnancy or following pregnancy in circumstances that might reasonably be attributable to the pregnancy (including abortion; full-term pregnancies before, during labour, or postpartum; and any operative procedure or complication. Death of fetus is not included; stillborn children are a separate category.),
4. suddenly and unexpectedly (represents majority of Coroners' cases—the significant word is *and*. Many deaths are sudden, but not unexpected and are not Coroners' cases. A family doctor can sign a death certificate; a Coroner should not become involved.),
5. from disease or sickness for which he or she was not treated by a legally qualified medical practitioner (no time limit is stated),
6. from any cause other than disease (i.e., drowning, no violence involved), or

7. under circumstances that may require investigation (this gives Coroners authority to investigate unusual circumstances)

will immediately notify a Coroner or a police officer of the facts and circumstances relating to the death, and where a police officer is notified, he or she will in turn immediately notify the Coroner of the facts and circumstances.

The location of death often determines whether a death is reportable. A sudden death occurring in a public place will likely be investigated by a Coroner. An expected death occurring in a home may be examined by the family physician. If the doctor believes that no further investigation is required, a Coroner will not be notified.

Once the Coroner has been notified, he or she has the following authorities:

1. Under s. 15, the Coroner may take possession or full control of the body until he or she releases it to the next of kin.
2. Under ss. 16(1) and (2), the Coroner has significant search and seizure authority. A Coroner may on reasonable grounds enter and inspect

    ▷ any place in which there is a dead body and any place from which the body was removed, and
    ▷ any place where the deceased person was before death.

    A Coroner may on reasonable grounds seize

    ▷ any records or writings relating to the deceased person, and
    ▷ anything relevant to the investigation.

    Sections 16(3) and (4) permit the Coroner to authorize police officers to exercise the above authority.[2]
3. A Coroner is the only person who can pronounce death. No other person (e.g., police officer, ambulance attendant) has the authority to do so under the *Coroners Act*.

Officers at a sudden death must assume that the victim is alive and make all efforts to preserve life and transport the victim to a hospital.[3] If death occurs at the hospital, the Coroner pronounces death there. Officers may assume death if the body is

▸ decapitated,
▸ decomposed, or
▸ in a state of rigor mortis.

Under these circumstances, the body should remain at the crime scene. A Coroner is called to the crime scene to pronounce death and a removal service must attend to take possession of the body. Each province has its own statute that governs the authority of a Coroner (or medical examiner, as they are called in western provinces).

IDENTIFICATION OF DECEASED PERSON

The first objective of a sudden-death investigation is to determine the identity of the deceased person. The victim must be identified before a post-mortem examination. The term **identification** has two meanings:

1. The victim's name must be identified. This requires facial recognition by a relative or friend, preferably next of kin, viewing the body at a morgue. The identification is made directly to a pathologist. A police officer should witness this identification.

2. The body must be identified as being the same body found at the specific location, for the purpose of proving continuity. The first officer should make this identification directly to the pathologist. The identification, by name, of an unknown victim or of remains cannot be accomplished simply by finding documents on the victim. A birth certificate, driver's licence, and so on greatly assist the process, but positive identification cannot be proven by these means. In addition, suspicion should always exist that documents had been planted on a victim for deceptive purposes.

Positive identification depends on a combination of two phases: (a) **general identification** (gender, age, race, height, weight, eye and hair colour, and blood type), and (b) **specific identification** (establishing positive examination by comparing autopsy findings with records made during life, depending on the existence of such records).

- A fingerprint examination is conducted by the Ident. officer. This examination depends upon the presence of the epidermis (outer layer of the skin).
- An autopsy of dental findings can be compared with dental records and X-rays. X-rays are preferable. The key points of dental comparison are that no two mouths are identical and that teeth are very resistant to heat. An accepted number of comparison points has not been established; however, comparison can result in a positive identification.
- X-rays of the skeletal system allow a comparison of old or recent injuries (e.g., healed broken bones).
- Tattoos are located in the dermis (deeper skin layers). They may be present if the body is moderately decomposed. Police arrest records of offenders describe tattoos.
- DNA typing.
- Jewellery.
- Clothes.[4]

CLASSIFICATION OF SUDDEN DEATHS

Every sudden-death investigation must determine by what means the victim died. Essentially, this process involves proving the classification of the death. Four classifications exist:

1. **homicide** (death resulting from an intentional criminal act)
2. **suicide** (intentional self-inflicted death; no criminal act)
3. **accidental** (no criminal act; not intentionally self-inflicted)
4. **natural causes** (none of the above apply)

Homicide

Section 222 C.C. defines **homicide** as causing the death of a human being, directly or indirectly. It divides homicide into two types:

1. **culpable** (the intentional causing of death, a criminal offence), and
2. **non-culpable** (the unintentional causing of death, no *mens rea* exists; not a criminal offence).

CULPABLE HOMICIDE

The following offences constitute culpable homicide:

1. **First-degree murder:** s. 231(2) C.C., which includes
   - a planned, deliberate, premeditated homicide,
   - a homicide where the victim is a police officer or prison employee, whether it was planned or not, and
   - a homicide occurring during the following offences, whether planned or not: (1) any type of sexual assault, (2) hijacking an aircraft, (3) kidnapping and forcible confinement, and (4) hostage taking.
2. **Second-degree murder:** s. 231(7) C.C., which includes all murder not classified as first-degree murder.
3. **Manslaughter:** s. 234 C.C., which includes all unlawful acts that result in a death. Specific intent to cause death is not a fact-in-issue (FII). The *mens rea* is simply the intent to commit an unlawful act. If death occurs, the offence of manslaughter has been committed. First- and second-degree murder require proof of a specific intent to cause death.
4. **Criminal negligence:** s. 219 C.C., which includes doing anything or omitting to do anything that is a person's duty to do and that shows wanton or reckless disregard for the lives or safety of others. Wanton or reckless is considered to be a "marked departure from the standard of a reasonable person."[5] Section 220 C.C. creates the offence of "causing death by criminal negligence."
5. **Infanticide:** s. 233 C.C., which includes the following FII:
   - a female person
   - by willful act or omission
   - causes the death of her child
   - the child must have been "newly born," which is defined in s. 2 C.C. as being under the age of one year
   - the death occurred when the female was not fully recovered from the effects of giving birth. It is necessary to prove that the female's mind was disturbed because of the effects of giving birth. Infanticide is the only form of culpable homicide that is not punishable by the maximum penalty of life imprisonment.[6]

AUTOPSY (POST-MORTEM EXAMINATION)

An **autopsy** or **post-mortem examination** is a medical operation of the deceased person that may help discover by what means a person died. This fulfills the objective of finding out how a person died. The decision to conduct an autopsy is made exclusively by the Coroner under s. 28(1) *Coroners Act*, which provides the authority for a Coroner to issue a warrant for a post-mortem examination.

The autopsy itself is conducted by a pathologist. Autopsies can be conducted by pathologists at a provincial forensic pathology branch, or at the pathology department of a local hospital. Before the autopsy is done, the CIB officer is responsible for informing the pathologist of all facts and circumstances learned from investigation. The Ontario Forensic Pathology Branch is located in Toronto. The decision to send a body there, as opposed to a local pathology branch, is made exclusively by the Coroner. The Toronto branch is available 24 hours a day; pathologists are available to attend the crime scene.

During an autopsy, the pathologist's objective is to find the mechanism and the manner of death. **Mechanism** of death refers to vital function disturbances generated by the cause of death. The **manner** of death refers to the means; that is, homicide, suicide, accidental, or natural.[7] Simplistically stated, there are only three mechanisms of death to consider:

1. The cardiovascular system suddenly lost its blood.
2. The breathing mechanism stopped working.
3. The heart stopped pumping.[8]

The **cause** refers to the "type of violence or disease which disrupted the vital processes of the body and brought about death."[9] Possible causes of death are:

1. **Sudden exsanguination:** the loss of blood occurring internally (i.e., within the body cavity) or externally. The usual causes of this are a ruptured blood vessel, an aneurysm, or the severing of a blood vessel by a bullet or knife.
2. **Cessation of respiration:** the respiratory centre is in the brain. A rapid respiratory shutdown is caused by
   - massive brain hemorrhage,
   - a bullet to the head,
   - a drug overdose,
   - spinal cord damage occurring during hanging, or
   - a lack of oxygen to the brain due to windpipe compression caused by strangulation.
3. **Cardiac arrest:** sudden ventricular fibrillation (irregular heartbeat) causes the heart to stop pumping blood to vital organs. It is caused by natural causes or electric shock.[10]

Time of Death

Determining when death occurred is very significant. To determine the means of death, by proving or disproving a sequence of possibilities during which homicide is the first stage, one must know the time of the assumed offence to speculate:

‣ who had the opportunity to commit an intentional act,

‣ who the potential witnesses are, and

‣ what the exact crime scene was to analyze it for physical evidence.

If homicide is proven, the time of the offence becomes an essential fact-in-issue that must be included in the Information, and is a crucial element in disproving alibis.

The easiest and most reliable method to prove the time of death is by eyewitness observation or by confession of a homicide offender. Otherwise, **post-mortem changes** must be relied on. These are defined as physical and chemical processes that cause tissue and cell disintegration. Examples of post-mortem changes include

‣ body temperature cooling,

‣ rigor mortis,

‣ post-mortem lividity, and

‣ decomposition.

No absolute, specific method exists to determine time of death by means of analyzing post-mortem changes. At best, only an estimate can be made.[11]

BODY TEMPERATURE COOLING

Body temperature cooling refers to the gradual decrease of a body's core (internal) temperature after death. This temperature decreases until it equals the temperature of its surrounding environment. Since pathologists know approximately how long a body takes to cool, they can calculate the approximate time of death. While other methods cannot be measured, body temperature is one of the few post-mortem changes that can be measured.[12] Therefore, body temperature cooling represents the single most meaningful indicator of time of death during the first 15 to 24 hours following death.[13]

For example, if environment temperature is 70°F (22°C), and body temperature is assumed to have been 98.6°F (37°C), the average rate of cooling is 1.5°F per hour (it may fluctuate from 1.0 to 1.5°C). A formula to estimate time of death is as follows:

normal body temp (degrees)
- rectal body temp (degrees)
÷ average heat loss rate (degrees/hour)
= 98.6°F (37.0°C)
- rectal temperature
÷ 1.5°F (1.0 to 1.5°C)
= estimated number of hours since death

The estimate can be fairly accurate if death actually occurred within 24 hours. However, the accuracy is affected by several factors:

1. The victim may have had a fever when death occurred.

2. Body temperature increases at the time of death, if death resulted from or was preceded by:

   ▷ physical activity,

   ▷ stroke,

    ▷ brain injury,

    ▷ strangulation, or

    ▷ asphyxia.

3. Obese bodies cool slower than those displaying average or thin physiques.

4. The amount of clothing on the victim.[14]

Core temperature and skin surface temperature will differ because their cooling rates differ. Skin surface temperature declines more quickly than core temperature declines. Skin will feel distinctly cool between two and four hours after death if the body is in a room-temperature environment. Core and skin temperature will generally equal environmental temperature 24 to 48 hours after death.[15] The body's internal (core) temperature does not drop much and may not change at all for up to three hours.[16]

RIGOR MORTIS

During the first two hours following death, muscles relax into a state of flaccidity, causing the body to conform to the contours of the surface it is on. **Rigor mortis** refers to the muscular stiffening that follows muscular flaccidity. It starts in the face and jaws and spreads to the upper body and finally to the hips and legs until the entire body is in a state of rigor mortis. Rigor mortis remains for a period of time and gradually disappears in the same order (top-down).[17]

A suggested theory relating rigor mortis and time of death is the **3-12s Rule**. It simply hypothesizes that rigor mortis takes 12 hours to develop fully, it remains for the next 12 hours, and then disappears gradually over a final 12-hour period.

Chronologically, the sequence of rigor mortis following death may occur as follows:

1. **0–12 hours:** no rigor mortis generally during the first two hours. It begins in the face and neck region between two and six hours and progresses downward. A total state of rigor mortis may exist between 10 and 12 hours.

2. **12–24 hours:** rigor mortis remains fully developed. It may remain beyond the 24-hour mark.

3. **24–36 hours:** rigor mortis recedes gradually, beginning in the face and neck, passing downward until completely gone.[18]

Rigor mortis development is the most inaccurate method[19] of estimating the time of death because of several factors that profoundly disrupt the chronological sequence:

1. Muscular development causes rigor mortis to begin sooner and remain longer.

2. Extreme muscular activity immediately before death (e.g., a violent struggle) quickens the development and spreading of rigor mortis.

3. Bodies of infants develop rigor mortis much earlier than those of adults.

4. Environmental temperature affects the rate at which rigor develops and spreads.

Post-Mortem Lividity (PML)

Post-mortem lividity (PML) refers to the settling of blood after death in parts of the body nearest the surface on which it is lying. PML helps to establish not only the time of death, but also the times at which the body may have been moved after death. After heart function ends, blood gravitates to the lower part of the body. Blood settles into small blood vessels, creating a visible purplish lividity stain. However, lividity stains will not form on parts of the body directly in contact with a firm surface; surface contact compresses blood vessels, preventing blood from entering and settling in the vessels. Therefore, these areas will have a white appearance.

Lividity stains become visible within one-half hour after death. The colour becomes more pronounced after about four hours. During this time, lividity stains are not fixed; blood is still mobile. If the body is turned over, the stains will relocate. Lividity stains become fixed between 8 and 12 hours after death. Moving the body at this point will not alter the stains. Factors may alter the time of these events. PML can permit a conclusion that a body was moved after 12 hours of death, creating a strong suspicion of a criminal act. For example:

1. If a body is found on its back and no lividity stains are visible on the front of the body, no suspicion exists that the body was moved after 12 hours from the time of death. The stains should be on the back. However, the body may have been moved within eight hours, before PML became fixed. A body moved between four and eight hours after death may have residual stains on the area of the body that had initially been in contact with a surface. Therefore, visible stains on the front and back create suspicion that the body was moved during the four- to eight-hour period.
2. If a body is found on its back and lividity stains are visible on the front and none on the back, suspicion exists that the body was moved after 12 hours.

Bruises and PML stains may have the same colour. They can be distinguished as follows:

- Bruises cause swelling, while PML does not.
- Bruises vary in colour (e.g., black, blue, yellowish green), while PML stains are uniformly purple.[20]

DECOMPOSITION (PUTREFACTION)

Decomposition or **putrefaction** refers to a phase during which the body rapidly disintegrates and gases are produced. Under average environmental conditions, decomposition may begin after 36 to 48 hours. Swelling of the body may distort facial features, preventing visual identification, and cause inaccurate weight estimation.[21]

After decomposition begins, **maggot collection and analysis** is another method to estimate the time of death. However, the results can only indicate a period of days (i.e., three to seven, eight to nine). Maggots are one part of the life cycle of bluebottle flies. They lay eggs, particularly in open wounds and orifices. After a couple of days, the eggs change into tiny jumping maggots. Maggots develop through four stages.

Finally, the maggot becomes dormant and spins a cocoon around itself (the third stage of the fly). The insect grows in the cocoon, develops into a fly, and breaks out of the cocoon. Examination by an **entomologist** (an insect specialist) can determine the stage of the fly's life cycle, which has a definite period.

In addition, **botanical examination** can be conducted in relation to decomposed bodies, or skeletal remains found in a field, to determine a general time of death estimate. A botanist from a forensic lab can examine vegetation beneath the body, which presumably stopped growing because of the body's weight. Comparison may be made with the vegetation surrounding the body. The botanist may determine a time difference (that is, when the vegetation beneath the body stopped growing). Also, plants growing through skeletal remains allow examination of the roots from which a botanist can determine the year that plant growth began (Smith, 1984).[22] However, these estimates simply indicate when the body was placed there and not necessarily the estimated time of death.

STOMACH CONTENTS

Stomach contents found during an autopsy are useless to estimate the time of death.[23]

OTHER EVIDENCE

In addition to analyzing post-mortem changes, other evidence may assist in estimating the time of death:

1. Interview witnesses to determine when the deceased person was
   ▷ last seen or heard alive, and/or
   ▷ found dead.
2. Notice an accumulation of mail and newspapers.
3. Check for a broken wristwatch.
4. Determine the type of clothes the victim was wearing.
5. Note specifics about food at the scene (e.g., breakfast, dinner, etc.).
6. Check to see whether lights were on or off in the area.
7. Note any disruptions of daily activities (e.g., work schedule, appointments, activities, etc.).

Case Study 21.1 Conclusion

An Ident. officer's examination of the crime scene revealed a bullet on the living room floor and one in the wall. The entry angle of the projectile determined an opinion of a path that indicated that the gunshot originated from the location where Jim was found.

The survivors were later interviewed.

Andrew admitted that Jim came to the apartment armed with a handgun. He argued with Matt about a past violent act. Jim opened fire. A struggle ensued. Jim was disarmed by Andrew, who then shot Jim in the chest.

Jennifer confessed that she took Jim's firearm and threw it in the river situated at the back of the apartment.

Matt confessed that he fabricated the report of the motorcycle gang members committing the offence.

An interview with Jim's wife revealed the make and calibre of Jim's gun. In addition, she saw the gun in Jim's possession about one half-hour before the shooting occurred.

Examination of the bullets created an opinion that the gun owned by Jim was capable of firing the seized bullets.

The river was searched by divers; the gun was not recovered.

ENDNOTES

1. Ontario Ministry of the Solicitor General, Public Safety Division, Forensic Pathology Branch, *Seminar on Forensic Pathology and Sudden-Death Investigation* (Toronto, 1984): J.W. Evans, "Introduction to Sudden-Death Investigation."

2. *Seminar on Forensic Pathology and Sudden-Death Investigation*, supra note 1: R.C. Bennett, M.D., Chief Coroner for the Province of Ontario, "The Role of the Coroner in Sudden-Death Investigation."

3. Ontario Police College, 1984.

4. F.A. Jaffe, *A Guide to Pathological Evidence* (Toronto: Carswell, 1991).

5. *R. v. Barron* (1985), 23 C.C.C. (3d) 544 (Ont. C.A.), as in E.L. Greenspan and M. Rosenberg, *Martin's Annual Criminal Code* (Aurora, ON: Canada Law Book, 2008).

6. *Martin's Annual Criminal Code*, supra note 5.

7. Jaffe, supra note 4, and *Seminar on Forensic Pathology and Sudden-Death Investigation*, supra note 1: F.A. Jaffe, "Pathological Evidence."

8. Bennett, supra note 2.

9. Jaffe, supra note 4, at 12.

10. Bennett, supra note 2.

11. Jaffe, supra note 4.

12. Jaffe, supra note 7.

13. *Seminar on Forensic Pathology and Sudden-Death Investigation*, supra note 1: H. Smith, "The Medicolegal Autopsy."

14. G.M. Chayko, E.D. Gulliver, and D.V. MacDougall, *Forensic Evidence in Canada* (Aurora, ON: Canada Law Book, 1991), and International Association of Chiefs of Police, *Criminal Investigation* (Arlington, VA: I.A.C.P., 1989).

15. Ibid.; Jaffe, supra note 4.

16. Smith, supra note 13; Jaffe, supra note 4.

17. Smith, supra note 13.

18. Ibid.; International Association of Chiefs of Police, supra note 14.

19. Jaffe, supra note 7.

20. Chayko, Gulliver, and MacDougall, supra note 14; Jaffe, supra note 4.

21. Jaffe, supra note 4.

22. Smith, supra note 13.

23. Ibid.

CHAPTER 22
Determining Means of Death

LEARNER SUMMARY

The worst consequence of a sudden-death investigation is to erroneously classify a homicide as a suicide, accident, or death by natural causes. An undetected homicide not only creates an obvious injustice to the victim, it poses a distinct public threat—a murderer will remain free. Therefore, the major objectives for investigating a sudden death are to classify the death and factually explain the reasonable grounds. If the death is classified as being anything other than a homicide, there is another objective: to factually explain the reasonable grounds that prove that a homicide did not occur.

These objectives are met by following an investigative sequence, by always assuming the worst, and by interpreting evidence properly to determine the means of death.

Case Study 22.1

On a Sunday afternoon at 1:30, officers responded to an unknown problem call at a suburban dwelling-house. Lindsay and Anthony (both age 45) met the police at a side door. Calmly, they informed the first officer, "He's downstairs," and directed him to a basement closet.

Nick, their 12-year-old son, was hanging from a rope around his neck.

(Refer to the end of Chapter 22 for the conclusion of this case study.)

INVESTIGATIVE METHODS

Investigators historically are taught to think the worst and assume every sudden death is a homicide when a sudden-death investigation begins. It is an excellent state of mind to have when investigating a sudden death. This attitude has nothing to do with pessimism; instead, it serves to keep investigators alert to the possibility of homicide indicators and, as such, it is crucial to fulfilling the investigative objectives of either classifying and proving a homicide or proving that a homicide did not occur. Especially in a case when an investigator has determined that a homicide did not occur, thinking the worst will result in making convincing explanations to support that conclusion. The sequence of steps that an investigation should follow is based on thinking the worst.

THE SUDDEN-DEATH INVESTIGATIVE SEQUENCE

Sudden deaths are investigated in four distinct phases. A phase cannot be abandoned until sufficient evidence exists conclusively to prove that the means of death, related to that phase, did not occur.

▸ **Phase 1** Prove the death was caused by an intentional criminal act (homicide). Move to Phase 2 only after evidence conclusively proves that a homicide did not occur.
▸ **Phase 2** Prove the death was intentionally self-inflicted (suicide). Move to Phase 3 only after evidence conclusively proves that a suicide did not occur.
▸ **Phase 3** Prove the death was the result of an accident. Move to Phase 4 only after evidence conclusively proves that an accident did not occur.
▸ **Phase 4** Prove that death resulted from natural causes, by means of (a) autopsy results and (b) the absence of evidence relating to homicide, suicide, and accident.

Phase 1: Homicide Assumption

Proving whether a homicide occurred can be accomplished by determining the existence or the absence of evidence of homicide indicators:

1. **Wounds or injuries indicating violence** Determine whether they are multiple or located in areas inaccessible to the victim. If injuries or wounds exist, officers should only visually examine the victim. They should not search the victim's clothing for a wallet, identification, and so on. Ident. officers will collect such evidence and examine it for fingerprints and trace evidence. Do not disturb the body unless it is decomposed, decapitated, or in a state of rigor mortis. In the absence of these three conditions, assume the victim is alive, despite the severity of the wounds or injuries; ensure the victim is taken to a hospital by ambulance; and ensure that all efforts are made to preserve his or her life.
2. **Weapons** The presence of wounds and the absence of a weapon are a strong homicide indicator. If a weapon is present, check whether it is a stolen item. If it has not been stolen, do not immediately assume that the victim purchased it to commit suicide.
3. **Domestic problems** Determine existence of a spouse, paramour, or family, then determine whether there was any history of domestic problems. A large percentage of homicides are committed by this group of people because of domestic disputes. Interview the victim's friends, because domestic problems are often discussed with acquaintances.

4. **Conflicting room condition** The appearance of a room may be meaningless unless the normal appearance is established first. This can be determined by interviewing people who were familiar with the usual appearance of the room. A contradicting appearance may indicate homicide. For example, disturbed furniture may obviously indicate that violence occurred, but the disturbed furniture may be the normal appearance of the room. Conversely, an impeccable room does not eliminate violence. The value of these appearances increases if they conflict with the norm.

5. **Theft of property** Search the interior, emphasizing the location of valuable property. The presence of a theft is a homicide indicator.

6. **Forcible entry** Search the exterior extensively (i.e., all entrances, windows). Ident. officers should examine any damaged area or unlocked area for physical evidence (e.g., fingerprints). The presence of forced entry is a homicide indicator, but the absence of forced entry does not eliminate a homicide. A relative or acquaintance may have murdered the victim while being lawfully present during a domestic dispute or sexual assault.

7. **Pathologist's opinion that violence and sexual assault occurred** If violence of any kind occurred, it is logical that homicide could have occurred.

8. **Motives for homicide** In addition to motives of domestic dispute, theft, and sexual assault, determine any vendettas and, in cases of infant death, parental frustration.

If all homicide indicators are absent, an officer can confidently prove that a homicide did not occur. The investigator may explain the absence of homicide indicators in the written police report as factual proof that a sudden death was not a homicide.

Phase 2: Suicide Assumption

Proving whether a suicide occurred can be accomplished by determining the existence or absence of the evidence of suicide indicators.

1. **Suicide note** If one is present, have the Ident. officer examine the paper for fingerprints. Ensure forensic analysis of handwriting. A handwriting comparison requires several samples of the author's handwriting. Search the victim's residence for at least 12 samples and prove that the victim was the author. One method is to obtain an eyewitness verification of the victim's writing. Another is to obtain the opinion of persons who frequently read the victim's writing. The handwriting must be proven to be the victim's before the suicide note can be considered as proof of suicide. If the note was typed, determine the machine used and examine it.

2. **Motive for suicide** A motive may or may not be immediately recognizable. Interview relatives, friends, and co-workers to establish whether any verbal intention had been made. Investigate the condition of the victim's

  ▷ relationships,
  ▷ physical health,
  ▷ mental health (medical and psychiatric history),
  ▷ police reports for prior suicide attempts,

    ▷ wrists for healed scars,

    ▷ finances,

    ▷ employment, and

    ▷ legal status (pending charges or sentencing).

3. **Weapons.**
4. **Self-inflicted injuries or wounds.**
5. **Autopsy reports that indicate the presence of a substance that suggests an overdose.**

If all suicide indicators are absent, an officer can confidently prove that a suicide did not occur.

Phase 3: Accident

Often, witnesses are present to prove an accident occurred. However, to prove that the death was accidental the circumstances must show that

- the manner of the accident was possible in relation to the surroundings, and
- homicide and suicide indicators are absent.

Phase 4: Natural Causes

Proving that a death resulted from natural causes depends on:

- compatible autopsy results, and
- absence of homicide, suicide, and accident indicators.

EVIDENCE INTERPRETATION IN RELATION TO MEANS OF DEATH

After specific evidence is found, its relevance to an investigation depends on the officer's ability to interpret the evidence and determine its significance in relation to the four classifications of sudden death.

Gunshot Wounds

Discharge of a firearm causes emission of the bullet, powder, carbon, and gas. These materials affect the appearance of gunshot wounds.

Gas temperature is about 1400 to 1500°F (760–816°C). A gun that is discharged while in hard contact with skin will burn the edges of the wound or clothing fibres. If the skin is bare, soot will be deposited and will be burned into the skin, blackening the wound edges. Soot resulting from a contact wound cannot be washed away with a wet cloth. A **contact wound** is a wound caused by a firearm that was discharged within two inches from the skin.

Soot can be deposited on skin in non-contact wounds (beyond two inches). The soot, however, will not be burned into the skin and can be removed by washing. Handguns and rifles can deposit soot up to 12 inches away; a shotgun has the same capacity up to 18 inches. Beyond these distances, no soot deposit should occur.

Silencers reduce the soot deposit distance to only two inches. Revolvers cannot be silenced because of a gap between the cylinder and barrel. Only automatic pistols can be silenced. In addition to the wound area, the victim's hands should be checked. Soot may be deposited on the non-dominant hand if it held the muzzle, as some suicide victims do.

Gas not only has extreme temperature, it emits pressure of 10,000 to 15,000 pounds (4536–6804 kg) per square inch. If discharged into air, the gas dissipates. However, if a gun is discharged during skin contact, with bone beneath it, gas will not penetrate the bone. Expansion between the skin and bone occurs. The skin may flare out, exceeding elasticity limits, resulting in irregular wounds. The irregularity depends on

- how hard the contact with the skin is,
- the elasticity of the skin, and
- the amount of gas produced by the weapon (variances exist among weapons).[1]

HOMICIDE INDICATORS

Homicide indicators are

- the range of the shot is beyond the victim's reach,
- the location of a wound on an inaccessible body part (this includes a location that contradicts the victim's dominant hand),
- the absence of the firearm at the crime scene (gun is nearby if the death was due to a suicide or accident), and
- multiple gunshot wounds.[2]

SUICIDE INDICATORS

The following are characteristics of self-inflicted gunshot wounds, which can be used to distinguish a suicide from a homicide or accident:

1. a wound self-inflicted from a range within the victim's reach, unless an elaborate method extends that reach,
2. a single wound, and
3. classic contact wound locations, which include
    - the temples,
    - the centre brow,
    - the roof of the mouth, and
    - over the heart.[3]

Stab Wounds

HOMICIDE INDICATORS

Homicide stab wounds are usually multiple, but a single wound should not be dismissed. The wound location can be anywhere on the body. Defence wounds may be visible on a victim's fingers, palms, or forearms. Other non-stabbing injuries may be visible. Wounds usually occur through clothing. The absence of the weapon is the strongest homicide indicator.[4]

SUICIDE INDICATORS

Suicide stabbings are not frequent. Wounds occur in accessible body areas, compatible with the victim's dominant hand. The chest area over the heart is a common area. Usually, a single wound exists; it may be surrounded by trial or tentative wounds. The victim often removes clothing or bares the targeted skin area.[5]

ACCIDENT INDICATORS

Accidental stabbings are rare. They usually consist of a single wound. No other injuries are present. Witnesses often exist. The weapon often remains and is found in the wound. Other homicide and suicide indicators must be absent to prove that an accident occurred.[6]

Incision Wounds

Compared with stab wounds, incision wounds are greater in length because they are caused by the horizontal movement of a sharp instrument. For example, cutting wrists with a razor blade causes incision wounds. They are characterized by being deep at the beginning of the wound and shallow at the end. Bruising does not usually accompany them.[7]

SUICIDE INDICATORS

The victim's dominant hand must be established and the wound beginning or the wound itself should be on the opposite side. For example, a right-handed person having a slashed left wrist, with a greater depth on the left side of the wound, represents a compatible suicide situation. A clean wound may have minute tags of skin on the edge, indicating the direction of the blade. An incision wound on the wrist may be accompanied by superficial wounds indicating additional attempts.

Suicide by a cut throat is not common. A suicide neck incision usually is characterized as follows. If the victim is right-handed, the incision is higher on the neck due to the tendency to lean the head back. The wound commonly starts on the left side below the ear, angles downward, and straightens under the chin to the other side of the neck. Many suicide neck incisions are performed with great violence, causing semi-decapitation. Men are six times more likely to commit suicide by incision wound than are women.[8]

HOMICIDE INDICATORS

Homicide neck incisions do not resemble suicide incisions. The incision is lower on the neck and is straight; the suicide incision is usually curved. No tentative scratches usually exist. Cuts on hands and forearms acquired during defence attempts may be visible.[9]

Asphyxia

Twenty percent of the air we breathe is oxygen. Oxygen is the fuel that enables the brain and vital organs to function. Asphyxia is a sudden stoppage of oxygen. Hangings, strangulations, and drownings are examples of asphyxia deaths.

Hemoglobin is the protein matter in the blood cells that acts as an oxygen carrier. However, hemoglobin has an affinity for carbon monoxide; it prefers to carry carbon monoxide 300 times more than carrying oxygen. Transporting carbon monoxide results in a rapid asphyxia death. Commonly, this death involves an idling motor vehicle either in a closed garage or in a public place with an attachment to the vehicle's exhaust pipe.[10]

SUICIDE INDICATORS

An attachment (e.g., a plastic hose) to an exhaust pipe can yield evidence that indicates suicide. If the attachment is new, the victim's fingerprints should exclusively be present. Establish the location of purchase and attempt to identify the victim as being the purchaser.

If the attachment is old, search the victim's house for an appliance (e.g., a clothes dryer) with its tubing missing. Examine the areas of detachment for fingerprints. If fingerprints of family members are found, a strong homicide indicator is established (dryer hoses do not require frequent replacement or repair). The absence of an attachment requires the essential homicide, suicide, or accident indicators to classify the means of death.[11]

Neck Injuries

Hangings are usually suicide deaths. If the victim is not decomposed or in a rigor mortis state, death cannot be pronounced by the first officer or ambulance personnel. The victim must be assumed to be alive and must be taken to a hospital. The rope should be cut between the neck and the knot, for the purpose of keeping the knot intact for forensic examination.

Although hanging is a strong indication of suicide, the possibility of a disguised homicide strangulation must be investigated.[12]

SUICIDE INDICATORS

The victim's face is pale and placid due to a rapid death, which causes no convulsions. An incomplete mark is formed around the neck. It is characterized as being straight along the front, sloping upward toward the ears, and with an absence of marks on the back of the neck. The surroundings should contain a means to allow elevation (a chair or a box). These items should bear the victim's fingerprints exclusively. An autopsy should find no other injuries resulting from violence.[13]

HOMICIDE INDICATORS

Homicide indicators represent evidence of strangulation. Death by strangulation takes longer than death by hanging. A build-up of carbon monoxide causes convulsions that may cause other injuries or a disturbance to items surrounding the location. Victims of strangulation may have a spotty, bluish, congested face. The spots are referred to as **pinpoint hemorrhages**, which are visible on the forehead, cheeks, upper eyelids in particular, and in the white portion of the eyes. Strangulation neck marks tend to be horizontal, possibly completely around the neck, and are low on the neck.[14]

Drowning

Approximately two-thirds of all drownings are accidental. Most of the rest are suicidal. Despite the fact that homicidal drownings are rare, the Ontario Forensic Pathology Branch examined 15 conclusive homicidal drowning victims between 1980 and 1984.

The difficulty in distinguishing the means of death of a drowning victim increases because of the usual severity of injuries found on the victim's body. The injuries must be classified as either:

1. **ante-mortem** (before death), which is a homicide indicator, or
2. **post-mortem** (after death), caused by circumstances during submergence. A conclusive classification may not be possible.

A successful method of determining whether drowning was the means of death is to ask the question: Was the body alive when it entered the water? If the answer is "no," a strong homicide indication exists. The question can be answered as follows.

1. **Visual examination** Froth or foam emitted from the mouth and nose of a body quickly recovered (i.e., not decomposed) indicates the body was alive when it entered the water. A decomposed body may have similar indicators; the froth or foam may have changed to a viscous, bubble-like fluid. The absence of this emittance may indicate that death occurred prior to entering the water.
2. **Visible post-mortem lividity on the front of the body** This, on a quickly recovered victim, indicates a face-down position while submerged. This suggests that the body was alive when it entered the water.
3. **Water-laden lungs** An autopsy of a quickly recovered body that finds water-laden lungs indicate that the body was alive when it entered the water.
4. **Diatom test** Diatoms are microscopic forms of plant life found in most types of naturally occurring water. They have a similar appearance to snowflakes. If the body is alive when it enters the water, water inhalation allows diatom access into the lungs. Lungs expand because of excessive water and this causes blood vessels to burst in the lungs. Water and diatoms enter the bloodstream and are dispersed to and lodge in the organs as the heart pumps.

A test is required to determine the presence of diatoms. The test requires examination of an enclosed organ, one not easily contaminated by other water samples. Therefore, the bone marrow of the thigh is used. The thigh bone is usually intact and its marrow is protected from contamination. The thigh bone is sawed open lengthwise and the marrow is examined for diatom presence. Diatoms are easily recognizable.

A positive test (diatoms are present) means that the body was alive when it entered the water, indicating any classification of sudden death. A negative test (diatoms are absent) suggests that the body was dead when it entered the water, therefore strongly indicating a homicide. A negative test may also indicate that the body of water did not contain diatoms. A sample from the body of water must be analyzed for its diatom content.

A positive test usually finds 12 to 15 diatoms in the bone marrow. An excessive number may indicate that the bone marrow was contaminated by other water samples during analysis.[15]

Fire Deaths

When investigating a fire death, a similar question to the one asked in a drowning death must be asked: Was the victim alive or dead at the start of the fire? If the victim was dead before the onset of fire, a strong homicide indicator exists. If the victim was alive before the fire started, indicators exist for accident, suicide, or homicide.

The mechanism of death by fire is circulatory shock caused by skin burns. Blisters accompany skin burns. Fluids fill the blisters, causing excessive body fluid loss, which then results in circulatory shock. Rarely can death be attributed to the effects of the actual flame and heat on air passages.

Indicators that the victim was alive at the time of the fire are revealed by autopsy results, which find the presence of

- carbon monoxide levels in blood (asphyxia),
- inhalation of soot,
- thermal burns deep in lung tissue, and
- burn blisters.

The absence of these conditions suggests the body was dead at the time of the fire, which strongly indicates homicide.

Injuries to fire victims must also be classified as ante-mortem or post-mortem. Ante-mortem wounds or injuries may be caused by accident (e.g., a collapse of building structures) or by a criminal act.[16]

Electrocution

High-voltage current refers to an excess of 1000 volts of electricity; **low-voltage current** is less than 1000 volts. Domestic voltage usually is 120, and this causes approximately 60 percent of electrocution deaths.

Low-voltage deaths are due to ventricular fibrillation, a fluttering or irregular heartbeat caused by the passing of electricity through the body. High-voltage deaths are caused by electrothermal injury or electricity burns; therefore, high-voltage deaths leave more evidence on the victim's body.

Current marks (skin penetration) may be present on the victim. If present, they can indicate (a) that death was caused by electrocution, (b) the entry and exit wounds showing path of the current, and (c) the shape of the conductor.

An exit wound may be similar to a laceration wound. Thus, examination of the body is necessary to determine the presence of an entry wound.

Penetration of skin increases with (a) the amount of voltage, (b) moisture, and (c) the duration of contact with the conductor.[17]

Case Study 22.1 Conclusion

The body was not in a rigor mortis state or decomposed. The rope was cut beneath the knot. Nick was taken to the hospital, where he was later pronounced dead by a Coroner.

A chair was situated beneath the rope. No foreign fingerprints were found. The parents were extensively interviewed. An autopsy revealed that the neck marks were conducive to hanging, as opposed to strangulation. No injuries were found indicating violence.

In the absence of homicide indicators, this death was classified as a suicide.

ENDNOTES

1. Ontario Ministry of the Solicitor General, Public Safety Division, Forensic Pathology Branch, *Seminar on Forensic Pathology and Sudden-Death Investigation* (Toronto, 1984): V. Dimaio, "Gunshot Injuries."
2. Ibid.
3. Ibid.
4. *Seminar on Forensic Pathology and Sudden-Death Investigation*, supra note 1: J.H. Smith, "The Medicolegal Autopsy."
5. Ibid.
6. Ibid.
7. Ibid.
8. Ibid.
9. Ibid.; International Association of Chiefs of Police, *Criminal Investigation* (Arlington, VA: 1.A.C.P., 1989).
10. Smith, supra note 4.
11. Ibid.
12. Ibid.
13. Ibid.
14. Ibid.
15. Ibid.
16. Ibid.
17. Ibid.

Table of Cases

Bibliography

Abrams, S., "The Validity of Polygraph Technique with Children" (1975) vol. 3, no. 3 *Journal of Police Science and Administration*.

Abrams, S., and E. Weinstein, "The Validity of the Polygraph with Retardates" (1974) vol. 2, no. 1 *Journal of Police Science and Administration*.

Agnew, R., "The Origins of Delinquent Events: An Examination of Offender Accounts" (1990) vol. 27, no. 3 *Journal of Research in Crime and Delinquency*.

Arcaro, G., *Basic Police Powers: Arrest and Search Procedures*, 4th ed. (Toronto: Emond Montgomery, 2009).

Arcaro, G., *Principles of Law Enforcement Report Writing*, 3rd ed. (Toronto: Emond Montgomery, 2009).

Aubry, A.S., Jr., and R.R. Caputo, *Criminal Investigation* (Springfield, IL: Charles C. Thomas, 1965).

Bartol, C.R., *Criminal Behavior: A Psychological Approach* (Englewood Cliffs, NJ: Prentice Hall, 1980).

Bellemare, D., *How to Testify in Court* (Montreal: Les Éditions Yvon Blais, 1985).

Bothwell, R.K., J.C. Brigham, and K.A. Deffenbacher, "Correlation of Eyewitness Accuracy and Confidence: Optimality Hypothesis Revisited" (1987) vol. 72, no. 4 *Journal of Applied Psychology*.

Boyanowsky, E., *Psychological Bases of Criminal and Deviant Behaviour Study Guide* (Burnaby, BC: School of Criminology, Centre for Distance Education—Continuing Studies, Simon Fraser University, 1990).

Brehm, J.W., and A.R. Cohen, *Explorations in Cognitive Dissonance* (New York: John Wiley and Sons, 1962).

Buchanan, D.R., "Enhancing Eyewitness Identification: Applied Psychology for Police Officers" (1985) vol. 13, no. 4 *Journal of Police Science and Administration*.

Budnick, J., K.G. Love, and L. Wisniewski Jr., "Predictors of Liar/Nonliar Status: Birth Order, Age, Reason for Polygraph Investigation, and Previous Arrest" (1983) vol. 11, no. 4 *Journal of Police Science and Administration*.

Chayko, G.M., E.D. Gulliver, and D.V. MacDougall, *Forensic Evidence in Canada* (Aurora, ON: Canada Law Book, 1991).

Cleckley, H., *The Mask of Sanity* (St. Louis: C.V. Mosby Company, 1976).

Cooper, T.G., *Crown Privilege* (Aurora, ON: Canada Law Book, 1990).

Cowger, J.F., *Friction Ridge Skin* (New York: Elsevier Science Publishing, 1983).

Cox, H.J., *Criminal Evidence Handbook* (Aurora, ON: Canada Law Book, 1991).

Deadman, H.A., "Fiber Evidence and the Wayne Williams Trial" (March 1984), *F.B.I. Law Enforcement Bulletin.*

Dukelow, D.A., and B. Nuse, *Pocket Dictionary of Canadian Law* (Toronto: Carswell, 1991).

Ehrlich, E., et al., *Oxford American Dictionary* (New York: Oxford University Press, 1980).

Fattah, E.A., *Introduction to Criminology* (Burnaby, BC: Simon Fraser University, 1989).

Festinger, L., *A Theory of Cognitive Dissonance* (Stanford, CA: Stanford University Press, 1957).

Festinger, L., *Conflict, Decision and Dissonance* (Stanford, CA: Stanford University Press, 1964).

Fisher, R.P., E.R. Geiselman, and D.R. Raymond, "Critical Analysis of Police Interview Techniques" (1987) vol. 15, no. 3 *Journal of Police Science and Administration.*

Gall, G.L., *The Canadian Legal System* (Toronto: Carswell, 1990).

Gerber, S., and O. Schroeder Jr., *Criminal Investigation and Interrogation* (Cincinnati: W.H. Anderson Co., 1962).

Gibson, J.L., *Canadian Criminal Code Offences*, rev. ed. (Toronto: Carswell, 1991).

Gibson, J.L., *Criminal Law Evidence, Practice and Procedure* (Toronto: Carswell, 1988).

Gleitman, H., *Basic Psychology* (Toronto: George J. MacLeod Ltd., 1983).

Greenspan, E.L., and M. Rosenberg, *Martin's Annual Criminal Code* (Aurora, ON: Canada Law Book, 2008).

Griffiths, C., and S.N. Verdun-Jones, *Canadian Criminal Justice* (Don Mills, ON: Butterworths, 1989).

Hill, S.C., "Recent Search and Seizure Issues—A Charter Overview," paper presented to the Canadian Bar Association Institute of Continuing Legal Education (Toronto, March 4, 1989).

Horvath, F.S., "Verbal and Non-Verbal Clues to Truth and Deception During Polygraph Examinations" (1973) vol. 1, no. 3 *Journal of Police Science and Administration.*

Hunter, F.L., and P. Ash, "The Accuracy and Consistency of Polygraph Examiner's Diagnosis" (1973) vol. 1, no. 3 *Journal of Police Science and Administration.*

Inbau, F.E., and J.E. Reid, *Lie Detection and Criminal Investigation* (Baltimore: Williams & Wilkins Co., 1953).

International Association of Chiefs of Police, *Criminal Investigation* (Arlington, VA: I.A.C.P., 1989).

Jaffe, F.A., *A Guide to Pathological Evidence* (Toronto: Carswell, 1991).

Krishnan, S.S., *An Introduction to Modern Criminal Investigation* (Springfield, IL: Charles C. Thomas, 1975).

Leippe, M.R., A.P. Manion, and A. Romanczyk, "Eyewitness Memory for a Touching Experience: Accuracy Differences Between Child and Adult Witnesses" (1991) vol. 76, no. 3 *Journal of Applied Psychology.*

Macintosh, D.A., *Fundamentals of the Criminal Justice System* (Toronto: Carswell, 1989).

Marin, R.J., *Admissibility of Statements* (Aurora, ON: Canada Law Book, 1989).

McWilliams, P.K., *Canadian Criminal Evidence*, 3rd ed. (Aurora, ON: Canada Law Book, 1991).

Mende, L., D.P. MacKinnon, and E.R. Geiselman, "Memory for License Plates as a Function of Exposure Time" (1987) vol. 15, no. 1 *Journal of Police Science and Administration*.

Milgram, S., "The Small World Problem" (1967) vol. 2 *Psychology Today*.

Moenssens, A.A., *Fingerprint Techniques* (Don Mills, ON: Chilton Book Co., 1971).

Ontario Ministry of the Solicitor General, Ontario Police College, *Criminal Investigation Course Lecture: Arrest, Search and Seizure* (Toronto: Queen's Printer, 1984).

Ontario Ministry of the Solicitor General, Ontario Police College, *Evidence for Senior Officers: Book 1* (Toronto: Queen's Printer, 1984).

Ontario Ministry of the Solicitor General, Ontario Police College, *Evidence for Senior Officers: Book 2* (Toronto: Queen's Printer, 1984).

Ontario Ministry of the Solicitor General, Ontario Police College, *Evidence for Senior Police Officers* (Toronto: Queen's Printer, 1984).

Ontario Ministry of the Solicitor General, Ontario Police College, *Physical Evidence* (Toronto: Queen's Printer, 1984).

Ontario Ministry of the Solicitor General, Public Safety Division, Centre for Forensic Sciences, *Laboratory Aids for the Investigator* (Toronto: Queen's Printer, 1984).

Ontario Ministry of the Solicitor General, Public Safety Division, Forensic Pathology Branch, *Seminar on Forensic Pathology and Sudden-Death Investigation* (Toronto, 1984). The following lecturers spoke:
- R.C. Bennett, "The Role of the Coroner in Sudden-Death Investigation."
- V. Dimaio, "Gunshot Injuries."
- J.W. Evans, "Introduction to Sudden-Death Investigation."
- F.A. Jaffe, "Pathological Evidence."
- C.W. Kirk, "Crime Scene Investigation" and "The Scene of Sudden Death."
- H. Smith, "The Medicolegal Autopsy."
- D. Wiecking, "Natural Deaths Occurring Under Unnatural Circumstances" and "Physical Evidence."

Parker, E.S., I.M. Beinbaum, and E.P. Noble, "Alcohol and Memory" (1976) *Journal of Applied Psychology*, as in Yuille and Tollestrup, 1990.

Patrick, C.J., and W.G. Iacono, "Psychopathy, Threat and Polygraph Test Accuracy" (1989) vol. 74, no. 2 *Journal of Applied Psychology*.

Patrick, C.J., and W.G. Iacono, "Validity of the Control Question Polygraph Test: The Problem of Sampling Bias" (1991) vol. 76, no. 2 *Journal of Applied Psychology*.

Pigott, M., and J.C. Brigham, "Relationship Between Accuracy of Prior Description and Facial Recognition" (1985) vol. 70, no. 3 *Journal of Applied Psychology*.

Reed, T.E., "Eyewitness Identification of an Armed Robber Within a Biased Police Lineup" (1984) vol. 12, no. 3 *Journal of Police Science and Administration*.

Reik, T., *The Compulsion to Confess* (New York: Grove Press, 1959).

Roach, K., P. Healy, and G. Trotter, *Criminal Law and Procedure: Cases and Materials*, 9th ed. (Toronto: Emond Montgomery, 2004).

Robbins, A., *Awaken the Giant Within* (New York: Summit Books, 1991).

Robbins, A., *Unlimited Power* (New York: Ballantine Books, 1986).

Rodrigues, G.P., *The Police Officer's Manual*, 15th ed. (Toronto: Carswell, 1998).

Rogers, C. *Client-Centered Therapy: Its Current Practice, Implications and Theory* (London: Constable, 1951).

Russo, J.E., and P.H. Shoemaker, *Decision Traps* (New York: Fireside, 1989).

Salhany, Hon. R.E., *Canadian Criminal Procedure*, 5th ed. (Aurora, ON: Canada Law Book, 1989).

Salhany, Hon. R.E., *A Basic Guide to Evidence in Criminal Cases*, 2nd ed. (Toronto: Carswell, 1991).

Saxton, B.J., and R.T. Stansfield, *Understanding Criminal Offences*, 2nd ed. (Toronto: Carswell, 1990).

Scrivener, E., and M.A. Safer, "Eyewitnesses Show Hypermnesia for Details About a Violent Event" (1988) vol. 73, no. 3 *Journal of Applied Psychology*.

Slowik, S.M., and J.P. Buckley, "Relative Accuracy of Polygraph Examiner Diagnosis of Respiration, Blood Pressure and GSR Recordings" (1975) vol. 3, no. 3 *Journal of Police Science and Administration*.

Smith, V.L., and P.C. Ellsworth, "The Social Psychology of Eyewitness Accuracy: Misleading Questions and Communicator Expertise" (1987) vol. 72, no. 2 *Journal of Applied Psychology*.

Smith, V.L., P.C. Ellsworth, and S.M. Kassin, "Eyewitness Accuracy and Confidence: Within- Versus Between-Subjects Correlations" (1989) vol. 74, no. 2 *Journal of Applied Psychology*.

Von Hentig, H., "The Contribution of the Victim to the Genesis of Crime," in *The Criminal and His Victim* (New Haven, CT: Yale University Press, 1948), chapter 12. Reprinted in 1967 by Archon Books.

Waltman, J.L., "Nonverbal Communication in Interrogation: Some Applications" (1983) vol. 11, no. 2 *Journal of Police Science and Administration*.

Wells, G.L., *Eyewitness Identification* (Toronto: Carswell, 1988).

Wells, G.L., "Verbal Descriptors of Faces from Memory: Are They Diagnostic of Identification Accuracy?" (1985) vol. 70, no. 4 *Journal of Applied Psychology*.

Wells, G.L., and R.C.L. Lindsay, "Methodological Notes on the Accuracy–Confidence Relation in Eyewitness Identifications" (1985) vol. 70, no. 2 *Journal of Applied Psychology*.

Wells, G.L., and E. Loftus, *Eyewitness Testimony* (Cambridge: Cambridge University Press, 1984).

Wilkins, L., *Social Deviance* (London: Tavistock, 1964).

Wood, S., et al., *The World of Psychology*, 2nd Cdn ed. (Scarborough, ON: Prentice Hall, 1999).

Woods, R.S.M., *Police Interrogation* (Toronto: Carswell, 1990).

Yuille, J.C., and P.A. Tollestrup, "Some Effects of Alcohol on Eyewitness Memory" (1990) vol. 75, no. 3 *Journal of Applied Psychology*.

Index